TRADITIONS IN TRANSFORMATION

TRADITIONS IN TRANSFORMATION

Turning Points in Biblical Faith

Edited by

BARUCH HALPERN
JON D. LEVENSON

WINONA LAKE, INDIANA
EISENBRAUNS

Copyright © 1981 Eisenbrauns
Printed in the United States of America

Library of Congress Cataloging in Publication Data

Traditions in transformation.

 Festschrift honoring Frank Moore Cross.
 Bibliography, p. 405.
 Includes index.
 CONTENTS: Miles, J. A., Jr. Radical editing—
L'Heureux, C. E. Searching for the origins of God.—
Halpern, B. The uneasy compromise.—[etc.]
 1. Bible. O.T.—Criticism interpretation, etc.—Addresses,
essays, lectures. 2. Cross, Frank Moore—Addresses, essays,
lectures. I. Halpern, Baruch. II. Levenson, Jon Douglas. III.
Cross, Frank Moore.
BS1188.T7 221.6   80-29112
ISBN 0-931464-06-4

To

Frank Moore Cross

on the occasion of his sixtieth birthday
July 13, 1981

עד מאה ועשרים

CONTENTS

ABBREVIATIONS

AASOR	Annual of the American Schools of Oriental Research
AB	Anchor Bible
AfO	*Archiv für Orientforschung*
AnBib	Analecta biblica
ANET	*Ancient Near Eastern Texts*
ATANT	Abhandlungen zur Theologie des Alten and Neuen Testaments
ATD	Das Alte Testament Deutsch
AV	Authorized Version
BA	*Biblical Archaeologist*
BASOR	*Bulletin of the American Schools of Oriental Research*
B. Bat.	*Baba Batra*
BBB	Bonner biblische Beiträge
BDB	Brown-Driver-Briggs, *Hebrew and English Lexicon of the Old Testament*
BETL	Bibiotheca ephemeridum theologicarum lovaniensium
BH	Biblia Hebraica
BHI	Bright, *A History of Israel*
Bib	*Biblica*
BibOr	Biblica et Orientalia
BibS(n)	Biblische Studien (Neukirchen, 1951-)
BJRL	*Bulletin of the John Rylands University Library of Manchester*
BKAT	Biblischer Kommentar: Altes Testament
BR	*Biblical Research*
BWANT	Beiträge zur Wissenschaft vom Alten und Neuen Testament
BZ	*Biblische Zeitschrift*
BZAW	Beihefte zur *ZAW*
CAH	*Cambridge Ancient History*
CBQ	*Catholic Biblical Quarterly*
CD	Cairo (Genizah text of the) Damascus (Document)
CIL	*Corpus inscriptionum latinarum*
CMHE	*Canaanite Myth and Hebrew Epic*
CTA	*Corpus des tablettes en cunéiformes alphabétiques*
DBSup	*Dictionnaire de la Bible, Supplément*
DDS	*Deuteronomy and the Deuteronomic School*
EI	*Eretz Israel*
EvT	*Evangelische Theologie*

Exp Tim	Expository Times
FRLANT	Forschungen zur Religion und Literatur des Alten und Neuen Testaments
HAT	Handbuch zum Alten Testament
HB	Hebrew Bible
HDR	Harvard Dissertations in Religion
HHI	Herrmann, *A History of Israel in Old Testament Times*
HKAT	Handkommentar zum Alten Testament
HNT	Handbuch zum Neuen Testament
HNTC	Harper's NT Commentaries
HSM	Harvard Semitic Monographs
HTR	*Harvard Theological Review*
HTS	Harvard Theological Studies
HUCA	*Hebrew Union College Annual*
ICC	International Critical Commentary
IDB	*Interpreter's Dictionary of the Bible*
IDBSup	Supplementary volume to *IDB*
ILOT	*Introduction to the Literature of the Old Testament*
JAAR	*Journal of the American Academy of Religion*
JAOS	*Journal of the American Oriental Society*
JBL	*Journal of Biblical Literature*
JCS	*Journal of Cuneiform Studies*
JJS	*Journal of Jewish Studies*
JNES	*Journal of Near Eastern Studies*
JQR	*Jewish Quarterly Review*
JRS	*Journal of Roman Studies*
JSS	*Journal of Semitic Studies*
JTS	*Journal of Theological Studies*
JWH	*Cahiers d'Historie Mondiale / Journal of World History*
LD	Lectio divina
LSJ	Liddell-Scott-Jones, *Greek-English Lexicon*
LTK	*Lexikon für Theologie und Kirche*
LXX	Septuagint
MeyerK	H. A. W. Meyer, Kritischexegetischer Kommentar über das Neue Testament
MNTC	Moffatt NT Commentary
MT	Massoretic Text
NHI	Noth, *The History of Israel*
NICOT	New International Commentary on the Old Testament
NovT	*Novum Testamentum*
NTD	Das Neue Testament Deutsch
NTS	*New Testament Studies*
OA	*Oriens Antiquus*

OLZ	*Orientalische Literaturzeitung*
OTL	Old Testament Library
OTS	*Oudtestamentische Studiën*
PEQ	*Palestine Exploration Quarterly*
Q	Qumran
1QH	*Hôdāyôt* (*Thanksgiving Hymns*) from Qumran, Cave 1
1QM	*War Scroll* from Qumran, Cave 1
1QS	*Manual of Discipline* from Qumran, Cave 1
1QSa	*Rule of the Congregation* from Qumran, Cave 1
4QTestim	*Testimonia* text from Qumran, Cave 4
11QMelch	*Melchizedek* text from Qumran, Cave 11
RelSRev	*Religious Studies Review*
RevQ	*Revue de Qumran*
RHR	*Revue de l'historie des religions*
RNT	Regensburger Neues Testament
RQ	*Römische Quartalschrift für christliche Altertumskunde und Kirchengeschichte*
RSR	*Recherches de science religieuse*
RSV	*Revised Standard Version*
Sanh	*Sanhedrin*
SBLSCS	SBL Septuagint and Cognate Studies
SBLDS	SBL Dissertation Series
SBT	Studies in Biblical Theology
SJLA	Studies in Judaism in Late Antiquity
SP	Samaritan Pentateuch
STDJ	Studies on the Texts of the Desert of Judah
SUNT	Studien zur Umwelt des Neuen Testaments
Tg	Targum
TLZ	*Theologische Literaturzeitung*
TU	Texte und Untersuchungen
TWAT	*Theologisches Wörterbuch zum Alten Testament*
TZ	*Theologische Zeitschrift*
UT	*Ugaritic Textbook*
UUÅ	Uppsala universitetsårsskrift
VS	Verbum salutis
VT	*Vetus Testamentum*
VTSup	Vetus Testamentum, Supplements
WD	*Wort und Dienst*
WMANT	Wissenschaftliche Monographen zum Alten und Neuen Testament
WZKMUL	*Wissenschaftliche Zeitschrift der Karl-Marx-Universität*
ZAW	*Zeitschrift für die alttestamentliche Wissenschaft*
ZDPV	*Zeitschrift des deutschen Palästina-Vereins*

ZKT	*Zeitschrift für Katholische Theologie*
ZNW	*Zeitschrift für die neutestamentliche Wissenschaft*
ZTK	*Zeitschrift für Theologie und Kirche*

Preface

How to Use This Book

This book is designed to open the world of modern biblical scholarship to a wider audience.

In each chapter, the scholar does not simply present the results of his research, but guides the reader through the process of advanced biblical study with sensitivity to those points in the argument where the layperson is likely to get lost. The goal of the volume is to offer the intelligent non-specialist a sense of active participation in the dynamics of contemporary research. Hence, these essays make no attempt to disguise the assumptions from which they proceed and the plurality of approaches that presently exists in the area of biblical studies. The volume is designed to offer the student of the Bible a richer and more advanced experience of his subject than introductory textbooks can provide.

After Chapter 1, which deals with the general issue of the assumptions underlying the critical study of the Bible and their relationship to the Jewish, Catholic, and Protestant understandings of scripture, the book proceeds in roughly chronological order, from the Bronze Age world preceding the emergence of Israel until the separation of the tradition into the Samaritan, Rabbinic, and Christian religions which endure to this day. Along the way, the focus shifts from chapter to chapter so as to give the reader a taste of the varied interests of contemporary biblical scholarship. For example, Chapter 3 deals primarily with political history, Chapter 6 with poetics, Chapters 7 and 11 with theology, and Chapters 12 and 13 with the development of sects. Hence, this volume presents the reader with a sample not only of each period of biblical history, but also of the variety of foci at the cutting edge of contemporary scholarship. In spite of this overall design, each chapter can be read without reference to the others.

Traditions in Transformation is a joint project on the part of Catholic, Jewish, and Protestant scholars. What unites them is a desire to honor their teacher, Frank Moore Cross, Hancock Professor of Hebrew and other Oriental Languages at Harvard University. Some of the chapters in this volume are explications and extensions of the work of Professor Cross; all of them stand in debt to him as scholar and teacher. The following appreciation by his friend and collaborator of many years, Professor David Noel Freedman, should give a sense of the magnitude of Professor Cross's achievement. We dedicate this book to Frank Moore Cross on the occasion of his sixtieth birthday, July 13, 1981.

BARUCH HALPERN
JON D. LEVENSON

Frank Moore Cross, Jr.
An Appreciation

It is not often that a scholar's preeminent place in the history and dynamics of his field of study is assured while he is still active and a long way from retirement, but that is clearly the case with Frank Moore Cross, Jr., Hancock Professor of Hebrew and Other Oriental Languages at Harvard University. Recognition of his extraordinary and varied skills and capabilities came early, and an unparalleled sequence of major achievements has indicated the promise of his high potential, and even the extreme expectations of teachers and colleagues over the years. These circumstances make it altogether fitting to honor Professor Cross with a festschrift on the occasion of his 60th birthday consisting entirely of contributions from his own students, and only a small but select group of them. They may be described as belonging to the most recent classes of successful doctoral candidates, and the confidence and force with which they support and defend their several theses reflect accurately the source and stimulus behind their work. I leave to others, especially the readers, to peruse the papers following, and pursue the leads and challenges which they provide, and will instead add some words about the central figure of this scholarly tribute, whom I have known for many, many years (it will be 35 by the time this volume appears, and Frank Cross observes his 60th anniversary), and admired as fellow-student, colleague, collaborator, critic, and mentor throughout all of them. That we have been close friends for all these years, bound by ties of personal affection as well as scholarly interests, is well known and should be duly weighed in what follows.

From the beginning of his career in the field of biblical studies, Frank Cross set a high standard and a fast pace. Not only his attainments, but the apparently effortless ease with which they were attained, were the despair and envy of his fellow-students, as they have been of his colleagues and his own students ever since. It was expected that he would win the Nettie F. McCormick Fellowship in Old Testament studies at McCormick Theological Seminary, as in fact he did in 1946. What was less expected but not less consistent with his scholarly qualities and extraordinary concentration was that the paper submitted at the fellowship competition proved to be publishable and a highly original, and convincing contribution to a major issue in Old Testament research. The principal judge of the competition was reported to have informed the McCormick faculty that the paper was of doctoral caliber, and except for the formal requirements (e.g. residency, examination, and the like), the author could be awarded the Ph. D. degree forthwith. His first serious article, on the Tabernacle, which appeared in the *BA* in the fall of 1947,[1] was not only an important reconsideration and basic revision of the standard scholarly view of this subject, but stands as a major contribution to the analysis and evaluation of the priestly source of the Pentateuch, a subject to which Cross has returned again and again. Considering that his weighty article appeared in print in an important scholarly journal while Cross was a graduate student at Johns Hopkins University, the awe and astonishment, not to speak of the consternation and dismay, of his fellow-students can easily be imagined. That was only the beginning and proved to be the rule rather than the exception. His experience at Johns Hopkins was characterized by more achievements, more honors, and continuing publication. By the spring of 1948, both doctoral dissertations in which Cross collaborated with me were completed, even though the dissertation assigned to Cross on Ancient Yahwistic Poetry was not formally submitted until 1950. In the meantime, however, a segment of that dissertation, a detailed study of the Testamentary Blessing of Moses (Deuteronomy 33) in the tradition of Paul Haupt and W. F. Albright, Cross's teacher, appeared in *JBL*, then as now the leading American scholarly journal in the biblical field, in the fall of 1948. Other articles derived from the dissertation appeared in *JBL* (in 1953 on 2 Samuel 22 = Psalm 18) and *JNES* (in 1955, on the Song of the Sea, Exodus 15) confirming a strong and ongoing engagement with early Israelite poetry. The full dissertation was issued later on, while the earlier one on Hebrew orthography was published in 1952 as a monograph in the *AOS* series. It provided a detailed orthographic analysis of all the major Northwest Semitic inscriptions then known from Phoenicia, Aram, Moab, as well as Israel and Judah, the latter two receiving special emphasis, from the pre-exilic period (i.e. between the 10th and 6th centuries B.C.E.). In spite of extended and occasionally sharp criticism, the book has served as a basic guide in this field for thirty years and is still functional. Although about as many more new inscriptions have turned up in the period since publication as were available before, the operating principles derived from the inductive study of the extant inscriptions have proved viable and usable with new ones. Aside from minor adjustments occasioned by new dates, the soundness of the approach and the effectiveness of the method have been vindicated by the evidence of the whole corpus. Studies of a great variety of individual inscriptions by Cross have demonstrated both the reliability and the

---

[1]See the bibliography note of Frank Cross at the end of this volume, p. 405.

adaptability of the observations and principles embodied in the dissertation.

Cross's longstanding interest in and mastery of the esoteric science of epigraphy stem from the extensive studies of inscriptions associated with that dissertation. This also was a major emphasis in Albright's work, and Cross has carried on the tradition in majestic style. He is widely and rightly recognized as the foremost epigrapher of Northwest Semitic in the world. His own studies and those of his students, including many doctoral dissertations completed under his supervision, have set the standards, established both the relative and absolute chronology of the inscriptions themselves, and supplied the master chart for the evolution of the Northwest Semitic alphabet in its variety of types and variations.

Other abiding interests and long-range accomplishments stem from the same years at Johns Hopkins. The story of his first exposure to the Dead Sea Scrolls has been told often and need not be repeated here. But the fascination of those first photographs which arrived in Baltimore early in 1948 was overwhelming and ensured all-abiding and continuing concern with them. Initially the interest was primarily orthographic and epigraphic, the latter culminatively, as seen in an appendix to the monograph on Hebrew orthography, and in the monumental study of the Jewish scripts of Qumran (in the festschrift in honor of Albright edited by G. E. Wright under the title *The Bible and the Ancient Near East*, which appeared in 1961.) Later when Cross became a member of the team of experts assigned responsibility for the publication of the Dead Sea Scrolls, he added text-critical study to the other disciplines. Such interest also had its roots in graduate study at J.H.U., and Cross was superbly equipped as linguist and scientist to undertake one of the most important tasks of his career, namely exposing and elucidating the complex patterns and development of the transmission of the text of the Hebrew Bible. The discovery of the now famous Samuel manuscripts from Cave 4 with their non-Massoretic Hebrew text provided a major breakthrough in this discipline. On the basis of the evidences at hand, Cross was able not only to reconstruct something of the earlier history of the text of Samuel, and by implication that of the former Prophets, but also to develop a theory to account for the appearance of three distinctive text-types, all of which were known at Qumran. While much controversy surrounds the central and many of the peripheral issues, there can be no doubt that Cross's studies have been the most original and stimulating, not to say the most important in the field of textual studies, and particularly the character of the Hebrew and Greek texts of the Old Testament and their relationship to each other (especially in regard to the Pentateuch and former Prophets).

In the course of these detailed examinations of the scrolls, Cross did not neglect the wider considerations of the people who wrote and preserved them, and in time produced an authoritative work on the *Ancient Library of Qumran*, in my view still the best single volume on the subject of the people of the scrolls, their life and times. Cross first achieved international status and prominence through his work on the Dead Sea Scrolls, and when he has completed the work on the texts assigned to him, and published the multi-volume series from Cave 4, undoubtedly this will be regarded as his major accomplishment, or certainly among the most important of his career.

There has always been another side to Cross as scholar and thinker. Along with his technical skills and capacities, as epigrapher and linguist, orthographer and text critic, he has an uncommon theoretical breadth, and wide-ranging interests in philosophical and mythological matters, combined with literary and historical considerations. While he has not yet produced that massive synthesis of *The Bible and The Ancient Near East*, of which he clearly is capable, and for which many of his colleagues and students look with high expectation as well as some anxiety, samples and preliminary sketches of this great work have appeared irregularly through the years but in sufficient quantity and of impressive merit to justify the publication of a widely acclaimed volume — *Canaanite Myth and Hebrew Epic* (1973). Cross has attacked the two ends of Israelite history with great verve, on the one hand doing for our generation what the great Albrecht Alt did for his in an intricate and convincing study of patriarchal religion, and on the other, proposing new solutions to old problems of the age of Ezra-Nehemiah. The interest in poetry is reflected in his continuing studies in the Ugaritic epic materials, and in the poems of the Pentateuch and other biblical books. His series of connected essays on the priestly traditions of the Pentateuch and his reconstruction of the tangled history of Aaronid-Mushite relations form a landmark in biblical criticism. While his views in this matter are highly controversial, they are also eminently defensible. The same is true of his investigation of the complex Deuteronomic materials and his proposed solution to the literary-historical questions concerning the foundation of the vast corpus. At the other end, notice should be taken of his creative approach to the post-Exilic period and the resolution of the Ezra-Nehemiah debate. In his presidential address to the Society of Biblical Literature, he announced a reversion to the traditional order of the two heroes and the rejection of the position advanced by Albright and others, namely that Nehemiah preceded Ezra. By combining text critical analysis of the various Ezra traditions in both Hebrew and Greek (especially 1 Esdras), and applying the well-established principle of papponymy to a difficult crux in the genealogy of the high priests, Cross has established the traditional position firmly, although hardly on traditional grounds.

To sum up: In the course of a remarkably fruitful career, which has many years to run, Cross has achieved major results, attained large goals. Already in his student days at Johns Hopkins the parameters of his later accomplishments were drawn, and the interests cultivated there under the tutelage of W. F. Albright have been pursued ever since, but with remarkable extensions and variations. The emphasis on inscriptions and texts has remained constant as has the special interest in literature, and in particular Israelite poetry. There are many other achievements and attainments to report or record, but these will be attested elsewhere, and there will be more in time to come: deserved honors, awards, and the recognition of colleagues, students, and admirers around the world. In the end, perhaps his most important work will be in the achievement of his students and of their students afterwards. Already there is an impressive list of these, and their publications have not only extended the range and scope of their teacher, but have consolidated his exploratory and innovative efforts. Probes have become bridge-heads, and bridge-heads have opened the way to larger territories, until the region and the country bear the stamp of his genius. The learned and provocative articles which have been assembled in this volume are the work of a group of his more recent students; they bear eloquent testimony to the breadth of his learning, the depth of his scholarship, and the stimulus of an active questing mind. It is altogether fitting that his friends and followers salute this man, meritorious incumbent of the oldest and most distinguished chair in our field.

DAVID NOEL FREEDMAN

University of Michigan

Radical Editing:
Redaktionsgeschichte and the Aesthetic of Willed Confusion

JOHN A. MILES, JR.
UNIVERSITY OF CALIFORNIA PRESS

AVANT-PROPOS

In his journal, Max Ehrmann tells of the first lecture he attended at Harvard. The lecturer was Josiah Royce, the first sentence, "Philosophy is a sad study." Ehrmann says that he remembered little of the rest of the lecture but never forgot that sentence. In the first course I attended at Harvard, the lecturer was Frank Moore Cross, Jr., the first sentence, "The history of Bible interpretation is the history of Western thought."

I write as a former Bible scholar, at least a formerly aspiring Bible scholar, who has now become an editor. But if all Bible scholars, to the extent that they are preoccupied with redaction, must become editors, then I hope I may still have something in common with my former colleagues. In the course of this paper, I hope to compare ancient and modern editing and to ask whether the difference between them makes any difference for contemporary Bible interpretation. I think it does.

By answering this question, however, I hope to get at a larger question. Why has criticism of other literatures had so slight an impact on the criticism of the Bible as literature? It has not been so for the study of the Bible as history or as religion or as folklore. It has not been so for the many ancillary disciplines: philology, linguistics, archaeology, etc. In the latter, borrowing has been the rule, not the exception. But I think few will quarrel with my assertion that borrowing from modern critical theory or other literary studies has been exceptional in Bible studies. Why so? What has got in the way?

In the body of this paper I shall argue two theses that may answer that question. My first thesis is that modern Bible critics, whether

Christians, Jews, or unbelievers, have shared a quasi-religious commitment to history. Their belief in the possibility of rendering the Bible historically coherent has seemed distinct from and, privately, often more important than their commitment to any traditional creed. In any event, that belief has been only part of their belief in the larger possibility of rendering an historically coherent account of all reality. I am not aware that any historian has said of history what I. A. Richards in a weak moment said of poetry; namely, that it can "save us." But I submit that something more has been at stake for historians, most particularly for Bible historians, than learning from the past so as not to repeat its mistakes.

If history and literature are rivals for the privilege of saving us, then it is plain with which of the rivals Bible scholarship casts its lot. Bible scholarship as taught and practiced in the best American universities is not skeptical, much less derisive, about the possibility and value of history, and so it finds the mood of modern literature—and by derivation the mood of modern literary theory—which is indeed skeptical and sometimes derisive about history most unlike its own mood.

But the mood is now shifting. Interest in history and skepticism about literary studies are giving way to skepticism about history and interest in literary studies. Bible critics have begun to apostatize from history as a quasi-religion; and as they have done so, they have begun to recognize in the preoccupations of modern poetry, fiction, and literary criticism their own preoccupations. Apostasy from history is by no means reappropriation of traditional Jewish or Christian faith. When Bible historians, however, stare exhausted and defeated at the subject of their study, they are engaged in a contemplation that is, at the least, religiously interesting.

Let us turn now to the promised consideration of ancient and modern editing and see whether and how we may be led thence to the conclusions just stated.

The Bible is arguably unique among the world's religious literatures for the self-consciousness that it displays *vis à vis* editorial processes and their importance. Later Jewish tradition has tended to conceal the Hebrew plural *torah nevi'im uketuvim* ("Law, Prophets, and Writings") beneath the opaque acronym *tanakh* ("Laprow"). Western Christian tradition has lost the Greek plural *biblia* ("Books") in the Latin singular *Scriptura* and vernacular singulars like the English *Bible*. But against this tendency, the separate attributions of separate books within the Bible have not been suppressed; moreover, within a single book—the Book of Psalms, for instance—there may be indications of significantly varying social contexts. Modern scholarship may challenge attributions, make further separations within books traditionally regarded as units, and further specify the contexts. We should bear in mind, however, that the recognition of division and subdivision within the collection was as strong at the beginning as it is now and has survived all efforts at forced harmonization.

In short, a concern with editorial questions of the sort that turn the Good Book into a shelf of books whose goodness varies is not fundamentally alien to the tradition that wrote and has continued to read the Bible. Particular editorial answers may be rejected, but editorial questions are as scriptural as Scripture itself. The very rationalist spirit of modern scholarship has its antecedents in the biblical text to the extent that the multiplication of attributions, glosses, and the like bespeaks a determination that the real raggedness of the collection not disappear wholly into the seamless unity of God. A truly sacralized, hypostatized text, a text turned into a fetish or an idol, could risk no such specificity about its origins. It would have to be—as so many myths are—anonymous and undated. The identification of so many biblical authors has offered critics not just in modern times but from the beginning that many opportunities and more to ask the questions that kept the genealogy of the Bible in view. It is not true, therefore, that the King James Version of the Bible is the only masterpiece ever produced by a committee. The Bible itself is such a masterpiece, a masterpiece of editing that has paraded its editing almost from the start.

In its analysis of editing, its *Redaktionsgeschichte*, contemporary Bible criticism usually assumes the universality of the classical principle *Ars est celare artem*, "Art is the hiding of art." The ancient editors of the biblical texts are assumed to intend—as the editors of a modern work would intend—to conceal their editorial handiwork as much as possible. A work attributed to one man should be made to read as the work of one man. A work purporting to deal with only one subject should be made to deal with that subject alone. A work dealing with times and places should be kept coherent as to chronology and geography. When it is not so, contemporary critics commonly "detect" an inconsistent editorial hand, the implication being that what has now been discovered was not intended for discovery.

Now, I concede that some of the editorial work in the Bible was not intended for discovery. I would point out, however, that the Bible may be most striking among ancient religious writings not for the editorial information it withholds but for the editorial information it provides. If the biblical editors knew so well how to provide information when they chose to, then when they do not, we should not assume that the cause is simple carelessness. It may rather be the operation of another aesthetic principle than *Ars est celare artem*. What is this principle?

Often, the impression the biblical text gives is that of incomplete editing. When two accounts of one event are included, there will often, yes, be an attempt at harmonization, an indication that someone, some editor, was indeed aware that the presence of two accounts constituted a problem. But the harmonization is rarely thoroughgoing. (I say "rarely" because, obviously, when it *is* thoroughgoing, we do not know about it.) It was this sense of incomplete or interrupted editing that led the late William Foxwell Albright to characterize ancient Israelite society as "proto-logical," taking that term to be a midpoint between "pre-logical" and "logical." Ancient Israelite society was neither happily primitive, wholly undisturbed about logical matters, nor yet as careful about them as the Greeks would be and as we are. If the Greek invention of logic was a revolution, then, as Albright saw it, ancient Israel, meaning a culture whose continuity was not broken until A.D. 135, was in a restive, pre-revolutionary state of mind. Our question must be: what aesthetic, if any, was proper to that state of mind?

When a contemporary critic comes across an original composition reflecting a plainly primitive mentality, he is quite content to leave it alone. Indeed, such compositions have their deepest appeal in our day precisely by virtue of their distance from logic. But primitive *editing*—or much worse, half-primitive, half-sophisticated editing—is less respectfully dealt with. Of an editor, even an ancient editor, the modern sensibility demands logic, precisely so that the absence of logic may shine forth at the appropriate moment. There is a chamber of unreason within the modern mind, and the portal opening upon it bears the warning: "Let him who is without logic *and him only* enter here." Accordingly, when a logical mind observes a style of editing that mars a pre-logical literary effect on what may now appear poorly conceived or badly implemented logical grounds, the logical mind is offended and wants to step in. In effect, the contemporary, fully logical critic wants to defend the ancient pre-logical writer against the bad taste of the ancient, partially logical editor.

Until now, Bible criticism has not produced an edition of the Bible purporting to correct all the errors of this order that Bible critics claim to have detected in the work of the ancient Israelite editors. Annotations pointing out the errors, yes, but corrected editions, no. But times may be changing. Doubleday has just published Stephen Mitchell's *Into The Whirlwind*, a translation of the Book of Job from which an ancient editor's addition, the speeches of Elihu, has been excised.[1] The first author or at least an earlier editor doubtless intended us to hear the first words of God in Ch. 38 directly after the last words of Job in Ch. 31. The effect of reading the text in this way is undeniably powerful. But by what right, many would ask, does this modern translator tamper so drastically with a text hallowed by history and by religious tradition? Can he really call such a tampering a translation at all? Is it not rather a

[1]S. Mitchell, *Into the Whirlwind* (New York: Doubleday, 1979).

selection from the Book of Job, or at most a condensation of the Book of Job? The answer, I submit, is that *Into The Whirlwind* is, in the unapologetic contemporary sense, an edition of the Book of Job.

Historical critics of the Bible should not be surpised to see their work used as Mitchell has used it. It is of the essence of critical Bible scholarship to seek to discern a better Bible within the received Bible. Critical commentaries—as they analyze the accidents of physical transmission and seek to undo the effects of cultural oblivion—are all in effect memos to some future, bolder scholar-editor, explaining to him what a true edition of the Bible would require, what portion of the original text he should put in footnotes, what in an appendix, what in the margin, etc., and what, perhaps, he should set in bold type with a dateline as the reconstituted original.

A few years ago, a well-regarded British scholar, Joseph Rhymer, published a translation with commentary entitled *The Bible in Order*, suggesting, plainly enough, that what we had all been reading was the Bible out of order.[2] James Charlesworth, director of the Duke University pseudepigrapha project, has suggested publicly that the canon be revised to include some of the writings his group studies.[3] Written by Jews, preserved by Christians, some of the pseudepigrapha, Charlesworth would maintain, are intrinsically worthy of as much respect as the canonized writings that antedate and postdate them.

If I may digress for just a moment on the subject of the Bible canon, I would point out that there are currently at least four canons in use. The Samaritans reject what the Jews added, the Samaritans and Jews reject what the Christians added, and the Catholics retain what the Protestants subtracted. It is hardly to be ruled out in principle that some further revision in one or more of these canons could take place. The Samaritans could admit the Jewish prophets as apocrypha. The Protestants could admit the present Apocrypha as Scripture. The Jews could canonize the *Pirke Abot*. Catholics and Protestants together could decanonize the Pastoral Letters. To borrow a popular expression that seems quaintly appropriate, the canon as canon is not written in stone.

And let us bear in mind that no less than the redaction of any individual biblical book, the question of the Bible canon as a whole is an editorial question. The layman thinks of the professional editor principally in his involvement with the revision of manuscripts, but revision is a second stage. The first stage is acceptance or rejection. Each editor in a book publishing company has his own list—his canon if you will—which he compiles according to criteria that are usually intuitive

[2] J. Rhymer, *The Bible in Order* (New York: Doubleday, 1975).
[3] J. Charlesworth, in interview in the Memphis *Commercial Appeal* (Dec. 25, 1977) Section F, p. 3.

and certainly never publicized as such. Though no editor troubles to do it, any editor could compile a list of noteworthy rejected books, a secular *Tosefta* of works unpublished or, if published, judged unworthy of a given imprint. Be that as it may, rivalry can arise between the ancient and modern editor over the canon as a whole as easily as it does over the redaction of a given book. If the modern editor can produce a better canon than the ancient editors did, why should he not do so?

Three reactions to the prospect of such radical editing are both possible and coherent. First, one may simply endorse it, as if to say, "This is just the kind of scholarship we need. Now at last we shall see what the intentions of the biblical authors really were." A second reaction is to endorse radical editing only as a stage. Such editing may show us the intentions of the biblical authors as separate agents, but a further act of criticism, it is confidently believed, will show us the intentions of the editors who created the collection as a collection. This I take to be the intent and the hope of *Redaktionsgeschichte*. A third reaction is to reject radical editing as theoretically possible, yes, but out of keeping with the general mission of Bible criticism; namely, that of preserving and promoting the Bible in the form in which it has actually been operative in Western religious and cultural history.

The last reaction, though coherent, is in context an evasion of responsibility. The entire thrust of critical Bible scholarship has been author-based, not reader-based. Religiously orthodox criticism has been, by intent at least, supremely author-based, studying the Bible as the Word of God, not as a mere artifact in the ongoing life of a human community. One may, of course, take the role of the Bible as canonized and influential over time for the object of one's study, but such study is not Bible criticism, strictly speaking, however appealing it may be.

By contrast, the first reaction of the three, that which would simply endorse radical editing, is a good deal more responsible. Radical editing does stand in direct continuity with all that has been most active and most serious in critical scholarship. There can be and possibly will be a good deal more of it than we have seen. The suggestion in it that the leap to *Redaktionsgeschichte* has been hasty may well be a good one. The shocking implications of historical criticism have probably not yet been adequately tasted. We have not yet gazed long enough on the peculiar new Bible that a legion of scholars, each re-constructing a separate portion of the text, has written for us. Radical editing may make that contemplation possible to the enrichment of later criticism. And yet there is an evasion in radical editing too. The ancient editors, particularly the very last editors, who created the collection as a collection, are not to be simply ignored. Responsible criticism must at least ask why those editors included so much that radical editing in our day would drop out.

To ask that question is, of course, to choose the second alternative, *Redaktionsgeschichte*, but let us not minimize the difficulty of this alternative. In reconstructing early stages in the history of a text that has gone through many editings, the critic may always blame confusion on some later stage, some later editorial hand. But when the very last stage is reached, the remaining confusion must be dealt with directly. Did the last editor simply do his work badly? If so, then radical editing is vindicated as we find that there is, yes, a final stage but one that has added nothing but only detracted. Or has the last editor somehow embraced confusion as an aesthetic principle in itself? I shall argue below that the literary experience of our own day should teach us that confusion can be artistically willed. But if the last editors of the Bible were operating on such a principle, if the proto-logical aesthetic allows for willed confusion, the practical consequences for interpretation are considerable. To begin with, how—at such a cultural remove—is the modern interpreter to distinguish artistically willed confusion from mere ignorance or carelessness? If he can do so at all, he surely cannot do so easily. More challenging still, if an artistically willed confusion characterized the last stage, may it not have characterized some earlier stage as well? If so, then *Redaktionsgeschichte* is possible only via a painstaking re-examination of the putatively assured results of all earlier historical criticism.

Of the aesthetic of willed confusion, we shall have more to say later, but that aesthetic is surely familiar enough to require little introduction. It is trite as primitive art in a skyscraper office or a collage of magazine photographs in a high school student's room, as familiar as rapid cutting during the opening seconds of a television police drama or the newscast that gradually drowns out Paul Simon's voice in his recorded version of "Silent Night." The question we must ask is not whether such an aesthetic is possible but why it seems never to have occurred to Bible critics to seek some variant of it in the Bible. Was this a rational conclusion that no such modern aesthetic could operate in an ancient text? I think not.

It was rather the effect of the allegiance of several generations of scholars to history against the claims of religion. The most recent generation of Bible scholars, trained in historical criticism, seems obscurely to know that the fight for the legitimacy of historical against theological criticism has been won. An earlier generation may have had to be alert against the intrusion of theological concerns into historical debate. Today, a more common objection is against the intrusion of prosaic historical concerns into literary appreciation. Or, if it is too much to speak of intrusion, historical criticism is faulted for ineloquence, an invincible blandness in speaking of the literary beauty of Scripture, or the literary quality of it, beautiful or not. The standard works of historical scholarship now seem halting and crude in literary sense, content with generalities that their authors would never countenance in linguistic or historical analysis. Diachronic, historical criticism was to have been a *mise en scène* for synchronic, literary appreciation. But the *mise en scène* seems to have become the performance. Why? And what is to be done?

The notion, sometimes bruited about, of breaking altogether with historical criticism and reading the Bible with fresh literary (or psychological or anthropological) eyes is naiveté of the worst kind. The present state of Bible scholarship, however, may well call for a patient *ad hominem* examination to see whether historical scholars' long struggle with authoritative, even authoritarian, religious interpretation has not left them with attitudes that block or slow literary appreciation. History may have had to become religion to resist religion. If historical critics now abandon their larger ambitions, their solemn responsibilities, then they may perceive a chaos in the Bible that they would once have resisted perceiving. With smaller responsibilities, in other words, Bible scholars may be free to take larger risks. If they do and as they do, the large achievement of a century of coherently pursued Bible scholarship may be further enlarged with what has been most authentically prophetic in the poetry and fiction of our own day.

From the point of view of the religious authorities from whom modern historical critics received the "received text," some of the most famous modern scholars have been outright apostates. One thinks among Christian exegetes of the vilified David Friedrich Strauss, and two generations later, of the celebrated Albert Schweitzer. But apostasy, it must be borne in mind, is a religious vocation of a sort. The Christian church has understood itself to be Christian by its careful preservation of certain memories. In some sense, then, those among the Christians who have been most Christian have been those who were most directly charged with deciding what to remember and what to forget. And as these were editorial decisions, we may say that the text of Scripture and its editors or students have consecrated one another reciprocally. The original editors, by their actions of redaction, exclusion, inclusion, etc., consecrated the text. But thereafter, they—and still more their followers —remained holy by association with the holy text. An apostate critic—a Strauss, a Schweitzer—by bringing a new set of criteria for redaction made by implication a new selection among the memories and provided a new and distinct impulse toward religious community. Some modern historical critics have embraced this vocation freely, others greedily; still others have had it thrust upon them, administering a revelation in spite of themselves. But in the religious context in which they began their work, all have been affected to some extent by this inherent power in their work. As in the Old Testament itself, it is sometimes the unwilling prophet who has the inescapable vocation.

How does an apostate become a prophet? Consider the following speech, written into *Ulysses* by James Joyce, as an address by an Irish patriot defending his language against the imperial claims of English:

> Mr. chairman, ladies and gentlemen: Great was my admiration in listening to the remarks addressed to the youth of Ireland a moment ago by my learned friend. It seemed to me that I had been transplanted into a country far away from this country, into an age remote from this age, that I stood in ancient Egypt and that I was listening to a speech of some high priest of that land addressed to the youthful Moses. . . .
>
> -Why will you Jews not accept our culture, our religion and our language? You are a tribe of nomad herdsmen; we are a mighty people. You have no cities nor no wealth: our cities are hives of humanity and our galleys, trireme and quadrireme, laden with all manner of merchandise, furrow the waters of the known globe. You have but emerged from primitive conditions: we have a literature, a priesthood, an agelong history and a policy. . . .
>
> -But, ladies and gentlemen, had the youthful Moses listened to and accepted that view of life, had he bowed his head and bowed his will and bowed his spirit before that arrogant admonition, he would never have brought the chosen people out of the house of bondage nor followed the pillar of cloud by day. He would never have spoken with the Eternal amid lightnings on Sinai's mountaintop nor ever have come down with the light of inspiration shining in his countenance and bearing in his arms the tables of the law, graven in the language of the outlaw.[4]

Is this a proud or is it a humble speech? Taken as the statement of an Irish patriot, it is proud. Taken as the statement of a speaker of English, a thrillingly eloquent and self-conscious speaker of English, it is humble. The speaker's eloquence is a confession of the pride he has taken in his language, a pride that he recognizes as excessive. His defense of Irish is an act of repentance. That he makes it publicly means he hopes others will follow his lead. Corporate vanity is still vanity. Corporate honesty must begin with one honest individual who, in context, will appear arrogant. It is in this way that the apostate becomes by stages the prophet.

In the passage quoted, the implicit and shocking question is "Why English and not Irish?" even though the speaker knows how large and noble the literature of English is and how small and almost casual the literature of Irish. In the situation we must now consider, the question, as it might be put by a young Jewish historian, an historical critic of the

---

[4]J. Joyce, *Ulysses* (New York: Random House, 1922) 185.

Bible, not arrogant but rather humble on behalf of many, is "Why Moses and not me?"

What is at issue in that question is not respect for Moses. A Jew need not think himself in any personal way superior to Moses to ask the question. Nor for that matter need he ever formulate the question to feel the tension in it. Choosing oneself over Moses is a matter of principle, not of personality: of the principle that all knowledge is subject to real revision and that even the written Torah and the oral Torah together are not adequate for all Jews for all time. It is the suspicion that the Torah, however magnificient, may in principle become a contribution to some larger, later whole, a brick in some subsequent Jewish edifice. This is the alternative criterion that points toward alternative editions of Scripture and ultimately toward alternative structures of memory and community. The sense, however obscure, that such alternatives are opened by historical scholarship is what has left at least some historical critics of the Bible with a paralyzing sense of their own responsibility. An appreciation of the chancy and the chaotic calls for the certain playfulness of spirit. Nothing could be further from the spirit of play than this sense of responsibility.

To normative Judaism, of course, the notion that the Torah is just one noteworthy lawcode among many is what the notion that Jesus is just one admirable human being among many is to normative Christianity. It is heresy and betrayal. The negation of this spirit of revision from the Jewish side is the line from the hymn *Yigdal*, after Deut 34:10: *lōɔ yāqûm kĕmōšeh ᶜôd*: there will not be another Moses, nor will there be a new and improved Torah from a radical Jewish editor more able than *rabbēnû*, "our teacher." The negation of the critical spirit from the Christian side might stand in formulation of the Letter to the Hebrews (13:8): *Iēsous Christos echthēs kai sēmeron ho autos kai eis tous aiōnas:* "Jesus Christ yesterday and today and the same forevermore." I set the Christian attitude toward the permanent significance of Jesus alongside the Jewish attitude toward the permanent significance of the Torah because I think it important to recognize that both of these religious communions are committed to the significance of an unrepeatable past over against all imaginable futures.

Pre-modern Judaism and pre-modern Christianity were concerned with the future. Neither, however, thought that the essential truths of human living were still to be revealed, much less that they were still to be constructed. Though Christianity did intend to revise Judaism, it did not intend to introduce revision itself as a principle. It understood God to have offered mankind a new covenant revising the old covenant with the Jews; but it did not expect its own, new covenant to become obsolete in its turn. Herbert N. Schneidau, in a remarkable work entitled *Sacred Discontent*, does maintain that the principle of endless revision is at the heart of the tradition that began at the burning bush.[5] This principle explains, he says, why Israel begat a Catholic Church, why the Catholic Church begat a Protestantism, Protestantism an Enlightenment, and the Enlightenment a cultural pluralism that so stimulates and exhausts us. Whether or not Schneidau is correct, it certainly is *not* the case that either Judaism or Christianity has publicly celebrated the joy of revision. Both have endured revision, all right; but only in rationalism is revision made something like a sacred principle in its own right.

Because rationalism—the spirit of the Enlightenment—arose in a generally Christian context, it has been natural, I think, for some Jewish traditionalists to think of secular scholarship as Christian; i.e., not to recognize that the rationalist spirit is as opposed to traditional Christian exegesis as to traditional Jewish exegesis. In Chaim Potok's novel *In the Beginning*, David, fresh from his rabbinical ordination, informs his father of a change in his plans:

> "A degree in Bible," I said, speaking English and using the English word. "I want to study Bible." I had already applied to a university, I said. I was waiting for an official answer. But I had been promised acceptance.
>
> . . . I apologized for doing that behind his back. I had felt the need to have it done before I spoke to him, I said.
>
> . . . He waved aside my words with a brusque movement of his arm. "I am not interested in hearing your apology." He leaned forward in the chair. "Tell me what it means to study Bible in a university. Your teachers will be goyim?"
>
> "And Jews."
>
> "The Jews are observers of the commandments?"
>
> "I don't know. They may be. I'm not certain."
>
> "It is unimportant to you that they may not be observers of the commandments? . . . You will study the Torah with goyim and with Jews who are like goyim? What do they know of the Torah?" . . .
>
> I wanted to say, It was beautiful; listening to the voices of the centuries teaching me Torah—that was beautiful. But, Papa, listen. The medieval commentators used the most advanced knowledge of their day to understand the Torah. But they did not have the tools we have today. They did not have anthropology, archeology, comparative religion, linguistics, a true grasp of the texture of history. I do not know what kind of commentaries Rashi, Ibn Ezra, the Ramban, and the others might be writing were they alive today. . . . I wanted to say all that, but I remained silent. . . .
>
> "I could forgive you anything," he said without preliminaries. "But I cannot forgive you going to the goyim to study Torah. Do the goyim come to us to learn their—what do you call it?—New Testament?"[6]

[5]H. Schneidau, *Sacred Discontent, The Bible and Western Tradition* (Baton Rouge: Louisiana University, 1976).

[6]C. Potok, *In the Beginning* (New York: Knopf, 1975) 444.

David's father undoubtedly knows in some notional way that not all goyim are Christians and that many goyim would find laughable the thought that the Christian New Testament belonged to them. When there are fights in Israel between practicing and non-practicing Jews, the *dātîyîm* and the *lō' dātîyîm*, lines are drawn between rationalists and believers: Christianity plays no part. It is only in Europe and America that at least some older Jews manage to see rationalists and Christians as part of one undifferentiated *goyishe THEM* over against the *yiddishe US*.

Potok's David not only avoids this error, he also believes that he can enlist the non-Christian kind of goyishe learning in defense of Jewish tradition. All those things that he wants to tell his father but cannot—about the kind of commentary Rashi would write were he alive today—reflect a trust on the boy's part that rationalism has no religious program of its own. Just as a rationalist may study Judaism without becoming a Jew, so a Jew may study rationalism without becoming a rationalist. Or so David thinks. His father, not without reason, is skeptical. The older man fears that David will start out wanting to be a new Rashi and end up wanting to be a new Moses.

Now, there is a real difference between a Jewish exegete who wants to be a new Rashi, even if he uses modern methods, and one who wants to be a new Moses, just as there is a difference between a Christian exegete who wants to be a new Luther and one who wants to be a new Christ. This difference is the difference between traditional exegesis, beholden to a community and opposed in principle to revision, and non-traditional exegesis, beholden to no community and in favor only of the paradoxical principle of continuous revision. Any philosophical arguments that can be adduced for traditional rabbinic exegesis, beholden to the Jewish community, are likely to serve equally well as arguments for traditional ecclesiastical exegesis, beholden to the Christian church. Luther is the same sort of boast and the same sort of embarrassment to the Lutheran that Rashi is to the Jew. A Jewish scholar who wants to study anthropology, archeology, and other modern disciplines without abandoning Rashi is very like a Christian scholar who might want to study the same disciplines without abandoning Luther. But is such an enterprise in double citizenship possible?

David's father asks him, pointedly, "Do you want to mix Yiddish-keit with goyishkeit? Do you think that will make Yiddishkeit stronger?" But translating this situation into Christian terms, we might just as easily imagine a pious pastor in the Bible Belt asking his college-trained son, "Do you think the Gospel needs your fancy education?" Both young men answer in the affirmative: yes, this will make Yiddishkeit stronger; yes, the Gospel needs my education. Both see the techniques of modern scholarship as just that: techniques. Both imply: we are free to use them; we need not fear that we will be used by them; modern scholarship is a medium that may be made to carry any message, even a traditional one; it has no message of its own.

Against this confidence, we may range the skepticism of the old rabbi and the old pastor, on the one hand, and, on the other, the reverse skepticism of rationalist scholars who believe that the logic of scholarship itself rules out any programmatic interest in the needs of a given religious community. Not long ago, the president of the Society of Biblical Literature made the following statement:

> . . . so-called scientific biblical scholarship, by and large, took up arms against traditionalism in the castle of Sacred Scripture and ended up by occupying the castle itself, while denying that it had done so.[7]

Or in the language we have been using, . . . so-called scientific biblical scholarship, by and large, took up arms against Rashi and Luther in defense of Moses and Jesus and ended by replacing Moses and Jesus with itself, all the while denying that it had done so.

If the only real alternatives are unreformed traditionalism, on the one hand, and, on the other, the kind of scientific scholarship that "takes over," then the implied advice for the devout, whether Jewish or Christian, is to avoid scholarship, as if the optimism of Potok's David were misplaced, as if the young man must inevitably end up doing something he did not intend to do, all the while denying that he had done it.

It may be well to ask at this point just what, on such a pessimistic hypothesis, a young ministerial or rabbinical student is likely to end up doing if he undertakes critical biblical scholarship. I submit that he is likely to end up writing history—and offering his work as a modest contribution to that comprehensive account of reality from its beginning to its end, from its top to its bottom, that history in our day intends to be. The British philosopher R. G. Collingwood, author of both *The Idea of Nature* and *The Idea of History*, regarded our western idea of history as finally including our idea of nature.[8] Nature, as we know now, is not constant. An astrophysicist like Lloyd Motz, author of *The Universe: Its Beginning and Its End*, can provide you the history of a single element; he can tell you when and under what circumstances the element iron first appeared in the universe and when and under what circumstances it will disappear.[9] Relative to the quick changes of a love

---

[7]R. Funk, "The Watershed of the American Biblical Tradition: The Chicago School, First Phase, 1892-1920," *JBL* 95 (1976) 7.

[8]R. G. Collingwood, *The Idea of Nature* (Oxford: Clarendon, 1945); *The Idea of History* (Oxford: Clarendon, 1946).

[9]L. Motz, *The Universe: Its Beginning and Its End* (New York: Scribner's, 1977).

affair, iron seems durable, but it is not immutable: it has a life cycle of a sort. Motz reports that the very scientific laws operative since the Big Bang and until the collapse of matter may obtain only for that interval; i. e., after the next Big Bang, if there is one, there may be an entirely new set of scientific laws. Of such changes, the only sense that can be made is not scientific but historical. The idea of history then, as including all conceivable changes and charting all provisional stabilities for as long as they obtain is our largest, most inclusive idea. As such it is nothing less than an alternative revelation.

Perceiving it as that, we can appreciate the difficulty that faces any contemporary critic who would amend the Bible text on religious grounds but by historical methods; viz., if history taken as a whole is an alternative revelation, then when an editor uses the methods of the historian to improve the Bible, he corrects one revelation by the methods of another. One need not deny that his correction is possible or even, subjectively, a devout act. One must insist, however, that the religion it serves is not the religion that the original editors served. Those ancient editors saw no larger context into which the Bible could be inserted. The context that, by stages, the biblical writers had created—the context that stretched in time from the first day of creation to the Day of the Lord and in space from Jerusalem outward to the Nations—was, literally, the largest context they could imagine. It was the cosmos. To create a larger context would have been then, as it is now, to found a new religion, or at least to challenge, radically, the adequacy of the old. It would be to consecrate a new clerisy of history holy in a new reciprocal relationship with the emerging sacred text of universal history itself. A critic who wished to take his stand with the old clerisy rather than the new might well decline, for that reason, to deal too critically with the text. Pre-critical exegesis has survived and will survive; on its own ground, it has not been defeated by critical exegesis. However, even on its own ground, its self-awareness has been modified by the silent presence of an alternative. Even where it is authoritative still, it exercises its authority in a new way.

But how authoritative, for those who know it best, is this new alternative? I submit that the authority of the historical criticism of the Bible can be no stronger than the authority of history itself in the broadest sense and that history in just that sense, i. e., as a comprehensive, organizing discipline, a field of fields, marshalling the forces of learning, is in trouble. The more Bible critics are skeptical about history, the less aggressively they will be inclined to use the tools that historical criticism has placed at their disposal. I sense that many Bible critics are indeed increasingly skeptical about history, not because of shortcomings in Bible historians themselves but because of what I can only call a mood swing in higher learning. This mood swing affects all higher learning but particularly those fields that are, like history, highly synthetic.

In the recent past, the metaphor that best caught the mood of learning was that of *avant-garde*: a metaphor of direction, landscape, compass, and armies on the march. A far more appropriate and, appropriately, a far more common metaphor today is that of *wavelength*: a metaphor of signal and interference that we hear in such American slang as *tuned in, tuned out, turned on, static, vibrations,* and *on my wavelength*. A given signal plays my whole radio so long as I tune to that signal. Different signals while simultaneously possible for me are not complementary but mutually exclusive. When the organizing metaphor was military and geographic, several avant-gardes could be wonderfully visible to one another: there could be and there were avant-garde art, avant-garde poetry, avant-garde politics, avant-garde child-rearing—all part of the same brave vanguard advancing across the same terrain toward the same retreating enemy. But different frequencies on my FM dial do not relate the way different battalions did in that advancing army. The different battalions of an avant-garde remain elaborately, urgently in touch. Radio stations on different wavelengths act as if each were the only station on the air.

The difference between these two metaphors, I think, points up a crucial skepticism in contemporary thought, a defeated privatization that now affects Bible scholars' confidence in historical criticism. This mood of privatization, I hasten to add, has not been created by radio or TV. Radio as a medium may have its own message. I speak of radio only as a metaphor for a message. For a fuller statement of the same message, I turn to a student of communications theory, Michel Serre.

In his provocative book *Interférence*, this French thinker has written: "We must read interference as inter-reference."[10] But Serre is ironic: he knows that one must also read inter-reference as outright interference, as static. Interdisciplinary cooperation is mutual obstruction, pursued to strained smiles at best. By what intellectual right does any intellectual presume to *situate* another intellectual's work within his own intellectual synthesis! *Situation* bespeaks compass and terrain. But that is the language of the past. One cannot situate one frequency on another frequency. Simultaneously valid, the two are mutually exclusive. Serre writes:

Il n'y aurait pas de science-reine, de théorie des théories en référence à quoi le savoir, dans sa totalité mouvante, dessinerait son arborescence: et comme reine, et comme science. Qui parle bien de l'ordre est dans l'ordre, ou son

---

[10]M. Serre, *L'interférence* (Paris: Les Editions de Minuit, 1972) 157.

langage est mal formé; la science des sciences est l'une d'elles—génitif partitif—ou elle n'est pas science. Une politique.[11]

There is no queen science, no theory of theories in relation to which knowing, in its ongoing totality, would work out its ramifications both as queen and as science. You cannot speak of order without being in the order you speak of. Anything else is misuse of language. The science of sciences is one *of* the sciences—the genitive is partitive—or it is not a science but only politics.

That there is no *science des sciences* but only a kind of politics is another way of announcing the collapse of the nineteenth-century, Hegelian ideal of universal history. The great systematic thinkers of the nineteenth century—Conte, Hegel, Dilthey—did believe that the various disciplines could be assigned their proper places in a common intellectual undertaking. Theology had once been the queen of the sciences, philosophy the *ancilla,* the handmaiden. When philosophy became queen, it was as philosophy of history. Serre describes our day as one in which the proliferation of autonomous scientific and humanistic disciplines has led to the abolition of monarchy itself, as if to cry, "History is dead."

But with the failure of history as universal arbiter, who *is* to mediate conflicting claims among disciplines? Within each discipline, there are those who entertain—as reactionaries, as crypto-monarchists—illicit ambitions. Who is to restrain them? Linguists conquer history by studying the language of history. Historians conquer language by studying the history of linguistics. Philosophers study fiction as philosophy. English professors study philosophers as writers. And so it goes. Whose discipline is properly regarded as most inclusive? The absence of any agreed upon answer to that question is the determining condition of all thought in our day, as of all thoughtful art, and finally of all Bible criticism as well. History is no longer the study to which the various specializations within Bible scholarship all eventually contribute. History is no longer the discipline of choice for an aspiring student of the Bible. There is no discipline of choice, for there is no basis on which to choose. The choice of research paradigm is a matter of faith or whim or, as Serre would have it, of politics.

I submit that, consciously or unconsciously, most Bible scholars have made crucial professional choices for no compelling intellectual reasons. This is not to fault them. Why should they be the exception to so general a rule? The question to ask about them is *ad hominem*; namely, as they grow aware of the arbitrary in their professional, intellectual lives, what is it about the Bible that they are most likely to

[11]Ibid., 20.

notice? I answer: they are likely to see the arbitrary in it, the fragmentary, the contradictory, the accidental, and the stylistically ill-assorted.
I suggest: in some ironic way the Bible scholarship of the future is likely
to celebrate these erstwhile embarrassments.

Why? Well, why is it that poet-prophets of our era like Ezra Pound
have been so drawn to the fragmentary and the unfinished in art and to
the juxtaposition in language of past and present, high culture and low,
sacred and profane? In a remarkable bit of literary sleuthing, Hugh
Kenner explains one example of this fascination in Pound as follows:

> What Sappho conceived on one occasion on Mitylene is gone beyond
> reconstitution; the sole proof that she ever conceived it is a scrap from a
> parchment copy made thirteen centuries later on; on an upper left-hand
> corner learning assisted by chemicals makes out a few letters; in *Berliner
> Klassikertexte*, V-2, 1907, pp. 14-15, type stands for those letters with
> perhaps misleading decisiveness:
>
> > . P 'A[. . .
> > ΔΗΡΑΤ.[. . .
> > ΓΟΓΓΥΛΑ.[. . .
>
> . . . plus the beginnings of perhaps a dozen more lines: very possibly, so
> modern editions indicate, the first aorist of the verb *to raise* (conjecturing
> ἦρα), and a word unknown, and the name of a girl of Sappho's. Or you
> can remember from Alcaeus and Ibycus ἦρ, the contraction for *springtime*,
> and derive the unknown word from δηρός, *too long*, and write
>
> > Spring. . . . .
> > Too long. . . . .
> > Gongula. . . . .
>
> heading the little witticism "Papyrus" and printing it in a book of poems
> called *Lustra* as an exemplum for resurrection-men. And wait decades for
> someone to unriddle it.[12]

Why did Pound write this cryptic poem? Why, having written it, did
he not at least entitle it, "After a fragment in the *Berliner Klassike
Texte*"? Was it really intended only for Kenner or a reader like him? I
think not: I think it was intended equally for all of us, for all the readers
who would *not* understand it. It was given no more informative title
because the author did not wish to inform more than he did. And why
did he write it in the first place? Is the world not full enough of
fragmentation and misinformation and half-truth and puzzlement already? Why add wantonly to the confusion?

The reason why, I think, is that when we are bold enough to create
confusion for our own pleasure, we tell ourselves that the confusion

[12] H. Kenner, *The Pound Era* (Berkeley and Los Angeles: University of
California, 1971) 5-6.

inflicted upon us by circumstances is bearable and even enjoyable. We
tell ourselves that we can defeat it, that we are as tough as it is, that it
doesn't scare us much. After long labors at beating chaos by drawing
order from it, we collapse in exhaustion and then, for the first time, see a
way to beat chaos by embracing a disorderly beauty within it and
creating a manageable, pet chaos of our own. Pound's poem may have
many meanings or none. It is quintessentially the kind of poem that
does not mean but is.

Though redaction criticism has arisen within the historical criticism of the Bible, its implication is that at times the Bible too does not
mean but simply is. The earlier techniques of Bible criticism—source
criticism, form criticism, tradition criticism, etc.—were relentlessly preoccupied with the author and the coherence of his vision. The author
was often anonymous and had to be named after the text he had written.
The critic was, nevertheless, intensely involved with the author and had
implicit faith in his rationality. Poor man, his work may have suffered
at the hands of copyists. It may have been distorted by the addition of
material that conflicted factually with his own. It may have been
stylistically modernized or archaized, added to, subtracted from, violated
in a hundred ways. But a sensitive critic could undo all the damage and
permit the ancient author to speak with his own calm ardor. If there
were two authors, both voices could be heard. If an intervening, harmon-
izing author, three voices. If an inhibiting ideology was detectible, that
too could be assessed. And redaction criticism ultimately could isolate
the elusive point of view—the editorial intent—of the last mind to have
shaped the work before its transmission became a matter of copying. But
in the search for this last elusive working, I submit that the reasonability
of historical criticism as a whole has to be reappraised.

It must be so because, as noted earlier, when the last redaction is
reached, there is no longer any later editor on whom to blame remaining
inconsistencies. The redactor may seem to be motivated by a concern for
surface smoothness in conflated texts—but only sometimes: sometimes
he cares more about reverence for received accounts, no matter how
many or how badly at variance with each other. Or a theological bias
may control him—but not at every point. Or a political allegiance—but
only residually. When such inconsistency is discovered in a supposed
written document or an oral tradition, it can be blamed on the redactor.
But if in the end the remaining inconsistencies must be simply accepted
as unexplainable, then one must object: why could the same inconsistencies not be accepted on the same basis at some earlier stage?

How odd it is to reflect that during the same decades when American and British Bible scholarship was so determinedly naming the
anonymous writers of the Bible, our own vernacular poetry was in

headlong pursuit of anonymity. In the "New Criticism," now no longer new, the text was to stand alone, as if authorless, a brute fact of language. If there were abrupt changes of voice or mood in it, these were all part of it and were not to be gainsaid by any reference to an author and his delicate intentions. The appeal that the Bible continued to have for the poets of that generation owed much to the ancient redactors' failure quite to eliminate the rough, the abrupt, the quizzical, the *hapax legomena*, the pointlessly repetitive, the unglossed and unglossable, the impenetrable. And thus the question arises now: if our best poets were so taken with this editorial failure, can we be sure it was a failure?

Owen Barfield has spoken of early man's sense of oneness with the cosmos as "original participation" and of the sense of oneness to which contemporary man may aspire as "final participation." But language is a part of the cosmos, a physical thing of throats and tongues and teeth and tympana. Final participation must include reacquaintance with all that. The shift of attention in recent poetry from poetic intention to verbal fact seems calculated to get this reacquaintance under way. The brain, after all, is a physical thing, and recent writers have listened to their own brains as a man might listen to his own pulse, palpate his eyeballs beneath their lids, or know the noise of his own excretion. We are all familiar, at least by report, with eastern meditation techniques in which the purposeful, organizing portion of the mind is neutralized by being assigned a topic without content: a nonsense syllable, the sound of one's breathing, or an unanswerable riddle. I submit that the parade of images, memories, etc., that occurs in meditation is a physical, participative experience of the brain. I can touch my hand when I am not using it. This is how I "touch" my brain.

And, when a Joyce writes in the stream of consciousness or an Eliot splices together passages from crazily assorted sources, it is to this that they invite their readers. This is physical participation in the experience of being an intelligent animal, both intelligent and an animal. But again, ancient texts, notably the Hebrew Bible, often create a similar splicy effect. Doubtless we are right to assume that the ancient author was not striving, as Eliot and Joyce were, for spliciness as such. But *unconscious does not mean unfelt.* An ancient redactor may not have sought the jarring and the truncated the way some modern poets have, and yet his tolerance of it may have been artistically motivated. That it didn't bother him enough for him to eliminate it must mean that to some extent, he simply liked it. Paul Ricoeur is celebrated for coining the phrases "first naiveté" and "second naiveté" for the interpretation of myth. But for Bible interpretation, I prefer Barfield's "final participation," extended now to cover the primitive flow of the Bible's language and the half-intended disarray of its contents.

The very last thing I want to suggest is that poets are the unac-
knowledged legislators of the race or that artists are theorists of nature.
Artists have a job to do like everybody else. Sometimes changes in mood
that eventually will touch everyone actually touch them last. In this
particular case, however, I do believe that modern poets felt first something that contemporary Bible critics are only now about to feel. It is the
critics' inability to imagine an aesthetic of disorder, or of deliberately
mingled order and disorder, that may separate them most sharply from
the ancient writers and editors they study. As they acquire this ability,
perhaps by relinquishing what in modern times has been their quasi-
religious vocation, they may find that they have less taste for the
harmony and smoothness that historical scholarship would impose on
the text. This is a matter of taste, but I think it a matter of great
consequence too.

Let me now bring this paper to a conclusion by reflecting briefly on
a line from Montesquieu which the Catholic theologian Hans Urs von
Balthasar invokes in his study of the Protestant theologian Karl Barth.
The line is: "The Catholic religion will destroy the Protestant religion,
and then Catholics will become Protestants."[13] If by the Catholic religion, one understands that form of Christianity that set human authority,
the church, over scriptural authority, then it is plain how the Catholic
religion has now destroyed the Protestant religion. The Protestant
principle of solā Scripturā, "By Scripture alone," that led to the modern
critical study of Scripture has now concluded that what lies behind the
Bible text at every point is not a revelatory event but a believing
community. Those ancient editors, those ancient redactors, those ancient
canonizers—they were, after all, a very human authority. That the
critical methods that sought to exalt Scripture have ended by exalting
these editorial nobodies, these ancient anonymities, is in archetypal
terms a victory for Catholicism over Protestantism.

Though Montesquieu did not have Bible criticism in mind, I fancy
that in his sly, rationalist way he did foresee that the Protestants,
however ardent they were in his day, would in the end despair of the
attempt to obey God directly and would create an intermediate human
authority as cold and scandalous as the papacy. In other words, he saw
that rationalism was inevitable in religion and that Catholicism, earlier
and worse infected with rationalism, was thereby the wave of the future.
Matthew Arnold paid the Church of Rome the same oblique compli-
ment in a comment on Pope Pius IX, the nineteenth-century pope
whose Vatican Council defined the doctrine of papal infallibility:

[13]H. U. von Balthasar, *Karl Barth: Darstellung und Deutung seiner Theologie* (Koeln: Hegner, 1951) 29-30.

The infallible Church Catholic is, really, the prophetic soul of the wide
world dreaming on things to come; the whole race, in its onward progress,
developing truth more complete than the parcel of truth any momentary
individual can seize. Nay, even that amiable old pessimist in St. Peter's
Chair, whose allocutions we read and call them impotent and vain,—the
Pope himself is, in his idea, the very Time-Spirit taking flesh, the
incarnate "Zeit-Geist"! O man, how true are thine instincts, how overhasty
thine interpretations of them![14]

Catholicism was an offense to Protestantism because of the way in
which the popes seemed to make up their Christianity as they went
along, but obviously, this was no special offense to rationalism, which
was convinced in any event that *all* religions were made up by men as
they went along. There was, in effect, a pope lurking in the bushes of
even the most primal, archetypal religion. There was no escaping him
because there was no escaping the scandal of human responsibility for
human behavior, even in religion.

Catholicism, I hardly need add, has never laid claim to first honors
in acknowledged rationalism. Views tending very delicately in this
direction were condemned by Rome in the Modernist controversy at the
turn of the nineteenth century. For two generations, every Catholic
priest had to take a formal oath against Modernism before his ordination. But centuries earlier, the French priest Richard Simon, sometimes
called the father of Pentateuch criticism for his separation of the
Yahwist and Elohist styles, had written:

> Si l'Écriture & la Tradition venoient également de Dieu, comme les Juifs
> prétendent, on devroit sans doute préférer la Tradition, qui explique
> nettement les Mystères, à un Texte qui est rempli d'obscurités & d'équi-
> voques.[15]

> If Scripture & Tradition come equally from God, as the Jews claim, then
> one must surely prefer Tradition, which explains the Mysteries clearly, to a
> text which is full of obscurity and equivocation.

And elsewhere:

> Les Catholiques, qui sont persuadés que leur Réligion ne depend pas
> seulement du Texte de l'Écriture, mais aussi de la Tradition de l'Église, ne
> sont point scandalisés de voir que le malheur des tems & la négligence des
> Copistes ayent apporté des changemens aux Livres Sacrés, aussi bien

---

[14]M. Arnold, *Literature and Dogma* (Boston: Osgood, 1873) xxxv-xxxvi.
[15]Cited in D. Knight, *Rediscovering the Traditions of Israel* (Missoula: *SBL*,
1973) 50 n. 10.

qu'aux Livres profanes. Il n'y a que des Protestans préoccupés ou ignorans
qui puissent s'en scandaliser.[16]

The Catholics, who are persuaded that their religion does not depend on
the text of Scripture alone but also on the Tradition of the Church, are not
at all scandalized to see that the misfortunes of time and the negligence of
copyists have brought about alteration in Sacred Books as well as in
profane. Only anxious or ignorant Protestants could be scandalized at such
a thing.

Simon's words could have been prophetic for Catholicism. They were
not. He was silenced. They remain prophetic, however, for Bible criticism today.

In what sense now can it be said that, the Catholic religion having
destroyed the Protestant, Catholics will become Protestants? In this
sense: Catholic and Protestant Bible scholars alike, having become
rationalist historians, will now become Protestants *vis à vis* history. The
aspirations of history to comprehensive, harmonious explanation—to a
full and final accounting—are exposed for them in redaction criticism in
a way that they have not been exposed earlier. This exposure, on the one
hand, and that new and general skepticism to which I earlier alluded, on
the other, are an invitation to something new, a new appreciation,
foreshadowed perhaps in some modern literature. And Jewish Bible
scholars, to the extent that they too have become believers in history,
will also break with the old faith. As (I think) Heine put it, *Wie es sich
christelt, so jüdelt es sich.*

The very broadest sweep of Western thought has been from cosmology to epistemology and now, hesitantly, back to cosmology again; or if
you will, from the object to the subject and now back to the object. Pre-
critical exegesis took the Bible almost as a natural fact. Critical exegesis,
preoccupied with religious subjectivity, took it as an historical fact and
sought to expose the complex human intent behind it. Post-critical
exegesis may take it again as a natural fact just as post-modern thought
takes the human being himself as a natural fact. The language of man,
written or spoken, is like his spoor, his scent, his gait, his distinctive
laughter—a part of the natural reality of him. It was by remembering
this about language, by feeling again the way it felt in the mouth—Yeats
said of one of his poems, "I made it of a mouthful of air"—that the great
poets of this century are guides to the Bible.

The Bible as we have it is messy. Should we clean up the mess?
Cleanliness is next to Godliness, a British and American proverb claims.
The Boy Scout promise (one recalls that the Scouts began in England) is:
"On my honor I will do my best to do my duty to God and my country,

---

[16]Ibid., n. 9.

to be clean, and to obey the Scout Oath." [Emphasis added.] In this spirit, should we clean up the biblical mess?

I do not mean to mock the impulse to cleanliness. All science owes much to it. But the best modern literature reminds us that life is not science and that literature, made of life, cannot ever be as clean as science would have it. The cosmos, it seems to claim, is finally messy. One who believes in a messy cosmos may find a messy Hebrew text oddly cosmetic. Science is most often a matter of solving the puzzle, but literature, like religious faith, is a matter of being drawn into the game. I take it that this was one of Kierkegaard's objections against Hegel. It may also be the correction that literary sensibility may provide to historicist criticism of the Bible.

The questions that arise about writing are as endless as the questions that arise about man—and as legitimate in their endlessness. The critical attempt to answer them will not be called off. New critical editions of the Bible in the radical sense earlier indicated may begin to appear and may well be the crown of critical scholarship. But there may also grow up around that critical enterprise something like what has begun to grow up around critical scholarship in other kinds of literature; namely, an accompanying, postcritical love for the physical and accidental and primitive beauty of the thing, this Bible thing, a love that leaves the critic no less free to improve the text but slightly more inclined to enjoy it as it is.

Searching for the Origins of God

CONRAD E. L'HEUREUX
UNIVERSITY OF DAYTON

INTRODUCTION

THIS essay has two principal parts. The first traces the historical developments in the early religion of Israel which resulted in the understanding of God which came to prevail in the Bible. The second part raises questions about the theological implications of the prior investigation. One way of formulating the relationship between the two parts would be to say that the first is historical while the second is theological. Since, however, the kind of history involved is precisely the history of religious and theological ideas, there is a sense in which even the first part is theological. A helpful way of expressing these relationships is provided by the terminology employed by K. Stendahl in a well known discussion of biblical theology.[1] He suggested that the study of theology involves two stages which he labeled "descriptive" and "normative." A descriptive analysis is one in which the scholar leaves behind his own theological convictions and attempts to *describe* as accurately and objectively as possible the theological and religious ideas of other persons. Naturally, in the study of ancient religions, the descriptive phase of work is primarily a historical investigation. In the normative phase, on the other hand, one consciously brings in one's own theological convictions in order to evaluate, criticize, accept, modify, or reject the concepts which have come to light as a result of the descriptive analysis. In other words, whenever one begins to *interpret* the material within the framework of a living contemporary world view—whether or not it is explicitly religious—one has started to make normative statements.

Although the descriptive part of this paper deals with quite specific questions, the problems of normative reflection which arise are similar to those which might emerge from the study of other issues in the wider field of biblical studies. The specific area chosen for descriptive analysis was selected because it is one in which significant and creative work has been done by Prof. Frank M. Cross, Jr., whom the contributors to this volume hope to honor by their participation. Moreover, the material

---

[1] K. Stendahl, "Biblical Theology, Contemporary," *IDB* 1 (1962) 418-32.

under review raises the normative theological problems in a particularly acute fashion.

It will also be noticed that the second part of the article is more tentative and less amply documented than the first part. This is because scholarship in this field of study has concentrated almost exclusively on descriptive analysis and has only rarely ventured into the normative questions. There are several reasons for this imbalance. For one thing, concentration on descriptive study has made it possible for a great deal of progress to be made within an inter-faith perspective. Scholars with widely differing religious beliefs—even with no religious beliefs at all— are able to exchange ideas within a common forum and in a relatively peaceful and amicable way as long as the normative issues are not raised. It may also be that the desire of scholars in biblical studies (or religious studies in general) to demonstrate to the rest of the university community that they are engaged in a legitimate and respectable academic pursuit promotes concentration on the descriptive phase which gives a greater appearance of "scientific objectivity." Finally, since the implications of this kind of research sometimes appear to threaten traditional religious concepts, a scholar's reluctance to become embroiled in controversy may hamper the fuller discussion of the issues. It perhaps seems safer and more comfortable to deal with rarefied descriptive problems and to keep one's normative reflections private.

Whatever the reasons for the relative neglect of normative theological discussion in current scholarship, it is quite paradoxical that one can listen for many hours to discussions of such topics as God, the purpose of human existence, and the relation of the individual to society and to the cosmos, without having the least notion of the speaker's own views on these subjects. The second part of this paper intends to make a modest contribution towards making up for this deficiency. Perhaps it will stimulate others to do more.

PART ONE

THE HISTORY OF ISRAELITE YAHWISM

Before venturing into our topic, which is part of the history of the religion of Israel, it is appropriate to comment briefly on the broader area of the history of Israel. The principal source for that history continues to be the Hebrew Bible, even though much help comes from comparative materials, especially those unearthed by the archaeologist and coming from the same historical and geographical context as the Bible itself. When a historian uses ancient documents for the reconstruction of history, the first step is to understand the nature of those documents in order to judge what kind of useful information, if any, is contained in them. It is especially true for the earliest history of Israel that the records we have are not purely objective contemporary records. In other words, even the so-called historical books of the Hebrew Bible do not contain the kind of history which is the concern of the modern historian. This means that the use of the biblical material by the historian is absolutely dependent upon the prior *literary* problem of the Bible.[2] This involves questions such as the date of composition of each relevant unit, the identification of the type of literature to which it belongs, an understanding of the prejudices and preconceptions of the author of the material, the pre-literary history of traditional materials, etc. It is obviously impossible even to summarize the results of such study in this essay. Nevertheless, it will be helpful to mention some general tendencies which are particularly important for the problem we are addressing.

For the period which begins with the monarchy, the Bible contains a great deal of reliable historical information. For the early periods, the biblical traditions have definitely preserved historically important information; however, this information was very heavily subjected to theological interpretation at a later period. One of the most significant processes involved was the generalization of historical experiences which befell small groups so that they were reinterpreted as having been experienced by all Israel. A helpful and frequently used analogy to this process is the ideology accompanying Thanksgiving Day in America. A broad spectrum of Americans feel free to say that they celebrate this holiday in continuity with "our ancestors" the pilgrims who came over on the Mayflower and found freedom from persecution in a land of abundance and opportunity. Many persons are able to identify with this story even though it deviates from the facts of "scientific" history. They identify with the story because it is analogous to the experience of their own "real" ancestors and because it richly symbolizes the feelings they have about their country.

The realization that the history of Israel as presented in the Bible is a *construct* which simplifies the actual course of events is based upon internal biblical evidence as well as comparison with the way in which national and religious traditions develop and grow in other cultures which can be studied more directly. The end product of this process was a "history" which was thought to have begun with Abraham and his son

---

[2]A good introduction to the various methodologies employed by contemporary scholarship may be found in a series entitled "Guides to Biblical Scholarship. Old Testament Series," published by Fortress Press. The following volumes in the series are now available: *Literary Criticism of the Old Testament*, by N. Habel; *Form Criticism of the Old Testament*, by G. Tucker; *Tradition History and the Old Testament*, by W. Rast, *The Historical-Critical Method*, by E. Krentz; and *The Old Testament and the Historian*, by J. M. Miller.

Isaac, continued in the latter's son Jacob (also named Israel), who had twelve sons, each of whom was the ancestor of one of the twelve tribes. These tribes are said to have migrated to Egypt as a result of the experiences of Joseph and, after having become slaves, were led out by Moses, entered into covenant with God at Mt. Sinai, wandered in the wilderness forty years, and were finally led to invade and occupy the promised land in the time of Joshua. The creation of this "national history" involved a process of simplification in which the experiences of smaller groups were selected, because of their symbolic power, and generalized as the experience of all Israel. The early history of Israel, therefore, was far more complex than the biblical record lets on. This is recognized by all modern historians of Israel, though they vary in the degree to which they are willing to depart from the construct which became canonical.[3] This means that the biblical genealogy which sees each Israelite as the descendant of a tribal ancestor who was one of the twelve sons of Jacob (Israel), the son of Isaac, the son of Abraham, must be regarded as artificial. So if one is to insist upon *biological* kinship as the sole parameter of truth, the family tree of Israel must be regarded as fictional. Anthropological research suggests, however, that in the formation of clans and tribes it is the *experience* of kinship which counts as real and a genealogy "constructed" on that basis seems false to us only because of the prejudices inherent in the modern outlook on reality.

A consequence of the above is that we can not really speak of a history of Israel until the time of the Judges. It is at that time that there existed a confederation of tribes jointly designated "Israel" and commonly committed to the worship of the God Yahweh as their patron. Before that time we can speak only of a variety of pre-Israelite groups, that is, groups which would eventually merge to form the entity we call Israel. This general observation concerning the history of Israel also applies to the history of Israelite religion. The understanding of God which became canonical and authoritative in ancient Israel must be understood as a fusion of different religious concepts with different sources and originally transmitted by different groups of pre-Israelites.

There are, in the Hebrew Bible, a variety of names used for God. One of these, the name Yahweh, appears to be unique to Israel. The Bible uses this name only in reference to the one God it recognizes. The other names have exact or approximate correspondances in the cognate

---

[3]The two standard histories most widely used today are J. Bright, *A History of Israel* (2d ed.; Philadelphia: Westminster, 1972) and M. Noth, *The History of Israel* (2d ed.; New York: Harper & Row, 1960). Bright tends to follow the canonical history unless there is strong evidence against it. Noth exhibits much greater freedom in this regard. A useful survey of the many divergent schools of thought may be found in *Israelite and Judaean History* (ed. J. H. Hayes and J. M. Miller; Philadelphia: Westminster, 1977).

languages. In some cases, for example the word ʾĕlōhîm, the Bible itself recognizes that the term can be applied to other gods. That is, ʾĕlōhîm can be either "God," "a god," or "gods." Of all the pre-Israelite religious concepts which entered into the biblical tradition, it is the Yahweh concept which predominated and absorbed all the others. The descriptive task which lies before us, therefore, is to analyze the process in which the various theological ideas merged under the dominance of the Yahweh tradition to result in the canonical understanding of God. The general model implied in this study is that of a number of streams flowing together and merging to form the canonical understanding of Yahweh.

The starting point for the modern discussion of the early religion of Israel is a study published in 1929 by the distinguished German scholar Albrecht Alt.[4] He argues that, although the J materials in Genesis regularly use the name Yahweh in referring to God, the actual history of Yahweh worship is more accurately reflected in the P and E sources, especially at Exod 3:13-15 and 6:2-3.[5] In these two texts, it is made clear that the name Yahweh was unknown to the Israelite ancestors before the time of Moses. In fact, the authors of these passages thought it was very important to *insist* that Yahweh was identical with the God worshipped by the Patriarchs. There would not have been the need to insist upon this identity if it had been an obvious fact. In other words, these passages strongly suggest that a significant religious change occurred in the time of Moses, a change which might have appeared to involve a new God and therefore elicited from Israel's theologians an insistence upon continuity with the past.

If the religion of the Patriarchs did not involve the worship of Yahweh, then of what did it consist? Alt found, in the stories of the Patriarchs preserved in the book of Genesis, two types of reference to the deity which are relatively rare in the rest of the Bible. He then took these as the real clues to the pre-Yahwistic religion of Israel's forebears.

The first type of reference to the deity is the "god of the fathers" type where the deity is not given a name but is identified by reference to the ancestor who worshipped him. We can speak of two subtypes here. In sub-type (a) the ancestor is not named: "the God of my/thy/your/ his/their father," Gen 26:24; 28:13; 31:5, 29, 42, 53; 32:10 (*bis*); 42:23; 46:3; 47:1; 49:25; 50:17; Exod 3:6; 15:2; 18:4.[6] In sub-type (b), on the other

---

[4]A. Alt, "The God of the Fathers," *Essays on Old Testament History and Religion* (Garden City, N.Y.: Anchor Books, 1966) 1-100.

[5]Readers not familiar with the meaning of the symbols J, E, D and P will find a brief introduction in the book by Habel mentioned in note 2.

[6]Some of the examples listed here are combinations with sub-type (b), viz., "God of my/his father Abraham/Isaac/Jacob," Gen 32:10 (*bis*) and Gen 46:1; "God of Abraham thy father," Gen 26:24 and 28:13.

hand, the name of the ancestor is given: "God of Abraham," Gen 31:42, 43; "God of Isaac," Gen 28:13; "the Fear of Isaac," Gen 31:42; "God of Nahor," Gen 31:53; "Bull of Jacob," Gen 49:24. The fullest formula, "The God of Abraham, the God of Isaac, the God of Jacob," in Exod 3:6, 15, 16; 4:5, appears to be a later development.

Alt compared this material with Palmyrene and Nabataean inscriptions from roughly 100 B.C. to 400 A.D. The inscriptions in question frequently refer to gods by using the formula "God of PN," where PN is a person's name. The person named would have been the first person to whom this god, who was himself anonymous, had revealed himself. Alt took the evidence of these inscriptions as providing an exact parallel to the religion of the Patriarchs. A god who was otherwise anonymous revealed himself to a clan leader or ancestor. The ancestor, then, could be understood as the founder of that particular cult. The only name the god had was "God of PN," and this is how he was remembered by the descendants of the cult-founder who understood this particular deity as the patron of their clan or tribe. Alt believed that this religious type belonged explicitly to a nomadic way of life which he thought characterized the early Nabataeans as well as the Patriarchs. The clan god, having a special relationship with the community, guided them in their day to day lives and especially in the wanderings characteristic of nomadism.

Alt's reconstruction has been very widely accepted, though with some important correctives. Archaeology has produced other texts which come from a time closer to that of the Patriarchs.[7] On the basis of these texts, it has been insisted by Prof. Cross, among others, that the "god of the fathers" was by no means anonymous but could in fact be identical with one of the great gods who were worshipped in the temples and about whom stories were told in the myths. The importance of this point will become apparent below. In spite of minor reservations, it must be acknowledged that Alt made a very important contribution by discovering that the type of religion associated with the god of the fathers was one of the important streams which entered into the biblical understanding of God.[8]

The second type of reference to God pointed out by Alt consisted of two or more words, the first of which was the Hebrew word ʾēl. In contrast to the god of the fathers type, the El-deities appeared to be linked with specific places: El-roi at Beer-lahai-roi (Gen 16:13); El Olam at Beersheba (Gen 21:33); El-elohe-Israel at Shechem (Gen 33:20); El

[7] J. Lewy, "Les textes paléo-assyriens et l'Ancien Testament," RHR 110 (1934) 29-65; H. Hirsch, "Gott der Väter," AfO 21 (1966) 56-58.

[8] The gods of the fathers may be placed within a larger religious context by comparing them with the so-called "personal god" in Mesopotamia. A large sampling of the relevant material is found in H. Cazelles, "Patriarches, V. La religion des Patriarches," DBSup 7 (1966) 141-56.

Bethel at Bethel (Gen 31:13; 35:7; cp. Gen 28:10-22); El Elyon at Jerusalem (Gen 14:19, 22). El Shadday (RSV: "God Almighty") is not geographically limited, but this seems to be the result of the P author's desire to select one name as characteristic of the whole patriarchal period.

The exact significance of each of these names, and hence its translation, is open to a variety of interpretations. The element ᵓēl is very widely documented in the Semitic languages with the meaning "god." An expression like ᵓēl ᶜôlām, therefore, might be either "the god Olam," or "the eternal god." In any case Alt assumed in his work of 1929 that the whole group of El names referred to local numina, that is, minor deities each of which was the "spirit" of a particular place and whose worship was confined to that place. Shortly after the publication of Alt's work, the newly discovered texts from Ras Shamra (ancient Ugarit) on the coast of Syria, were successfully deciphered. Some of these texts, written in a language which is closely related to biblical Hebrew, have a bearing on the significance of ᵓēl. The documents in question were written about 1400 B.C., though they contain religious traditions several centuries older than that. In these texts, the word ᵓilu, which corresponds to Hebrew ᵓēl, does indeed occur with the meaning "god." Far more frequently, however, it stands as the proper name of the god El. This El is the creator, father of gods and men, and head of the Ugaritic pantheon.[9] These texts from Ugarit, therefore, open the possibility, if not the likelihood, that the word ᵓēl in the divine names studied by Alt, refers to the high god El. In that case, ᵓēl ᶜôlām would mean "El, the Eternal One." Among the ᵓēl-names listed above, one at least, ᵓēl ᵓĕlōhê yiśrāᵓēl, appears to be grammatically unambiguous and must be translated "El, the God of Israel." Prof. Cross has argued that some of the other terms used in the ᵓēl-names (ᶜôlām, ᶜelyôn and šaddāy) are particularly appropriate from what we know of El.[10]

When Alt's analysis is viewed in the light of the Ugaritic texts, therefore, it becomes apparent that the El traditions constitute a second major stream which merged with others to produce the biblical understanding of God. This view is confirmed when one looks beyond the patriarchal stories of Genesis, for there are a number of other indications

[9] The two principal works on El are O. Eissfeldt, *El im ugaritischen Pantheon* (Berlin: Akademie, 1951) and M. Pope, *El in the Ugaritic Texts* (Leiden: Brill, 1955). A critique of some aspects of Pope's work is found in my *Rank among the Canaanite Gods: El, Baᶜal, and the Rephaᵓim.* (HSM 21; Missoula: Scholars, 1979) 3-93.

[10] Cross first published his views in "Yahweh and the God of the Patriarchs," *HTR* 55 (1962) 225-59. That article is revised and updated in *Canaanite Myth and Hebrew Epic* (Cambridge: Harvard University, 1973). See also his article "אל," *TWAT* 1 (1973) 259-79.

of the presence of El traditions within the Bible. For example, when the Hebrew word ʾēl, identical with the name of the Canaanite god El, is used to refer to Yahweh, there is no suggestion that such usage is theologically ambiguous or suspect. There are also a number of characteristics which are shared by Yahweh and El: each is said to be creator and father,[11] he is old and wise,[12] patient and merciful,[13] and eternal king.[14] Both Yahweh and El are described as head of the council of the gods who assigns patron deities to the nations.[15] They are both called "bull," and the connection between El and the bull may lie behind the imagery of the golden calf in the Bible. It has also been suggested that the traditions of the wilderness tent (ʾōhel môʿēd) may be derived from the tent in which El dwelled, and that the description of Yahweh as a warrior may be connected with El traditions which differed in emphasis from those preserved at Ugarit.[16] Finally, a recent study suggests that theological concepts linked to ʾēl were responsible for the development of a universalistic perspective within the Bible,[17] thus confirming the extraordinary influence which the cult of El has had on the biblical understanding of God.

In addition to the god of the fathers concept and the El concept, scholars have generally presupposed that there was one other major source of input flowing into the biblical mainstream and producing the canonical understanding of God. That was, of course, the Yahweh tradition. Here one must at least allow for the possibility that this Yahweh tradition had a history of its own *before* it was merged with the other two traditions we have discussed. We can thus speak of a primitive or pre-canonical Yahweh tradition which had not as yet been affected by

[11]Most striking is the parallel between *ṯr ʾil ʾabh ʾil mlk d yknnh*, "Bull El his father, King El who created him," of CTA 3.5.43; 4.1.5; 4.4.47; and *hălôʾ hûʾ ʾābîkā qānekā hûʾ ʿāśěkā wayěkōněnekā*. "Is he not thy father who created thee, he formed thee into being"? of Deut 32:6.

[12]For El see *CTA* 10.3.6; 4.4.41; 3.5.38; 4.5.66. Compare biblical ʾēl gibbôr ʾăbî ʿad in Isa 9:5 and the "ancient of days," in Dan 7:9.

[13]A standard epithet of El is *lṭpn ʾil dpʾid*, "the kind one, the god of mercy." Compare Exod 34:6.

[14]The title *mlk ʿlm*, "Eternal King," is applied to El in *Ug* 5 2.1. The identical title is applied to Yahweh at Jer 10:10 and Ps 10:16. For a discussion of the Ugaritic text, see *Rank among the Canaanite Gods* 169-81.

[15]For a summary of the evidence with further bibliography, see R. J. Clifford, *The Cosmic Mountain in Canaan and the Old Testament* (HSM 4; Cambridge: Harvard University, 1972) 42-48.

[16]R. J. Clifford, "The Tent of El and the Israelite Tent of Meeting," *CBQ* 33 (1971) 221-27, and P. D. Miller, "El the Warrior," *HTR* 60 (1967) 411-31.

[17]J. Blommendaal, *El als fundament en als exponent van het oudt-testamentisch universalisme* (Utrecht: Elinkwijk, 1972). See also my review of this book in *CBQ* 37 (1975) 240-42.

the god of the fathers concept or the El concept. The origin of this primitive Yahweh tradition may be thought of in two ways. First, it might be strictly limited to Israel and have arisen from the unique historical and religious experiences of either an individual (e.g., Moses), or of a group (e.g., the Exodus group). On the other hand, these primitive Yahweh traditions might have been taken over or borrowed from a non-Israelite source. In line with the second possibility, one must give serious consideration to the proposal that the name Yahweh and the basic religious ideas associated with that name were taken over by Moses from his Kenite or Midianite in-laws. The fact that it was precisely while in the territory of the Midianites or Kenites that Moses received the revelation from Yahweh (Exodus 3), that his father-in-law (rather than Moses or Aaron) offers a sacrifice to Yahweh (Exod 18:10-12), and that a place named after Yahweh appears to have existed in the vicinity of the Midianite domain long before the time of Moses, all point in this direction.[18]

The attempt to define and characterize this primitive Yahwism is extremely difficult for two reasons. First, unlike the situation regarding the god of the fathers and the cult of El, we have no extra-biblical sources which could help us understand what this primitive Yahwism was like. Secondly, as far as the Bible itself is concerned, it has combined the various streams which flowed into its concept of God with Yahweh as the principal and unifying factor which absorbed everything else. Therefore the picture of Yahweh which became canonical is a composite, and there is no simple way of sorting out which features of the biblical Yahweh were characteristic of the primitive Yahwism whose existence we have postulated. We can probably assume that, in addition to the name Yahweh itself, the terror-inspiring aspect reflected in passages such as Exod 19:16-25 is an original Yahweh feature which contrasts sharply with the character of both El and the god of the fathers. In addition it seems plausible that the "jealousy" of the biblical God, that is, his unwillingness to tolerate the worship of other gods alongside himself, is a feature of primitive Yahwism. Finally, it is not unlikely that the Bible has accurately remembered the historical development by associating the introduction of Yahweh with the time of Moses and with a specific geographical setting: Mt. Sinai.

We have seen that the tendency in contemporary scholarship is to understand the biblical concept of God as the result of a merging of

---

[18]For a discussion of the evidence supporting the Kenite hypothesis, see H. H. Rowley, *From Joseph to Joshua* (London: Oxford University, 1950) 148-63. The place name in question is discussed by R. de Vaux, "The Revelation of the Divine Name YHWH," *Proclamation and Presence* (ed. J. I. Durham and J. R. Porter; Richmond: John Knox, 1970) 48-75.

three major streams of religious tradition: the god of the fathers type of
religion, the cult of Canaanite El, and a primitive form of Yahwism. But
exactly how did these three streams come to merge? A variety of pro-
posals have been made. In these reconstructions, differing degrees of
significance have been assigned to the various contributing streams.
Victor Maag, for example, deemphasized the El traditions while stressing
the god of the fathers concept which he found similar in important
respects to the primitive conception of Yahweh. The merging of the god
of the fathers with Yahweh, in his view, took place in two stages. First,
in the pre-Exodus period, at least one tribe had already combined the
god of the fathers with Yahweh who was the unpredictable and earth-
shaking God of Sinai who produced the thunder and lightning. This
tribe would have been one of those which was subjected to slavery in
Egypt and escaped along with at least one other tribe whose knowledge
of Yahweh had been limited to the Exodus experience itself. A second
stage would have taken place in the land of Canaan where the gods of
the fathers had already been localized at various shrines and had assimilated some Canaanite ideas. After the formation of the twelve tribe
league in the settled land, Yahweh absorbed the gods of the fathers by
being identified with them. Though the El concept had exercised some
influence upon the understanding of gods of the fathers while the latter
were attached to local shrines, this influence, according to Maag, was
limited in extent and by no means did El worship ever replace the cult of
the gods of the fathers as claimed by O. Eissfeldt. Indeed, it was only
with the incorporation of Jerusalemite traditions during the United
Monarchy, argued Maag, that the El imagery exercised significant influence on Israelite religious development.[19]

Greater emphasis on El is found in Eissfeldt's reconstruction. He
argued that the deities having names compounded with $^{\jmath}\bar{e}l$ were local
hypostases or manifestations of the god El known from the Ugaritic
texts. When the Patriarchs settled in Canaan, according to Eissfeldt, the
El cult completely replaced the gods of the fathers. The latter, in fact,
would have been the gods who were put away in Josh 24:14-15 and Gen
35:1-7. On the other hand, the Yahweh cult would have been introduced
either by the last wave or by one of the last waves of incoming tribesmen
who encountered previously settled kinfolk among whom El had become
dominant. Though El was at first thought to be distinct from and
superior to Yahweh, the El cult gradually came to be understood as an
older stage of the cult of Yahweh. In this way, Yahweh acquired El
characteristics, especially the roles of King and Creator. The process of

---

[19]V. Maag, "Der Hirte Israels," *Schweizerische Theologische Umschau* 28
(1958) 1-28, and "Sichembund und Vätergötter," *VTSup* 16 (1967) 205-18.

assimilation would have taken a certain length of time, but, according to Eissfeldt, was complete by the end of the United Monarchy.[20]

The most comprehensive claims for the role of the El cult have been made by Prof. Cross. He has insisted, to begin with, that the "god of the fathers" was never anonymous but could in fact be identical with one of the high gods. This allows the possibility that even before they settled in Canaan, the ancestors of Israel worshipped El as their ancestral God. Thus the two major types distinguished by Alt are brought into harmony by Cross.[21] However, the most creative contribution made by Cross in this discussion is his claim that Yahweh was an El figure right from the start.[22] That is to say, the name Yahweh would have been part of a longer liturgical title applied to El in worship. As the religion of the Israelites, or perhaps we should speak of proto-Israelites, developed more and more in that distinctive direction which would come to expression in the Bible, more importance was attached to the name Yahweh and the God called by that name was regarded as an independent God in his own right. In other words, Yahweh split off from El. In a bold piece of reconstruction, Cross postulates behind the phrase *ʾehyê ʾăšer ʾehyê* (Exod 3:14) a full cultic name: *ʾil ḏū yahwī ṣabaʾōt*, "El who creates the (heavenly) armies." This analysis is a highly controversial one. Nonetheless, the basic thesis that Yahweh was originally a cult name of El has much to recommend it. The strongest argument in its favor is that it makes it easier to understand how the worshippers of El and/or the gods of the fathers were willing to accept Yahweh as *the* God of the tribal league during the period of the Judges. The sense of discontinuity which this innovation could have produced was muted by the lingering consciousness of the affinity between El and Yahweh.

[20]O. Eissfeldt, "El and Yahweh," *JSS* 1 (1956) 25-37; "Israels Religion und die Religionen seiner Umwelt," *Kleine Schriften* 5 (1973) 1-20; "Der Kanaanäische El als Geber der den israelitischen Erzvätern Geltenden Nachkommenschaft-und Landbesitzverheissungen," *Kleine Schriften* 5 (1973) 50-62. See also R. de Vaux, "El et Baal, le dieu des pères et Yahweh," *Ugaritica* 6 (MRS 17; Paris: Geuthner, 1969) 501-17. Like Eissfeldt, de Vaux attaches major significance to El, with whom the patriarchs associated the god(s) of the fathers. The rest of de Vaux's reconstruction, however, is closer to Maag's.

[21]*Canaanite Myth and Hebrew Epic*, 44-75. The fusion of the cults of El and the god of the fathers is also maintained by T. C. Vriezen, "The Study of the Old Testament and the History of Religion," *VTSup* 17 (1969) 1-24.

[22]*Canaanite Myth and Hebrew Epic*, 68-71. The identity of El and Yahweh is also affirmed by G. Ahlström, *Aspects of Syncretism in Israelite Religion* (Lund: Gleerup, 1963) 13. The identity of Yahweh and the *original* El is claimed by U. Oldenburg, *The Conflict Between El and Baʿal in Canaanite Religion* (Leiden: Brill, 1969). His motivation, however, appears to be primarily theological and will be discussed below.

It will be clear from the above discussion that a variety of theories have been proposed to illustrate how the different streams flowed together to form the biblical understanding of God. Either Yahweh was originally identical with El (Cross, Oldenburg, Ahlström) or Yahweh absorbed the El cult either in the pre-monarchial period (Eissfeldt, de Vaux) or during the United Monarchy (Maag). The problem as to how the god of the fathers concept entered in is open to a variety of solutions. Moreover, these are not the only theological traditions which found their way into biblical thought. For example, Cross has shown that the very early poem contained in Exodus 15, the Song of the Sea, has made use of imagery which is connected with the storm god (Baal-Hadad in the Ugaritic texts).[23] The historical picture is therefore a complex one and many uncertainties remain.[24] Nonetheless, reflection on the theological implications of this historical material cannot wait until the last word has been said by descriptive scholarship. It is quite appropriate, therefore, for us to move on to the normative stage of discussion in spite of the tentative nature of much of the foregoing.

PART TWO

THEOLOGICAL IMPLICATIONS

How does one go about making the transition from descriptive study to normative theological reflection? If it were not for historical criticism, the answer would be quite simple: "The 'plain meaning' of the Bible discloses truths which are authoritative and binding upon the believer. Normative theology is just a restatement, within a confession of faith, of the results of descriptive study." A position of this type is still possible today only if one wishes completely to reject critical methodology in favor of a fideistic affirmation of the "old time religion." In this paper, however, it is assumed that Fundamentalism is not a viable alternative, and that, in one way or another, the results of historical critical study must be dealt with.

The reason why historical criticism greatly complicates the problem of normative reflection is essentially related to the theological concept of revelation. The discussion of revelation by contemporary theologians, however, exhibits a great variety of approaches and a bewildering complexity of issues.[25] Fortunately, it will be adequate for the purpose at

---

[23]*Canaanite Myth and Hebrew Epic*, 112-44.

[24]Already it is being claimed that the divine name Yah, which would be an early form of Yahweh, can be documented in texts dating from 2400 B.C. See G. Pettinato, "The Royal Archives of Tell-Mardikh-Ebla," *BA* 39 (1976) 44-52, esp. p. 50. Most scholars are, however, highly skeptical of this claim.

[25]For surveys of the history of scholarship on revelation, see A. Dulles,

hand to simplify somewhat and to speak of one element which is at least implicitly present in most of the theologies of revelation—that is, the insistence upon the uniqueness of the Bible.

The uniqueness which is claimed for the Bible goes beyond what we mean when we say, "Every snowflake is unique," or "Every human being is a unique person." The Bible is usually thought to be more than a unique arrangement of basic components which can be found elsewhere in other equally unique arrangements. It is said to be or to contain something which is exclusively its own—as a matter of *principle*, that unique aspect can not be found anywhere else. This basic tendency seems to be quite pervasive even though there are a number of different emphases when it comes to specifying precisely what constitutes this exclusive uniqueness. One of the most important areas of emphasis, especially in view of the descriptive questions dealt with in this paper, is the uniqueness of the biblical God. He is said to be the only true God. All the other gods we read about in the religious literature of other peoples are not only false and illegitimate, they don't even really exist. Another focus of uniqueness widely insisted upon by recent scholarship is that only the Bible understood God as acting in *history* rather than in the cycles of nature.[26] One can therefore stress the uniqueness of the great events reported in the Bible as the saving acts of God (*magnalia dei*). It would be these events which uniquely reveal the will of God and his way of acting with his chosen people. For Christians, of course, the uniqueness of Jesus is emphasized with the insistence that his life, death and resurrection constitute the one great event which has effected salvation for mankind. This entails the accompanying idea, applied more or less strictly, that it is exclusively by adhering to this Gospel that the individual person can be saved.

The problem posed for theology by descriptive historical scholarship can be regarded as revolving to a large extent about this question of the uniqueness of the Bible. The style of normative theology will depend upon how an individual reacts to the question of uniqueness. The majority of students of the Bible who accept historical criticism also

---

Revelation Theology: A History (New York: Herder and Herder, 1969) and G. O'Collins, *Foundations of Theology* (Chicago: Loyola University: 1970).

[26]There have been a number of critiques of this position in recent years. For a summary, see J. Barr, "Revelation in History," *IDBSup* (1976) 746-49. The work of Prof. Cross, especially on "The Song of the Sea," (see above, n. 23), provides a way out of the rigid opposition between myth and history. According to Cross, it is a feature of biblical thought to use mythological imagery applied to historical events. The function of the myth is to give transcendent meaning to certain historical events. Seen in this way, the absolute dichotomy between myth and history is superseded.

continue to insist upon uniqueness. There are many ways in which this can be done without departing too radically from traditional concepts of revelation. Other persons, both experts and those who do not claim expertise, are willing to leave behind the insistence on uniqueness, though within a religious perspective which feels itself to be in essential continuity with the Jewish and/or Christian tradition. Finally, there will be interpreters of the Bible who do not consider themselves religious but still want to engage in normative reflection on the Bible. There are, in other words, a number of different *stances* from which normative thought can begin.

In what follows, we will outline four such basic stances. These are not just abstract possibilities, but are based upon positions which have actually been espoused in reaction to the kind of descriptive study reviewed in Part One of this paper. It should be clear that these are not the only possible stances, nor are they necessarily exclusive of one another. A more conservative thinker, for example, might be able to accept and integrate within his general perspective some of the insights arising from the normative reflections of a less traditional interpreter. It is nonetheless helpful to differentiate these stances in order to illustrate how each one will tend to produce a certain *type* of normative reflection. Furthermore, this approach intends to highlight something which may not be immediately apparent—namely, that normative theologizing about the Bible is possible and necessary within stances which are far from traditional. Of course, it is not possible here to outline a whole normative theology for each of the stances. All that is attempted is an indication of the directions in which one might move, illustrated with a few examples.

1. Primitive Revelation

If something which has been regarded as unique to the Bible becomes apparent elsewhere, in seeming independence of the biblical tradition, what can be done to preserve the theological claim of uniqueness for the Bible? In the history of Christian thought, such a problem has in fact been encountered several times. Some of the Church Fathers, for example, were very much impressed by the fact that they could find in the writings of Plato many truths which were identical with the teaching of the Bible as they interpreted it.[27] For them, this did not threaten the uniqueness of the Bible. They simply argued that Plato had read the five books of Moses and had learned these truths from the Bible!

---

[27]Actually, the biblical thought patterns are quite different from Platonism. It was the philosophical ambience of their own culture which caused the Fathers to read the Bible with Platonic spectacles.

This is a kind of preemptive manoeuvre which preserves the Bible's exclusive claim to truth.[28]

An analogous problem arose when Catholic missionaries discovered that there existed among "pagans," certain conceptions of God and of human origins which seemed to them quite similar to biblical teachings. How could it be that "outside of revelation" some of the truths of revelation had already been known? Again, a preemptive solution was found. These truths would have been preserved through a primitive or primeval revelation of the biblical God. This primitive revelation, or *Uroffenbarung*, could be linked with biblical stories which presume that God manifested himself to the ancestors of the human race, including Adam and Eve as well as Noah, from whom all living persons are descended. They regarded this as a genuinely "supernatural" revelation, the memory of which would have been kept alive among many peoples of the world. More recently, an attempt was made to give empirical support to the theory of an *Uroffenbarung*. This is found in the monumental study of W. Schmidt entitled *Der Ursprung der Gottesidee*. He argued that among primitive peoples surviving into modern times, there was, beyond the superficial polytheism and superstition, a belief in a high god corresponding to the God of the Bible. This belief, in his view, was a relic of the *Uroffenbarung*, the existence of which would thus receive support from anthropological studies.[29]

The appeal to a kind of *Uroffenbarung* has actually been proposed as a way of dealing with the problems arising from the study of the history of Israelite religion. Both G. B. Roggia and U. Oldenburg were convinced from their study of the Ugaritic texts that the God of the Bible is in some way identical with the Canaanite god El, about whom we have stories in the Ugaritic literature. How to deal with the conclusion that the one true God, who revealed himself to ancient Israel, appears to have been known in earlier times by other peoples? The solution proposed by Roggia and Oldenburg, though they do not use this word, is to appeal to an *Uroffenbarung*. According to this theory, the true God revealed himself in pre-biblical times as El. The understanding of El, however, became corrupt among most peoples by combination with mythological concepts, especially those derived from the fertility religion. Only one small group, namely the patriarchs, preserved the true and original understanding of El. By the time of Moses, the conception of El had been so corrupted by the Canaanite culture, that it was necessary for the true God to reveal himself anew, this time under a new name, Yahweh, which served to differentiate him from the degenerate El

---

[28] See the comments of Justin Martyr, a second century Church Father, in his *Apology* 1. 44.

[29] See J. Heislbetz, "Uroffenbarung," *LTK* 10 (1965) 565-67.

48 CONRAD E. L'HEUREUX

worshipped by the Canaanites. In other words, the Mosaic revelation was a re-affirmation of the earlier revelation of the true God. The presence, in mythological texts, of some of the features of the biblical God is therefore explained, while at the same time, the uniqueness of the God of the Bible is preserved. One can continue to insist that this God is known only through his self-disclosure which, today at least, is found exclusively in the Bible.[30]

Oldenburg does not indicate *when* he thinks this original revelation of the true God as El took place. The first proponents of an *Uroffenbarung* situated it at the time of Adam and Noah. Obviously, modern scientific knowledge of the antiquity of the human race makes it difficult to maintain that religious ideas were preserved from the first ancestors down to historical times. Though Oldenburg does not comment on this, one might suspect that a contemporary theologian would have to be satisfied with a relative *Uroffenbarung* situated within historical times.

The appeal to *Uroffenbarung* is a clever idea which allows one to preserve, with minor adjustment, the traditional understanding of the truth and uniqueness of the Bible. The kind of normative theological reflection which results can be a simple reaffirmation of the way in which the Bible has traditionally been interpreted and the potentially threatening aspect of historico-critical study is nullified.

Unfortunately, the attempt of Roggia and Oldenburg to demonstrate that the earliest non-Israelite records concerning El are the purest and truest and that the El concept degenerated as time went on is simply unconvincing.[31] The existing evidence concerning El does not indicate such a process of degradation. Thus the appeal to a kind of primitive revelation to handle the problems raised in the study of the origins of Yahwism encounters the same objection as the above-mentioned attempts to explain the "biblical" ideas of Plato and the worship of a high god by primitive peoples: historical evidence simply does not support the theories. Moreover, this approach, at least as manifested by Roggia and Oldenburg, does not deal with the evidence that the name of Yahweh and some of the theological concepts linked with that name may also have had a pre-Israelite history.

2. Developmental Approaches to Revelation

The appeal to primitive revelation allows one to recognize that the biblical understanding of God is related to other ancient religious ideas while continuing to insist upon the uniqueness of the Bible. The same

[30]G. B. Roggia, "Alcune Osservazioni sul culto di el a Ras-Samra," *Aevum* 15 (1941) 559-75, For Oldenburg, see above, n. 23.
[31]For details, see my monograph, *Rank among the Canaanite Gods*, 3-108.

result can be achieved by understanding revelation as a developmental phenomenon. What is meant by "developmental" is that throughout the biblical period, the truth would have been revealed in gradual and progressive fashion because God took account of the limited capacity of people at any given stage of the unfolding of His plan.[32] This means that the earlier parts of the Bible contain many expressions of the truth which are partial and imperfect and must therefore be seen in the light of the fulness of revelation which came later.[33]

In Christian theologies of revelation, there is at least one sense in which the developmental concept is virtually indispensable, that is, in the description of the relationship between the Old Testament and the New Testament. The New Testament is taken to be the final and ultimate revelation which fulfills and at times *supersedes* the partial and temporary revelation of the Old Testament. The developmental concept can also be applied within the Old Testament to deal with problems such as the apparently barbaric attitudes to non-Israelites exhibited in the stories of the conquest. One can argue that such an imperfect grasp of the truth was later superseded by the more perfect revelation of universality found, for example, in Second Isaiah.

The developmental idea may be extended backwards in time to deal with the historical evidence that the Israelite patriarchs understood the "god of the fathers" in much the same way as did other ancient people, and that they called God "El" without being fully conscious that this El was other than the El worshipped by the Canaanites. All of this can be explained in terms of the divine "condescension" by which God manifested Himself to the patriarchs by means of concepts which were familiar to them, the only concepts which they were capable of grasping. Furthermore, it can be claimed that it was not by accident that these religious concepts were present at the right time, but rather that a divine providence had prepared the necessary background so that the revelation to the patriarchs would be possible from the human side. Some theologians might even be comfortable in affirming that this providential

---

[32] The *Dogmatic Constitution on Divine Revelation* of the Second Vatican Council (para. 13) quotes St. John Chrysostom in speaking of the marvelous "condescension" of eternal widom "that we may learn the gentle kindness of God, which words cannot express, and how far He has gone in adapting His language with thoughtful concern for our weak human nature."

[33] This view is reflected in the *Dogmatic Constitution on Divine Revelation*, (para. 15), which says, "Now the books of the Old Testament, in accordance with the state of mankind before the time of salvation established by Christ, reveal to all men the knowledge of God and of man and the ways in which God, just and merciful, deals with men. These books, though they also contain some things which are incomplete and temporary, nevertheless show us true divine pedagogy."

preparation was itself genuine revelation, though at a still less perfect and less complete stage.

When we ask what kind of normative theology flows from the developmental stance, it must be noted that we are not dealing with a single specific theological system, but a perspective which is shared by many theologians who might differ significantly in other respects. In fact, it seems likely that among those scholars who accept historico-critical methodologies, the majority would identify with the developmental stance in one way or another. The differences between them will be due, in large part, to the precise manner in which they apply historical criticism. The latter is, after all, only a tool. As with any tool, it may be used more conservatively or more radically.

The developmental approach works most cohesively when (as seems to be envisaged by the Second Vatican Council, for example) criticism is rather cautious and leads, on the descriptive level, to conclusions which do not depart dramatically from the picture of Israel's history which is presented in the Bible. The normative end-product is not so much a new theology as a way of adjusting to the results of historico-critical study without requiring a radical revision of traditional theology. In other words, theologizing can go on pretty much as it always has

When critical methods are used less conservatively, on the other hand, the reconstruction of Israel's history (including its religious history) which emerges tends to be significantly different from the picture presented in the Bible. One becomes aware that within the Bible itself there is a *variety* of theologies. Scholars can still attempt to find a developmental process within the Old Testament as is done, for example, by Gerhard von Rad in his *Old Testament Theology*.[34] However, the discussion of von Rad's work by other scholars illustrates the state of chaos which currently exists in the field of Old Testament theology. While it is generally recognized that von Rad had made a very important contribution, his theological synthesis has a highly idiosyncratic stamp which makes it quite different from what other biblical theologians are proposing.[35] The main reason for such differences is that researchers are not able to agree in identifying a unified developmental process which would characterize the essence of the Old Testament taken as a whole. There does not seem to have been a unilinear evolution in which the truth was revealed more and more perfectly as time went on. On the contrary, at any given stage of biblical history, there was a *variety* of theological movements, some of which were in conscious conflict with

[34]G. von Rad, *Old Testament Theology* (2 vols; New York: Harper & Row, 1962-1965).

[35]For a review of scholarship in this area, see G. Hasel, *Old Testament Theology: Basic Issues in the Current Debate* (Grand Rapids: Eerdmans, 1975).

one another. Moreover, the processes of change did not always involve progress. There were ups and downs in the development, and it cannot be assumed that the later the stage, the more perfectly the truth was grasped.

The more radical critical conclusions which find it impossible to identify a single coherent process underlying the history of Israelite religion and theology seem to be characteristic of recent developments in biblical scholarship.[36] In the face of this dominant trend, it will be difficult to prevent the developmental model from breaking down. In any case, it is clear that theologians who think of themselves as having a moderate attitude towards critical study of the Bible have a number of urgent tasks before them. They will have to determine just what it is in the Old Testament that should become the ground of modern religious commitment. They must work out explicitly and self-consciously just how the results of biblical criticism bear upon contemporary theological thought. In dealing with these problems, they might well collaborate with theologians representing the less traditional stance which will be discussed next.

3. Relativizing the Biblical Traditions

We have seen two possible stances which allow one to accept the results of historical criticism while continuing to insist upon the uniqueness of the Bible and remaining relatively close to its traditional interpretation. Many students of the Bible, however, will agree that exclusive claims to possession of the truth and insistence on superiority relative to other religious traditions should be left behind. It certainly is highly dubious whether a completely detached and objective study of the historical facts can support the view that the so-called Judaeo-Christian tradition is superior to other religions of the world; that the New Testament is superior to the Old Testament; and that the Old Testament is superior to the other religions of the ancient Near East.[37] Furthermore,

[36] In this country, for example, the dominant school of thought twenty years ago was the so-called Albright school which was relatively conservative where the historicity of biblical traditions is concerned. How far things have changed may be seen by reviewing the volume edited by Hayes and Miller, referred to above, n. 3. As evidence that the more radical trend is underway among Roman Catholic scholars too, one may point to T. L. Thompson, *The Historicity of the Patriarchal Narratives* (*BZAW* 133; Berlin: de Gruyter, 1974) and B. Zuber, *Vier Studien zu den Ursprungen Israels* (Orbis biblicus et orientalis 9; Göttingen: Vandenhoeck & Ruprecht, 1976). See also my review of the latter in *CBQ* 40 (1978) 110-11.

[37] In *The Meaning and End of Religion* (New York: Mentor, 1964), W. C. Smith demonstrates that the claim to an exclusive kind of uniqueness is found only in Christianity, Islam and, to a lesser extent, Judaism. One might argue

the claim to superiority will seem to many persons a sign of arrogance and chauvinism which has been the cause of intolerance and persecution including, though by no means limited to, the tragic manifestations of anti-Semitism in modern times. The third stance which we are describing is one which affirms that a vital faith, nourished and clarified by the biblical tradition, is possible without claims to a kind of uniqueness which involves exclusivity and superiority. This essay, while striving to be fair to the other options, avowedly favors this third stance.

An analogy may be drawn between the developing attitude of children to their parents and our attitude to the Bible. Most of us, when we were very young, idealized our parents, viewed them as without fault, and insisted that they were the best parents in the world. Upon growing older we became aware of the limitations of our parents, some of them serious limitations which adversely affected our own lives. Fortunately, most of us can overcome the shock which comes when our parents become relativized. We continue to love them, find support from them and enjoy a unique relationship with them. They are still the "only" parents for us. This relationship is not threatened by the awareness that for someone else, other parents are just as "unique." It no longer makes sense, however, to speak about "the best parents in the world." This relativization is analogous to the relativization of one's own religious tradition which is not only possible but, according to Wilfred Cantwell Smith, strongly to be desired.[38] While some will regard such a step as a betrayal of the biblical tradition, to others it will be a necessary step towards a fuller and more mature life of faith.

It was suggested earlier that the conflict experienced between traditional belief and historical criticism was due in large part to the insistence upon an exclusivistic kind of uniqueness for the Bible which is part of most theologies of revelation. It is possible, however, to have a theology of revelation without exclusivism. Revelation may be regarded as the encounter with transcendence which includes, but is not limited to, religious insight. This encounter is experienced as "grace," that is, it is not commensurate with our finiteness but is conferred upon us as a gift which is received in gratitude. These fundamental aspects of religious experience are preserved and expressed in the theological concept of revelation. The Bible itself is not a kind of objectified revelation. It is rather the written record of individuals in the past who experienced revelation. It is possible that study and reflection upon the Bible will become the occasion for revelation to happen today. But the Bible's quality as the product of revelation and its potential to elicit revelation

---

that this claim is due to culturally conditioned factors and can be abandoned without giving up essential fidelity to the tradition.

[38]Smith, *Meaning*, 174-81.

need not be viewed as quantitatively or qualitatively superior. Its superiority is a relative one dependent upon the reader's relationship with the Bible and with the communities which have preserved it and handed it down. Exclusivism, therefore, can be abandoned while maintaining a viable and meaningful theology of revelation.[39]

What kind of normative theologizing results from this stance which relativizes the biblical tradition? To begin with, the same urgent questions facing more traditional theologians must be addressed, from a somewhat different point of view, by persons identifying with this third stance: just what is it in the Old Testament which has meaning and value for today, and just how does one make the transition from the study of ancient texts to contemporary thought?[40] However, rather than discussing the areas of overlap between this and other theological perspectives, we will concentrate here on the possibilities which lie open for this specific stance.

In the descriptive part of this essay, we saw that the concepts of the "god of the fathers" and of El were common to early Israel and to other peoples of the ancient Near East. Moreover, the name Yahweh and related ideas may have had a non-Israelite source. When these conclusions of historical study are reflected upon from a stance which does not feel compelled to prove the uniqueness of the Bible, more attention can be paid to the element of continuity between the religion of Israel and that of its ancient contemporaries.[41] This continuity invites a fresh and more positive evaluation of what is too often scornfully rejected as "Canaanite religion" or "the fertility cult."[42] Liberated from the need to prove the Bible's superiority, scholars could attempt a fair and sympathetic understanding of ancient religious traditions of which we are indirect heirs, whether we admit it or not. Such an investigation would

---

[39]I believe that the view advocated here is in fundamental harmony with the position of Gabriel Moran in *The Present Revelation* (New York: Herder and Herder, 1972). The perspective represented by his earlier *Theology of Revelation* (New York: Herder and Herder, 1966) is based upon the documents of the Second Vatican Council and stands squarely within the developmental approach discussed above.

[40]For an illustration of my own approach to these questions, see my short book on Genesis 2-3, which will be published soon by Paulist Press.

[41]Works on comparative religion which stress the continuity between the Bible and other religious traditions frequently have the result (at times intentionally, it would appear) of "debunking" the biblical faith. If the compulsion to prove uniqueness is given up, however, the presence of biblical concepts outside of the Bible can be taken as *confirming* the value of what is found in the Bible.

[42]See, for example, Bright's description of Canaanite religion in his *A History of Israel*, 116-17.

strengthen our perception of the universality of the religious quest of humankind and the sisterhood and brotherhood of humanity. It would constitute a broader interpretation of what is truly ecumenical. It might also be, that by better understanding the reasons for the biblical (especially prophetic) rejection of non-Israelite religious concepts, we could find room for re-admitting within our theological horizon the religious significance of our relation to nature and of the feminine aspect of the divine. Perhaps we might even grasp the positive contribution which is made by a polytheistic perspective. The above are merely suggestions, but it is hoped they are enough to demonstrate that there are fruitful new directions which biblical scholarship could explore.

The question may be asked, finally, whether historico-critical methodology leads, by its own inner logic, to the kind of stance presently under discussion. The empirical evidence would appear to lead to a negative answer, since the majority of critical biblical scholars appear to prefer a more conservative position. Nonetheless, it is suggested that this third stance is indeed the natural outcome of historical criticism and that the apparent resistance of a large number of scholars is due to deeply ingrained predispositions which have not been subjected to rigorous scrutiny.[43]

4. Non-Religious Approaches

The third stance, which we have just discussed, rejects any absolute and exclusive claims for the Bible, but is a professedly religious position which considers itself to be in profound continuity with the biblical tradition. Among biblical scholars, however, as well as among the students who sit in their classes, there are many who do not consider themselves religious and do not find that the concept of God or of any transcendent reality has any meaning for them. Persons in this category also make normative judgments on the basis of the conclusions of descriptive study. It seems to be a natural inclination of the human psyche to want to sharpen its own self-understanding by comparison and contrast with the views of others, including the ancients. Even apart from this, however, every teacher has a responsibility to encourage and facilitate the process by which students can integrate the results of descriptive study with their own understanding of reality, even if that understanding is not explicitly religious. Whether or not, in this case, the normative reflection ought to be called "theology" is debatable. Since the very nature of the material studied descriptively involves questions of ultimate meaning and value, the normative reflection takes place within the context of the individual's own understanding of what

---

[43]See the reflections of Smith in n. 9, pp. 339-40.

is ultimate. This may be sufficient to merit the label "theology," but that need not be insisted upon.

In their normative reflection upon the history of Israel's ideas of God, surveyed earlier in this paper, there are a number of questions which can be asked by students who do not consider themselves religious. Is the language about God purely illusory and misguided, or might it be an indirect way in which a society expresses its understanding of something other than God? Something which *is* real and important? If so, then what was ancient Israel really thinking about when it spoke of God? Do the relatively unique features of Israelite God-talk reflect some unique understanding of human nature and human society? If so, is there something of value here which can be affirmed and appropriated by persons who are not religious in any traditional sense?

Reflection of this type could focus, for example, on some of the ideas in Norman Gottwald's article, "Biblical Theology or Biblical Sociology?"[44] In this article, Gottwald examines the arguments supporting the prevalent view that Israel's understanding of history and of God were absolutely unique. He finds the arguments unconvincing. While Israel was unique in exluding the worship of any God but Yahweh, all of the other features of the biblical God can be found elsewhere in the ancient world. According to Gottwald, what was unique about Israel was its understanding of human society. It was a movement against the socially stratified life of the monarchical city-states and an attempt to reassert tribal values of sharing and community. In other words, it was a socio-political drive towards the creation of an egalitarian society. He believes that it is because of Israel's conviction that it differed from neighboring societies that it felt obliged to differentiate its God so strongly from the gods who served to provide the ideological underpining of the *status quo* in the city-states. Yahweh, therefore, symbolizes the unity and the driving power of a community geared to political and social liberation. It is not clear whether Gottwald himself believes that the *only* truth in God-talk consists of what it has to say about societal self-understanding. Even if such an extreme position is taken, however, a whole area is opened up for normative reflection. If the historical process in which Israel arose consisted essentially of a movement of liberation, then it becomes possible for persons who are not "religious" to define their own convictions over against the biblical material. Some may even find a feeling of identity with this aspect of the Bible and

---

[44]N. K. Gottwald, "Biblical Theology or Biblical Sociology? On Affirming the 'Uniqueness' of Israel," *The Bible and Liberation* (Berkeley: Radical Religion, 1976) 42-57. A revised form of the article now appears in *The Tribes of Yahweh* (Maryknoll, N. Y.: Orbis, 1979) 667-709.

appropriate it as significant in their own struggle to become more fully human.

Even if the evaluation of the biblical material is more negative in tone, the possibilities for normative reflection are many. One can ask whether in the history of Israel, concern for God was helpful, harmful, or neutral in encouraging them to achieve their human potential. If it was harmful, then why is it that human beings persist in speaking about God? (No simplistic answers allowed!) What is it about these students' understanding of humanity which makes them regard concern for God and religion as harmful in humankind's search for fulfillment? How do their reactions to the views of ancient Israel relate to their here and now relations with persons who are deeply committed to the truth of the Bible? Are they satisfied with the latter relationship? If not, why? If they are satisfied with it, then what does that tell them about their understanding of human society and the relationship between human individuals? The list of questions could go on, but enough has been said to demonstrate that there is plenty of room for normative reflection, no matter what the theological views of the interpreter.

CONCLUSION

The title of this article was intended to be both provocative and ambiguous. It is provocative in that religious experience testifies that God is precisely the Unsearchable. The very idea of "Searching for the Origins of God" sounds like a challenge directed at the very center of the way in which God has been understood. This impression appropriately fits the article which, in both its descriptive and normative parts, will seem, at least to many readers, to challenge the traditional understanding of God and the Bible.

The title is also ambiguous. It could be taken to refer to an investigation which seeks to find the origin of the *ideas* used in speaking of God while recognizing that deity itself is mysterious and without origin. On the other hand, the title might seem to imply that once we have explained the origin of the *ideas* connected with God, deity itself has been explained away. The author is personally committed to the former of these two alternatives. The content of the essay, however, is intended to be meaningful to adherents of either of the two options.

More concretely, it has been the purpose of this essay to make accessible to a wider reading public the principal conclusions of the historical study of the early religion of Israel, with special emphasis on the contributions made by Prof. Frank M. Cross, Jr. It was insisted upon that there is a need for normative theological reflection on the results of descriptive study and that this normative phase has been neglected. Furthermore, in order to promote normative reflection, it is important to be aware of the variety of basic theological stances from which such reflection can begin. The personal integrity of the scholar and the demands of his vocation as a teacher require him to take on the responsibility of promoting such discussion. If it stimulates both teachers and students to accept this responsibility, the essay will have been a success.

The Uneasy Compromise: Israel between League and Monarchy

BARUCH HALPERN

YORK UNIVERSITY

I.

T HE ancient Israelite lived a life more like our own than different from it. He ate, drank, walked and talked. He fretted over his livelihood. He worried about politics. He concerned himself generally with the hundreds of disparate forces and faces that affected his personal weal. He lived, that is, in a world of three dimensions. Yet perhaps because we see him silhouetted against the horizon of history, we tend to perceive only two. Modern treatment of Israelite history has reduced it in turns to history of religion, to the history of saints, to the history of books, and so forth.[1] The notion of a "history of Israel" has advanced, by contrast, little beyond the stage already represented by biblical texts themselves. Specifically, the notion that a whole social dynamic underlay the religious or theological or literary evolution of Israel commands from most treatments no more than a curt nod in passing.

Ironically, the ancient Israelite engaged in a similar endeavor. But the terms in which he conceived it were wholly different. He looked first to the "history of Israel," and only later to that of ideas. Ideas for him were expressed through parable, paradigm or precedent. They were tangible, still there to that day. Yhwh, "he who causes to be,"[2] the god

---

[1] Primarily, interest has concentrated on the history of religions, to the extent that that has become, and was esp. in the 19th c., the ground from which to construe "history." See esp. J. Wellhausen, *Prolegomena to the History of Ancient Israel* (Cleveland: World, 1957), which was the first volume of his *History of Israel* (1878). Wellhausen uses his understanding of the history of religion (pp. 17-167) as a basis for investigating socio-political history.

[2] See F. M. Cross, *Canaanite Myth and Hebrew Epic* (Cambridge: Harvard, 1973) 68-71 (hereafter cited as *CMHE*). The translation stretches back at least to P. Haupt, "Der Name Jahwe" *OLZ* 1909 211-14. See also W. F. Albright, "Contributions to Biblical Archaeology and Philology" *JBL* 43 (1924) 363-93; "Further Observations on the Name Yahweh and its Modifications in Proper Names" *JBL* 44 (1925) 158-62; for a review of scholarship, W. H. Brownlee, "The Ineffable Name of God" *BASOR* 226 (1977) 39-46.

who defines himself "I cause to be what I cause to be,"[3] is no airy theologian. He is known by his works, and only by his works.[4] He affirms the priority of event over idea. The principle of the thing is secondary to the thing itself.

To say that Israel's was an historical religion, a cliche so worn that it might clothe any emperor, is to say, too, that politics were Israel's religion. History, for the Israelite, was politics, and so was theology. Yet Giorgio Buccellati strikes home with the complaint, "While the bibliography about the *religious* nature of the monarchy can cover several pages, hardly anything has been written on the *political* nature of the same institution."[5] Scholarship has not sought Israel's essence, her political heart, but only her religious outcroppings. Scholarship has sought the principle, arrived at *ex posteriori*, not the thing itself.

This practice—of discussing Israel's history from a theological standpoint—blinds the historian to political dynamic. The history of religion must rest on the prior basis of socio-political history. To investigate the latter on the basis of the former is to contaminate it. Simply, one cannot proceed from a theological history to an historical theology. Yet this is precisely what biblical historians have traditionally essayed.[6]

Nowhere is this methodological arrogance more egregious than in treatments of Israel under the early kings. Current research knows only the poverty of Saul's "capital"[7] and the glory of Solomon's claims. Kingship has never, since Alt and before, represented a radical break in

---

[3]See esp. D. N. Freedman, "The Name of the God of Moses" *JBL* 79 (1960) 151-56, for the revision of the AV translation. Granted the translation above, the change in Exod 3:14 is a clear possibility.

[4]Thus, in Deut 18:21-22, if the prophet is right, he is inspired; if wrong, he is uninspired. Nothing could be more practical as a test. It is worth adding that Num 12:8 suggests even prophets received only a refracted, or, as in Jonah's case, Delphic revelation (hence the angelic interpreter, e. g., of Zechariah 1-6). On the problem in general, see G. E. Wright, *God Who Acts. Biblical Theology as Recital* (*SBT* 8; London: SCM, 1952).

[5]G. Buccellati, *Cities and Nations of Ancient Syria. An Essay on Political Institutions with Special Reference to the Israelite Kingdoms* (*Studi Semitici* 26; Rome: Istituto di Studi del Vicino Oriente, 1967) 241. Buccellati's work, which requires sophistication, is a pioneer volume in the historical approach to ancient Israel. See also the type of study undertaken in Cross, *CMHE*, 195-215.

[6]As Wellhausen, *Prolegomena;* M. Noth, *A History of Pentateuchal Traditions* (Englewood Cliffs: Prentice-Hall, 1972), among others.

[7]See E. L. Sinclair, *An Archaeological Study of Gibeah (Tell el-Ful) AASOR* 34-35 (1954-1956) 1-52; *BA* 27 (1964) 52-64; P. W. Lapp, "Tell el-Fūl" *BA* 28 (1965) 2-10; Noth, "Rezens." *ZDPV* 78 (1962) 91-94. But see below, n. 16.

Israel either politically or historically.[8] The scholar, however, brings it to life as the enemy of the prophets, the corrupter of primitive Yahwism, an eventual pimp of paganism. It is viewed in theological terms.

The three histories of Israel currently in widespread use in North America—those of M. Noth, J. Bright, and S. Herrmann[9]—typify the problem. All agree that Philistine hegemony in Canaan contributed substantially to the constitutional change from league to monarchy.[10] They agree further that Saul came to power because his victory over Ammon demonstrated his "charisma" (1 Samuel 11).[11] 1 Sam 9:1-10:16 and 1 Sam 8; 10:17-27; 12, they divide off as belonging to separate sources. The former, in which Samuel anoints Saul nāgîd (AV "captain;" 1 Sam 9:16; 10:1), is treated vaguely as pro-monarchic; it is regarded as secondarily bound up with the account of the Ammonite campaign in 1 Samuel 11.[12] The latter account, in which Saul is chosen by lot, contains material critical of monarchy (e. g., 8:7-8). It is therefore characterized as a retrojection of later disillusionment.[13] At the same time, Noth makes the concession that some contemporary opposition to the monarchy probably did exist.[14]

There are some strong points to this collective reconstruction. Particularly, there should be little doubt that the Philistine pentapolis exerted considerable military-economic pressure on Israel before Saul's rise. This is attested not only in the battle narrative of 1 Samuel 13-14, but also by the tradition that the Philistines displayed Saul's and Jonathan's corpses in Beth Shean (1 Sam 31:8-13). This report implies Philistine control of the Jezreel Valley; 1 Sam 31:7 may be accurate in reporting extension of that control to include the King's Highway in

---

[8]See A. Alt, "Die Staatenbildung der Israeliten in Palästina" *KS* 2. 1-65 (esp. p. 12), translated in "The Formation of the Israelite State in Palestine," *Essays on Old Testament History and Religion* (Garden City: Doubleday, 1968) 225-309.

[9]Noth, *The History of Israel* (2d ed.; New York: Harper and Row, 1960), hereafter *NHI*; Bright, *A History of Israel* (2d ed.; Philadelphia: Westminster, 1972), hereafter *BHI*; Herrmann, *A History of Israel in Old Testament Times* (Philadelphia: Fortress, 1975), hereafter *HHI*.

[10]*NHI*, 165, 171; *BHI*, 180-81; *HHI*, 124, 132, 138.

[11]*NHI*, 168-71; *BHI*, 183-84; *HHI*, 131-34.

[12]*NHI*, 168-69; *BHI*, 183, 185; *HHI*, 135-36. This view derives from Wellhausen's (e.g., his *Prolegomena*, 245ff.) twisted source analysis of 1 Samuel.

[13]*NHI*, 172 n. 2, which sees 8:1-22; 10:17, 27a; 12:1-25 as "deuteronomistic" (for Noth, exilic); *BHI*, 183 (more non-committal); *HHI*, 134, which sees chaps. 8; 12 as "artificial" framework for chaps. 9-11.

[14]*NHI*, 172-73; *BHI*, 185 and *HHI*, 183 n. 10 intimate a similar position.

Transjordan.[15] Given the convincing nature of the tradition that Saul met his death fighting the Philistines at Gilboa (1 Samuel 31; esp. 2 Sam 1:18-27), and the geopolitical verisimilitude of the materials cited above in their suggestion of Philistine dominance on the plains—where chariotry would bestow a premium advantage—it is difficult to indict the text's testimony regarding the Philistine problem.

In addition to Jezreel, the Philistines may well have garrisoned the Aijalon Pass through the Benjaminite hill country. According to 1 Sam 13:2-4, Saul struck first against the Philistine installation at Gibeah.[16] By this action, he could guarantee Benjaminite access through Gilgal to Transjordan. At the same time, it is a likely inference that the garrison there was meant to disrupt and regulate that access. Certainly, the ensuing encounter at Michmash lends weight to such a construction (1 Samuel 14).

It seems likely, whatever the character of Philistia's hegemony, that Ammon sought simultaneously to expand at Israel's expense. 1 Sam 31:8-13; 2 Sam 2:4-7; 21:12-14 strongly corroborate the battle account of 1 Samuel 11. The Jephthah story further attests to its verisimilitude. In that account, Ammon's putatively rivanchist ambitions also embrace primarily the settlements of Gilead (Judg 11:12-33). Thus the histories are correct insofar as they locate Israel's shift from league to monarchy in an era of military pressure from her peripheries.

On the other hand, beyond this single insight, the treatment of the period has been inadequate. Prominent in all the reconstructions is the notion that Saul must have demonstrated his "charisma" before becoming king.[17] One must ask, however, whether "charisma" is the sort of commodity in which historians ought freely to trade. Granted that rare

---

[15]See H. W. Hertzberg, *I & II Samuel* (2d ed.; *OTL*; Philadelphia: Westminster, 1976) 232-33, for limited, but cautious discussion. Possibly, the presence was not Philistine specifically, but Sea-People.

[16]See Hertzberg, *Samuel*, 101-5, for the location of the garrison in Geba (strategically a sounder location). Cf. H. Seebass, "I Sam 15 als Schlüssel für das Verständnis der sogenannten königsfreundlichen Reihe I Sam 9:1-10:16; 11:1-15 und 13:2-14:52" *ZAW* 78 (1966) 148-79, esp. pp. 161-68; J. M. Miller, "Geba/ Gibeah of Benjamin" *VT* 25 (1975) 145-66; cf. also A. Demsky, "The Genealogy of Gibeon (I Chronicles 9:35-44)" *BASOR* 202 (1971) 16-23; "Geba, Gibeah, and Gibeon—an Historico-Geographic Riddle" *BASOR* 212 (1973) 26-31. 1 Sam 13:4 indicates that Saul reduced the garrison, mentioned in 10:5, at Gibeah. 13:3 reads Geba, and gives the credit to Jonathan. But with the apocope of fem. *-t* in Heb. *status rectus*, Gibeah and Geba were for a time indistinguishable in the script, and thereafter readily confused. With regard to Jonathan, the problem is no greater. Napoleon conquered Portugal; but Junot led the army. This text probably records Saul's conquest of his future capital.

[17]See *NHI*, 171. Bright (*BHI*, 185) suggests that Saul was never more than

individuals have it, that in a Gracchus or a Caesar it may influence profoundly the course of an era, nevertheless, one must not permit the idea to restrict the play of political, sectional, factional or economic issues. In biblical studies, the term has been used in just that way. It expresses a theological notion residual from Max Weber's understanding of the Israelite judges: Weber referred to the judges called by Yhwh (the "major" judges) as charismatics. The term thus embodies certain theological predispositions toward the text—predispositions now validated with the *imprimatur* of the sociologist—that excuse the scholar from hard, historical research. Worse yet, these predispositions have been applied, by rather a curious principle of transitivity, directly to historical reconstruction. That is, it is one thing to claim that the text portrays the judge as a figure hurled by some heavenly catapult from obscurity into prominence. It is another altogether to claim that historically this was the case. And it is an exercise in methodological abandon to insist that the historical Saul conform to a mold present at best in literary convention, and in the literature concerning only some of the judges at that.

It is of course true that Israel initiated a monarchic system, under pressure from the Philistine pentapolis, at Saul's time. But Israel had suffered military and economic constraint before. What was the impetus at Saul's time? Who supported the departure from the constitution of the league? Surely some groups opposed the change. Who were the opposition? And what restraint did the league then impose on the king? The view that emerges from the histories is one of a whole nation rushing down to Gilgal, swept along in the grip of some spontaneous mass inspiration, to enthrone an obscure Benjaminite. But this is precisely how nations do not function. Cool heads, and entrenched elites, do exist. In short, the shift from league to monarchy must be reconstructed on the basis of Israel's politics, of domestic and foreign relations, and not as it has in the past—as a gift dropped from heaven, as a *machina ex deo*, or as a case of historical ergatism.

The first step in investigating Saul's election is, as the histories recognize, a division of the sources in 1 Samuel 8ff. This division, however, cannot be founded on the texts' attitudes toward monarchy. Use of that criterion is circular: if text Y is antagonistic to kingship, it belongs by definition to the anti-monarchic source; since the source contains texts like Y, it must be opposed to kingship. The logic is irrefutable, given only the premise that one of the sources is uniformly anti-monarchic. That, however, is hardly responsible source criticism.[18]

"military leader on a permanent basis," and that 1 Sam 10:1 preserves the post's original name (*nāgîd*).

[18]It is, however, typical. See Wellhausen, *Die Composition des Hexateuchs und der historischen Bücher des Alten Testaments* (3rd ed.; Berlin: deGruyter,

The basic criterion for source-division is the presence of doublets, or slightly divergent repetitions of stories or sequences of events. Contradictions, inconcinnities, even clear disjunction may sometimes indicate the presence of an editorial hand; only the doublet demonstrates the presence of a second source. This has profound relevance to the situation in 1 Samuel. There, close reading discloses a number of doublets. But at no point whatever are more than two sources in evidence.[19] Given that there is no need to posit a third source, and given, as I have tried to show elsewhere, that two continuous sources can be recovered without doing violence to the text,[20] it is safest to refrain from multiplying documentary sources unnecessarily.

The same situation obtains in 1 Samuel 8-12. If one discards the criterion of views on monarchy, it becomes clear that literarily only two sources are present. In the first place, critics are correct to isolate 1 Sam

---

1963 [=1899]) 240-43; R. Press, "Sauls Königswahl" *Theologische Blätter* 43 (1933) 234-48; Seebass, "Traditionsgeschichte von 1 Sam 8; 10:17ff. und 12" *ZAW* 77 (1965) 286-96; J. A. Soggin, *Das Königtum in Israel* (*BZAW* 104; Berlin: Topelmann, 1967) 29-31, J. Blenkinsopp, "The Quest of the Historical Saul," in *No Famine in the Land*, ed. by J. W. Flanagan and A. W. Robinson (*Festschrift* for J. L. McKenzie; Missoula: Scholars, 1975) 75-99; esp. T. Ishida, in his generally superlative *The Royal Dynasties in Ancient Israel. A Study on the Formation and Development of Royal-Dynastic Ideology* (*BZAW* 142; Berlin: de Gruyter, 1977) 31 n. 34. Wellhausen (and, derivatively, the histories) thinks 1 Samuel 11 was removed from 9:1-10:16; 13:1-14:52 and integrated into 8; 10:17-27; 12. Press and Seebass maintain 8:11-18 were inserted into an originally pro-monarchic source. So, the "anti-monarchic" source was originally pro-monarchic, but was subject to anti-monarchic redaction, after which pro-monarchic materials from the originally "pro-monarchic" source were secondarily introduced into it. Even this parody fails to do justice to the difficulties created by "doctrine-criticism."

[19]E.g., 1 Sam 10:10-12//19:18-24. The reading of the proverb in 10:11, 12; 19:24 is "Is Saul, too, among the prophets?" (*hă-gam šā'ûl ban-nĕbî'îm*), which might also be rendered, "Is it (not) asked also of/among the prophets?" But the quip in 10:12, "And who is their father?" plays on the couplet, "What is it that has happened to the son of Kish?/ Is Saul, too, among the prophets?" and also on the expression "son(s) of the prophet(s)" (Amos 7:14; 1 Kgs 20:35; 2 Kgs 2:3, 5, 7, 15; 4:1, 38; 5:22; 6:1; 9:1; cf. 1 Sam 10:10; 19:20), *bn nb'(m)*. This last reading may be called for, though the *bon mot* may simply be a pun. Contrast the theological ramifications of Hertzberg, *Samuel*, 86; S. R. Driver, *Notes on the Hebrew Text and the Topography of the Books of Samuel* (2d ed.; Oxford: Clarendon, 1913) 83. Also 1 Sam 13:8-15a//15:10-26; 1 Sam 18:10-11//19:9-10; esp. 1 Sam 23:19-24:23//26:1-25, etc.

[20]See my *The Constitution of the Monarchy in Israel*, forthcoming in *HSM*. The rough outline of the division there, which cannot be fully rehearsed, is:

9:1-10:16 as a unit. Regardless of problems in the pre-history of the narrative, it now proceeds logically throughout.[21] Though the final vv of the tale do create some difficulty, they, too, are closely integrated in the current recension: Saul's uncle brings attention back to the vagrant asses with which the story commenced (10:14-16: cf. 9:3, 5, 20; 10:2).[22]

Similarly, it has long been recognized that 1 Sam 10:17-27 picks up the narrative thread of 1 Samuel 8.[23] Thus, 10:18-19 regurgitate the tone and sentiment established in 8:7-8: the sacred history of Israel illustrates that to request a king is to reject the deity. In effect, 1 Sam 9:1-10:16 see Saul's appointment as standing in continuity with the history of the "judges." Saul arises to deal with a particular problem—the Philistine "oppression" (9:16; 10:1, reading with OG). By contrast, 1 Sam 8:7-8; 10:18-19 see this as a moment to recapitulate. It is the end of an era, the inception of a new relationship between Israel and her god. The very notion that kingship implies a rejection of god is incompatible with the idea (in 1 Sam 9:1-10:16) that Yhwh inspired the constitutional change.

The actual selection of Saul is also important. His appointment in 1 Sam 10:17-27 depends purely on the lot. It is not proved there, as in 9:1-10:16, by a series of signs. As a result, the hellions'[24] doubt (10:27) is

---

A. 8; 10:17-27; 11; 12; (13:1); 15-16; (17:1-11, 21-22a, 25, 32-39, 40d, 42-47, 50, 52-53); (18:14-16); 18:20-30; 19; 25-28:2; 29-30; 2 Sam 1ff.

B. 9:1-10:8 (16); 13:2-14:52; (17:12-20, 22b-24, 26-31, 40a-c, 41, 48-49, 51, 54-58); (18:1-5, 6-13, 17-19); 20:1b-42; 21:1-24:23; 28:3-25; 31.

Each source seems to have undergone editing independently; but little editing is evident after the combination (20:1a; prps. 10:14-16; 28:17-18). Possibly, or even probably, 9:1-10:8; 13:2-14:52; 28:3-25; 31 are the sole texts of source B. In that case, substantial accretion of traditions is witnessed (and some of the materials in source A must be ejected in favor of those classified here as belonging to B).

[21]Note 10:14-16, where Saul reports to his uncle, not his father (cf. 9:3). That the "man of god"/"seer" is unnamed in 9:6-13 has also inspired speculation that Samuel was not originally involved. But this might also be literary technique. See, e.g., M. Buber, "Die Erzählung von Sauls Königswahl" *VT* 6 (1956) 113-73.

[22]Note 9:12-13 lead to 9:22-24. 9:14, 18-19 tie back to 9:6-11. 9:20 links 9:3 with 10:14-16. 10:2 refers to 9:5. Cf. Seebass, "Traditionsgeschichte," 286-96; "I Sam 15," 148-79; "Die Vorgeschichte der Königserhebung Sauls" *ZAW* 79 (1967) 155-71.

[23]See nn. 13, 18, and K. Budde, "Sauls Königswahl und Verwerfung" *ZAW* 8 (1888) 223-48; Noth, *Überlieferungsgeschichtliche Studien* (2d ed.; Tübingen: Mohr, 1957) 56-58; J. Gray, "The Kingship of God in the Prophets and Psalms" *VT* 11 (1961) 1-29, esp. p 12, etc.

[24]*běnê bĕlîyaᶜal*. Note the important doublet 9:2//10:23, and that 10:20-21 again introduce Saul by tribe, clan and patronym (cf. 9:1). I owe the translation "hellions" here to Professor Cross, who suggested it in another context as a replacement for my original "sons of bitches."

entirely appropriate. This takes on significance in view of the fact that
11:12-13 presume precisely 10:27. In addition, the timetable of chap. 11[25]
presumes the dismissal of the assembly (10:25). The location of Saul in
Gibeah (11:4-5) also depends on 10:26.[26] Finally, the renewal of the
kingship by Samuel and the people (11:14) implies its prior initiation
(10:17-27). In sum, therefore, 1 Samuel 11 must be recognized as the
continuation of 10:17-27. It represents the sign that follows Saul's
designation (cf. 10:9-12 after 9:1-10:8), a confirmation of his divine
vocation.

From 1 Samuel 8; 10:17-27; 11, chap. 12 follows logically, as
Samuel's address at the "renewal" of the kingship (11:14-15). It rehearses
elements of 1 Samuel 8 (12:2; cf. 8:1ff.); it reviews once more the sacred
history (12:6-7, 8-11).[27] Finally, 12:6ff. lead directly to the formulation in
12:12 that Saul's elevation came in response to Ammon's threats. Since
this cannot be detached from the rehearsal that precedes, the chapter as a
whole must be linked to chap. 11, as well as to 8; 10:17-27. In
other words, chap. 12 confirms the association of chap. 11, with 8;
10:17-27.

In fact, a number of aporias arise from the isolation of 1 Sam 11
from 8; 10:17-27; and 12. First, 11:12-14 must arbitrarily be sundered
from their context.[28] More important, though the narrative of the
Ammonite war has close connections with 1 Sam 31:8-13; 2 Sam 2:4-7, it

---

[25]Professor Cross informs me that 4QSam[b] confirms Josephus' text on 10:27,
or the beginning of chap. 11. MT *wyhy kmhrys* should be read *wyhy kmw hds*
(already OG, 4QSam[b]), "a month later . . . ;" but this material introduces an
account of Ammonite aggrandizement which chronologically antedates Saul's
elevation. On the problem of simultaneity, here in point, see S. Talmon, "The
Presentation of Synchroneity and Simultaneity in Biblical Narrative" *SH* 27
(1978) 9-26.

[26]1 Sam 9:1-10:16 do not locate Saul specifically in Gibeah; it seems likely
therefore that in source B, Gibeah is first taken in 1 Sam 13:3-4 (hence "Gibeah
of Saul"—paradoxically only in A in 1 Sam 11:4; 15:34; 2 Sam 21:6; Isa 10:29—
parallel to calling Jerusalem "the city of David"). It is important to note here
that 2 Sam 21:14 indicates that the familial burial plot of Saul did not lie in
Gibeah.

[27]See again above, n. 25. The name Bedan in 1 Sam 12:11 may allude to
Abdon (Judg 12:13-15), as some suggest. More likely, however, is the Manassite
clan eponym (1 Chr 7:17).

[28]See above, n. 23 and O. Eissfeldt, *Die Komposition der Samuelisbücher*
(Leipzig: Hinrichs, 1931) 7-10; Noth, *Studien*, 56-58; H. Wildberger, "Samuel
und die Entstehung des israelitischen Königtums" *TZ* 13 (1957) 442-69, esp.
p. 468; K. D. Schunck, *Benjamin. Untersuchungen zur Entstehung und Geschichte
eines israelitischen Stammes* (BZAW 86; Berlin: Töpelmann, 1963) 107ff.; Hertzberg, *Samuel*, 94. Cf. Ishida, *Dynasties*, 42, 46-47.

appears, according to this hypothesis, in a vacuum. There is no introduction of Saul, either by tribe or by patronym;[29] there is no continuation beyond the now sundered coronation at Gilgal (11:14-15).[30] The
result is that Saul, who the histories claim must demonstrate "charisma"
to become king, needs do nothing of the sort to assemble the entire
league army of Israel, under his own leadership. A side of beef suffices to
call out all the tribes.

The integration of 1 Samuel 11 into the so-called anti-monarchic
source resolves all these difficulties. It satisfies additionally the literary
evidence adduced above. Questions about the narrative's character, however, necessarily assert themselves. For instance, what relation has the
elevation of Saul in 10:17-27 to the renewal of the kingship in 11:14-15?
Why does the sequence 1 Samuel 8; 10:17-27; 11; 12 appear to be both
critical of and positive toward monarchy? These questions cannot be
answered without reference to the ideological and historiographic background of the monarchic era. The sole clear literary deposit here is the
book of Judges.

II

The most advanced literary work on Judges stems from Wolfgang
Richter, appropriately enough. Richter has established, in two masterful
monographs, that the formula set down in Judg 2:11-19 was systematically worked into the narratives from Ehud to Gideon; to these was
prefaced the account of Othniel (3:7-11), an exmple of the pattern in
pure form, with only names plugged in. In deuteronomistic and other
redaction, chaps. (9)10-21 accrued.[31] The book in its most pristine form
comprehended chaps. 3:12-8:29, the history of the "major" "judges."

It is worthwhile outlining the formula of 2:11-19, which does little
violence to the text on which it was imposed. The Israelites, under
foreign rule, cry out to Yhwh. Yhwh raises a savior, who liberates them,

[29]Cf. 9:1-2; 10:20b-21; David in 1 Sam 16:1-13, 18; 17:12. Note also Judg
3:15b; 4:4a; 6:11; 11:1, etc. See W. Richter, *Traditionsgeschichtliche Untersuchungen zum Richterbuch* (*BBB* 18; Bonn: Hanstein, 1963) 12-13, 37-38.

[30]Soggin (*Königtum*, 41-47) leaves chap. 11 intact, tied for no good reason
only to 13:1-4; 14. Cf. B. C. Birch, "The Choosing of Saul at Mizpah" *CBQ* 37
(1975) 447-57; in *The Rise of the Israelite Monarchy: The Growth and Development of 1 Samuel 7-15* (*SBLDS* 27; Missoula: Scholars, 1976) 54-63, Birch
leaves 11:1-11, 15 as independent. However, his literary-critical arguments lack
force.

[31]Richter, *Untersuchungen; Die Bearbeitung des "Retterbuches" in der
deuteronomischen Epoche* (*BBB* 21; Bann: Hanstein, 1964). Possibly 2:11-19 and
the Othniel account, and even chaps. 9-12, belong to a second pre-deuteronomistic
edition of the book.

and rules thereafter uneventfully. The editor imputes the foreign rule to Israel's unfaithfulness. This is of little moment. Key is the idea that the "major" judge rescues his people from foreign hegemony, thereby earning power.

This pattern recalls the sequence of events in *Enuma Eliš* (Ee), the Babylonian creation epic. There, the assembly of gods is threatened by Tiamat. They seek a champion, finally entering into agreement with Marduk that if he meets Tiamat they will enthrone him (Ee 2:120-129; 3:55-65, etc.). Before the battle, they acclaim him king—in terms identical with those in which Absalom (2 Sam 15:10-13) and Adonijah (1 Kgs 1:5-11, 13, 23-25) are acclaimed (Ee 4:28).[32] On his victorious return, they enthrone him again, forever (Ee 4:133-134; 6:45-47; cf. 1 Sam 11:14-15). The pattern is identical to that of the "major" judges. Given only the nuance of Israel's monotheism, the judge is the avatar of the Divine Warrior.

Signal in this regard is the story of Jephthah. The account, in Judges 11, stands outside the oldest edition of Judges; still, it has closer links to that edition than the other materials appended after chap. 8. In it, Jephthah is approached by Gilead's elders.[33] He demands, like Marduk, ascendancy over the assembly in return for leadership at war. The elders offer him military leadership (*qāṣîn*),[34] which Jephthah rejects (11:6-7). The elders then offer civil leadership (*rō^ɔš*). Jephthah states, "If you restore me to fight the Ammonites, and Yhwh gives them over before me, I shall be your chief." Still, as in Marduk's case, Jephthah is installed before he goes out to war (Judg 11:8-11). In other words, he is provisional leader. Like Marduk's, Jephthah's subsequent ascendance depends on his martial success. He will return from battle with his shield, or on it.

A key difference between the Jephthah account and those of previous "major" judges is that the former lacks any notice of Yhwh's election. This has more literary than historical significance. Were one to rewrite the Jephthah account from the theological standpoint, one might well omit the details presented in 10:18; 11:5-11. It would be easy

---

[32] *marduk-ma šarru*, "Marduk is king." Note also Ps 47:9; 93:1; 97:1; 99:1. See further S. Mowinckel, *The Psalms in Israel's Worship* (New York: Abingdon, 1967) 1. 107-92.

[33] Note the role of the "elders" (*něśî^ɔîm* in priestly literature are elders in deuteronomistic literature) in Joshua 9; 1 Samuel 8; 1 Kings 12, etc. See esp. A. Malamat, "Organs of Statecraft in the Israelite Monarchy" *BA* 28 (1965) 34-65, and below.

[34] On *qāṣîn*, cf. Josh 10:24; Isa 3:1-7; 22:3; Dan 11:18. Micah 3 juxtaposes "head" and "leader" as in Judges 11; Prov 25:15 probably plays on Jephthah's leadership (*yěputtê qāṣîn*).

enough to substitute the catch-phrase, "And Yhwh raised up a savior
. . ." (Judg 2:16; 3:9, 15; cf. 4:1-6; 6:7-12, 33-40). The account, thus
revised, would not necessarily deny the negotiations between Jephthah
and the elders. It would de-emphasize them. It would assert that Yhwh
had worked his will through elders and assembly. Just this view underlies Epic traditions that the elders were inspired (Exod 24:9-11; Num
11:16-17, 23-29). Thus, the formulae applied to the "major" judges
reflect literary and theological usage. This usage draws attention away
from historical processes in effect among the tribes. For the Israelite, for
whom history represents Yhwh's judgment, the head of the muster is by
definition Yhwh's protege. Concrete political processes, therefore, remain implicit—in just such statements as, "Yhwh raised up for them a
savior."

The same historiographic contrast—between the objective, political
reporting of the Jephthah story and the more colored accounts of the
"major" judges—surfaces in the versions of Saul's rise. Thus 1 Sam 9:1-
10:16 present a shift to kingship in which everything is inspired by
Yhwh. Initiative descends from heaven; seers and god (and note 9:16;
10:1, 5-6, 7[35]) make the decisions throughout.[36]

1 Samuel 8; 10:17-27; 11 provide a stark contrast. There, the elders
demand kingship. Samuel consults with Yhwh, who orders him to
comply. The prophet then proposes, in hopes of persuading the assembly
to desist, a kingship of virtually unlimited power.[37] But the people
vote even for the despotism he initially offers. Samuel, now faced down,
consults again with Yhwh and agrees to install a king. This he does, at a
second convention, selecting Saul by sortition. Saul is acclaimed, the
constitution of kingship legislated. Some time thereafter, Saul summons
the muster, defeats Nahash, and wins his confirmation.

This narrative reports, as does the Jephthah narrative, negotiations
in assembly, the stuff of which politics were made. Regardless of the
historical value placed on the report, one ought not doubt that some

[35]Cf. "do what comes to hand" in Judg 9:33; note Ps 21:9; 1 Sam 23:17; Isa
10:14. Like "god is with you" (cf. Judg 6:12), this implies the reduction of the
Philistine garrison. Fulfillment comes in 13:2-4.

[36]The folkloristic character of 9:1-10:16 has inspired spirited debate. See, e.g.,
M. Bič, "Saul sucht die Eselinnen" *VT* 7 (1957) 92-97; Birch, "The Development
of the Tradition of the Anointing of Saul in 1 Sam 9:1-10:16" *JBL* 90 (1971) 55-
68; *Rise of Monarchy*, 29-42; D. R. ap-Thomas, "Saul's Uncle" *VT* 11 (1961) 241-
45; Buber, "Sauls Königswahl," 113-73; H. J. Stoebe, "Nochmal die Eselinnen
von Kiš" *VT* 7 (1957) 362-70.

[37]Note in 8:11 Samuel's remark, "This would/will be the *mišpāṭ* (legal due,
constitutional power) of the king who will/would reign over you." Samuel is
formulating a motion designed to frighten off support for monarchy (cf. Thucydides vi 20ff.). The assembly pass it nevertheless.

such negotiations occurred, and, as the source has it, between the elders, Samuel and the people. The narrative in 9:1ff., like the narrative concerning the "major" judges, skips over the deliberations of Israel's political organs, imputing initiative and disposal to the deity. 9:1-10:16 are pro-monarchical. But this theological disposition has worked itself into the form of the narrative. Kingship is not the issue: it is, rather, a premise. Not so in chap. 8. Here, the issue is tackled directly, as part of the narrative's content. The elders are not "wicked" for the narrator. Yhwh and Samuel stigmatize their behavior. But these are characters in the story, not the narrator himself. The result, if the facts are correct, is good history. Hence the contrast between the anti-monarchic sentiments of 1 Samuel 8 and the neutrality of 1 Samuel 11. The narrator records the participants' sentiments. Samuel (Yhwh) may have opposed the idea of monarchy. But he allowed it and himself designated the king. Kingship thus stands in the peculiar position of a relative evil embraced by the god. Such an attitude, if too sophisticated for most source-critics, demonstrates at least the complexity of the source.

This historiographic divergence makes it all the more impressive that a thorough structural congruence characterizes 1 Samuel 8; 10:17-27; 11; 12 and 1 Sam 9:1-10:16; 13-14. Briefly, in each account, Saul is designated and in some way acclaimed (9:22-24 with 10:1; 10:21-24). He wins a victory (10:9-11; 13:2-4; 13-14; and, 11). And, he settles down thereafter to rule as king (note the accession formulae of 14:47-52; cf. 11:14-15; 12).

This sequence is identical to that of the Jephthah narrative, and of the pattern in Judg 2:11-19. It is implicitly present in the narratives of all the major judges. Indeed, Gideon, after his victory, has the honor to refuse dynasty over Israel's confederacy (Judg 8:22-23). The fact is, a fairly clear pattern emerges from Israel's literature generally: there is a two-tiered process of designation and accession (cf. esp. Joshua 1; 3:7-10; 4:14; 2 Kings 9-10), interrupted, in some cases at least, by success on the battlefield or some ritual substitute. The exception is Adonijah, who is designated ritually (1 Kgs 1:5-11, 13, 23-25; cf. 2 Sam 15:10-13), but fails to win the throne. In this case, Solomon obtains a rival designation and acclamation (1 Kgs 1:38-39), and assumes power (1:49-53). But Solomon's accession proper ensues only on David's death (1 Kgs 2:10-12).[38]

[38]Curiously, the parallel account 1 Chr 23-2 Chr 1:1 is in substantial agreement. Chronicles omits the coup attempt by Adonijah, and exaggerates the dignity of Solomon's designation. But note 1 Kgs 1:42-53. The conflict is over matters of detail. On the two-tiered process delineated here, see also Alt, "Formation," 253-54; Soggin, Königtum, 43-44; recently, the very stimulating work of T. N. D. Mettinger, King and Messiah. The Civil and Sacral Legitimation of the Israelite Kings (Coniectanea Biblica Old Testament Series 8; Lund: Gleerup, 1976) 112-13, perhaps strongest to date.

This configuration has a bearing on the interpretation of the term *nāgîd*, a center of controversy since the middle of the century. The term occurs eleven times in the "deuteronomistic history" (1 Sam 9:16; 10:1; 13:14; 25:30; 2 Sam 5:2; 6:21; 7:8; 1 Kgs 1:35; 14:7; 16:2; 2 Kgs 20:5). In nine of these, the appointer is Yhwh.[39] In all eleven, the designee succeeds, or has succeeded, to the throne. Alt and others therefore concluded that the *nāgîd* was the divine designee for kingship.[40] Albright, however, who saw the *nāgîd* as a military leader,[41] and Richter, who argued that the title described a leader in the pre-monarchic era, dissented. Richter maintained that since Saul's anointment to be *nāgîd* was unique, that since Saul's commission corresponded to that of savior-judge (viz., Gideon), the "office" itself must be early and northern.[42]

Albright's position, based on comparison to a cognate term on the Nora stone and at Sefire, has not carried conviction. As for Richter's, Solomon's anointment as *nāgîd* (1 Kgs 1:35-40; 1 Chr 29:22), and David's anointment (1 Sam 16:1-13), very probably as *nāgîd* (see Sir 46:13) present something of an embarrassment. Richter's argument, in fact, that the position of *nāgîd* merged with monarchy after Saul's time assumes enthymematically that it was originally distinct from monarchy. This is not the understanding of 1 Sam 10:14-16; 13:2-14:52, let alone of any other passage in the Former Prophets (see also esp. 2 Chr 11:22).[43]

There is some merit in Richter's description of the position as "an office tied to Yhwh and filled through a prophet for the rescue of Israel,"[44] as 1 Sam 9:16ff.; 10:1ff., among other texts, suggest. This in no

---

[39]2 Kgs 20:5 refers to Hezekiah simply as "*nāgîd* of my (Yhwh's) people." The phrase is omitted in Isa 38:5. 1 Kgs 1:35 is anomalous in that David appoints the *nāgîd*. But Zadoq performs the unction (1 Kgs 1:38-40), implying divine appointment (to which David's is parallel).

[40]Alt, "Formation" 254 and n. 54; *NHI* 169 and n. 1, among others.

[41]W. F. Albright, *Samuel and the Beginnings of the Prophetic Movement* (Goldenson Lecture; Cincinnati: Hebrew Union College, 1961) 15-16. See Sefire III 10; Nora 3-8 in F. M. Cross, "An Interpretation of the Nora Stone" *BASOR* 208 (1972) 13-19.

[42]Richter, "Die *nāgîd*-Formel" *BZ* 9 (1965) 71-84.

[43]I have undertaken a systematic critique in my *Constitution*. See Ishida, *Dynasties*, 50-51. Professor A. Malamat has kindly called my attention also to Ishida's article on the subject in *JABS* 3. This, however, is unavailable to me. See, further, Mettinger, *King and Messiah* 151ff., esp. pp. 155-58, for highly sound discussion. Mettinger is in my view too hasty, however, in inferring from his (correct) association of 1 Kgs 1:35 with 1:20 that the root "to tell" is in point: the possibility of a pun is still open (p. 161).

[44]Richter, "Formel," 83. See now Cross, *CMHE*, 220 n. 5; *BHI*, 185; *HHI*, 137; Birch, *Rise*, 38-39, 119 n. 68.

way constitutes a license, however, to ignore or dismiss the associations between the *nāgîd* and kingship, evident in Samuel and Kings, as well as in 2 Chr 11:22.[45] The "office" is the position of heir-apparent, of official designee for the kingship. While the passages in Samuel and Kings indicate that Yhwh must make the designation, it is safe to assume that a secure dynasty would relegate the deity to a rubber-stamp role.[46]

This construction finds support in the analysis of 1 Sam 10:17-27; 11 and 1 Sam 9:1-10:16; 13:2-14:42 undertaken above. The *nāgîd* is Yhwh's designee for the crown before he wins the battle by which he proves his worth. Thus, Albright and Richter are correct in distinguishing as primary the military aspect of the position. In Jephthah's, Marduk's and Saul's cases, the designee is promised permanent power provided he saves the people. Saul, like divine king and Israelite judge, undergoes a two-tiered accession process.[47] It is as *nāgîd* that he proceeds against the Philistines (note 1 Sam 14:47a). This is also Saul's position in 1 Sam 10:17-27, though the alternate appellation "king" (cf. Ee 4:28) appears there. He must defeat Ammon in order to receive his confirmation (1 Samuel 11). Some confirmation comes from the story of Solomon's succession: Solomon is acclaimed in the same terms as is Saul at Mizpeh (*yĕḥî ham-melek*, lit. "Let the king live!" 1 Kgs 1:34, 39; 1 Sam 10:24); but he has actually become *nāgîd* (1 Kgs 1:35). His accession comes later.[48]

In this respect, then, kingship arose in Israel in continuity with the traditions and theological conceptions of the pre-monarchic league. Like the savior-judge, the king-elect was designated by Yhwh. Like the savior-judge, he proved his "charisma" by defeating a foe. And, like the savior judge as Israel's tradition recalled him, he assumed power thereafter permanently. The narratives of Saul's rise represent historiographic

---

[45]Read *kî ḥāšab lĕ-hamlîkô* with the versions. Cf. 1 Chr 5:2; 28:4.

[46]See my *Constitution*. In an important statement, Mettinger (*King and Messiah*, 162-79) has argued the term was originally a secular one, and acquired theological associations only after the Solomonic schism. His characteristically persuasive arguments demand a full response, which, unfortunately, cannot here be undertaken.

[47]Hence the correspondence noted by Richter between Saul's vocation and that of Gideon. See above. For a possible Mesopotamian parallel to kingship contingent on victory in the field, see T. Jacobsen, *Toward the Image of Tammuz* (W. L. Moran, ed.; Cambridge: Harvard, 1970) 373 n. 17.

[48]1 Kgs 2:12. Cf. E. Ball, "The Co-regency of David and Solomon" *VT* 27 (1977) 268-79; also I. Engnell, *Studies in Divine Kingship in Israel and the Ancient Near East* (2d ed.; Oxford: Blackwell, 1967) 17, for a parallel to the *bît ridūti* at Asshur. On this, cf. R. Labat, *Le caractère religieux de la royauté assyro-babylonienne* (*Etudes d'Assyriologie* 2; Paris: Adrien Maisonneuve, 1939) 40-80. On the formula *yĕḥî ham-melek*, see Mettinger, *King and Messiah*, 134-37.

implementations of the pattern for a leader's accession. One presumes, however, that as Israel's first king, Saul needed historically to conform to the same pattern.

III

Beyond this, it becomes difficult to trace the monarchy's introduction, primarily because of our ignorance of the structure of Israel's league. Noth's theory that ancient amphictyonies provide an apt model on which to construe Israel has fallen recently from favor.[49] The book of Judges itself evinces little internal political or sociological interest. And gleanings from the Pentateuch, though common enough in scholarship, remain unalterably scant and uncertain. The period of the judges is a dark alley in Israelite history. The critic enters it at his peril; and once in he must go slow to avoid unseen obstacles—many of them the corpses of his colleagues.

It is safe to assert the existence of some sort of alliance among the Israelite tribes in Canaan. Thus, the song of Deborah (Judges 5) summons ten of the tribes to war as "the people of Yhwh" (5:11). One confederate, Meroz, is cursed for evading its duty (5:23).[50] Reports of Ephraimite claims in Judg 8:1-7; 12:1-6 and the legal reprisals of Gideon in Judg 8:8-9, 14-17 bear the implications of Judges 5 out. Israel's unity under Saul, Ishbaal, David and Solomon provides confirmation.

On the other hand, Judah's (and therefore Simeon's) affiliation with the league is not entirely clear. Neither Judah nor Simeon appears in the song of Deborah, something of a damning circumstance given that Meroz is cursed for neglecting her obligations. All the other tribes, except Levi, are enumerated. Moreover, when one detaches the Othniel account from Judg 3:7-11 (following Richter),[51] the tribe plays no part in any of the central narratives of the book. In this case, the first reference to Judah after Judges 1 occurs in the Samson story: Judah extradites the Danite to the Philistines (Judg 15:8-19). Even if historical—a dubious

---

[49]Noth in *Das System der zwölf Stämme Israels* (*BWANT* 4/1; Stuttgart: Kohlhammer, 1930). Against him, H. Orlinsky, "The Tribal System of Israel and Related Groups in the Period of the Judges" *OA* 1 (1962) 11-20; G. Fohrer, "Altes Testament — 'Amphiktyonie' und 'Bund'?" *TLZ* 91 (1966) 801-16, 894-903; esp. R. de Vaux, *The Early History of Israel* (Philadelphia: Westminster, 1978) 695-749. Also, A. D. H. Mayes, *Israel in the Period of the Judges* (*SBT* 2/29; London: SCM, 1974).

[50]Probably a city or clan, Meroz may have been a tribe, or even, as my father, Prof. S. Halpern, observes (in correspondence), another name for an existing tribe.

[51]See above.

possibility—the passage indicates a loose relationship between Judah
and the north at best.

Scholars have adduced further texts to argue Judah's independence
of the league, and even of Saul.[52] For instance, 2 Sam 19:44 has Israel
claim "ten portions" in the king, against Judah's single portion (cf.
Judges 5). The civil war after Saul's death (2 Samuel 2-3), David's
wooing Judah's elders during Saul's reign (1 Sam 30:26-31), Judah's
exclusion from Solomon's districting system (1 Kgs 4:7-19) and the
division of the kingdom all point to a sharp differentiation between
Israel and the south. Still, one cannot discount Judah's definition of
herself as Israelite, even today, or the fact of unification under Saul,
David and Solomon. Broadly speaking, at least, Judah was Israelite.

Even within the northern league, however, distinctions are evident.
Meroz' expulsion (Judg 5:23), for example, finds a parallel in Gideon's
assault on Succoth and Penuel, motivated by their refusal to cross
Midian (Judg 8:5-9, 14-17). Presumably, the cities were obligated, as
members of the league, to sustain Gideon's offensive. At the same time,
the Transjordanian element seem to have followed a line in conflict with
that of their Cisjordanian allies.

The same narrative discloses tension between Manasseh and the
northerly tribes on the one hand and Ephraim on the other. Gideon calls
on Manasseh, Asher, Zebulun and Naphtali (6:34-35). He then pares his
force to three hundred men (7:2-8). The tribes involved border on the
Jezreel Valley. All participate in Deborah's victory, too (Judg 5:14c-d,
17c-18).[53] Yet Gideon's muster omits the other tribes. This leads to

---

[52]See, e.g., A. Jepsen, "Zur Überlieferungsgeschichte der Vätergestalten"
WZKMUL 3 (1953-1954) 265-81; de Vaux, "The Settlement of the Israelites in
Southern Palestine and the Origins of the Tribe of Judah," in *Translating and
Understanding the Old Testament*, ed. by H. T. Frank and W. L. Reed
(Nashville: Abingdon, 1970) 108-35; Herrmann, "Autonome Entwicklungen in
den Königreichen Israel und Juda" *VTSup* 17 (1969) 139-58; Mayes, *Israel*, 107;
J. W. Flanagan, "Judah in All Israel" in *No Famine*, 101-16; Freedman, "Early
Israelite History in the Light of Early Israelite Poetry" in *Unity and Diversity.
Essays in the History, Literature and Religion of the Ancient Near East*, ed. by
H. Goedicke and J. J. M. Roberts (Baltimore: Hopkins, 1975) 3-35.

[53]Issachar is absent from the list (cf. Judg 5:15a-c), which has cast suspicion
on the tribal muster as a whole. Thus W. Beyerlin, in "Geschichte und
Traditionsbildung im Alten Testament" *VT* 13 (1963) 1-25, has adduced strong
argument against its historicity. See also Richter, *Untersuchungen*, 114-20.
Richter's argument that the reduction of the muster proves there was no muster
is tendentious; in a league situation, participation of each group, even through
relatively few representatives, would have political consequence. By the same
token, there is no apparent reason for an editor to have added the northern tribes
to Abiezer, and omit Issachar: the notice in Judg 6:34-35 may therefore be

trouble particularly with the Ephraimites, who intercept Midianite elements fleeing across the Jordan (7:24-25). The account here is consonant with the subsequent "neutrality" of Gilead: in this account, Gilead is to Midian what until 1970 Cambodia was to the NVA, or Hashemite Jordan to the PLO. At any rate, Gideon's placation of Ephraim (8:1-3) implies both a treaty relationship and a rivalry. It suggests that a closer confederation existed among the tribes north of Ephraim than among the north as a whole. And it testifies strongly to the relative independence of Trans- from Cisjordan.

With its hints of dialectal difference (12:5-6) and further Ephraimite pressure—this time on Gilead (12:1ff.)—the Jephthah story bears these impressions out. The Israelite "league" was a segmented entity—its components stood in varying relations to one another, just as one should expect. Possibly, the sectional differentiation of 2 Sam 2:8 represents an accurate depiction. At any rate, the relationship was loose, sectionally defined, and probably in constant flux. It is the long-term cohesion, not the disunity of the tribes that should command wonder.

Unanimity on the government of this amoebic community is the last thing one should expect from historiographic or modern critical circles.[54] Still, several instances are recorded in which the "league"

---

authentic. 7:23 is not evidence to the contrary; it picks up the strand of 7:8 (cf. 7:22 and 7:8). Zebulun's omission from 7:23 is probably due to haplography (homoioarcton).

[54]With the exception of Baraq, the "judges" seem to be largely local. Scholars have therefore tried to generate some sort of national network from the contrast between the major and minor judges. See, e.g., Noth, "Das Amt des 'Richters Israels,'" *Festschrift Alfred Bertholet*, ed. by W. Baumgartner *et al* (Tübingen: Mohr, 1950) 404-17; D. A. McKenzie, "The Judge of Israel" *VT* 25 (1975) 118-21; K.-D. Schunck, "Die Richter Israels und ihr Amt" *VTSup* 15 (1966) 252-62; H. W. Hertzberg, "Die kleinen Richter" *TLZ* 79 (1954) 285-90. But the list of minor judges does not bear this out. The list (10:1-5; 12:7-15) can be identified only by its form. It plainly includes Jephthah (12:7), whose story is inserted at the point in the list where his name would have occurred (10:6-12:6). It seems also to include Gideon (8:30, 32; 8:31 is an insertion proleptic of chap. 9, and the expected "he judged Israel X years" has been displaced by the *Retterbuch* conclusion in 8:28). Thus, even disregarding the fact that Yair (10:3-5) is identical with the conqueror of the Bashan (Num 33:41; Deut 3:14; 1 Kgs 4:13; 1 Chr 2:21-23), and Tola (10:1-2; cf. Gen 46:13; Num 26:23; 1 Chr 7:1-5) and Elon (12:11-12; cf. Gen 46:14; Num 26:26), and very likely the enigmatic savior *bdn* of 1 Sam 12:11 (1 Chr 7:17) with clan eponyms (against Noth, "Amt," 408-12), it is impossible to distinguish historically "minor" from "major" "judges." Samuel, in fact, may be the last figure on the list (1 Sam 7:15; 8:1-2; 25:1=28:3; Mayes [*Israel*, 59-60] is too quick to dismiss Samuel and Gideon among a host of less

probably did assemble. The first is the case of Deborah; a second is the assembly of Saul's election. In each, the presiding authority is sacral. The same holds true for the account of the battle against the Philistines at Ebenezer (1 Samuel 4). And Judges 20, though historically suspect, provides a fourth instance. Historiographically, therefore, and perhaps historically, the league went to war at the behest, or with the approval, of a central sacral authority (cf. Exod 17:8-16; Num 10:35-36; 14:40-45).[55] Such an authority probably presided regularly over the league council. Thus Gideon refuses dynasty (Judg 8:22-23) in order to don the cloth: his predilection for priesthood (8:24-27) represents a preference for a position independent of popular approval.[56]

Here the Jephthah account assumes real significance. A number of passages (e.g., Deut 21:1-9, 18-21; 22:13-21) confirm the elders' and assemblies' control over local politics suggested in Judg 11:1-11. That a local council might refuse to dispatch troops to a league war (e. g., Judg 5:23; 12:2; 21:5-9; cf. Judg 8:5-8; 1 Sam 11:7, etc.) corroborates the point. The confederacy was sufficiently loose that each region could exercise control over its own relationship to the whole. A similar arrangement obtained in the United States before the Civil War. At the same time, as in the United States, the central regime, conditions permitting,[57] could impose its will by force (Judges 19-21; prps. Judg 8:1-7; 12:1-6; also 8:8-17; 5:23),[58] or the threat of force (1 Sam 11:7). The inference is sensible, therefore, that regional dignitaries represented tribal and local units at some sort of confederate assembly. Over their deliberations, the priesthood evidently exercised presidence.

These considerations lend added significance to Gideon's establishment of a priesthood. His action, viewed against 1 Samuel 8, confirms that the king in Israel was regarded as the creature of the confederate assembly. The same is true for Jephthah on a tribal level. The national

---

cogent cases). Thus, to distinguish on this basis is to assume the offices were different because the sources concerning them were different. See further Richter, "Zu den 'Richtern Israels'" *ZAW* 77 (1965) 40-72; J. Dus, "Die 'Sufeten' Israels" *Archiv Or.* 31 (1963) 444-69; de Vaux, *Early History*, 751-73.

[55] The custom of asking divine approval for war, of course, persisted. See *CMHE*, 226-27.

[56] See my "The Rise of Abimelek ben-Jerubbaal" *HAR* 2 (1978) 79-100.

[57] Given the confederates' willingness to participate. We should not think of an active, administrative and legislative central government. A national assembly would be rare, with government largely local, all within the guidelines of an inter-tribal treaty (the covenant).

[58] Prof. T. Gaster has suggested to me that the "angel of Yhwh" who orders the reviling of Meroz in this last passage may be a ranking member of the league sacral establishment.

"judge," by contrast, is consistently characterized as Yhwh's creature.[59] Thus, in the same sense as that in which Deborah appoints Baraq,[60] it seems likely that the priesthood (i. e., Yhwh) might designate any figure of stature to assume civil and military imperium. If the office of "judge" did in fact exist on the national level, its incumbent derived his imperium most likely from the god (i. e., the priesthood), and not from the assembly. As an appointee, the "judge" would not enjoy the dynastic rights exercised on the one hand by the priesthood, and, on the other, by the king.

This conclusion rests largely on those accounts in which the league assembles as a body (Judges 4-5; 19-21; 1 Samuel 4; 8; 10:17-27; 11; 12). In this connection, another consideration deserves special note: as Israel emerges into the era of the kings, its last two "judges" are Eli, a priest of Shiloh (1 Samuel 1-4, esp. 4:18) and Samuel, Eli's protege (1 Samuel 7ff.).[61] This is the period in which a fully united Israel is most likely to have existed. This is the era closest to the time of the monarchy. Like the Greek amphictyony, therefore, Israel's confederacy apparently convened under the auspices of a central, priestly establishment.

IV

The materials above shed considerable light on 1 Samuel 8; 10:17-27; 11; 12. There, the elders approach the priest. After a consultation with Yhwh, the priest presents a motion, on which the people pass (1 Sam 8:1-20). This sequence is characteristic of assembly transactions both before and during the monarchy. Thus, Ahab consults with the elders over the appeasement of Ben-Hadad; subsequently, "all the elders and all the people ($^{c}\bar{a}m$)" reply (1 Kgs 20:7-8). David negotiates to become king with the elders of Judah (1 Sam 30:26-31); the "men of Judah" enthrone him (2 Sam 2:1-4).[62] When David seeks restoration after

[59]See, e.g., Judg 2:11-19 and above. I differentiate here between Jephthah's appointment as "head and commander" of Gilead and his tenure as "judge" of Israel. Note, though, that Saul's imperium is divine only as $n\bar{a}g\hat{i}d$, divine designee for kingship. In Jephthah's case, priestly designation may be implicit in Judg 11:11. Cf. 1 Sam 10:25; 11:15).

[60]Deborah represents a divine presence (accompanying Baraq to battle—Judg 4:8-9) and may actually have led the league sacral establishment. This is blatantly conjectural, however.

[61]Even J. L. McKenzie ("The Four Samuels" *BR* 7 [1962] 3-18), arguing that Samuel was only a seer, not a priest, prophet or "judge," leaves Samuel some of his religious functions.

[62]See H. Tadmor, " 'The People' and the Kingship in Ancient Israel: The Role of Political Institutions in the Biblical Period" *JWH* 11 (1968) 46-68. Tadmor establishes that this is probably the body of citizenry under arms, representing the ·constituent assembly.

Absalom's revolt, he again negotiates with the elders (2 Sam 19:12-14); again, the "men of Judah" elect him (19:15-16, 41-44). Jephthah negotiates his appointment with "the elders of Gilead" (Judg 11:5-10); but "the people ($^c\bar{a}m$) placed him over them" (11:11). The leader formulates the resolution on which the assembly must pass in consultation with the elders; the assembly have the final decision to make.[63]

A glance at 1 Kings 12 brings the point home. Israel demands that Rehoboam promise to reduce taxes. Rehoboam consults with the elders, and with the "children" with whom he grew up (non-tribal officers).[64] He rejects compromise, and the assembly vote against his succession. In Israel's patriarchal society, the elder's view would carry substantial weight.[65] Thus, in 1 Samuel 8, where the elders carry the tribes's position to Samuel, Samuel makes concession to their viewpoint. The tribes ratify it duly. The narrative observes with scrupulous care the form of the Israelite polity.

The treatment of the issues in 1 Samuel 8 boasts a similar verisimilitude. Two groups participate: the assembly, and Samuel, representing the president sacral authority. With their request, the assembly threaten this polar configuration. The king, like Jephthah, is to be a civilian head and a warlord (esp. 8:20; cf. Judg 8:22) His permanent enthronement, at the levies' head, and in all likelihood with a qualified dynastic guarantee,[66] could come only at the expense of some of Samuel's prerogative. As the assembly's creature, his primary allegiance would be to the people. In the new arrangement, it was the priesthood that stood to lose most.

[63]See Deut 21:18-21; 1 Kgs 21:8-11 (elders bring the charge; the people pass judgment; and the observation of legal forms indicates legal restraint on the king); Jer 26:1-24; Exod 19:7-8; 2 Kgs 23:1-2. I have discussed this issue in detail in my *Constitution*. Especially noteworthy is 2 Chr 30:2-4, where king and assembly exercise sacral control; cf. 1 Sam 14:36-45 (read with OG throughout) for a case where the assembly alone do so. Note that there is no case in HB in which the "people" and "elders" are at odds.

[64]See Malamat, "Organs of Statecraft," 41-50, and bibliography there. Cf. G. Evans, "Rehoboam's Advisers at Shechem and Political Institutions in Israel and Sumer" *JNES* 25 (1966) 273-79. Evans correctly denies the typological equivalence Malamat saw between Israel and Sumer. Malamat's conclusions, however, are sound.

[65]Note that Absalom's advisors contend in council for the elders' favor (2 Sam 16:20-24; 17:1-15). Here again, final approval comes from Absalom and the assembly (cf. 2 Chr 30:2-4).

[66]Though kingship was from the first dynastic in Israel, scholars have commonly maintained the opposite. Ishida (*Dynasties*), however, has now laid even the ghost of the dispute to rest.

The reports of Samuel's opposition to monarchy in 1 Samuel 8, therefore, deserve considerably more credence than those of his silence, even enthusiasm, in 1 Sam 9:1-10:16. Samuel's very remarks in the chapter are almost equally authentic. That is, the notion that a demand for monarchy amounted to apostasy is a natural one for a priest, and is grounded somewhat already in the Gideon story. Similarly, Samuel's "'manner' (mišpāṭ) of the king" to be installed (8:11-18), spoken publicly, addresses the tribes' concerns, concerns that no doubt asserted themselves in contemporary debate—those of taxation. Plainly, these were at issue at the time of the Solomonic schism (1 Kings 12), and probably already earlier in Solomon's reign.[67] They are present already in early traditions of opposition to the census (2 Samuel 24; 1 Chronicles 21) in David's reign. It would be less than surprising, too, if resistance to David's temple-building plans (2 Samuel 7; 1 Chronicles 17), and, indeed, the revolts of Absalom and Sheba (2 Samuel 15-20) arose not so much out of ideological conflicts as from economically based opposition to public works.

Scholars have been quick to assign Samuel's anti-royalism to the "deuteronomist(s)," or to an originally anti-Solomonic polemic displaced by the "deuteronomist(s)."[68] This is untenable. There is no incontestably deuteronomistic context in which such sentiments appear.[69] There is no evidence of "anti-monarchic" sentiment in Israel after David—the north, seceding at Solomon's death, installs a king, in fact. And there is no king or reign to which the "deuteronomist" applies the language used here. Even in Solomon's case, the "deuteronomist" avoids recalling Samuel's polemic; his polemic simply indicts David's heir for apostasy (1 Kings 11), somewhat a more serious problem. Indeed, the Solomonic schism flatly contradicts Samuel's concluding prophecy, "You will cry out on that day because of your king, whom you have chosen for yourselves; but Yhwh will not answer you on that

[67]See my "Sectionalism and the Schism" *JBL* 93 (1974) 519-32.

[68]See Noth, *Studien*, 57; Birch, *Rise*, 23-29. Worst is R. E. Clements, "The Deuteronomistic Interpretation of the Founding of the Monarchy in I Sam. VIII" *VT* 24 (1974) 398-410. Clements argues the anti-Solomonic polemic was displaced to Saul because the "deuteronomist" regarded Davidides as sacrosanct. Even ignoring various condemnations of Davidic kings in 1-2 Kings, Dtr is precisely anti-Solomonic, as comparison of 1 Kings 1-11 with 1 Chronicles 22-2 Chronicles 9 illustrates. Further, Clements fails to explain why accusations of oppression were excised (except from 1 Kings 12, where they are historical: see my "Sectionalism") while those of apostasy were not. Again, the ideological argument is insufficiently subtle for the sources.

[69]See esp. A. Weiser, "Samuel und die Vorgeschichte des israelitischen Königtums" *ZTK* 57 (1960) 141-61.

day" (8:18). Thus, the text seems to antedate the division. When to these considerations one adds the fact that 1 Sam 8:11-18 paint an accurate picture of contemporary Canaanite kingship,[70] it seems somewhat frivolous to detach the material from its historical context.[71]

Historiographically, Samuel's remarks represent his effort to dissuade the assembly from adopting monarchy: he adopts the subtle strategy of formulating a proposal stronger than the proponents of change would like (cf. Thucydides vi 20ff.). Concentrating on the economic costs of kingship, he suggests that the government will burgeon, expanding beyond control. Ultimately, this would pose a second, political threat to the conservative tribal elders: central government could grow only at their expense, and at that of their clans and families.[72] The suggestion, of course, was as accurate as, no doubt, it was telling. Thus, the probability is that the historiographic recollection is accurate as well.

Simultaneously, Samuel's expatiation paves the way for a full formulation of monarchic power. The deliberations recorded in 1 Samuel 8 lead to the passage of a resolution introducing kingship into Israel. The form of the kingship, however, remained a matter for debate. The remarks of 1 Sam 8:11-18 indicate that Samuel, reluctantly prepared to accommodate a constitutional change, desired to set some limitation on the king. The opportunity to do so was set into the very structure of the inauguration. First, the king must be Yhwh's candidate, offering Samuel, and, so far as he knew, his successors among the Shilonite priesthood, at least some control over the politics of succession. On the other hand, under what influence a king might fall after his designation would be impossible to divine.

The second source of limitation was a legal one. To judge from Judg 11:1-11; 2 Sam 5:1-3; 2 Kings 11, and especially 1 Kings 12, election of officers in Israel involved negotiation and contract; it involved mutual obligation. For kings, similarly (and see Judg 9:8-20), the assembly's consent, and their entry into a covenant, was the necessary culmination of the accession process (again, 2 Samuel 19).[73] Wielding the threat of

[70]The study of I. Mendelsohn ("Samuel's Denunciation of Kingship in the Light of Akkadian Documents from Ugarit" *BASOR* 143 [1956] 17-22) remains sound. Frequently cited, it seems rarely to be weighed.

[71]See now Soggin, *Königtum*, 33-37; M. Tsevat, "The Biblical Narrative of the Foundation of the Kingship in Israel" *Tarbiz* 36 (1966-1967) 99-109 (Hebrew); Ishida, *Dynasties*, 36-41.

[72]See below, and, for Solomon's district system, my "Sectionalism" 528-31.

[73]See Fohrer, "Der Vertrag zwischen König und Volk in Israel" *ZAW* 71 (1959) 1-22; G. Widengren, "King and Covenant" *JSS* 2 (1957) 1-32; Soggin, *Königtum*, 43-47; cf. Tadmor, " 'People' and Kingship," 59-62. Note 2 Sam 5:1-3; D. J. Wiseman, *The Vassal-Treaties of Esarhaddon* (London: British School of

refusal to ratify the king's nomination, the assembly were in a position to extract political concessions (so 1 Kings 12). An identical theoretical mechanism obtained at Rome, where the senate had the power to delineate the emperor's powers at his accession.[74] Simply, the electorate in an elective autocracy could extract campaign promises before installing the king, and endow them with legal status.

The process of this legal limitation is reported in 1 Sam 10:25. Samuel, at Saul's designation (not his confirmation), "spoke to the people the 'manner' (*mišpāṭ*) of the kingship and wrote it in a scroll (*sēper*) and laid it up before Yhwh." Presumably, this scroll limited the king's authority—both for Samuel's sake, and for that of the tribal elders. No other text refers to this one. The report itself creates the question, what did the "constitution of kingship" contain? It is difficult to suppose that the author of the account did not have a specific, recorded text in mind. In any other event, 1 Sam 10:25 is a gratuitous, even foolish assertion.[75] This report, which squares so nicely with its historical, as well as with its historiographic context, is accurate.

Granting that some document enjoining moderation on the king is envisioned in 1 Sam 10:25, the "law of the king" in Deut 17:14-20 suggests itself as a likely possibility. This ordinance, responding almost explicitly to the concerns that motivate 1 Sam 8:11-18, is the only text in HB regulating kingship:

> When you come to the land that Yhwh your god is giving to you, and you inherit it, and inhabit it, and say, "Let me place over me a king like all the nations that are around me," do indeed place a king over you, whom Yhwh your god chooses. From among your brothers you may place over you a king; you will not be able to put over you a foreign man, who is not your brother.

> But, let him not multiply for himself, *nor send the people back to Egypt in order to multiply horses; Yhwh has said to you, "You shall not continue to return this way again."* Let him not multiply wives for himself, *that his heart not turn;* and silver and gold let him not multiply for himself (too) much . . . (Deut 17:14-17).[76]

Archaeology in Iraq, 1958) lines 41-72, 188-97; *ABL* 1239, as exemplars of related Assyrian practice.

[74]*CIL* 6, 1, 167 n. 930; see J. B. Bury, *The Constitution of the Later Roman Empire* (Cambridge: Cambridge, 1910) 25-27.

[75]No other reference to a "scroll/book" in HB appears to be fraudulent. See my "Chronicles' Thematic Structure: Indications of an Earlier Source," forthcoming in *The Creation of Context*, ed. by R. E. Friedman, for argument that tends to substantiate the authenticity of source references found in Chronicles.

[76]The material underlined seems to be secondary. After "horses," the text shifts from an address to "you" (singular) to one referring to the people in the

Thereafter, the law urges the king to read the book of the law; by observing it, he can extend his and his children's days on the throne (17:18-20).

This text has occasioned extensive debate.[77] However, numerous considerations tie it to the inception of the monarchy. First, it is literarily associated with the elder's request (1 Sam 8:4, 20; cf. 10:19; 12:12). Second, in offering kingship as a possibility, not as a given, the statute refers to its adoption. Third, the Court History of David twice responds to the demand that the king be an Israelite (2 Sam 5:1-3; cf. 1 Chr 11:1-3; 12:23-41; and, 2 Sam 19:11-13; cf. also Judg 9:2; elsewhere, Gen 2:22; 29:4). No such concern surfaces at any time after the accounts of David's reign; the formula of compliance there disappears after the 10th century.[78]

In addition, Deut 17:14-20 understand the people to place over themselves a king, who must be designated by Yhwh. This is the understanding of 1 Samuel 8; 10:17-27; 11; 12 as well. In the Former Prophets, records of the whole process are rare (1 Sam 10:17-11:15; 2 Kings 11). Thus the law has its primary reflex in Saul's case. Fifth, the tenor of the law is identical to that of 1 Samuel 8ff.: kingship, an evil created by the assembly, is to be accepted reluctantly as a fact of life.

A sixth, historical piece of evidence is David's hamstringing the horses of Aram (2 Sam 8:4). Previous explanations have harped on David's supposed, but rather dubious, inability to integrate the chariot animals into his military establishment. Far more likely is the explanation that David was adhering to the "law of the king."[79] Chariot horses were valuable spoil: David did not hamstring them for lack of outlets either among his subjects or among distant foreign nations.

---

third person. This is rare in the law-code (Deuteronomy 12-26), being elsewhere only in 13:10; 16:18; 17:7, 13; 18:3; 20:2-9. It is used to distinguish some subsection of the people from the corporate body under address. That this is also the case in 17:16 suggests it may belong to the same legal layers as the laws cited above. Note allusions to it in Isa 2:6-8; 30:2; 31:1. Deut 17:16 then addresses Israel in the plural. V 16b is paranetic; it lends a polysyndetic awkwardness to the whole. Like much of the hortatory material in the code, it is probably an accretion. On the plural as secondary, see G. M. de Tillesse, "Sections 'tu' et sections 'vous' dans le Deutéronome" *VT* 12 (1962) 29-87. On 17:18-20, cf. M. Weinfeld, *Deuteronomy and the Deuteronomic School* (Oxford: Oxford, 1972) 5 n. 1.

[77]See Ishida, *Dynasties*, 37-41.

[78]The phrase in Gen 2:22 is different and perhaps should not be considered here. Still, it expresses kinship (2:24). Assuming that J is 10th c., the phrase is not witnessed thereafter. See Malamat ("Organs," 170) for some corroboration.

[79]I wish to thank Prof. R. E. Friedman for bringing this case to my attention.

It is the context of "the law of the king" that affords greatest confidence in this regard. Deut 17:8-13 erects a high court of Levites and appointees, independent of the king. After the law of the king, Deut 18:1-8 establishes a national priestly order. The law treats the " 'manner (*mišpāṭ*)' of the priests," regulating the priests' due from sacrifice (18:3). Here, it calls to mind 1 Sam 2:13-14, where the priests' "manner (*mišpāṭ*)" is wholly different. In point, in the law, is the "legal right," a substantial concession.[80]

The ensuing legislation, establishing a prophetic office, is of signal import. 18:9-14 ban the traditional mantic arts, presumably with the intention of creating some sort of "prophetic" monopoly over sooth-saying in Israel. A notice in the histories dates this legislation to some extent: 1 Sam 28:3, 8-14 (cf. 1 Chr 10:13) credibly assert that Saul initiated the prosecution of necromancers among the tribes. That is, the law came into force specifically in Saul's reign. Yet one cannot detach it from the "law of the prophet" (18:15-22), which follows. The injunctions of 18:9-14, set into effect by Saul, clear out the prophet proper's competition.

Frank Moore Cross has had the insight—characteristically, it may be added, it is the sort of ground-breaking insight upon which a lesser scholar might found a whole career, but which in Cross is born of that intuition of history that can be cultivated, but rarely sewn—that the institution of prophecy in Israel arose and declined with monarchy. In his view, the prophet appointed the *nāgîd*, denounced the king's excesses, and initiated the Holy War.[81] Thus the prophet in the monarchy imposed a sacral restraint—in theory—on the king's secular power. Such an office represents precisely the concession one would expect the priestly establishment to extract from the assembly in return for the erection of a monarchy. Moreover, in its creation of an officer "like (Moses)" (18:15), the ordinance ties itself to the league: the "judge" is very much an undifferentiated executive and cultic leader, "like Moses" (and cf. 1 Sam 12:1-5 with Num 16:15),[82] an officer both civil and military (and note the military organization of the subsidiary judiciary in Exodus 18). That of the four monarchic offices—those of king, priest, judge and prophet—the prophet should inherit the Mosaic mantle, that the role of "Prophet" is precisely that which Samuel himself assumes

---

[80]The remarks in 1 Sam 2:15ff. accuse Shiloh of aberration from the *mišpāṭ* here laid out. But the law is considerably more generous than the priests' practice there. Cf. Lev. 7:34.

[81]*CMHE*, 223-29.

[82]See Cross, *CMHE*, 219-20 n. 3; and de Vaux's extremely solid treatment in *Early History*, 751-73.

(and to no recorded detriment to Saul),[83] suggests that this law should be located in the era of the shift to kingship.[84]

The provisions of Deut 17:8-18:22 thus work to limit and to hedge the powers of the monarch. In so doing, they reflect the concerns that assert themselves in 1 Samuel 8-12. Even more, Deut 18:1-8, along with much of the other legal material in Deuteronomy, reserve the cult to the Levites only. Given the well-known priestly diversity of pre-monarchic Israel (including Judg 8:22-27; 17:1-6), and the pallor of the evidence for such diversity after the inception of the kingship,[85] it is perhaps too daring, but not unreasonable to suggest that this, too, was a concession that Samuel extracted: he obtained, in exchange for the king, a Levitic monopoly on the cult. That is, the individual elements of Deut 17:8-18:22 saw enforcement during the United Monarchy, even during Saul's reign.[86] The program as a whole makes eminent historical sense if located at the transition to kingship. The implication is, the Deuteronomic text is the authentic prescription for the constitutional shift to monarchy.

V

With this as background, a new synthesis of the accounts of the early monarchy is possible. The Israelite tribes in the 11th c. B.C.E. found themselves confronting a series of problems. To the north, a series of Aramean kingdoms were beginning to crystallize in Syria. Phoenicia was awakening from a relative dark age that came on her in the 14th c. To the south, in a period of Egyptian weakness, Amaleq seems to have been

---

[83] See Cross, *CMHE*, 223-29; Albright, *Samuel.* For general discussion, see also Clements, *Prophecy and Covenant* (*SBT* 43; London: SCM, 1965).

[84] I therefore moot here the admittedly speculative notion that Moses was regarded in the early tradition as a "judge," motivating Exodus 18 (E) when the sense "ruler" was attenuated, because this was the model available by which to construe his role. The tradition—already in Hos 12:14—that Moses was a "prophet" arose with the "prophet's" assumption of his (in reality, rent) mantle in the constitutional arrangements for monarchy.

[85] Note my contrary remarks in "Rise" 84-88. Note A. Cody, *A History of Old Testament Priesthood* (*AnBib* 35; Rome: P. B. I., 1969) 52ff.; de Vaux, *Ancient Israel* (N. Y.: McGraw-Hill, 1965) 2.358ff.. Note, finally, that Deut 18:6-8 has a reflex in 1 Sam 2:36, adumbrating a Shilonite (i.e., Samuelic) origin for the text and its surroundings. Isa 2:6-8 perceives the unity of the whole.

[86] Deut 18:20-22 is in effect in 1 Kings 22. The king of Israel imprisons Micaiah after calling the people to witness. If Micaiah's prophecy proves false, the king will, quite rightly, kill him (vv 27-29). The historian, portraying the king as a blackguard, neglects the fact that he acts in accordance with the law. The tradition therefore rests on prior, possibly historical materials, attesting to the precedence of the Deuteronomic ordinance. See further my *Constitution.*

engaged in marauding across settled territories (1 Samuel 15; 27:8; 30). David's treatment of Edom (2 Sam 8:13-14; cf. 1 Kgs 11:14-22) suggests that it either participated in Amaleq's ventures (cf. Deut 25:17-19) or posed a signal independent threat of its own. To the west, Ammon was entering a period of military strength (1 Samuel 11, esp. *apud* Josephus), threatening the very existence of the inhabitants of Gilead. And, in Canaan, Philistia maintained an iron grip on the lowlands and passes.

Confined to the hills, only loosely organized, Israel was in no position to resist her more sophisticated neighbors. Moreover, the refinement of iron-working techniques was bringing with it a progressive dominance of cataphractic warfare (see 1 Sam 17:5-6 in context; 21:16). To this circumstance, the Philistines responded by establishing a monopoly on metal-working in Canaan (1 Sam 13:19-21), and by creating a professional soldiery skilled in contemporary tactics. To judge from Ammon's success in the same period, and from the fact that she functioned under a monarchy, a similar situation obtained in Transjordan. However, geography was most conducive to the growth of a professional army in the plains in which the Philistines were located; chariotry, the use of which required trained and subsidized specialists, was the major weapon there in shock combat from early times. With a tradition, therefore, of a professional military, the Philistines stood at a sharp advantage over other peoples in the region.

The introduction of iron into the hills, however, opened whole new areas for cultivation. It must have led to an explosion in agriculture, and may have led to a population increase as well. Ultimately, these factors contributed to Solomon's public works; perhaps they provided at the time an incentive to settle more thickly lowlands previously infested with disease. In Samuel's day, however, it seems likely that they produced an accumulation of capital—human and financial—whose reinvestment was to produce the expansion of the next fifty years.[87]

Israel had no tradition comparable to that of Philistia, and no mechanism by which to erect a standing force. In order to throw off Philistine domination, in order to expand into the valleys and passes, in order to participate in the resurgence of the region, she needed to restructure her very essence. The tribesmen agreed to submit to a strong

[87]Compare the remarks of C. H. J. de Geus, *The Tribes of Israel. An Investigation into Some of the Presuppositions of Martin Noth's Amphictyony Hypothesis* (*Studia Semitica Neerlandica* 18; Assen: van Gorcum, 1976) 180-81. De Geus's fine study, which came into my hands just as this piece was going to press, deserves systematic response. It should be noted, however, that the centrality of the clan to daily life does not mitigate the administrative reality of the tribe; nor does this second reality mitigate the institutional self-expression of the "people, Israel."

central administration. They appealed to an indigenous military element familiar with the new technology and tactics (1 Sam 13:22; 16:21; 17:38-39; 18:4; cf. Judg 11:1ff.), the class to which Saul, Jonathan, and David evidently belonged. The sources recall—and the recollection is probably reliable—that these Israelites eluded Philistine shock tactics by resorting primarily to missile warfare, using the sling and bow (esp. 1 Chr 12:2; also 1 Sam 17:40-51; cf. 21:10;[88] 1 Sam 31:3; 2 Sam 1:22). Ultimately, in order to descend into the plains, Israel would need to assimilate all the arms and tactics of the new age (and note 2 Sam 2:12-16).

At the same time, the tribes cannot have been unanimously disposed toward the innovation. Kingship involved a profound sociological change to which the elders, no less than Samuel, would have been alert. Once in charge of a professional army, the king would represent a formidable force in internal, as well as external affairs. The cost of maintaining even a modest royal establishment must have figured prominently in the minds of men unaccustomed to taxation, if perhaps learned in extortion. Moreover, certain areas of the countryside would have reaped from the innovation benefits minute in comparison to those of a Benjamin, suddenly in control of the mountain passes, or of a Manasseh, now expanding into the Jezreel Valley. Social and economic considerations therefore asserted themselves in council.

The kingship that emerged from the Ramah and Mizpeh proceedings took its shape from all these factors. Saul was appointed to assemble a professional army (1 Sam 8:20; 13:2; 14:52). Its first task was the unification of the Israelite tribes: Saul's early actions cleared the Philistines from the Aijalon Pass (1 Sam 13:2-14:46), securing communications between himself and Judah, and guaranteeing Benjaminite access to Transjordan, and, on the other hand, established league protection over Gilead (1 Samuel 11).[89] What offensives would have ensued had Saul not met his death on Gilboa it is impossible to tell. At any rate,

---

[88]The sling represented a highly advanced weapon at the time. See Y. Yadin, *The Art of Warfare in Biblical Lands* (New York: McGraw-Hill, 1963) 2.252. Yadin asserts that the Philistines did not use the bow, but did employ the javelin for medium-range engagement. Thus, for 1 Sam 17:40-51, the analogy to the duel between Yankee and knight in Twain's *Connecticut Yankee* would not be inappropriate. But cf. 1 Sam 31:3. On 1 Sam 17:40-51, see A. Deem, " '. . . and the stone sank into his forehead.' A note on 1 Samuel xvii 49" *VT* 28 (1978) 349-51. Citing T. Jud. 3:1 as a parallel, Deem argues *mṣḥ*, "forehead," is an error for *mṣḥt*, "greave," in 17:49 (cf. 17:6), and that David actually kneecapped Goliath. This remains hypothetical.

[89]On 1 Samuel 13-14, so, too, Mayes, *Israel*, 102-3. See also C. E. Hauer, "The Shape of the Saulide Strategy" *CBQ* 31 (1969) 153-67. Hauer suggests that Saul turned from west (1 Samuel 11) to his center (13-14) to the south (15), to the north (29-31), the last abortively, in an effort to clear Israel's highlands. He is

though Saul had the power to tax, and to pay his professionals through land grants (e.g., 1 Sam 22:6-7), the assembly enjoined him from collecting wealth, from creating a large cavalry (chariotry) arm, which would involve the creation of a strong feudal aristocracy not answerable to the assembly, and generally from erecting an immodest administrative or personal establishment (hence the poverty of Saulide Gibeah). In a sense, these strictures resulted in Saul's death at Gilboa: the assembly refused the king the materiel he needed to meet the Philistines on equal terms. They did so, however, if primarily on account of the cost, also out of the fear that he would turn his materiel on them.

Over against the kingship, during the time of Saul, stood the Levitic priesthood, and more specifically, that of Shiloh, under the leadership of Samuel. Very probably, it was, as the text reports, at Samuel's instigation that Israel built into the accession process an opportunity to impose conditions on the king's election (1 Sam 10:25; cf. 2 Samuel 19; 1 Kings 12, etc.). This element dovetails with Samuel's initial opposition to the constitutional change. If finds further corroboration in the recurrent traditions that Samuel early broke relations with Saul (1 Sam 13:8-15a; 15:10-26; 16:1-13; 19:18-24; 28:11-19), though none of these appears reliable in its details. Starker, but more believable, is the report that Saul actually attempted to eradicate the Shilonite priests at Nob (1 Samuel 21-22);[90] this act propelled the Elide heir, Abiathar (or his father Ahimelek/Abimelek) into David's bosom.

Simultaneously, Saul waged an equally bloody campaign against the Hivites of the Gibeonite cities (2 Sam 4:2-3; 21:2). This was no coincidence: Joshua 9 already provides an etiology for the Gibeonites' affiliation with the cult; the presence in Qiryath Yearim in this period of the ark of the covenant, the special charge of the Shilonites, fleshes this picture out. The vendetta against Gibeon cannot be set into isolation from that against Shiloh.[91] Opposed by the sacral establishment, tempted

---

correct, except in that the last campaign was actually an effort to move down onto the plains, possibly to isolate Beth Shean. On 1 Samuel 13-14, see also H. J. Stoebe, "Zur Topographie und Überlieferung der Schlacht von Mikmas, I. Sam. 13 und 14" *TZ* 21 (1965) 269-80; *NHI*, 173; *BHI*, 184; J. M. Miller, "Saul's Rise to Power: Some Observations Concerning 1 Sam 9:1-10:16; 10:26-11:15 and 13:2-14:46" *CBQ* 36 (1974) 157-74; Blenkinsopp, "Quest," 75-100.

[90] See R. Frankena, "The Vassal Treaties of Esarhaddon and the Dating of Deuteronomy" *OTS* 14 (1965) 122-54; J. Greenfield, "Stylistic Aspects of the Sefire Treaty Inscriptions" *Acta Orientalia* 29 (1965) 1-18, esp. p. 5, citing VTE lines 143-44; Sefire III 5-13 on the destruction of Nob. Cf. Judg 9:23-45, 46-48.

[91] But see Schunck, *Benjamin: Untersuchungen zur Entstehung und Geschichte eines israelitischen Stammes* (*BZAW* 86; Berlin: Töpelmann, 1963) 132-33; Blenkinsopp, "Did Saul Make Gibeon his Capital?" *VT* 24 (1974); A. Demsky,

by a governmental system that created a "Prophet" but gave him no
military prop to lean on, Saul waged war upon the Levitic cult itself.

Apart from this, however, Saul seems to have succeeded in uniting
Israel's tribes (esp. 2 Sam 2:8-9). The sole question mark is Judah. There
are some indications that Judah did belong to Saul's kingdom.[92] Most,
like the traditions of Ziphite collaboration with Saul against David
(1 Sam 23:19-24:23//26:1-25), are open to plausible indictment. However,
David's own relationship with the court of Saul is not so easily gainsaid.
Since David came of a family of stature and, it seems of wealth (1 Chr
2:10; Num 1:7; 2:3; 7:12, 17; 10:14; Ruth 4:20; 1 Sam 16:20; 17:17-20), and
since, as his career as "captain of Ziklag" illustrates, he was a part of
that (presumably wealthy) warrior class that it was Saul's aim to
consolidate, it seems likely that David came to Saul's court as an almost
princely hostage (esp. 1 Sam 18:2; 20:5ff.) from a key Judahite family.
Indeed, David apparently gained a marriage alliance with Saul's house
(1 Sam 18:17-19//20-30; 19:1-24; cf. 2 Sam 3:14-15; 6:20-23; 21:8). It is
uncertain whether David was betrothed to Merab, or married to Michal,
or both.[93] But the marriage of one of them to Adriel ben-Barzillai the
Meholathite suggests that Saul sought by his marital diplomacy to
strengthen his ties not just with Judah (David and Michal? 1 Sam 18:20-
30; cf. 1 Sam 25:44; 2 Sam 3:15-16), but also with northwestern (possibly
Transjordanian) Manasseh (? 1 Sam 18:19). David's inclusion in this
scheme testifies to his political importance on the tribal, or regional
level.

"The Genealogy of Gibeon (I Chronicles 9:35-44)" *BASOR* 202 (1971) 16-23;
"Geba, Gibeah, and Gibeon—an Historico-Geographic Riddle" *BASOR* 212
(1973) 26-31, for other views.

[92]Most are explored in Schunck, *Benjamin*, 124-26.

[93]In 2 Sam 21:8, Michal is said to be the wife of Merab's husband (1 Sam
18:19)—Adriel ben-Barzillai (!) the Meholathite. This may be the Barzillai of
2 Sam 17:27; 19:32-35; 1 Kgs 2:7, whose offspring established a priesthood (Ezra
2:61; Neh 7:63). J. J. Glück ("Merab or Michal" *ZAW* 77 [1965] 72-81) has
opposed the emendation of Michal in 2 Sam 21:8 to Merab. But cf. the levelling
through of "Mephibaal" in G[B] of 2 Samuel 4 for "Ishbaal." Michal's marriage
to "Paltiel ben-Laish who was from *gallîm*" (1 Sam 25:44; 2 Sam 3:15-16) is
sufficiently attested. But this husband may prps. have come from the old
territory of Laish (Dan). It is suspicious, at all events, that Barzillai is from
rōgĕlîm (prps. also in Meholah?). Laish may have entered the Gileadite's pseudo-
genealogy. Indeed, the location of (ᶜên?) *rōgĕlîm* near Laish is tempting (see esp.
Judg 18:14). Its confusion with *gallîm* could result from simple script lapse.
Prps. Isa 10:30 plays on this complex. In any case, one should not ignore the fact
that by marital diplomacy, Saul sought to consolidate his ties with Gilead, the
north, and Judah. Though it might mean spreading his daughters thin, his
purpose, again, was unification.

It is worth speculating, therefore, whether David's flight from Saul also signified the withdrawal of Judah's support from the league. The tales of Ziphite collusion with Saul are more than counterbalanced by reports of David's wooing the elders of Judah during Saul's lifetime (1 Sam 30:22-31). The story of Nabal, in which David works a protection racket and acquires in the end the wife of a Calebite chieftain,[94] presents another, more realistic instance of the same phenomenon (1 Samuel 25). The fact of Judah's desertion of Israel to make David king (2 Samuel 2-4), and the very suspicious notices that David reigned seven years in Hebron (2 Sam 2:11; 5:5), while Ishbaal reigned only two over Israel (2 Sam 2:10),[95] contribute to the impression that Judah left Saul at about the time that David fled.

The possibility thus exists that David came to the Philistines in much the same capacity as that in which he originally came to Saul. Given that he seems to have enjoyed amicable relations with the king of Moab (22:3-4), and with Saul's nemesis Nahash the Ammonite (2 Sam 10:2; 17:27; 23:37—here, it is no coincidence that one of Joab's armor-bearers is Ammonite, the other a Gibeonite), one may justifiably suspect David of pursuing—if inadvertently, then felicitously—the diplomatic encirclement of Israel. His marriages to the daughter of the king of Geshur (2 Sam 3:3), as well as to the Jezreelitess Ahinoam (1 Sam 25:43; 2 Sam 3:2), provide some confirmation.[96] It is not coincidental, thus, that David found sanctuary from Absalom in Gilead. It was precisely such peripheries that he characteristically played off against the center.

David's whole early policy, in fact, falls into perspective if one regards him as a Judahite leader concerned with Israel to the north, and prepared, for that reason, to come to a *modus vivendi* with his other neighbors. Of these, the Philistines posed the greatest threat. At the same time, they seem traditionally to have confined their military activity to the plains and passes, encircling Israel.[97] Apart from the tradition of their having collaborators in Judah (Judg 15:9-14), there is no record whatsoever of Philistine garrisons in Judahite territory. Indeed, a strong Philistia might also serve Judah in providing a buffer against possible

[94]See J. D. Levenson, "1 Samuel 25 as Literature and as History" *CBQ* 40 (1978) 11-28.

[95]See Levenson, "1 Samuel 25," 27; Freedman, "History," 16.

[96]On Ahinoam, though, see Levenson and Halpern, "The Political Import of David's Marriages," forthcoming in *JBL*.

[97]See G. E. Wright, "Fresh Evidnece for the Philistine Story" *BA* 29 (1966) 70-86. The possibility, still open, that some of the materials recovered by archaeologists are Sea-People, but not Philistine, in no way alters matters, since ethnic, religious and political factors would very likely have created a relatively homogeneous community anyway.

Egyptian or nomadic raids from the south. To the north, they might buffer her against Israel: the Judahite hills would be a prize more tempting to Saul than to Achish. That is, were Saul seeking to consolidate the central mountain ridge as a prelude to expansion into the plains, Judah might first extract territorial concessions by collaborating with Benjamin in the Pass, then consolidate her position by making overtures to the Philistines.

Judah's affiliation with Ammon (see above), and her close relationship with Philistia (and see further 1 Kgs 2:39-40, with an extradition treaty implied), when conjoined with David's favor among the Gibeonites and the Shilonite priesthood, paint a vivid picture. In alliance with the two peripheral powers that had pressured Israel into accepting kingship in the first place, David made Judah a partner in the containment of the north. Driving Abner's army from the Aijalon Pass (2 Sam 2:12-32), David gradually brought Israel to her knees (2 Samuel 3-4). It is noteworthy that no tradition of Davidic conflict with the Philistines during his tenure at Hebron surfaces in the records. Probably, David's aggressive posture toward Israel satisfied the pentapolis (cf. esp. 1 Sam 29:3-5). It is only after David's unification of Israel and Judah (2 Sam 5:1-3), and his seizure of Jerusalem that Philistia intervenes (2 Sam 5:17-25), precisely to take the Aijalon Pass; yet this had apparently been in David's hands throughout the preceding period of Israel's civil war. The suggestion is, David as king of Judah was Philistia's ally or vassal. David as king of Israel was a menace.

David's reign took its departure from Saul's in a variety of ways. Externally, the extensive conquests reflected the king's exploitation of the potential that Saul had only begun to tap. Internally, David's election conformed precisely to the program fixed by Saul's: the elders covenanted to him their allegiance (2 Sam 5:1-3). The notices of 2 Sam 8:4ff. indicate that the "'manner' of the kingship" remained in effect. Moreover, the list of 1 Chr 27:16-22 indicates that tribal organs remained in operation, that taxation took place through existing structures of officialdom. In the list, the tribe of Manasseh is broken into two segments (27:20-21). Gad and Asher do not appear, though Aaron does (27:17). It is possible to maintain that the list is late and worthless;[98] if it is not, however—and 2 Samuel 24; 1 Chronicles 21; 27:23 are quite clear in the assertion that no census was ever completed to allow David to circumvent the elders[99]—then Gad's absence, at least, may relate to

[98]Recently, de Vaux, *Early History*, 732, for reasons that are threadbare. "Aaron" has probably crept in secondarily (prps. inserted by Chr), as there are 13 sections. Note the Levitic head Hashabya ben-Qemuel. This may be the Hebronite of 1 Chr 26:30.

[99]Joab's opposition here (2 Sam 24:3) is most telling. Joab's character is clear from 2 Samuel, and a fascinating study. His loyalty throughout is to David

Barzillai's allegiance during Absalom's revolt (2 Sam 17:24-29), or perhaps to the fruition of the negotiations reported in 2 Sam 2:4-7.[100]

Some attempts to aggrandize monarchic power did occur. Apart
from the census, to which the prophet Gad, as a protector of tribal
rights, correctly objected, David evidently initiated a period of expansion
in the military. Administration, too, must have burgeoned, as David
based his government in the newly won Jerusalem, and coordinated an
extensive territorial and diplomatic perimeter. Moreover, the religious
establishment, too, set up shop in the capital: the ark came from Qiryath
Yearim, to the charge of the Shilonite Abiathar (1 Sam 22:9, 11, 20; 1 Kgs
2:27; note 1 Sam 14:3). Here, David also appointed Zadoq, an Aaronid.
Cross has maintained the Zadoq and Aaron generally had close ties with
Hebron: he cites Num 26:58a, an old genealogy dividing Levi into five
clans—Libni (Gershonite in P and Chronicles), Hebron and Qorah
(Kohathite in P and Chronicles), and Mushi and, perhaps, Mahli (Me-
rarite in P and Chronicles). Presumably Aaron is subsumed in the
Hebronite designation; this is particularly likely given Aaron's administration of Hebron as a Levitic city (Josh 21:10, 13; 1 Chr 6:42). The
suggestion is, Aaron was primarily affiliated with Judah. David's appointment of an Aaronid enfranchised the south in the cultic establishment.[101] In so doing, he no doubt enlarged that establishment, going so
far as to obtain a site (but not a prophetic permit) for a temple (2 Samuel
24; 1 Chronicles 21; 2 Samuel 7; 1 Chronicles 17).

Despite David's eminent moderation, the tribes grew restive under
his control. Absalom's revolt indicates first that David had not seriously
impaired the traditional tribal structures, and second, that his policies
created widespread discontent. The text reports that Absalom won his
support by a combination of charisma and cajolery (2 Sam 15:1-12), a superficial analysis indeed. Succeeding materials clarify the character of the
revolt. Absalom's force consisted of the "men (ʾanšê) of Israel" (2 Sam
15:2-6, 13; 16:15, 18; 17:14, 24; 19:42-44; 20:2) and "of Judah" (2 Sam
19:15-17, 42-44; 20:4-5—up to chap. 19, these are included in the broader

---

personally. His support of Adonijah (1 Kings 1), therefore, may indicate that
son's legitimacy. At any rate, Adonijah's opponent, Solomon, was big government incarnate.

[100]On these, see Soggin, *Königtum*, 65, and esp. n. 12, citing Moran, "A
Note on the Treaty Terminology of the Sefîre Stelas" *JNES* 22 (1963) 173-76.

[101]See Cross, *CMHE*, 206-15 on this and for further discussion, esp. of
Zadoq's ancestry; my response, in "Levitic Participation in the Reform Cult of
Jeroboam I" *JBL* 95 (1976) 31-42, with the retractions of "Rise," 87 and n. 21.
See also M. Haran, "Studies in the Account of the Levitical Cities II. Utopia and
Historical Reality" *JBL* 80 (1961) 156-65, esp. p. 161. Cf. B. Mazar, "The Cities
of the Priests and Levites" *VTSup* 7 (1960) 193-205, esp. p. 197. For a review, see
Cody, *History*, 88-93.

term, "men of Israel"); he had, that is to say, the whole muster of the
tribes behind him. David's force consisted of the professional army
(2 Sam 15:18), possibly augmented with aid from Gilead and Ammon
(2 Sam 17:27-29). The war is thus a battle of the tribal system against the
central government. In fact, Mephibaal, on hearing of Absalom's coronation, apparently thought he might be awarded his grandfather's
throne over Israel (2 Sam 16:3).[102] At issue was the ongoing expansion of
David's government; the tribes, while, as they thought, they still had the
strength, felt compelled to resort to force in order to dismantle it.

David's professionals, of course, smash the muster, apparently avail-
ing themselves of the rough terrain in "the forest of Ephraim," in which
unskilled troops would prove unmaneuverable. 2 Sam 18:8 suggests
either command control loss or desertion among the conscripts. The
result is a victory that proves paradigmatically the standing army's
superiority over the tribes. Moreover, in the Sheba ben-Bichri revolt that
ensued on Absalom's—a rebellion inspired by anti-Jessianic sentiment
similar to that attributed to Mephibaal (2 Samuel 20)—David and Joab
find occasion to explore yet another advantage of the royal guard. After
Absalom's revolt, in a concession to Judah's elders, David had installed
Amasa, Absalom's general, at the head of the tribal musters (see below).
The Sheba insurrection provides the pretext for the removal of this
encumbrance. Thus David orders Amasa to call out the Judahite muster
immediately after having dismissed it, setting a near-impossible three-
day time limit (20:4-5). Meanwhile, the quickly-mustered imperial guard
appear at Gibeon; Joab assassinates Amasa professionally (20:6-10; cf.
3:27), squelches the revolt, and returns to his former post (20:11-23).
With the professional army on duty, there is little risk of an outbreak by
the militia. David's almost public murder of Amasa depends for its
success on the speedy mobilization of the regulars.

What is remarkable about David's actions after Absalom's revolt is
not his arrogance in the case of Amasa. Rather, David actually cam-
paigns for the allegiance of Judah and Israel, in much the same sense as
he did before his initial enthronement (2 Sam 19:5-11). Thus, David
promises command of the muster to Amasa, Absalom's general (19:14).
He obtains, by this concession, the support of the tribe of Judah (19:12-
16). Next, David negotiates with the Saulide heirs, Shimei, Mephibaal

---

[102]The accuracy of Ziba's accusation is less important than its credibility (see
2 Sam 19:25-31). This construct depends on the reliability of the source. But the
account has the ring of honesty to it; nor does it display any obtrusive dull axes.
Note esp. the call to insurrection involves Hebron only, the capital of Judah
(2 Sam 15:10), leaving room for Mephibaal's delusion. 2 Sam 16:4; 19:25-31, and
the northern secession attempt of 2 Samuel 20 all confirm the historicity of the
report. Note esp. vv 23-24 before 19:25ff. On the terms "men of Israel/Judah,"
see again Tadmor, "'People' and Kingship," 50-66.

and Ziba (19:17-31). And he makes promises to the Gileadite Barzillai (19:32-39). David comes to terms with each of the premier sections of the country. Only afterward does he, as Saul did, cross the Jordan to Gilgal (2 Sam 19:41; cf. 1 Sam 11:14-15; 2 Sam 2:8-9). That is, like Saul, and, very probably Ishbaal, David affords the tribes an opportunity to place conditions on his election, even despite their abortive coup. In liquidating Amasa, his concession to Judah's elders, David continues to toe the line: as usual, Joab assumes the blame;[103] the forms remain intact.[104] In David's reign, at least, the domination of the regular army does not lead to the breakdown of the old constitutional forms.

It is only in Solomon's time that the lessons of the Absalom revolt assert themselves in the text. Solomon comes to the throne with the support of Zadoq and Benaiah ben-Jehoiada against Adonijah, Abiathar and Joab. Benaiah, an Aaronid whose father is listed in Chronicles as having been head of the clan (1 Chr 12:28; 27:5), apparently assumed command in the standing army during the latter part of David's reign (1 Chr 18:17; 2 Sam 8:18; 20:23; 2 Sam 23:20-23).[105] Solomon, thus, controlled the Zadoqite priesthood and the professional army (1 Kgs 1:8-10, 44). After the Absalom experience, Adonijah's partisans among the "men of Judah" (1 Kgs 1:9), his supporters among Israel (1 Kgs 2:15)[106] are no match for Solomon's pretorians.

Solomon's power is plain from his accession purges (1 Kings 2). He made it even plainer to the tribes by his erection of a district system of taxation, from which the elders were disenfranchised. Here, Azaryah ben-Nathan, probably Zabud ben-Nathan's brother (1 Kgs 4:5; 4:7-19) was placed in charge. His officers, a majority of whom are identifiable as associates of Solomon's imperial court,[107] presided over a series of

---

[103] Joab murders Abner, Absalom (2 Sam 18:10-15) and Amasa, according to the text on his own initiative. On the other hand, he acts as David's instrument to murder Uriah quite deviously (2 Sam 11:14-25). In this case, David's motives are transparent (11:26-27), and Nathan cracks the case (2 Sam 12:1-12—not, of course, for a political murder). But the instance suggests Davidic instigation in the other instances. In none could David afford to shoulder the blame.

[104] Cf. Augustus' preservation of the forms of republicanism during the empire, and, recently, F. Millar, "Triumvirate and Principate" *JRS* 63 (1973) 50-67.

[105] He replaced Abishai (1 Sam 26:6-9; 2 Sam 10:10-14; 16:9-11; 18:2-12; 20:6, etc.). Benaiah doesn't participate in the narratives of 1-2 Samuel.

[106] This is an authentic report, which Mettinger is wrong to neglect (*King and Messiah*, 119-20). His observation that Solomon's anointment is virtually private, however, (pp. 120-21) is more typical of his acuity.

[107] See my "Sectionalism," 529-30. On 1 Kgs 4:7-19 as an old, slightly effaced tablet, see Wright, "The Provinces of Solomon" *Sukenik Memorial Volume* (*EI* 8; Jerusalem: I.E.S., 1967) 58*-68*.

territories having nothing to do with the original tribal divisions preserved under David's rule. Indeed, of the tribes, only Benjamin (1 Kgs
4:18) and Naphtali (4:15), if even they, seem to have remained intact. On
the other hand, Judah seems simply to have evaded the scheme altogether. That is, Solomon's schemes circumvented or disenfranchised the
Israelite elders. They did not threaten, so far as we can tell, the tribal
structures of Judah.

Other Solomonic acts typify his imperial administration. Solomon
built the temple, a permanent site for the ark.[108] His establishment was
of enormous proportions by contemporary standards (1 Kgs 10:14-21, 27-
29; 9:19; 5:6; 11:1-3), violating every manner of restriction imposed
previously by Israel's assembly. Most shocking of all, Solomon actually
bartered off part of the tribe of Asher in order to raise capital to fortify
Judah against the Egyptian threat (1 Kgs 9:10-14). This measure specifically motivated Jeroboam's coup attempt (1 Kgs 11:26-40).[109] It motivated ultimately the division of the Israelite kingdom (1 Kings 12).

Grossly speaking, then, Israel adopted her peculiar form of kingship
as a compromise between the tribal power structures and the sacral
authority wielded over the tribes by the ark-priesthood. Each of these
entrenched communities therefore retained much of its power into the
monarchic era. In Saul's time, however, the monarchy joined with the
tribes to deprive the priesthood of its temporal authority, precipitating
the league authority structures into turmoil. The result was the emergence of a new tension, this time between the king, or the central regime,
and the tribesmen. The "prophet," a constitutional fetter on the king,
would traditionally side with the latter (as 1 Kgs 12:21-24).

In almost every respect, it is David's reign that marked the turning-
point in the monarchy's formation. Succeeding Ishbaal, about whom
nothing is known, David tied himself to the old ark-priesthood, introducing the Judahite Aaronides into the cultic establishment of the
nation. After making his peace with the elders, he embarked on a
forward policy, subjecting or evicting all the neighboring peoples,
bringing "wealth and honor" to his constituents. Nevertheless, the
strong and large administrative apparatus required and implied by
David's successes took its toll among the tribes. David's creation of a
new, feudal class of professional warriors, and of a new, central bureau-
cracy, posed an imminent threat to older, traditionally decentralized
tribal power structures. At some mid-point in his reign, his son, Absalom aligned Caleb and Judah and the northern tribes against him.
This was to prove the watershed in monarchic history.

[108]See esp. Cross, *CMHE* 237-41.
[109]See my "Sectionalism" 522-26.

David's victory in "the forest of Ephraim" proved and reinforced the ascendance of the professional army over the tribal musters, laying the groundwork for Solomon's regime. The attempted census, the acquisition of the future temple site, the building of Jerusalem all pointed the way to the events of the coming years. At the same time, David paid lip-service to the old league traditions. He preserved the forms prescribed by the priests and tribes at the time of Saul's coronation. Thus it is that it was in his reign that Israel's democratic, covenantal traditions began to accommodate, and to accommodate themselves to, the more centralized necessities of nationhood.

Solomon came to the throne with the backing of the professional army. There is no indication that he had popular support. He erected what Engels would have called an oriental despotism in a country whose terrain was peculiarly unsuited to it. Thus, Solomon's disenfranchisement of the tribal authorities, and his sale of land to Hiram of Tyre repudiated thoroughly Israel's inherited notions of communal, perpetual land-ownership. His building projects—both with regard to the temple and palace, and elsewhere—meant forced labor and heavy taxes. Solomon's administrative centralization was far-seeing, anticipating the developments of the next hundred years. But with regard to his conservative constituents, David's heir was myopic: unwilling to suffer exploitation as a virtual crown colony, enraged by their peremptory dismissal as a major political force, and fearful that Rehoboam would follow his father's footsteps in neglecting the northern borders, the elders and tribes of the north reacted. At Rehoboam's accession, they exercised their right to refuse to confirm the king.

This stark break is every bit as surprising as David's campaign for re-election after Absalom's revolt. It is an awesome affidavit, following on forty years of imperial rule, to the survival and the viability of the tribal structures, to the survival and the centrality of the forms of a constitutional monarchy. Later reports bear it out: prophecy, as a limit on the kingship, persisted (esp. 1 Kgs 12:21-24; Jeremiah 26, among many other texts).[110] The elders and assembly continued to influence national policy and the succession (esp. 2 Kings 9-10; 11; 21:23-24; 23:30; even 1 Kgs 21:1ff.!). Throughout the monarchy, at least the theoretical limitations legislated by Samuel remained in force. That is, just as Israel's egalitarian, covenantal religion assimilated and transformed

---

[110]See also, e.g., Beyerlin, *Die Kulttraditionen Israels in der Verkündigung des Propheten Michas* (*FRLANT* 72; Göttingen: Vandenhoeck & Ruprecht, 1959) 42-64; H. W. Wolff, "Hoseas geistige Heimat" *TLZ* 81 (1956) 83-94; K. Baltzer, "Naboths Weinberg (I. Kön. 21). Der Konflikt zwischen israelitischem und kanaanäischem Bodenrecht" *WD* 8 (1965) 73-78.

royal, messianic elements, Israel's tribes came to terms with the fact of a central administration. In the process, both the religion of the covenant, and the tribes, were profoundly transformed. But it is precisely that transformation that produced the ancient Near East's profoundest contributions to the human race. It is that synthesis from which much of the modern world has been shaped.

Withholding the Word

WALDEMAR JANZEN

CANADIAN MENNONITE BIBLE COLLEGE

I.

A MONG the diverse media of revelation the prophetic messenger-word[1] is especially suited to safeguard God's transcendence while initiating a mode of divine-human communication which is both intimate and versatile. Unencumbered by the mechanism of divination and the fixity of canonized scriptures, it spans the distance between God and man on the analogy of the most centrally human encounter, speaking and hearing, albeit through the medium of a third party, the messenger. It is in the mystery of the messenger's psychology, in its conscious and unconscious dimensions, that the translation of the numinous message into human words occurs.[2]

The price for this completely personal and non-mechanical revelatory channel is the impossibility of subjecting it to any fully adequate controlling principle. Claim and counter-claim meet each other, leaving it to history to judge between true and false prophet.[3] Even at that, the

---

[1] The understanding of the prophet as messenger, discovered independently by L. Koehler and J. Lindblom, and expanded by C. Westermann and others, is assumed throughout this study. See C. Westermann, *Basic Forms of Prophetic Speech* (Philadephia: Westminster, 1967). Cf. also W. E. March, "Prophecy," *Old Testament Form Criticism* (ed. J. H. Hayes; San Antonio: Trinity University Press, 1974) 141-77; and J. F. Ross, "The Prophet as Yahweh's Messenger," *Israel's Prophetic Heritage* (ed. B. W. Anderson and W. Harrelson; New York: Harper, 1962) 98-107.

[2] For an extensive study of prophetic psychology, see J. Lindblom, *Prophecy in Ancient Israel* (Oxford: Basil Blackwell, 1962) chap. III. Our particular concern is illuminated helpfully by H. W. Robinson, *Inspiration and Revelation in the Old Testament* (Oxford: Clarendon, 1962) 173-86, esp. p. 184.

[3] A forceful presentation of this tension has been given by J. L. Crenshaw, *Prophetic Conflict: Its Effect Upon Israelite Religion* (BZAW 124; Berlin/New York: de Gruyter, 1971). However, Crenshaw overburdens the case when he concludes that this struggle led to the demise of prophecy due to the absence of any valid criteria. Even the major religions in their totality have not been able to advance such validation, without coming to their demise on this account. Ultimately every believer holds to his faith with "subjective certainty," buttressed

much-discussed phenomenon of "false" prophecy[4] does not nearly exhaust the possible ambiguities of divine self-disclosure inherent in
prophetic speech. The whole plethora of nuanced possibilities of communication and miscommunication which resides in human oral-aural
interchange accompanies the word into the divine-human context as
well.

The unreceptive hearer, who hears yet does not hear, is a familiar
figure in the story of prophecy. Less attention has been given to the
unwilling speaker, i.e. the prophet who withholds the revelatory word
given to him. It is well known, of course, that attempts to ward off the
prophetic calling are found within the call pericopes. Further, the
laments of Jeremiah tell the story of a prophet's inner struggle with, and
at times against, his compelling charisma. The story of Jonah epito-
mizes the dynamics of refusal to deliver the divine word. In these
instances, however, the problem is viewed from the vantage point of the
prophet, with little attention to the fact that the possibility of his
withholding the message might also constitute a problem for its potential hearers.

An Israelite exposed to the message of someone claiming to be a
prophet faced two basic questions. The first comes to mind immediately:
Is the claimant really a true prophet? Does his word actually derive from
divine revelation, or is he—consciously or unconsciously—making a
false claim for it? However, our Israelite might well have done some
reflecting in the inverse direction: If the prophet has indeed received
some revelation from God, has he perhaps received more? Could he be
withholding something from us? Or at least from me, while he might
share it with his intimate circle?[5]

---

by objective criteria and data, but not finally validated by them. The same
was true—and quite properly so—with respect to the acceptance of any given
prophecy as divine revelation. S. H. Blank's address *"Of a Truth the Lord Hath
Sent Me"* (Cincinnati: Hebrew Union College, 1955) is a fine illustration of
criteria available to a prophet (here Jeremiah) in support of his claims, without
removing the need for the hearer to make an existential decision of faith. Cf. also
H.-J. Kraus, *Prophetie in der Krisis* [BibS(n) 43; Neukirchen-Vluyn: Neukirchener, 1964].

[4]See Crenshaw, *Prophetic Conflict*, 13-22, for the various attempts to define
this complex phenomenon; also T. W. Overholt, *The Threat of Falsehood* (SBT
2/16; London: SCM, 1970) 37.

[5]Von Rad reckons with the possibility that many apparent discrepancies
within the same prophetic book may be due to a difference in audience; words of
woe were addressed to the sinful crowd, while oracles of blessing and promise
were spoken to the inner circles. (G. von Rad, *Old Testament Theology: The
Theology of Israel's Prophetic Traditions* [New York: Harper & Row, 1965],
2. 171, and Crenshaw, *Prophetic Conflict*, 73 n. 38). This would certainly have

Actually, the situation with respect to the spoken word differs little from that which applies to writing. Copyists and transmitters have always been wary of the two basic dangers to their manuscripts, namely adding and subtracting. The two-pronged warning formulae at the end of inscriptions and manuscripts are ubiquitous and well-known.[6] From within the Bible, Rev 22:18-19 offers a perfect example:

> I warn every one who hears the words of the prophecy of this book: if anyone adds to them, God will add to him the plagues described in this book, and if any one takes away from the words of the book of this prophecy, God will take away his share in the tree of life and in the holy city, which are described in this book.[7]

While the motif of adding has received ample attention from interpreters under the catchword "false" prophets/prophecy, its companion motif of taking away, or withholding, appears to have fallen short of explicit scholarly investigation. The present study is an attempt to remedy this neglect.

It may be well to begin our inquiry into the theme of withholding the word by considering a passage with a fairly clear setting and context, Jer 42:1 6. Here Jeremiah is being implored by the remnant of Judean splinter groups, gathered at the court of the assassinated governor Gedaliah, to seek guidance from the Lord.

> Jeremiah the prophet said to them, "I have heard you; behold, I will pray to the LORD your God according to your request, and whatever the LORD answers you I will tell you; *I will keep nothing back from you*" (v. 4; italics mine).

Jeremiah appears here to give more assurance than is asked of him. Perhaps his protestation of utter openness is conditioned by the circumstances; he must neutralize the suspicions of people who have for many years regarded him to be a trouble-maker and national enemy. Even if

---

contributed to popular suspicion that a prophet might be withholding a good word from his hearers.

[6]The widespread maledictions against altering, defacing or abolishing an inscription are well illustrated by the conclusion to the Code of Hammurabi, *ANET*, 178, col. II, 11, 7ff. Tablet I of *Enûma Elish* closes with a colophon containing the words: "He who fears Marduk and Sarpanî[tu shall not take it away illegitimately]/Or withhold (it) from use." A. Heidel, *The Babylonian Genesis* (2d ed.; Chicago/London: University of Chicago, 1972) 25, 11. 4-5; similarly 30, 1. 2.

[7]Biblical quotations are given according to the Revised Standard Version, unless otherwise indicated.

recent events have justified his preaching, total confidence may well be lacking yet.[8]

However, the fact that the people make a formal commitment by oath in return (vv 5-6) should caution against the assumption that Jeremiah's commitment to full communication was prompted by the circumstances of the moment. A more formalized transaction may be involved. We may well be witnessing here a procedure of assurance that had resulted from the century-old tension between prophet and community. In this tension the prophet's strength lay solely in the access to the divine word, and to pronounce it or to withhold it was the only leverage he could exert. We may hypothesize that formal ways had been developed to insure for the community the full benefit of the prophetic gift and to protect it from false prophecy. Jeremiah may be volunteering here to resort to such procedures.[9] This would have strengthened his claim to legitimacy as a prophet by offering formal assurance against any suspicion of conscious falsification of the divine revelation. It might also have involved a certain guarantee of personal safety for him, no matter what the message. That the men in our passage later respond to Jeremiah's unfavorable message with the accusation "You are telling a lie" (43:2) and break their sworn commitment is undoubtedly the reason why the writer calls them "insolent men" (Hebrew: הזדים האנשים, 43:2).[10]

This hypothesis finds support from other passages in the book of Jeremiah and in the Deuteronomic History. Jer 38:14-16 exhibits elements very similar to those just discussed, though with greater emphasis on the bartering position of the prophet:

[8]Weiser sees here a psychological-pastoral concern of Jeremiah for the dejected and discouraged remnant (*Das Buch Jeremia* [6th ed.; ATD 20/21; Göttingen: Vandenhoeck & Ruprecht, 1969] 360). Similarly, he explains Jer 38:14-23 (see below) on the basis of Zedekiah's psychological state of mind (ibid., 340).

[9]H. G. Reventlow (*Liturgie und prophetisches Ich bei Jeremia* [Gütersloh: Gerd Mohn, 1963] 143-49) sees here, as also in 37:1ff. and 21:1ff. (why not 38:16ff.?), a liturgy of inquiry—שרד is used in 21:2 and 37:7, though not here—by means of prophetic intercession, concerning a divine directive. He argues that a propitious oracle is naturally desired, but cannot be taken for granted. This undergirds my assumption of a formal setting and transaction for this passage. However, while it makes good sense that the inquirers would wish to insure their chances of receiving a desirable oracle against being frustrated by a potentially hostile prophet-intercessor (cf. also 1 Kings 22, where שרד is used in vv 5 and 7), my postulation of a formal procedure to avert the danger of "prophetic withholding" is by no means tied to the setting of a liturgy of inquiry.

[10]BDB: ". . . elsewh. used substantively, as term. techn. for godless, rebellious men."

King Zedekiah sent for Jeremiah the prophet and received him at the third entrance of the temple of the LORD. The king said to Jeremiah, "I will ask you a question; *hide nothing from me.*" Jeremiah said to Zedekiah, "If I tell you, will you not be sure to put me to death? And if I give you counsel, you will not listen to me." Then King Zedekiah swore secretly to Jeremiah, "As the LORD lives, who made our souls, I will not put you to death or deliver you into the hands of these men who seek your life" (italics mine).

The passage begins with a formal request for that unreserved openness which Jeremiah volunteered in the context discussed above (42:4). The prophet clearly uses the bartering power he has by his access to the divine word, motivated by fear of persecution and by frustration at the prospect of ineffectiveness. The king accedes to the plea for Jeremiah's safety with an oath, remaining non-committal, however, with respect to heeding the word. A similar plea by Jeremiah for his safety, or perhaps a variant recording of the same incident,[11] is reported in Jer 37:16-21.

Before leaving Jeremiah, some tentative remarks on chap. 26 may be in order.[12] In v 2 we read:

"Thus says the LORD: Stand in the court of the LORD'S house, and speak to all the cities of Judah which come to worship in the house of the LORD all the words that I command you to speak to them; do not hold back a word"(אל־תגרע דבר).

Here it is Yahweh himself, rather than human inquirers, who enjoins full proclamation upon the prophet (cf. 1:7), forbidding him to withhold anything.[13] Obedience to this command almost costs him his life. Vv 12, 14-15 report his self-defense before the assembled court.[14] There can be no doubt that we are dealing here with the testing of a specific

---

[11]According to J. Bright, 37:11-21 and 38:1-28a may be variant accounts of the same event (*Jeremiah* [AB; Garden City: Doubleday, 1965] 232-34).

[12]For a survey of several recent interpretations of this chap., see F.-L. Hossfeld and I. Meyer, "Der Prophet vor dem Tribunal: Neuer Auslegungsversuch von Jer 26," *ZAW* 86 (1974) 30-31.

[13]Hossfeld and Meyer reckon *die "halbe Kanonformel"* (p. 34), i.e. the phrase "do not hold back a word," among the deuteronomistic additions of this chap. (p. 41f.). In view of the incidence of גרע in related formulae in Deut 4:2; 13:1, this is plausible, but it makes little difference to our argument, since we are concerned with the existence of a procedure, not the historicity of a particular event.

[14]G. W. Ramsey ("Speech Forms in Hebrew Law and Prophetic Oracles," *JBL* 96 [1977] 45-58) has reviewed Jeremiah 26 in the light of H. J. Boecker's *Redeformen des Rechtslebens im Alten Testament* (WMANT 14; 2d ed.; Neukirchen-Vluyn: Neukirchener, 1970). He finds vv 12-15 to be one of two types of defense-speeches, namely that of self-defense.

prophecy by a human tribunal.[15] Jeremiah pleads his innocence on the grounds that he has not withheld God's word, and he appears to imply that such action on his part as in those instances where a human agreement not to withhold was involved (42:1-6; 38:14-16), and those transgressing this understanding would be guilty, just as the men named in 43:2. Thus, while no human agreement of non-withholding has been procured, it seems plausible nevertheless that a formal frame of reference for a proper response to prophetic openness is assumed to be known and valid.

A slightly different, yet related pattern is found in 1 Kgs 22:15-17. Micaiah ben Imlah withholds his divine commission by substituting a word favorable to Ahab. The reason may be fear, or perhaps polite observance of court protocol.[16] The king replies:

> "How many times shall I adjure you (מַשְׁבִּעֶךָ) that you speak to me nothing but the truth in the name of the LORD?"

These words imply a history of adjuration to overcome Micaiah's reluctance to speak unreservedly to Ahab (cf. also 22:8). The Hiphil of שׁבע generally involves the imposition of an oath on another party in connection with some matter. Its use in 1 Kgs 18:10 is particularly interesting for our purpose, as it concerns the extraction of information withheld, by means of adjuration. Ahab's minister Obadiah says to Elijah:

> ". . . there is no nation or kingdom whither my lord has not sent to seek you; and when they would say, 'He is not here,' he would take an oath (וְהִשְׁבִּיעַ) of the kingdom or nation, that they had not found you."

We cannot but assume that such an action must have required recourse to formal procedures of international diplomacy. While it is not warranted, of course, to treat Ahab's adjuration of Micaiah as closely analogous, 1 Kgs 18:10 does appear to lend support to an understanding of Ahab's action towards Micaiah as a formal procedure for procuring

---

[15]Thus also Hossfeld and Meyer, 43f., but these authors deny the historicity of this event and question in principle whether such "tests of orthodoxy" ("*Lehrzuchtverfahren*") could ever have taken place in Israel. They consider Jeremiah 26 a construct analogous to Deut 18:15-22. However, does it make any sense to assume that the widespread need for criteria for true prophecy should have spawned fictitious and theoretical solutions without actual attempts to deal with concrete cases?

[16]Thus F. M. Cross, *Canaanite Myth and Hebrew Epic: Essays in the History of the Religion of Israel* (Cambridge, Mass.: Harvard University, 1973) 242, incl. n. 98; cf. 2 Sam 7:3 and Jer 28:5, 11 in this connection.

information which might otherwise have been withheld.[17] One can only speculate as to whether Ahab's order to imprison Micaiah until his own safe return (22:27) constituted an indirect form of protection by way of milder punishment than might have been meted out.

Our hypothesis that formal procedures had developed to assure the community of the full benefit of the prophetic message, while perhaps protecting the prophet to some extent, finds further confirmation in a little scene between Eli and Samuel, according to 1 Sam 3:15b-18:

> And Samuel was afraid to tell the vision to Eli. But Eli called Samuel and said, "Samuel, my son." And he said, "Here I am." And Eli said, "What was it that he told you? Do not hide it from me. May God do so to you and more also, if you hide anything from me of all that he told you." So Samuel told him everything and hid nothing from him. And he said, "It is the LORD; let him do what seems good to him."

The elements of our hypothesis are present with the exception of a promise of protection, which would obviously have been out of place in this context. Samuel receives a vision, but withholds it out of fear. Eli exhorts him not to hide anything, invoking God in an oath. Samuel shares the message. Eli accepts it. The redundant and formulaic quality of this passage, including the conditional curse, seems extremely heavy-handed when deployed against the young boy who is portrayed as inexperienced, but trusting and devotedly serving the aging, fatherly priest. This incongruity diminishes, however, if we remember that the materials concerning Samuel's childhood are paradigmatic in their presentation of the prophetic call.[18] Then Samuel's adjuration by Eli

---

[17]For a thorough traditio-historical analysis of 1 Kings 22, see E. Würthwein, "Zur Komposition von I Reg 22:1-38," *Das ferne und das nahe Wort* (ed. F. Maass; Rost-Festschrift; Berlin: Alfred Töpelmann, 1967) 245-54. The significance of the Micaiah-scene for our hypothesis is enhanced by Würthwein's conclusion that 1 Kings 22:5-28 is concerned throughout with the criteria of true prophecy. The interest does not lie with the individual features of Micaiah ben Imlah, but with the type of the true prophet (p. 253). Similarly B. O. Long ("Reports of Visions Among the Prophets," *JBL* 95 [1976] 353-65), who refers to the "partly obscure compositional history that probably began with reflection on pragmatic tests for legitimate prophets (vv 5-9, 13-17, 26-28), then included material concerning the test of spirit possession (vv 10-12, 24-25) and lastly raised the possibility that even the spirit was no guarantee of legitimacy (vv 19-22)" (p. 362).

[18]See M. Newman, "The Prophetic Call of Samuel," *Israel's Prophetic Heritage*, 86-97; Cross, *Canaanite Myth and Hebrew Epic*, 223 ("The figure of Samuel in the Deuteronomistic history provides a paradigm of a prophetic leader."); and Crenshaw, *Prophetic Conflict*, 85, n. 79.

depicts an experience which typically formed a part of the ministry of a prophet.

The passages discussed belong to the Jeremianic-Deuteronomistic literature. It is tempting to draw the conclusion that our hypothesis, if valid, should be applied mainly or exclusively to the late pre-exilic era. It would indeed be plausible to think that formal procedures for insuring the full delivery of the prophetic word would have developed gradually along with the unfolding of prophecy in Israel, until a certain consensus and formal firmness was achieved by the time under discussion. We must be cautious, however, in identifying the substance of our concern with the dates of the literary sources cited.

Testing procedures for authenticating prophecy—to be sure, without specific reference to the withholding motif—are attested already in the "prophetic" texts from Mari. In one such text an official reporting the message of an *assinnu* of the goddess Annunitum to the king, adds the following comment: "Before (sending) the report of Ili-haznaya [the *assinnu*] I interrogated [him] for five days. [The re]port which Annuni-[tum se]nt to you and my interrogation agree."[19] Huffmon suggests that the prophetic word, being a new and unconventional mode of revelation, was tested here, as well as in some other instances, by means of the more familiar and accepted practice of divination.[20] He relates the frequently-referred-to practice of sending the prophet's "hair and hem" to the king to the fact that prophecy was still new and therefore suspect. This practice itself may have served the purpose of establishing the prophet's identity, but Huffmon considers it more likely to be "a symbolic subjection to royal authority." He adds: "The statement in X.81 'let them declare (me) free (of guilt),' further suggests that the hair and hem might have been used to represent the person in some ritual that examined, in a more proper way, his or her reliability."[21] Moran cites one instance where a prophetess volunteers her hair and hem with the request that she be declared "clean," meaning in all likelihood that her case should be tried and upheld by the haruspex. While her oath could not, of course, authenticate the ultimate source of her message, it could establish her personal sincerity.[22] We are reminded of Jeremiah's volunteered affirmation (Jer 42:1-6).

The importance of all this for our hypothesis lies in the fact that the interrogation of prophets is already attested in this early extra-Biblical setting and that it shows a certain tendency to crystallize into a pattern:

---

[19]H. B. Huffmon, "Prophecy in the Mari Letters," *BA* 31 (1968) 111.

[20]Ibid., 109, 115f., 120ff.

[21]Ibid., 121. Cf. Ahab's cruder order for Micaiah (1 Kgs 22:26-28).

[22]W. L. Moran, "New Evidence from Mari on the History of Prophecy," *Bib* 50 (1969) 22-23.

interrogation, sending of hair and hem, verification by divination. Unfortunately we know nothing of the content of the interrogation, though adjuration may well have formed a part of it. While the possibility that the prophet might be withholding some of his message is not the concern of the Mari documents, we may nevertheless suggest, with all caution, that the evidence from Mari enhances the plausibility of the early development of formal testing practices for various aspects of prophecy in Israel.

Our hypothesis includes the use of adjuration. The practice of adjuration to extract information is in itself neither novel nor reserved for prophets. We have already referred to Ahab's tactic reported in 1 Kgs 18:10. Joshua (7:19) questions Achan with the words:

> "My son, give glory to the LORD God of Israel and render praise to him; and tell me now what you have done; do not hide it from me (אל־תכחד ממני)."

David addresses the wise woman of Tekoa with the same formula: "Do not hide from me (אל־נא תכחדי ממני) anything I ask you" (2 Sam 14:18). And Zedekiah posits the possibility that his officers might come and interrogate Jeremiah concerning his secret interview with the king, saying, "Tell us what you have said to the king and what the king said to you; hide nothing from us (אל־תכחד ממנו) and we will not put you to death" (Jer 38:25). An oath is not mentioned here. One is tempted to speak of an interrogation formula, although formulaic and contextual firmness are not sustained throughout. Interestingly, we meet the formula also in the context of a divine exhortation to proclaim the word:

> "Declare among the nations and proclaim, (. . .)[23] conceal it not (אל־תכחדו), and say: 'Babylon is taken . . .'" (Jer 50:2).

A similar divine exhortation is directed at Jeremiah in 26:2.[24] Here, however, the use of the verb גרע, generally meaning "to diminish," constitutes a variation in wording, if not in substance (cf. Deut 4:2; 13:1). In these two examples (Jer 50:2; 26:2) the possibility of withholding is posited, not by the potential hearers of the messages, as elsewhere in our study, but by the sender himself.

II.

Whether or not the evidence presented is sufficient to support a pattern of interrogating prophets, often by adjuration, to extract the full

---

[23]Omit "set up a banner and proclaim it," with LXX, as a gloss.
[24]See above, 101.

divine message from them, it demonstrates clearly that the possibility of a prophet's withholding the word revealed to him was a troubling one.[25]

(1) Among the reasons for such withholding, fear of reprisal is the most obvious one. "And Samuel was afraid to tell the vision to Eli" (1 Sam 3:15). Jeremiah draws on his own experiences, but also on the history of prophecy generally (1 Kgs 19:2, 14; Jer 11:21; Jer 26:20-24), when he replies to Zedekiah, "If I tell you, will you not be sure to put me to death?" (Jer 38:15). To kill a prophet was more than the violent expression of personal hostility; it must have appeared at times as the ultimate protection against his powerful and potentially destructive word. To bring his word fully into the open through adjuration, perhaps with the assurance that then death would no longer be necessary as an act of self-protection by society, may have been a milder substitute procedure.

(2) Fear is not the only reason for withholding the word. According to Jer 43:2-3, the people suspect the prophet of ill-will towards personal enemies:

> "You are telling a lie. The LORD our God did not send you to tell us,[26] 'Do not go to Egypt to live there'; but Baruch the son of Neriah has set you against us, to deliver us into the hand of the Chaldeans, that they may kill us or take us into exile in Babylon."

Ill-intentioned diplomacy may be substituted by the prophet for divine revelation. Conceivably a prophet might himself have been tempted in that direction, even if the passage cited attributes the origin of the supposed deceit to Baruch.

There is evidence indeed that lying to achieve one's desired end was not only one of the persistent attributes of "false" prophets, but that it could actually be employed—albeit marginally—with the approval of the canonical scriptures in the service of God. God answers Elisha's prayer by striking a band of Syrian soldiers with blindness, so that the prophet can guide them into captivity by means of a lie (2 Kgs 6:18-20). The deception of the man of God from Judah by an old prophet in Bethel (1 Kings 13), while difficult in its details, suggests clearly that God used one true prophet to test another by means of a lie.[27] An interesting parallel from the realm of wisdom is the undoing of the wise counsel of Ahitophel through the deceptive—but God-willed—counsel of Hushai (2 Samuel 17, esp. v 14).

---

[25]Crenshaw's assumption (*Prophetic Conflict*, 62-77) that there is evidence of transition from true to false, and vice versa, within the same prophet further underscores this uncertainty.

[26]With LXX, against MT.

[27]See Crenshaw's detailed discussion (*Prophetic Conflict*, 39-49).

We have been concerned so far with instances where the human agent is aware of using deceit. These could conceivably be subject to adjuration to tell the whole truth and not to withhold anything. It is an article of canonical faith that such instances of divinely approved lying are few and exceptional. Deception as such does not normally belong to the image of the canonically approved prophet. He is truthful and reflects in this the truthfulness of the God who sent him.[28] The instances of God-inspired falsehood belong to Israel's radical affirmation of God's sovereignty, to the point where evil itself could not be seen as outside of his service. The God who hardened Pharaoh's heart (Exod 7:13; 9:12; etc.) and sent an evil spirit upon Saul (1 Sam 16:14-15; 18:10; etc. cf. 2 Kgs 19:7; Isa 37:7) could also make the wise into fools and prophets into liars. "I make weal and create woe" (Isa 45:7). For the contemporaries of the prophets, however, the distinction between true and false prophet was difficult to make, and no one was above the suspicion of withholding the truth. The situation is different again, of course, where God in his sovereignty uses someone to become his unconscious agent of testing or punishment by means of lying (1 Kgs 22:19-23; Ezek 14:9). No adjuration could insure the hearer of the truth in this case.

Lying represents only one method of withholding the divine word in order to bring calamity upon an adversary. Jonah's flight from his mission represents another means. His negative motive is stated in Jonah 4:2:

"I pray thee, LORD, is not this what I said when I was yet in my country? That is why I made haste to flee to Tarshish; for I knew that thou art a gracious God and merciful, slow to anger, and abounding in steadfast love, and repentest of evil."

The intent of withholding the divine word from Nineveh by means of his flight, then, was to allow evil to come upon Nineveh, just as Jeremiah's contemporaries suspected of that prophet.

Malicious withholding of the divine word may also have been suspected where a known and acknowledged prophet failed to speak. The three-year drought in Elijah's time is linked explicitly to the absence of that prophet's word:

[28]Crenshaw (*Prophetic Conflict*, 77-90) overemphasizes the "demonic"—and therefore unpredictable—element in Yahweh, even if he mitigates the offense by placing the demonic into the wider framework of benevolent divine providence. This is not to minimize the need to recognize the presence of this element in Yahweh. Cf. F. Hesse (*Das Verstockungsproblem im Alten Testament* [BZAW 74; Berlin: Alfred Töpelmann, 1955] 96), who rightly states that this dimension of the divine image plays a minor role in the context under discussion ("Aber dieses Moment [the deceptive, demonic] der Gottesauffassung spielt in unserem Fragenbreich eine nur sehr untergeordnete Rolle").

"As the LORD the God of Israel lives, before whom I stand, there shall be neither dew nor rain these years, except by my word" (1 Kgs 17:1).

Elijah's intermittent unavailability (1 Kgs 17:1-3; 18:1) may have been interpreted no differently by Ahab from the behavior and lack of straight-forwardness of Elijah's contemporary Micaiah (1 Kgs 22:15-17). Absence of prophecy as such constituted something like a national calamity analogous to drought, famine, or devastation in war (1 Sam 3:1; Amos 8:11-12; Lam 2:9); could not a prophet bring on such a state for a time, by withholding the word entrusted to him? Such fear is justified by Ezek 14:1-11. Here a prophet is instructed not to speak a word from the Lord to those who come to inquire while idolatry reigns in their hearts. Should a prophet fail to be silent in that case, the Lord himself will provide a deceptive word, for the punishment of both the inquirer and the prophet (cf. Ezek 20:1-3, 31; Jer 23:33-40). An unrepentant inquirer could only see such prophetic silence as a malicious act of withholding the word due to him. Ezekiel's long silence (Ezek 3:25-26; 24:25-27; 33:21-22), enigmatic as it is, may also belong into this realm of thought.[29]

If an Israelite may thus have felt in danger of being deprived of the Word of God, his fear is substantiated by Jeremiah's stance towards the "false" prophets of his time. Reventlow has argued convincingly that Jeremiah's chief charge against his opponents is not, as is often believed, that they preach peace where there is no peace, but that they announce peace or blessing to those whose moral conduct violates the covenant stipulations of Yahweh. Consequently, they cast the pearls before the swine (Matt 7:6).[30] Jeremiah does not dispute the genuineness of oracles of weal as such,[31] but he accuses his opponents of not withholding these from the unworthy. Reventlow sees this situation in analogy to the cult, where the blessing of God is also screened from the unworthy, as the testing liturgies at the gate (e.g. Psalm 15; Ps 24:3-5) demonstrate.[32] In a similar vein, Kraus formulates the chief mark of the false prophets as that of pronouncing salvation upon those who do not deserve it: "They strengthen the hands of evildoers" (Jer 23:14).[33] Thus Jeremiah appears to be calling on his prophetic "colleagues" to exercise a judicious withholding of the word where the moral state of the potential hearers warrants it. From the vantage point of these hearers, assuming that they

[29]For a review of this problem, see E. Vogt, "Die Lähmung und Stummheit des Propheten Ezechiel," *Wort-Gebot-Glaube* (ed. H. J. Stoebe; Eichrodt-*Festschrift*; ATANT 59; Zürich: Zwingli, 1970) 87-100.

[30]H. G. Reventlow, *Liturgie*, 121-26.

[31]Reventlow argues this in spite of Jer 28:7-9, which he dismisses, with Quell, as not compelling (*Liturgie*, 126).

[32]Reventlow, *Liturgie*, 132-34.

[33]Kraus, *Prophetie in der Krisis*, 114.

were unrepentant, such a withholding could only be seen as deliberately malicious.

(3) Fear of reprisal and ill-will towards enemies does not exhaust the motives for withholding the word, attributed rightly or wrongly to prophets. Jeremiah, having stated his fear of death at the command of Zedekiah, adds a further hesitation to speak openly: "And if I give you counsel, you will not listen to me" (Jer 38:14). A sense of futility may close a prophet's lips. Elijah's discouragement may have been of the same sort (1 Kgs 19:4-10).

It must be said, however, that withholding the word appears to have been only the momentary temptation of the great prophets, rather than their sustained response to the ineffectiveness of their preaching. On the contrary, it is remarkable how Isaiah, Jeremiah, and Ezekiel persisted in their apparently futile prophetic mission through many decades. They continued to deliver the divine word in spite of their repeated experience that their preaching was not only ineffective, but counterproductive in the life of the people. Jeremiah's laments afford an insight into the personal suffering and struggle that was the consequence.

In this continuous tension between their divine commission and their unreceptive audience the prophets were sustained, not only by the compelling certainty of their call (Amos 3:8; Jer 20:7-9), but also by the doctrine of the hardening of hearts.[34] Rooted in the sovereignty of Yahweh even over the powers of evil,[35] it finds its classical expression for the prophetic context in Isaiah 6:9-10:

And he said, "Go, and say to this people:
'Hear and hear, but do not understand;
see and see, but do not perceive.'
Make the heart of this people fat,
    and their ears heavy,
    and shut their eyes;
lest they see with their eyes,
    and hear with their ears,
and understand with their hearts,
    and turn and be healed."

It is unnecessary for our purpose to enter into the debate as to whether Isaiah received this perspective on his proclamation literally in connection with his call, or whether he arrived at it gradually as he experienced the inexplicable resistance of his hearers to the divine word.[36] In either

---

[34]Hesse, Das Verstockungsproblem is the classical treatment of this motif.

[35]Hesse, Das Verstockungsproblem, 90; Crenshaw, Prophetic Conflict, 88f.

[36]The latter is held by Hesse (Das Verstockungsproblem, 84); the former by von Rad (Old Testament Theology, 2. 151-55); O. Kaiser (Isaiah 1-12 [OTL;

case the prophet could draw reassurance, at least at some point in his career, from the belief that God himself was ultimately responsible for the ineffectiveness of his word. Moreover, the prophet could accept this ineffectiveness as only apparently so, since in reality God's purpose— namely to bring punishment upon the people—was actually being achieved in a twofold manner: The hardening of heart effected by the prophetic preaching in itself constituted punishment, and at the same time it made the people culpable and ripe for further punishment.[37] Hesse discusses related thoughts in Amos and Hosea and traces the history of the impact of Isaiah 6:9-10 in Jeremiah, Ezekiel, and elsewhere.[38]

Thus the prophets could feel justified in continuing their proclamation in the face of its blatant rejection and apparent futility, where they might well have been tempted to fall silent. Such a perspective, however, of necessity altered the quality of the prophetic proclamation. Where a message is spoken from the duty to enunciate it, rather than the hope to elicit assent for it, the dynamics of communication are broken, and this justifies our inclusion of the hardening motif in our discussion of withholding the word. The abdication of the messenger's original purpose of communicating stands out starkly in the formulaic and unconditional command to Ezekiel to speak "whether they hear or refuse to hear" (Ezek 2:5; 3:11).

If enunciation rather than reception by the hearers is ultimately the important goal, it becomes less and less necessary to reckon with the response, and eventually with the presence, of those addressed. Interpreters generally recognize that rejection and persecution provided an impetus for recording prophetic oracles in writing, both to propagate them among contemporaries (Jeremiah 36) and to preserve them for the judgment of posterity (Isa 30:8-11; cf. Job 19:23). The latter was undoubtedly facilitated by the decreasing sense of need to elicit response, which resulted from the hardening motif. It was no longer so urgent to address the divine message to the populace, as long as it was spoken (or written down) at all.[39]

Philadelphia: Westminster, 1972] 82-83). According to H. Wildberger (*Jesaja* [BK X/1; Neukirchen-Vluyn: Neukirchener, 1972] 254-56), this passage, instead of commanding the prophet what he should preach, describes the state of the people, so that the prophet would not doubt his commission when increasing hardness of heart, instead of success, would meet his message.

[37]Hesse, *Das Verstockungsproblem*, 59f.; Wildberger, *Jesaja*, 256.

[38]Hesse studies this theme in Hosea and Amos (*Das Verstockungsproblem*, 56-59) and traces the aftereffects of Isa 6:9-10 in Jeremiah, Ezekiel, and elsewhere in the OT (60-62).

[39]A substratum of belief in word magic may have facilitated this turn; cf. Jer 51:60.

As a consequence, Isaiah was ready to restrict his proclamation to the circle of his disciples:

Bind[40] up the testimony, seal the teaching among[41] my disciples. I will wait for the LORD, who is hiding his face from the house of Jacob, and I will hope in him. Behold, I and the children whom the LORD has given are signs and portents in Israel from the LORD of hosts, who dwells on Mount Zion (Isa 8:16-18).

This smaller circle is the kernel of the future remnant, according to Hesse,[42] which has not been drawn into the hardening of hearts. While the verbs of v 16 are perhaps employed figuratively here to express restricted communication, Isa 30:8-11 reports that the prophet actually committed his message to the future in writing, as a result of the hardened condition of his contemporaries:

And now, go, write it before them on a tablet,
    and inscribe it in a book,
that it may be for the time to come
    as a witness[43] for ever.
For they are a rebellious people,
    lying sons,
sons who will not hear
    the instruction of the LORD;

[40]Wildberger (Jesaja, 342-43) interprets חתום and צור as inf. abs. forms and translates: "I bind up . . . seal. . . ."

[41]The difficult בלמדי has been rendered "with my disciples," i.e. the testimony is left in their keeping; "among my disciples," i.e. the testimony is bound up and sealed in their presence, or "through my disciples," i.e. with their help. Wildberger insists that the expression must be understood as an image, rather than literally. Isaiah wants to deposit his testimony in the persons of his disciples as one deposits a treasure in a bag (Jesaja, 344-45). Similarly T. Lescow, "Jesajas Denkschrift aus der Zeit des syrisch-ephraimitischen Krieges," ZAW 85 (1973) 225-26. Kaiser (Isaiah 1-12, 120), on the other hand, visualizes the wrapping and sealing (in an earthen jar) of a scroll. The disciples witness the process. The whole procedure is designed to insure against later suspicions that the prophet might have adapted his words to the events of history that he expects to substantiate his message. For the purpose of our study, these differences need not be resolved. It is the deliberate restriction of the message, whether to a smaller circle of hearers or to a scroll actually bound up and sealed, that concerns us.

[42]Hesse, Das Verstockungsproblem, 90.

[43]See BH mg.

who say to the seers, "See not;"
    and to the prophets, "Prophecy
        not to us what is right; . . ."[44] (vv 8-10a).

Thus the prophet hands the hardened hearers over to their perdition by committing to the future a divine message which has already, in effect, become sealed for them (cf. Isa 29:9-14). Hesse emphasizes that salvation is restricted to the remnant. The people as a whole are made ripe for destruction by means of the hardening of their hearts, so that the way can be cleared for the breaking in of the era of salvation for the remnant.[45]

Contrary to Hesse, von Rad[46] holds—rightly, I believe[47]—that the doctrine of hardening in Isaiah must be seen as the basis for God's total redemptive "work." In a marvelous way a small circle is receptive to this work even now (Isa 8:16-18). In the days to come, the word which can only be seen in its hardening effect on the people as a whole at present will become instrumental in God's saving work. Thus the hardening must be seen, paradoxically, as the beginning of a salvation-oriented course of divine action.

However one may view the nature and finality of the hardening in Isaiah, it is clear that both this prophet and others after him understood the hardening to perform a limited and temporary function. It would be followed by a new receptivity for the divine word which would ultimately issue into the age of salvation.[48]

The confidence that the divine word, though rejected for a time, remained a part of the divine economy of salvation even in their time,

---

[44]The structural relationship of these vv to their context, as well as their authenticity, are debated. (See O. Kaiser, *Isaiah 13-39* [OTL; Philadelphia: Westminster, 1974] 292-95.) If secondary, they nevertheless reflect Isaiah's theology faithfully. The scope of what is to be written down is not clear, either, but for our purpose it is, once again, the fact of withholding that matters, rather than the content of what is withheld.

[45]Hesse, *Das Verstockungsproblem*, 89-91.

[46]Von Rad, *Old Testament Theology*, 2. 164-66.

[47]Isaiah's proclamation carries an appeal that is generally recognized as being serious in its intent (see Wildberger, *Jesaja*, 256). For Hesse, who recognizes this, too (*Das Verstockungsproblem*, 82f.), it becomes the basis for seeing the hardening as an insight gradually gained by the prophet in a long and fruitless ministry; for how could he have preached repentance genuinely if the hardening motif had already been a part of his call? One could ask, however, whether the hardening motif in this context does not highlight God's autonomous work of grace, just as the murmuring in Israel's exodus and wilderness wandering tradition?

[48]Isa 11:9b; 29:18; 30:19-22; 32:3; 34:16; Ezek 11:19; 18:31; 36:26f.; 37. Also, Hesse, *Das Verstockungsproblem*, 92f.

encouraged and compelled the prophets to sustain its proclamation. The defiant quality of this proclamation ("whether they hear or refuse to hear"), the occasional restriction of it to a smaller circle, and the recourse to writing it down and "sealing" it for the future must therefore be seen as features of the divine-human interaction in their own time, and not as expressions of total abdication of all hope in that era. Nevertheless, these gestures of holding back the word are pointing the way to the apocalyptic tendency to see the present aeon as one of waiting for history to catch up with the divine word delivered (in veiled form) to the elect few, while the hopelessly hardened majority cascaded down its wicked path to the end in ignorance:

> But you, Daniel, shut up the words and seal the book, until the time of the end (Dan 12:4).

> He said, "Go your way, Daniel, for the words are shut up and sealed until the time of the end. Many shall purify themselves and make themselves white, and be refined; but the wicked shall do wickedly; and none of the wicked shall understand; but those who are wise shall understand" (Dan 12:9-10).

The present study must limit itself to the canonical books of the Old Testament. The theme of withholding the word, however, continues far beyond these. Its point of contact with the veiling and unveiling of the divine plan in apocalyptic literature has just been shown.[49] Millar Burrows considers it possible that the reticence of the Qumran community to denounce the "evil generation" of its time—in sharp contrast to the prophets' vehement condemnation of their contemporaries—was related to Isaiah's decision to bind up the testimony and to seal the teaching among his disciples (Isa 8:16-17).[50] Rabbinic torah exposition, on the other hand, had its own assumptions about the hidden dimensions of scripture waiting to be unlocked by its learned interpreters of the latter days.[51]

In the New Testament, many pericopes suggest themselves as standing in some continuity with the withholding theme. Jesus' silence before the Sanhedrin (Matt 26:63; Mark 14:55-62; Luke 22:67-68),[52] before Pilate

---

[49]Cf. also I. Willi-Plein, "Das Geheimnis der Apokalyptik," *VT* 27 (1977) 62-81.

[50]M. Burrows, "Prophecy and the Prophets at Qumran," *Israel's Prophetic Heritage*, 225-26.

[51]My attention was drawn to this by my colleague, Dr. David Schroeder. Cf. also Willi-Plein, "Das Geheimnis," 77, 79-80.

[52]It is interesting to note in Matthew's account that Jesus answers only when adjured (vv 63-64), and that his tormentors wish to make him "prophesy" to them (vv 67-68). The Luke-pericope bears considerable resemblance to Jer 38:14-16.

(Matt 27:11-14; Mark 15:2-6), and before Herod (Luke 23:8-9) come to mind immediately. Further, there are Jesus' admonitions to the disciples not to cast their pearls before swine (Matt 7:6), and to leave an unresponsive house or town, shaking the dust from their feet (Matt 10:14). Isa 6:9-10, the key passage of the theme of hardening one's heart, makes its appearance in various contexts.[53] Two important facts are linked to it explicitly (Matt 13:3-17; Mark 4:3-13; Luke 8:5-10): First, it is the hardening of the hearers' hearts which accounts for Jesus' recourse to parables.[54] Secondly, this hardening is not equally present in the disciples, so that they can receive Jesus' message in unveiled form. Elsewhere, however, the disciples are also characterized as not immune to it (Mark 8:18; John 12:37-41). Finally, we must mention the complex of motifs which has come to be known as "the messianic secret," in the wake of W. Wrede's classical work by that name.[55]

This must remain a mere hint at some avenues along which the withholding motif could be pursued. The reflective reader might move on beyond them to our own time. Does the absence of the word from God loom large among the spectres of our time? Could it be that there are those among us who withhold it, moved by dynamics not altogether different from those traced in this study?

---

[53]Hesse traces the impact of this passage upon the NT (*Das Verstockungsproblem*, 64-66).

[54]Cf. W. Wrede (*Das Messiasgeheimnis in den Evangelien* [4th ed.; Göttingen: Vandenhoeck & Ruprecht, 1969] 200), who writes: "Aber geht nicht durch die meisten Reden Jesu etwas Figürliches, Mysteriöses? Jesus bedient sich wie absichtlich einer andeutenden, doppeldeutigen, das Missverständnis geradezu provozierenden Ausdrucksweise."

[55]Wrede, *Das Messiasgeheimnis*, first published 1901.

Yahweh Recalls Elijah

ROBERT B. COOTE
SAN FRANCISCO THEOLOGICAL SEMINARY

T HE story of Elijah's visit to Horeb, his encounter there with the "silent sound," and his return to appoint Elisha is the third in the Deuteronomist's train of stories about Elijah. The first is a group of three short tales that demonstrate what the widow of Sarephath says when Elijah intercedes for the life of her child: "Now I know . . . for certain that the word of Yahweh is in your mouth." Her authentication of Elijah's prophetic authority goes back to the very beginning of his story, to his claim to have stood in the presence of Yahweh (1 Kgs 17:1; compare 18:15). The second story demonstrates that Yahweh is God of the weather, not Baal, and again that Elijah is his prophet. Yahweh responds to Elijah's summons with the *"fire* of Yahweh" which consumes even the water around the altar, with the *"sound"* (*qôl*) of the impending downpour (18:41), the *wind* (18:45), and finally the downpour itself. In the third story, at Horeb, Yahweh is not with the wind, not with the shaking, not with the fire, and, implicitly, not with the thunderous sound, but with the "thin, silent sound."

Following Eissfeldt, Jeremias, and Steck, Frank Moore Cross[1] interprets this reversal in terms of the history of traditions. The purpose of the reversal is to affirm that Yahweh not only can best Baal on Baal's terms, as god of the weather whose voice (*qôl*) is the thunder, but also holds a distinctive authority as the divine judge, counsellor, and commander whose voice (*qôl*) speaks the intelligible word. According to Cross, in the time of Elijah the character of Yahweh as god of the storm is too close to the character of Baal for Yahweh to be recognized as the distinctive deity he is, with claims on his people quite different from the claims of Baal. In the context of the competition between the two gods, confusion must be avoided. In this setting the characteristics of Yahweh that go back to El rather than Baal come to the fore to be emphasized, and the characteristics held in common with Baal recede to the background, or, as in 1 Kings 19, are denied. Cross and others who hold this

---

[1] F. M. Cross, *Canaanite Myth and Hebrew Epic* (Cambridge: Harvard University, 1973) 190-94. To the bibliography available there one should add E. von Nordheim, "Ein Prophet kündigt sein Amt auf (Elia am Horeb)," *Bib* 59 (1978) 153-73.

view may well have put their finger on a significant level of meaning in the story of 1 Kings 19 as it was told in the ninth and eighth centuries. Even in its Deuteronomistic context, it supports Yahweh's uniqueness.

But what about Elijah? The story of Yahweh's besting of Baal in 1 Kings 18 can be understood as a story mainly about Yahweh; but the story of Elijah's visit to Horeb in 1 Kings 19 is not simply, or even mainly, a story about Yahweh, but about Yahweh's prophet. The tradition of the denial of Baalistic theophanic language and conception to which Cross points is but a part of the story. To see what meaning it now has within the story, it is necessary to come to some understanding of the story as a whole.

Elijah's visit to Horeb is the centerpiece of a three-part story. Like the stories of 1 Kings 17 and 18, with which it is inextricably interwoven, the story takes place at three locales: a day's journey into the wilderness, at Horeb, and near the home of Elisha. Each of the three parts is marked at the beginning by the phrase "and he went (to the respective locale)," in the middle by an encounter in which a repeated expression resolves a hesitancy ("great" and "rise, eat"; Yahweh's inquiry; "go, return" and "kiss"), and at the end by a preservation (of Elijah, the remnant of seven thousand, the people) These marks reflect the story's chief theme: Yahweh induces Elijah to return to service as Yahweh's prophet, with life-saving results. Everything that occurs between Elijah's flight from Jezebel to Elisha's feeding of the people contributes to this theme.

Enraged over Elijah's killing of 450 prophets of Baal at Carmel, their patroness Jezebel threatens to make Elijah's "life (nepeš) like the life of one of them," a threat Elijah describes with the words, "They seek to take my life." Elijah goes for his life, leaves his lad in Beersheba (he will get another helper), comes to a place where there is a bush, and asks for death: "Enough (rab), Yahweh. Take my life." Does Elijah want to save his life (he flees) or lose it (he asks to die)? The story immediately raises this question not to have it answered right away, but to focus attention on a crisis: Will Elijah serve as Yahweh's prophet or not? The issue is a life or death matter, since without Moses or the "document of the torah" he dictated, Elijah alone exists to mediate between Yahweh and the people.

The story portrays this crisis in terms of Elijah's intent. It does not, however, tell what is going on inside Elijah's mind; instead, it represents Elijah's intent through formal or symbolic means. Elijah lies down at the bush and goes to sleep, entering a state that in Hebrew conception hangs midway between life and death. The man who twice before has claimed "I have stood (in service) before Yahweh" and who will again stand before Yahweh now wants only to lie down.

Suddenly a genie appears, who touches Elijah and commands him to get up and eat. Elijah eats and drinks. To eat and drink is to revive the *nepeš*, so Elijah is saved. To Elijah's request "Take my *nepeš*" Yahweh has in effect responded, "Eat, and keep your *nepeš*." A second time Elijah goes to sleep—he has not yet given up his desire to die—and a second time the genie touches him and commands him to get up and eat, "for the way is too great (*rab*) for you." A second time Elijah eats and drinks and, unbidden, goes on. For the time being he keeps his life. But has he changed his mind about being a prophet?

Elijah, of course, resembles Moses. Once Moses, having killed an enemy, fled from those who sought his life into the wilderness, came to a bush, and there encountered a genie. There Yahweh called Moses to represent him to the people, to lead them out of slavery and into life. Moses hesitated, but eventually he acceded to Yahweh's command, "Go, return" (Exod 4:19). Once Moses asked to die in the wilderness (Num 11:15) because he was dismayed that he could not provide meat for his people. On that occasion Yahweh provided meat and distributed the spirit of prophecy that Moses "alone" (11:14) possessed among 72 other Israelites.

With the strength gotten from food and water, Elijah journeys back through the wilderness for forty days and forty nights until he arrives at Horeb. There he comes to the cave to spend the night. Having traveled for forty nights, presumably he is now more ready than ever to lie down. But Yahweh forestalls his sleep: "What is your business here, Elijah?"

The incident in the life of Moses to which the cave alludes is the concealment of Moses in the "cleft" (Exod 33:22) and the "passing" of Yahweh (33:22; 34:6). But the "cave" (rather than "cleft") has already played a role in the story of Elijah. Twice it has been said that in the cave (where it was is not told) Obadiah concealed one hundred prophets of Yahweh from persecution by Jezebel and preserved them with food and water. Elijah claimed, despite the preservation of these prophets in the cave, to be the sole prophet of Yahweh left (18:22). To be concealed in the cave and preserved with food and water is to remain alive, but not, according to Elijah's own words, to remain a prophet. In answer to Yahweh's question, "What is your business here?" Elijah now claims (with multiple references to the preceding story) to be the only one left. Only this time he, too, is concealed in the cave! The wording of Elijah's answer conveys the irony: in contrast to his statement in 18:22, he omits the word "prophet," precisely because it is questionable whether at this point Elijah is a prophet. Yahweh commands, "Get out of the cave and stand before Yahweh" if you intend to be a prophet.

What induces Elijah to come to the entrance of the cave? So far he has eaten food, drunk water, traveled to Horeb, concealed himself in the cave, and made a (doubtful) claim to be a prophet—steps that show he is progressively more willing to resume his service as Yahweh's prophet. How is he to be induced to take the final step?

Not by means of a great wind, quaking, or fire. Yahweh desires to return Elijah to service, not to kill him. These phenomena, so effective in demonstrating Yahweh's superiority over Baal in Carmel, are lethal, sure agents of death, to persons at Horeb. They occurred there during the life of Moses. While all the people stood before the mountain to hear God's commandments, the mountain shook (Exod 19:18), lightning flashed (19:16; 20:18), the mountain smoked (19:18; 20:18), and Yahweh descended in the fire (19:18). Above all, as is repeated many times over, there was a great qôl—thunder, noise, and voice.

The Deuteronomist's description of this moment, with all its phenomena, serves as the very basis of his understanding of Moses as the preeminent prophet whom all other prophets would resemble as they serve as the indispensable means of Yahweh conveying his voice to his people (Deut 5:1-30; 18:15-18). The third phenomenon, fire, is the most significant one: "We have heard Yahweh's voice from the midst of the fire," the people say at Horeb. "Today we have seen that God can speak with persons and they live. But now, why should we die? For this great fire will consume us; if we continue to hear any more the voice of Yahweh, we will die" (5:21-22).

After the fire, rather than from its midst, there occurs a qôl. It is not the voice of Yahweh, nor the noisy thunderings of the storm at Horeb, but a "thin, silent sound." The significance of this strange phrase has three aspects: it expresses at one and the same time Yahweh's solicitude, the dire crisis, and the anticipated outcome of the story.

As an expression of Yahweh's concern for the life of his intended prophet, the silent sound is the climax of the sequence of phenomena. If at Horeb above all the noise of thunder and God's booming voice threatened to kill the people, then Yahweh conveys his intent to preserve Elijah by the reversal of this noise. It is not appropriate in this story to say that Yahweh is not in the qôl, since in an important way the opposite is about to be the case. The alternative is to say that, for the moment, the lethal qôl of Yahweh's appearance at Horeb is silenced. Through this silence Yahweh allows the prophet-to-be to live.

"Silent sound" is an oxymoron, a combination of seemingly contradictory words. Which is it, the phrase demands, silence or sound? The oxymoron thus represents the crisis. Will Elijah remain silent in the cave and leave Yahweh, who speaks through the prophet, silenced, or will Yahweh's word again sound through Elijah's voice? The oxymoron confronts Elijah with the nature and weight of his choice.

By means of an allusion, the phrase anticipates the outcome of the story. The silent sound is said to be "thin" (daqqâ). This description recalls to the ear of the hearer the description of manna as a "flaky thin thing (daq), a thin thing (daq) like hoarfrost" (Exod 16:14), and as the "insubstantial, or perhaps contemptible (qĕlōqēl), food" (Num 21:5). Why this allusion to manna? Because there was a tradition in Israel that God's intelligible word, by which one lives, was food, like manna. Moses said that Yahweh fed Israel manna in the wilderness in order to make them know that human beings do not live solely by food, but by everything that issues from the mouth of Yahweh (Deut 8:3), all of which is heard from the prophet. The same tradition lies behind Amos 8:11: "The days are on their way . . . when I will send a famine into the land—not a famine for food or a thirst for water, but for the hearing of the words of Yahweh." The prophet is less the one who is fed and more the one who feeds, and one thing he feeds to the people is the qôl . . . daqqâ, the manna-like, life-giving word of Yahweh. (As the third part of this story makes clear, neither can Yahweh's people subsist on this voice-bread alone.)

Upon hearing the silent sound and realizing the concern, the crisis, and the result it represents, Elijah covers his face with his mantle, recalling the time when Yahweh covered Moses as he passed by so that Moses would not die (Exod 33:20). Elijah protects himself as he emerges from the cave: he wants to live. Through the thin, silent sound Yahweh has induced him to stand once again before Yahweh in service. The question raised by the first part of the story, whether Elijah wants to save his life or lose it, is now clearly answered. This time Elijah's response to Yahweh's repeated inquiry is entirely true.

Elijah's mantle is equivalent to Moses' rod. Elijah uses the mantle to part the waters of the Jordan (2 Kgs 2:8), and Elisha does the same (2:13-14), repeating Moses' parting the Reed Sea with his rod (Exod 14:16). This equivalence applies to the present story as well. Given the similarity of the first part of the story to Exodus 3, and of the command about to be given, "Go, return," to Exod 4:19, it appears that, just as Moses' rod functions in Exod 4:1-17 to persuade Moses to abandon his reluctance to serve Yahweh, so Elijah's mantle functions as a symbol of his own persuasion to be recalled to Yahweh's service. The mantle has the same significance when Elijah tosses it to Elisha in the third part of the story.

Yahweh commands Elijah to "Go, return" the way he came—his return to the land signifies his return to service (compare Jer 15:19)—and to anoint Hazael, Jehu, and Elisha. Hazael will kill many; whoever escapes from the sword of Hazael Jehu will kill; whoever escapes from the sword of Jehu Elisha will kill, except for a remnant of seven thousand who neither bow to nor kiss Baal. However the apparent contradiction between this command and its later execution is to be explained, within the context of this story the command makes one thing clear: by one ordained person or another all those who want to take Elijah's life will be killed. Elijah's preservation is assured, and at least one prophet will be preserved in his stead when Yahweh takes him.

Yahweh's command to Elijah both concludes the second part of the story and begins the third part. The phrase "and he went" and the change of locale occur after Yahweh's command, but the command is the repeated expression that resolves Elisha's hesitancy in the third part. Hence the beginning of the third part is correctly represented by the Masoretic *setuma* division. Although the second and third parts overlap, nevertheless their marks retain their distinctiveness and function.

Elijah finds Elisha plowing with twelve oxen, a fantastic show of wealth—his father's, it must be assumed. Elijah commences to play Yahweh to Elisha's Elijah. He "passes by" the twelve oxen, tosses his mantle to Elisha to call him to be a prophet, and keeps on running, like Yahweh in Exodus 33-34. Elisha hurries after, but hesitates: "Let me kiss my father and my mother; then I will go." Like Yahweh Elijah says, "Go, return," which because it also means "repent" is ironic, and like Yahweh he queries him: "What have I done to you?" The question directs Elisha's attention to the call to which he must give a decisive response. His response shows his acceptance. Returning, he slaughters the oxen belonging to his father, whose person and property—and values—he need no longer regard, since Elijah is now his father (2 Kgs 2:12; compare 1 Sam 10:11-12). He cooks the flesh of the oxen "and gives to the people and they eat."

This last bare phrase in its present literary context is elucidated by the story it prefigures in which Elisha feeds the one hundred men (2 Kgs 4:42-44), which repeats, "Give to the people that they may eat . . . Give to the people that they may eat . . . And he gave . . . and they ate." Through the motif of excess that story alludes to the giving of manna during the life of Moses (Exodus 16), suggesting that the third part of the story in 1 Kings 19 follows the second and first parts in also alluding to the giving of manna. Yahweh's word is food. If Yahweh's chosen prophets heed their call, then Yahweh's word will be proclaimed. If the word is proclaimed and obeyed, the people will be fed—the Deuteronomistic stipulations will come into effect and everyone will share in the blessing of the land.

Elisha follows after Elijah and serves him, replacing the lad whom Elijah left at Beersheba. The story has progressed from one extreme to the other, from the intent of the last prophet in existence to die to Elijah's and Elisha's acceptance of their calls and the consequent preservation of the people of Israel, or a remnant of them.

In Zion and David a New Beginning: An Interpretation of Psalm 78

WESTON SCHOOL OF THEOLOGY

A Psalm of Asaph

[1] Hear, o my people, my teaching;
   Attend to my words.
[2] I will speak in story form;
   I will draw a lesson from olden times.
[3] Stories told to us, we are familiar with them,
   Our forefathers have repeated them to us.
[4] We will not keep them from our children,
   We will tell them to the next generation:
   The praiseworthy acts of Yahweh and his might,
   The wonders which he has performed.
[5] He established a decree in Jacob;
   Ordained a law in Israel.
These he commanded our forefathers;
   They were to command them to their children;
[6] So that the next generation might come to know,
   Children yet to be born,
[7] Who in turn were to tell their children,
   Were to put their trust in God,
   And not forget the works of God,
   And keep his commandments.
[8] They were not to be like their forefathers,
   A wayward and defiant generation,
A generation whose heart was inconstant,
   And whose spirit was not faithful to God;
[9] (Like) the children of Ephraim, shooters of the bow,
   Who retreated in the day of battle.
[10] They did not keep God's covenant,
   They refused to walk in his law.
[11] *They forgot his works,*
   The wondrous deeds which he showed them.

[12] In the sight of their forefathers he did wonders,
   In the land of Egypt, the plain of Zoan
[13] He split the sea and led them through it;
   He made the waters stand like a heap.

[14]He led them by a cloud by day,
   And by night with the light of fire.
[15]He split cliffs in the wilderness,
   He provided water to drink as from the great abyss.
[16]He brought floods forth from rock,
   He brought out water in rivers.
[17]But they persisted in sinning against him,
   In rebelling against the Most High in the arid land.
[18]They tested God in their hearts
   By demanding food for themselves.
[19]They spoke against God, saying,
   "Is God able to spread a feast in the wilderness?
[20]True, he smote the rock and waters flowed,
   The wadis overflowed.
   But has he power to provide food,
   To give meat to his people?"
[21]Yahweh heard and grew angry,
   Fire blazed forth against Jacob,
      Anger flared up against Israel.
[22]For they did not believe in God,
   Did not trust in his saving power.
[23]So he commanded the skies above,
   The portals of heaven he opened.
[24]He rained upon them manna for food,
   Bread from heaven he gave them.
[25]Each man ate a hero's meal,
   He sent them food in abundance.
[26]He set the east wind moving from heaven,
   He guided by his power the south wind.
[27]He rained meat upon them like the dust for abundance,
   Winged fowl, as many as the sands of the sea.
[28]He brought them down in the midst of the camp,
   All around their tents.
[29]They ate, they were sated to the full;
   He gave them what they craved.
[30]This craving had not yet left them,
   The food was still in their mouths,
[31]Then the anger of God attacked them,
   It killed their sturdiest,
      Struck down the youth of Israel.
[32]In spite of all this they persisted in sinning,
   They did not believe in his wonders.

[33]He ended their days in futility,
   Their years in sudden death.
[34]When he slew them, they sought him,
   They again inquired of God.

[35]They remembered that God is their Rock,
That God Most High is their redeemer.
[36]But they deceived him with their mouths,
By their tongues they lied to him.
[37]Their hearts were inconstant toward him,
They were not faithful to his covenant.
[38]But he is merciful,
He forgives iniquity,
He does not annihilate.
He restrained his anger time and again,
He did not give full vent to his wrath.
[39]He remembered that they are flesh,
A passing breath that does not return.

[40]How often they rebelled against him in the wilderness,
Grieved him in the wasteland.
[41]They tested God again,
Provoked the Holy One of Israel.
[42]They did not remember his power,
The day he redeemed them from distress,
[43]When he displayed his signs in Egypt,
His wonders in the plain of Zoan
[44]He changed their rivers to blood,
Their streams they could not drink.
[45]He sent insects to devour them,
Frogs to destroy them.
[46]He yielded their crops to the caterpillar,
The fruits of their labor to the locust.
[47]He killed their vines with hail,
Their sycamores with frost.
[48]He gave over their flocks to hail,
Their cattle to lightning bolts.
[49]He sent the heat of his anger among them,
Wrath, anger, distress,
A band of deadly messengers.
[50]He spared not their very life,
He delivered their souls to deadly pestilence.
[51]He smote every first born in Egypt,
The fruits of their vigor in the tents of Ham.
[52]He set his people moving like sheep,
He guided them, a flock, in the wilderness,
[53]He led them in safety so that they were unafraid,
As for their enemies, the sea covered them.
[54]He brought them to his sacred precinct,
The mountain which his right hand created.
[55]He drove out the nations before them,
He apportioned them the heritage by lot,
He settled the tribes of Israel in their tents.

⁵⁶They tested, they rebelled against God Most High,
His covenant they did not observe.
⁵⁷They fell away, they were deceitful like their fathers,
They proved false like a treacherous bow.
⁵⁸They angered him by their high places,
With their idols they angered him.
⁵⁹God heard and grew angry,
He vehemently rejected Israel.
⁶⁰He forsook the tabernacle of Shiloh,
The tent where he dwelt among men.
⁶¹He gave up his might to captivity,
His glory into the hands of the foe.
⁶²He yielded his people to the sword,
He was wrathful toward his heritage.
⁶³His young men were consumed by fire,
His maidens had no wedding song.
⁶⁴His priests fell by the sword,
His widows made no lamentation.

⁶⁵The Lord awoke as from sleep,
Like a warrior shaking off wine.
⁶⁶He beat back his enemies,
Everlasting shame he dealt them.
⁶⁷He rejected the tent of Joseph,
He chose not the tribe of Ephraim.
⁶⁸He chose the tribe of Judah,
Mount Zion which he favored.
⁶⁹He built his shrine like the heavens,
Like the earth, he founded it forever.
⁷⁰He chose David his servant,
He took him from the sheepfolds,
⁷¹From tending the ewes he brought him,
To shepherd Jacob his people,
Israel his heritage.
⁷²He shepherded them with a pure heart,
With skillful hands he guided them. (Psalm 78)

P SALM 78, the longest review of Israel's historical traditions in the psalter, is in many ways puzzling as a liturgical poem. In the introduction, vv 1-11, the speaker promises a profound interpretation of the ancient traditions revered by the Israelite congregation. There is a sober lesson to be learned from the infidelity of past generations. The speaker next retells two stories of Israel's past. In both, the ancestors provoked God to angry punishment. The stories, however, are not in the order in which they are found in the Pentateuch, nor do they function in the same way. The desert wanderings come *before* the exodus from Egypt. The miracle of water in the desert is bound in with the crossing of the Red Sea, unlike the Pentateuchal tradition. The story of the manna, which in the Pentateuch is a story of grace, is joined to the narrative about the quail, becoming the instrument of God's punishment upon disbelief. More puzzling even than the recasting of ancient traditions is the intention of the psalm. What is the new reading of the liturgical recitation of old familiar stories promised in v 2? It cannot be simply a restatement that Israel has a sinful past. The old traditions already declared that. To find the purpose of the poem one must review scholarly opinions and make a fresh examination of the psalm itself.

Reputable scholars of the last half-century differ widely among themselves on the psalm's genre, or type, date, structure and aim. It has been dated as early as the tenth century,[1] within the period of the divided monarchy[2] (922-587 B.C.E.), and as late as the post-exilic period.[3] In genre, it has been called "a mixture of genres . . . legend, hymn, prophetic warning, and wisdom poem,"[4] a historical psalm,[5] a wisdom

[1]O. Eissfeldt, "Das Lied Moses Deuteronomium 32:1-43 und das Lehrgedicht Asaphs Psalm 78 samt einer Analyse der Umgebung des Mose-Liedes," *Berichte über die Verhandlungen der Sachsischen Akademie der Wissenschaften zu Leipzig* (Phil.-hist. Klasse 104, 5; Berlin: Akademie, 1958) esp. pp. 34-37. Eissfeldt gives insufficient attention to the rhetoric of the whole poem. J. Hofbauer ("Psalm 77/78: ein 'politisch Lied,'" *ZKT* 89 [1967] 41-50) attributes the psalm to Asaph in the time of David. However, too little is known of Asaph and of superscriptions generally in the psalms to date by this means. Like Eissfeldt, he neglects the poetry and does not deal adequately with the deuteronomic language. The most recent treatment, which contains a competent presentation of arguments for an early date, is A. F. Campbell, "Psalm 78: A Contribution to the Theology of Tenth Century Israel," *CBQ* 41 (1979) 51-79.

[2]H. Junker, "Die Entstehungszeit des Ps. 78 und des Deuteronomiums," *Bib* 34 (1953) 487-500; M. Dahood, *Psalms II* (AB 17; Garden City: Doubleday, 1968) 238; E. Podechard, *Le Psautier* (Lyon: Facultes Catholiques, 1954) 2. 49-50; A. Weiser, *The Psalms* (Old Testament Library; Philadelphia: Westminster, 1962) 540; A. F. Kirkpatrick, *The Book of Psalms* (The Cambridge Bible for Schools and Colleges; Cambridge: Cambridge Univ., 1921) 463; D. N. Freedman, "Divine Names and Titles in Early Hebrew Poetry," *Magnalia Dei: The Mighty Acts of God* (ed. F. M. Cross, *et al.*; Garden City: Doubleday, 1978) 81; J. Schildenberger, "Psalm 78 (77) und die Pentateuchquellen," *Lex Tua Veritas* (Festschrift für H. Junker; Trier: Paulinus, 1961) 231-56.

[3]H. Gunkel dated the psalm to post-exilic times because of the mixture of genres (for him a sign of late date) and the alleged dependence on already formed OT historical books, in *Die Psalmen* (HKAT 2/2; 4th ed.; Göttingen: Vandenhoeck & Ruprecht, 1926) 342. For an effective criticism of Gunkel's second criterion, see Campbell, "Psalm 78." H.-J. Kraus, while sympathetic to a pre-exilic dating, remains open to a post-exilic composition date, *Psalmen* (BKAT 15/2; 4th ed.; Neukirchen-Vluyn: Neukirchener, 1972) 541.

[4]Gunkel, *Die Psalmen*, 342.

[5]Kraus, *Psalmen*, 539, and E. Podechard, *Le Psautier*, 2. 44.

poem.[6] Its structure has been variously outlined but a consensus has not emerged regarding its divisions.[7] Its intention has been interpreted in widely different ways. The late 19th century scholar, Bernhard Duhm, thought the purpose was to show simply that the Ephraimites had always been a rejected tribe.[8] Herman Gunkel, who founded modern psalm criticism, does not propose a single aim. He sees the work as a depiction of the repeated infidelity of the ancestors so as to warn the contemporary generation, with a mention at the end of the election of Jerusalem and David.[9] H.-J. Kraus, in his theologically perceptive commentary, describes the thought of the psalm rather than settling on a single intention. He suggests that the psalm attempts to fit the traditions about the choice of Zion and David into the old sacred epic (*Heilsgeschichte*) but expresses himself cautiously about the reason for the linking of the two tradition complexes. He asks whether it was a polemic against the refoundation on Mount Gerizim of the old northern shrine under the Samaritans in the late post-exilic period, but leaves the question open.[10] The Scandinavian, Sigmund Mowinckel, sees the psalm as a theodicy, "to testify to the faithfulness of Yahweh and the breaking of the covenant on the part of the people, proving the justice of punishment and disaster."[11] For J. Hofbauer, the work is political, an announcement of the rejection of the north and the selection of David, Judah and Zion.[12] In a recent study, R. P. Carroll explains it as "a charter myth explaining how Judah was the rightful heir of the exodus movement and therefore could claim the leadership of the people of Israel. The polemic against the north involved the rejection of the leadership of the Joseph clans and the denial of their legitimate claims to be the bearers of the Heilsgeschichte."[13] A. F. Campbell argues that the psalm is concerned "how to understand and interpret theologically

---

[6]Eissfeldt, *The Old Testament: An Introduction* (New York: Harper, 1965) 125.

[7]To give a sampling: Gunkel, vv 1-11 (1-4, 5-11), 12-16, 17-31, 32-39, 40-51, 52-55, 56-58, 59-64, 65-72, in *Die Psalmen*, 341; E. Podechard, vv 1-11, 12-16, 17-31, 32-39, 40-51, 52-55, 56-58, 59-64, 65-72, in *Le Psautier*, 40-44; H.-J. Kraus, vv 1-11, 12-31, 32-41, 42-53, 54-64, 65-72, in *Psalmen*, 540; G. W. Coats sees the following sections, vv 1-8, 9-16 + 44-66, 17-41, 65-72, in *Rebellion in the Wilderness* (Nashville: Abingdon, 1968) 223-24.

[8]*Die Psalmen* (Kurzer Hand-Commentar zum Alten Testament 15; Freiburg i. B.: J. C. B. Mohr, 1899) 201, 206.

[9]*Die Psalmen*, 341.

[10]*Psalmen*, 2. 548.

[11]*The Psalms in Israel's Worship* (New York: Abingdon, 1967) 2. 112.

[12]"Psalm 77/78," 43.

[13]R. P. Carroll, "Psalm LXXVIII: Vestiges of a Tribal Polemic," *VT* 21 (1971) 150.

the events from Shiloh to Jerusalem," i.e. the destruction of Shiloh, interpreted in the light of the people's religious history, is a rejection of Yahweh. Matching that rejection is the election of David and Zion.[14] Campbell's general interpretation, though not his dating, is in most respects similar to mine.

Given such diversity of opinion, the expectation of uncovering the authentic structure and intention of the poem may appear foolhardy. In my opinion, previous scholars have not given sufficient attention to the rhetoric of the work, i.e., how the psalm works as a piece of liturgical poetry. Study of the poem as illustrating northern and southern tribal relations, or a particular typology of historical traditions, genres, or Hebrew language, have generally taken precedence over examination of the poetic techniques. Literary questions such as the function of the extraordinarily long "wisdom" introduction (vv 1-11), of the two separate historical recitals, of the relation of the Zion-David section in vv 65-72 to the rest of the poem, of the much discussed reference to the Ephraimites in v 9 and of the rather elaborate system of cross references of words and word plays have been insufficiently addressed.

I intend in this paper to study first of all the structure of the poem, making as much use as possible of formal criteria drawn from within the psalm. The individual sections will then be analysed for their contribution to the purpose of the entire poem. I shall then make suggestions regarding its date, setting and relationship to Israel's history and literature.

It is a pleasure to dedicate this study to my mentor, Frank Moore Cross, who has contributed so significantly to our understanding of Hebrew poetry and of the relationship between liturgy and the literature of the Bible.

My argument depends in large measure upon the overall arrangement of the material. Fortunately the author's outline can be discerned by the aid of formal devices such as repetition of key words and phrases, chiasm, paronomasia or word play, and especially in the parallel structure of the two historical recitals.

Gunkel[15] and Kraus[16] have correctly perceived vv 1-11 to be introductory to the rest of the poem. As can be seen graphically in the translation given above, the thirty cola[17] are divided into three stanzas of ten cola (vv 1-4, 5-7, 8-10) all of which end with similar substantives,

---

[14]"Psalm 78," 76-77. An earlier formulation is contained in his *The Ark Narrative* (SBLDS 16; Missoula: Scholars, 1975) 225.

[15]*Die Psalmen*, 341-43.

[16]*Psalmen*, 540-43.

[17]In this paper, colon designates the verse. Bi-colon (plural: bi-cola) are parallel verses.

"the wondrous deeds of Yahweh" or the like (italicized). The important word "forefathers" (ʾăbôt-), underlined in the above translation, gradually ascends in each stanza to become the topic sentence of the climactic third stanza on the rebellious generation. The word also links the introduction to v 12 which introduces the first recital. V 12 is transitional. The first part of the verse, "In the sight of their fathers he did wonders," links back to v 11b and forward to the first story in the wilderness, while the second part of the verse, "in the land of Egypt, the plain of Zoan," refers one to the second recital (vv 40-64) where the sites are repeated as introduction in v 43, ". . . in the land of Egypt . . . in the plain of Zoan." Within the frame that is thus established, the first narrative is played out.

That vv 13-32 portray a unified drama is shown by two facts. The presumptuous questions in vv 19-20 presuppose the miraculous outpouring of water in vv 15-16. And vv 17-32 contain a chiasm which draws the verses together.

v 17 ʿôd laḥăṭôʾ lô, "continue to sin against him"
   v 21 ʾap ʿālâ běyiśrāʾēl, "wrath went up against Israel"
      v 25 laśōbāʿ, "unto satiety"
      v 29 wayyiśběʿû měʿōd, "they were thoroughly sated"
   v 31 ʾap ʾĕlōhîm ʿālâ bāhem, "wrath of God went up against them"
v 32 ḥāṭěʾû ʿôd, "they continued to sin"

In addition to these poetic unifying devices, one should note that vv 13-16 form a diptych, or two matching pictures, united through the use of the verb bāqaʿ "to split," and the parallelism of the various terms for water in both parts of the diptych. Also the phrase wayyamṭēr ʿălêhem, "He rained upon them," in vv 24 and 27 is a device to bring together the two traditions of manna and quail. V 32, "For all this, they continued to sin, and they did not believe in his wonderful acts," by its position in the chiasm concludes the section. The phrase "for all this . . ." is a concluding formula elsewhere (Isa 5:25; 9:11, 16, 20; 10:4; Jer 3:10; Job 1:22 and 2:10). V 40, "How often they rebelled against him in the wilderness, angered him in the wasteland," evidently begins the second recital of history because it repeats the site of the wilderness events, "in the wilderness" and "in the wasteland." The verses between vv 33-39 appear to be a meditation on the events narrated in vv 12-32, showing that the punishment in the desert is not the end, that God's mercy makes a new beginning possible.

A second presentation of historical traditions is found in vv 40-64. Here I differ from Gunkel, Kraus and most other commentators who do not see these verses as a unified whole. Few disagree that v 43 which speaks of Egypt and the plain of Zoan is the proper heading for the plague narrative. My reason for taking the whole section as unified is based on the close resemblance of vv 44-55 to the old poem Exod 15:1-18 in vocabulary and poetic logic, and from parallelism with the first recital of vv 12-32 in the sequence of miracle, sin, divine anger, and punishment. The plagues in Egypt, vv 44-50, are part of a single action. The divine assault and victory over the Egyptians is but the first act of a drama leading to the procession in the wilderness and the settling in the land conceived as a mountain. In Exod 15:1-12, Yahweh's battle against Egypt is not to be separated from the consequent procession to the holy land and settlement on the holy mountain in vv 13-18.[18] This fruitful parallel will be explored later. The description of the people's sin, divine anger, and punishment in vv 56-64 follows naturally from the settlement and is clearly paralleled in the first story (vv 12-32) where the sequence is demonstrable by formal devices.

Commentators agree that vv 65-72 are a coherent section, the account of Yahweh's military intervention to reject Ephraim and choose Judah, Zion and David. This, like vv 33-40, seems to be a sequel to vv 42-64, drawing conclusions from venerable and ancient traditions.

The outline may be summarized.

Introduction: vv 1-11 (30 cola)
Liturgical officer addresses all Israel to reveal the true meaning of the covenantal traditions, to instill fidelity to those traditions, and to provide a negative example of infidelity.

First Recital:	*Second Recital:*
Wilderness Events	*From Egypt to Canaan*
vv 12-32 (47 cola)	vv 40-64 (55 cola)
Gracious act (vv 12-16)	Gracious act (vv 44-55)
Rebellion (vv 17-20)	Rebellion (vv 56-58)
Divine anger & punishment	Divine anger & punishment
(manna and quail) vv 21-32	(destruction of Shiloh) vv 59-64
Sequel vv 33-39 (16 cola)	*Sequel* vv 65-72 (17 cola)
total cola: 63	total cola: 72

Analysis of the structure of the poem has shown two recitals each followed by a sequel in which divine merciful response is depicted. Detailed examination of the parts is now called for. From vv 1-2, which in style resemble some passages in wisdom literature (Prov 3:1; 4:2; Pss 49:2-5; 119:171) some commentators conclude the poem is a didactic instruction.[19] "Wisdom" elements do not appear outside of the first two

---

[18]A parallel already noted by Campbell, *The Ark Narrative*, 214, n. 1.
[19]Mowinckel, *The Psalms in Israel's Worship*, 2. 112, and Eissfeldt, *Introduction*, 125, and to some extent Kraus, *Psalmen, passim.*

verses. A more appropriate comparison is with the book of Deuteronomy, that store of Mosaic retrospective historical speeches. The Song
of Moses, Deut 32:1-43, resembles Psalm 78 especially in its "wisdom"
beginning to a historical review and warning.

> [1]Give ear, o heavens, and I will speak,
> And let the earth hear the words of my mouth.
> [2]May my teaching drop as the rain,
> My teaching distill as the dew,
> As the gentle rain upon the tender grass,
> And as the showers upon the herbage.
> [3]For the name of Yahweh I will proclaim
> Ascribe greatness to our God.

The excerpt illustrates a style of speech which was thought appropriate
in retelling the history of the people. More significant than similarities
of style is the general Deuteronomic picture of Moses as the authoritative
speaker of the ancient traditions, rebuking, exhorting, promising. The
third speech of Moses, Deut 29:1-30:20 (English translation [ET] 29:2-
30:20), is a good example of the Mosaic tradition of liturgical preaching:

> And Moses summoned all Israel and said to them, "You have seen all that
> Yahweh did before your eyes in the land of Egypt, to Pharaoh and to all
> his people and to all his land, the great trials which your eyes saw, the
> signs and those great wonders. But Yahweh has not given you a heart
> to know and eyes to see and ears to hear unto this day" (Deut 29:1-3;
> ET 29:2-4).
> ". . . You stand this day all of you before Yahweh your God . . . (v 9; ET
> 10) . . . that you may enter the covenant with an oath . . . (v 11; ET 12) . . .
> the anger of Yahweh and his jealousy would smoke against that man (v 19;
> ET 20) . . . See I have set before you this day life and good, death and evil"
> (30:15).

The verses excerpted from the speech show that Moses speaks to all
Israel in a liturgical gathering ("this day" Deut 29:3; ET 4, and v 14; ET
15) selecting only those national traditions which would be appropriate
to the aim of the speech. Of significance is the repeated stress on divine
wrath (Deut 29:17-20; ET 18-21; 24-27; ET 25-28), a theme that is
repeated in Ps 78:21, 31, 49, 59. Important here too is the well-known
passage Deut 18:15, "Yahweh your God will raise up for you from the
midst of your brethren a prophet like me. To him shall you heed." The
verse, when taken with vv 16-17, with which it forms a whole, seems to
legitimate later officials with the Mosaic mantle. Deut 18:16-17 seems to
be a quotation from the unit Deut 5:1-6:3, a passage which has as its
intention the authorization of liturgical successors of Moses to mediate
covenantal traditions. The speaker of the psalm, then, is not a wise man

solving riddles or merely teaching a lesson from history. He authoritatively restates the ancient traditions so that Israel will be able to decide
for Yahweh. The story/lesson of v 2 is the true meaning of the traditions
which only one vested with authority can disclose—in this case the
choosing of a new shrine and new dynasty as the divinely appointed
successor to Shiloh.[20]

The thought of the introduction progresses from the identification
of the speaker who announces himself as authoritatively retelling the old
traditions of Yahweh's glorious deeds to the present generation (vv 1-4),
to the insistence on fidelity as this generation's proper response to the
covenant (vv 5-7), and to the sober illustration of the infidelity of the
forefathers, among whom the Ephraimites offer a dramatic example (vv
8-11). V 9, literally according to the Hebrew, "the children of Ephraim
armed with shooters of the bow, retreated in the day of battle," is
redundant with its double description of the armaments of the Ephraimites. Fortunately paranomasia, i.e. word-play, in v 57 makes possible the
recovery of the original text. V 57 clearly alludes to v 9, reading *nhpkw
kqšt rmyh*, "they turned like a deceitful bow," thus showing that v 11
should be read *rmy qšt hpkw*, "shooters of the bow, they retreated," and
that *nwšqy*, "armed," is a secondary variant.[21] The entire verse, "(Like)
the children of Ephraim, shooters of the bow, who retreated in the day of
battle," is deliberately general. The phrase "day of battle" is general also
in Job 38:23 and Zech 14:13. As will be explained below, the verse

[20]Wisdom literature and the business of the court and temple are intimately
related in the ancient Near East. One finds so-called wisdom language in
international treaties and also in liturgical language. The occurrence of wisdom
language is not therefore always a sign of instructional purpose in the narrow
sense.

[21]H. Gunkel's radical emendation in *Die Psalmen*, 343, has not been
followed by the majority of commentators. Nonetheless, many scholars regard
the verse as doubtfully related to its immediate context: Podechard, *Le Psautier*,
2. 50-51 and Kraus, *Psalmen*, 538. Dahood (*Psalms II*) explains the *y* of *nwšqy* as
the third person singular suffix ("his bowmen"). However, final *y* for the third
person singular suffix is a Phoenician phenomenon in nouns or verbs ending in
long vowels and in singular nouns in the genitive case. It should not be read
into Hebrew. Weiser (*The Psalms*, 540) interprets the verse as a reference to the
day of battle when Saul fell in battle (1 Samuel 31 and cf. 1 Samuel 15). The
verse is too vague to be so explained without further support from within the
psalm.

The most likely explanation of the word *nôšĕqê* in 9 is that it is an ancient
variant. The phrase *rômēh qešet* also occurs in Jer 4:29. The phrase *nôšĕqê qešet*
occurs in the late texts 1 Chr 12:2 and 2 Chr 17:17. For a recent discussion of
ancient variants, see S. Talmon, "The Textual Study of the Bible—A New
Outlook," *Qumran and the History of the Biblical Text* (ed. F. M. Cross and
S. Talmon: Cambridge: Harvard, 1975) 344-57.

probably describes the series of military defeats of the second half of the eighth century leading to the destruction of Samaria and the loss of Ephraim in 722. But it should be stressed against the dominant trend in interpretation that the Ephraimite defeat is only an instance of all Israel's infidelity. The word "their forefathers" in v 8 designates all the tribes. In vv 21, 31, 33, 55, 59, 72, Jacob/Israel designates the whole people, not only the northern tribes. The poem's view that all Israel has sinned is important. To anticipate somewhat, the destruction of Shiloh, the national shrine before its destruction in the mid-eleventh century, is a punishment dealt to all Israel. The tribe of Ephraim/Joseph is no longer the site of the shrine. Judah is the new location. The northern tribes *per se* are not rejected.[22]

That all Israel is the concern of the poem and not the northern tribes alone is clear also from the echoes of vv 8-11 in the rest of the poem. These introductory verses have to do with the ancestors in general. The many cross references between these verses and the other parts of the poem show that the general infidelity of the ancestral generation is illustrated in the specific sins of the recitals. The word play linking v 9 and v 57 has already been noted. V 8cd *dôr lō⁾ hēkîn libbô wĕlō⁾ neɔemnâ ɔet ɔēl rûḥô*, "a generation whose heart was inconstant, and whose spirit was not faithful toward God" reappears in the sequel to the first recital, v 37, *wĕlibbām lō⁾ nākôn ᶜimmô wĕlō⁾ neɔemnû bibrîtô*, "and their heart was not constant toward him, and they were not faithful toward his covenant." Other instances: "like their fathers" of v 8b in v 57; "rebellious" of v 8b in vv 17, 40, 56; "they did not keep the covenant" of v 10 in v 56; "his wonders" of v 11 in v 32.

It is now time to look at the first presentation of history, vv 12-32. It narrates traditions also found in the Pentateuch, arranging them so that the crossing of the Reed Sea and the water in the wilderness constitute one great miracle, making all the more heinous the consequent rebellion. In Exod 17:1-7 and Num 20:2-13, Moses strikes the rock for water in response to the murmuring of the people. Psalm 78, however, makes the miracle one of pure grace. God's initiative, not the people's sin, provokes the outpouring. It has been made into two matched pictures: the splitting (*bqᶜ*) of the sea and the splitting (*bqᶜ*) of the rocks. Yahweh controls the sea which they cross (v 13) and the rivers which they drink (v 16) for the benefit of his people. "Sea" and "river" are often parallel in Hebrew poetry. The stunning miracle only leads the people to test Yahweh. "True, he smote the rock so that waters flowed, so that wadis overflowed. But can he provide bread, can he supply meat for his people?" (v 20).

[22]So also Campbell, *The Ark Narrative*, 219.

Vv 17-32, drawn together by the chiasm which has been pointed out, unite traditions which in the Pentateuch (Exodus 16 and Numbers 11) are separate and there function differently: the manna, the quail, and the outpouring of divine wrath in the act of eating.[23] "They continued to sin against him" alludes to the last stanza of the introduction, vv 8-11, which states that the ancestral generation forgot the wonders which they had seen. The desert generation "forgot," i.e. were not faithful to the divine act of the miraculous waters. Before the manna and quail are actually given, God is incited to anger and flames out against Israel in vv 21-22 (cf. Num 11:10, 33). Unlike the Pentateuchal traditions of the graceful gift of manna, manna is here given under the sign of divine wrath, like the quail of Num 11:31-35. "While the flesh was still between their teeth, before it was consumed, the anger of Yahweh burned against the people, and Yahweh smote the people with a very great plague" (Num 11:33).

Vv 33-39 appear to be a reflection on the miracle and punishment of vv 12-32. The verses do not describe a specific event. The people's repentance in the face of punishment is not sincere. In their infidelity they fail to recognize the God who is willing to make a new beginning. "But he is merciful, he forgives sin, and he does not destroy."

Vv 40-64 is the second arrangement of sacred lore clearly intended to be juxtaposed to the first, vv 12-32. V 40, "in the wilderness . . . in the wasteland," resumes the first recital and links it to the second, "in Egypt . . . in the plain of Zoan," of v 43. The author has arranged his traditions in vv 44-55 in the ancient pattern found also in Exod 15:1-18, a divine assault against the hapless Egyptians followed by a procession of the victorious entourage back to the holy mountain dwelling of the deity. Exod 15:1-12 describes the battle, "Yahweh is a warrior, / Yahweh is his name. / Pharaoh and his army / he hurled into the sea. / His elite troops / he drowned in the Reed Sea" (vv 3-4). The divine weapon is "a storm at sea, a storm blown up by the blast of wind from his dilated nostrils."[24] Passages suggesting a storm include "At the blast of your nostrils / the waters were heaped up. / The swells mounted up as a hill, / The deeps foamed in the heart of the sea" (15:8); "You blew with your breath, / Sea covered them. They sank like a lead weight / In the dreadful waters" (15:10). Exod 15:13-18 depicts the procession of the victorious god with his clients back to the sanctuary on the holy mountain. "You faithfully led (nāḥîtâ) / the people whom you re-deemed; / You guided in your might / to the holy encampment" (15:13).

---

[23]Formally the linking of the two traditions is accomplished by the verb yamṭēr, "he rained," which is the first word in both v 26 and v 28.

[24]Cross, *Canaanite Myth and Hebrew Epic* (Cambridge: Harvard, 1973) 131. In what concerns the Song of the Sea, I am indebted to Cross' analysis, pp. 112-44.

The peoples are terrified (15:14-16). "You brought them, you planted them / In the mount of your heritage (*běhar naḥălātěkā*) / the dais of your throne / which you made, Yahweh, / the sanctuary, Yahweh, / Which your hands created" (15:17).

In Ps 78:44-55, vv 44-51 depict the divine attack, corresponding to Exod 15:1-12, while vv 52-55, the procession, parallels Exod 15:13-18. There is common vocabulary.[25] The plagues are arranged in a series of seven bi-cola, with the killing of the first born in the climactic seventh place. The terms for the plagues, and their number, are the same as in the Yahwist source in the Pentateuch (Exodus 7-12). However, the Yahwist's second and third plagues, insects and frogs, are combined into one bi-colon (v 45). Instead of a specific sixth plague, there are two tri-cola (vv 49-50) portraying divine wrath against Egypt and providing a transition to the slaughter of v 51. Moses and Aaron do not appear. In this assault against the land of Egypt the Lord alone is the warrior.[26]

The procession to the holy mountain, described in vv 52-55, is the second movement of a unified drama, true also for Exod 15:1-18. F. M. Cross has shown that the ancient poem in Exodus 15 is a transformation of an ancient polytheistic story of the storm god's victory over sea and his triumphant return to his royal seat.[27]

> [52]He set his people moving like sheep,
> He guided them, a flock in the wilderness.
> [53]He led them in safety so that they were unafraid.
> As for their enemies, the sea covered them.

[25]*těšallaḥ ḥărōněkā yōʾkělēmô qaqqaš*, "You sent forth your fury, / It consumed them like stubble" (Exod 15:7) is reflected in Ps 78:49 *yěšallaḥ bām ḥărôn ʾappô*, "He sent among them the fury of his wrath"; *nôzělîm*, "swells, streams," in Exod 15:8 and Ps 78:16, 44; *nāḥîtā, wayyanḥēm*, "you led," "he led them," in Exod 15:13 and Ps 78:53; *ʿam, ʿammô*, "people," "his people," in Exod 15:13, 16 and Ps 78:52; *něwēh qodšěkā, gěbûl qodšô*, "your holy encampment," "his holy precinct," in Exod 15:13 and Ps 78:54; *těbîʾēmô, wayěbîʾēm*, "You brought them," "he brought them," in Exod 15:17 and Ps 78:54; *naḥălātěkā, naḥălâ*, "Your heritage," "heritage," in Exod 15:17 and Ps 78:55; *miqdāš ʾădōnāy kôněnû yādêkā, har zeh qānětâ yěmînô*, "the sanctuary, Lord, which your hands created," "the mountain which your right hand created," in Exod 15:17 and Ps 78:54.

[26]For detailed comparison of Pentateuchal narrative and Psalm 78, see the valuable survey of A. Lauha, "Die Geschichtsmotive in den alttestamentlichen Psalmen," *Annales Academiae Scientiarum Fennicae* B 56 (Helsinki, 1945; Helsinki: Suomalainen, 1946), especially pp. 50-54. Lauha's assumption that Psalm 78 depends on the Pentateuch is unlikely, as is demonstrated most recently by Campbell, "Psalm 78," 64-70.

[27]Cross (*Canaanite Myth*, 135-44) gives a number of examples of Israelite adaptations of the ancient traditions, e.g. Ps 77:17-20, Isa 51:9-11, Psalm 114.

[54]He brought them to his sacred precinct,[28]
The mountain which his right hand created.
[55]He drove out the nations before them,
He apportioned them their heritage by lot,
He settled the tribes of Israel in their tents.

In the logic of the poem, the sacred mountain of v 54 is not Mount Zion, contrary to the opinion of many commentators. H.-J. Kraus, for example, writes, "The exodus tradition leaps over in 54 to the Zion tradition. This sudden transition, in which the conquest is focused exclusively in Zion, also holds true for Exod 15:17."[29] Kraus' position is unlikely for Exod 15:17[30] and untenable here. That Shiloh is the shrine of v 54 is shown by vocabulary cross references to v 60, where the shrine is clearly Shiloh. V 60, "He forsook the tabernacle (miškan) of Shiloh / the tent (ʾōhel) where he dwelt (šikkēn) among men," takes up words descriptive of the unnamed shrine and the surrounding land of v 55c. V 62, "He gave his people (ʿammô) to the sword, / and at his heritage (naḥălātô) he became enraged," refers back to vv 52 and 55 where the same words appear in the procession and land distribution. Similar vocabulary is also used of Jerusalem in vv 68 and 71, showing the poem sees Shiloh and Jerusalem as successive central shrines for all Israel. V 68, "Mount Zion which he loves," echoes v 54, "the mountain which his right hand created," while ʿammô "his people," and naḥălātô "his heritage" in v 71 refers one back to ʿammô in v 52 and naḥălâ in v 55. The destruction of one shrine does not mean that God will not choose another.

As in the first recital, the act of God is followed by infidelity:

[56]They *tested*, they *rebelled* against God *Most High*;
His covenant they did not observe.
[57]They fell away, they were deceitful *like their fathers.*
They proved false like a treacherous bow.
[58]They angered him by their high places,
With their idols they angered him.

[28]M. Dahood has revived the old suggestion of A. B. Ehrlich that gĕbûl "boundary, territory," means "mountain" here on the basis of Ugaritic gbl "mount, hill," and Arabic jabal, "hill, mountain," in *Psalms II*, 245. This is possible but not compelling. Exodus 15 shows that har "mountain," in v 17 is parallel to miqdāš, "sanctuary." Also in Ugaritic, qdš, "shrine," and nʿm, "chosen, favored spot," appear to be in parallel to ǵr, "mountain," and gbʿ, "hill," in *CTA* 3.3.26-28 (= *UT* ʿnt).

[29]*Psalmen*, 2. 574. Other commentators allow for both Zion and Canaan considered as a mountain, e.g. Gunkel, *Die Psalmen*, 346, Podechard, *Le Psautier*, 2. 48, Dahood, *Psalms II*, 245.

[30]Cross, *Canaanite Myth*, 142-43, for the evidence that the mountain in Exodus 15 was only later applied to Jerusalem.

The use of the roots *nsh*, "test," *mrh*, "rebel," of the words ᶜ*elyôn*, "the Most High" and "like their fathers," of the word play in "they proved false like a treacherous bow," which are paralleled in other descriptions of Israel's sin, show that the infidelity in the land is but one more outbreak of the rebellion mentioned in the introductory vv 8-11. In addition to the links to other parts of the poem the italicized words in the above verses are found frequently in Deuteronomy or the Deutero-nomistic history, a relation that will be explored below in dealing with the date and setting.

Vv 60-64 describe the Philistine capture of Shiloh in the mid-eleventh century. The Ark Narrative, examined in the classic study by L. Rost in 1926,[31] and recently restudied by A. F. Campbell[32] (1 Sam 4:1b-7:1 + 2 Sam 6:2-23) is a prose account of the battle, the capture of the ark and its entry into Jerusalem. Though similar in theology to the psalm, the ark narrative is not its source. The divine dwelling in the poem is correctly the old tent (v 60) and not the *bêt* or *hêkāl*, "temple," of the folkloristic narratives of 1 Samuel 1-3.

Corresponding to the sequel of the first recital of history in vv 33-41, vv 65-72 describe the intervention of the Lord in a new battle for Israel, his rejection of the tent of Joseph//tribe of Ephraim, and the choosing of a new shrine—Zion in the tribe of Judah, and a servant—David. The divine warrior wakes from sleep,[33] conquers the enemy, then chooses a new shrine for his dwelling. God chooses Zion and David, and rejects Joseph and Ephraim, in language reminiscent of 1 Sam 15:26-28 and 16:1-13. There, God rejects (*māᵓas*) Saul, a man of non-Judahite origins, and chooses (*bāḥar*) David in order to start anew. In language evocative of the earlier choice of the holy precinct on the mountain after the defeat of the enemies, God chooses a new shrine.

> [54]He brought them to his holy precinct,
> The mountain which his right hand created.
> [68]He chose the tribe of Judah,
> Mount Zion which he loves.

The first sequel, vv 33-40, spoke in general terms of Yahweh's merciful intent to forgive sin and not to destroy, his willingness to live with a

---

[31]*Die Überlieferung von der Thronnachfolge Davids* (BWANT 3/6; Stutt-gart: Kohlhammer, 1926), reprinted in *Das kleine Credo und andere Studien zum Alten Testament* (Heidelberg: Quelle und Meyer, 1956).

[32]*The Ark Narrative.*

[33]The waking of the warrior from a drunken sleep is a topos elsewhere attested. Isa 51:9-11 is a cry to Yahweh to awake and come forth as a warrior to save Israel. Isa 42:13-16 (though vv 14-16 are often wrongly separated from v 13) similarly describes the rousing of the deity.

persistently sinful people. Here, that same merciful intent is specified in the selection of Judah, Zion and David. The destruction of Shiloh does not mean the end of the sanctuary in Israel's midst. God begins a fresh mercy in Zion-Jerusalem.

It should be stressed again, in the face of scholarly consensus, that the northern tribes are not rejected. Joseph//Ephraim in v 67 as the site of the central sanctuary is rejected. And Judah is chosen in v 68 only under the same qualification: as the site of the new sanctuary, Jerusalem//Zion. The new sanctuary, however, is greater than the old. "He built his sanctuary like the heavens, like the earth he established it forever," v 69.[34]

H AVING examined the rhetoric of the piece, it is now appropriate to ask about the intention of the psalm. It certainly is not to show the corruption of the northern tribes (B. Duhm)[35] because the two recitals portray all Israel's sins. Nor is it a celebration of the rejection of the northern tribes in favor of the southern. A celebration of fraternal strife is otherwise unexampled in the psalms. The psalms have as their ideal all Israel worshipping in Jerusalem. It is not didactic, unless didactic be shorn of its school-masterish and non-liturgical overtones. It is rather a liturgical celebration of God's merciful choice of Zion and David as the continuation today of the ancient shrine celebrating the exodus and conquest tradition. It unites the old sacred epic with the new religious tradition of the choice of Zion and David. At the same time there is a warning: to continue to worship in the northern sanctuary is to repent falsely because God has definitively rejected the northern shrines in their destruction in the eighth century. God's mercy is shown in the new beginning at Zion. This warning is apparent when one reads vv 65-72 alongside the first sacred story in vv 33-40. As has been seen in discussing the Mosaic speech in Deuteronomy and the Mosaic authority of the liturgical spokesman, Israel is given a choice. Will they recognize the true meaning of their traditions which point to David and Zion as the goal of the exodus-conquest and the new means of unity, or will they continue to rebel and worship in a divinely rejected northern shrine? Psalm 78's closest analogues in the psalter are those psalms which celebrate Zion (e.g. Psalms 2, 46, 48, 76) and the Davidic ruler (Psalms 2, 18, 110, 132).

One has the impression that of the two recitals in the poem the exodus-conquest story in vv 41-72 is more central to the final meaning of

---

[34]Cf. Ps 89:3, and v 38, "Forever is (thy) steadfast love established, / (like) the heavens is your fidelity made firm." The eternity of David's line is linked to the eternity of the heavens.

[35]Die Psalmen, 201, 206.

the poem. The focus of attention is Zion as the ultimate goal of the victorious procession. Why then is the first recital prefaced to the second, more important narrative? Possibly the poet wanted to establish by means of the wilderness traditions that no matter how heinous the infidelity, God stands ready to begin again. More subtly, it shows that God can make even the graced gift the instrument of his anger. If he did not hesitate to make the manna and the quail into means of punishment, he would not hesitate to make holy Shiloh into an arena of slaughter and reject it outright as a holy place.

So to state the intention of the psalm is to situate it in a time of division between north and south. Eissfeldt's and other scholars' dating of the psalm to the time before the northern secession under Jeroboam in the late tenth century makes overly specific the deliberately generalized introduction, especially v 9. Moreover, it does not reckon sufficiently with the Deuteronomic language. On the other hand, a post-exilic date suggested by Gunkel for stylistic reasons, and by other scholars for historical reasons, seems excluded by the lively role of the Davidic shepherd as the unifying agent in vv 70-72. Of course, the psalm could have been utilized in the late period against Samaritan claims. It seems certain then that the psalm was composed, using older traditions perhaps, sometime between the schism in 922 and the destruction of Jerusalem in 587 with the consequent loss in significance of the classically stated Israel-Judah enmity. The Deuteronomic language and the concern of the psalm to unite all Israel under the Davidic monarchy in a single place of worship suggests a time during the Hezekian reform of the late eighth century (cf. 2 Chr 30:1-12) or the Josianic reform of the late seventh century. Both reforms invited the northern tribes to return to unity under David with worship in Jerusalem.

Although the Hezekian reform is literarily less well attested than the Josianic, it is in fact a more likely situation for Psalm 78.[36] The successive military defeats of Ephraim in 734-732 and the destruction of Samaria, the capital city, in 722, well illustrate the Ephraimites' "turning back on the day of battle" of v 9, the proof of Yahweh's abandonment of the shrine. The liturgy combines into one divine action the rejection of Shiloh and later northern shrines. The instability of the kings from Zechariah in 746 to Hoshea in 722 makes more attractive the eternal promise to the Davidic shepherd in vv 70-72. The northern victims of Assyrian destruction in 722 are told their shrine has been superseded by Jerusalem where a fresh beginning can take place. They

---

[36]For a convenient discussion of Hezekiah's reform, see J. Bright, *A History of Israel* (2d ed.; Philadelphia: Westminster, 1972) 280-82, and F. L. Moriarty, "The Chronicler's Account of Hezekiah's Reform," *CBQ* 27 (1965) 399-406. For the reform of Josiah, see Bright, *History*, 318-21.

should not be like their forefathers who trusted in a divinely rejected shrine.

2 Chr 30:1-27 describe the Hezekian reform to unite all Israel around one sanctuary after the destruction of Samaria in 722.

[1]Hezekiah sent to all Israel and Judah and wrote letters to Ephraim and Manasseh that they should come to the house of Yahweh the God of Israel . . . [6]So couriers went with letters from the king and his princes through all Israel and Judah as the king commanded. "Children of Israel, return to Yahweh, the God of Abraham, Isaac and Israel, that he may turn again to the remnant of you who have escaped from the Assyrian kings. [7]Do not be like your fathers and your brothers who were unfaithful to Yahweh the God of your fathers so that he made them a desolation as you see. [8]And now do not be stiff-necked like your fathers. Yield yourselves to Yahweh, and come to his sanctuary which he has sanctified forever, and worship Yahweh your God, so that his fierce anger may turn away from you . . . [9]For gracious and merciful is Yahweh your God" (2 Chr 30:1-27).

The seventh century Josianic reform is much better attested literarily than the Hezekian, and it is to three documents from that time that we must go for parallels to Psalm 78. The first is the Deuteronomistic meditation on the fall of Samaria and the northern kingdom in 722, contained in 1 Kgs 17:7-23:

[7]And this [the fall of the north and the deportation] happened because the children of Israel sinned against ($ḥṭ^ɔ$ cf. Ps 78:17) Yahweh their God, who brought them out of the land of Egypt, from under the power of Pharoah the king of Egypt and they reverenced other gods. [8]And they walked according to the rites of the nations whom Yahweh had cleared out of the way of the children of Israel . . . [9]And they built high places ($bāmôt$, cf. Ps 78:58) in all their cities . . . [11]And they burned incense there in all the high places like the nations whom Yahweh had sent into exile at their coming. And they did evil things to anger (hk^cys, cf. Ps 78:58) Yahweh . . . [13]And though Yahweh admonished Israel and Judah by every prophet and seer, saying, "Turn from your evil ways and observe ($šmr$, cf. Ps 78:10, 56) my commandments, my statutes, according to the law ($tôrâ$, cf. Ps 78:1, 5) which I commanded ($ṣwh$, Ps 78:5) your fathers (Ps 78:1-11) and which I sent by my servants the prophets. [14]And they did not listen and were as stiff-necked as their fathers ($ɔăbôtām$, Ps 78:8, 58) who did not believe ($h^ɔmynw$, Ps 78:22, 32) in Yahweh their God. [15]And they rejected his statutes and his covenant ($běrît$, Ps 78:10) which he made with their fathers (Ps 78:1-7) and his covenant stipulations (^cēdôt, Ps 78:56) with which he warned them . . . [17]And they sold themselves to do evil in the eyes of Yahweh to incense him (hk^cys, Ps 78:58) [18]so that Yahweh grew exceedingly wrathful ($wayyit^ɔannap$ and cf. $ɔap$ in Ps 78:21, 31) and drove them from his sight. Only the tribe of Judah ($šēbeṭ Yěhûdâ$, cf. Ps 78:68) was left. [21]When he tore Israel from the house of David, they made Jeroboam

the son of Nabat the king. He drove the Israelites away from Yahweh, causing them to commit a great sin. [22]And the children of Israel walked in all the sins which Jeroboam committed and did not turn from them, [23]until the time when Yahweh put Israel away out of his sight, as he had foretold by his servants the prophets. And Israel went into exile from their native land to Assyria, an exile lasting to the present (1 Kgs 17:7-23).

Noteworthy is language common to this meditation and Psalm 78; the continuity seen between the sins isolating Israel from Judah in the events of 922 (the sin of Jeroboam) and those of 722 (the fall of Samaria); and the singling out of the tribe of Judah as the remnant. The purpose of the first edition of the Deuteronomic history of which this chapter is a product is similar to that of Psalm 78, the examination of the sins of Israel as a lesson, to show that all Israel still exists in the tribe of Judah, and that God's mercy is shown in this new period in his election of Zion and David.

From the same Josianic period come two texts from Jeremiah. In his temple sermon (Jer 7:1-15 and cf. 26:1-24) Jeremiah makes use of a parallel between Shiloh/Israel and Zion/Judah similar to that in Ps 78:41-64.

[12]Go now to my shrine in Shiloh, where I caused my name to dwell at first and see what I did to it because of the evil of my people Israel. [13]And now, because you did not listen, though I spoke to you untiringly, because you did not answer though I called you, [14]I will do to this temple called by my name, in which you trust, and to this shrine, which I gave to you and to your forefathers as I did to Shiloh. [15]And I will scatter from before me just as I scattered your brethren, all the seed of Ephraim.

The passages from Jeremiah and the Psalm both presuppose that Shiloh was the legitimate shrine for all Israel before Jerusalem. Jeremiah now uses the fact that Jerusalem succeeded Shiloh as a warning. Just as the first shrine was rejected, so too can the second be rejected. Implicit in the Jeremiah passage is the suggestion that the destruction of the shrine means a scattering of the people. This is not unexpected since the shrine is the place where the people are settle by their victorious god, and where they unite in worship.

The third Josianic passage is Jeremiah's "Book of Consolation," chaps. 30-31. Though the passages have been retouched in the sixth century to address the situation of the Babylonian exile by the addition of "Judah" to the oracles, there are no convincing grounds for denying it to Jeremiah. It is addressed to the northern tribes to return to worship in Jerusalem.[37] The original reflects Jeremiah's vision of a single Israel

---

[37]I follow W. Rudolph, *Jeremia* (HAT 12; 3rd ed.; Tübingen: J. C. B. Mohr, 1968), esp. 188-89.

gathered again in the holy land. "Yes, there is to be a day when the watchmen will cry out on Mount Ephraim, 'Rise and let us go to Zion, to Yahweh our God'" (Jer 31:6).

The psalm is thus a liturgical expression of the ideal of a united Israel worshipping at a single shrine. It retells the ancient traditions common to both north and south, so as to show that the divine abandonment of the old northern shrine is not the end of God's love of the north. Zion in Judah is the successor to Shiloh and is the divine dwelling for all the children of Israel.

From Temple to Synagogue: 1 Kings 8

JON D. LEVENSON
WELLESLEY COLLEGE

I

T HE Bible has been the object of intensive study as long as it has
been in existence. The study of the Bible grew up hand in hand
with the great religious traditions genetically derived from it, Judaism
and Christianity. For almost eighteen centuries, all who studied Scripture did so within a context established by one or the other of those
faiths. The result of their labors is a rich and exciting body of literature,
as anyone who has ever dipped into the exegetical material such as
midrash or the medieval commentaries, like Rashi or Radaq, knows
well. Part of the irresistible charm of this literature lies in the way the
commentators interpret biblical passages according to the beliefs of their
religious tradition as it stood in their own age. Thus, it was normal for
Christian exegetes to see references to Jesus and even to the sacraments,
as their particular group understood them, throughout the Old Testament. For the Jewish side, the same proclivity, although with a different
thrust, is equally evident. For example, a midrash in the Talmud
presents King Hezekiah's deliverance from the Assyrian enemy, Sen-
nacherib, as owing to the Judean monarch's zeal for the study of
rabbinic law in synagogues and Houses of Study (b. Sanh 94b), this
despite the fact that the origin of these institutions lay in an era many
centuries after Hezekiah's death. But the life of the pious Jew of
Talmudic times centered on the synagogue and the House of Study. It
was only natural to him that the life of a biblical hero like Hezekiah
should have had the same focus.

Underlying this inclination toward anachronism is the profound
conviction that, grossly put, revelation is literal truth (although its
meaning does not lie on the plane of literalism alone), and that truth is a
unity. Thus, what God reveals in one verse he alludes to in many.
Scripture thus becomes "an endlessly self-referential system of divinely
revealed truth existing in the simultaneity of an exegetical eternity."[1] In
the process, the question of the temporal relationships between passages,

---

[1]R. Alter, in an untitled response to letters to the editor, *Commentary* 61:3
(March, 1976) 20.

which preceded which in composition, becomes pointless. In fact, the rabbis (the men of the first several centuries of the common era who transformed Judaism and gave it its normative shape) even had a dictum to express the absurdity of seeking literary relationships of a chronological nature in the holiest literature: "There is no 'earlier' or 'later' in the Torah."[2] To be sure, like all principles man devises, this one often failed to be applied. One can, if he looks for them, find in rabbinic commentary instances of acute, often almost heretical, historical speculation.[3] But these are the exception that proves the rule. To ask how men's beliefs about God grew and changed in time is already to assume that revelation is not of a piece, to impugn, in other words, what was the underlying conviction of Jewish and Christian exegesis until virtually the last two centuries. The history or religion could only be the history of other men's religions, that is, of error.

It was inevitable that biblical studies would be affected by the consciousness of history, of the growth and change of ideas in time, of the contingent nature of all human enterprises, which has marked the intellectual history of the last two centuries. No longer would scripture be universally regarded as immune to the flux of history, nor would change in religious ideas be presumed to be disproof of their validity. But how could one recover the stages of growth behind the texts we have received? Unfortunately, the process of religious homogenization reigned in biblical times themselves, so that no text can be presupposed to be free of anachronism. The only option for the historian of the religion of Israel was to sort out the texts in order to recover earlier documents, unencumbered by later elaborations of distortions. This process, called somewhat misleadingly "literary criticism," was the hallmark of biblical criticism in the last century. It was principally applied to the Pentateuch, which was found to be composed of essentially four documents, hence the "Documentary Hypothesis." It has been many decades since literary criticism dominated critical biblical scholarship, for, indeed, many weighty arguments have been delivered against the technique it employs. For one example, we now know enough about the oral transmission of literature in societies like ancient Israel to be skeptical of so much talk about written documents. For another, one can ask what is left when we have finished analyzing a passage into its components. Surely the canonical text has a reality to it which no hypothetical document or oral unit can claim to match. Finally—although more criticisms can be adduced—we can cite the highly disputatious nature of

---

[2]See the use of this principle, for example, in the Rashi to Exod 19:11.

[3]This was amply demonstrated and documented in a paper by N. Sarna, "Medieval Biblical Commentary and the Modern Jewish Bible Scholar," at the Association for Jewish Studies annual conference, Dec. 19, 1975.

the field of literary criticism, its persistent lack of consensus, as proof of the inability of modern man to attain a sure enough grasp of the literary mind of Semitic antiquity to carry on the endeavor of documentary analysis.

Despite its recession from the center of biblical scholarship, literary criticism has not disappeared, nor can it, for the history of theology, no matter how many other tools it employs, still requires a technique for the recovery of texts submerged within others in our Bible. Moreover, despite all the work that has been done on the curious psychology of "primitives," the fact remains that some contradictions in the Hebrew Bible are so blatant and the attempts to reconcile them so forced that they can be understood only under the assumption that we have before us two or more disparate documents, secondarily and imperfectly meshed.

II

The complex that extends from Joshua to 2 Kings is a case in point. Already in the nineteenth century, it was noticed that throughout these six books an idiom recurs which is closest to that of Deuteronomy. Thus, earlier generations of critics spoke of a redactor whom they labelled "D," in other words, an editor who was either identical with or under the immediate influence of the Deuteronomic source whose hand they detected, along with essentially three others, in the Pentateuch. Almost forty years ago, the great German critic Martin Noth argued with winning cogency for the idea that the contribution of "D" in Joshua— 2 Kings was more than a random assortment of editorial glosses; instead, Noth spoke of a "Deuteronomistic history" which extended from Moses' deathbed address at the beginning of Deuteronomy until the fall of the Kingdom of Judah at the close of 2 Kings.[4] After Noth, one hears little or nothing about a Deuteronomic glossator, but much about a self-conscious theological historiographer whose work exhibits breath-taking scope.

What was the theological purpose of the Deuteronomistic historian (Dtr)? According to Noth, it was to show the stricken Israel of the Exile (587-539 B.C.E.) the divine justice behind their doom. Not very encouraging tidings! Against Noth, other scholars argued for a counter-balancing optimism to this grim theme. Thus, Hans W. Wolff saw a note of hope in the emphasis upon human repentance, which in turn could bring Israel back to their land.[5] Somewhat more convincingly, Gerhard von

[4]M. Noth, *Überlieferungsgeschichtliche Studien* (Darmstadt: Wissenschaft-liche Buchgesellschaft, 1963) 3-110. This is a reprint of the original (1943) treatise.

[5]H. W. Wolff, "Das Kerygma des Deuteronomistischen Geschichtswerks," *ZAW* 73 (1961) 171-86.

Rad saw a ground for hope in the reiterated stress upon the promise to
David, the founder and ancestor of the recently defeated and exiled royal
house of Judah.[6] Surely God could not have withdrawn the promise to
Solomon, whose language we find echoed throughout Dtr:

> I will establish your royal throne over
> Israel forever, as I promised David your
> father, saying "You shall never lack a
> man upon the throne of Israel" (1 Kgs 9:5).

According to this theology, any separation of the House of David from
the throne of Israel must be a parenthesis in history, an aberration which
cannot endure, since it defies God's pledged word. The function of this
continual recollection of the divine promise to David within Dtr is to
encourage hope centering upon the Davidic claimant of the early Exile,
Jehoiachin, presently a captive in Babylonia.

Frank Moore Cross argued against von Rad on the grounds that
there is no basis for the latter's assumption that significant messianic
expectation focused upon Jehoiachin, who was after all, a pathetic
prisoner under at least house arrest until his death.[7] Instead, Cross sees
the Davidic hope as most fully realized in Josiah, the vigorous reform-
minded monarch of the Israelite religious and political renaissance a
generation before the Exile (640-609 B.C.E.) It was Josiah alone who "did
what was right in the eyes of YHWH and walked in the ways of David
his forefather and did not turn aside to the right or the left" (2 Kgs 22:2),
Josiah alone whose successful purgation of the perversions of the schismatics of the Northern Kingdom had been prophesied long ago (1 Kgs
13:2-3). In short, Cross sees the origins of Dtr as pre-Exilic. He does
appreciate, however, that the history continues into the Exile, to which
it appears to allude in many places. Thus, the logic of his analysis leads
Cross to detect two strands in Dtr, which he calls Dtr 1 and Dtr 2. Dtr 1
is an optimistic work of the late monarchy written to glorify Josiah. Dtr
2 is a work of the Exile, whose themes include the doom upon Judah for
generations of idolatry and the modest hope for restoration after repentance.[8] In light of my dependence upon Frank Cross' theories throughout the remainder of this study, it is fitting that I dedicate this small
contribution to him with gratitude for the paths he lit for me.

One difficulty with the royalist motivation which both von Rad and
Cross find in the history is that the frontispiece and guiding light of the

---

[6]G. von Rad, *The Problem of the Hexateuch and Other Essays* (New York:
McGraw-Hill, 1966) 205-21.

[7]F. M. Cross, *Canaanite Myth and Hebrew Epic* (Cambridge: Harvard, 1973)
278-85.

[8]Cross, *Canaanite Myth*, 285-87.

whole work, the book of Deuteronomy, is critical of the monarchical institution, which it discusses in only one passage, the famous "Law of the King" (Deut 17:14-20), an obvious effort to limit the royal office. How could Cross's Dtr 1 be both a royalist propagandist and Deuteronomistic? Acting on an insight of William L. Moran, I began to investigate the placement of the Deuteronomic code (Deuteronomy 12-26) and its parenetic prologue (chaps. 4-11) and covenantal epilogue (chaps. 27-32) within Dtr. By carefully examining the language of Deuteronomy, I came to see that there is an exilic framework which interrupts the account of Moses' installation of Joshua as his successor in Deut 3:21-28, which resumes in our present text in Deut 31:1.[9] Detailed verbal comparisons showed that the first bracket was Deut 3:29-4:40 and the second, Deut 29:21-28; 30; 31:16-22, 24-29; 31:30-32:44, and probably 29:16 as well. Remove these brackets and the core of Deuteronomy, and you are left with a continuous historical narrative about Moses' last words and his ordination of a successor. In other words, there is no reason to assume that Dtr always included the parts of Deuteronomy which are not historical narrative. When did the framework and what it brackets come into Dtr? Our study of the language of the framework definitely established that it is Dtr 2. Hence, the introduction of the Deuteronomic code and what immediately surrounds it into the history it abruptly interrupts is the work of an Exilic redactor.

To the theologian we call Dtr 2, the monarchy could no longer mean what it did to Dtr 1. Living in Babylonia, whither the scion of the House of David had been dragged as a captive, he could no longer believe the words of the promise to David which are the refrain of Dtr 1, words which say that even a sinful king God will not reject in order that the faithful dynastic ancestor David might always have a descendant on the throne (2 Sam 7:8-16).[10] Instead, he saw the welfare and independence of the people Israel as a frightfully fragile plant, nourished by their willingness to perform the stipulations of covenant, but killed by their straying from the divine commands which are their life and the length of their days. His keynote could not be the covenant with David, but rather the very different covenant on the plains of Moab of Deuteronomy, which starkly sets forth the awesome choice of obedience or apostasy, the land or exile, blessing or curse, life or death.

---

[9]J. D. Levenson, "Who Inserted the Book of the Torah," *HTR* 68 (1975) 203-33.

[10]The promise is reiterated in 1 Kgs 11:12, 13, 32, 34, 36; 15:4; 2 Kgs 8:19; 19:34 (cf. Isa 37:35); 20:6.

III

A salient characteristic of Dtr, according to Noth and his critics both, is a tendency to punctuate his narrative with formal speeches that provide historical retrospect and recapitulation at times of painful transition and innovation. Such speeches include Joshua's farewell in Joshua 23, the theology of the era of the judges in Judges 2, Samuel's great address in 1 Samuel 12, Solomon's temple dedication speech in 1 Kings 8, and the solemn meditation on the fall of the Northern kingdom in 2 Kings 17.[11] Of all these fascinating compositions, the most fruitful for the purposes of source analysis and history of theology is Solomon's speech upon his dedication of the Temple, for in that text, from the mouth of the first descendant of David to become king, we should detect, if our theories are correct, the tensions which ultimately divide Dtr 1 and Dtr 2. We expect to hear therein a vigorous statement of the theology of the Davidic dynasty, that is, if Dtr 1 is as truly monarchistic as von Rad, Cross, and the author of this study have believed. But if we have isolated a Dtr 2 and identified his theology accurately, we should not be surprised to detect his more sober and tempered view of the promise to David in the same speech. Before we turn our literary-critical scissors to 1 Kings 8, let us read it in its entirety first so as to experience the full measure of its rhetorical power:

[1]Then Solomon summoned the elders of Israel, all the heads of tribes, the chieftains of the ancestral houses of the Israelites, to an assembly in Jerusalem, in order to bring the ark of the covenant of YHWH up from the city of David, that is, Zion. [2]All the men of Israel assembled in King Solomon's presence, in the month of Ethanim, at the festival, which is the seventh month. [3]When all the elders of Israel had come, the priests lifted the ark [4]and carried it up with the Tent of Encounter and all the sacred apparatus which was in the Tent; it was the priests and the Levites together who brought these up. [5]King Solomon and the whole congregation of Israel, assembled with him in the presence of the ark, sacrificed sheep and oxen too numerous to be tabulated or counted. [6]Then the priests brought in the Ark of the covenant of YHWH to its place in the inner sanctum of the Temple, the Holy of Holies, under the wings of the cherubim. [7]For the cherubim spread their wings over the place of the Ark, forming a screen over the Ark and its poles. [8]The poles projected in such a way that their ends were visible from the Holy Place just in front of the inner sanctum, but not from outside. They have been there to this day. [9]There was nothing in the Ark except the two stone tablets which Moses deposited there on Mount Horeb, the tablets of the covenant[12] which YHWH made with the Israelites when they came out of the Land of Egypt.

[11]Noth, *Überlieferungsgeschichtliche Studien*, 5-6.
[12]Insert "the tablets of the covenant" with LXX.

[10]Then the priests left the Holy Place, since the cloud filled the Temple of YHWH, [11]and they were unable to stand and discharge their duties because of the cloud; the glory of YHWH filled his Temple. [12]Then Solomon said:

> "The sun YHWH fixed[13] in the sky,
> But said he would dwell in deep darkness;
> [13]But I have built a regal house for you,
> A fixed place for your throne for all eternity!"

[14]As the whole assembly of Israel remained standing, Solomon turned around and blessed them, [15]saying, "Blessed be YHWH, the God of Israel, who spoke directly with David my father and commissioned him, saying, [16]'From the day I brought my people Israel out of Egypt, I have never chosen a city out of all the tribes of Israel to build a Temple for my name to be there, but I have chosen David to be in charge of my people Israel.' [17]David had it in mind to build a Temple in honor of the name of YHWH, God of Israel, [18]but YHWH said to David my father, 'You did a good thing to have it in mind to build a Temple in honor of my name, [19]but you will not build it. Rather, your son, who will issue from your loins—he will build the Temple in honor of my name.' [20]YHWH has now fulfilled the promise he made: I have succeeded David my father, assuming the throne of Israel, as YHWH predicted, and I have built the Temple in honor of the name of YHWH, the God of Israel. [21]I have assigned therein a place for the Ark containing the covenant of YHWH which he made with our fathers when he brought them out of the land of Egypt."

[22]Solomon stood before the altar of YHWH in the presence of all the congregation of Israel and, spreading out his palms to heaven, [23]he said, "YHWH, God of Israel, there is no god like you in heaven above or earth beneath, keeping covenant with your servants and showing them love while they continue faithful to you with all their heart. [24]You have fulfilled for David my father everything you promised him. You spoke with your mouth and with your hand you have brought it about this very day. [25]And now, YHWH, God of Israel, keep the promise you made to David my father when you said to him, 'You shall never lack a man appointed by me to sit on the throne of Israel, if only your sons guard their ways and walk before me as you have walked before me.' [26]Now, therefore, YHWH,[14] God of Israel, let the word you spoke to David my father be confirmed.

[27]But can God really dwell on earth when heaven itself, even the highest heaven, cannot contain you? How much less the Temple I have built! [28]Yet attend to the prayer of your servant and to his supplication, YHWH, God of Israel, that you may hearken to the cry and the prayer which your servant prays before you today, [29]that your eyes may be open

---

[13]Read *hēkîn* for the *hēbîn* which underlies the LXX. Otherwise, this colon is to be read with LXX.

[14]Insert *YHWH* with LXX.

toward this house night and day, toward the place of which you said, 'My name shall be there,' so that you may listen to the prayer your servant prays toward this place. [30]Hear the supplication of your servant and of your people Israel when they pray toward this place. May you hear from the place where you dwell, from the heavens,[15] and, when you hear, may you forgive!

[31]When a man sins against his neighbor and he takes upon himself an oath and he comes and makes the adjuration[16] before your altar in this Temple, [32]then hear in heaven and act: be your servants' judge, condemning the guilty man and bringing his deeds upon his own head, vindicating the innocent man, rewarding him as he deserves.

[33]When your people are defeated by an enemy because they sinned against you, and they come back to you, confessing your name and praying and making supplication to you in this Temple, [34]then hear in heaven and forgive the sin of your people Israel, and restore them to the land you gave their forefathers.

[35]When the skies are closed so that there is no rain, since they have sinned against you, and they pray toward this place, confess your name, and forsake their sin when you have afflicted them,[17] [36]then hear in heaven and forgive the sin of your servants and your people Israel. May you show them the good path in which to walk and give rain to the land you gave your people as a possession.

[37]If famine there be in the land, or plague, or smut, or mildew, or locusts; or if their enemy besiege them in any[18] of their cities, or if any plague or illness strike them, [38]then hear every prayer and every supplication which any man in all your people Israel makes when he recognizes the source of the affliction within and spreads out his hands toward this Temple, [39]hear in heaven, the place of your dwelling, and forgive, and act. May you, who know a man's heart, reward each according to his ways, for you alone know the heart of every man, [40]so that they will fear you all the days that they live in the land you gave their fathers.

[41]Also the foreigner, who is not from your people Israel, but has come from a distant land because of your fame ([42]for men shall indeed hear of your fame and your strong hand and outstretched arm), when he comes and prays toward this Temple, [43]then hear in heaven, the place of your dwelling, and act whenever the foreigner calls to you, so that all the peoples of the world may know your fame and, like your people Israel, fear you and learn that this Temple which I have built bears your name.

[44]When your people goes out to war against their enemy on the road upon which you send them, and they pray to you[19] turning in the direction of the city which you have chosen and of the Temple which I have built in

[15]Read *mimmĕqôm* and *min-haššāmayim* with 2 Chr 6:21.
[16]Read *wĕʾālâ* with LXX.
[17]Read *tĕʿannēm*.
[18]Read *bĕʾaḥad* for *bĕʾereṣ* with LXX.
[19]Read *ʾēlêkā* with LXX.

honor of your name, [45]then hear in heaven their prayer and their supplication, and do them justice.

[46]When they sin against you (for there is no man who does not sin),
and you become enraged against them and hand them over to an enemy
who carries them captive to his own land, far or near, [47]if in the land in
which they have become prisoners they reconsider and repent, making
supplication to you in the land of their captors, saying, 'We have sinned,
we have acted perversely, we have been wicked,' [48]and they come back to
you with all their heart and all their soul in the land of their enemies who
captured them, and they pray to you turning in the direction of the land
you gave their fathers and the city[20] you have chosen and the Temple I
have built in honor of your name, [49]then hear in heaven, the place of your
dwelling, their prayers and their supplication, and do them justice. [50]For-
give your people, who have sinned against you, all their rebellions which
they have undertaken against you, and put pity for them in the hearts of
their captors, so that they will be merciful with them. [51]For they are your
people and your possession, whom you brought out of Egypt, out of the
midst of the smelting furnace. [52]May your eyes be open to the prayer of
your servant and to the supplication of your people Israel to listen to them
whenever they cry to you. [53]For you singled them out for yourself, as a
special possession, from among all the peoples of the earth, just as you
promised when you took our forefathers out of Egypt, O Lord God."

[54]When Solomon had finished this prayer and supplication to YHWH,
he rose from before the altar of YHWH, where he had been kneeling, with
his palms spread out to heaven. [55]He stood and blessed the whole assembly
of Israel in a loud voice, saying, [56]"Blessed is YHWH who has provided
rest for his people Israel, as he promised; nothing from all the good things
he promised through his servant Moses has failed. [57]May YHWH our God
be with us as he was with our father; may he neither leave us nor abandon
us. [58]May he turn our hearts toward him so that we shall walk in all his
ways and observe his commands, his laws, and his judgments, which he
commanded our fathers. [59]And may these words of mine which I utter in
supplication before YHWH be near YHWH our God day and night, so
that, as the need arises, day by day, he will do justice to his servant and
justice to his people Israel, [60]so that all peoples of the earth may know that
YHWH is God; there is no other. [61]May your heart be complete in loyalty
to YHWH our God so that you walk in his laws and observe his
commands as you are doing this day."

[62]The king and all Israel with him offered sacrifices before YHWH.
[63]Solomon offered as share-offerings to YHWH twenty-two thousand oxen
and one hundred twenty thousand sheep. Thus did the king and all Israel
dedicate the Temple of YHWH. [64]On the same day the king consecrated
the center of the court which lay in front of the Temple of YHWH, for
there he offered the whole-offering, the grain-offering, and the fat portions
of the shared-offering, since the bronze altar located in front of YHWH

[20]Read $h\bar{a}^c\hat{i}r$ with LXX.

was too small to hold the whole-offering, the grain-offering, and the fat portions of the shared-offering.
[65]And so Solomon and all Israel with him, an immense assembly from Lebo-Hamath to the Wadi of Egypt, celebrated the festival at that time before YHWH our God seven days.[21] [66]On the eighth day, he dismissed the people, and they blessed the king and went to their tents happy and in good spirits over all the prosperity which YHWH had granted David his servant and Israel his people (1 Kings 8).

Critical opinion on the composition of this chapter is bewildering. The only thing it establishes definitively is that the field of literary criticism is as deficient of consensus as we said in Section I. To the great pioneer Julius Wellhausen, the issue was relatively simple: the final redaction of 1 Kings 8 was clearly Exilic.[22] His contemporary, Karl Marti, argued for a very complicated process of redaction of a pre-exilic base into and beyond the Exile.[23] C. F. Burney, on the other hand, held out for the pre-Exilic composition of the entire passage, maintaining that the patent references to exile and the hope of return in vv 44-53 referred to the ten lost tribes of the Northern kingdom and not to the Babylonian Exile of a century and a half later. Burney noted, interestingly, that vv 46 and 48 presuppose the existence of the Temple, which was razed in 587.[24] James Montgomery also saw 1 Kings 8 as basically pre-Exilic, although he, unlike Burney, conceded the Exilic origin of vv 44-53.[25] Alfred Jepsen's theory is quite interesting, although exceedingly complicated. Put simply, he believed that vv 44-53 are the work of an Exilic redactor who was under the influence of a prophetic, anti-monarchical theology, a redactor, in other words, who sounds very much like our Dtr 2.[26] In support of this idea, Jepsen developed a few semantic points about these ten verses, which he argued proved their divergence from what precedes them. We shall examine these points in depth in the next section. Against scholars of Jepsen's bent, Arnold Gamper attempted to demonstrate the integrity of vv 31-53 by indicating the seven-fold structure of this section, which has often been divided in two

[21]Omit the rest of the clause with LXX.
[22]J. Wellhausen, *Die Composition des Hexateuchs und der historischen Bücher des Alten Testaments* (Berlin: Georg Reimer, 1899) 270-71.
[23]K. Marti, *Die Bücher der Könige* (Kurzer Hand-Commentar zum alten Testament 4; Freiburg, Leipzig, and Tübingen: J. C. B. Mohr [Paul Siebeck], 1899) 56.
[24]C. F. Burney, *Notes on the Hebrew Text of the Book of Kings* (Oxford: Clarendon, 1903) 113-14.
[25]J. Montgomery, *A Critical and Exegetical Commentary on the Book of Kings*, edited by H. S. Gehman (ICC; Edinburgh: T. and T. Clark, 1951) 185-203.
[26]A. Jepsen, *Die Quellen des Königsbuches* (Halle: Max Niemeyer, 1953) 15-17.

between v 43 and v 44. Seven references to the Temple and seven appeals to "hear then" the prayer of the supplicant structure this passage—impressive testimony to its unity.[27] Finally, Noth saw vv 44-53 as tacked on, although, given his belief in the Exilic date of his Dtr, it is not clear why.[28] Cross sees vv 46-53 as Dtr 2, hence Exilic, but refrains from comment on the verses preceding these.[29]

Where does all this leave us? In total confusion, for in places like this biblical scholarship in the modern mode shatters the integrity of the reader's response to the Hebrew Bible, which it renders less rather than more accessible—surely the most damning thing one can say of a method that calls itself "literary criticism." In Section IV, I shall try to move the discussion onto less subjective and more rational ground.

IV

The first thing to notice about Solomon's addresses in 1 Kings 8 is that there are four of them. Vv 10-12; 14-15; 22-23; and v 55 constitute introductions to three distinct speeches. It remains to ascertain the nature and source of each address and the presence or absence of influence of one on others among them.

The first speech is found in vv 12-13, where it is unfortunately in such garbled condition that one must reconstruct the form given above from various ancient versions. When we have done so, it becomes obvious that the two verses are in poetry, unlike anything else in the chapter.[30] They seem to be a mere excerpt from some longer poem, an idea given added support by the introduction to them in some ancient Greek manuscripts: "Is this not written in the *Book of the Song?*"[31] In any event, vv 12-13 show no sign whatever of redaction at the hands of any editor, Dtr 1 or Dtr 2. They are most likely the oldest piece in 1 Kings 8.

The second address is found in vv 15-21. Its great theme is the present fulfillment of the promise to David which is first articulated in 2 Samuel 7. In fact, if the reader will compare these verses with 2 Sam 7:8-16, he will immediately recognize that the author of this second address of Solomon had the very words of Nathan's prophecy in mind as he composed. The likeness is too strong to admit any other conclusion.

[27]Gamper, "Die Heilsgeschichtliche Bedeutung des Salomonischen Tempelweihegebets," *ZKT* 85 (1963) 55-61.

[28]M. Noth, *Könige* (BKAT 9; Neukirchen-Vluyn: Neukirchener, 1968) 174.

[29]Cross, *Canaanite Myth*, 287.

[30]Using syllable count as a very rough gauge of metrical symmetry, we find here a quattrain (9:8:9:9).

[31]Perhaps the Hebrew that lies behind the Greek here read *hayyāšār* ("the upright") instead of *haššîr* ("the song"), as in Josh 10:13 and 2 Sam 1:18.

Two themes the passsages share, the previously unprecedented divine singling-out of David and the prediction that not he, but his son and rightful successor will build Israel's first truly legitimate temple. The second address closes with the reflection that what YHWH had predicted to David, he has now fulfilled in Solomon (1 Kings 8:20-21).

In light of Cross's theory about the redaction of Dtr, the dependence of 1 Kgs 8:15-21 upon 2 Sam 7:8-16 cannot be inconsequential, for the latter is the keynote, as we have seen, of Cross's Dtr 1. Nowhere is this keynote dwelt upon at greater length than in Solomon's second speech. In fact, it is more accurate to say that 1 Kgs 8:15-21 does not dwell upon 2 Sam 7:8-16 so much as it recreates it, or most of it, without deviation or innovation. Nothing in these verses adds to what we find in Nathan's original prophecy. The natural conclusion is that Solomon's second speech upon the dedication of his Temple is Dtr 1, pure and unalloyed.

Solomon's third speech is 1 Kgs 8:23-53. It is within these verses that the critics we examined in Section III are most inclined to discover multiple sources. Before we can discuss the theology and origin of the third speech, we must examine the arguments for and against its unity.

We have already seen that Gamper argues for the unity of vv 31-53 on the basis of the seven-fold rhetorical structure he discerns therein.[32] The reader can see the units of this structure in the seven paragraphs, all very similar in structure, of our translation of these verses. In light of this internal similarity and of the importance of the number seven as a symbol of completeness and perfection in Hebrew thought, it seems arbitrary to separate vv 44-53, as many critics do, from vv 31-43, simply because vv 44-53 speak of exile. Against what was to be Gamper's argument, however, Alfred Jepsen brought less subjective evidence. He notes some verbal discrepancies in vv 44-53 from what we see in vv 31-43. These are essentially five. First, the expression we translate "then hear" is in a different form in vv 45 and 49 ($w\check{e}\check{s}\bar{a}ma^c t\bar{a}$) from vv 32, 34, 36, 38, and 43 ($w\check{e}^{\,\jmath}att\hat{a}\ ti\check{s}ma^c$).[33] The meaning is identical, but the grammatical form is different. Second, Jepsen noticed that in vv 44 and 48 we read "turning in the direction of the city" or "turning in the direction of the land," whereas in vv 31, 33, 35, 38, and 42, we find "this Temple" or "this place (or sanctuary)" (v 35).[34] Again, the meaning is substantially the same, but the diction is not. Third, the paragraphs introduced by vv 44 and 46 begin with the particle $k\hat{\imath}$, which we render "when," unlike any of the other five paragraphs. Jepsen conceded, however, that v 37 includes the same particle, although not as the first word.[35] Fourth,

[32]Gamper, "Die Heilsgeschichtliche Bedeutung," 56.
[33]Jepsen, Die Quellen, 15.
[34]Ibid.
[35]Ibid.

Jepsen observed that in vv 49-50, "hear them in heaven, the place of your dwelling" is separated from "forgive," whereas the two are contiguous in vv 34, 36, 39. Fifth and finally, he noted that in vv 51-53, the word we translate "special possession" (*naḥălâ*) refers to the people Israel, whereas in v 36 it refers to the land of the same name.[36] In short, Jepsen develops five stylistic points to buttress the already prevalent idea that vv 44-53 are an Exilic appendix to Solomon's third speech.

Each of the five points deserves examination. As to the variation between *ʾattâ tišmaᶜ* and *wĕšāmaᶜtā*, what difference does it make? The meaning, even the literal translation, is unaffected. It is only the impressive similarity of the two paragraphs of vv 44-53 to the five of vv 31-43 which caused Jepsen to fix on such a minute variation. I feel no cogency in his first argument.

As to the difference between "turning in the direction of this city (land)" and "toward this Temple (place or sanctuary)," again one is inclined to wonder whether without the mention of exile in vv 44-53 any scholar would have even noticed this variation. Exiles by definition cannot pray in the Temple, only in the direction (*derek*) of the spot on which it stood. The difference in language proves nothing.

The use of *kî* in vv 44 and 46 is another argument. There is no uniform introduction to the first five paragraphs; therefore, the fact that the last two begin with the same word cannot be cited as proof of their divergent origin. The fact that the fourth paragraph of the seven also begins with a *kî* clause is more damaging to Jepsen's thesis than he recognized. Once more, one has the impression that he was picking at gnats.

All that need be said about Jepsen's fourth point is that the fact that the words of the last paragraph are so similar to those of earlier paragraphs is much more important than the fact that they are not in exactly the same relative positions. The similarities are immense; the differences, minute.

Finally, on Jepsen's last point, note that the word *naḥălâ* has different referents in different places. Why assume that its use in reference to the people in vv 51-53 contradicts its use in reference to the land in v 36? Israel is the "special possession" of YHWH; he has given them the land as a "special possession." Note also that in the sermon of Deut 4:1-40, which I consider Dtr 2, *naḥălā* can refer to either the people (v 20) or the land (v 38).

One more argument against the unity of vv 23-53 must be answered before we can proceed to discuss evidence in favor of it. Montgomery noted a contradiction in the description of Solomon's posture at the beginning and at the end of the speech. In v 22, the king is standing,

[36]Ibid., 16.

whereas in v 54 he is on his knees.[37] The first thing to note about this is that the alleged contradiction is not within the speech, but within the narrative which frames it. Montgomery provides at best an argument for a multiplicity of authorship in the narrative, which is necessarily later than the speech it introduces and concludes. But why assume a contradiction at all? Is it somehow unlikely that Solomon fell to his knees in the course of his prayer? On the contrary, nothing could be more natural in a speech which increasingly talks of sin and repentance, themes for which the prostration of the worshipper was appropriate. Nor is there reason to believe that the narrator would have interrupted a rhetorical masterpiece to apprise us of the uneventful fact that just here Solomon kneeled. Only the hypercritical eye of a literary critic can see a contradiction between v 22 and v 54.

In the absence of persuasive arguments for the composite nature of Solomon's third address on the occasion of the dedication of his Temple, it is useful to see whether there is positive evidence for its unitary composition. For this purpose, it is interesting to note the expression "that your eyes may be open" (lihyôt ʿênêkā pĕtūḥôt) in v 29. Except in the parallel passage 2 Chr 6:20, which is dependent upon 1 Kings 8, this expression occurs in this precise form only in 1 Kgs 8:52, in other words, later in the same speech. In a slightly different construction, it can be seen in Neh 1:6 and 2 Chr 7:15 (2 Chr 6:40 parallels and depends upon 1 Kgs 8:52). The expression is otherwise unattested. Given its rarity, it is surely worthy of notice that it occurs twice in the same speech, once in a passage that has very often been thought an appendix, vv 44-53. Some might argue here that we have two very similar authors, or that one is deliberately imitating the other. A more sensible conclusion is that vv 44-53 stem from the same source as the main body of the address.

Another piece of evidence for the unitary composition of 1 Kgs 8:23-53 is the marked tendency, elucidated in detail by C. F. Keil,[38] for this speech to reflect Lev 26:14-45 and especially Deut 28:15-68, two collections of covenant curses upon an apostate Israel. Read against the latter passage, Solomon's third address moves from topic to topic in the most natural of ways; there is nothing extraordinary in closing with a discussion of the agony of exile, for Deuteronomy 28 closes likewise (vv 47-68). Of course, it can be argued that these verses are, like 1 Kgs 8:44-53, an Exilic appendix.[39] But it is imperative to remember that exile had been a covenant curse long before the Babylonians sacked Jerusalem in

---

[37] Montgomery, *A Critical and Exegetical Commentary*, 194.

[38] C. F. Keil, *The Book of Kings* (Biblical Commentary on the Old Testament; Grand Rapids: Eerdmans, 1950) 128-32.

[39] Von Rad, *The Problem*, 176.

587 B.C.E.[40] There is every reason to believe that Israel knew of and dreaded exile long before she experienced it. As we shall see in the next section, 1 Kgs 8:44-53, unlike Deut 28:47-68, presupposes an Exilic setting, although its dependence on Deuteronomy 28 is a strong argument against its assignment to a later hand.

V

Curiously, to John Gray, vv 44-53, the very passage that most critics see as an Exilic addendum, is proof of the pre-Exilic composition of the speech. He regards the exile of v 46 as "an" exile, not "the" Exile of the sixth century. In support of this, he and other critics note that v 48 presupposes the existence of the Temple. Hence, the exile of v 46 is most likely that of the "ten lost tribes" of the Kingdom of Israel in the eighth century.[41]

Gray's theory is unlikely. Prayers for return from exile in the Hebrew Bible almost always derive from "the" Exile, which has left us a rich library of its theology in books like Lamentations, 2 Isaiah (Isaiah 40-55), and Ezekiel, all of which are marked by a fervent hope and plea for restoration to the land. We have no counterpart to this from the earlier deportation. The burden of proof lies upon those who would identify the setting of our prayer as earlier, not upon those who see it as of the sixth century. Furthermore, Wellhausen scored a telling point against the theory of a pre-Exilic origin for this material when he noted that the concern for the Temple in Jerusalem of this speech belies any Northern origin for it.[42] Wellhausen's argument thus would force Gray to hold that the prayer speaks of an exile other than that of its author, in other words, that a Southerner here envisions the repentance of the North, which then will reembrace the Temple in Jerusalem which it once spurned. Again, the position, although logical in a way, is too forced to merit our credence. Nor does the argument that v 48 presupposes the existence of the Temple carry weight. All that verse says is that the exiles will pray "turning in the direction . . . of the Temple. . . ." Nothing here implies that the Temple is other than a ruin. Note that Jer 41:5 speaks of eighty men bringing sacrifices "to the Temple of YHWH" after its destruction. To this day, Jews speak of facing the Temple in prayer.

What stamps vv 44-53 as Exilic is not that it speaks of exile, but that it strives to awaken in its audience the hope for restoration, secured

[40]See D. R. Hillers, *Treaty-Curses and the Old Testament* (Rome: Pontifical Biblical Institute, 1964) 33-34.

[41]J. Gray, *I and II Kings: A Commentary* (OTL; London: SCM, 1964) 197.

[42]Wellhausen, *Die Composition*, 271.

through repentance. This unambiguous hope of return makes sense only within a community already in exile. It is significant that the notion of return is not limited to these ten suspect verses. V 34b stresses the same point. If the third speech is indeed a unity, and if these two pleas for restoration indicate Exilic composition, then it follows that the speech dates in its entirety from the sixth century.

Are there characteristic Exilic themes in 1 Kgs 8:23-53 further to buttress our dating of it? One such theme is that of the foreigner who, "converting" (the word is a bit anachronistic at this point) to YHWHism, makes a pilgrimage to the Temple in Jerusalem (vv 41-43). The closest parallels to this are all from the Exile or the immediate post-Exilic era. In Second Isaiah, for example, we read:

> A people you do not know you shall summon,
> A people who do not know you will run to you,
> For the sake of YHWH your God,
> The Holy One of Israel, who has made you glorious (Isa 55:5).

In Third Isaiah (Isaiah 56-66), from the early Restoration (ca. 520 B.C.E.), we hear that:

> [10]Foreigners shall rebuild your walls,
> Their kings shall serve you,
> For in my wrath I struck you down,
> But in my favor I have shown you mercy.
> [11]Your gates shall always be open,[43]
> Day and night they shall not be closed,
> To bring you the wealth of nations,
> And their kings under escort (Isa 60:10-11)

And when 1 Kgs 8:42 tells us that "men shall indeed hear of your fame (*šiměkā haggādôl*)," we immediately think of the post-Exilic book Malachi, which stresses that "my fame is great (*gādôl šěmî*) among the nations" (Mal 1:11).

The theology of the Temple in 1 Kgs 8:23-53 is another characteristic Exilic note. Classically, the Temple served two functions: it was the locus of legitimate sacrifice and of divine revelation. Thus, Deuteronomy 12 sounds the great Deuteronomic call for sacrifice in Jerusalem and in Jerusalem alone, and Isaiah 6 narrates the great prophet's vision of his holy God in the Temple. But Solomon's third address on the occasion of the dedication of the same shrine presents a different focus. Here, the Temple is principally a place of prayer. Time and again Solomon speaks of "prayer" (*těpillâ*) and "supplication" (*těhinnâ*) (vv 28, 29, 30, 33, 35, 38, 42, 44, 45, 47, 48, 49, 52). In fact, the narrative frame

---

[43]Read *wěniptěhû* with LXX.

describes the address itself as precisely a "prayer and supplication" (v 54). I shall discuss the theological significance of this in Section VII. Here, I want to note only that the reinterpretation of the Temple as a place of prayer is known from other sixth century literature, most prominently from Third Isaiah:

> [6]And the foreigners who swear allegiance
> To YHWH, to serve him,
> And to love the name of YHWH,
> To become his servants.
> All who keep the sabbath undefiled,
> And hold fast to my covenant:
> [7]Them I will bring to my holy mountain,
> And gladden them in my House of Prayer.
> Their offerings and sacrifices
> Shall be acceptable upon my altar;
> For my Temple shall be called
> "A House of Prayer for All Nations."
> [8]An oracle of YHWH,
> Who gathers the outcasts of Israel:
> I will yet gather the exiles[44]
>   who remain to be brought in (Isa 56:6-8).

This theology of the Temple as a place of prayer is implicitly a polemic against the idea that God is literally, even physically present therein, as he was in Isaiah 6. Thus, we hear in 1 Kgs 8:23-53 a continual emphasis upon God's true dwelling, the heavens, from which he hears the prayers uttered on earth (vv 27, 32, 34, 36, 39, 43, 45, 49). When Solomon exclaims in v 27, "But can God really dwell on earth when the heaven itself, even the highest heaven, cannot contain you?" we can only think of the polemic of Third Isaiah:

> [1]Thus spoke YHWH:
> Heaven is my throne,
> And earth is my footstool.
> What is this Temple
> You would build for me,
> What is this resting-place for me? (Isa 66:1)

Surely Claus Westermann is right that "these words from the Deuteronomic account of the prayer at the consecration of the temple may come from about the same time as Isa 66:1f."[45] Only, I say not "may," but "must." 1 Kgs 8:23-53 is distinctly Exilic.

---

[44]Read gōlâw with Tg.

[45]C. Westermann, *Isaiah 40-66: A Commentary* (OTL; Philadelphia: Westminster, 1969) 413.

VI

The Exilic hand in the complex that extends from Deuteronomy through 2 Kings we have designated Dtr 2. It was this hand, we have argued, to which we owe the insertion of the central portion of Deuteronomy and the composition of the frame around it. If, as we suggested in the previous section, the third address of Solomon at the dedication of his Temple dates in its entirety from the Exile, then it is likely that its author is the person or school we call Dtr 2. Of course, it is quite possible that there are other Exilic passages within the complex in question than Dtr 2. In order to verify the hypothesis that the speech under discussion is indeed Dtr 2, we must compare first its idiom and then its theology with the passages already identified as Dtr 2.[46] If there is a manifest similarity, this discovery will add fuel to our argument for a unitary Exilic context for 1 Kgs 8:23-53.

I begin with verbal comparisons, as this realm is more objective than that of theology. My method is to present an expression in combination with its parallel in Dtr 2 and then to comment statistically upon the comparison.

1 Kgs 8:23.   "There is no god like you in heaven above or on earth beneath."
($^{)}\hat{e}n$-$k\bar{a}m\hat{o}k\bar{a}$ $^{)}\check{e}l\bar{o}h\hat{i}m$ $ba\check{s}\check{s}\bar{a}mayim$ $mimma^{c}al$ $w\check{e}^{c}al$-$h\bar{a}^{)}\bar{a}re\d{s}$ $mittahat.$)

Deut 4:39.   "YHWH is God in heaven above and on earth beneath. There is no other."
($YHWH$ $h\hat{u}^{)}$ $h\bar{a}^{)}\check{e}l\bar{o}h\hat{i}m$ $ba\check{s}\check{s}\bar{a}mayim$ $mimma^{c}al$ $w\check{e}^{c}al$-$h\bar{a}^{)}\bar{a}re\d{s}$ $mittahat$ $^{)}\hat{e}n$ $^{c}\hat{o}d.$)

The only close parallel in phraseology is Josh 2:11, which Burney, interestingly, calls D^2, the later Deuteronomic redactor.[47] In any event, the parallel is striking.

1 Kgs 8:41.   "The foreigner [who] has come from a distant land"
($hannokr\hat{i}$ . . . $\hat{u}b\bar{a}^{)}$ $m\bar{e}^{)}ere\d{s}$ $r\check{e}h\hat{o}q\hat{a}$)

Deut 29:21.   "The foreigner who comes from a distant land"
($hannokr\hat{i}$ . . . $y\bar{a}b\bar{o}^{)}$ $m\bar{e}^{)}ere\d{s}$ $r\check{e}h\hat{o}q\hat{a}$)

The only other use of the expression is found in 2 Chr 6:32, which is a quote from the speech in 1 Kgs 8:41. The expression is exclusive to the passages above.

[46] See Levenson, "Who Inserted," *HTR* 68 (1975).
[47] Burney, *Notes*, 116.

1 Kgs 8:47.	"If they reconsider" (wĕhēšîbû ʾel-libbām)
Deut 4:39.	"And you shall reflect" (wahăšēbôtā ʾel-lĕbābekā)
Deut 30:1.	"If you take to heart." (wahăšēbōtā ʾel-lĕbābekā)

The expression is difficult to translate into English, but it is identical in these three passages in Hebrew. Those are the only occurrences of it in all Dtr. It is interesting that all other attestations of it are demonstrably Exilic (Lam 3:21; Isa 44:19, 46:8; 2 Chr 6:37 quotes 1 Kgs 8:47).

1 Kgs 8:48.	"And they come back to you with all their heart and all their soul." (wĕšābû ʾêlêkā bĕkol-lĕbābām ûbkol-napšām)
Deut 30:10.	"For you will come back to YHWH your God with all your heart and all your soul." (kî tāšûb ʾel-YHWH ʾĕlōhêkā bĕkol-lĕbābĕkā ûbkol-napšêkā)

The verbal similarity is unmistakable and unparalleled. The emphasis on repentance is the hallmark of Dtr 2. It is expressed in somewhat similar language in Deut 4:30; 30:2; 30:8.

1 Kgs 8:51.	"Out of the midst of the smelting furnace." (mittôk kûr habbarzel)
Deut 4:20.	"Out of the smelting furnace." (mikkûr habbarzel)

The only other attestation of the expression is Jer 11:4. The Exilic passage Isa 48:10 offers a similar idiom, "in the furnace of affliction" (bĕkûr ʿōnî).

1 Kgs 8:52.	"Whenever they cry to you" (bĕkōl qorʾām ʾēlêkā)
Deut 4:7.	"Whenever we cry to him." (bĕkol-qorʾēnû ʾēlāw)

These two verses may be the only attestations of kōl plus the infinitive construct of qārāʾ with a subjective suffix. In Pss 86:5 and 145:18, the suffix is objective.

1 Kgs 8:51.   "For they are your people and
               your possession."
               (kî ʿammĕkā wĕnahălātĕkā hēm)

Deut 4:20.   "To be his people and his possession."
               (lihyôt lô lĕʿam nahălâ)

In my earlier study of Dtr 2, I argued that the emphasis upon God as
Israel's "possession" (nahălâ) and Israel as God's was a major point in
the theology of this Exilic source, one conceived under the influence of
the old poem of Deuteronomy 32 (see v 8).[48]

Let me now state the results of our inquiry into the relationship of
the language of 1 Kgs 8:23-53 to that of Dtr 2. We have uncovered fully
seven close parallels in idiom between the two, some unique to the
passages in question. Significantly for our argument in favor of the
unity of the third speech, the parallels are not simply with the obviously
Exilic end of the address (vv 44-53), but with the core of it as well. The
verbal research tends to support the hypothesis that Dtr 2 composed
1 Kgs 8:23-53.

What about theology? Does the third address present us with the
themes we have already identified as characteristic of Dtr 2? Certainly,
the whole passage resonates with the notions of repentance and the
openness of YHWH to Israel's anguished cry, major items in the
theological inventory of Dtr 2. In fact, to see the common centrality of
these themes, one need only compare 1 Kgs 8:23-53 with the speech I
think it most closely resembles, Deut 4:1-40. Five of our seven verbal
parallels relate these two great addresses; it is well-nigh impossible to
hold that the unique relationship between the address of Moses and that
of Solomon is coincidental. In each case, the speaker drives home with
symphonic effect the possibility of return, both literal and metaphorical,
in spite of Israel's sorry history of sin. The two discourses rank among
the finest sermons ever composed.[49]

The theology of monarchy in Solomon's speech supports even more
my attribution of it to Dtr 2. In Dtr 1, the royal theology of the House of
David became a major theme, one first articulated in 2 Sam 7:8-16 and reiterated almost as a refrain throughout Kings. "You shall never lack a
man," YHWH had promised David, "on the throne of Israel." In the
aftermath of the events of 587, as we have seen, it became impossible to
maintain faith in this pledge in the same way as before the Davidic family had been deposed. In his other great sermon, the Mosaic discourse of
Deut 4:1-40, Dtr 2 can avoid the whole issue of the monarchy. But he
cannot allow Solomon to pass over the problem of monarchy, especially

[48] Levenson, "Who Inserted," HTR 68 (1975).
[49] W. L. Moran points out to me that 1 Kgs 8:53 may be an allusion to
Deut 4:20.

after Solomon had just reiterated Nathan's promise to David almost verbatim in 1 Kgs 8:15-21, the second speech. And so Dtr 2 upholds the great pledge to David, but with a rider of momentous import.

> [25]And now, YHWH, God of Israel, keep this promise you made to David my father when you said to him, 'You shall never lack a man appointed by me to sit on the throne of Israel, if only your sons guard their ways and walk before me as you have walked before me' (1 Kgs 8:25).

What an "if!" It is that final conditional clause that we do not hear in Dtr 1's Davidic refrain.[50] On the contrary, in a case like that of King Joram of Judah, the Davidid was able to retain his fief, even though he turned as blatantly away from the ways of YHWH and toward idolatry as had his father-in-law, Ahab—all this "for the sake of David my servant." (2 Kgs 8:16-19).[51] In Dtr 2's theology, by contrast, so stunning a promise to the royal dynasty could never be the real meaning of YHWH's pledge, for it disregards, and even belittles, the Torah from Mount Sinai, especially in its classic recapitulation in Deuteronomy. The eternal pledge to David had to be harmonised with the promise that Israel would be blessed *only if* she observed the commandments from Sinai (Deuteronomy 28). The hand that inserted the core of Deuteronomy could not suffer that its threats be treated so lightly. Eternity and contingency, conditionality and unconditionality, promise and offer all were to be reconciled, however lamely, in that one clause at the end of 1 Kgs 8:25. Its "if" is a major point in the history of biblical theology.

A few remarks about the fourth speech of Solomon at the dedication of his Temple (1 Kgs 8:56-61): It is more difficult to ascertain the origins of this speech than those of the previous three. Its language being for the most part a collection of Deuteronomic clichés, it is difficult to tell whether we are hearing Dtr 1 or Dtr 2, both of whom are Deuteronomic in diction. Two points suggest that this last brief address is also Dtr 2. First, the expression of faith in the eventual universal recognition of YHWH's unique divinity in v 60 recalls v 23 and its striking parallel in Deut 4:39. (Note also the clause "so that all the peoples of the world may know" in v 60 and in v 43.) Second, the emphasis of this fourth speech upon YHWH's promise of blessing for Israel through the mediation of

[50]See now Levenson, "The Davidic Covenant and Its Modern Interpreters," *CBQ* 41 (1979) 205-19.

[51]Here, I must dissent from the thinking of M. Weinfeld ("The Covenant of Grant in the Old Testament and in the Ancient Near East," *JAOS* 90 [1970] 195), who believes that Dtr has made conditional the promise to David, for whose heirs "the covenant is eternal only if the donee keeps his loyalty to the donor." The conditional statement of the promise to David is indeed to be found (e.g., 1 Kgs 9:1-9), but it is much more logical to attribute it to a different hand, that is, to Dtr 2.

Moses (v 56) is a fitting focus for the document that introduces the core of the Mosaic revelation of Deuteronomy and has been so profoundly influenced by the blessings and curses of Deuteronomy 28. I suspect that this fourth is in reality the continuation of Solomon's third address once he has risen (v 55) after his more penitential prayer in vv 23-53.

VII

We saw above that the third address does not speak in the tones of the older Temple theology, which stressed the physical manifestation of God in his earthly house and his ordination of an acceptable liturgy there, one to which animal sacrifice was central. In that better known conception of the shrine at Jerusalem, the Temple was a cosmic, even mythical institution,[52] inviolable to attack (Psalm 48), the sacred source of the miraculous fresh waters of Israel (Ezekiel 47), and, most importantly, the place of a unique encounter with God, from which a prophet like Isaiah emerged transformed (Isaiah 6). In 1 Kgs 8:23-53 (61), in contrast, the Temple is a house of prayer, for God is in heaven, and it is from above, as the refrain will not let us forget, that he hears our supplications (vv 27, 32, 34, 36, 39, 43, 45, 49). In fact, not only is the Temple a place for prayer and supplication, but its very inauguration was a ceremony most notably of prayer and supplication (v 54). The Hebrew words for these two acts of worship (*těpillâ* and *těḥinnâ*), or their verbal counterparts, recur unremittingly throughout the third address (vv 28, 29, 30, 33, 35, 38, 42, 44, 45, 47, 48, 49, 52). It is as though the author does not want us to forget that this is the one true and enduring aspect of the Temple. And, indeed, in the era of the Exile, when the great shrine lay in ruins, what other function could it serve than as a place toward which a captive Israel could face in anguished acknowledgement of their sins and humble request for an unmerited restoration (v 48)? A new institution has begun to move into the quarters Isaiah knew and psalmists celebrated. Its name is the "synagogue."

1 Kgs 8:23-53 (61) is thus a pivotal text in the transition from Israelite faith to Judaism and Christianity. It is a great paradox that both these communities are descended from a Temple-centered faith, yet have no Temple in them. Their understanding of the Temple must be explored very carefully if we are to comprehend them in a profound way. It is well known that the Church harbors a polemical relationship with

---

[52]On the concept of the cosmic mountain, see R. J. Clifford, *The Cosmic Mountain in Canaan and the Old Testament* (HSM 4; Cambridge: Harvard University, 1972); M. Eliade, *The Myth of the Eternal Return, or, Cosmos and History* (Bollingen Series 46; Princeton: Princeton University, 1971); and Levenson, *Theology of the Program of Restoration of Ezekiel 40-48* (HSM 10; Missoula: Scholars) chaps. 1-3.

the Temple, as seen, for example, in those passages in the Synoptic Gospels in which Jesus prophetically predicts the destruction of the Temple (Matt 24:1-2; Mark 13:1-12; Luke 21:5-7). What is less often remarked is the favorable attitude that is clear, for instance, in John 2:21-22, where the body of Christ is identified with the Temple, and in 2 Cor 6:16, where the Christian community appears as the Temple of the living God. We can relate these two apparently contradictory thrusts by saying that in early Christian theology, the Temple had not been abolished, but fulfilled in Christ. It is probably fair to say that in an authentic Christian understanding, wherever the community gathers to pray to Jesus, there the Temple is, in a sense, recreated.

As for Judaism, the first thing to be said is that the tradition did not halt in place in the first century of the common era. The belief that it did is still too often seen in Christian treatments, which tend to mistake Judaism for the religion of the "Old Testament,"[53] a mistake reassuring to Christians since it implies that Judaism is at best merely the part of which Christianity is the whole, a part that failed to develop spiritually after the death of Jesus. The truth is, however, that Judaism is the tradition of the synagogue and the yeshivah, not of the Temple, the tradition of prayer and learning rather than of sacrifice. The replacement of sacrifice by prayer must not be seen as an example of simple progress, as if the rabbis somehow came to view the Temple as unenlightened. Rather, prayer and learning were viewed as the temporary and imperfect continuation of the sacrificial practices once the destruction of the Temple rendered the latter incapable of literal fulfillment. Thus, in a Talmudic discussion of the correct times for certain prayers, Rabbi Joshua ben Levi stated, "The obligatory prayers were instituted to correspond to the daily sacrifices" (b. Ber. 26b).[54] What is more, prayer is not only the successor to sacrifice; prayer is sacrifice. The equation has been made explicit in Jewish theology from Talmudic antiquity until the present.[55] It is ominously implicit in 1 Kings 8. The Temple which Solomon consecrated amidst sacrifice and prayer is, once again, in a sense made real and its deepest purpose fulfilled when Jews pray.

In Jewish theology, the liturgical order that the rabbis made normative is only a temporary institution while we await the final consummation of the divine plan. When that occurs, the Temple is to be rebuilt and its sacrificial liturgy resumed in the Land of Israel, to which all Jews are to be miraculously restored. In other words, the present condition of Jewry, their living in the Diaspora, is a parenthesis in the history

[53] E.g. H. Smith, *The Religions of Man* (New York, Evanston and London: Harper and Row, 1958) 225-65.

[54] The prayer in question is the *tĕpillâ* or *ᶜămîdâ*.

[55] A. J. Heschel, *Man's Quest for God* (New York: Scribner's, 1954) 70-72, and the references there.

of redemption which will one day be closed. In the meantime, in the "in-between time" which lies after the destruction of the Second Temple and before the construction of the Third, the Jew prays that the promised day will come soon and in his own time. Prayer, therefore, links the Jews spiritually with the past liturgy which it replaces and partially fulfills and with the coming order, which is typologically and literally related to the past, and yet surpasses anything so far experienced. As Solomon's speech at the dedication of his Temple from the hand of Dtr 2 makes so clear, prayer is the proper response for the Jew in spiritual or physical Exile, whom God has neither rejected nor restored altogether. Prayer is the first step in the redemption of the world.

From Egypt to Egypt: Dtr[1] and Dtr[2]

RICHARD ELLIOTT FRIEDMAN
UNIVERSITY OF CALIFORNIA
SAN DIEGO

F OR a hundred years since Wellhausen, scholars have concentrated
upon the task of uncovering the sources of which the books of the
Bible are composed. The initial focus has been far more on the sources
themselves than on the final united literary products, more on the
authors of the component texts than on those author/editors who
created from those inherited texts the larger works which survive as the
Holy Scriptures, more on the historical milieu of each of the sources
than on the historical process which brought the sources together in
creative syntheses. The redactors have remained elusive, figures whose
backgrounds and purposes are unclear. This is problematic not only
intrinsically—as a serious gap in our understanding of the final stages of
the creation of the Biblical text—but also retroactively, preventing our
fullest possible apprehension of the sources themselves, because the
activity of identifying the sources and uncovering the process of redaction of them is dialectical.

This avenue of Biblical scholarship is another of the areas in which
we are indebted to Frank Moore Cross. In his treatments of the Priestly
work and the Deuteronomistic history, Professor Cross has examined the
process and the artistry involved in the growth of these works out of
sources.[1] Cross's analysis of the Deuteronomistic history came in response to the work of Martin Noth. The initial notion of a "Deuteronomistic history" was Noth's. In the *Überlieferungsgeschichtliche Studien*
(1943) Noth argued for the editorial unity of the sequence Deuteronomy-
Joshua-Judges-Samuel-Kings, all developed by an Exilic figure who
collected source documents and elaborated upon them with the perspective of the Deuteronomic law as pivotal. That figure, both a writer and
an editor, selected source materials and wrote passages at all times
developing this perspective, occasionally referring the reader back to the
sources for data which did not serve the writer/editor's interest.[2] He thus

---

[1]*Canaanite Myth and Hebrew Epic* (Cambridge: Harvard University Press,
1973) 274-325.

[2]Including the Chronicles of Solomon, the Chronicles of the Kings of
Judah, and the Chronicles of the Kings of Israel.

assembled a particular account of Israel's story from Moses to the Davidic king Jehoiachin in Babylonian Exile, attributing Israel's current homelessness to the centuries of failure of the people and its kings to fulfill that which had been demanded of them in Moses' book.

Cross perceived a more complex development of the Deuteronomistic corpus, arguing that the original construction of the work out of sources plus newly composed material was an event of the reign of Josiah. It was a work which praised that king, portraying in him a return to fidelity to Yhwh and his (Deuteronomic)[3] law, as well as preservation of the nation through the force of the Davidic covenant. The full version of the Deuteronomistic history, covering the years subsequent to Josiah, down to the Babylonian exile (plus the notation of the release of Jehoiachin), together with other elaborative insertions, was the result of a second redaction, an updating of the work to record and account for the striking historical turns of fortune which followed the Josianic years. Cross marked the Josianic edition of the Deuteronomistic history Dtr^1 and the Exilic edition Dtr^2.

Identifying and separating Dtr^1 from Dtr^2 is a more complex task than e.g. distinguishing P from D. The characteristic Deuteronomistic style is as consistent as it is striking. The bank of characteristic Deuteronomistic terminology is uniform as well.[4] Cross's view of Josianic and Exilic editions of the history is rather based on literary and thematic considerations. Chief among these is the Deuteronomistic treatment of the Davidic covenant. Here, in a work which commences with threats of destruction and exile in the event of betrayal of the Mosaic covenant and concludes with a portrayal of that destruction and exile, stands a series of passages developing God's promise of eternal security for the Davidic dynasty and for David's city Jerusalem. The tension between the "unconditional" Davidic covenant and the multiconditional Mosaic covenant is itself a common concern in theological and history-of-religion studies.[5] As difficult as it is to reconcile the two traditions in those disciplines, it is harder still, from a literary-historical perspective, to picture an Exilic writer composing an account of a divine promise of a never-ending

---

[3]In this discussion, the term *Deuteronomic* is used to refer exclusively to the book of Deuteronomy, as opposed to the term *Deuteronomistic*, which is applied to the entire Deuteronomistic history.

[4]For a collection of Deuteronomistic phraseology, see Moshe Weinfeld, *Deuteronomy and the Deuteronomic School* (London: Oxford University, 1972) Appendix A, 320-65 (hereafter cited as *DDS*).

[5]See Weinfeld, "The Covenant of Grant in the Old Testament and in the Ancient Near East," *JAOS* 90 (1970) 184-203; M. Tsevat, "Studies in the Book of Samuel, III," *HUCA* 34 (1963) 73; J. Levenson, "Who Inserted the Book of the Torah?" *HTR* 68 (1975) 203-33.

kingdom together with an account of the destruction and exile of that kingdom.

The Davidic dynastic promise is portrayed as such in only a few passages, but their import is patent. The initial declaration of the commitment to David, pronounced by the prophet Nathan, is powerful:

> YHWH will make a House[6] for you. When your days will be full and you will lie with your fathers, I shall establish your seed, who will come from your insides, after you. He will build a house for my name, and I shall sustain the throne of his kingdom forever. I shall be a father to him, and he will be a son to me, whom I shall chastize with the rod of humans and the lashes of men when he does wrong, but my *ḥesed*[7] will not turn from him as I turned from Saul, whom I turned out from before you. Your house and your kingdom will be secure before you forever; your throne will be established forever.
>
> (2 Sam 7:11b-16)

The wording is clear and unequivocal. The prayer of David which follows (vv 18-29) underlines the point, as do three later notations in the history of the dynasty. When the prophet Ahijah announces that the offenses of Solomon against Yhwh are to result in forfeiture of reign over Israel to Jeroboam, he declares:

> But I shall not take the whole kingdom from his hand, for I shall make him a prince all the days of his life for the sake of David my servant whom I chose, who kept my commandments and laws. I shall take the kingdom from the hand of his son and give it to you—the ten tribes. But I shall give one tribe to his son so that there may be a fief[8] for my servant David always before me in Jerusalem, the city which I have chosen for myself to set my name there.
>
> (1 Kgs 11:34-36)

Despite the offenses of Solomon's successors, Rehoboam and Abijah, Yhwh continues to sustain the throne in Jerusalem because of the merit of David. Abijah

> went in all the crimes of his father which he had done before him, and his heart was not whole[9] with YHWH his God as the heart of David his father.

[6]Hebrew *bayit* refers to dynasty.

[7]The untranslatable *ḥesed* refers to the kindness shown in fidelity to a covenant relationship, almost always coming from the stronger of the covenant parties.

[8]On the meaning of the term *nîr*, see Paul Hanson, "Song of Heshbon and David's *NÎR*," *HTR* 61 (1968) 297-320.

[9]For examples of *whole heart* as covenant fidelity terminology, cf. the treaties: Mursilis II of Hatti and Niqmepa of Ugarit, line 20, J. Nougayrol,

> But for the sake of David YHWH his God gave him a fief in Jerusalem to establish his son after him and to establish Jerusalem.
>
> (1 Kgs 15:3f)

The Davidid Jehoram likewise receives undeserved divine protection on David's account.

> He went in the path of the kings of Israel . . . and he did evil in the eyes of YHWH, but YHWH was not willing to destroy Judah for the sake of David his servant, as he had promised him to give a fief to him and to his sons always.
>
> (2 Kgs 8:18f)

The equation to the kings of the Northern kingdom here is particularly of interest. Cross noted that the theme of the Davidic promise in Judah is balanced against the ongoing theme of the crimes of Jeroboam and his successors in Israel. Even when the Davidid commits the very crimes of his Northern peer, his kingdom is not condemned to the same fate as that of Israel. Judah, on the contrary, survives long past the destruction of Israel and, in Josiah, seems to be entering upon a new golden age like that of David. Cross saw in this milieu the background of the first edition of the Deuteronomistic history (Dtr[1]). The paired themes of apostasy leading to destruction in the North and Davidic fidelity leading to preservation and ultimate restoration of the North to the Davidic line are precisely the interests of the Josianic reform. Cross attributed to the Exilic Deuteronomist (Dtr[2]) the two-and-a-half chapters which follow the Josiah pericope, together with certain passages which seem to be addressed to exiles, as well as passages which seem to soften the certainty of the Davidic promise, including Deut 4:27-31; 28:36f., 63-68; 29:27; 30:1-10; Josh 23:11-13, 15f; 1 Sam 12:25; 1 Kgs 2:4; 6:11-13; 8:25b, 46-53; 9:4-9; 2 Kgs 17:19; 20:17f.; 21:2-15. In addition to the theme of the eternal maintenance of the kingdom, a rather strange theme for one to develop after 587, Cross pointed to the notation of earlier literary critics that the expression "to this day" occurs regularly, often referring to circumstances which obtained only while the kingdom of Judah was still standing.[10] The matter of the re-acquisition of the North under Josiah seems likewise to be a datum which one would hardly expect an

---

Palais royal d'Ugarit IV, 84ff. (RS 17.353); Ashurnirari V and Mat'ilu of Bit-Agusi, Col. IV, line 3, E. Weidner, *Archiv für Orientforschung* 8, 16ff., also in D. J. McCarthy, *Treaty and Covenant* (Rome: PBI, 1963) 195; Esarhaddon's Vassal Treaty, lines 53, 387, in McCarthy, *Treaty and Covenant*, 199. See also Weinfeld, "The Covenant of Grant in the Old Testament and in the Ancient Near East," 184-203.

[10] 2 Kgs 8:22; 16:6; see also 1 Kgs 8:8; 9:21; 10:12; 12:19; 2 Kgs 10:27; 14:7; 17:23.

Exilic writer to emphasize so. The greater length of the narrative devoted to Josiah than to other Deuteronomistically-approved kings is another clue to be reckoned with. Indeed, since the verdict for the destruction of the kingdom is traced to the crimes of Josiah's grandfather Manasseh (2 Kgs 21:12-15; reckoned by Cross among the Dtr² insertions) the attention given to Josiah is a strange anticlimax. What one would expect to find, if the history were the work of a single Exilic tradent, Cross observed, would be a peroration on the fall of Jerusalem, comparable to that upon the destruction of the North (2 Kgs 17:7-23). One might expect, as well, a concluding indicator of hope for restoration of the people to its land and a suggested repentance. But these are lacking. The prophecy of 1 Kgs 13:2, on the other hand, which predicts Josiah by name is, Cross noted, a striking literary anticipation which particularly points to the Josianic perspective.

Following are my own observations which I believe add compelling evidence for the existence of two editions of the Deuteronomistic history, the first Josianic, the second Exilic.

First, literary evidence indicates that not only did someone design the work to accord a singular status to Josiah out of all the kings of Israel and Judah, but, further, that figure consciously framed the work within an *inclusio* constructed of associations between Moses and Josiah. A number of matters in Deuteronomy echo in the Josiah pericope in 2 Kings 22 and 23 both in theme and phraseology.

The closing reference to Moses following his death in Deuteronomy commences with the words, "There did not arise a prophet again in Israel like Moses . . ." (*lʾ qm nbyʾ ʿwd byśrʾl kmšh*), Deut 34:10. This precise expression, "none arose like him," is not applied to any other biblical personage but one. The closing reference to Josiah following the account of his reform reads, "There was no king like him before him turning to Yhwh with all his heart and with all his soul and with all his might according to all the Torah of Moses, and after him none arose like him" (2 Kgs 23:25).[11] The parallel occurrence of the phrase appears to be more than a chance colloquy when one notes that a second parallel occurs in the same verse. The well-known command of Deut 6:5, "Love Yhwh your God with all your heart and with all your soul and with all your might," appears in precisely this threefold form including fidelity to Yhwh with all of one's *měʾōd* in only one other verse in the Scriptures, this Josiah eulogy of 2 Kgs 23:25.[12]

The judgment command of Deut 17:8-12 requires that one "enquire" (*drš*) via a priest or judge, at the place which Yhwh chooses, what course

[11] Jack R. Lundbom, "The Lawbook of the Josianic Reform," *CBQ* 38 (1976) 301-2, notes this parallel.

[12] I am grateful to Baruch Halpern for sharing this observation with me.

to take in a difficult judgment. The only king who is ever portrayed as having thus enquired (drš) of Yhwh via a priest at the chosen place on any matter is Josiah, who enquires via the priest Hilkiah concerning the book which Hilkiah has found (2 Kgs 22:13, 18). The passage in Deuteronomy, interestingly, is immediately followed by the Deuteronomic law of the king, vv 13-20. The drš command warns the enquiring party, "Do not turn from the thing which they will tell you, to the right or left," (v 11). The law of the king, requiring that the king write a copy of the Torah and read regularly, likewise explains, ". . . so that he will not turn from the commandment to the right or left," (v 20; cf. also Deut 5:29; 28:14). This caution in the form "Do not turn to the right or left" is attached to obedience to the book of the Torah of Moses in two passages in the book of Joshua as well (1:7; 23:6). It occurs nowhere else in Scripture except in the Deuteronomist's evaluation of Josiah, reporting that Josiah did what was right in the eyes of Yhwh, went in the path of David, "and he did not turn to the right or left" (2 Kgs 22:2).

Josiah's zeal in regard to the book (sēper) of the Torah is itself another link between Deuteronomy and the Josiah pericope. Indeed, the sēper of Moses is mentioned in only three passages in the Deuteronomistic history outside of Deuteronomy and the story of Josiah: Josh 1:8, 8:31, 34; 23:6. Two of these passages are already familiar to us as those relating to obedience without "turning to the right or left" (cf. above).

The Deuteronomist's intended linkage of Moses and Josiah is further manifest in several more parallels of action and phraseology. Moses commands that the Torah be read every seventh year "in the ears" of all the people, תקרא את התורה הזאת נגד כל ישראל באזניהם (Deut 31:11). Josiah gathers all the people and reads the words of the book in their ears, ויקרא באזניהם (2 Kgs 23:2). The idiom occurs only once elsewhere in the history.[13] Moses burns and smashes the golden calf "thin as dust," daq lᵉᶜāpār, and casts the dust on the wadi, (nahal), (Deut 9:21). At the site of Jeroboam's golden calf of Bethel, Josiah smashes the bāmâ and burns it, "and he made it thin as dust (hēdaq lᵉᶜāpār)" (2 Kgs 23:15). The dependence of the episode of Aaron's golden calf in JE and Deuteronomic tradition upon the matter of Jeroboam's golden calves at Dan and Bethel has long been noted in scholarly discussion. This equation of the fate of Aaron's calf and that of the calf (or bāmâ) of Bethel especially underlines the association of the two in the Deuteronomist's perspective.[14] The particular phraseology occurs twice more in the description of Josiah's zealous actions. Josiah burns

[13] Judg 7:3; the verb qrʾ is used here in its sense of to call rather than to read in the other passages.

[14] And, as noted above, it is in 1 Kings 13, the account of the inauguration of Jeroboam's Bethel altar, that Josiah's coming zeal is explicitly predicted (v 2).

the statue of Asherah which Manasseh had set in the Temple, at the wadi (*naḥal*) Kidron, "and he made it thin as dust (*wayyādeq lĕ°āpār*)" (23:6). The phrase *daq lĕ°āpār* occurs nowhere but in the passages noted here. Josiah also smashes the altars which his ancestors had made and casts their dust into the wadi (v 12).

This treatment which Josiah accords the altar and statue of Asherah has other direct parallels in the Torah of Moses. The Mosaic law of Deuteronomy 12 specifically commands, "you shall smash (*nts*) their altars . . . and burn (*śrp*) their Asherim with fires . . ." (Deut 12:3). Josiah, as remarked above, smashes (*nts*) the altars and burns (*śrp*) the Asherah.[15]

The prohibition of making any graven image (*pesel*) occurs repeatedly in Deuteronomy, both in the Decalogue (Deut 5:8) and elsewhere (4:16, 23, 25; 27:15), including an order that a *pesel* of a foreign god be burnt (7:25). The term rarely occurs thereafter—outside of the book of Judges, the only reference to a *pesel* is among the Samaritans—until Manasseh sets the *pesel* of Asherah in the Temple (2 Kgs 21:7). Josiah removes this image and burns it.

The list of associations between Moses' book and the Josiah narrative must certainly include the matter of the *sēper hattôrâ* itself. As remarked above, the *sēper* as such is only mentioned in this particular series of passages. The connection, however, is more than terminological. In Deuteronomy, Moses summons the Levites who bear the ark and he instructs them: "Take this book of the Torah (*sēper hattôrâ*) and place it at the side of the ark of the covenant of Yhwh your God, and it will be there as a witness against you" (31:26). The book then ceases to be an issue in the history until Hilkiah says, "I have found *sēper hattôrâ* in the house of Yhwh" (2 Kgs 22:8).[16]

Whatever the actual historical circumstances, we can discern the Deuteronomistic writer/editor's design in his portrayal of history. He did more than compose a particularly positive entry on Josiah's reign for a record of the kings of Israel and Judah. He constructed a history of the nation which pointed to Josiah, first by setting a blatant prediction of Josiah by name in the account of the inauguration of the Northern cult, i.e. he embedded the anticipation of Josiah at the point of inception of the portrayal of the Israelite heresy, against which the history of Judah is juxtaposed. Second, he fashioned an *inclusio* which tied Josiah, as no other king, to Moses and to the law of Moses' book. In this *inclusio*, that which begins with Moses approaches its culmination at last in Josiah.

Still, one may admit the importance of the figure Josiah and acknowledge the focus upon him in the literary construction of the

---

[15]One should observe that the treatment of Hezekiah's similar measures (2 Kings 18) does not portray them in the language of Deuteronomy.

[16]Cf. 1 Kgs 8:21.

work, but at the same time argue that a single Exilic historian could nonetheless have been responsible for this construction, choosing to focus upon Josiah for reasons of ideology or simply because he held that monarch in special esteem. The character of the text itself, however, suggests a break and addition following the Josiah pericope. Changes in the fundamental perspective of the narration occur at this juncture. The discussion begins with an observation of Gerhard von Rad's. Von Rad noted that the criterion by which the Deuteronomistic historian regularly evaluated the kings of Israel and Judah was their fulfillment or transgression of the requirement of centralization of worship. The Deuteronomist thus classified every one of the kings of Israel's two-century history as evil for having retained the alternate worship which Jeroboam had initiated at Dan and Bethel. The Deuteronomist likewise faulted all of the kings of Judah, except Hezekiah and Josiah, for having built or retained *bāmôt* outside the Jerusalem Temple. Hezekiah and Josiah draw the tradent's praise for having destroyed the *bāmôt*. Von Rad did not note, however, that in the account of the four kings who follow Josiah not a word about *bāmôt* appears, even though the *bāmôt* were revived in this period.[17] Why would an Exilic writer apply this criterion to every king except the four in whose reigns the calamities finally occurred?

Von Rad also noted a recurring prophecy/fulfillment pattern through the course of the Deuteronomistic history, pointing out eleven examples.[18] But this pattern likewise ceases after Josiah: the fulfillment in him of the Bethel prophecy, discussed above, is the last occurrence of the phenomenon in the Deuteronomistic history.

Another notable disappearance occurring after the Josiah pericope is that of the reminiscences of David. Not only is the Davidic promise no longer an issue, but the regular rating of Judean kings in comparison to their father David ceases. Toward the end of the history one finds this family standard in the evaluation of Ahaz, Hezekiah, Manasseh, Amon (by implication) and Josiah, after which the criterion ceases.

These matters constitute more than arguments from silence. This is a proper change of perspective and manner of presentation of history. The last four kings receive the shortest of ratings; they "did evil in the eyes of Yhwh according to all that their fathers had done"—an unthoughtful choice of wording if the writer who described these kings was the same writer who had just described the career of their father Josiah.

The reign of Josiah is more than *important* to the history. It is the original culmination of the work. Any remaining thoughts that the

---

[17]Cf. Jer 17:3; Ezek 6:3, 6.

[18]Von Rad, "The Deuteronomic Theology of History in I and II Kings," in *The Problem of the Hexateuch* (New York: McGraw-Hill, 1966) 205-21.

present structure of the work might reflect only a single Exilic historian's presentation should end when one examines the text itself for evidence of secondary expansion. In this examination the consistency of the Deuteronomistic style and language noted above requires that we have more than phraseological grounds for identifying a passage as Exilic expansion of an earlier text. We must rather find convergences of such factors as terminology, theme, grammar, syntax, literary structure, and comparative data to make such identification. This is possible in all of the following passages:

1 Kgs 9:6-9. The full pericope 1 Kgs 9:1-9 is the portrayal of Yhwh's second appearance to Solomon. Cross's discussion of conditional and unconditional covenant traditions is in point here, as the pericope seems to include both the notion that Solomon's Temple will stand forever and that the Temple may be destroyed. V 3 expresses the former notion in the formula of what has come to be known as the "Deuteronomistic Name theology,"[19] i.e. the expression of Yhwh's setting his name in the Temple as an available channel to him for humans. The Name theology formula is associated with the eternal survival of the Temple (1 Kgs 9:3; 11:36; 2 Kgs 21:7), an unlikely theme for an Exilic Deuteronomist to have developed. Vv 7 and 8, meanwhile, threaten the rejection of the Temple.

The first step to unraveling the literary history of this pericope comes in vv 4 and 5. In these two verses God promises that the throne of David will be securely attached to the Davidids forever, but only on condition that they observe the laws of Yhwh. This sounds like the conditional sort of covenant formulation that Cross identified as Exilic. The case here is, however, still more complex. Two other passages likewise attach conditions of observance of the law to the promise of the Davidic family's eternal hold on the throne, 1 Kgs 2:4 and 8:25. But the common element of all these three passages is the formula *l$^{\circ}$ ykrt lk $^{\circ}$yš m^{c}l ks$^{\circ}$ yśr$^{\circ}$l*, "there will not be cut off from you a man upon the throne of Israel." It is the throne of *Israel* which is conditional. The references to the eternal dynastic promise, on the other hand, refer to the "throne" or to the "Kingdom," but never say "throne of Israel" or "Kingdom of Israel" (so 2 Sam 7:11b-16; 1 Kgs 2:45). The passages cited above (pp. 169f.) concerning the fief which the Davidids retain despite the offences of Solomon, Abijah, and Jehoram, on the other hand, clearly identify that fief as only Jerusalem/Judah, i.e., the original holding of the Davidic family. This critical distinction between the thrones of Israel and Judah is not a more subtle one than the historian intended. On the contrary, the Deuteronomistic history maintains the distinction both before and

---

[19]". . . the House where Yhwh will set his name forever"; see S. D. McBride, "The Deuteronomic Name Theology" (dss. Harvard, 1969).

after the division of Jeroboam.[20] There is thus no contradiction between the eternal promise concerning the Temple of Solomon in v 3 and the conditional promise of Solomon's retention of the whole of Israel in vv 4, 5. The difficulty comes rather in the next verse, where, following this conditional offer to Solomon, a strange shift in the address occurs. In the middle of this second person singular address, suddenly Yhwh is addressing a plural audience which in context can only be the entire people (vv 6-9).[21] This passage threatens that if the people commit apostasy they will be cast out of their land and the Temple will be destroyed. It is with the arrival of this second passage that covenant traditions collide. The Name theology of the earlier passage (vv 3-5) with its assurance of the eternal survival of the Temple has been followed with a blatant discarding of that eternal commitment. The grammatical juncture and the thematic juncture converge, mutually pointing to a secondary insertion. The literary history of the pericope is: a first stage, depicting a divine promise of eternal security for the Temple in Jerusalem without stipulation, together with a conditional offer of eternal Davidic reign over all of Israel (thus accounting for the loss of the North for failure to fulfill the conditions; cf. 1 Kings 11[22]); plus a second redactional stage, wholly conditional, adding the notions of (1) divine rejection of the Temple and (2) exile of the people. The united pericope argues for the presence of the Dtr[1] and Dtr[2] editions.

2 Kgs 21:8-15. Cross pointed to thematic grounds for regarding this passage, which predicts destruction and exile[23] in the midst of the Manasseh pericope, as an Exilic editor's addition, namely: the unspecific reference to unnamed prophets' oracles against Manasseh and the nation, the lack of any prior prophecies concerning Manasseh's sin and its consequences, the conflict with the portrayal of the eternal Davidic promise, and the question of "Why Manasseh?" In addition to these factors, one may discern a syntactical irregularity in the text which

[20] Cf. 2 Sam 3:10; 5:5; 1 Kgs 1:35; 11:38; 12:19ff.

[21] The well-known singular/plural problem in source identification in the book of Deuteronomy is not an issue here. There it is the nation which is addressed in singular or plural. Here the case is a change to plural in the midst of an address to Solomon. The problem in Deuteronomy is discussed by G. Minette de Tillesse, "Sections 'tu' et sections 'vous' dans le Deutéronome," *VT* 12 (1962) 29-87. The position of de Tillesse is summarized in E. W. Nicholson, *Deuteronomy and Tradition* (Philadelphia: Fortress Press, 1967) 27-31.

[22] One should note that the offensive places of worship which Solomon erects (1 Kgs 11:5-8) *Josiah* destroys (2 Kgs 23:13f.).

[23] The prediction of exile does not itself call for an Exilic provenience. It was a common entry in seventh-century treaty curse lists. See D. Hillers, *Treaty-Curses and the Old Testament Prophets* (Rome: PBI, 1964) 33-34.

points to the precise juncture at which the Exilic editor intervened. The first seven verses of the chapter describe the crimes of Manasseh in terms which relate to the activities of Josiah, i.e., the writer names the wrongs which Josiah set right. Manasseh rebuilds the *bāmôt*; Josiah smashes them. Manasseh sets up the Asherah; Josiah burns it. Manasseh sets altars "to all the host of heaven" in the Temple precincts; Josiah smashes them. The record of the offences of Manasseh is thus consistent with the interests of the Josianic edition discussed above, a fact which is further confirmed by the reference to the Temple as "the house where Yhwh would set his name forever," (v 7), the formula of the Deuteron-omistic Name theology once again. The theme of the text subtly shifts immediately following this verse, the shift occurring amidst some syn-tactical awkwardness, thus:

> (v 7) He set the image of Asherah which he had made in the house of which Yhwh had said to David and to Solomon his son, "In this house and in Jerusalem which I have chosen from all the tribes of Israel I shall set my name forever (v 8) and I shall not cause the foot of Israel to wander from the land which I gave to their fathers only if they will take care to do according to all that I have commanded them and to all the Torah which my servant Moses commanded them."

The matter of concern in v 7 is the *house*, and the quotation of Yhwh which begins in the middle of that verse indeed does focus on the house. The second half of the quotation (v 8), however, has nothing to do with the house, even though the quotation is specifically introduced in v 7 as being the words of Yhwh with regard to the house (". . . in the *house of which Yhwh had said* . . ."). This second half of the quotation rather limits the *forever* of the Name Theology formula with an "only if," the *forever* being precisely what is the issue between the two editions of the work.

From this juncture through v 15, the perspective changes. The center of attention becomes the people instead of the king. The historian is only interested in Manasseh as a *maḥăṭîʾ*, i.e., as one who causes the others to transgress. The unnamed prophets predict the utter destruction of the nation like the destruction of the Northern kingdom. The text then returns in v 16 to the personal crimes of Manasseh (= Dtr^1). The thematic friction between two portions of the pericope coincides with the juncture at which syntactical friction occurs. Together they point, once again, to an Exilic editor's need to soften the portrayal of an eternal divine commitment to preservation of the Temple in his received text. The Exilic editor's revision was brilliant with regard to structure. Taking advantage of the portrayal in his received text of the crimes of Manasseh and of Josiah's horror at the pending consequences, he expanded the implications of the crimes, emphasized the role of the

178   RICHARD ELLIOTT FRIEDMAN

people, and rendered the eternal Name theology conditional, all without
apparently deleting a word of the received edition. The Exilic editor also
began the updating epilogue of the Exilic edition (2 Kgs 23:26-25:26) by
stating—immediately following the notice in the received edition that
there arose none like Josiah—that Josiah's short-lived reform did not
suffice to offset the crimes of Manasseh. Judah would suffer a fate like
that of the Northern kingdom, and Yhwh would reject the house of
which he had said, "My name will be there." One should note that in
this Exilic version of the Name theology formula the word *forever* is no
longer used.

Deut 31:16-22; 28-30. This chapter is one of the most difficult in the
Pentateuch for identification, for three layers are present. A number of
scholars have observed that the chapter divides neatly into thematic
units[24] thus:

vv 1-8	Moses encourages Joshua and the people
9-13	Moses charges that the Torah be read publicly every seven years
14f., 23	Yhwh charges Joshua
16-22	Introduction of the Song of Moses
24-27	Moses charges that the book of the Torah be placed beside the ark
28-30	Introduction of the Song of Moses (continued)

The first two units, vv 1-13, are consistent with the themes of the
Josianic edition discussed above. The instruction that the Torah be
"read in the ears" of the people is discussed above[25] in thematic and
phraseological association with the Josiah pericope. Vv 14f. are anomalous amidst Deuteronomic materials. These verses contain the only
mention of the Tent of Meeting (ʾōhel môʿēd) in Deuteronomy, and
they have been identified as JE.[26] The instruction that Moses bring
Joshua to the Tent to be charged is carried out in v 23, which is from the
same hand. The intervening verses, 16-22, however, break the context
and are patently in the Deuteronomistic style. This passage introduces

[24]G. E. Wright, *Deuteronomy, The Interpreter's Bible* II (Nashville: Abingdon, 1953) 515; Nicholson, *Deuteronomy and Tradition*, 19; S. R. Driver,
Introduction to the Literature of the Old Testament (Gloucester: Peter Smith,
1972) 71-72, (hereafter cited as *ILOT*).
[25]P. 172.
[26]Driver, *ILOT*, 31; Weinfeld, *DDS*, 191n.

the Song of Moses (Deuteronomy 32) and is modeled upon the song at certain points. The expression "I shall hide my face from them" (31:17f), for example, derives directly from the striking words of the old song[27] "I shall hide my face from them/I shall see what their end will be" (32:20). The preceding line of the song states, "and Yhwh saw and spurned," an expression which likewise appears in the introduction, thus: ". . . and they caused me to spurn (or spurned me) . . ." (31:20). In the introduction, Yhwh declares that he will one day leave his people and hide his face from them.[28] This is not presented as a *threat* of Exile (which, as noted above, could be pre-Exilic composition) but as a revelation of an actual future event. It is the work of an Exilic hand.

Following these JE and Exilic units, the text returns to the matter of Moses' instructions regarding the *sēper hattôrâ* (vv 24-27). The writer explains in v 24 that what follows is the instruction which Moses had made at the time of his completion of the book. Some scholars have regarded this passage (vv 24-27) as a doublet of vv 9-13, but it is certainly not. Both the charge to read the Torah publicly and the charge to set the book beside the ark as a witness were integral to the Deuteronomistic (Dtr¹) interest, and each has a reflex in the Josiah narrative, as discussed above. The awkward double notice of Moses' completion of the book (31:9, 24) is an epanalepsis which meets a particular editorial need: on the one hand, the Song is cast as a *witness* against the people, and so it is inserted adjacent to the portion of the received text in which Moses speaks of the Torah itself as a witness; on the other hand, this arrangement now leaves Moses writing the Song into the scroll after he has already handed the scroll over to the Levites. The epanalepsis (v 24; "And it came to pass, *as Moses was finishing writing* the words of this Torah on a scroll to their conclusion"[29]) solves the editorial problem.

V 28 begins with Moses' instruction to the Levites to summon all the elders of the tribes. But, in the Dtr¹ account, all the elders of Israel are already standing in front of Moses. The theme of vv 28f. and its language further confirm that this is once again the hand of the second editor. The subject is once again the song which Yhwh has instructed Moses to teach the people. Moses now fulfills this instruction and presents the song as a witness against Israel. Again the tradent's choice

---

[27] On the date of the Song of Moses, long preceding Dtr¹ and Dtr², see G. E. Wright, "The Lawsuit of God: A Form-Critical Study of Deuteronomy 32," in *Israel's Prophetic Heritage*, B. Anderson and W. Harrelson, eds. (New York: Harper, 1962) 26-67; W. F. Albright, "Some Remarks on the Song of Moses in Deuteronomy XXXII," *VT* 9 (1959) 339-46; Cross, *CMHE*, 264n.

[28] On the phrase "I shall hide my face," see R. E. Friedman, "The Biblical Expression *mastîr pānîm*," *HAR* 1 (1977) 139-47.

[29] Cf. the reference to Moses' reciting the words of the Song "to their conclusion" (vs 30).

of wording is based on the words of the song. Moses announces that he
will call heaven and earth to witness (v 28). This of course corresponds
to the opening bicolon of the song, which does just that:

> Give ear, O heaven, and I shall speak,
> And hear, O earth, the words of my mouth.
>
> (32:1)

The causative *šḥt* (to corrupt) of 31:29 matches the *piel* form of that verb
in the song, 32:5. The reference to the end of days (*ʾaḥărît hayyāmîm*)
and the angering of Yhwh (31:29) probably relate to terms in the song as
well; cf. 32:16, 19, 20.

Driver observed this break between Deut 31:24-27 and 28-30 and also
ascribed them to separate authors[30] but failed to identify the latter as
more than an unknown redactor. Others[31] regarded the two passages as a
unity, thus forcing themselves to postulate emendations in the text to
resolve difficulties. The similarity of the thus-united passage to vv 16-22
led many commentators to replace the word *Torah* in v 24 with the word
song. Von Rad expressed confidence that the case was the reverse; the
word *song* in vv 16-22 was to be replaced with *Torah*.[32] Such emendations are utterly unnecessary in the light of the evidence for the work of
two editions here. In the case of this chapter, comparative thematic and
terminological evidence point together to the presence of two redactions
of the text, and the literary structure (narrative sequence, epanalepsis)
further confirms this analysis.

Following the introduction of the Song of Moses, the second editor
inserted the text of the song itself (Deut 32:1-43), the insertion being
marked by a single-verse resumption of the narrative (32:44; cf. 31:30).

Deut 4:25-31. The thematic grounds for regarding this passage as
Exilic are patent—apostasy leading to exile and national dispersal,
followed by repentance leading to restoration—as scholars have long
noted. A. Bertholet (1899) regarded vv 25-31 as an Exilic addition
and noted that vv 32ff. continue comfortably from vv 1-24.[32a] Even
N. Lohfink, who regards Deuteronomy 4 as a unity (wholly Exilic), notes
a thematic division of the chapter into units of vv 1-24, 25-31, and 32-40,
and he further notes the particular Exile/restoration orientation of the
second unit. He nonetheless associates this second unit with the one

---

[30]See above, n. 24.

[31]Nicholson, see above, n. 24.

[32]Von Rad, *Deuteronomy, A Commentary* (Philadelphia: Westminster,
1966) 190.

[32a]*Deuteronomium* (Leipzig: J. G. B. Mohr, 1899) 13-15.

which precedes it on the grounds that the second unit naturally continues the discussion of the prohibition of making a *pesel* (v 25), which
is the final concern of the first unit (v 23).[33] In response to Lohfink, one
must simply recognize the possibility that the Exilic Deuteronomist was
clever-enough an editor to think of associating his insertions with his
received text. As seen in the texts which we have examined thus far, this
Exilic tradent was expert at just this. In the present text, nothing of vv 1-
24 thematically demands an Exilic date. On the contrary, the prohibition
of the *pesel*, as noted above,[34] finds dramatization in the Manasseh/
Josiah pericopes. Vv 25-31, moreover, generates a significant thematic
interference with the units which precede and follow it. These units
emphasize the angry side of the character of Yhwh, characterizing him as
ʾēl qannāʾ ("jealous God"; v 24) and particularly emphasizing the
image of his consuming fire repeatedly (vv 11, 12, 15, 24, 33, 36 *bis*). But
in the midst of this fiery warning comes a promise that even in the event
of exile the people may seek Yhwh and find him, he will not destroy
them, he will not forget his covenant with them, because he is *ʾēl raḥûm*
(merciful God; v 31)! The text then reverts to fiery warning.

Converging with these thematic and structural observations, certain
matters of phraseology further indicate the Exilic character of vv 25-31.
Notably, the words "I call heaven and earth to witness against you"
(v 26) are a recurrence of the expression cited above as deriving from the
Song of Moses. Also recurring are the reference to the end of days and
the notion that troubles will "find" the people in the absence of the
protection of Yhwh (v 30), both of which occur in the Exilic portions of
Deuteronomy 31. The notion of Yhwh's scattering (*hēpîṣ*) the people
among the nations (v 27), as well occurs only in passages in the
Deuteronomistic history which, on other grounds as well, may be
identified as Exilic,[35] as we shall see.

Another indicator that this passage was addressed to an Exilic audience is its extreme similarity to the letter which Jeremiah sends to the
exiles in Babylon shortly before the fall of Jerusalem. Moses declares:

---

[33]Norbert Lohfink, "Auslegung deuteronomischer Texte, IV," *Bibel und
Leben* 5 (1964) 250-53. See also Levenson, "Who Inserted the Book of the
Torah?" 203-33.

[34]See above, p. 173.

[35]Levenson has identified phraseological parallels which, he suggests, argue
that the whole of Deuteronomy 4 is Exilic. See his "Who Inserted the Book of
the Torah?" 203-33; cf. my "The Impact of Exile upon the Character of Biblical
Narrative," (dss. Harvard, 1978) 32-35.

ובקשתם משם את ה' אלהיך ומצאת
כי תדרשנו בכל לבבך ובכל נפשך

And you will seek Yhwh your God from there and
you will find him, when you seek him out with all
your heart and all your soul.

(Deut 4:29)

Jeremiah writes:

ובקשתם אתי ומצאתם
כי תדרשני בכל לבבכם

And you will seek me and you will find me, when
you seek me out with all your heart.

(Jer 29:13)

On structural thematic, phraseological, and comparative grounds, therefore, Deut 4:25-31 must be regarded as an Exilic addition to a received
text.

Deut 29:21-27. Lohfink and Levenson have noted the Exilic character of this passage.[36] The syntactical indicator of the insertion is the
changeover of subject. From a threat concerning an individual man or
woman who might sin (29:17, 19) and the consequences for that individual (bā²îš hahû²), the text suddenly turns in v 21 to speaking as if the
subject had been the entire nation. The nation is pictured as having been
cast out of its land. As in the insertion into the Jerusalem revelation of
Solomon discussed above, the author here portrays some one as asking,
"Why has Yhwh done thus to this land?" (Deut 29:23 = 1 Kgs 9:8), to
which the response is:

> And they will say, "Because they left the covenant of
> Yhwh the God of their fathers which he made with them
> when he brought them out of the land of Egypt, and
> they went and served other gods and bowed to them . . ."
> (Deut 29:24, 25a)

> And they will say, "Because they left Yhwh their God
> who brought them out of the land of Egypt, and they
> took hold of other gods and bowed to them and served
> them . . ."
> (1 Kgs 9:9a)

Syntax, theme, and comparative evidence mutually suggest that the hand
of an exilic writer/editor was at work here.

[36]Lohfink, "Auslegung deuteronomischer Texte," 44-45; Levenson, "Who
Inserted the Book of the Torah?" 208.

Deut 30:1-10, 15-20. G. E. Wright has pointed out that, following the passage just discussed, the last verse of Deuteronomy 29 connects properly to vv 11-14 of Deuteronomy 30.[37] Thus united, the passage 29:29; 30:11-14 compares "the hidden things," which belong to Yhwh, to the commandment of Yhwh, which is "close to you, in your mouth and in your heart, to do it." The text which intersects the unity of this passage, Deut 30:1-10, is clearly from the same writer as the other Exilic additions identified thus far. Some affinities of this pericope to the Exilic portion of Deuteronomy 4 are present, leading H. W. Wolff and Levenson to speak in terms of a late bracketing of the original Deuteronomic corpus.[38] Terminologically, the expression of Yhwh's scattering (hēpîṣ) the people among the nations occurs in both of these pericopes. Thematically, as well, the words of Deut 30:1-10 look strikingly Exilic, addressing an exiled community, declaring that restoration is possible, referring to the mercy of Yhwh, pointing to the return to Yhwh which is necessary in order to bring about this reconciliation.

Following the passage which was noted above to be intersected by the Exilic 30:1-10, a second Exilic passage has been added in 30:15-20. Many scholars have regarded 30:1-20 as a unity, apparently without taking notice of the continuity of 29:29 to 30:11-14. The fact is that there is good evidence for identifying 1-10 and 15-20 with other Exilic passages, and little for 11-14. This fact is especially underlined by Lohfink's having had to look for such evidence in comparing the notion of the nearness of the commandment in 11:14 with the notion of the nearness of God in Exilic (sic!) Deut 4:7.[39] The comparison is weak; and in any event the view of this portion of Deuteronomy 4 as Exilic has been questioned above.

The wording of 30:15-20 is certainly consistent with other Exilic passages. The declaration "I call heaven and earth to witness against you" recurs (v 19), which certainly derives from the Exilic editor's presentation of the Song of Moses and occurs in Deut 4:26 as well. Also recalling 4:26 is the infinitival emphatic ᵓābōd tōᵓbēdûn of 30:18. The theme of the passage is the duration of the nation on the land and the threat of apostasy to that duration.

Thus theme and terminology join with syntax and literary structure in Deuteronomy 29 and 30 to point to the presence of two editorial layers.

Deut 28:36f. These two verses break context with the portions of the Deuteronomic curse list which surround them. In the midst of a group

---

[37]Wright, Deuteronomy, 507.

[38]Wolff, "Das Kerygma des deuteronomistischen Geschichtswerkes," ZAW 73 (1961) 182-83.

[39]Lohfink, "Auslegung deuteronomischer Texte," 42n.

of curses which relate to miseries of the body and of the land comes this
threat of exile for the people and their king among many nations. The
curses which follow, however, do not relate to exile at all, but rather
presume the presence of the people in the land. The intrusion of these
verses into the structure of the pericope, together with the exilic theme of
the intruding verses, suggests secondary Exilic addition.

Deut 28:63-68. At this juncture in the curse list of Deuteronomy
there appears an exception to the specific curses which have filled the
chapter. V 63 is rather a terrifying dramatization of the attitude of Yhwh
toward the people if they will break his covenant.

> And it will be that, as Yhwh rejoiced over you to do you good and to
> multiply you, so will Yhwh rejoice over you to destroy you and annihilate
> you.

What follows is a threat of eviction from the land and scattering of the
people among the nations. This is the third encounter with the phrase
"scatter (hēpîṣ) among the nations," and this exhausts their appearances
in the Deuteronomistic history. As for the rejoicing of Yhwh, first to do
good and then to do harm, the hope which is offered in the Exilic
passage Deut 30:1-10 includes the turnaround: "Yhwh will turn back to
rejoice over you for good as he rejoiced over your fathers." This
particular parallel must be regarded cautiously, for the 30:1-10 passage
also turns around some of the older curses of Deuteronomy 28. Still, this
particular expression occurs only in these two places and in the prison
speech of Jeremiah, which is dated in the text to within a year of the fall
of Jerusalem (Jer 32:41). While a threat of exile does not necessarily
mark a passage as Exilic,[40] the combination of the theme of exile
intimidation, the phraseological associations, and the juncture at v 63
suggests again an Exilic updating of a received text.

The last curse of the list is the ultimate threat in the story of the
people of Israel, namely that Yhwh will cause them to return to Egypt.
This extraordinary statement of a return to the *status quo* which existed
prior to Israel's meeting with Yhwh and formation as an independent
people concludes with the horror: "and you will sell yourselves there to
your enemies as slaves, and no one will buy" (v 68). The implications of
this curse, which has never been properly weighed and reckoned with,
will be discussed at length below.

Deut 8:19f. The text of Deut 8:1-18 forewarns the people that when
prosperity prevails in their new land they are not to attribute their
wellbeing to their own powers. They must remember the power of Yhwh

---

[40]See above, n. 23.

which brought them out of Egypt and maintained them in the wilderness; this is the power which provides plenty for the land. Deuteronomy 9 similarly forewarns the people not to attribute the coming conquest of the land to their own merit. The short passage which intervenes between these related pericopes is a two-verse threat concerning apostasy. The consequence is destruction. The language is familiar. The expressions "I [call heaven and earth to] witness against you" and $^{\jmath}\bar{a}b\bar{o}d$ $t\bar{o}^{\jmath}b\bar{e}d\hat{u}n$ recur, and this exhausts their appearances. Structure, theme, and phraseology converge here to identify this two-verse passage as secondary.

In addition to these evidences that the individual passages discussed above are editorially secondary in their respective contexts, one should note their thematic consistency as a group. The theme of apostasy occurs in every passage. The consequence is consistently destruction, exile, dispersal. Emphasis on eternal witness of these things frequently recurs. The unity of outlook of the group of passages is patent.

One should note the *locations* of the passages as well. All occur at structurally significant junctures in the Deuteronomistic history: (1) at the beginning of the work, among the opening remarks of Moses' final address (Deut 4:25-31; 8:19f); (2) in the Deuteronomic curse list, particularly the last curses of the list (28:36f., 63-68); (3) among Moses' closing words to the people before their entry into the land (29:21; 30:1-10, 15-20; 31:28-30); (4) in Yhwh's last words to Moses before summoning him to his death (31:16-22); (5) following the dedication of the Temple, on the last occasion in the Deuteronomistic history on which Yhwh is said to have appeared to a human (1 Kings 9:6-9); (6) in the Manasseh pericope (2 Kings 21:8-15); (7) at the conclusion of the work (2 Kings 23:26-25:26). This is no randomly situated collection of passages. Rather, these passages, which on thematic, syntactical, grammatical, structural, phraseological, and comparative grounds suggest a second redaction of a received text, are distributed through the Deuteronomistic history at precisely the points where they would have the strongest impact on the work's depiction of Israel's history, from entry into the land to exile from it.

The cumulative effect of all of the above data is, I believe, a compelling case for seeing the literary history of the Deuteronomistic history as comprising two editions, the first Josianic (Dtr[1]), the second Exilic (Dtr[2]).

Now let us consider how the Exilic redactor was able to remodel the Josianic edition of the Deuteronomistic history so successfully. First, of course, he retained the marked style of the received edition, as observed above, drawing on a body of terms and phrases which were hallmarks of the parent work. So much do the new and received editions share in style and vocabulary that it is not really proper to speak of Dtr[2] as *imitating* the style of Dtr[1] so much as *continuing* it; i.e. the two perhaps derive from a single school, perhaps from a single family. Indeed, there is no reason why the two editions could not be the work of a single literary figure, an individual who updated his own work some thirty to forty years after the original.

One must also note that, beyond the continuity of style and language, a continuity of ideas informs the two stages of redaction. The differences of concern between the two are not conceptual, but historical. The passages attributed to Dtr[2] above do not develop a new theology, they do not revamp the principles of structure of the Mosaic covenant—or even refer to the Davidic covenant—they do not include any premise which constitutes a radical break with the fundamental views of God and the people of Israel in Dtr.[1] The creation of Dtr[2] was rather a response to a new historical circumstance. The literary-theological enterprise of the writer/editor of Dtr[2] was to integrate that new circumstance into the old work, i.e. to deal with the catastrophe of 587 within the terms of the received document.

A case in point is the Dtr[2] focus upon Manasseh as the primary precipitator of the nation's downfall. The exceptional record of transgression in the reign of Manasseh was already developed in the received edition (Dtr[1]). The Exilic writer's task required only a six-verse insertion in the Manasseh pericope, elaborating upon the crimes of that reign and upon their impending consequence (2 Kgs 21:8-15), plus a two-verse notation, following the Josiah pericope, that the Josianic reform was not sufficient to prevent that consequence (2 Kgs 23:26f.). He did not choose to develop a wholly new treatment, tracing the destruction and exile to the sins of any or all of the last four kings. Rather, as Cross observed, the Exilic figure's additions to the received text were quite limited, only a few brief units, associated in language and theme with the contexts into which their author set them. Thus the Exilic figure drew his explanation of the catastrophe from material already present in the Josianic edition, viz. the Manasseh indictment.

His consistent development of apostasy as the crime which brought about the national disaster was of course no innovation either. The exclusive worship of Yhwh was already fully developed in Dtr[1], emphasized in every book of the work. Worship of *ʾĕlōhîm ʾăḥērîm*, whether as alternative or as supplemental to the service of Yhwh, is regularly and forcefully forbidden in Dtr[1], as opposed to, for example, the Pentateuchal source P in which, for whatever reason, the phrase *ʾĕlōhîm ʾăḥērîm* never occurs.[41] Thus Dtr[1] provided the crime and the perpetrator for Dtr[2] treatment of the destruction and exile.

---

[41]Its appearance in the Decalogue (Exod 20:3) is common to the P and D versions and is the "*Grundsatzerklärung*" of the covenant formula. See K. Baltzer,

Another Dtr[1] element which the Exilic writer/editor preserved in the service of the Exilic edition of the work was testimony of things to come. Von Rad has observed the frequency of specific prophecy/fulfillment notices in the history.[42] The composer of Dtr[1] was careful to demonstrate that the word of Yhwh does not fail to realize. This was crucial to the climax of the first edition of the work, because the issue was the words of Moses' book. Moses instructs the Levites to set the book beside the ark, ". . . and it will be there as a witness against you" (Deut 31:26). In Dtr[1], written witness has been present during the entire course of the national history. Dtr[2] continues to develop the Dtr[1] concern that a properly witnessed warning has been given to Israel. The author of the Exilic version, however, chose new witnesses. The problem for the composer of Dtr[2] was that its interests were not confined to the past but rather looked forward to restoration as well. The book's being *"there* as a witness" was less than inspiring after 587, when *there* no longer existed. The Exilic additions to Deuteronomy therefore repeatedly summon heaven and earth, eternal witnesses, to testify. The Song of Moses thus provided Dtr[2] with an old revered foundation for any future promises. The Exilic Deuteronomist inserted the Song, together with his prose portrayals of Moses' summoning heaven and earth as witnesses, into the received text in the midst of the Dtr[1] portrayal of Moses' handing the book of the Torah to the Levites to be kept as witness. Again we have a view of the Exilic Deuteronomist's redactional technique, trying as much as possible to align his own additions with concerns in his received text.

His most difficult obstacle in this respect was the Dtr[1] depiction of the Davidic covenant. Here, as nowhere else in the received text, theology took a slap in the face from history. The eternal promises of Davidic sovereignty over Jerusalem/Judah and sanctity of Solomon's Temple left little room for explaining 587. As we have already seen, the Exilic Deuteronomist's *modus operandi* was to elaborate upon, not eliminate portions of, the received text. His first step, therefore, was to focus above all on the people and not on the kings. The Exilic additions to the book of Deuteronomy have little to say of the monarch. The one reference seems to include the king only in passing, while the statement itself, threatening the curse of exile, is directed to the people (Deut 28:36f.). All responsibility is placed upon the people in every Exilic passage. In the latter books, the Dtr[1] monarchical focus is deliberately redirected into a concern for the course of the nation. The Exilic addition of 1 Kgs 9:6-9 blatantly turns a specifically dynastic revelation to Solomon into a threatening warning to the people to keep the commandments. The

---

The Covenant Formulary (Philadelphia: Fortress, 1971) 12-13, 21-22. It is thus part of the received text and not the work of the author(s) of P.

[42]N. 18 above.

Exilic prediction of the fall of Judah, set in the midst of the Dtr[1] reckoning of the crimes of Manasseh, places responsibility completely on the people, so that Manasseh is blamed primarily as a catalyst. The *issue*, in Dtr[2], is much older than Manasseh. The nation is to suffer "because they did evil in my eyes and have been angering me from the day that their fathers went out of Egypt until this day," (2 Kgs 21:15). Only in two Exilic notices which follow the death of Josiah (23:26; 24:3f.) are the provocations of Manasseh himself an issue, but this is possible only because the Exilic Deuteronomist has already remodeled the Manasseh pericope as described. The whole of the post-Josiah record has little to say about the kings; as noted above, the kings are treated succinctly and nearly identically.

This concern for the people more than for the rulers is apparent in the treatment of the covenants as well. It is in the Exile that the tension between the national (Mosaic) covenant and the monarchic (Davidic) covenant becomes critical.[43] For the Exilic treatment, nonetheless, it becomes as if there were no dilemma at all. The Davidic promise is not mentioned, no theological justification of the abandonment of the commitment is attempted. Dtr[2] simply pulls the carpet out from under the feet of the Davidids. The last Davidic kings suffer the fate of their nation. From one point of view we may say that the Davidic covenant promise of eternal sovereignty became meaningless with no nation over which to be sovereign. To be more accurate politically though, we should take note that in the Dtr[2] edition of the work the notion of the king as *maḥăṭîʾ*, i.e. as a force who can cause the people to break the *national* covenant, is consciously developed. This notion links the two covenants organically and thus provides the catch through which the Davidic ideology could be short-circuited. The notion of king as *maḥăṭîʾ* was already developed in Dtr[1] (1 Kgs 14:16; 15:26, 34; 16:26; 22:53; 2 Kgs 17:21). The Exilic Deuteronomist then twice characterized Manasseh in this way (2 Kgs 21:9, 11) and added to the Deuteronomic curse list the inclusive: "Yhwh will send you *and your king which you will set over you* to a nation which you have not known . . ." (Deut 28:36). Dtr[2] is concerned with the covenant of Yhwh and Israel. The only indication of a concern with the future of the royal line lies in the final four verses of the work, noting the release of Jehoiachin from prison and maintenance in Babylon. This is, as Cross has observed, "a thin thread upon which to hang the expectation of the fulfillment of the promises to David."[44] These last verses in fact may not even be from the hand which produced the Dtr[2] edition, as will be discussed presently.

[43]See Levenson, "Who Inserted the Book of the Torah?" 203-33; Tsevat, "Studies in the Book of Samuel, III," 73.

[44]*CMHE*, 277.

The re-editing of the work was above all designed to deal with the circumstance in which the people found itself, namely Exile. Almost all of Biblical scholarship relating to the Exile has focused on the portion of the community which was deported to Babylon. This is unfortunate, especially in the light of Scriptural notations that only a very small fraction of the people was taken in the Babylonian deportations.[45] As noted above, Dtr² additions to Deuteronomy refer to the scattering (hēpîṣ) of the people. The number of refugees to neighboring countries is unkown. The number of those who remained in Judah under the authority of the Babylonian appointee Gedaliah is unknown. Whatever the actual historical situation, however, there can be no doubt of the Exilic Deuteronomist's intended portrayal of the fate of the people. The final sentence of the story of the people states:

> And all the people, young and old, and the officers of the soldiers arose and came to Egypt, for they feared the Babylonians.
>
> (2 Kgs 25:26)

This statement of the flight of the remnant of Israel to Egypt is an abbreviated version of the account in Jer 43:4-7.

> But Johanan ben Kareah and all the officers of the soldiers and all the people did not listen to the voice of Yhwh to live in the land of Judah. And Johanan ben Kareah and all the officers of the soldiers took all of the remnant of Judah which had returned from all the nations to which they had been driven to dwell in the land of Judah, the men and the women and the children and the daughters of the king and all the souls which Nebuzaradan, captain of the guard, had left with Gedaliah ben Ahikam ben Shaphan, and Jeremiah the prophet and Baruch ben Neriah. And they came to the land of Egypt, for they did not listen to the voice of Yhwh, and they came to Tahpanhes.

So simply does the Deuteronomist report the extraordinary fate of the people that it simply has never been properly reckoned with in modern scholarship. The nation which was born in redemption from Egypt, and which was forbidden by Torah (Deut 17:16) and prophet (Jeremiah 42) to return there, now seeks its security there. Now the horror of the final curse of Deuteronomy 28 can be understood:

---

[45] 4,600 by the reckoning of Jer 52:28ff.; approximately 11,600 in the light of 2 Kgs 24:14. See W. F. Albright, *The Biblical Period from Abraham to Ezra* (New York: Harper, 1963) 85; John Bright, *A History of Israel* (Philadelphia: Westminster Press, 1952) 2d edition, 345; A. Malamat, "The Twilight of Judah: In the Egyptian-Babylonian Maelstrom," *VTSup* 28 (1974) 133-34.

> And Yhwh will cause you to return to Egypt in boats, in the way
> concerning which I said to you, "you will never see it again," and you will
> sell yourselves there to your enemies as slaves, and none will buy.
>
> (v 68)

The meaning of the reference to boats is an enigma. It may be an *alef/ayin* scribal error for ᶜ*nywt* (afflictions), though the form is unattested. It may be a plural form of the rare ᵓ*ăniyāh* (mourning; cf. Isa 29:2; Lam 2:5). It may refer to some historical circumstance. In any case, the concern with Egypt which becomes critical in the second edition of the Deuteronomistic history is another example of the way in which the concerns of the Josianic edition served the latter version. Egypt is a regular and fundamental interest of Dtr[1]. Beside the fact that Egypt is regularly a political and military issue through the course of history, the experience of Egyptian bondage and Exodus are ever a temporal and thematic focus of the historian and of his sources. The Exodus from Egypt is the premise of the Decalogue (Deut 5:6), the only historical datum of the historical prologue.[46] The covenant itself is associated with the Exodus (1 Kgs 8:9, 21; cf. Deut 4:20). The most blatant difference between the Decalogue as it appears in Deuteronomy and its counterpart in the Priestly work is that the Deuteronomic Sabbath command bases the observance of the Sabbath not on the seven-day creation, as in the Priestly work, but on the memory of slavery in Egypt (Deut 5:15; cf. Exod 20:11). Numerous other laws are followed by this same formula: "And you will remember that you were a slave in Egypt, therefore I command you to do this thing," (Deut 16:12; 24:18, 22);[47] and in the famous passage which has appropriately become a part of the Jewish Passover *seder*, Deut 6:20-25, the entire body of law is predicated upon Yhwh's having brought Israel out of Egyptian slavery. Passover is of course the key celebration of the Josianic reform as well (2 Kgs 23:21-23). The memory of Yhwh's power against Egypt is posited as a source of confidence in future battles (Deut 1:29f.; 7:18; 20:1). The law of the king forbids the monarch to bring the people back to Egypt "for Yhwh has said to you 'you will not ever go back this way again' " (17:16). The historical creeds of Deut 26:5-9 and Josh 24:2-13 which, together with that of Deut 6:20-25 (mentioned above), were regarded by von Rad as

[46]Baltzer has particularly stressed the role of the historical prologue as the grounds on which the covenant relations are built in the Hittite covenant models (though absent in the later Assyrian type). Personal communication. See his study of Near Eastern and Biblical covenant, *The Covenant Formulary*, and G. E. Mendenhall, *Law and Covenant in Israel and the Ancient Near East* (Pittsburgh: The Biblical Colloquium, 1955).

[47]See also 16:1-3.

central to understanding Israel's *Heilsgeschichte* both set Egyptian bondage and Exodus at the heart of Israel's birth.[48] Both versions of the story
of Samuel's installation of Saul set the institution of the monarchy in
the light of the salvation from Egypt. The building of the Temple is
twice discussed in reference to Yhwh's not having required a house since
the day he brought Israel out of Egypt (2 Sam 7:6; 1 Kgs 8:16), and the
dedication of the Temple is dated to the year of the Exodus (1 Kgs 6:1).
Jeroboam is bound to identify his new cult with the "God(s) who
brought you up out of the land of Egypt," (1 Kgs 12:28). Even more
telling are the numerous references to Egypt and the Exodus which are
gratuitous to their immediate contexts (Deut 4:45f.; 6:12; 8:14; 9:12; 13:6,
11; 23:5; 24:9; 25:17; Judg 2:12; 19:30; 2 Sam 7:23; 1 Kgs 8:51; 2 Kgs 17:7).

Egypt is plainly fundamental to the perspective of Dtr[1]; and so, in
the full Dtr[2] edition, Egypt becomes a constant and ominous presence,
the setting of the last and worst of the Deuteronomistic curses. When
that curse realizes in the final verses of the Deuteronomistic history—
suddenly, and without referring back to Deuteronomy 28 blatantly—it is
as powerful and ironic an ending as in any book of the Bible. It accounts
for the lack of a peroration on the fall of Judah which concerned Cross,
for this is at least as powerful a conclusion. It raises the possibility that
Dtr[2] is even a product of the Egyptian community, a possibility which is
enhanced by the extreme similarity of style and interest between the
Deuteronomistic history and the book of Jeremiah,[49] summoning to
mind the Rabbinic claim of Jeremiah's authorship of the books of
Kings.[50] It further raises the likelihood that the last four verses of the
history (2 Kgs 25:27-30), referring to the release of Jehoiachin, are not the
work of the author of Dtr[2], but are possibly the addition of a member of
the Babylonian community. Whatever the situation with regard to
authorship, the Deuteronomistic history, in its final form, tells the story
of Israel from Egypt to Egypt.[51] It is the story of the failure of the
covenant relations of Yhwh and his people. The words of the old Song
of Moses, "I shall hide my face from them, I shall see what their end will
be," repeated and emphasized by the Exilic Deuteronomist (Deut 31:17f.)
in the mouth of Moses, now impose a direction upon the earlier edition
of the history which points to Yhwh's ultimate abandonment of his
people.

[48]Von Rad, "The Form-Critical Problem of the Hexateuch," in *The Problem
of the Hexateuch*, 3-8.

[49]See above, n. 4.

[50]B., *B. Bat.* 15a.

[51]Jer 44:1 identifies the places of settlement in Egypt as Tahpanhes, Noph,
and the region of Pathros, all of which lay in the general area of the land of
Goshen.

And my anger will burn at them in that day, and I shall leave them, and I shall hide my face from them, and they will be consumed, and many evils and troubles will find them, and they will say in that day, "Is it not because our God is not in our midst that these troubles have found us?"

The predictions of Deuteronomy match the events of 2 Kings and so produce the image of a unified work, this image being enhanced by the very few, but artful, insertions in the body of the history. Dtr^2 thus over-encloses the inclusion of Dtr^1, and a story of rebuilding and reform is revamped into an account of a people whose God abandons them to disaster because of their breaking covenant, leaving them now back where they started, to repent and hope for restoration. There is hardly a more awesome depiction of Yhwh's power in Biblical narrative.

Reporting Speech in the Book of Deuteronomy: Toward a Compositional Analysis of the Deuteronomic History

CARLETON UNIVERSITY

THE DEUTERONOMIC HISTORY

THAT corpus of the Hebrew Bible that stretches from the Book of Deuteronomy through 2 Kings is called the Deuteronomic History. It consists of seven books: Deuteronomy, Joshua, Judges, 1-2 Samuel, and 1-2 Kings. The analysis that follows concerning the reporting speech of the Book of Deuteronomy will attempt to uncover the various points of view that make up its compositional structure. The term, "composition," therefore has to do with the relationships of various points of view, on a number of levels, that make up a literary work. I will assume from the start that the Deuteronomic History is a unified literary work; I do not base this assumption upon previous historical critical analyses. By the term "Deuteronomist" I mean that person or persons, functioning in an authorial or editorial role, and responsible for the final form of the Deuteronomic History. There may actually have been no single individual or recognizable group to whom this term refers. I use it heuristically to designate that imagined personification of a combination of literary features that seem to constitute the literary composition of the Deuteronomic History. For me, the text creates the Deuteronomist's features as much as it creates those of Moses. The Deuteronomist is the "implied author" of this work.[1]

One way to get at a useful framework within the text is to attend to the various shifts that occur within the text and within the various levels of the text. These shifts often indicate the implied author's devices for framing his work and, once identified, can help us understand how he may be said to manipulate and program his readers' responses. The various points of view realized in the text are represented there in a

---

*It is with pleasure and gratitude that I dedicate this article to Frank M. Cross.

[1] I understand "implied author" in a somewhat different way than Wayne Booth does in *The Rhetoric of Fiction* (Chicago: University of Chicago, 1961).

number of ways that are interrelated, and an attempt to articulate a framework is the first step in analyzing what a text or its author seems to be saying. Much of what is written, its "author" does not subscribe to. He may, for example, be offering up a position to ridicule. A framework helps us articulate what an author's stated position is, as distinct from statements he transmits for various other reasons.[2]

If we begin with V. N. Voloshinov's demonstration of the crucial importance of "reported speech" in language analysis,[3] we are immediately able to segment the Deuteronomic History into two basic units which, although not quantitatively balanced, are amazingly complementary from a compositional point of view. It has long been emphasized that basic to the viewpoint of the Deuteronomist is "that system of prophetic prediction and its exactly observed fulfilment which pervades the whole work of this writer."[4] If we apply this obvious aspect of the Deuteronomist's position to his work *in toto*, we see that a compositional device occurring innumerable times within it—that is, first the word of God is reported by a prophet, then a description of events follows with the explicit statement that these events happened "according to the word of God" (or a statement similar in meaning)—appears to be operating in the relationship between the two largest segments of the work. The first segmentation of the Deuteronomic History results in separating the Book of Deuteronomy from Joshua-2 Kings. We thereby see that Deuteronomy, in that it is almost totally a number of Mosaic speeches, functions as an expression of the prophetic word of God, and that Joshua-2 Kings mainly recounts events that constitute "its exactly observed fulfilment."

The balanced nature of this first division is seen when one applies Voloshinov's distinction between reporting and reported speech to the two basic sections of the Deuteronomic History. The Book of Deuteronomy contains thirty-four chapters. Almost all of the book consists of reported speech, mostly in direct discourse and mostly of Moses, whereas only about fifty-six verses are reporting speech, the Deuteronomic narrator's, which forms the context for Moses' direct utterances. On the other hand, Joshua-2 Kings is predominantly reporting speech, that of the narrator, with a significantly smaller amount of reported speech scattered throughout. (Here, however, the disproportion between reporting and reported speech is not so great as in Deuteronomy.) In Deuteronomy, reported speech of its hero is emphasized; in Joshua-2 Kings, the

[2]My goal, therefore, is to begin the task of literary interpretation programmatically outlined by B. Uspensky in *A Poetics of Composition* (Berkeley: University of California, 1973).

[3]*Marxism and the Philosophy of Language* (New York: Seminar, 1953).

[4]G. von Rad, *The Problem of the Hexateuch and Other Essays* (New York: McGraw-Hill, 1966) 208-9.

reporting speech of its narrator is dominant. It is as though the Deuter-onomist is telling us in Deuteronomy, "Here is what God has prophe-sied concerning Israel," but in Joshua-2 Kings "This is how God's word has been exactly fulfilled in Israel's history from the settlement to the destruction of Jerusalem and the Exile."

Another significant aspect of the relationship between Deuteronomy on one hand and Joshua-2 Kings on the other is seen in the internal arrangement of reporting and reported speech within each of the two segments themselves. In Joshua-2 Kings it is not enough to chronicle Israel's continual disobedience and the countless disastrous events that resulted from such disobedience. As von Rad has detailed for us with regard to 1-2 Kings,[5] the narrative systematically singles out the reported speech of prophets who periodically arise to announce to various indi-viduals the punishing word of God. Thus, for example, intermittent recurring reported prophetic speech interrupts the narrative at least eleven times in 1-2 Kings, apparently to reinforce what appears to be the general point of view of Joshua-2 Kings taken as a whole: how Israel's history is dependent upon the word of God that is the Book of Deuter-onomy. In Joshua-2 Kings, the reporting narrator is intermittently supported in his basic story of Israel's history by the occasional reported words of various prophets. The preponderant reporting narrative of the narrator and the intermittent reported speech of a number of prophets within the narrative help to articulate the same evaluative point of view.

When we look at the Book of Deuteronomy, the relationship between the reporting narration and reported prophetic speech is reversed. Re-ported prophetic speech absolutely predominates, with reporting nar-ration at a minimum and on occasion a confusing interruption. We will discuss this last point in the third section of this paper, but for now it is enough to underline how the respective roles of narrator's word and prophetic word in Deuteronomy form a mirror image of their roles in Joshua-2 Kings. In Deuteronomy the unobtrusive reporting speech of the retiring narrator reinforces and supports here and there the prepon-derant reported speech of the greatest prophet of them all, Moses. In Joshua-2 Kings, lesser prophets occasionally appear to reinforce by their reported speech the now preponderant and highly visible reporting speech of the narrator.

If we first divide up the Deuteronomic History into Deuteronomy on one hand and Joshua-2 Kings on the other, the concept of reported speech, primarily in the form of direct discourse, allows us to see that in the first section, according to quantity and distribution, Moses' words are to the narrator's words as, in the second section, the narrator's words

[5]*The Problem*, 205-21.

are to the words of a number of lesser prophets. The significance of this first compositional relationship is great.

The distribution of reported speech and its reporting context has helped form a preliminary criterion that allowed us both to segment the text into its two largest main sections and to discover a couple of complementary relationships between these sections. This criterion can now be used to help us articulate a central problem confronting any attempt at a literary interpretation of the Deuteronomic History: *wherein does the ultimate semantic authority of this complex lie*? By the phrase, "ultimate semantic authority," we mean the basic ideological and evaluative point of view of a work,[6] the unifying ideological stance of a work's "implied author." Do we find it in the speech of the narrator, forming the slight frame of the Book of Deuteronomy and the main body of Joshua-2 Kings, or is it present in the reported speech both of Moses, forming the bulk of Deuteronomy, and of other mouth-pieces of God scattered throughout the rest of the history?

Another way to express the problem is this: there are two kinds of speech in the Deuteronomic History, the word of the narrator and the reported words of those individuals who form part of his story. What is immediately obvious from even a superficial reading of the text (and to be expected) is that among the figures in the story preeminent place is given to the figure of God himself, and that the preeminent speech the Deuteronomic narrator reports is speech purported to be from God himself. Therefore, is the implied author's stance to be found in the words of the narrator or in the words of God found in the narrative? Or, as a third possibility, is it found somehow synthesized both in the narration that quantitatively predominates and in the quoted words of God that are quantitatively much less dominant in the Deuteronomic History?

All three of the possibilities just mentioned assume that the Deuteronomic History is indeed a *monologue*, that is, its ideological evaluation is carried out from a single dominating point of view which subordinates all others in the work. The Deuteronomic History, viewed as the juxtaposition of two principal utterances, that of its narrator and that of God, is constructed as an utterance within an utterance: the reported word of God is found within the reporting word of the narrator. Stated in these terms, the ideological composition of this work appears to be overtly monologic, since the immediate obvious message of the narrator is, "God has said 'such and such' to Israel, and the events of Israel's history have happened in the way I am now describing them: as a fulfilment of God's word." This is the narrator's obvious conclusion

---

[6]Cf. M. Bakhtin, *Problems of Dostoevsky's Poetics* (Ann Arbor: Ardis, 1973).

about the history of Israel. He says to the reader, "In terms of what God and myself say, 'I and the Father are one.'"

Bakhtin summarizes the characteristics of a novel that is basically monological in structure; his words are equally valid for a work such as the Deuteronomic History:

> How and in what elements of the verbal whole is the author's ultimate semantic authority realized? For the monologic novel this question is very easily answered. Whatever types of word the novelist-monologist may introduce and whatever their compositional distribution may be, the author's interpretations and evaluations must dominate all others and must comprise a compact and unambiguous whole.[7]

Viewed from this perspective, the central authority figure of the history is God and, consequently, the prophets of God within the narrative who are described as reporting His words. In addition, since the history purports to show how this divine speech has been verified in history, we may say that the narrator's general position may be understood as one that is in agreement with the ideological positions of the central authority figures of his story. It is apparent therefore that if the Deuteronomic History is viewed as the intersection of two words, God's and the narrator's, the overall picture presented therein is one in which, concerning the ideological plane, the narrator's word is presented as subordinate to God's word which the narrator reports. The Deuteronomic History is not the intersection of two equally weighted words, but the conjoining of God's word to the narrator's word in a dominant to subordinate relationship respectively.

When we inquire further into the overtly monologic structure of the history on the plane of ideology, we find that the question is not quite so simply answered. For even if we can say that the narrator clearly intends to subordinate his position to the word of God which he reports to us, we still must inquire what precisely does God say within the work, and how precisely is His word said to be fulfilled in it? For clearly even a

[7]Ibid., 168. For those who question the validity of putting the genres of novel and history together in the same semantic boat in regard to the concept of monologic/dialogic structure, it should be noted here that, apart from the ambiguities of calling the Deuteronomic History "history," this study proceeds in wholehearted agreement with the views of Hayden White (*Metahistory* [Baltimore and London: Hopkins, 1973]) and Roland Barthes ("Historical Discourse" in *Structuralism: A Reader*, Michael Lane, ed. [London, 1970] 145-55) on the nature of historical discourse and its relation to literary interpretation. Both authors underline, from different perspectives, the similarities between the interpretive elements and imaginative constructions found in historiographic works and those found in other genres such as the novel.

monologue may contain a variety of ideas and viewpoints that may or may not compete with one another with equal weight or authority. This raises the question of whether the history, as an overt monologue in which the Deuteronomist has subordinated his narrator's voice to God's voice as its echo, actually may contain a *hidden dialogue* within the word of God itself and/or within the "subordinate" word of the narrator. There is not just one utterance of God but a number of them reported to have been said by God throughout the historical period covered by the narrative. There is not just one utterance of the narrator interpreting God's word, but a number of them.[8]

Therefore the possibility exists that, whatever may be the obvious monologic composition of the Deuteronomic History taken as a unity, a closer reading of the text may reveal a hidden dialogue between competing voices within the various utterances of God both in themselves and as interpreted by the Deuteronomic narrator. Bakhtin describes theoretically what would be the case if a work were indeed a true dialogue:

> The weakening or destruction of the monological context occurs only when two equally and directly object-oriented utterances come together. Two equally and directly object-oriented words within a single context cannot stand side by side without dialogically intersecting, regardless of whether they corroborate one another or on the contrary contradict one another, or have any other sort of dialogical relationship (the relationship of question and answer, for example). Two equal-weighted words which speak to the same subject, once they have come together, must become oriented one to the other. Two embodied thoughts cannot lie side by side like two objects—they must come into inner contact, i.e., must enter into a semantic bond.[9]

An attempt to answer such a basic question as whether we have in the history a monologue or a dialogue, in the sense employed by Bakhtin, ought not, at first, to be based upon the historical-critical approaches of modern biblical scholarship. From a methodological point of view, historical criticism is ill-suited for beginning attempts at understanding the important questions that an interpretation of the Deuteronomic History involves, however necessary such approaches are for an adequate understanding. Therefore, the present study begins at a point that is operationally prior to the kinds of historical critical stances

---

[8]Indeed, the basic issues that I am raising here have been set out by Wayne Booth in *The Rhetoric of Fiction*. Booth's discussion, in the manner with which he exemplifies his conclusions with countless examples from modern western literature, complements the more methodologically oriented analyses of Bakhtin more than thirty years earlier.

[9]Bakhtin, *Problems*, 156.

that up to now have divided biblical scholars on the structure of the Deuteronomic History, e.g., the question of the existence and description of at least two editions of this work. For, whatever might be the Deuteronomic History's genesis, what we are now asking is where does a close compositional reading of this work place it within the dynamic poles of a dialogue on one hand and a monologue on the other? Whatever the answer may turn out to be, no help is at this preliminary point relevant, since both a predominantly dialogic and a predominantly monologic ideology could conceivably be the final result of either one or more editions of the Deuteronomic History. At the same time, I fully recognize that historical-critical analyses are methodologically useful, indeed necessary to refine further and even, in some cases, to alter preliminary approximations of a dialogic or monologic composition of our text.

It does seem clear that even with regard to the overtly monologic nature of the Deuteronomic History, it would be too simplistic to say that the ultimate semantic authority is to be found solely in the words of God reported in the history, or solely in the words of the narrator that form the controlling narrative. For clearly, even though the narrator assumes that his words are subordinate to God's words, by the very fact that he "takes over" what God has said and uses it for his own purposes, to this extent he is subordinating God's words to his own. Therefore, it seems that we would be more faithful to an intuitive first impression of the work to assume that ultimate semantic authority, be it predominantly monologic or dialogic, will be found somehow synthesized in the narration that quantitatively predominates, but by authorial plan is subordinate, and in the quoted words of God that are quantitatively subordinate, but by authorial plan dominant.

Another way of describing the position just stated would be to say the following: the ultimate semantic authority of a work, the implied author's "intention,"[10] a text's basic ideological perspective, can be realized not only by a narrator's direct word, but as Bakhtin puts it, ". . . with the help of the words of others, created and distributed in a specific way as belonging to others."[11] Moreover, if it is possible to find the author's voice in the words of others, conversely, it is also possible to find in the author's words, or in those of his narrator, reflections of points of view that are subordinate or even contrary to his basic ideological position. In other words, the specific composition of a work on the ideological plane is not always concurrent with its composition

[10]Confer on this point Bakhtin (*Problems*, 160-61) and Uspensky (*A Poetics*, 8-16). I should point out here that when I write of the implied author's *intention*, I use this term in its phenomenological sense. The intentionality of the text is as much my own reconstruction as the implied author of a text is.

[11]*Problems*, 155.

on less basic levels such as the phraseological level of reporting/reported speech.

The above point is especially relevant to our discussion of the compositional structure of the Deuteronomic History in general and of its two basic sequential sections in particular.[12] An adequate explanation of the Deuteronomic History's framework must begin to delineate which of its utterances are single-voiced and which are double-voiced, on a number of compositional planes. Moreover, on the basic plane of a work's ideology, a proposed framework ought to be able to describe which of the text's utterances or words express its dominant ideological voice(s), which its subordinated or dependent ideological voice or voices, and which utterances express both kinds of voices. Furthermore, the framework constructed ought to illuminate the various relationships between competing voices of whatever level in the text, and between various levels themselves, that is, the concurrence or not of the compositional structure of different planes.

The basic requirements of an adequately constructed framework are further complicated by the object we are investigating. The Deuteronomic History is an especially complex arrangement of messages within a message, so that it would be especially helpful to construct a satisfactory description of how its internal messages interrelate to form that message we call the Deuteronomic History.

MOSES AND THE DEUTERONOMIC NARRATOR AS HERO AND "AUTHOR" OF THE BOOK OF DEUTERONOMY

1.   Concerning the attribution of utterances in Deuteronomy, most of the book is a series of direct quotations of Moses. Within this body of Mosaic utterances, in one instance, 27:1-8, Moses and the elders of Israel speak as one in direct discourse, and in another instance in the same chapter, 27:9-10, Moses and the Levitical priests are quoted in direct discourse. In all other cases in the reporting of Moses' words, Moses speaks alone. In addition, the Deuteronomic narrator, like Moses, is able to quote God in direct discourse: five times toward the end of the book, 31:14b; 31:16b-21; 31:23b; 32:49-52; and 34:4b.

The book is more than just Moses' utterances within the narrator's utterances: Moses' utterances continually quote, with direct discourse, other utterances, as for example throughout chapters two and three which are mostly various quotations within a quote. Here Moses is

---

[12]The Russian structuralists have already worked out many of the implications of the fact that "within a single utterance there may occur two intentions, two voices." Cf. Bakhtin, *Problems*, 153ff.

quoted by the narrator as quoting a number of others. Each of these cases can be described as an utterance (of the person quoted by Moses) within an utterance (of Moses) within an utterance (of the narrator).

It is sometimes more complicated than this. For example, 1:28 has the narrator quoting Moses quoting Israel quoting Israel's scouts at Kadesh Barnea. And in 2:4-5; 32:26; and 32:40-42, we find the narrator quoting Moses quoting Yahweh quoting Himself, all in direct discourse. In such cases, we have examples of an utterance within an utterance within an utterance within an utterance.

The varying complexities of quotes within quotes that make up most of Deuteronomy is further enhanced by a complicated temporal scheme relating the quotes to their context. At first, Moses' words look mostly to past events and past statements, as in the first address of Moses in 1:6-4:40. Then in his second address, 5:1b-28:68, Moses starts to turn his attention to the future, and a much larger proportion of other people's utterances found within this address expresses what they will, should, or should not say in the future, e.g., 6:20-25; 7:17; 9:4. Then in the third address of Moses, 29:2-31:6, whenever Moses quotes anyone directly, it is their *future* utterances he quotes, coinciding with this address's almost complete orientation toward the distant future. Finally, the group of Moses' sayings that ends the book's collection of his utterances, 31:7-33:29, also emphasizes the future in its quotes, as 31:17b and 32:37-42 show.

The temporal relations of Moses' inclusion of utterances within his own utterances is occasionally even more complex, as for example in 9:26-29. In this pericope the narrator is quoting Moses who, in the valley of Beth-Peor, is quoting what he (Moses) had said at Horeb to the effect that he had prayed that the Egyptians would not say "such and such" at some time subsequent to the events at Horeb.

One of the immediate results of this exceedingly complex network of utterances within utterances is the deliberate representation in Deuteronomy of a vast number of intersecting statements, sometimes in agreement with one another, sometimes interfering with one another. This enables the book to be the repository of a plurality of viewpoints, all working together to achieve an effect on the reader that is multidimensional. We should not be surprised that such a sophisticated work has come down to us from the first millennium B.C. This complex intersecting of viewpoints deserves to be taken seriously and analyzed carefully by the modern reader.

The immediate hero of the book is Moses as the spokesman of God. The only other person who is quoted by the narrator is God. (We have already mentioned that Moses speaks with the elders of Israel in 27:1-8, and that he speaks with the Levitical priests in 27:9-10.) Thus there are only two direct voices[13] which the narrator asks us to attend to in the book: Moses' and God's. Deuteronomy may be described therefore as the speech of the Deuteronomic narrator in which he directly quotes only two figures in the story, predominantly Moses and sometimes God.

As far as Moses is concerned, none of the words of God which he quotes are described as also having been heard by the people, except for the Decalogue (5:6-21). In fact, in chapter five, Moses makes the point that only when God spoke the Decalogue was He heard by the people: all the other words of God were deliberately avoided by the people as directly heard words, and were to be transmitted indirectly to them through Moses' reporting. As for the narrator, he like Moses directly reports God's words. In 31:14b he relates, in direct discourse, God's words to Moses; he does so again in 31:16b-21; 32:49-52; and 34:4b. He also directly reports God's words to Joshua in 31:23b. *In all these cases, he is a privileged observer and reporter of God's words, just as he describes Moses describing himself to be in chapter five.* The point is unavoidable that only two personages in the book directly hear and relate God's words (apart from the Decalogue): Moses and the Deuteronomic narrator.

2.   If only Moses and the narrator are privileged to hear God's word in the book, and even though Moses reports the bulk of God's words found therein, only the words of God that are reported by the narrator are *immediately* reported there. The preponderance of God's words found in Deuteronomy are on another level, a secondary or mediate level. That is, the narrator quotes Moses as quoting God. One might begin therefore one's analysis of the book by articulating a problem similar to the one made above concerning the entire Deuteronomic History. There it was asked whether the ideological position of the Deuteronomist as implied author is to be found in the words of God or in the words of the Deuteronomic narrator. Here we may ask an

[13]I use the term "voice" sometimes to refer to a text's own distinction between reporting and reported speech. In this instance the expression plane of a narrative itself distinguishes the voice or words, say, of its narrator from those of various characters in the story. At other times I use "voice" to refer to distinguishable perspectives on the ideological plane of the text. In this instance I am concerned with the implied author's ideological position as I have reconstructed it from the interrelationships discovered between the utterances of narrator and characters in the text. This stance of the implied author may be complex enough to warrant talking about two or more ideological voices and the specific order of subordination and/or equality apparent among them. Distinction of voice on the expression plane is the construction of a text's author. Distinction of voice on the ideological plane is the construction of the interpreter; this construction is what we call "the implied author."

analogous question. How reliable a narrator do we have here, and how is his voice related to the voice of the book's implied author?

The emphasis in Deuteronomy is on the legislative and judicial word of God, and the conveyors of this word are two: Moses and the narrator. In interpreting the book, do we understand Moses' word as subordinate to the narrator's, or is the narrator's word subordinate to that of Moses? The narrator might be said to be the main carrier of the implied author's ideological stance since he alone conveys to us Moses' conveying of the words of God that constitute most of the book. But if so, one notices that, as vehicle for the book's ultimate semantic authority (he alone can tell us what Moses says that God says to the reader of the book), the narrator seems at great pains to impress upon his reader that it is Moses, and Moses alone, who possessed the type of reliable authority to convey accurately and authoritatively the direct words of God that form most of the book. We find ourselves in a dilemma: we are asked by the narrator to accept his assertion that "there has not arisen a prophet since in Israel like Moses, whom the LORD knew face to face . . ." (34:10), at the same time as it is only the Deuteronomic narrator who knows Moses face to face! If the path to God is through Moses, the path to Moses is through the text's narrator. Does the reader interpret the reported words of Moses by means of the reporting context: "Moses was God's greatest prophet, therefore believe *him* when he says . . ."? Or does one interpret the reporting words of the narrator by means of the reported words of Moses: "Moses said such and such, therefore believe *me*, as narrator, when I say . . ."?

In our brief introductory remarks to the Deuteronomic History above, we made the assumption that ultimate semantic authority in the work, that is, the implied author's main ideological stance, probably should be looked for both in the words of God and in the words of the narrator. We can apply this assumption to the Book of Deuteronomy itself by stating that the ultimate ideological stance of the book ought to be looked for both in the reporting words of the narrator, its "author's" spokesman, and in the reported words of Moses, its hero. We may note that in Deuteronomy we find both the narrator and Moses utilizing the formula that is the basic constituent of the whole history: "God said 'such and such'; therefore this event happened precisely to fulfill His word." For example, Moses is quoted as saying:

> "And the LORD heard your words and was angered, and he swore, 'Not one of these men of this evil generation shall see the good land which I swore to give to your fathers . . .'" (1:34-35).

In the next chapter, Moses is then quoted as saying:

"And the time from our leaving Kadesh-Barnea until we crossed the brook
Zered was thirty-eight years, until the present generation, that is, the men
of war, had perished from the camp *as the LORD had sworn to them*"
(2:14, emphasis added).

We find the Deuteronomist employing the same compositional device in
the narrator's portions of Deuteronomy. Thus the narrator says:

And the LORD said to Moses, "This is the land of which I swore to
Abraham, to Isaac, and to Jacob, 'I will give it to your descendants.' I have
let you see it with your eyes but you shall not go over there" (34:4).

to which he immediately adds in 34:5:

So Moses the servant of the LORD died there in the land of Moab,
according to the word of the LORD (emphasis added).

These pericopes illustrate very well how elements of the ultimate semantic stance of the Book of Deuteronomy (as of the whole history), to
which is subordinated everything else in the text, are to be found both in
the utterances of the narrator and in the utterances of Moses as hero of
the book.

We may expect to find characteristics of the narrator's speech in the
hero's speech, and vice-versa, on any or all compositional planes of the
book. Both words will be "double-voiced," and to this extent the
question must be raised about Deuteronomy which was previously raised
about the whole Deuteronomic History: if it is clear that this book is an
overt monologue (its narrator is clearly stating, "As far as our basic
stance is concerned, Moses and I are one."), to what extent may we
characterize the book, in its compositional structure, as a hidden dialogue or even as a hidden polemic? Are there competing and equally
weighted points of view represented in Deuteronomy on a number of
compositional planes? Concerning the ideological plane of the book, the
four pericopes quoted above show that it is probably misguided to
attribute dominant viewpoints solely to the narrator or solely to Moses.
It is possible, I believe, to determine by careful rhetorical analysis
elements of the text that can be said to belong to the ultimate ideological
stance of the book, just as one can discover and describe other elements
that are clearly subordinate to this viewpoint.

THE REPORTING SPEECH OF DEUT: THE
NARRATOR'S DIRECT UTTERANCES

The reporting context of Deuteronomy comprises only about fifty-
six verses: 1:1-5; 2:10-12, 20-23; 3:9, 11, 13b-14; 4:41-5:1a; 10:6-7, 9; 27:1a,
9a, 11; 28:69; 29:1a; 31:1, 7a, 9-10a, 14a, 14c-16a, 22-23a, 24-25, 30;

32:44-45, 48; 33:1; 34:1-4a, 5-12. The remainder of the book is composed of utterances of various individuals, mostly Moses, reported in direct discourse.

1.   What is the position of the Deuteronomic narrator and what is his voice like?[14] The obvious relation of reporting to reported speech shows that, on the phraseological plane at least,[15] Moses' words are to some extent subordinated to the narrator's. Although the narrator has deliberately put himself in the background and Moses in the foreground, the narrator's word, for very specific reasons, remains visibly separate on the surface of the text. Since the book's surface is constructed mostly in two voices, and since the implied author could have chosen completely to merge his narrator's voice with the voice of his hero, as seems to be the case in the Book of Qoheleth, it is clear that Deuteronomy emphasizes, even on the phraseological plane, a distinction between the word of Moses and the word of the narrator. What are the implications of such an arrangement?

The most obvious functions of the narrator's words are that they situate the words of Moses in time and space (when, where, and in what circumstances Moses spoke the words reported by the narrator), and that they define the pre-eminent position Moses held as leader and legislator of his people. It is also clear that the narrator does not attempt to interpret the words of Moses to any great extent in the Book of Deuteronomy. This is to be expected since the other main section of the history, Joshua-2 Kings, so clearly and so often indicates that it functions as the Deuteronomist's main interpretation of the word of Moses found in Deuteronomy. The *overt* function of the narrator's direct utterances in Deuteronomy is to represent to his readers the word of Moses as pre-eminent, and Moses himself as the greatest prophet in Israel's history.

On the other hand, there are clear indications, even within the brief scope of fifty-six verses, that the content and distribution of the narrator's direct utterances serve to exalt his importance as one who is as necessary to his contemporaries as Moses was to his, and to legitimate that self-serving claim by means obvious and subtle. We now want to explain how, within the narrator's apparently monologic utterances, there are in fact two ideological perspectives that interfere with one another to such an extent that the narrative carries within itself (just as Moses' utterances do) a hidden tension concerning the pre-eminence of Moses.

---

[14]Here "voice" is used to refer to the expression plane of our narrative; it is not a reconstruction as "voice" on the ideological plane would be.

[15]In Uspensky's perspectival scheme the phraseological, spatial-temporal and psychological levels are on a text's surface or plane of expression; the ideological level refers to the deep structure or composition of a text.

Most of the narrator's words provide a suitable frame for the words of Moses in that the former do not distract the reader, either by their quantity or in their emotional power, from attending to the preponderantly powerful words of the book's hero. Examples of the narrator's respectful reticence are found in 1:1-5 and 4:41-48 in the first Mosaic address, 5:1a and 28:69 (Hebrew versification) in the second address, and 29:1a in the third.

But there are other words of the narrator which in fact serve to "break frame,"[16] either by distracting the reader from Moses' main message through the insertion of a number of apparently pedantic, explanatory side-remarks, or else by simply interrupting Moses' words without apparent reason, such as within Moses' third short address: "So Moses continued to speak these words to all Israel, saying . . ." (31:1). What do these narrative "interruptions" of Moses' speech mean?

A typical explanation of these occasional frame-breaks points to some sort of editorial activity aimed at (haphazardly) bringing the text up-to-date, either by explaining archaic terms for contemporary readers or by artificially adding other words of Moses that the editor felt were sufficiently important. If it cannot be decided whether these verses indicate the activity of an author or rather of an editor, an argument for their not being crude or haphazard interruptions of the text can still be articulated. Historical-critical explanations of these verses as crude editorial additions may be considered premature, since it can be plausibly argued that such frame-breaks perform an integral and important function in the text. Rather than indications of sloppy editorial tampering, these breaks in the text serve to represent the narrator's subtle but powerful claim to his audience to be the sole authentic interpreter of Moses' words. Let us look at some of these passages.

2.   In Moses' first address, 1:6-4:40, the text abruptly shifts from Moses' utterance to the narrator's comment, and back again, five times. For example in chapter two, Moses is recalling to the Israelites how they had avoided passing through Edom at the command of the LORD, and had turned toward Moab. Then the text suddenly shifts to another voice:

> The Emim formerly lived there [Moab], a people great and many and tall as the Anakim; like the Anakim they were also known as Rephaim, but the Moabites call them Emim. The Horites also lived in Seir formerly, but the sons of Esau settled in their stead: as Israel did to the land of their possession which the LORD gave to them (2:10-12).

Four other interruptions, similar in pedantic tone and content, appear

---

[16]Erving Goffman, *Frame Analysis. An Essay on the Organization of Experience* (Cambridge MA: Harvard University, 1974).

in this first address: 2:20-23; 3:9, 11, 13b-14. What strikes one immediately is how relatively minor appear to be those points of Moses' speech that the Deuteronomist feels important enough to interrupt with explanatory background information from his narrator. Somehow, what Moses at this point is saying is especially important to the Deuteronomist's audience, and so the text is interrupted with information whose contemporary importance is indicated within these interruptions by phrases such as, ". . . even to this day" (2:22); "is it [Og's bedstead] not in Rabbah of the Ammonites?" (3:11); and ". . . Havvoth-jair, as it is to this day" (3:14). Given these verses' nature as explanations of relatively minor aspects of Moses' speech, why are they there at all, if we are to assume that they are not disruptive to the text?

As Uspensky brings out[17] and Booth amply illustrates,[18] shifts such as these often indicate an author's device for manipulating and programming his readers' responses. Specifically then, even if we might have lost, over the ages, historical information that would help us see the importance that the content of these interruptions might have had to the Deuteronomist and his audience, it still must be pointed out here that frame-breaks of this kind are a frequent device by which an author/editor, even of an ancient work, may *involve* his readers more in his message. In the case of Deuteronomy, this would involve shifting the reader back and forth a number of times between the "that day" of Moses and the "this day" of the Deuteronomist. By breaking frame five times, the Deuteronomist may very well be forcing the reader to shift back and forth a number of times between narrated past and narrator's present.

We are suggesting that the Deuteronomic narrator is pictured here as subtly reinforcing the *difference* between Moses' audience and his own audience so that the latter, while attending focally to Moses' powerful authority and message, is subsidiarily and intermittently kept aware of the distance between the two audiences. These frame-breaks force the Deuteronomic audience to shift from a subsidiary awareness that they are descendants of these earlier Israelites, and therefore distant hearers of Moses' teaching, to a momentary focal awareness of this situation, and then back again to the continuing focal awareness of the earlier context of the story.

By chapter four, principally by means of these five breaks, the reader of the Deuteronomist's day has begun to *feel*, inchoately and almost without being aware of it, what he will by the end of the book consciously apprehend, that the book's author, through his narrator, is as important to him as Moses was to those earlier Israelites.

[17]*A Poetics*, 148.
[18]*The Rhetoric of Fiction, passim.*

We can be more specific than this. The function of these frame-breaks appears to be a chief means by which the narrator begins to program his audience to realize that he is indeed the Moses of his generation. In this first address Moses looks to the past and invokes it as the interpretant for his audience's present and future. If we look at the utterances of Moses to make a point, we will see that the perspective of Moses' first address involves a shifting back and forth between "the day that you stood before the LORD your God at Horeb" (4:10) and the "this day" when "I set before you . . . this law in Moab" (4:8). Moses uses "that day" at Horeb to help him cement "this day's" interpretation of that law. We are suggesting that just as Moses is described as doing this explicitly in his first address, so also the Deuteronomist, by taking Moses' "this day" and transforming it into "that day" (1:3) when Moses set forth the law, uses it to cement "this day's," that is, the Deuteronomist's interpretation of Moses' law, namely, the history from Joshua to 2 Kings as recounted by his narrator.

The deliberate comparison made between how Moses taught and how the Deuteronomic narrator teaches is all the more impressive when we consider that he here implies it by subtle compositional means rather than by bald and bold statements. Were we to look closely at Moses' addresses, we would see that this same comparison between Moses and the narrator is much more boldly stated. The difference is instructive. Given the overt message of the history, "Moses was the greatest prophet of God: I the narrator am just his interpreter," if the narrator is to convey to his audience an analogous status in regard to Moses as interpreter of the Law, he will be more inclined to represent such a point of view more or less clearly through *Moses'* utterances, while leaving to his own utterances more subtle ways of manipulating his audience in the same direction.

The implication of the foregoing analysis is that parts of the narrative which serve either as a frame for the Mosaic utterances or as a statement of Moses' eminence are to be distinguished from other parts of that narrative which break frame in order to prepare the reader to accept authorial claims for eminence, or at least for a status equal in his own generation to Moses' status in the latter's generation.

3.   The frame-breaks that interrupt Moses' second address (5:1b-28:68) also function as interruptions designed to put the narrator on the same level as Moses, and even to *limit* the authority of Moses. The first interruption occurs in 10:6-9. Here, after the narrator relates information about Israel's itinerary and about Aaron's death in verses six and seven, we read:

> *At that time* the LORD set apart the tribe of Levi to carry the ark of the covenant of the LORD, to stand before the LORD to minister to him and

> to bless in his name *to this day*. Therefore Levi has no portion or inheritance with his brothers; the LORD is his inheritance, as the LORD your God said to him (10:8-9; emphasis added).

There are a number of features worth noting in this frame-break, besides the function it has of jolting the reader back to a focal awareness of another time and circumstance. In verse eight, the italicized words recall the typical Mosaic device of using "that day" to clarify "this day"; only in this example it is not clear who is supposed to be employing the device. Second, the list of levitical functions, to carry the ark, to stand before the LORD to minister to him, to bless, seems to be a summary of God's words, here apparently rendered in indirect discourse which continues on into verse nine. Then, in verse 9b, "as the LORD your God said to him" suddenly shifts the report into direct discourse again, as the phrase, "the LORD your God" shows. Verses eight and nine sound very much like a continuation of Moses' speech in verse five. On the other hand, the phrases, "At that time . . . to this day," are ambiguous enough to make us wonder whether in fact verses eight and nine are a continuation of the frame-break of verses six and seven.

The very ambiguity of verses eight and nine serves to underline what we have been noticing all along: the utterance of Moses and the utterance of the narrator are in many respects indistinguishable. Both employ the device, "God said such and such; such and such an event fulfils God's word." As we have already noted, 1:34-35 and 2:14 have Moses speaking this way, and 34:4-5 has the narrator speaking in exactly the same way. Again, as we have seen, since both use the "that day . . . this day" device in their utterances, verse eight could have been spoken by Moses just as well as by the narrator. We should point out here that verse 9b, if attributed to the narrator, would be a rare instance in Deuteronomy of the narrator's speech employing "quasi-direct discourse."[19] Here, the presence of "as the LORD your God said to him" does not indicate the narrator's utterance (since he never uses the second person to indicate the audience for whom he is writing) but rather Moses' reported speech in some kind of direct discourse. Verses eight and nine are a good example of how the voices of Moses and narrator echo one another.

Chapter twenty-seven contains three narrative interruptions:

> Now Moses and the elders of Israel commanded the people . . . (27:1a)
> And Moses and the levitical priests said to all Israel . . . (27:9a)
> And Moses charged the people the same day . . . (27:11)

It is possible to regard chapter twenty-seven as an obvious and awkward

---

[19]Cf. Voloshinov, *Marxism*, 137-59.

interruption of Moses' second address only if one forgets that the whole book shows signs of an intricately planned composition. What is important here is that Moses speaks in conjunction with the elders of Israel and with the levitical priests. If we have faith in the deliberate compositional complexity of the book, we are led to see the frame-breaks of 27:1a, 9a as further diminishing the uniqueness of Moses' authority at a key place in the text.

The frame-break of 27:11 is similar to the frame-break within the third address, 31:1. Both appear to continue the Deuteronomist's practice of shifting the reader back periodically to the narrator's present in order to reinforce the reader's experience that it is the narrator who is the vital link between Moses and the "this day" of the reporting speech.

Within the narrator's direct utterances, it is by means of the distribution of the frame-breaks we have just discussed that the unique status of Moses, emphasized in the other parts of the reporting narrative, is undermined. The narrator's utterances are spoken in two ideological voices which interfere with one another: an overt, obvious voice that exalts Moses and plays down its own role, and a hidden voice that will soon exalt itself at the expense of Moses' uniqueness.

1.   In summary, our analysis of the distribution and content of the various "authorial" interruptions by the narrator in Moses' three addresses indicates a subtle but effective strategy on the part of the Deuteronomist gradually to diminish the unique status of his hero at the very same time as the retrospective elements of Moses' own utterances are enhancing that status. Already by the end of Moses' first address, during which we hear Moses deftly rehearsing past events and utterances to prepare his audience to heed "the statutes and the ordinances which I teach you" (4:1), the Deuteronomist by means of five narrative interruptions of apparently inconsequential nature is beginning to accustom his audience to listen to his narrator's voice, a voice that also rehearses past events and utterances as a means of inclining his audience to heed what *he* is teaching them.

In Moses' second address, a series of narrative interruptions furthers the process of diminishing Moses' unique status at the same time as it is being augmented by the account of his magisterial actions and utterances. In 10:6-9 the normal signals that up to now have so clearly separated reported from reporting speech in the book are so muted that it is not possible to say for sure whether verses eight and nine are the reporting utterance of the narrator or the reported word of Moses. The effect of this compositionally is to reinforce in yet another way what has been accomplished by the previous frame-breaks. Once again brought back by 10:6-7 to a brief focal awareness that it is the narrator who is transmitting the words of Moses, not Moses speaking directly, the reader of 10:8-9 now experiences the narrator's utterance and the hero's word as

indistinguishable in tone, style, and content: the voice of the Deuteronomic narrator merges for a brief moment with Moses'.

By the time we reach the last word of the narrator in the book, 34:5-
12, we are well disposed to interpret this first explicit and direct
evaluation of Moses' unique status in the proper perspective. The soft,
still voice of the narrator has deftly drawn attention to itself throughout
the book with such subtle persistence that when we come to the words
that frame the end of the narrative, and read therein:

> And there has not arisen a prophet since in Israel like Moses, whom the
> LORD knew face to face . . . (34:10)

we are tempted to disagree and to say in reply:

> On the contrary, the LORD our God *has* raised up for us a prophet like
> Moses from among us, and God *has* put His words in his mouth, and he
> *has* spoken to us all that God commands him. And whoever of us do not
> give heed to God's words, which this latter prophet speaks in His name,
> God will require it of us.

This dissenting reply to 34:10, which comes to us somehow through the
book itself, is expressive of another voice which has entered into a gentle
but effective dialogue with the first. The author's narrative frame-breaks
have allowed us to introduce this other voice.

The dissenting reply I have just quoted above is actually adapted
from the words of *Moses* in 18:15-18. We are thus led into a consideration of the reported speech of Moses. Here too, as 18:15-18 illustrates,
what appears to be the monologic word of the greatest prophet of them
all perhaps contains a hidden dialogue between two "Mosaic" voices, to
some degree in conflict. The first, most obvious Mosaic voice functions
in exactly the same way as 34:10 does in the reporting context: to exalt
the hero of Deuteronomy and to subordinate its "author." At the same
time, a second Mosaic voice speaks in the book to exalt the narrator at
the expense of Moses' uniqueness, just as the frame-breaks do within the
reporting context. The main question there as here is whether these two
voices are of equal weight.

Satire and Symbolism in the Song of Jonah*

JAMES S. ACKERMAN
INDIANA UNIVERSITY

BIBLICAL scholars have had as much difficulty digesting Jonah's song as the great fish had with Jonah. Despite sophisticated application of traditional methodologies, the result has usually been an unceremonious regurgitation that removes Jonah's song from its narrative context. Although the following list is not exhaustive, some of the main reasons for separating the song from the body of the work may be noted:

(1) There are examples in other parts of the Hebrew Bible in which prayer material has been secondarily incorporated into prose narrative (cf. 2 Kgs 20:11-12 and Isa 38:7-39:1).

(2) The verb in 2:2 describes Jonah as appealing for help in the belly of the fish, but the song shows him thanking God for help already rendered. The present song would make sense only after 2:11, when Jonah has been returned to dry land.

(3) Jonah's appeal describes the danger of drowning, not his peril in the belly of the fish.

(4) The word for "fish" in 2:2 is feminine, whereas it is masculine in 2:1—suggesting either careless editorial work or a conflation of two separate sources.

(5) The song's sincere expression of heartfelt thanks does not correspond to any of Jonah's other prayers or speeches in mood or in length. He seems to be seeking death in chap. 1, and in the story's last scene he still wants to die. Why does the song express sudden relief that he has been saved from death? Such a meandering song is inappropriate in a story that otherwise has a tight narrative structure.

(6) The song makes no reference to incidents in chap. 1. From the perspective of the song, for example, it was YHWH, not the sailors acting at Jonah's request, who cast Jonah into the sea. Also, the song concludes by expressing the desire to return and worship YHWH in the

*This essay is dedicated with gratitude and affection to Frank Moore Cross, my esteemed professor, for teaching me more about the study of the Hebrew Bible than any other person.

holy temple—rather strange for a prophet who had been fleeing God's presence in chap. 1.

(7) In 2:9 the song looks down on idolaters, yet the sailors were described most sympathetically in chap. 1; and it is "violence," not idolatry, that is the essence of Nineveh's sin in chap. 3.

(8) The language used in the song of thanks is quite different from that of the prose narrative, whereas it would have been easy for the song to pick up and develop *Leitwörter* from the story (e.g., chap. 1 uses "hurl," the song has "cast"). Also, there are Aramaisms thought to be typical of late Hebrew narrative style in the prose sections, whereas the song has none.

A recent trend in biblical scholarship has been to focus on literary artistry, probing the means by which the story's craftsmanship elucidates its meaning. Significant advances have been made using this method with the Jonah story; and, not surprisingly, most of these scholars have argued for the literary unity of the song with its narrative context.[1] Although literary analysts differ somewhat, some of their main arguments are:

(1) The story has many other incongruities. What other biblical prophet commanded to arise and go eastward immediately arises and flees westward? What other biblical prophet gets angry as a result of the greatest success ever achieved by a prophet? From Jonah expect the unexpected—why not sing a song of thanks when in the belly of a fish?

(2) Chap. 2 actually describes two prayers: (a) the prayer for help described in 2:2, and (b) the prayer of thanks in 2:3-10. The former prayer is alluded to in vv 3 and 8, which bracket the flashback description of Jonah's near-drowning experience.

(3) The fish plays a positive role as a vehicle of deliverance in the story and should not be seen as a monster. The writer uses the neutral

---

[1]G. M. Landes, "The Kerygma of the Book of Jonah," *Int* 26 (1967) 3-31; G. H. Cohn, *Das Buch Jona im Lichte der biblischen Erzählkunst* (Te Assen Bij: Van Gorcum, 1969); A. Jepsen, "Anmerkungen zum Buche Jona," *Wort-Gebot-Glaube: Walter Eichrodt Zum 80. Geburtstag* (ATANT 59; ed. J. J. Stamm, E. Jenni, and H. J. Stoebe; Zürich: Zwingli, 1970) 297-305; O. Kaiser, "Wirklichkeit, Möglichkeit und Vorurteil: ein Beitrag zum Verständnis des Buches Jonas," *EvT* 33 (1973) 91-103; J. Rosenberg, "Jonah and the Prophetic Vocation," *Response* 22 (1974) 23-26; T. S. Warshaw, "The Book of Jonah," *Literary Interpretations of Biblical Narratives* (ed. K. R. R. Gros Louis, J. S. Ackerman and T. S. Warshaw; Nashville: Abingdon, 1974) 191-207; L. C. Allen, *The Books of Joel, Obadiah, Jonah and Micah* (NICOT; Grand Rapids: Eerdmans, 1976) 175-235; J. Magonet, *Form and Meaning: Studies in Literary Techniques in the Book of Jonah* (Beiträge zur biblischen Exegese und Theologie 2; Bern and Frankfort/M: H. and P. Lang, 1976); T. E. Fretheim, *The Message of Jonah* (Minneapolis: Augsburg, 1977).

term *dāg* rather than the mythical term *tannîn*. The three days and three nights refer to the time it took the fish to bring Jonah back from the underworld of near drowning to the safety of dry land. Therefore the prayer in vv 3-10 is quite properly a song of thanks, because Jonah knows he has been rescued.

(4) Unlike the prose narrative, the song has several instances of archaic language, and the switch in the song between second and third person reflects its use in an actual worship situation at one time. Although it frequently mentions water and drowning, it does not refer to other incidents in the story. Since the song is not specific to the story, it originated before the story within a liturgical context—inserted by the prose narrator to describe Jonah's grateful response to deliverance.

(5) The song does not indicate psychological inconsistency. 4:6, describing his mercurial response when God ordains the *qîqāyôn* tree to shade him, shows that Jonah can be quite exhilarated when he receives favorable treatment. He becomes grumpy only when others get a similar break.

(6) Although one would expect differences in language, themes, style, and structure between prose narrative and the poetic song of thanks, there is a surprising number of parallels. In terminology, both prose and poetry refer to going down, calling out, steadfast love, vows, and sacrifices. Thematic parallels include casting, presence of God, idol worship, and the notion of God's doing as he wills. Stylistic and structural parallels also suggest that the prose narrative and the song of thanks are a well integrated unity.

Although some of the arguments given above are more convincing than others, I agree with this second group of scholars that Jonah's song of thanks is integral to the story. But I do not think that they have moved in the right general direction in their interpretation of the song's function within the story. Several of them allude to the ironies in the song: e.g., there is no indication of Jonah's repentance or readiness to resume his commission to Nineveh; thus his proud contrast between himself and the idol-worshipers in vv 9-10 is somewhat ridiculous. They further ask how Jonah can rejoice in God's deliverance while begrudging it to the Ninevites when he concludes the song with "deliverance is YHWH's." But, strangely, by interpreting the song as expressing limited, yet growing insight on Jonah's part, these scholars have not fully integrated the prayer into its prose narrative context.

Three representative quotations follow:

> Weder wird (Jona) von aussen ohne sein Zutun gerettet, noch rettet er sich selbst. Die Wiedergeburt des Jona ist weder ein Akt, den er allein durch eigene Aktivität errang, noch ist Jona an ihm unbeteiligt. Vielmehr ist es das Zusammengehen einer inneren und äusseren Rettung. Durch sein

Gebet bahnt sich Jona den Weg hinaus zu Licht und Leben. Durch die
Unterwerfung unter Gottes Ratschluss, der dem Menschen seinen Weg
verzeichnet, rettet Jona sein Selbst.[2]

So ausgestossen, sagt er ja zu Gottes Gericht und nimmt es auf sich; er
sieht das Ende vor sich und liefert sich ihm, nein, liefert sich Gott aus
("resignatio ad infernum"). Grade im Gericht aber erfährt er Gottes
Erbarmen und Rettung, und zwar, als er betet und im Gebet sich diesem
Gott beugt. Der verschlingende Fisch ist zugleich der rettende Fisch.[3]

. . . the 'psalm' is also a necessary complement to the actions of the prophet
described in the book. If one had only an account of his behaviour, it
would be almost impossible to take Jonah seriously, and remarkably
difficult to understand why God bothers with him. Yet for all his selfish-
ness and absurdity, even Jonah has an inner life; he is capable of crying to
God and of a limited degree of change in response to God's command and
teaching.[4]

Taken in and of itself, the song does express genuine piety; and it
has been so interpreted for the past century. Yet we see that even those
scholars who are arguing for the literary unity of the Book of Jonah
have succumbed to the song's traditional interpretation. They see it as at
least a partial expression of real piety—either as a radical turning point
in which the prophet is delivered when he accepts divine judgment, or as
bringing out heretofore hidden dimensions of positive piety in Jonah's
erratic personality.

My main thesis is that the song of Jonah plays a most important
function in the story: it establishes major dissonances between the
prophet's perception of reality and that of his narrative world. These
dissonances, I suggest, are set in the context of the bizarre and unexpected. Thus, they move the entire work in the direction of satire and
compel an ironic reading throughout. Therefore, the song performs two
functions. It helps to establish an appropriate genre (i.e., satire) through

[2]Cohn, *Das Buch Jona*, 84. "(Jonah) is not saved by external forces apart
from his own efforts, nor does he save himself. The rebirth of Jonah is neither a
deed which he accomplished by his own activity, nor is Jonah uninvolved. It is
much more a confluence of an internal and external deliverance. Through his
prayer Jonah winds his way out towards light and life. Through his capitulation
before God's verdict, which points the way for mankind, Jonah delivers himself."

[3]Jepsen, "Anmerkungen," 300. "Thus thrust out, he says yes to God's
judgment and takes it upon himself. He sees the end before him and hands
himself over to it—no, hands himself over to God ('resignatio ad infernum'). But
precisely in the judgment he experiences God's forgiveness and deliverance.
Indeed, as he prays and bows himself in prayer before this God, the devouring
fish is at the same time the delivering fish."

[4]Magonet, *Form and Meaning*, 53.

which the story can be understood. It is also the crucial vortex into and out of which all of the story's main images move, helping us to integrate and properly interpret the symbolism with which the work abounds.

The prose narrative jars us to amusement with the unexpected, showing us a protagonist who is consistently out of step with his surroundings. Other prophets fled the land, sang prayers to God, preached judgment in wicked cities, argued with God, and sought death while sitting under a shade tree. But Jonah's actions and speeches come through as caricatures of the prophetic tradition, and the result is a farce. Commanded to go, Jonah flees. With everyone else scurrying and praying to save the swamping ship, Jonah sleeps. Commanded to pray by the captain, Jonah rolls over and snores on. Asked by the sailors his land and occupation, the prophet who had sought to escape God's domain on the high seas chants a confession of faith in YHWH "who has made the sea and the dry land." Jonah hits the water, and the sea calms instantly. Jonah hits Nineveh, mounts the first available street corner soap box, and proclaims the city's impending doom (not even giving the people a fair break by introducing the oracle with a "Thus says YHWH"). And the lone voice becomes a booming command rattling the rafters of Nineveh, making the king come down from the throne, plunging the city into the widest ranging sackcloth-and-ashes routine ever heard of in the ancient Near East, including even the animals. The king commands "no food, no water—everyone cry out to God with gusto." Think of the racket unwatered animals can make. So God's anger cools down. What does Jonah do? His anger heats up. As he had lectured the sailors about fear of the creator god, he now proceeds to lecture God (in proper prayer-complaint form, of course) that God is simply too full of love for his own good. It makes him come through as wishy-washy—a capricious Oriental monarch. When a city deserves zapping, zap it! God asks whether it's proper for Jonah to be so hot-angry and proceeds to heat things up further—bringing on worm, sun, and sirocco. Now Jonah is hot over the lost *qîqāyôn* plant—hot enough to die. "Look here," says God, "you pity qiqayons, I pity cities—people who don't know up from down, including their kids and cattle."

*   *   *

Before studying Jonah's song in this narrative context, I would like to give several relevant non-biblical examples to illustrate three ways in which context is crucial in determining meaning.

First, regarding the location in which a song is sung:

And the rocket's red glare, the bombs bursting in air, gave proof through the night that our flag was still there.

Think of the difference in meaning when these lines are sung at a Veteran's Day celebration or at a late 60's rally protesting the American military presence in Vietnam. We must deal seriously with the fact that Jonah's song is sung inside a great fish and with the circumstances that preceded and followed that song.

Second, context helps us evaluate analyses which conclude that a song is not an original part of the setting because its language is more archaic or because it represents a later corruption of a particular genre. Some scholars have argued for prior authorship of Jonah's song because of the archaic, non-Aramaised language. On the other hand since the individual song of thanks genre that Jonah uses has been corrupted—the original setting being the fulfilling of a vow by performing a sacrifice—other scholars have argued that Jonah's song reflects a later hymnic development in which prayers, detached from their original cultic setting, have been spiritualized.

Could one not reach similar conclusions regarding J. B.'s prayer in Scene One of MacLeish's play:

> Our Father which art in Heaven
> Give us this day our daily bread.[5]?

One could point to the archaic language and broken genre of this statement and proceed to interpret the prayer out of context. But MacLeish has given it a context—through the preceding commentary of Zuss and Nickles and followed by the older children and maids saying "Amen!"; Rebecca and Ruth saying "Amenamen."; Sarah saying "That was short and sweet, my darling." The point need not be labored that MacLeish is in total control of his material and that J. B.'s truncated prayer is a way of introducing and calling attention to the theological position that will be taken up by the protagonist. Should we then be so surprised if stylized, archaic language occurs in Jonah's song? May we not also assume that the broken genre, jolting us with its unexpected pattern and unusual setting, reflects conscious literary artistry?

Third, context helps us determine the sometimes obscure line between genuine religious expression and its parody. Take this example:

> O Thou that in the Heavens does dwell,
> Wha, as it pleases best Thysel,
> Sends ane to Heaven an' ten to Hell
>   A' for Thy glory,
> And no for onie guid or ill
>   They've done before Thee!

---

[5]A. MacLeish, *J.B.* (Boston: Houghton, Mifflin, 1956) 25.

> I bless and praise Thy matchless might,
> When thousands Thou hast left in night,
> That I am here before Thy sight,
>   For gifts an' grace
> A burning and a shining light
>   To a' this place.
>
> ....
>
> But, Lord, remember me and mine
> Wi' mercies temporal and divine,
> That I for grace an' gear may shine
>   Excell'd by nane;
> And a' the glory shall be Thine—
>   Amen, Amen![6]

As Gilbert Highet points out, "some of the best material parodies are those which might, by the unwary, be accepted as genuine work of the . . . style parodied."[7] We do not have a prose narrative context for these lines. Linguistic analysis might show that the language is traditional middle-class 18th century Scottish. If this were an artifact devoid of other context, we might be tempted to interpret it as a product of 18th century lay piety existing within Scottish Presbyterianism. It closely parallels one stanza in an Isaac Watts hymn:

> Lord, I ascribe it to Thy grace,
>   And not to chance, as others do,
> That I was born of Christian race,
>   And not a Heathen, or a Jew.[8]

But when we learn that the poem's title is "Holy Willie's Prayer," that its author is Robert Burns, and when we read the intervening lines, we see that the "prayer," though couched in correct form, is a brilliant parody of Calvinist Presbyterianism.

Let me turn to a biblical example to make the same point about context and parody:

> Come, let us return to YHWH;
> for he has torn, that he may heal us;
> he has stricken, and he will bind us up.
> After two days he will revive us;

---

[6]R. Burns, *The Complete Poetical Works of Burns* (Cambridge, MA: Riverside, 1897) 109-10. Example cited in G. Highet, *The Anatomy of Satire* (Princeton: Princeton University, 1962) 71-72.

[7]*The Anatomy of Satire*, 72.

[8]Pointed out by Highet (*The Anatomy of Satire*, 72).

on the third day he will raise us up,
that we may live before him.
Let us know, let us press on to know YHWH;
his going forth is sure as the dawn;
he will come to us as the showers,
as the spring rains that water the earth.

This passage occurs in Hos 6:1-3. How are we to interpret it? Is the prophet urging Israel to return to YHWH? Is it a repentance liturgy of the people, expressing faith in God's healing power and willingness to restore the relationship once they return? The context gives us the interpretation. The prayer is hypothetical, placed by YHWH in the people's mouths (5:15); and in 6:4-6 we see YHWH's response to it: "What shall I do with you, O Ephraim . . . your love is like a morning cloud, like the dew that goes early away. . . ." The repentance liturgy of the people, we see, is heavily ironic. YHWH is exasperated by it because Israel perceives her god as a vegetation deity whose return is as sure as the spring rains—not dependent on Israel's return to and respect for covenant law. Biblical literature is also capable of highly sophisticated irony which, taken out of context, can be missed entirely.

* * *

The context that introduces Jonah's song is provided by the final verses of chap. 1 and the first two verses of chap. 2. The sailors, having desperately tried to save Jonah's life by rowing toward land against the storm, finally concede the futility of countering the divine will. They "call out" to YHWH, praying to be released from the blood guilt that otherwise would come upon them for their role in Jonah's execution. If Jonah is allowed to drown, the sailors could be held responsible. The sea calms, and while the sailors respond in turn by preparing sacrifices and uttering vows, YHWH assumes responsibility for the errant prophet's fate.

When YHWH ordains the great fish to swallow Jonah, the context does not lead us to expect that he will survive. The term bl^c, meaning "gulp, swallow, devour," never has a positive meaning in the Hebrew Bible: Korah's followers are swallowed up by the earth, as are Pharaoh and his chariots;[9] the psalmist begs YHWH not to allow the deeps to swallow him up.[10] Just as YHWH had sent a lion to destroy the disobedient prophet in 1 Kings 13, the larger context of the Jonah story leads us to assume that our prophet is destined for extinction within the

[9]Num 16:30,32,34; Exod 15:12.
[10]Ps 69:16.

fish. The three days and three nights motif, indicating the time it takes to reach the world of the dead, confirms our worst fears.[11]

Anyone caught in such a situation, even a fleeing prophet, might be expected to appeal to God for help; and this is precisely what Jonah seems to do.[12] His song is replete with snippets from the Psalter, the first verse closely paralleling the opening lines of Psalms 120 and 130.

> 120:1 Unto YHWH in my straits I call out, that he might answer me.[13]

> 130:1, 2a From the depths I call out to you YHWH, O Lord, hear my voice.[14]

Both psalms are individual laments, with Psalm 130 proceeding to express an eloquent confession of sin and of hope in God's mercy. Given Jonah's fearful predicament and the writer's indication that he is appealing for help (*wayyitpallēl*), one first encountering the Book of Jonah could legitimately expect that the song would continue as an individual lament. The 3:2 lament meter dominates. And the Psalter segments, from beginning to end, are drawn from individual laments.[15] Even the song's

---

[11]It is true that "three days" can indicate a longer or shorter time span in the Hebrew Bible, especially in the context of a journey, and that "three days *and three nights*" seems to stress the length of the period. But G. M. Landes ("The 'Three Days and Three Nights' Motif in Jonah 2:1," *JBL* 86 [1967] 446-50) has demonstrated the mythological background of the motif through his interpretation of "The Descent of Inanna to the Nether World" story. As interpreted by Landes, the story does not describe the goddess' being raised from the dead after three days and three nights. The time-span instead refers to the time needed to reach the nether world. Landes proceeds to interpret the fish as *delivering* Jonah in 2:1, accounting for the prophet's song of thanks as the fish *brings him back* from the nether world. I would argue just the opposite: the use of *blᶜ* and "great fish," as well as the motif of the punishment of the disobedient prophet in 1 Kings 13, establishes a strong context that invites the reader to picture the prophet being carried to his death. For further discussion of "The Descent of Inanna" text, see S. N. Kramer, "'Inanna's Descent to the Nether World': Continued and Revised," *JCS* 4 (1950) 199-214; 5 (1951) 1-17; F. Nötscher, "Zur Auferstehung nach 3 Tagen," *Bib* 35 (1954) 313-19; J. B. Bauer, "Drei Tage," *Bib* 39 (1958) 354-58.

[12]The Hithpael of *pll* always denotes a lament or petition.

[13]The context of Psalm 120 points toward translating the perfect tense of *qrᵓ* as present-durative. The appeal quoted in v 2 may have been made in the past; but it clearly has not yet been answered.

[14]The grammar of Ps 130:1-2, in which the perfect tense of *qrᵓ* is linked to the imperative of *šmᶜ*, forces a present-durative translation of that line.

[15]Pss 42:8; 31:23; 69:2; 71:20; 142:4/143:4; 5:8; 31:7; 41:5.

conclusion, "Deliverance is YHWH's" echoes the last line of the individual lament in Psalm 3.

Instead of giving an appeal for help, however, the prophet shifts gears, and the prayer veers crazily towards a song of thanksgiving—the usual context of which is carrying out vows and performing sacrifices in the temple. Such a sudden shift forces the reader to go back and see these earlier lines in a new light, since the song-of-thanksgiving genre recounts *past* troubles from which the singer has been delivered. "I call*ed* out of my straits. . . . From the belly of Sheol I appeal*ed*, and you hear*d* my voice." These choice words are being sung by a man snugly ensconced in the entrails of a fish! Through this ingenious incongruity we have been forced to ponder the dissonance between Jonah's perception of reality and that of the narrative.

What turns out to be a song of thanksgiving begins with what appeared to be an individual lament. Why were we misled? Normally a song of thanksgiving begins with the singer praising God (or exhorting his fellow worshippers to praise God) for his goodness and mercy, and Jonah skips this part.[16] Instead he opens with the second part of the form, using stereotyped metaphors (e.g. "from the belly of Sheol") to describe the distress from which he thinks he has been rescued. By omitting the opening formula of praise and by focusing on his own plight, Jonah makes us see his self-centeredness. We now realize that *he* is mistaken rather than the reader; and to confirm our perception Jonah is made to attribute his deliverance to *his* "calling out" (*qārā᾿tî* 2:3a)— the *Leitwort* around which the first cluster of ironic incongruities can be found. Jonah may well have gurgled out an unreported appeal for help as he thrashed in the water; but the story suggests that the great fish was sent in response to the *sailors'* "calling out" to be freed from the bloodguilt associated with Jonah's death (*wayyiqrĕ᾿û* 1:14a).

Not only are we forced to question Jonah's perception of reality; we are also left wondering whether we have been given some new insight into Jonah's character. In chap. 1 Jonah had been unwilling to "call out" when it concerned Nineveh or the floundering ship. YHWH had commanded (*qûm . . . ûqrā᾿* 1:2), and this command was echoed by the desperate sea captain (*qûm qĕrā᾿* 1:6). Indeed, Jonah had no great regard for his own life, either (1:12). Why did this prophet, who had been so oblivious to the fate of others and himself, finally call out to YHWH? What was he seeking through his appeal, and why would he give thanks that his prayer had been answered while he was still in the fish's belly? We will return to these questions in the final part of this paper.

---

[16]See especially F. Crüsemann, *Studien zur Formgeschichte von Hymnus und Danklied in Israel* (WMANT 32; Neukirchen: Neukirchener, 1969) 210-82.

The second group of ironies centered in the song relates to Jonah's perception that YHWH had cast him into the depths—that the prophet had been driven from the divine presence (2:4-5). The word "cast" in 2:4 is not the same word as "hurl" used four times in chap. 1, but the change in term is appropriate: "cast" (*hišlîk*) is the proper word in a liturgical context, where "cast" (never "hurl" *hēṭîl*) is used by the psalmists to refer to being thrown into the depths or removed from God's presence.[17] Jonah asserts that YHWH had done the casting; but if we look back at chap. 1, the only thing YHWH had hurled was his wind/spirit. As a matter of fact, it was the sailors who, against their will, had hurled Jonah into the depths; and they had acted at Jonah's request. Now in the song, ironically, he attributes his plight to YHWH.

Furthermore, Jonah had not been driven from YHWH's presence. On the contrary, he had fled. The opening scene of chap. 1 makes it quite clear that Jonah's chief purpose was to abrogate his prophetic office of standing before YHWH's presence by escaping from YHWH's domain.[18] One might perhaps argue that Jonah's song reflects the realization that his disobedience had provoked a divine reaction of judgment, and that 1:12 shows Jonah's willingness to accept the punishment he had coming. But the larger context leads us in another direction. There are several allusions in the prose narrative which suggest that, from the beginning of the story, Jonah's conscious flight from YHWH's presence has been simultaneously an unconscious pursuit of death. Thus his offer to the sailors in v 12 is not a sacrificial act for innocent bystanders; it is a further stage in the pursuit of death, which Jonah had unconsciously initiated in 1:3.

In the opening verses of chap. 1, the word "go down" is repeated three times: Jonah goes down to Joppa, goes down into the ship, and finally goes down into the innermost parts of the ship. He then lies down and falls into a deep sleep—the latter word (*wayyērādam*) being a word play on the root *yrd* "to go down" or "descend." Throughout the Bible *yrd* is used—especially in the psalms—to describe a descent into Sheol, the underworld. As George Landes has pointed out, the motif of descent is continued in the song to describe Jonah's descent to the belly of Sheol.[19] The prose narrative lets us see that Jonah has descended toward the depths—at his initiative—*before* he is hurled into the waters. The point of view reflected in Jonah's song—that it was YHWH who cast him—confirms our perception that the darkness in the great fish's

---

[17]Ps 51:13; 71:9; 102:11; Isa 14:19; 34:34.

[18]For "standing before YHWH's presence" as a designation of the prophetic office, see 1 Kgs 17:1; 18:15; 2 Kgs 3:14; 5:16; Jer 15:19.

[19]"The Kerygma of the Book of Jonah," 25.

belly has not given Jonah much illumination. We will discuss the motif of Jonah's descent in more detail in the final section of this paper.

The final irony in vv 4-5 is the assurance Jonah now feels that he will be returned to the divine presence, again looking upon YHWH in his holy temple. Should this be a comforting thought for our runaway prophet? The entire song gives no indication of Jonah's repentance for turning away from his commission. Nor is there in the song any expression of his willingness to resume the journey to Nineveh; for Jonah the end result will be the return to the temple, where he can pay his vows and make his sacrifices. The prose narrative leaves us wondering if the cozy security expressed in Jonah's song concerning a return to the temple is warranted. In the song Jonah affirms only deliverance *by* YHWH's power, whereas the prose narrative suggests he should be fearing deliverance *into* YHWH's power for his disobedient flight. This is hardly a song to be sung by a prophet who had smugly confessed his fear of YHWH to the sailors in 1:9!

The next cluster of ironies centers on vv 9-10 of the song. Again at the end Jonah breaks the individual song of thanksgiving form. The normal setting for the song, as was mentioned, is during the carrying out of a temple sacrifice in fulfillment of earlier-made vows. Jonah might have made his vows, but he is in no position to carry out the sacrifices, which suggests that he is in no position to sing such a song. The song of thanksgiving genre traditionally moves back and forth—sometimes giving thanks directly to YHWH for the singer's reversal of fortune, sometimes recounting to the rest of the worshipping community what YHWH has done, instructing them concerning the lesson one can learn. The singer's cohorts in such a liturgy are traditionally referred to as the "pious ones" (*ḥăsîdîm*) or the "fearers of God."[20] Both of these motifs become important *Leitwörter* in the Jonah story.

In chap. 1 Jonah inappropriately confesses his fear of God, but the real fearers are the sailors—whose fear is at first directed at the raging tempest and is at the end, through Jonah's unwitting help, transformed into fear of YHWH. The language of the song's conclusion (v 10) forces us to make the parallel between what Jonah promises he will do once he returns to the temple and what the sailors already have done on board the ship: "And the men feared YHWH a great fear. And they sacrificed a sacrifice to YHWH. And they vowed vows" (1:16).

Given this striking parallelism which contrasts actual piety with piety deferred, we are ready to look at 2:9, where the *ḥesed* motif is introduced:

---

[20]Ps 30:5; 32:6; 116:15. Ps 15:4; 22:24; 31:20; 66:16.

The ones who watch over helpless idols
They have forsaken their *hesed*.

Hesed in the Hebrew Bible often is used to describe a dominant characteristic of YHWH that is usually translated as "steadfast love" or
"mercy." It refers to a generous, loving response—carried out in the
context of a covenant relationship. Interestingly, the term *hesed* in the
songs of thanksgiving also can denote God himself.[21] Given the context
of the story, v 9 is highly ironic. The idol-worshipping sailors have
deserted their individual *ʾĕlōhîm*; they have not forsaken YHWH. They
had moved beyond their gods in 1:5-6 when they saw that appealing to
them did not work and when they learned where the true power lay.
They had rowed desperately to save Jonah's life. Finally, they had feared
YHWH and carried out the proper sacrifices, even making the appropriate prayer to be spared from blood-guilt. Instead it is Jonah who has
forsaken his *hesed*.

We will see that *hesed* is a key theme of the entire story; in 4:2 Jonah
finally gives us the reason for his flight from YHWH's presence. It is
precisely that he realizes that God is too full of *hesed* and compassion.
Jonah perceives this as inappropriate in a world which, according to
covenant tradition, is to be ruled on the principle of justice. In chap. 4
YHWH responds to Jonah's lament-appeal with actions and questions
that are meant to serve as lessons for his recalcitrant prophet. Since there
are structural parallels between chaps. 2 and 4,[22] we return to the end of
chap. 2 to note YHWH's response to the lament/appeal-become-song of
thanks. It is a very muted response, which is nevertheless full of
eloquence. What does YHWH think of Jonah and his song? The great
fish is commanded to vomit!

An alternative interpretation of 2:11 would stress the absurd more
than the ironic. We as readers have been prepared by 2:1 for Jonah's
death. We have been puzzled and amused by the prophet singing his
song of thanks as he plunges to the bottom. Clearly the great fish is not
equipped with a depth gauge. Why would YHWH reverse Jonah's
descent, so that the fish is transformed in a moment from a vehicle of
destruction to a means of deliverance? Even though Jonah never knows
the full implications of what he says throughout the story, sometimes he
is capable of telling more truth than he is aware of. In chap. 3 he will
proclaim that Nineveh will be "overturned," and it will be—though not

[21]H. W. Wolff, *Obadja und Jona* (BKAT 14/3; Neukirchen: Neukirchener,
1977) 103, 113.
[22]Landes, "The Kerygma of the Book of Jonah," 16-18; Cohn, *Das Buch
Jona*, 48-51; Magonet, *Form and Meaning*, 55-63.

in the manner he thinks—because he unwittingly provides the key for
the Ninevites' reversing their situation. He had done the same for the
sailors, again unwittingly, with his condescending confession of faith.
Here in chap. 2, in the absurd context of reciting a song of thanksgiving
as he heads to the bottom, he ends almost by accident (or by tradition?)
with a line that relates to *ḥesed* and sounds the key theme of the entire
story: "deliverance is YHWH's." Structurally and thematically, this
parallels the last statement of the sailors in the storm scene: ". . . according as you have pleased, so you have done." YHWH will rephrase this
idea one more time in chap. 4 to make sure we all get that point (vv 10-
11). Chaps. 1 and 3 had ended with marvellous acts of grace that are
hoped for yet not counted upon by petitioners who earnestly changed
their way of life. In chap. 2 Jonah's "petition" gives no indication of
willingness to change his ways and is in fact a secure song of thanks for
a "rescue" which is bringing him toward the underworld. Then: "Deliverance is YHWH's." The effect of Jonah's rescue is similar to that of a
television show where contestants unwittingly stumble onto the secret
key word. Bells ring, lights flash, and buzzers buzz as the sponsor makes
all their unarticulated dreams suddenly come true. Jonah, almost by
accident, hit the key phrase—and paradoxically he is belched forth from
his false sense of secure deliverance into a potentially real deliverance to
be sought in resuming his neglected commission.

There is one final point of irony in this song, learned from an
excellent article by John Miles that scholars working on the Book of
Jonah should not ignore.[23] In commenting on Jonah 2, Miles begins
with the obvious point that in all the other liturgical material in the
Bible, the motif of descending into Sheol or being cast into the depths/
heart of the seas is clearly metaphorical. These motifs are intended to
cover the entire range of human suffering, sense of weakness and
isolation, and feeling of the absence of God. Humor occurs often, he
notes, when traditionally metaphorical language is used in a setting
where it must be interpreted literally. It would be akin to the effect on an
audience in which the first scene of a film was a close-up of the word
"Titanic" emblazoned on what seems to be the side of a ship. In the
distance we hear a hymn being sung, and as the camera moves slowly
toward the passengers we hear the words more distinctly

> Rock of Ages, cleft for me, let me hold myself to Thee.

The focus comes in on one or two faces, and we are overwhelmed by the
blend of exuberant faith and joyful expectation as the song grows louder

[23] J. A. Miles, "Laughing at the Bible: Jonah as Parody," *JQR* 65 (1974-75)
168-81.

in sounding its great affirmation. Then the camera pans back, and we see that it is a great ship after all—impaled securely on a great rock in the midst of a raging ocean! When metaphor is given a literal context, one moves toward the absurd; and the effect is a parodying of that which in its normal setting would have a totally different meaning.

*   *   *

Thus far the discussion of Jonah's song and its narrative context has centered on incongruities in the story that can only be explained through verbal and dramatic ironies. But irony is a mode or rhetorical device that can be used in a wide variety of literary genres. Scholars have long debated the genre of the Jonah story, calling it prophetic narrative, *Novelle*, short story, midrash, etc. Burrows has proposed satire, and Wolff tentatively follows by referring to elements in the story as "satiric."[24] Although there is no evidence that such a category was an integral part of Jewish culture at the time of the story's composition, satire provides the best hermeneutical key for my reading of the song in its context: a lament/appeal-become-song of thanks sung by a man descending towards the nether world. As the man's "ascending" piety becomes sickeningly sweet or unwittingly perceptive, he is burped out towards deliverance just as he hits bottom. Such a reading brings the story close to farce, but the Book of Jonah is far too serious for farce. Only satire permits such a blend of wild improbabilities with ironic incongruities.

Neither Burrows nor Wolff incorporated background on satire into his discussion of the Jonah story in order to strengthen his arguments. Briefly, the first known satirist was Archilochus in the 7th-6th centuries B.C.E. Behind him was a cultic setting (known in cultures ranging from Greek to ancient Near Eastern to Arabic to Irish) of developed curse rituals to expel the evil powers with all types of (often bawdy) humor intended to laugh them out of town.[25] As in ancient curse ceremonies, the satire often develops the theme that the particular evil characteristic in the villain may be intensified in a way that will lead to his destruction. We see, for example, the prophet who descends as he flees being swallowed by a fish that takes him all the way down. Also, as Jonah

---

[24]M. Burrows, "The Literary Category of The Book of Jonah," *Translating and Understanding the Old Testament* (ed. H. T. Frank and W. L. Reed; Nashville: Abingdon, 1970) 80-107; Wolff, *Obadja und Jona*, 62-64. See also E. M. Good, *Irony in the Old Testament* (Philadelphia: Westminster, 1965) 39-55.

[25]R. C. Elliot, *The Power of Satire: Magic, Ritual, Art* (Princeton: Princeton University, 1960) 3-48; R. Paulson, *The Fictions of Satire* (Baltimore: Johns Hopkins, 1967) 6.

becomes hot-angry when Nineveh is spared, God heats things up further through sun and east wind.

In the classical period various types of satire developed: Juvenalian, which is sharp, biting, told to wound and denounce; Horatian, which is whimsical, mellow, told to bemuse and heal. In both of these, however, the satirist addresses the readers directly. The closest parallel to the Jonah story is Menippean satire, in which the characters speak for themselves and are made to look ridiculous through their actions.[26]

In classical satire the events are wildly incongruous and distorted.[27] The writer uses a mishmash of literary genres, often swinging from narrative prose to a song interlude and inverting those forms through parody. At the heart of the satire is an unforgettable image of violence. Some of its typical narrative settings are the dinner party, the ship of fools, and the journey. There is very little plot or character development in this genre, the end leaving us pretty close to the beginning.[28] In Northrop Frye's terms, satire denies us the happy ending of comedy in which the blocking agent is either expelled from or incorporated into the new society.[29] Since satire is an inversion of the ideal themes of journey-quest and victorious struggle over the powers of evil, Frye places it at the opposite pole from romance.

Satire is one of the most difficult of all literary genres to write successfully. The hero will not change much, and the artist must use great imaginative power to convince us that the caricature is more real than the ideal type we know is being caricatured. Furthermore, the writer must create considerable distance between the hero and the readers. If we become overly identified with the hero and his/her fate, the genre shifts into an adventure story. Finally, the satirist must walk the narrow path between invective (in which the moral message dominates) and farce (in which comic fantasy for its own sake takes over).

A rhetorical device that helps the satirist achieve these ends is irony. Booth claims that irony's purpose is to deceive all readers for awhile,

---

[26]J. P. Cèbe, *Varron, Satires Menippées: Édition, Traduction et Commentaire* (Collection de l'École Française de Rome 9; Rome: Palais Farnèse, 1972-77).

[27]For discussions of satire, see A. Kernan, *The Cankered Muse* (New Haven: Yale University, 1959); Elliott, *The Power of Satire*; Highet, *The Anatomy of Satire*; R. Alter, *Rogue's Progress* (Cambridge: Harvard University, 1965); S. Sacks, *Fiction and the Shape of Belief* (Berkeley: University of California, 1966) 7-15, 31-49; Paulson, *The Fictions of Satire*; L. Feinberg, *Introduction to Satire* (Ames: Iowa State University, 1967).

[28]It would be an insult to the reader to point out the applicability of these characteristics of satire to the Jonah story.

[29]N. Frye, *Anatomy of Criticism* (Princeton: Princeton University, 1957) 223-39.

and, once they discover what has happened, force them to deal with their deception.[30] Irony puts distance between the hero and the reader, as we ponder the incongruities between words and actions. Irony also moves the story away from invective, taking the sting out of the punch. Satire excludes more people from its new society than does comedy, whose role is incorporation of almost everyone into it. But the effect of blending irony into satire is to reach out and be as inclusive as possible. It allows the readers sufficient distance so that they can judge the object of ridicule; but it also helps them to acknowledge the kinship between themselves and the object of ridicule with a laugh of recognition.[31]

*   *   *

The Book of Jonah contains recurring images that help to express the central themes of the story. Because these images relate to one another in a coherent pattern, we can speak of the story's symbolism.[32] But when irony is a dominant mode in the satire, as in the Jonah story, the symbols can mis-represent more than they represent.[33] My thesis is that a central symbol system in the Jonah story relates to the protagonist's misguided attempts to avoid certain enclosures, which he perceives negatively, by searching for other shelters that he perceives as sources of security. As stated earlier, Jonah's song plays a central role in the patterning of these symbols so that major thematic statements of the story can be articulated.

To begin with the obvious: Jonah's song teems with underworld imagery. A key to interpreting this imagery and the role it plays in the story lies in the opening verses of chap. 1. We have already noted that the *yrd* descent pattern that describes Jonah's flight in chap. 1 recurs in chap. 2 to describe his perilous encounter with the world of the dead. Also, as already noted, in the context of prophetic narratives Jonah's flight "from before YHWH's presence" is an attempt to evade his role of service. The opening verses of chap. 1 describe Jonah's flight as a *yrd* descent: to the seaport of Joppa, into the ship, and finally into the ship's hold.

The careful reader will note that the culmination of Jonah's descent in 1:5 is ʾel-yarkĕtê hassĕfînâ ("unto the innermost parts of the ship")—an unusual term that is also a word play[34] on the mythic yarkĕtê

[30]W. C. Booth, *A Rhetoric of Irony* (Chicago: University of Chicago, 1974) 106; see also Good, *Irony in the Old Testament*.
[31]Booth, *A Rhetoric of Irony*, 27-30.
[32]See Frye, *Anatomy of Criticism*, 71-128.
[33]Feinberg, *Introduction to Satire*, 198-201.
[34]The technical term for this type of word play is "paronomasia."

ṣāfôn ("the innermost parts of Zaphon/the north"). A second word play is on the Hebrew root ṣfn, meaning "to hide, treasure up." Thus at one level the word play is re-enforcing Jonah's search for a secure hiding place in his flight from YHWH.

At another level, Zaphon is also Baal's dwelling place in the Ugaritic literature.[35] Although Baal must descend periodically from Zaphon to enter the jaws of Death, the ṣrrt/mrym ṣpn is the location of his mountain fortress where he sits enthroned—from which he cannot be expelled by his enemies. Baal reaffirms his life-giving power and cosmic authority by driving back and vanquishing those forces that would overthrow his rule. Richard Clifford has described the "translatio" process by which the Zaphon Völkersturm motifs have been incorporated into the Zion traditions.[36] In Psalm 48, for example, har-ṣiyyôn yarkĕtê ṣāfôn ("Mt. Zion, the innermost parts of Zaphon," v 3) is described as the ᶜîr ᵓĕlōhênû ("the city of our God," v 2)—the ultimate refuge for God's people against the assault of the nations.

In his interpretation of Job 26:6-9 J. J. M. Roberts has demonstrated another important aspect of Zaphon in the biblical tradition—its intimate relationship to "earth" (ᵓrṣ), both of which are suspended above Sheol/Abaddon/Tohu.[37] That is, Zaphon includes both the heights and the base of a sacred mountain, with its foundations, as described in Job, extending to the underworld. Isa 14:12-15 depicts the innermost parts of Zaphon and the world of the dead as related, yet ultimately antithetical. Day Star had thought he could ascend to the heavens, taking his place "in the innermost parts of Zaphon" (bĕyarkĕtê ṣāfôn). But "unto Sheol you will be made to descend (tûrād) . . . unto the innermost parts of the pit (ᵓel-yarkĕtê-bôr)."

Thus when set in its cultural context, Jonah's flight from YHWH's presence/service is not only described as a descent; the subtle mythic allusion suggests that Jonah has searched out a secure hiding place against which cosmic furies might not prevail. The literary context, however, also forces us to see him plummeting to the nether world. The prophet is, consciously or not, pursuing a course towards death. When the story tells us that Jonah ends up in the yarkĕtê . . . , the context forces us to assume it will be the yarkĕtê-bôr ("innermost parts of the pit/ Sheol"). The incongruity is that yarkĕtê hassĕfînâ suggests that Jonah has "descended to the heights." The attentive reader is being told two things: (a) Jonah's flight from YHWH—his descent—has not removed

[35]UT 49:II:29, 34; 51:IV:19; ᶜnt:I:21-22, etc.

[36]R. J. Clifford, The Cosmic Mountain in Canaan and the Old Testament (HSM 4; Cambridge: Harvard University, 1972) 131-60.

[37]J. J. M. Roberts, "Ṣāpon in Job 26:7," Bib 56 (1975) 554-57.

him as far from the deity's presence as our prophet might think; but, more importantly, (b) since Jonah's movement is downward, his comfortable enclosure in the ship's hold will not provide the *ṣāfôn*-like security from threatening powers for which he is hoping.[38]

Jonah's activity in the ship's hold continues the "pursuit of death" theme. He lies down (*škb*) and falls into a deep sleep (*wayyērādam*—a word play that reinforces the *yrd* pattern). The motif of lying down and sleeping is common in descriptions of death. In Psalm 88 the psalmist claims that YHWH has placed him in the pit (*bôr*). Using the same imagery and language that we find in Jonah's song "dark regions of the deeps" (*bimṣōlôt*), where he is crushed by "all your breakers" (*kol-mišbārêkā*) the psalmist states that he has been made like the slain who lie (*škb*) in the grave (cf. Ps 88:7f and Jon 2:4). In the Ugaritic poem 1 Aqht (150f), Aqhat is concerned about Daniel's sleep being disturbed as he lies in his grave:

> If they fly over the grave of my son;
> if they disturb him in his sleep (*bšnth*)

Finally Job 14:12: "A man lies down (*škb*) and does not "arise" (*qûm*), until the heavens are nought they will not awake, nor will they be roused from their sleep (*miššĕnātām*)."

The unusual word in Jon 1:5 for "deep sleep" can have polar connotations in the Bible. It is a divinely induced sleep that can be preparatory to death (Jud 4:21), the creation of life (Gen 2:21), or the giving of revelation (Gen 15:12). With the storm lashing the ship, we might assume that the deep sleep is the first stage of Jonah's death. But the sea captain appears, and his words—echoing the divine revelation of 1:2 (*qûm qĕrā*ʾ)—show us that Jonah can still "arise" (*qûm*) from the land of the dead that he is entering if he fulfills YHWH's command to call out (*qĕrā*ʾ). Jonah's refusal to comply shows us the direction in which he is seeking his security. The language suggests the relationship between obedience and rising from the nether world toward which he is heading.

The world of the dead is described not only as the place from which one cannot "arise," but also the land from which there is no "return" (*šûb*). Job 7:9b-10a reads "thus the one who descends (*yrd*) to Sheol does not come up; he does not return (*šûb*) to his house" (cf. Job 10:21). In Akkadian the underworld is also called *erṣet lā tāri*: "the land of no return." In Jon 1:13 the *šûb* motif symbolically parallels the captain's

---

[38]Even Psalm 48, which had glorified the security of Zion/Zaphon, goes on to describe what YHWH does with ships of Tarshish: he shatters them with wind from the east!

use of *qûm*. By using *qûm* the captain was appealing to Jonah to "get up" and pray to his god; but the larger context echoes the divine command, pointing out the way through which he can "arise" (*qûm*) from his death descent. The use of *šûb* in v 13 describes the sailors' attempt to "steer" the ship back home, because they have perceived that the storm was caused by Jonah's flight from his commission. They are trying to get the ship and Jonah to "return" to dry land so that he can obey. But the larger context suggests a voyage to the land from which there is no return. The ship is doomed unless Jonah decides to obey. Jonah, however, has made his decision; he prefers death in the sea to the alternative of undertaking his commission to Nineveh.

Is there a relationship between Jonah's search for shelter in the hold of the ship and his choice of death in 1:12? The former suggests a return to womb-like security:[39] *yarkĕtê* means "inward parts." Clifford points out that "both Hebrew and Ugaritic use organs of the middle of the body for 'in the midst of' e.g. *beṭen, lēb, kabid, qirbu*"[40]—the last term meaning "female sexual organs" in one Ugaritic text and *beṭen* meaning "womb." Ps 139:13-15 poetically links the formation of the embryo in the mother's womb with being fashioned in the depths of the earth, and Job 1.21 completes the metaphor by describing death as a return to the earth-womb: "naked I came from my mother's womb, and naked shall I return." Thus both in Jonah's flight-descent and in his request to be hurled into the sea, his disobedience is depicted as a search for womb/death-like security.

Because there are too few descriptive attestations of "Tarshish" in the biblical corpus, one cannot be overly precise regarding its symbolic significance. Its location is across the sea, but scholars are not agreed as to the specific location. Frequent reference is made to "ships of Tarshish," which Albright interprets as "refinery fleet."[41] It seems also

[39]In a chapter titled "The Nature of Symbolic Language" Erich Fromm writes "We find a sequence of symbols which follow one another: going into the ship, going into the ship's belly, falling asleep, being in the ocean, and being in the fish's belly. All these symbols stand for the same inner experience: for a condition of being protected and isolated, of safe withdrawal from communication with other human beings. They represent what could be represented in another symbol, the fetus in the mother's womb. Different as the ship's belly, deep sleep, the ocean, and a fish's belly are realistically, they are expressive of the same inner experience, of the blending between protection and isolation" (*The Forgotten Language: an Introduction to the Understanding of Dreams, Fairy Tales, and Myths* [New York: Grove, 1951] 22). Cited by Warshaw, "The Book of Jonah," 202.

[40]Clifford, *The Cosmic Mountain in Canaan and the Old Testament*, 170n.

[41]W. F. Albright, "New Light on the Early History of Phoenician Colonization," *BASOR* 83 (1941) 21-22.

to have been a source of precious metals (Jer 10:9). A further connotation in Isa 2:16 is that of "luxury, desire, delight":

> all the ships of Tarshish
> all the craft of luxury/delight

C. H. Gordon concludes from this that "whatever the original identification of Tarshish may have been, in literature and popular imagination it became a distant paradise."[42]

Isa 66:19 gives another important characteristic of Tarshish in the biblical tradition: it is a place where YHWH is not known, on the periphery of his domain. Since Jonah is a servant fleeing his lord's kingdom, Tarshish would represent a place of security because it is also the point at which YHWH's sovereignty ends. Since YHWH is confessed in the story as the creator god, however, this point would also be at the ends of the earth where death and chaos begin.[43] The antipole to this would be the temple or cosmic mountain, the ultimate place of security.[44] For Jonah, therefore, Tarshish may paradoxically represent a pleasant place of security that borders on non-existence.

The geography of the underworld, as described in Jonah's song, has been sufficiently elucidated by other works; so there is little need for further comment. Clifford points out that the song is an excellent description of Mot's domain, as given in the Ugaritic literature.[45] Jonah depicts himself as having descended to Sheol—a miry place embraced by the chaos waters. One enters that realm at the base of the mountains— the pillars on which earth rests, extending into *tĕhôm*. Mot's land is named *Hmry* in Ugaritic, the same word used for Mot's gullet: "you shall go down the throat (*bnpš*) of Mot son of El, into the miry gorge (*bhmrt*) of El's beloved hero."[46]

There are other Ugaritic passages in which Mot is portrayed as a voracious monster into whose gullet one descends at the base of the mountains.[47] As pointed out above, the motif of being swallowed (*blꜥ*) by the underworld (*ꜣrṣ/šꜣl*) has also been incorporated into Israelite tradition:

> you stretched out your right hand,
> earth swallowed them (Exod 15:12)

[42]C. H. Gordon, "Tarshish," *IDB IV*, 517-18.

[43]O. Keel, *The Symbolism of the Biblical World* (New York: Seabury, 1978) 22-24, 42.

[44]Keel, *The Symbolism of the Biblical World*, 24.

[45]Clifford, *The Cosmic Mountain in Canaan and the Old Testament*, 79-86, esp. 81n.

[46]*UT* 67:I:6-8.

[47]*UT* 51:VIII:1-12; 67:II:1-12.

> . . . and the earth opened up its mouth
> and swallowed them . . . (Num 16:32)
>
> . . . like Sheol let us swallow them
> alive and whole, like those who descend into
> the pit (Prov 1:12)

By this time the dissonance has become overwhelming. As the build-up of imagery in Jonah's song gives increasing vividness to Sheol, with its contextual resonances as swallower (bl^c), we are forced to equate the dread world from which Jonah thinks he has escaped—the "womb of Sheol"—with the belly of the great fish in which he still remains. Since Jonah has been swallowed (bl^c) by the great fish, we are prevented from sharing his illusion that he has found deliverance in a secure place. We are at once amused by this total blindness, yet forced to ponder the ties constructed within the narrative between the ship, the fish, and the world of the dead.

As others have pointed out, Jonah's song describes Death's abode as a city.[48]

> I have descended the earth;
> her bars behind me forever (v 7)

In the Ugaritic texts *Hmry* is likewise called Mot's "city." Since a most prominent feature of cities was their gates, the biblical tradition expresses the "city of Death" motif by referring to its "gates"[49]:

> Have the gates of Death been revealed to you;
> have you seen the gates of deep darkness? (Job 38:17)
>
> To the gates of Sheol I have been
> consigned; the rest of my years (Isa 38:10)
>
> I raised my voice from earth;
> from the gates of Sheol my cry (Sir 51:9)

Keel shows a most interesting 12th century *kudurru* inscription depicting the huge walls of the city of Death, protected by an entwined serpent.[50] The city's towers are the pillars of the cosmos or the foundations of the earth.

As Ps 78:69 shows, there is a close connection between the foundations of the cosmos and the foundations of the temple. Such a parallelism

[48]For both Ugaritic and biblical texts, see N. J. Tromp, *Primitive Conceptions of Death and the Nether World in the Old Testament* (BibOr 21; Rome: Pontifical Biblical Institute, 1969) 152-54.

[49]For *běrîaḥ* "bars" (Jon 2:7) as designating city gates, see Deut 3:5; Judg 16:3; 1 Sam 23:7; 1 Kgs 4:13; 2 Chr 8:5; 14:6; Neh 3:3-15; Amos 1:5.

[50]Keel, *The Symbolism of the Biblical World*, 46.

between foundations of the cosmos and foundations of the temple allows the poet in Psalm 24 to move comfortably from one sphere to the other.[51] The fluidity between these spheres can be further illustrated in a wide range of hymnic literature. The foundations of the earth, however, are also sunk into the nether world. And this relationship allows the psalmist to depict the city of Death and the city of Zion as antipoles:

> Raise me from the gates of Death,
> That I may recount all your praises
> From the gates of daughter Zion (Ps 9:14b-15)

To summarize our results thus far: Jonah's flight from YHWH's service has been portrayed as a search for shelter that is paradoxically a descent toward death. The *yarkĕtê hassĕfînâ* of the ship had seemed to offer a womb-like security that would provide Jonah with Zaphon-like protection against cosmic assault. It was, however, a descent toward the sleep of death. YHWH's wind/spirit on the waters elicits attempts by the ship's personnel to get Jonah to "arise" and "return/ repent"; but he continues his course toward the sleep from which one does not arise, the land from which there is no return. This course is reinforced by his request to be thrown into the sea. His ultimate destination was "Tarshish," which may be a paradisiacal land of comfort and security—but also the point of non-existence because it lies at the periphery of YHWH's domain.

Once inside the belly of the fish Jonah absurdly bursts into song, thanking YHWH for deliverance from the womb of Sheol. Having experienced the proximity of death as chaotic and destructive (anything but the safe, enclosured comfort he had been pursuing), Jonah thanks YHWH for being raised up from the city of Death—secure in the knowledge that he will again worship in "your holy temple," the city of God. We know, however, that Death is the great swallower—that the fish, though perceived by Jonah as a means of deliverance, is in fact a continuation of the ship, with Tarshish and the oceanic depths representing variations of the same destination. The fish had swallowed (*blᶜ*) Jonah, in whose belly he remained three days and three nights. The prophet rejoices in the fish's belly because it provides him with the same false, death-like security that he had sought out in the *yarkĕtê hassĕfînâ*. *And this is why what should have been Jonah's lament-appeal becomes a song of thanks.* Based on a false sense of security, it is a hollow song sung in a hollow place. To make sure we get the point the male fish (*dāg*) that devoured Jonah in 2:1 becomes a female (*dāgâ*) for Jonah, once he enters her entrails. The point is forced upon us further as we

[51]F. M. Cross, *Canaanite Myth and Hebrew Epic* (Cambridge: Harvard, 1973) 91-111.

hear Jonah, from the innards of the female fish, sing a misguided song of thanks for deliverance from the "womb of Sheol."

We have dealt with two death-like images of enclosure—ship and great fish—that have been incorrectly perceived by the prophet as places of safety.[52] There is one more enclosure described as a safe haven in Jonah's song, with no negative associations whatsoever: YHWH's holy temple. In Jonah's song (as in Ps 9:14b-15 quoted above) it is the antipole of the city of Death, from which our prophet believes himself to have been rescued. But these enclosures—city of Death and holy temple— are only antipoles *if one takes the song out of context.* We have learned from chaps. 1-2 that Jonah feels secure in shelters that really lead to death. The larger context forces us to wonder whether in this story "YHWH's holy temple" does not represent Jonah's further quest for security in womb-like shelters that lead to death. Therefore, I would suggest that the larger context gives such dissonance to Jonah's joyful anticipation of the temple that the antipodal city of Death/temple relationship becomes complementary and the two spheres are equated. This interpretation, I think, is borne out because there is no indication in the song that Jonah is ready to "call out" (qr°) to Nineveh or return ($\check{s}\hat{u}b$) to his commission.

Jonah concludes "Deliverance is YHWH's," because he sees the fish as a secure place bringing him up from the destructive chaos of Death's raging breakers to the security of the temple. As the prose narrative picks up again in verse 11, we see that deliverance is indeed YHWH's. But it does not result in Jonah's return to the temple. It heads him again toward Nineveh—the place in which his original commission was to have been carried out.

Commentators have long pointed out the anachronism that during the time of Jonah in the early eighth century B.C.E. Nineveh was not yet the capital of Assyria. There is the further oddity that the king is designated as "King of Nineveh" rather than "King of Assyria." I would agree with those who have argued that the story makes no attempt to give the city a historical context. It is simply called "the great city," inviting the reader to de-historicize Nineveh and align it with other cities and enclosures referred or alluded to in the story.

The starting point, quite clearly, is given in the story's opening scene. Nineveh is the counterpart of Tarshish, lying in exactly the opposite direction. We are not told immediately why Jonah heads toward Tarshish rather than Nineveh. Tarshish perhaps suggests the paradoxical connotations of a pleasant spot which, because it lay at the

---

[52]Tarshish could be cited as a third parallel symbol, but the evidence is too enigmatic.

perimeter of YHWH's realm, was the point at which non-existence began.

We know from biblical history that Nineveh was anything but a never-never land for the people of Israel. And the allusions in the story force us to see the city as an embodiment of human evil. YHWH's statement "their wrong has come up before me" (1:2), Jonah's message "yet forty days and Nineveh will be overturned" (3:4), and the king's command that his people repent of "the violence which is on their hands" (3:8) are sufficient clues to point us both toward the Noah and the Sodom and Gomorrah stories.[53] The evil in Nineveh is comparable to the chaotic collapse of cosmic order that prompted God's decision to return the world to its primeval condition through the flood. The references to YHWH's taking note of evil and bringing overthrow also suggest Sodom and Gomorrah, paradigmatic of the total devastation that YHWH brings upon cities in which evil is absolute.

Nineveh is also related to Jerusalem in the Jonah story. It has long been accepted that chap. 3 is using Jeremiah 36 as a foil. YHWH expresses the hope in Jer 36:3 "it may be that when the house of Judah hears all the evil I am proposing to do to them so that they return—each man from his evil way, that I may pardon their iniquity and their sin." Jeremiah is also hopeful that it is not too late: "it may be that their appeal for mercy will fall before YHWH, and that they return—each man from his evil way, for great is the wrath and hot rage which YHWH has spoken unto this people" (36:7; cf. Jon 3:8-9). A further parallel has the citizens of both Nineveh and Jerusalem calling a fast before the judgment message reaches the king (Jon 3:5; Jer 36:9).

Here the similarities between the two episodes end. Whereas the king of Nineveh responds to the judgment message by proclaiming a more extravagant repentance than his people had initiated, Jehoiakim does not react the way YHWH and Jeremiah had hoped. Jerusalem soon falls; Nineveh is spared. The Jonah story thus likens Nineveh to Jeremiah's Jerusalem, but not with the result we might have initially expected.

In the story Nineveh is also related to the city of Death from which Jonah's song describes his escape. These are the only two enclosures in the story that Jonah regards as threatening. Jonah seems to perceive Nineveh in terms of its traditional biblical context described above. He is eager to get out of town the day he arrives, after giving his message. This action-reaction parallels his gratitude to YHWH for quick deliverance from the chaotic city of Death whose gates had banged shut behind him. The story equates the two cities in Jonah's mind, showing both to be

[53]Gen 18:20-21; 19:21, 25, 29; Amos 4:11; Gen 7:17; 6:11, 13.

central embodiments of that which destroys life. For Jonah the secure refuge and means of deliverance through which one can reach YHWH's presence have been the great fish and the temple. Since the story has associated the great fish with the Tarshish-bound ship by which Jonah was seeking to flee YHWH's presence/service, and since the great fish has devoured the prophet for a period of three days and three nights, we were forced to question Jonah's perception that the great fish had wrought deliverance and that the holy temple would offer ultimate protection.

The context of chaps. 1 and 2 suggests that the city of Death is not an antipole of the ship/great fish/temple, even though our prophet had thus perceived them. The latter three may offer the illusion of security, but it is a security leading to the inertia of deep sleep, bringing one to the portal of the city of Death. Chap. 3, with its play on Jeremiah 36, seems to confirm this interpretation. Here we see that Jerusalem and Nineveh are indeed antitheses, but not in the manner affirmed by biblical tradition. Whereas Jonah's song had equated Jerusalem's holy temple with the city of God, we see from the Jeremiah 36 allusion that appearances deceive. Jonah had made the traditional equation between Nineveh and the city of Death, but the story shows us that quite the reverse is true. Nineveh is not called "the city of God" in the story, but we are certainly pointed in that direction when the narrator describes it as "a great city for God" (3:3). And indeed the city of Nineveh lived up to its potential, as the conclusion of chap. 3 indicates.

A final question regarding the significance of Nineveh in this story: Are we being asked to ponder the parallels between the great fish and the great city? In 2:1 we are told that Jonah was in the fish's belly "three days and three nights." In 3:3 we learn that the city of Nineveh is "a journey of three days" in which Jonah gives God's message on the first day. Is the relationship between "great fish" and "great city" that both of these figures are traditional symbols of evil that are transformed to fulfill YHWH's purpose in the course of the story?

On the other hand, one could note that in both cases the time is specifically linked to Jonah's stay within the figure. Is each three days' duration an ordeal? P. Kyle McCarter has pointed out the Mesopotamian river ordeal background presupposed by Jonah's song.[54] If this is correct, there is further irony in the song because Jonah, although he has not repented, is giving thanks that he has been found innocent and raised up from the waters of death. Although perceived by Jonah as rescuing him from the ordeal and affirming his innocence, the great fish is in fact delivering him to his ordeal—the three days in Nineveh. And although Jonah is unwittingly successful despite himself, he lasts only one day; he

[54]P. K. McCarter, "The River Ordeal in Israelite Literature," *HTR* 66 (1973) 403-12.

does not endure the ordeal. The resolution of his guilt or innocence will have to be worked out east of Nineveh in chap. 4.

A second figure to be investigated in chap. 3 is the king of Nineveh. It has long been recognized that he plays a role quite parallel to that of the ship's captain in chap. 1 (cf. 1:6 and 3:9). Even more important, however, is the story's development of the king and Jonah as antitypes. Jonah's response to YHWH's word (*dābār*) is to flee in the other direction. When the *dābār* comes to the king he arises (*qûm*) and commands that the land rid itself of violence and return (*šûb*) unto God. These two actions were precisely what the ship's captain and crew had tried to get Jonah to do (cf. 1:6, 13). They were unsuccessful in their efforts, however, since the prophet was literally hell-bent on fleeing his commission. Furthermore, "arise" and "return" are also closely associated with the nether world, the state from which one does not arise, the place from which there is no return.

The key feature of Nineveh's reversal is its turning away from violence. However the larger context of this ethical activity is the symbolic association of the community with the world of the dead. Torn clothes, ashes/dust/earth on the head, sack cloth, and fasting were all forms of mourning and self-negation.[55] In Ugaritic literature El comes down from his throne to sit on the ground, strewing dust on his head, wearing a loin cloth, and gashing himself—to mourn the loss of Baal.[56] In Genesis 37 Jacob tears his garments and wears sack cloth, saying he will follow his dead son down into Sheol. Interestingly, these rites are forbidden to the Israelite priesthood because bringing them into contact with the world of the dead renders them unclean.[57]

As a further antitype to Jonah, the king of Nineveh plays a primary role in enacting his city's symbolic death. Upon hearing God's word the king "arises" from his throne—his place of security because it represents the rule of his god and is established upon the foundations of the earth—and associates himself with the world of the dead, undergoing a symbolic death. And paradoxically, by coming down and entering the world of the dead he "arises" and "returns" from the threat of death that had been laid on the city. Death is a sphere from which there is indeed the possibility of return, and the key to the symbolic death is a "return/repentance" from violence.

Whereas the king symbolically descends from his secure place to associate himself with the world of the dead, Jonah in chap. 1 had

[55]E. Kutsch, "'Trauerbräuche' und 'Selbstminderungsriten' im Alten Testament," *Drei Wiener Antrittsreden* (Theologische Studien 78; ed. K. Lüthi, E. Kutsch, and W. Dantine; Zürich: EVZ, 1965) 25-37.

[56]*UT* 67:VI:11-23.

[57]Kutsch, "'Trauerbräuche' und 'Selbstminderungsriten' im Alten Testament," 32.

descended towards the world of the dead—towards what he thought would be a secure place. Because his descent is carried out in the context of flight and disobedience, the evil from which Nineveh had delivered itself still hovers over Jonah and becomes the focus of YHWH's activity in chap. 4.

The interesting scholarly discussion concerning the location of the event described in 4:5 in the story's chronological sequence need not concern us here. Regardless of when Jonah built his *sukkâ*-booth, the description is appropriate here in the narrative because the theme of shelter is once again being developed, this time in conjunction with the super-shelter provided by God's *qîqāyôn* plant. As Magonet points out, we are asked to contrast two sitting figures: the king of Nineveh, stripped of his royal garb, clothed in sack cloth, sitting in ashes; and Jonah, east of the city, sitting securely and comfortably in the shade provided by the *sukkâ* that he had built for himself.[58] Cohn points out the symbolic contrast between the human-made *sukkâ* and the God-given *qîqāyôn*. Continuing the quest for death motif, Jonah's first outburst expresses a preference for death to living in a world without justice; when the God-given *qîqāyôn* perishes, however, Cohn sees Jonah's second outburst as expressing a preference for death to living in a world without divine grace.[59]

It seems to me, however, that a key theme running throughout the story is Jonah's misguided search for shelter, and this would lead to a different line of interpretation. In chap. 4 Jonah constructs the *sukkâ* to await the destruction of Nineveh. It "wrongs" Jonah "a great wrong" that this judgment is delayed or cancelled by YHWH's change of heart— wrought by the combination of Nineveh's comical response to impending judgment along with YHWH's inclination toward mercy. God then "ordains" the *qîqāyôn* to "deliver Jonah from his wrong." How so? The *qîqāyôn* represents a super-abundant shelter in this context, and sheltering enclosures have given Jonah a *false* sense of security throughout the story. Should we not be doubly suspicious when Jonah's being "wronged a great wrong" is quickly transformed to his "rejoicing a great rejoicing" by the appearance of the *qîqāyôn*? Is this his "deliverance"? Hardly. In fact, Jonah's rejoicing over the *qîqāyôn* is an exact parallel to his song of thanksgiving in the belly of the divinely "ordained" great fish—both reactions resulting from a death-like sense of security that inhibits a proper response.

The point I would stress is that in chap. 4 God "ordains" three events, not one, before the deliverance begins to occur. Just as Jonah's descent pattern had been reinforced by YHWH ordaining the great fish

[58]Magonet, *Form and Meaning*, 19-20.
[59]Cohn, *Das Buch Jona*, 87-88.

to devour him, Jonah's hot anger in response to YHWH's withholding his judgment upon Nineveh is not reinforced until all three chap. 4 agents have been ordained: wood, worm, and wind. Now Jonah's physical heat matches his spiritual heat. Only after all three events strike against our prophet can the deliverance from his wrong—the hot anger he feels—commence. Thus although it may be the growth of the qîqāyôn that will "shade" him, it is dealing with the *loss* of the secure shelter of the qîqāyôn that may "deliver" him.[60]

As pointed out above, there are allusions in the Jonah story that equate Nineveh with Sodom and Gomorrah. The hearers of the Jonah story will recall Abraham questioning YHWH on the nature of divine justice and how this relates to the cities' impending destruction. The contrast is obvious, with Jonah questioning YHWH on the nature of divine justice and how this relates to the possible sparing of Nineveh.[61] The final scene of the Sodom-Gomorrah story is of Abraham looking down upon the smoldering remains of the wasted cities (Gen 19:27-28). Jonah has gone east of Nineveh and built his *sukkâ* booth, hoping to experience a similar finale as an affirmation of God's ultimate justice.

The story had begun with Jonah's paradoxical "descent to a secure height." I would suggest that the biblical context has placed our protagonist on another imaginative height that is perceived as secure until all three ordinations take place. The biblical associations of the *sukkâ* booth are not only to provide shelter, but also as part of a larger context in which God can be worshipped. The Hebrew root *śmḥ* ("Jonah *rejoiced* over the qîqāyôn a great *rejoicing*") often appears in a liturgical setting describing worship.[62] One typical yet key example is the description of the festival of Booths, in which Israel is admonished to build *sukkôt* for themselves and celebrate in the place that YHWH will choose.[63] A result of this celebration, stressed in Deuteronomy and elsewhere, is *śimḥâ* ("rejoicing").[64]

I am not trying to locate the life setting of the Jonah story at the festival of Booths. I am, however, pointing out that the combination of *sukkâ* and *śmḥ* suggests a festal setting in the holy place chosen by God. In Ps 76:3 *sukkâ* is an epithet for the Jerusalem temple. And the term recurs in the psalms as an image of divine shelter and protection in connection with Zion (e.g. Ps 27:4c-5c: "that I may dwell in the house of

---

[60]The story develops the word play between "shade" (ṣēl) and "to deliver" (lĕhaṣṣîl). The LXX translation renders the word-play as a pun, reading lĕhāṣēl.

[61]L. Schmidt, "De Deo:" *Studien zur Literarkritik und Theologie des Buches Jona, des Gesprächs zwischen Abraham und Jahwe in Gen 18:22ff und von Hi 1* (BZAW 143; Berlin and New York: Walter de Gruyter, 1976).

[62]e.g., Deut 12:12, 18, 26; 27:7; Lev 23:40, etc.

[63]Deut 16:13-15; Neh 8:14-17.

[64]Deut 16:14; Neh 8:17.

YHWH, all the days of my life; to see the beauty of YHWH, and to inquire in his temple. For he will hide me (*yiṣpĕnēnî* [!]) in his *sukkâ* in the day of evil; he will conceal me under the cover of his tent . . .").[65] Is Jonah's *sukkâ* shelter a dim reflection of the secure heights of the holy city—of the temple that had been the final hoped for destination of his song?

What role, then, is the *qîqāyôn* plant playing in this interpretation? Let us not forget the development of the Zaphon/mountain of God/holy temple motifs in the Jonah story. Ancient Near Eastern iconography is replete with figures of the tree of life flourishing atop the divine mountain, yet being attacked by a serpent.[66] In Jonah, the "worm" does indeed destroy the *qîqāyôn*. If these parallels are intended, why not call it "tree of life" and "serpent"? Why "*qîqāyôn*" and "worm"? To this I would respond that the story is using irony to downplay its strong symbols, often reversing our expectations of the role they should be playing. It is for this very reason that the monster devouring Jonah is called a "great fish" rather than Leviathan, Tannin, Rahab, or the many other word choices to which the writer had access.

The "holy temple/mountain of God" motif reaches its culmination in the *sukkâ* that is temporarily shaded by the *qîqāyôn*. Once we accept an irony that undercuts its symbols, is there not a further contextual overlay that the narrator has incorporated through the plant/tree and the worm/serpent allusions? Ezekiel 28 equates "the holy mountain of God" with "Eden, the garden of God" and proceeds to describe the same kind of great wealth on that secure, paradisiacal mountain for which Tarshish was also renowned.

Jonah no longer has access to the plant, and still he has not been delivered. Will the *sukkâ* shelter that remains be sufficient to reach that goal? Not necessarily. The ancient reader would not have needed reminding that there is a long-standing traditional "other side" to the practice of *śmḥ*: rejoicing over the demise of one's enemies.[67] This is what Jonah had been prepared for, and it is in this context that YHWH gets in the closing lesson about *ḥûs* ("pity").

Jonah had complained to YHWH for having subverted the prophet's conception of what the covenant relationship entailed. YHWH's forgiveness of Nineveh "has wronged him a great wrong"; and paradoxically Jonah is to be delivered from this wrong by dealing with the loss of the *qîqāyôn* in which he had rejoiced. The prophet feels no positive emotion about anything beyond himself until YHWH gives him the benefit of the doubt by attributing his second round of hot anger to his "pity"

[65]Pointed out by Robert Alter in a personal communication.

[66]See Keel, *The Symbolism of the Biblical World*, 51-52 (Figs. 45, 46, and 47).

[67]Ps 35:15, 19, 24; 38:17; Job 31:29; Obad 12; Mic 7:8; Ezek 25:6; Eccl 5:19.

(*ḥûs*) for the dead *qîqāyôn* plant. The *qîqāyôn* plant had "perished," the term used for the fate that the ship's crew and the city of Nineveh were seeking to avoid. We are presented with the great irony that the prophet who would not arise to call out to his god to save the ship from "perishing," the prophet who headed west rather than bring a word that could save Nineveh from "perishing"—is the very person who has *ḥûs* when the *qîqāyôn* does indeed "perish."

At this point Jonah learns that his "pity" is misdirected. *Ḥûs* is an odd word, perhaps chosen as a pun on *ḥsh*—a recurring term in the Psalter for "seeking shelter" (in YHWH).[67a] Jonah had spent four chapters looking for cover. YHWH has stripped away his shelter and now points toward pity. *Ḥûs* may also have been used because of its phonetic associations with *ḥesed*.[68] It is important to note that the overwhelming biblical tradition enjoins that Israel *not* have *ḥûs* for the enemy, or the promised land will not become a secure possession.[69] The prophet must learn his lesson when he is asked to contrast his own feelings for "the great city" with the *ḥûs* of God. Is Jonah not being told, through God's discreet indirection, that if he cannot live covenant-ally tied to the world in *ḥesed*, he can at least emulate the Creator by responding to all things with *ḥûs*?

The *qîqāyôn* has perished. The secure proximity to the garden/mountain of God is gone. Jonah cannot remain safely enclosed in his *sukkâ* if he is to fulfill his divinely given commission. Nor can he, in a world in which one is banished from ultimate protection, hold back on *ḥûs*. Why? Because the world, though it can be perceived as a threatening city of Death, has the potential to *šûb* from its wrong, and because that world-city is ultimately the creation of the God who has *ḥûs* for the creatures—children and animals—who walk, toddle, urinate, and vomit in its streets. The *qîqāyôn* (like Tarshish, Eden, and Zion/Zaphon) is now part of a never-never land. Only when Jonah realizes that he must live out his days apart from its splendor and shade in the context of a *sukkâ* that will not bring the security he seeks; only when he learns the propriety of *ḥûs* will Jonah truly have been delivered from his evil by the *qîqāyôn*. This *anagnorisis* is an event that must transpire beyond the parameter of the narrative.

*   *   *

In commenting on satire in *Gulliver's Travels*, S. Sacks focuses on Gulliver's description of his first bowel movement in the land of

---

[67a]Discovered on the same day I received a personal communication from Robert Alter suggesting the same point!

[68]See Warshaw, "The Book of Jonah," 193-94, 198.

[69]Wolff, *Obadja und Jona*, 146-48.

Lilliput. Heretofore Gulliver had been quite terse and phlegmatic in recounting his wondrous adventures. "But," says Sacks, "when a bluff, good-natured Englishman, by nature circumstantial and unimaginative, waxes eloquent, we will take special notice. When that eloquence is employed in so dubious a cause, we are justified in believing that even the delusion of grandeur consequent upon his second voyage is less aberrant than his state of mind in Lilliput.[70] I have tried to show that the song of Jonah merits our special attention, because it is unusual in its rhetorical flourishes, depicting a part of the prophet's state of mind that is not elsewhere so extensively expressed. The song develops the story's satiric elements, forcing us to judge the prophet's perception of reality as illusory. It also provides a system of images (womb, chaos waters, city of Death, holy Temple) that both relates to and aids in the interpretation of the images in the prose narrative (ship, sea, great fish, great city of God, sukkâ, qîqāyôn, and worm). The ironic mode in which the satire is presented invites us to laugh at the prophet's erratic behavior while acknowledging in ourselves the impulses that motivate such behavior.

Our amused reaction to Jonah's spasmodic, disjointed activity is nicely explained by H. Bergson's argument that rigidity, is the key principle in humor.[71] Laughter is produced by "a certain mechanical inelasticity just where one would expect to find the wide awake adaptability and the living pliableness of a human being.[72] We are moved to laughter when humans act like machines, as, for example, when people make gestures that are not appropriate expressions of what they are saying. Thus humor has the function of helping society adapt to new circumstances as it perceives that certain long-learned responses are now ridiculously mechanical. People will turn against inelasticity—banishing it or bringing it into conformity—because they see it as possibly symptomatic of a slumbering death-like state. There is something exquisitely comic and movingly sad about the painted smile of a clown that remains frozen in position no matter what the circumstances. Scholes and Kellogg see satire as simultaneously attacking (a) the inelasticity of the smile—decrying the behavior and even ideals of the past for being no longer relevant; and (b) the new context which renders the smile inappropriate—depicting the present age as a falling away from the ideals of the past.[73]

[70]Sacks, Fiction and the Shape of Belief, 37-38.
[71]H. Bergson, Laughter: an Essay on the Meaning of the Comic (New York: Macmillan, 1914).
[72]Bergson, Laughter, 10.
[73]R. Scholes and R. Kellogg, The Nature of Narrative (London and New York: Oxford, 1966) 112-13.

Satire always has a target outside the work, and combining humor with unbridled fantasy is a most effective means of combatting that enemy. The best examples of this genre have historically come from "periods when ethical and rational norms were sufficiently powerful to attract widespread assent, yet not so powerful as to compel absolute conformity—those periods when the satirist could be of his society and apart from it; could exercise the 'double vision.' "[74] S. R. Hopper argues that irony directed against one's own culture develops rather late.[75] In the early period the archetypes of a culture are full of power, he claims, giving form to the world of a particular society. But eventually these archetypes become hardened into a canon, losing their depth dimension. When this happens, the creative artist must move into an ironic mode, stepping outside the culture to use the old forms in new ways.

Regarding the historical background in which the Book of Jonah was written, I agree with the reasons given by T. Fretheim for a mid-fifth century date.[76] Whereas the story contains allusions to Jeremiah and Elijah, it is not primarily a polemic against late Jewish prophecy. Nor is the issue unfulfilled prophecy. Jonah's anger in chap. 4 is not because YHWH has made him look foolish by turning his message into a lie. The primary issue is divine justice. How could YHWH possibly hold back judgment against nations that deserved it far more than Israel? Jonah's theological problem is the reverse of Job's. Whereas suffering had caused Job to probe the caprice of divine sovereignty, the sparing of Nineveh causes Jonah to express the same concern. For both protagonists YHWH's rule must be expressed through a well-ordered universe. A causal relationship between sin-punishment and obedience-blessing is fundamental to biblical religion. Jonah sees mercy as a threat to God's order. One must be able to count on oppression and violence having certain repercussions, or the god of biblical religion no longer controls human history. Jonah's yearning for justice is in fact a zeal for divine integrity. He is a man of faith whose tradition turns him against God. And before casting the first stone at Jonah, one should try to recall the feeling of moral outrage upon discovering that a new President, in the name of compassion, had issued a blanket pardon to his predecessor who had just stepped down.

Ironically, it is the divine ḥesed and ḥûs that separate Jonah from God. In the name of his interpretation of the Yahwistic tradition, he is driven toward a disobedience that is expressive not only of his separation

[74]R. C. Elliott, "Satire," *Princeton Encyclopedia of Poetry and Poetics* (ed. A. Preminger; Princeton: Princeton, 1974) 739.

[75]S. R. Hopper, "Irony—the Pathos of the Middle," *Cross Currents* 12 (1962) 31-40.

[76]Fretheim, *The Message of Jonah*, 13-38.

from the deity but from all others whom he encounters. Yet he does not
perceive his separation as disobedience. He believes that he has been
absolved of guilt through weathering the ordeal (of exile?); and he
yearns to return to the security of the temple, failing to realize that this is
no safe haven because his anger over divine injustice has not been
resolved.

The symbols of the story, as pointed out by Fromm, are all embodiments of protection and isolation.[77] Although the story has many levels
of meaning, it can be seen as a subtle critique of the re-establishment of
the Zion/temple emphasis in post-exilic Judaism. The temple is associated with the Tarshish-bound ship and the devouring great fish, as well
as the *sukkâ* with its withered *qîqāyôn* in which Jonah's hot anger
remains unabated. It will not bring the secure protection that Jonah's
Yahwism affirms. Instead it further isolates him from the divine creation.
This critique of temple religion contains an implicit universalism that
rebukes Jonah for searching out shelters that isolate him from others. In
chap. 1 he separates himself from the sailors who instantly worship
YHWH when given the chance. In chap. 3 he is isolated from "the great
city" that nevertheless shows its potential to adhere to the divine will.
And, as we learn in chap. 4, whether or not the "great city" fulfills its
potential or not, it can be included within the sphere of God's pity
because it too is part of God's creation. The combined anti-temple and
universalistic thrust may be aimed at the "Temple Presence" theology of
the post-exilic Zadokite priesthood, yet the Book of Jonah cannot be
easily set within the categories of "proto-apocalyptic" thought. This
must be left for others to resolve.[78]

Regardless of the story's original environment, its subtle, ironic use
of symbols gives the satire an archetypal power that has intrigued
countless generations ever since. The final word in its interpretation will
never be spoken.

[77] See above, footnote 36.
[78] See P. D. Hanson, *The Dawn of Apocalyptic* (Philadelphia: Fortress, 1975)
esp. 1-31, 161-86, 369-401.

The Origin of the Idea of Resurrection

LEONARD J. GREENSPOON
CLEMSON UNIVERSITY

I N the field of Biblical studies there is scarcely a position one can take that does not arouse opposition from some quarter or other. Interestingly, modern scholarly debate frequently reflects many of the same concerns that rose to the surface in early Jewish and Christian communities, at a time when questions of proper interpretation of the text often assumed the proportions of a life-and-death choice. Such is the case in connection with the belief in the resurrection of the dead.

Thus, the Jews of Jesus' time, so we learn from the New Testament, were divided over this issue. Some, and especially the Sadducees, a group whose leadership was centered among the priests in the Temple of Jerusalem, found no reference to resurrection in the literature they considered holy. Others, particularly the Pharisees, who as teachers were found in synagogues and other centers throughout the Land and beyond, found support for the doctrine of resurrection in texts they judged authoritative. It is probable that, from at least the second century B.C.E. on, the majority of Jews adhered to the Pharasaic position on this question.

The modern Biblical scholar has under investigation essentially the same Biblical texts as the Pharisees or Sadducees, but he is in the habit of bracketing (at least in scholarly publications) questions concerning his own stake in the authority or truth of any particular text. This should not mean, however, that a present-day scholar is any less serious about such texts than those who carried on the debate 2000 years ago. It does mean that he brings somewhat different concerns and very different methodologies to bear in the interpretation of passages from the Hebrew Bible.

Scholars have reached a consensus that a belief in resurrection can be detected only in the very latest portions of the Hebrew Bible. Almost all admit its presence in Daniel 12, which dates from the second century B.C.E., and a few are willing to locate it as well in material perhaps a century or two older than that. Along with this reluctance to see any trace of a belief in resurrection in earlier writings goes the understanding that the origins for this belief in Israel are to be sought in the influence of Persian doctrines or borrowings from the various pagan cults that centered on dying-and-rising fertility gods.

In discussions of origins for Biblical practices and beliefs (such as resurrection), one often encounters terms such as "inner-Israelite development" and "foreign influence/borrowing" used as if they were clearly-understood, mutually exclusive expressions. In our opinion, such a use is too restrictive, even misleading, for when properly defined these terms can describe complementary, and not opposing aspects of the same process. To us it is beyond question that the writers of the Hebrew Bible, in whatever way they were inspired, drew from the environment in which they and their predecessors lived. Thus they described God and many of His activities through the same epithets, motifs, imagery, and language that other cultures utilized to portray their deities.

However, none of this can be taken to mean that the Biblical writers were equating YHWH with such deities. Rather, divine activity can be translated into the human realm only through the human idiom, be it word or picture. Certain modes of representation become traditional, so that divine activity can be comprehended by man; thus, it is possible for different cultures to make even simultaneous application of shared modes of representation to define the activities of deities who nevertheless remain distinct entities in the minds of believers.

In the hands of Biblical writers, the creative use of such shared material was a particularly effective way to draw contrasts between the one God whom they worshipped and the numerous deities that populated the pantheons of their pagan adversaries. In reality, neither the crude term "borrowing" nor the seemingly loftier "inner-Israelite development" can do justice to the complex, creative process we have touched on. While we must restrict ourselves in this paper to those aspects of this process that relate to our topic, we are certain that a modern reader who gives consideration to such matters will find his understanding of, and appreciation for, the Biblical treatment of many topics greatly enriched.

Our analysis of the origin and development of the Biblical concept of bodily resurrection is divided into five main parts. After a discussion of the range of meanings Biblical writers allotted to the terms "life" and "death" (part 1), a study of words and phrases connected with the concept of resurrection in the Hebrew Bible (part 2), and a survey of previous hypotheses (part 3), we present our own hypothesis, which links the specific concept of resurrection with a dominant theme from Israel's earliest history on—YHWH as Divine Warrior (part 4).

Various connections suggested by this hypothesis are tested in a number of Biblical passages, through which we demonstrate that a belief in resurrection arose early in Israel and underwent rather profound development, as the people who held this belief themselves underwent change. It emerges that Dan 12:2, which is in general the starting point for any discussion of the Biblical concept of resurrection, is the end product of countless generations of speculation concerning man's place in the afterlife (part 5). In post-Biblical and Rabbinic Judaism and in early Christianity, Daniel 12 formed the basis for much further elaboration. While any detailed discussion of such developments falls outside the limits set for this paper, in our Conclusions we do have something to say about how our interpretation of the material from the Hebrew Bible might affect the way in which we view the endeavors of those Jews and early Christians to ground their beliefs concerning resurrection in the Biblical text itself.

1

The most successful attempt to put in order Biblical references to "life" and "death" has been that of Johs. Pedersen, whose *Israel: Its Life and Culture* remains remarkably fresh even though more than fifty years and countless trends have intervened since the publication of its first part.[1] What Pedersen says about "life" and "death" is part of his overall presentation of the Biblical view on the nature of man. As Pedersen reads the evidence, the Hebrew Bible presents man as a vital unity or totality. The comprehensive term *nepeš*, which corresponds to "man in the totality of his being," is frequently used in this connection. When one sees *nepeš* translated as "soul" in Pedersen's work, and at various points in translations of the Hebrew Bible, one must understand the English term in this comprehensive manner and not read into it any sort of body-soul division of the type encountered in later theological speculations.

Pedersen demonstrates that any and all parts of the human body have the capacity to act as "soul": "All that pertains to the life of the soul, *is* the soul, and this more particularly must hold good of its most important functions."[2] Thus it is that from "heart" to "bowels" the totality of a human can be summed up through reference to a particular feature. Man is a unity of all of these elements, none of which acts or is acted upon without reference to the total organism.

The body as "flesh" is not excluded from this pattern, for "every soul must have a body, a form in which it lives."[3] While in some passages "flesh" indicates the weaker nature of a human being, in other contexts it stands in synonymous parallelism with a term such as "heart." What is most significant for our purposes is that no matter what the context, "flesh" or "body" refers to "the human entirety, or in

[1] Johs. Pedersen, *Israel: Its Life and Culture* (London: Oxford University, 1926 [vol. 1], 1940 [vol. 2]).

[2] Pedersen 1, 171.

[3] Ibid., 176.

other words the soul." In sum, "the whole of the soul is in the reins, in the heart, in the flesh, just as, on the other hand, the flesh stamps the whole of the character of the soul."[4] There is simply no room here for the idea that in life the soul is of a higher, more divine substance than any or all of the body, or that the body is in and of itself a corruptive agent for man. What is true in life is, we shall see, true in death as well, for death involves the *totality* of man (Pedersen's "soul") just as does life.

What makes for life is the totality of man's being, his "soul." This totality can experience and be experienced through a myriad of physical manifestations, but while being a perfectly valid expression thereof, the physical does not exhaust the potentialities of man's entirety. There are other aspects of "soul" which are not so decidedly physical. While such aspects can be generally comprehended under the term "soul" or connected with any or all of the manifestations referred to above, descriptions of man in action frequently make use of the specific terms "heart" and "spirit."

Again, we must turn to Pedersen for definitions, if we wish to avoid reading back into the Biblical material concepts that we would almost naturally associate with such terminology. We must recall first of all that "heart" or "spirit" or any other term can be used to designate man's total existence. Yet, even so, nuances do tend to cluster around various of the terms. "*Nephesh* is the soul in the sum of its totality, such as it appears; the heart is the soul in its inner value . . . the heart is at the same time the centre of the soul and the substance gathering round it and determining its strength." The spirit "is more particularly the motive power of the soul. It does not mean the centre of the soul, but the strength emanating from it and, in its turn, reacting upon it."[5] It is important to realize that the use of terms such as "spirit" or "heart" does not suggest, any more than "soul" itself, something superior to "bowels" or "liver," or separable therefrom. To use a phrase from A. R. Johnson, man is a "psycho-physical unity."

When all aspects of man's being are functioning well, then there is a force or vitality that the Hebrews summed up through the word "life." Thus understood, "life" has a positive connotation which extends far beyond the mere functioning of certain organs of the body. As Pedersen explains it, "life is all that fills the soul, makes it 'wide' and full of matter."[6] Life then is fullness, activity, power. Anything that would siphon off this active, vital power so that the "soul," man's entire being, cannot function to its fullest capacities leads away from life.

[4]Ibid., 178.
[5]Ibid., 104.
[6]Ibid., 154.

As strength characterizes life, weakness becomes increasingly characteristic of those forms of existence lacking the fullness of life—and culminating ultimately in death. At this point I can do no better than to quote Pedersen on these matters:

> Life and death are not two sharply distinguished spheres, because they do not mean existence or nonexistence. Life is something which one possesses in a higher or lower degree. If afflicted by misfortune, illness or something else which checks the soul, then one has only little life, but all the more death. He who is ill or otherwise in distress may say that he is dead, and when he recovers, he is pulled out of death.[7]

The full implications of this statement will become clear as we proceed. Here it is important to point out that this weakness does not affect some parts of man's entirety (e.g., the body) to the exclusion of others (e.g., the spirit). Weakness to any part of the unity that is man is weakness to every part; unless checked, that weakness leads to death, when "*both* [my emphasis] soul and body lose their lives at the same time, because they are a unity."[8]

Thus death is marked by a losing of strength, an emptying out of the soul; it is not marked by the dissolution of the constituent aspects of man's totality, or by the liberating escape of one/more still-vital parts of man's being from the rest, or by the change of man from one form of existence to another. The unity that was man in life remains, in its weakest state, to man in death.

In what ways is the material presented from Pedersen important for the overall development of our own argument? First of all, it conveys a rather clear and, at least in its contours, accurate picture of the Biblical view of the nature of man, his life and death. If one wishes to say anything meaningful about the resurrection of the dead, then it is necessary to have at least a broad conception of the nature of the being involved [the human being]; the quality of his existence when he experiences (or might experience) resurrection [death]; and the state from which he has passed and to which he will return [life].

Such an overall view is valuable not only as it provides an appropriate context in which to discuss the concept of resurrection, but also as a corrective to certain confusions that may arise and/or erroneous solutions that may be advanced. To deal with the latter first, it is clear that any attempt to understand the Biblical conception of the afterlife which presupposes body-soul duality or the necessarily corruptive nature of "flesh" is at variance with the overwhelming evidence of the Hebrew Bible itself. While the Biblical text undoubtedly reveals development and

[7]Ibid., 153.
[8]Ibid., 180.

shifts of emphasis in these concepts during the lengthy period of its writing, editing, and compilation, we can find nothing to indicate that the view of man as a unity or totality underwent any fundamental change from the earliest to the latest accounts in the Hebrew Bible. In this respect, the story from the Talmud (b. Sanh. 91a-b) about the cripple and the blind man accords well with the Biblical view.

In the Hebrew Bible death is seen as something natural, although not to be longed for or precipitated. Since this is the case, it is confusing, even misleading, to lump together in the same discussion a general concern for the afterlife (which involves a host of issues), immortality, and resurrection. Immortality and resurrection especially must be kept separate, and furthermore, the appropriateness of the latter in the context of the Biblical worldview must be decisively underscored. The belief in resurrection affirms that at one time or another the dead (or at least some of them) will be revived in their bodies and live again. It is thus clear that resurrection means the start of life once again after death; i.e., life doesn't simply continue. This is totally consistent with our previous discussion concerning the nature of man from the perspective of the Hebrew Bible.

On the other hand, the belief in immortality, as the word itself implies, means continuance; i.e., in a general sense the "soul" is not subject to death. Also implicit in such a belief is the idea that the body is an impeding factor to be shed as quickly as possible so that the pure soul can make its ascent. While we would not argue that absolutely no trace of a belief in immortality is present anywhere in the Biblical text, it is obvious that such a conception, even in its most general sense, is not compatible with our understanding of what the Bible itself says about the nature of man. We might add that in what follows we keep to the specific issue of the resurrection of the dead.

Before leaving Pedersen, we should note that our acceptance of his account of certain aspects of the Biblical view of man is not a blanket endorsement of all of his views. On the contrary, we have serious reservations at a number of points. We have never been convinced, for example, that "what we call objective, that is to say inactive, theoretical thinking without further implications, does not exist in the case of the Israelite. He naturally knows mind-images, which are only flashes, or so peripheric as to leave no deeper impress upon the soul."[9] Or: "For the Israelite *thinking* was not the solving of abstract problems. He does not add link to link, nor does he set up major and minor premises from which conclusions are drawn."[10] All of this comes disconcertingly close to Levi-Bruhl's "primitive mentality" or the so-called distinction between

[9]Ibid., 106.
[10]Ibid., 108.

pre-logical (pre-/non-Greek) thinking and our own, more advanced thought processes.[11]

2

A belief in the concept of resurrection is the acceptance that at some time the dead will be revived in their bodies and live again. No one would deny that such a belief, in some form or other, is found somewhere in the Hebrew Bible. It is interesting then that there is no Biblical term for "resurrection of the dead." The phrase *thyt hmtym*, which is still used in modern Hebrew, is apparently of Rabbinic origin. It is essentially through verbs that Biblical writers expressed this concept, and an exploration of these verbs and associated lexical items should go far in advancing our understanding of what "resurrection" meant in the context of the Hebrew Bible.

That such an exploration is necessary becomes clear even after only momentary consideration of the very term "resurrection" that we use throughout this paper. It is hard for anyone acquainted with the New Testament to consider the concept of "resurrection" totally apart from THE resurrection. Moreover, both that event and the etymology of the word itself suggest that the spatial concept of "rising up" is somehow primary. Such associations, however, should not lead us to make Biblical "resurrection" conform to this pattern. An initial warning in this direction is supplied by the expression *thyt hmtym*, discussed above, which says nothing of "rising up," but rather means something like the "revivification of the dead."

On the other hand, an exploration of "resurrection" terminology is hardly a neutral one. By this we mean that one first must determine that a passage is dealing with resurrection before its vocabulary can be introduced into the discussion. At the same time, however, it is very much a matter of vocabulary and its interpretation that enables one to decide that a passage does indeed refer to resurrection. Furthermore, a word or expression associated with resurrection in one or two contexts may in the vast majority of its uses mean nothing more than (normal) "living" or "awakening" or "standing up."

To break out of the circle, one must examine an extremely wide range of passages, certainly those most commonly thought to refer to resurrection. John F. A. Sawyer has conducted an examination of this type, and a summary of his results is worth considering.[12] He finds that there are five sectors or lexical groups that form the core of resurrection

---

[11]For a recent evaluation of Pedersen's work, see J. R. Porter, "Biblical Classics III. Johs. Pedersen: Israel," *Exp Tim* 90 (1978) 36-40.

[12]John F. A. Sawyer, "Hebrew Words for the Resurrection of the Dead," *VT* 23 (1973) 218-34.

language. These sectors are represented by the verbs *ḥyh* "to live," *qwm* "to stand up," *ḥqyṣ* "to wake up," *šwb* "to come back," and *ṣyṣ* "to sprout forth." In addition, there are temporal expressions and forensic terms. It should be noted that Sawyer does not limit his selection of examples to the Hebrew Bible, but includes Mishnaic and Mediaeval Hebrew as well. Further, he brings in illustrations from what he calls "the rich immortality sector of the field." Even though, from our standpoint, these two procedures cause needless confusion, the gathering together of this material is most valuable.

Can we proceed a step further than Sawyer and locate in one of these terms what we might call the essence or the heart of the process we define as Biblical resurrection? I think we can. Even though many are skeptical of such a reductionist tendency, as if the very attempt necessarily leads to the oversimplification of a complex matter, we are confident that in this case an emphasis on one particular term is both supported by the Biblical text and of great aid in understanding the origin and development of the concept of resurrection in the Hebrew Bible.

As we see it, the term which best sums up what is especially characteristic of Biblical resurrection is *ḥqyṣ/yqṣ* "to awaken" (in the stative sense). If we may be allowed to anticipate specific arguments developed below, in certain contexts we would translate this verb "to be (again) in a waking (=living) state."

First of all, we should note that all of the other major sectors isolated by Sawyer are rather closely related to *ḥqyṣ* with the possible exception of no. 2, "to stand up." Although it is surely only happenstance that "to wake up" is in the central (third) position in Sawyer's listing, it is a coincidence of the most felicitous kind. Particularly important, as we shall see, is the connection with the "sprouting up or blossoming forth" of nature, although it must be admitted that verbal formulations with *ṣyṣ* referring to resurrection are absent from the Hebrew Bible itself.

We reserve for a later section detailed examination of specific passages. Here we simply note that it is the verb *ḥqyṣ* which is used in the sole undisputed Biblical reference to the resurrection of the dead, Dan 12:2: "And many of those who sleep in the land of dust *shall awake*." We ought not, however, to stress this point overmuch, since the emphasis on this particular passage in most discussions may not be warranted on the basis of all of the Biblical evidence.

We prefer to place far greater stress on the fact that the picture of awakening from the "sleep of death" is fully compatible with the overall Biblical view of life and death. When death is thought of as man's existence in its most weakened state, then one can without great difficulty liken it to other states wherein man's strength is "poured out" to a marked degree.

Two such states are sleep and sickness. Our emphasis on the former should not lead one to overlook the fact that the imagery of illness is an important element in the Biblical conception of life and death. This is especially true with serious illness, in which man is forced to confront at close quarters the realm of death (we might say today such a person "has one foot in the grave"). The Bible certainly recognizes, however, as do we, some quantitative and qualitative difference between even the most severe illness or other distress and the ultimate "pouring out" that is death. And it is to the imagery of sleep that more than one Biblical writer turns to describe and characterize this state of death.

Dan 12:2, which we quoted just above, is again the *locus classicus* in this context: "And many of those who *sleep*. . . ." Texts as diverse as Job 14:12, Jer 51:39, and Ps 13:3 are further witnesses to the same usage. In the Deuteronomistic histories we are generally informed in connection with each of the departed rulers of Israel that he "slept with his fathers." We should note further that the dwelling place of the dead, no matter what the precise relationship between the individual/family grave and Sheol might be, is said to be permeated with darkness and silence, both of which to a lesser degree likewise characterize sleep.

Not all of the Biblical texts that liken death to sleep do so in order to affirm the doctrine of resurrection. In fact, just the opposite is true. However, in certain contexts, such as Daniel 12, we hear the affirmation that just as man's everyday sleep normally ends as he awakens, with strength renewed, to an invigorated form of life, so that sleep which is death will be ended, at least for some, with a re-awakening to the full possibilities of life. We shall see that this imagery is drawn not only from the life cycle of mankind, for observations and beliefs concerning the world of plants and animals also supply a necessary, even crucial component in the origin and development of the Biblical conception of the resurrection of the dead. Discussion and elaboration of that component follows in a later section.

To conclude the present section, we want to sharpen the focus somewhat and at the same time hopefully eliminate any false impressions that may have arisen in our outline of what we consider to be basic in the Biblical view of resurrection. First of all, our interest in isolating what we call the essence or heart of the process of resurrection is not to discover that simple, primal element out of which a more complex, full-blown doctrine ultimately evolved. As we trace it, the concept of resurrection was always complex, and is itself the result and combination of strands from other complex conceptions, most notably the theme of YHWH as Divine Warrior. Thus the development of the Biblical view of resurrection is not to be charted in terms of growth from simple to complex, but rather in terms of changes of emphasis in response to changing historical and theological concerns. In all of this the image of death-resurrection as sleep-awakening remains a fairly constant and stable one. (We shall see that the number of contexts in which the language of sleep-awakening could reasonably refer to resurrection is very limited; we have no interest in finding a reference to resurrection each and every time someone goes to sleep or wakes up.)

Our emphasis on essential element(s) does have one other advantage: it allows us to identify and place in proper perspective other elements that are non-essential. For example, in reference to the resurrections effected by Elijah and Elisha (1 Kings 17; 2 Kings 4), it is often pointed out that the youths in question were not buried and therefore could not be resurrected in the "proper" sense of the term. We see no indication, however, that actual burial is a necessary and essential precondition for the process of resurrection to take place. In the normal course of events, the dead are buried, but if a resurrection intervenes before that event, the lack of burial should make no difference. The source of this type of objection is, in our opinion, an excessive preoccupation with the idea of "rising up" from the abode of the dead. (Of course, the youths do "stand up" after they are resurrected, but that is not good enough for some critics.)

In all of the above much has been said about the nature of man; little has been said about the Biblical view of the nature of God. Or, to put it differently, much has been said about Biblical man's perception of his own nature and of the process of resurrection whereby a re-awakening from the sleep of death to the vitality of life was envisioned; little has been said about the role of God in all of this. Although such a procedure is valid for the purposes of developing our argument, this must not obscure what is undoubtedly the basic affirmation of the Biblical writers: there is one and only one God who created the world and all that is in it; who was, is, and will always be; and whom alone it is proper to worship. For the Hebrew no conception of his own existence, from life through death to whatever follows, is possible apart from their belief in the Lord, God of Israel.

All the other peoples of the ancient Near East also had views about the nature of man; as with Israel, these concepts were not unrelated to the peoples' understanding of the divine powers or forces in which they believed. As we read the evidence, it is correct both to call the Hebrews' belief monotheistic and to characterize this belief as unique (by which we do not mean better/worse, more/less correct) among societies prior to or contemporaneous with the Israelites.

If we can accept the uniqueness of the Hebrews' beliefs concerning God, then it follows that, to a greater or lesser extent, their beliefs concerning man's life, death, and the possibility of resurrection will also be unique. It is the finished product, however, the arrangement of components, the ultimate initiator of action that are unique; at numerous points, some of them significant, we would expect that the Hebrews held views in common with many of their neighbors. We referred earlier to the fact that a common store of language, motifs, and beliefs was the shared property of the various cultures of the Near East and that authors from each of these cultures drew from this common store to describe deities and actions that were not identical.

In connection with the Biblical conception of the resurrection of the dead, the question of origins is frequently encountered, as we have already noted. Thus, it is appropriate to describe and comment upon, in survey fashion, some of the ways in which this question has been answered. To this we now turn.

3

In discussing the question of the possibility of non-Israelite influence, we may most profitably survey the evidence in terms of three geographical/cultural divisions: Mesopotamia, Canaan, Persia. Our primary aim here is to identify general scholarly trends and the types of evidence adduced to support them.

Scholars have introduced material from Mesopotamia in two separate, but related contexts. Thus, some researchers, citing material of which the following passage from the "Poem of the Righteous Sufferer" (ANET 437d) is typical, seek to draw a parallel between the activity of a god such as Marduk and the role of the God of Israel as initiator of the process of resurrection:

> Who but Marduk restores his dead to life?
> Apart from Ṣarpanitum which goddess grants life?
> Marduk can restore to life from the grave,
> Ṣarpanitum knows how to save from destruction.

A careful study of this entire poem, as well as similar phrasing elsewhere, leads to the conclusion that these passages do not refer to "death, the ultimate pouring out." Rather, they are affirmations that (1) one suffering from grave illness or other serious distress is already experiencing life-draining death and also that (2) one in such a situation may seek restoration to health and fullness from one or another of the divine powers. In this respect, such statements are similar to a number found in the Hebrew Psalter (e.g., Pss 31:12, 88:4 ff, 143:3, also Lam 3:6), where a sufferer, who often claims that he has been afflicted unjustly, calls upon the Lord to aid him in returning to his former strength (and at the same time to justify him in the face of his enemies). Such parallels are obviously not without worth, but do not deal directly with the question of the resurrection of the dead.

The second starting point for the introduction of Mesopotamian evidence is an interest in (a) so-called dying and rising gods; (b) the inclusion of related mythic material in certain cultic rites; and (c) the important role of humans, especially kings, in rituals conducted at these same cultic rites. Such concerns figure prominently in what is generally known as the myth-and-ritual "school," of which the English scholar S. H. Hooke is perhaps the best-known exponent. In general his understanding of the relationship between myth and ritual is identical to that of the Cambridge ritualist, Jane Harrison: a myth is "the spoken correlative of the acted rite, the thing done; it is *to legomenon* as contrasted with or rather related to *to dromenon*."[13] As elaborated by Hooke and various of his followers, the central mythic text for the Babylonian New Year emphasized the death and resurrection of the chief god Marduk. The action that accompanied this myth involved the ritual death and resurrection of the king, conceived of as divine, behind which there may lie an earlier practice of the actual slaying of divine kings.

That this was in fact the nature of the Babylonian New Year observance has been widely questioned, as has the interpretation of certain passages as references to Marduk's death and resurrection. Since Hooke connected the New Year festival, as understood by him, with an earlier observance in connection with Tammuz (Adonis), it is relevant to note that recent commentators on the texts dealing with Tammuz do not find any reference to that god's dying and rising. As best it is his sister Inanna (Ishtar) who manages to win her own freedom from the underworld at the expense of Tammuz' imprisonment therein.

In some form or other, this pattern of myth-and-ritual, so it is argued, is also visible in the Hebrew Bible, where the king in Jerusalem partook of such practices as sacred marriage. Some even speak of the death and resurrection of YHWH in this context, as well. We simply do not see evidence in the Hebrew Bible itself to support this "reconstruction."

However, we should note that if one does accept the existence of a pattern as that discerned by Hooke and others in Babylonia and further sees reflected in the Bible the Jerusalem version of this myth and ritual, then a connection with the Israelite concept of resurrection is suggestive. On the other hand, it does not follow that a belief in a dying-and-rising god and knowledge of related myths and rituals necessarily lead to the conception of the resurrection of the dead found in the Hebrew Bible.

---

[13]Quoted in J. W. Rogerson, *Myth in Old Testament Interpretation* (BZAW 134; Berlin: Walter de Gruyter, 1974) 68. Chapter 6 (pp. 66-84) of Rogerson's volume is entitled "Myth and Ritual."

First, it is not clear that there is any place in this Babylonian myth-and-ritual pattern for the hope of the average believer (as opposed, for example, to the king) in his own resurrection. Secondly, we do not see how the belief in a deity (whether it be Marduk, Tammuz, or some other) who is constrained periodically to suffer death could possibly lead to an understanding of God who Himself has power over death and specifically the power to awaken the bodies of His dead believers.

The objections raised just above to the attempt to establish too direct a link between any sort of belief in a dying-and-rising god and the Hebrew conception of resurrection also hold true for the Canaanite evidence. In general, Canaan has been most fertile ground as the source for a number of Israelite beliefs and practices as well as linguistic usages, especially since the discovery and decipherment of Ugaritic texts in the late 1920's. Recent finds at Ebla insure that this trend will show no abatement in coming decades. The Ugaritic texts from Ras Shamra vividly confirm the fact that in Canaanite mythology the god Baal played the role of the periodically dying and rising god.

We know that the worship of Baal was a forbidden fruit, ofttimes voraciously consumed by large numbers of the Hebrews. At the same time, we note that even within the Hebrew Bible itself God is in numerous contexts described with attributes and epithets remarkably similar to those used with reference to Baal in the Canaanite texts. In short, the connection of resurrection with Baal cannot automatically be taken to exclude its being taken up from Canaanite sources into the Hebrew Bible. What does exclude such appropriation, at least as stated so baldly, is that the death and resurrection of Baal are no closer to the Biblical concept of God's awakening of the dead than is the same or similar pattern elsewhere.

We must not overlook the possibility, however, that other beliefs connected with Baal might have exerted an influence on the origin and development of the Biblical concept of the resurrection of the dead. In fact, the hypothesis we develop below makes much of what we might term the "Baal-element" in the Biblical descriptions of God as Divine Warrior and the importance of this latter theme for the Israelite belief in resurrection.

When we turn to the texts from Persia/Iran, both the substance and the nature of the argument changes. In the first place, there is no doubt that the doctrine of bodily resurrection is found in at least some religious texts from Persia. Thus we are not confronted with the phenomenon of the belief in a dying-and-rising god, something we consider wholly out of keeping with the Hebrew Bible, but with a doctrine that is surely comparable to that found in the Bible.

It is just at the point of comparison, however, that much of the apparent similarity breaks down. We have seen that in the Hebrew Bible resurrection is the re-awakening from the sleep of death brought about by God for His people. In Zoroastrian (Persian religious) texts, however, resurrection is "a veritable recreation; it consists in a reconstitution of the body through the reunion of its several component elements . . . the Persians emphasize the physical reconstitution of the creature."[14] In this connection, supposed linguistic parallels between texts in the two traditions have not always been carefully drawn.

The Persian texts have another attraction, apart from the differences and similarities in the process and implications of resurrection in the two cultures; namely, in the matter of dates. The Jews would naturally have first become acquainted with Persian ideas at the end of the Exile and throughout the early post-Exilic period. And it is in Biblical passages dated from precisely this period that many commentators have found the beginnings of a clear expression of Hebrew belief in resurrection, as well as other eschatological features. From both sides, however, reservations must be expressed in this regard. Specialists in Persian religion are not in agreement as to the dating of the Persian texts, and the dating of much Biblical material is notoriously circular. For example, if one holds on whatever grounds that a text clearly expressing the concept of resurrection *cannot* be early, then he is generally led to a later dating of any such passage than would be considered by another scholar who remains more open and sensitive to all possibilities. We will return to the question of the dating of Biblical material when we discuss individual passages below.

Even if the dating of texts does not exclude the possibility of significant Persian influence at the point of origin or at some (other) crucial point in the development of the Biblical doctrine, we would question whether the Jewish community of the Exilic or early post-Exilic period would have had any need to resort to such "borrowing" in order to express their belief. Paul Hanson, a student of Frank Cross's at Harvard and now one of his colleagues, has produced a number of studies arguing that many aspects of Jewish apocalypticism, previously thought to have been drawn from Persian religious sources, are in fact developments from the pre-Exilic and Exilic prophetic tradition which were shaped in the sociological matrix of the post-Exilic Jewish

---

[14]Robert Martin-Achard, *From Death to Life* (Edinburgh: Oliver and Boyd, 1960) 192f. As the subtitle of Martin-Achard's work ("A Study of the Development of the Doctrine of the Resurrection in the Old Testament") indicates, his volume touches upon many of the same issues and passages with which we deal in the present study. While we generally do not follow his interpretations, we have found considerable value in his discussions, which frequently include a succinct "history of scholarship" on individual passages and particular problems.

community in the Land of Israel.[15] That is to say, with respect to (proto-) apocalypticism, there is, according to Cross and Hanson, no need to have recourse to an explanation which attributes a dominant role to Persian influence. In respect to the concept of resurrection, which shares certain features with apocalypticism, we hope to prove that the same is true.

When Hanson speaks of further development of the pre-Exilic prophetic tradition or when we refer to a connection between the belief in resurrection and the theme of the Divine Warrior, then it might seem that we are championing the cause of "inner-Israelite development" over against any sort of foreign influence. That this would be a misstatement of Hanson's position is clear when he speaks of the decisive influence of a renewed interest in old mythological motifs on the part of just those Biblical writers most responsible for the development of (proto-) apocalypticism. Earlier, we spoke of the significance of Baal-language and imagery as a major component in the Biblical portrayal of YHWH as Divine Warrior.

Nevertheless, the term "inner-Israelite development" does serve to remind us that, regardless of what the origin of the concept of resurrection may be, its development within Biblical Judaism represents a unique reaction to historical as well as theological forces. Just as clear is it that from the Biblical standpoint the belief in resurrection is meaningless apart from the existence of God and the revelation of His attributes, in this case especially His power and its consequences.

That YHWH has power over death is affirmed in a number of Biblical passages. That He can bring the dead back to life is stated in two very ancient songs of praise: Deut 32:39, the Song of Moses, and 1 Sam 2:6, the Song of Hannah. This power is thrice demonstrated in the resurrections miraculously brought about through Elijah and Elisha in the old material contained in 1 and 2 Kings. (Part 5 contains detailed discussion of each of these passages.)

4

Our survey of previous studies concerned with the origin and development of the Biblical concept of the resurrection of the dead included the outright rejection of some suggestions, but the partial or modified acceptance of others. After all, our hypothesis depends on no new textual or archaeological discovery, but rather on an approach which proceeds from a new starting point. And it is precisely in

---

[15]See Paul D. Hanson, *The Dawn of Apocalyptic* (Philadelphia: Fortress, 1975).

connection with this starting point that we are most indebted to Frank Cross.

Cross was not the first to identify the Biblical theme of the Lord as Divine Warrior, to place this theme within the larger context of Holy Warfare, or to draw parallels between Biblical and Canaanite concepts in this regard. In his *Canaanite Myth and Hebrew Epic* (especially in chapters 5-7), however, he succeeds in drawing together, synthesizing, and interpreting the relevant material in such a way that he has clearly set the tone for discussion of these topics for years to come.[16] We gratefully acknowledge our debt to Cross and to his student Patrick Miller who has also carried on extensive research in this area.

The Israelite community acknowledged the primacy of the Lord God in any and all of the workings of the world and its inhabitants. His hand could be viewed in the phenomena of nature and equally well in the activities, great or small, of mankind, particularly of His people Israel. It is in the context of this overarching affirmation of the Hebrew Bible that we place the conviction that God is also working His will when His people are at war. This was especially true with reference to the wars fought during the conquest of the Promised Land, as described in the books of Joshua and Judges. The conviction that God was fighting alongside His people, however, that in effect Israel's wars were God's wars, was not limited to any particular historical period or event and could be expressed as an open-ended hope for divine intervention as well as an interpretation of a contemporary or past event.

Within the Hebrew Bible itself the concept of Holy War and God as Divine Warrior did not free Israel from playing a major role in the battles that were to be fought. God fought *along with* Israel; His presence was not usually viewed as a substitute for the active participation of His people. In fact, the responsibility for human participation was subject to certain regulations, the infringement of which could lead to disastrous defeat for Israel (as in Joshua 7). Furthermore, the people were bound to suffer defeat whenever they turned from God by, for example, presuming that any military undertaking of their own was synonymous with Holy War.

At no point is the concept of God as Divine Warrior stated more succinctly or unambiguously than in the ancient song preserved in Exodus 15. Part of v 3 reads in the Hebrew *yhwh ʾyš mlḥmh*, which is most literally translated, "The Lord is a man of war." The "Song at the Sea" (Exodus 15) has been variously dated, but it is probable that it dates not much later than the events it describes. Joshua's farewell address (in Joshua 23) and the ceremony of covenant renewal (in Joshua 24) are

[16]Frank Moore Cross, *Canaanite Myth and Hebrew Epic: Essays in the History of the Religion of Israel* (Cambridge: Harvard University, 1973).

replete with statements like "it is the Lord your God who has fought for you" (23:3), "Then I brought you to the land of the Amorites . . . they fought with you, and I gave them into your hand, and you took possession of their land, and I destroyed them before you" (24:8), "the men of Jericho fought against you . . . and I gave them into your hand" (24:11).

At many specific points God's role as leader of His warring people is graphically portrayed. Sometimes this portrayal occurs in prose narrative, as at Josh 10:11, where "the Lord threw down great stones from heaven" against Israel's (and His) enemies. Characteristically, such a portrayal occurs in poetic passages, such as Exodus 15 quoted above. In another very old poem, the Song of Deborah (Judges 5; as with the crossing of the Sea of Reeds [Exodus 14 and 15], the victory of Deborah and Barak is told in a prose and poetic version in successive chapters), the advance of God is described as follows:

> Lord, when thou didst go forth from Seir
> when thou didst march from the region of Edom,
> the earth trembled,
> and the heavens dropped,
> yea, the clouds dropped water.
>
> The mountains quaked before the Lord,
> yon Sinai before the Lord, the God of Israel.
> (Judg 5:4-5, RSV)

We should also look at v 20 in this regard:

> From heaven fought the stars,
> from their courses they fought against Sisera.

In his role as Divine Warrior, YHWH does not fight alone; His Heavenly Host, here pictured as the stars, accompany Him in His activity here as well as in other contexts.

While still moored to a particular historical event, the descriptions in Judges 5 do take on what we might term "cosmic" dimensions. The term "cosmic," as we use it, refers to the introduction of descriptive language which not only affirms God's role at this particular moment, but connects it with the totality of God's action—both past and future— through which He manifests Himself. Thus, the imagery of Judge 5:4f links this event with the theophany and revelation at Sinai.

The full force of such imagery as Judg 5:4f depends in large part, to be sure, on its evocation of Israel's past encounters with God through the processes of history, but there is to this imagery an imaginative force which, while building on the recollection of history, is not totally bound or determined by it. Such a force is even more vividly apparent in

passages, notably in the Psalms, where the expression of belief in God as
Divine Warrior is not linked directly to any particular historical encounter. We may call this "mythic" or transhistorical language, if we
wish, but the faith which produced these passages was informed with the
same sense of God's acting in history that rose closer to the surface in the
examples previously discussed.
    One such passage is Ps 24:7-10:

> Lift up your heads, O gates!
> and be lifted up, O ancient doors!
> that the King of glory may come in.
>
> Who is the King of glory?
> The Lord, strong and mighty,
> the Lord, mighty in battle. . . .

Psalm 18 (2 Samuel 22), especially vv 9-14; Psalm 29; and others could be
quoted as well. Nor does this begin to exhaust the evidence from
material that is surely to be dated to the earlier period of Israel's history.
From a later period come such passages as Isa 24:19-23; 34; 35; Zechariah
9; Haggai 2; Job 26:5-14 and 38:1 (=40:6).
    Certain general developments and changes of emphasis are visible as
we move from the earlier to a later period, but that is not our concern at
this point. Our purpose has been to show the importance of the theme of
God as Divine Warrior, leading His Heavenly Host and His people in
Holy Warfare, for a proper understanding of the Hebrew Bible. At this
juncture it is appropriate to quote at some length from Patrick Miller's
evaluation, with which we fully agree, of the significance of this theme
within the overall structure of the Hebrew Bible:

> The conception of God as warrior played a fundamental role in the
> religious and military experiences of Israel . . . One can go only so far in
> describing the history of Israel, or its religion, or the theology of the Old
> Testament without encountering the wars of Yahweh. In prose and poetry,
> early and later materials alike, the view that Yahweh fought for or against
> his people stands forth prominently. The centrality of that conviction and
> its historical, cultic, literary and theological ramifications can hardy be
> overestimated.

Or again, "the view of Yahweh as warrior can hardly be a peripheral
matter in the effort to work out a Biblical theology. Rather, it lies at the
theological center. . . ."
    Near the end of his work Miller again calls attention "to the
centrality of the divine warrior imagery and language in the Old
Testament. . . . From beginning to end this theme in various forms and
with various ramifications comes to the fore. . . . The language and

understanding of God as warrior dominated Israel's faith throughout its course . . . wherever one turns one encounters this theme."[17]
The source of the language and imagery through which God's actions as Divine Warrior are described is at least twofold. The dominant element throughout, even when it is left largely unexpressed, is Israel's conviction that God's revelation is preeminently visible in the historical process. In their recitations of the history of mankind, the writers of the Hebrew Bible fused event and interpretation, since for them no meaningful description of, for example, the activities of the Exodus-Sinai-Conquest complex was possible without the acknowledgment of God's determinative role. God then is visible in the course of each series of wars conducted by the Israelites. Viewed in this way, the "military history" of Israel bears witness to numerous divine-human encounters, and supplies to the writers of the Hebrew Bible what is unique and most vital in their portrayals of YHWH as Divine Warrior. Thus, Israel's sense of its own history and of God's role in that history is central to its understanding of Holy Warfare and the Divine Warrior.

However, Israel was not the only people of the ancient Near East to believe that divine powers determined success or failure. In fact, there was hardly a group that did not invoke the help of the gods as an integral part of any military undertaking. In general, a people's defeat was judged as a defeat for its chief gods and was the occasion for a change of allegiance from the weaker to the stronger pantheon. In matters divine, as on earth, might makes right, so it seemed, and there was no reason to be overly concerned with deities who were unable to protect their human subjects.

In Israel the thrust of monotheism impelled the believers to look at their own failings, rather than to any weakness in their God, when hoped-for victory turned into defeat. It is true that many Hebrews, despairing of sole trust in a God who seemed to desert them, did indeed abandon YHWH or seek to combine His worship with that of other deities. Nevertheless, the prophets and other spokesmen of God repeatedly called upon Israel to remember the unique nature of YHWH. As was the case with other aspects of their belief, components of both unique and shared faith existed in an uneasy tension that sometimes threatened to overwhelm what was distinctly Israelite.

Even though there were such dangers in drawing from the common store of language and images to describe God as Divine Warrior, writers of the Hebrew Bible did so, especially in the earlier and the later periods. How else was Israel to comprehend God's action in the military sphere? Nevertheless, the writers of the Hebrew Bible were not indiscriminate in

[17]Patrick D. Miller, Jr., *The Divine Warrior in Early Israel* (HSM 5; Cambridge: Harvard University, 1973) 1, 7, 170f.

their use of such language. Detailed study of the Biblical and Canaanite
(Ugaritic) material has led numerous scholars, including Cross and
Miller, to conclude that the Canaanite myths dealing with Baal supplied
what we call the second element within Israelite descriptions of God as
Divine Warrior. To put it another way, various writers of the Hebrew
Bible sought to diffuse the supercharged language of their Canaanite
neighbors through the careful appropriation of just such language in
their portrayals of YHWH. In this way, they hoped to bring into greater
relief the very real differences that separated God from a so-called deity
with whom He seemed to share a number of attributes and characteristics.

It is not possible here to do more than outline, in a very schematic
way, the Canaanite material to which constant reference is made in the
works of Cross and Miller. In our discussion of the Canaanite evidence,
we reverse the procedure we followed in connection with the Biblical
material; i.e., here a general summary and evaluation drawn from
Miller's study precedes specific examples from the texts themselves:

> With regard to the Ugaritic texts, the emphasis [for a study of the divine
> warrior] is placed on the Baal and Anat [Baal's female consort] cycle. . . .
> Baal epic . . . furnishes the most information concerning divine warfare.

We learn that "Baal was understood to be the leader of an indeterminate
host apparently conceived in part as a military force," for Baal and Anat
are "the warrior deities par excellence in the Ugaritic texts."[18] After a
successful initial battle against Prince Yamm (the Sea, which "represented the unruly powers of the universe who threatened chaos"), Baal
engaged in combat with Mot (Death, which "represents the dark chthonic
powers which bring sterility, disease, and death").[19] In these major
battles of Baal, "kingship, sanctuary, and fertility [are] at stake. The
battle of the gods is the means whereby these three qualities of world
order—divine and human—are established."[20]

At first glance, it may appear that no sure link could possibly be
established between the Hebrew Bible and these Canaanite texts. After
all, God never appears with a consort, and we are accustomed to think of
His battles and those of His people more in terms of historical encounters. On the other hand, in the Hebrew Bible, as in the Canaanite
texts, the Divine Warrior is accompanied by his Heavenly Host,
frequently described in terms of natural phenomena; the Hebrew Bible
also supplies impressive testimony, often overlooked, that the enemies of
YHWH are not limited to hostile nations and tribes, for to God is

[18]Miller, 11, 20, 24.
[19]Cross, 116.
[20]Miller, 39.

emphatically ascribed responsibility for the banishment of chaos and the establishment and maintenance of order, both cosmic and terrestrial. An investigation of the available texts in this regard led Miller to conclude that:

> In many respects the imagery associated with Yahweh is the same as that associated with Baal, particularly with regard to Yahweh as warrior. He battles as the storm god, riding or driving the clouds. He sends forth his voice and the enemies flee. He battles the monsters of the deep who represent death and chaos, as does Baal.[21]

At one point in the Baal cycle from Ugarit, Kothar, the divine craftsman, gives the following prediction of Baal's victory over Yamm, his first adversary [Ugaritic texts are taken from Cross, *CMHE*]:[22]

> Let me speak to you, O Prince Baal,
> Let me recite (to you), O Rider of the Clouds:
>
> Behold, thy enemy, O Baal,
> Behold, thy enemy thou shalt smite,
> Behold, thou shalt smite thy foes.

To this we may compare several verses at the close of the Blessing of Moses (Deut 33:26f) [unless otherwise noted, all Biblical texts in this section are given in the form reconstructed by Cross; the reader is invited to compare this with a standard translation such as that found in the RSV]:

> There is none like the god of Jeshurun,
> Who rides the heavens mightly,
> Who gloriously rides the clouds.
>
> He drove out the enemy before you;
> Before you he smashed the foe.

We may also compare the similar effect that the voice of each is said to produce throughout the world, one might even say throughout the cosmos:

> Baal gives forth his holy voice,
> Baal repeats the utterance of his lips,
> His holy voice [shatters] the earth.

---

[21]Miller, 60.

[22]We have taken the liberty of altering Cross's rendering of certain proper names, in order to present such names in their more familiar, if less correct, form. The same is true in the material quoted from Miller above. Thus Cross's Baᶜl and Miller's Baᶜal become Baal, and so forth.

[At his roar] the mountains quake,
Afar [   ] before Sea,
the highplaces of the earth shake.

As described in Psalm 29 (vv2ff),

The god of the Glory thunders,
The voice of Yahweh is on the Waters,
Yahweh is upon the Deep Waters.

The voice of Yahweh is mighty; the voice of Yahweh
   is majestic.
The voice of Yahweh splinters the cedars;
Yahweh splinters the cedars of Lebanon.

Both Baal and God are able to enlist any or all of the forces of nature in their efforts to destroy the powers that oppose them. The following description of the activity of YHWH in this guise comes from Ps 18 (2 Sam 22):10ff:

He spread apart the heavens and descended,
A storm cloud under his feet,

He rode a cherub and flew,
He soared on the wings of the wind.

He set darkness round about him,
His pavilion is the raincloud.

Cloud-banks were before him,
Before him his clouds raced by,
Hail and coals of fire.

He shot forth his arrows and scattered them,
Lightning-bolts he flashed and put them in panic.

For Baal, we find passages such as the following:

Seven lightning bolts he casts,
Eight magazines of thunder;
He brandishes a spear of lightning.

Commenting on the prominence of storm imagery, here and elsewhere, Cross remarks that "fire and light, smoke and shining cloud, thunder and quaking are all elements intimately bound together in the poetic descriptions of the theophany of the storm god, or of the attack of the Divine Warrior."[23] The power of God is manifest in, though not limited to, the natural phenomena associated with a storm. Thus the

[23]Cross, 169.

writers of the Hebrew Bible, partly in dependence on similar descriptions from the surrounding Canaanite environment, could turn to storm imagery to picture God on the march against inimical forces.

As we noted above, the first of Baal's enemies was the untamed, chaotic force of Yamm, the Sea. Baal's victory is described as follows:

Sea fell,	He sank to earth,
His joints trembled,	His frame collapsed.
Baal destroyed,	Drank Sea!
He finished off Judge River.	

God is likewise portrayed as victor over the chaotic forces of the Sea in Ps 89:10f:

> You rule (enthroned) on the back of Sea.
> When his waves rise you calm them.
>
> You crushed Rahab [the Flood dragon] as a corpse,
> With your mighty arm you despatched your enemy. . . .

So also Isa 51:9f:

> Was it not thou who smote through Rahab?
> Who pierced Tannīn (the dragon)?
>
> Was it not thou who dried up Sea,
> The waters of the abysmal Deep?

Victory over death (Mot) is credited to Baal's consort Anat in the following passage:

> She seized El's son Mot.
> With a sword she sliced him;
> With a sieve she winnowed him;
> With a fire she burnt him;
> With millstones she ground him.

Isa 25:8, in the context of the Isaiah Apocalypse (chapters 24-27), says of the Lord that "He will swallow up death for ever."

Victory also brings for both Divine Warriors alike kingship and installation in their respective temples, which are situated on great mountains. Representative pictures of the victorious Baal include the following:

> My temple I have built of silver.
> My palace, indeed, of gold. . . .
>
> Behold, Mighty Baal lives;
> Behold, the Prince, lord of earth exists.

> Baal sits enthroned, (his) mountain like a dais,
> Haddu the shepherd, like the Flood dragon,
> In the midst of his mount, Divine Ṣapōn,
> On the mount of (his) victory.

From Ps 29:10 a similar picture of God emerges:

> In his temple (his) Glory appears!
> Yahweh sits enthroned on the Flood dragon;
> Yahweh is enthroned, king forever.

Exod 15:17 is also significant in this respect:

> You brought them, you planted them
> In the mount of your heritage,
> The dais of your throne
> Which you made, Yahweh,
> The sanctuary, Yahweh,
> Which your hands created.

We have concentrated our attention thus far on the implications of victory and defeat for the Divine Warrior and such foes as Chaos and Death. Already in these passages, however, we note that the actions of the Divine Warrior also have their ramifications in the world of nature; ultimately, all of nature is affected by Divine Warfare and thus has a stake in its outcome.

As the Divine Warrior marches off and engages his foes in battle, his anger has a devastating effect throughout nature. Thus, as Baal does battle with Lothan, the primeval dragon,

> (Then) the heavens withered (and) drooped
> Like the loops of your garment.

In like manner, Baal's absence can bring to a halt virtually all of the processes of nature on which the continued well-being of the world depends:

> Seven years Baal failed,
> Eight years the Cloud Rider;
> No dew nor shower,
> No surging of the double-deep,
> Nor goodly sound of Baal's voice.

Baal's eventual victory, on the other hand, produces a bounteous over-flow of nature's richest gifts:

> The heavens are raining oil,
> The wadis run with mead.

The Hebrew Bible contains similar descriptions. At God's wrath,

> The heavens roll up like a scroll,
> And all their hosts languish,
> As the vine leaf withers,
> As the fig droops.
>
> (Isa 34:4)

Hab 3:5f presents the following picture of the reaction of nature to the march of YHWH as Divine Warrior:

> Before him walked Pestilence,
> Plague marched at his feet.
> He stood and shook Earth;
> He looked and startled the nations.
> The ancient mountains were shattered,
> The eternal hills collapsed.

Ps 18:8f supplies our final example in this regard:

> The earth quaked and shook;
> The foundations of the mountains shuddered;
> They quaked when his wrath waxed hot.
>
> Smoke rose from his nostrils,
> And fire from his mouth devoured;
> Coals flamed forth from him.

Vivid descriptions of nature's joyous re-awakening at God's victory are also not lacking in the Hebrew Bible. Isaiah 35 serves as a companion piece to the preceding chapter, a portion of which we quoted just above. From Isaiah 35 comes the following depiction of nature's exuberant and vital response, a response which stands in marked contrast to the sombre and stark mood attending the collapse of nature:

> The desert and the steppe shall laugh,
> The wilderness shall rejoice and blossom;
>
> Like the crocus it shall burst into bloom,
> And shall rejoice, yea, rejoicing and singing. . . .
>
> Indeed waters shall break out in the desert,
> And streams in the wilderness.
>
> And glaring desert shall become a swamp,
> Parched earth springs of water.
>
> The abode of jackals shall become a pasturage.
> Open land (turn into) reeds and papyrus.
>
> (Isa 35:1-2, 6b f)

The movement of nature from dormancy to purposeful activity can be likened to the process of birth:

> Fall down before Yahweh who appears in holiness!
> He makes Lebanon dance like a bullcalf,
> Sirion like a young buffalo. . . .
> The voice of Yahweh makes the desert writhe;
> Yahweh makes the Holy Desert to writhe;
> Yahweh makes the hinds to writhe (that is, calve).
> (Ps 29:2, 6, 8)

With respect to the Ugaritic material Cross has delineated two complementary themes:
(A) The Divine Warrior marches off to war. Driving a fiery cloud-chariot, he uses the elements of nature such as the thunderbolt and the winds as weapons against his enemies. At his wrath, nature is in upheaval, with mountains tottering and the heavens collapsing; in effect, all nature wilts and languishes. In the foreground is the cosmogonic myth in which Chaos—represented by the deified Sea Yamm or by the flood dragon Lothan (Leviathan)—is defeated.
(B) The Divine Warrior, victorious over his foes, comes to his new temple on his newly-won mount. At the sound of his voice all nature awakens. As the mountains dance and the trees clap their hands, the fertility of the earth, of sea, and of womb manifests the rule of the life-sustaining Divine Warrior.

What Cross calls an archaic mythic pattern underlies both Canaanite and early Biblical texts. This significant pattern, which encompasses the two themes outlined just above, is made up of the following elements:

(A) March of Divine Warrior to battle
    (1) The Divine Warrior goes forth to battle against Chaos.
    (2) Nature convulses and languishes as the Warrior manifests his wrath.
(B) Return of Divine Warrior to take up kingship
    (1) Warrior returns to take up kingship among the gods on his mountain.
    (2) Nature responds to the victorious Divine Warrior; the earth is fertilized, there is festive glee among men and mountains, animals writhe in giving birth.

We have repeatedly emphasized that at the center of Israel's conception of God as Divine Warrior stands the conviction that YHWH does indeed reveal Himself through the processes of human history and natural phenomena visible in that history. Careful use of language shared by the Hebrews and Canaanites, among others, served to enhance descriptions of such events as the Exodus-Sinai-Conquest and to underscore what the Biblical writers considered the fullest implications inherent in the events themselves.

It seems to us that the writers responsible for the Hebrew Bible often reached the same goal from two quite different points of departure. Let us illustrate this with reference to the variety of descriptions of the Crossing of the Sea of Reeds. What lies behind them all is the fact that the Hebrews, escaping from the enslavement of Egypt to the promised freedom beyond, passed successfully through a body of water (Sea of Reeds) that the pursuing Egyptians were unable to negotiate.

In many cases, preeminent among them Exodus 15, the author begins with this historical occurrence itself. His description is not limited, however, to the human participants: it begins and ends with praise for God, and throughout it directs the readers' attention to the decisive and active role of God in the defeat of His people's (and His) enemies. All of this also serves to highlight the passive role of the Sea, which can act only as commanded by God:

> Your right hand, Yahweh,
> Shattered the enemy . . .
> At the blast of your nostrils
> The waters were heaped up.

> The swells mounted up as a hill;
> The deeps foamed in the heart of the sea . . .
> You blew with your breath,
> Sea covered them . . .
> You stretched out your hand,
> The underworld swallowed them.
>
>   (Exod 15:6, 8, 10, 12)

Let the Canaanites and others continue in the errors of their ways, when they attach to Sea/River active, independent divine power to produce Chaos or other disaster! The Hebrew knew, and continued recitation of God's actions at the crossing of the Sea reminded him, that God as Divine Warrior had met and conquered the waters of Chaos, which were now reduced to the status of one among many in the divine arsenal of weapons.

Other writers, among them the psalmist who composed Psalm 77, move from initial descriptions of God's defeat of the Waters of Chaos to the recollection of the Exodus from Egypt:

> The Waters saw you, Yahweh,
> The Waters saw you and writhed;
> Yea the Deeps shuddered.

The clouds streamed water.
The heavens roared,
Your bolts shot back and forth.

Your thunder was in the tempest,
Lightning lighted the world,
Earth shuddered and shook.

Your way was through the sea, Yahweh
Your path in the deep waters,
Your tracks beyond our understanding.

Thou didst lead thy people like a flock
by the hand of Moses and Aaron.
> (Ps 77:16-20, all but the last
> two lines are in Cross's recon-
> struction; see also Isa 51:9-11)

This psalmist holds in common with the author of Exodus 15 the belief that a full understanding of the Crossing of the Sea is impossible apart from the recognition of God's role as Divine Warrior both in the victory over the Egyptians and in the conquest of the forces of Chaos in any and all of their manifestations

The Biblical passages from which we have quoted thus far were composed over a period of at least 700 years. Our emphasis on the earlier material should not obscure the development and shifts of emphasis in the Biblical concept of the Divine Warrior from the pre-Exilic period through the Exile to the era of the early post-Exilic community. Undoubtedly, the theme of the Divine Warrior also underwent extensive reworking at Ugarit and elsewhere, but the charting of processes at work outside of Israel is not our purpose. Nor can we do justice to the wealth of evidence even within Israel itself. Rather, we limit ourselves here to two brief observations.

First, as Cross points out, the classical prophets rarely made explicit use of the concept of God as Divine Warrior; especially avoided was just that language, so prominent in our examples above, which had the closest links to Canaanite imagery associated with Baal. The figure of YHWH as Divine Warrior is visible, but only in muted tones, in the following passage from the first chapter of Amos:

Yahweh roars from Zion,
From Jerusalem he gives voice.
The pastures of the shepherds languished,
The peak of Carmel became sere.
> (Amos 1:2; see also Mic 1:3)

Is not the avoidance by the classical prophets of the most striking language drawn from the theme of the Divine Warrior to be understood as an indication of their negative judgment on the whole enterprise of attempting to differentiate the true God of Israel from Baal (and other pagan "pretenders") through the use of language and imagery common to descriptions of both? To be sure some would see the point, but there was just too great a danger that an equal or larger number would be seduced by the lure of shared attributes to equate God with Baal and either worship them both or shift primary allegiance to the Divine Warrior of the Canaanites.

In the late Exilic and post-Exilic period the complex of language and imagery surrounding the figure of the Divine Warrior once again became a widely-accepted vehicle for depicting significant aspects within the realm of God's activity. To this period belong such prophetic compositions as the Isaiah Apocalypse (chapters 24-27); Isaiah 34 and 35; several passages from Deutero- (and Trito-) Isaiah; Zechariah 9; and Haggai 2. Themes which had lain largely dormant for centuries suddenly produced fresh and exciting fruit, as if they themselves were responding to the march of a victorious Divine Warrior whose life-stimulating presence had for too long been absent in Israel.

What is especially taken up from the earlier concept of the Divine Warrior is the portrayal of nature's response as God enters into or returns from combat. In this respect, Isaiah 34 and 35, from which we quoted earlier, are typical.

Cross speaks of the recrudescence (i.e., the breaking out anew) of older, mythic motifs and language during this period. It was not limited to the theme of the Divine Warrior, but included significant aspects of apocalypticism and other eschatological features as well. The Biblical material in which one or more of these themes play a part is often referred to as proto-apocalyptic.

The re-introduction of this material during the late Exilic and post-Exilic period is the result of a combination of factors. Quite possibly the affinities of Biblical language with descriptions of Baal were no longer felt to be the danger that the classical prophets had perceived in their time. Such language had become sufficiently "domesticated" that many were unaware of its earlier and non-Israelite connections. Most importantly some in the post-Exilic community were no longer satisfied with the leadership provided by the priestly and lay Establishment. They reached far back to other ancient traditions, and what they came up with were themes such as the Divine Warrior, which they used to shape and justify their future course of action.

We now turn to that aspect of the theme of the Divine Warrior which is most suggestive of a connection between this larger complex and the specific belief that the God of Israel has power to reawaken the bodies of dead human beings: in his role as Warrior the deity has power over nature, over even such pervasive forces as Chaos and Death. This concept makes much of the divine role in creation and the establishment of order, over against the emphasis on the god's subjection to nature implicit in the belief in a dying-and-rising god.

It is to the second of Cross's complementary themes that we should turn our attention in this regard. At the return of the victorious Divine Warrior, once-dormant nature quickens in reaction: everywhere there is a surge of renewed vigor, evident in joyous activity, fertility, and the blossoming forth of life in a wide range of manifestations. It would hardly be too much to refer to all of this as a re-birth, brought about by the active stimulus of God Himself.

Man, as part of nature, could hardly remain unaffected. The Hebrew Bible makes this point clear in such passages as the following:

> Then the eyes of the blind shall see,
> And the ears of the deaf be opened.
>
> The lame shall leap as a gazelle,
> And the tongue of the dumb sing.
> (Isa 35:5f)

Was one limited, in depicting man's reaction, to references to healing and the like, or was it possible to go beyond this and affirm that man's reaction too involved a re-awakening from a dormant state to the vitality of life? The evidence strongly suggests that some Biblical writers did in fact take the latter course and draw from the larger picture of the quickening of all nature the conclusion that man, as a created being, would participate in this life-producing response.

There is everything in the Hebrew understanding of "life" and "death" and in the characteristic language of resurrection (e.g., sleep, re-awakening, sprouting forth), all of which we explored earlier, to suggest just such a connection. Further, as we detail below, the contexts in which references to resurrection appear in the Hebrew Bible and the humans, especially Elijah and Elisha, through whom God's power is manifest point quite clearly to this same connection. We admit that it is not possible to cite any one passage that demonstrates an undeniable link between the theme of the Divine Warrior and the concept of human resurrection, but this is to be expected, inasmuch as the latter belief is not a necessary or universal outgrowth of the former theme, but rather a particular development of an aspect of that theme as a result of Israel's theological and historical perspectives.

We have attempted to show that the resurrection of man can be fit into the overall portrayal of nature's response to the victorious Divine Warrior. What the Hebrew Bible says about the process of resurrection is consistent with this. We have not yet looked, however, at Biblical passages dealing with the relationship between man and nature. On the basis of that evidence, are we correct even to speak of man as "part of nature" and to envision that he would have the same stake in the Warrior's return as, for example, the trees, the deserts, and the animals of the field?

From first to last the Hebrew Bible maintains that man is but one of the creations of God and that humans thus share with all created beings a certain number of fundamental characteristics. The descriptions from Genesis of the origins of the first man, whose creation applies by extension to the birth of all mankind, make abundantly clear that humans stand in the closest relationship to both animals and the earth itself. Gen 2:7 states that "the Lord God formed man of dust from the ground [i.e., earth]." At his death man returns to the earth out of which he was formed:

> In the sweat of your face
> you shall eat bread
> till you return to the ground,
> for out of it you were taken;
> you are dust,
> and to dust you shall return.
> (Gen 3:19, RSV)

Commenting on the connection between man and the earth implicit in these passages, Hans Walter Wolff notes that this relationship "is documented linguistically in the original text through the consonance of $\ ^{\jmath}\bar{a}d\bar{a}m$ (man) and $\ ^{\jmath a}d\bar{a}m\bar{a}$ (earth), in which the common etymological root $\ ^{\jmath}dm$, 'to be red,' appears for man's reddish brown skin and for the reddish brown of the earth."[24]

Gen 2:19 provides a description of the formation of animals. In its language this verse forms a remarkable parallel to 2:7 (the formation of humans), thus emphasizing that mankind and the animal kingdom are to a large extent composed of the same substance: "So out of the *ground* the Lord God *formed* every beast of the field and every bird of the air. . . ." The close relationship between man and animals also emerges in Genesis 1. The formation of man is part of the same process of "creation" that produced the earth and all of the animals that inhabit the water, fly, and move on ground. In fact, terrestrial animals are a product of the sixth, and last, day of Creation no less than man himself.

Biblical writers did not favor extensive speculation into the workings of nature, of the sort from which a highly-developed scheme of the relationship between man and nature might have evolved. Points of connection between man and (the rest of) nature, however, do clearly

[24]Hans Walter Wolff, *Anthropology of the Old Testament* (Philadelphia: Fortress, 1974) 94.

emerge from a careful reading of the first chapters of Genesis, and some of these points receive confirmation elsewhere in the Hebrew Bible. The psalmist who composed Psalm 139 includes within his address to the Lord an account of his own birth, part of which reads as follows:

> It is thou who has formed my kidneys,
> who has woven me together in my mother's womb. . . .
>
> My bones were not hidden from thee
> when I was being made in secret
> wrought motley-wise in the depths of the earth.
> (Ps 139:13, 15; according to Wolff)

Wolff has offered several comments on the phrase "in the depths of the earth" that are relevant for the present discussion: "It is noticeable in this context that, besides the womb as man's chamber of development, the psalmist names the depths of the earth. . . . This is the reflection of an archaic view according to which man 'sprouted from the earth like corn.' "[25] (Cf. the explanatory note to this passage in the New Oxford Annotated Bible, which refers to the womb, "poetically called 'the depths of the earth.' ")

Wolff then brings in the following passage from the first chapter of Job (note: Job, who lies prostrate on the ground after having received the crushing news of his family's disaster, is the speaker):

> Naked I came from my mother's womb,
> and naked shall I return there.
> (Job 1:21, Wolff)

As understood by Wolff, this passage shows that "Job sees his mother's womb and the womb of the earth as, for man, belonging together." "There," which is absent from the earliest translations of the Hebrew text, "undoubtedly means the hidden places in the womb of the earth, in analogy to the mother's womb." He also speculates that "the ancient oriental form of burial in a squatting position may be a reminder of the position of the embryo."[26] In a later address, which like Psalm 139 deals in part with the birth of an individual man, Job calls upon God to:

> Remember that thou hast made me [Heb.: as] of clay;
> and now thou turnest me to dust again.
> (Job 10:9)

Thus, what was true with respect to the first man (Gen 2:7, 3:19) applies with equal validity to each and every individual human who

[25]Wolff, 96.
[26]Wolff, 96f.

follows. It is interesting to note that the closeness of the relationship between man and nature is affirmed alike in contexts dealing specifically with Creation and those in which the birth and death of man play a subsidiary, though important part in the overall development of a larger theme or argument.

In a few places in the Hebrew Bible we can detect a refinement of the belief that the relationship of *all* men to nature is the same. These passages, which need not be later than any of the preceding, contain the distillation of considerable reflection on possible correlations between varieties of human types and different conditions within nature at large. The two which follow are closely related in thought and language, and clearly derive from the same tradition:

> Blessed is the man
> who walks not in the counsel of the wicked . . .
>
> but his delight is in the law of the Lord,
> and on His law he meditates day and night.
>
> He is like a tree
> planted by streams of water,
> that yields its fruit in its season,
> and its leaf does not wither . . .
>
> The wicked are not so,
> but are like chaff which the wind drives away.
>   (from Psalm 1, RSV)

> Thus says the Lord:
> "Cursed is the man who trusts in man
> and makes flesh his arm,
> whose heart turns away from the Lord.
>
> He is like a shrub in the desert,
> and shall not see any good come.
> He shall dwell in the parched places of the wilderness
> in an uninhabited salt land.
>
> Blessed is the man who trusts in the Lord,
> whose trust is the Lord.
> He is like a tree planted by water,
> that sends out its roots by the stream,
> and does not fear when heat comes,
> for its leaves remain green,
> and is not anxious in the year of drought,
> for it does not cease to bear fruit."
>   (Jer 17:5-8, RSV)

We have quoted first from Psalm 1, which functions as a prologue for the entire Psalter, because it is more familiar to most readers of the

Bible. It is widely agreed, however, that the section from Jeremiah, whether composed by the prophet himself or written by another and inserted into the prophetic corpus, is the earlier of the two, and moreover that it served as a source for the author of Psalm 1. We note also that the contrasting descriptions drawn from nature are far more extensive in Jeremiah 17, while in Psalm 1 relatively more space is taken up with the characterization of a righteous man and the rewards and punishments allotted to the righteous and wicked respectively. In this respect, Psalm 1 represents a difference in emphasis which might well be explained as a further development from an earlier stage when the descriptive material, based on close familiarity with the natural phenomena themselves, was the stimulus for the comparison with the human situation.

The portrayal of the sterility of desert and wilderness and its comparison with the man who does not trust in the Lord are especially prominent in Jeremiah. (Psalm 1 substitutes the more commonplace picture of the separation of worthless chaff at the time of threshing.) Thus the state of the wicked is precisely that of nature at the time the Divine Warrior marches off to combat his foes. The righteous man, on the other hand, is like an ever-verdant tree firmly established and continuously nourished by waters which stand as the source of life against any onslaught that threatens the vitality and growth of nature. As we saw earlier, the return of the victorious Divine Warrior brought just such fertility and blossoming forth throughout nature.

In short, it is not all men, but only those whose righteousness is manifested through their trust in God, their study of divine law, and their avoidance of evil, that are worthy to participate as full partners with the rest of nature in that joyous response to the Divine Warrior which is Life. The wicked, by their own repeated attempts to cultivate "un-natural" fruit from the blighted trees of evil, forfeit their "natural" right to share in the renewal of life brought about by the Divine Warrior. They are, so to speak, locked in a self-imposed permanent state of darkness and dormancy, which even the life-sustaining creative activity of the Divine Warrior cannot penetrate. It is natural, as we saw, for all of nature, man included, to die; it is distinctly unnatural for any to miss the re-awakening promised to all of God's created beings.

If it is correct that this additional theme of the righteous man's kinship with nature vs. the wicked man's alienation from it flowed into the larger complex surrounding the Divine Warrior at an early period, then we should be able to find a reflex of this theme in the related belief in the resurrection of the dead. In fact, this additional theme may provide important aid in tracing the Biblical concept of resurrection, as, for example, when we look at the two passages, Dan 12:2 and Isa 26:19, which are invariably included in any discussion of resurrection in the

Hebrew Bible. Dan 12:2, which envisions the resurrection of both righteous and wicked, may be seen as a later typological development than Isa 26:19, which limits the process of resurrection to God's righteous people (cf. Isa 26:14).

To this and a host of other issues we turn, as we investigate a number of references and some supposed references to resurrection in light of the hypotheses we have developed above.

5

In our opinion, it is not necessarily the most desirable procedure, when speaking of development and even of origin, to move in strict chronological order from the (hypothetically) earliest material to that produced during successively later periods. Not only does such a procedure prejudice the evidence by frequently assuming absolute dates when even the relative ordering of material is unsure, but it also tends to substitute unilinear development for what ought to be viewed as a far more complex process. Our choice of Dan 12:2 as the starting point for this section may seem paradoxical, since we argue that it represents the latest and in some respects most developed statement concerning resurrection found in the Hebrew Bible. We trust, however, that the very familiarity of this passage, its wide use and study in previous discussions concerning the Biblical concept of resurrection, and especially the ways in which our consideration of Daniel opens up a number of other passages for investigation, all serve to justify our choice in this regard.

Dan 12:2

a   And many of those who *sleep* in the land of dust *shall awake*. ["the land of dust," with George Nickelsburg; cf. RSV: "the dust of the earth"][27]

b   Some to eternal life, and some to eternal contempt. [Further note: We agree with Nickelsburg that *lḥrph* (RSV: "shame") did not form part of the original text of this verse, but represents a later gloss on the very rare word *dērā'ôn* ("contempt").]

We have previously discussed the primary importance of the terms "sleep" and "awake" for a proper understanding of the Biblical concepts surrounding death and the (re-)awakening to life that is resurrection; there is no need for further elaboration on these points. Nor are we

[27]For this and subsequent references to Nickelsburg, see George W. E. Nickelsburg, Jr., *Resurrection, Immortality, and Eternal Life in Intertestamental Judaism* (HTS 26; Cambridge: Harvard University, 1972).

inclined to enter into the continuing debate concerning the scope of the anticipated resurrection or the precise identification of those for whom either the certainty of future reward or the equally sure prospect of punishment is an already-present reality in the mind of the author of this passage. Rather, we want to focus on the innovation in this passage; namely, the affirmation that through the process of resurrection not only the righteous, but also the wicked are re-awakened from the sleep of death (see our discussion immediately preceding in support of the view that such a belief is indeed an innovation vis-à-vis the earlier formulations of the Biblical concept of resurrection).

We can locate the sources for the distinctive formulation in Dan 12:2b in both the politico-religious situation at the time of its composition and in the absolute faith of its author that each and every one of God's words, as revealed through his prophets, must ultimately be fulfilled. This section of Daniel reflects the tumultuous period during which the Maccabees and their followers were engaged in bitter, often bloody combat against the Syrian forces of Antiochus IV (Epiphanes) and his allied sympathizers among the Jewish population itself. The modifications in the ancestral religious practices which Antiochus and his supporters sought to introduce throughout Israel would have led, in the eyes of the Maccabees, to nothing short of the total destruction of Judaism through its submersion in the all-encompassing ocean of Hellenism. Since the author of this section of Daniel apparently knew of the beginnings of the Maccabean uprising in 167 B.C.E., but not of the re-taking and re-dedication of the Temple at Jerusalem in December, 164, we can date Daniel 12 with some precision to this three-year period.

There are some who hold that all of the book of Daniel arises out of the Exilic period in which the first six chapters are set. To argue thus, especially with respect to the visions and interpretations contained in chapters 7ff, is to drain them of just that sense of steadfast trust, in the context of immediate and profound danger, which made this material so powerful a vehicle of faith in its contemporary second-century setting and which also served as an exemplar for countless later generations.

The Jewish people had experienced numerous disasters prior to the Maccabean period; the prophets had been able to explain them as God's judgment on His disobedient people, who in turning away from Him had in effect brought their own deserved punishment on themselves. It was a simple matter, particularly from the vantage point of Jerusalem, to view the fall of Northern Israel in this light. It was surely more difficult for the citizens of the Southern Kingdom to be made to comprehend that the fall of their beloved Jerusalem and the subsequent captivity and Exile were likewise the result of their own presumptuous trust in self, in place of the faith owed to God alone; such prophets as Jeremiah and Ezekiel made valiant efforts at that time as well.

What, however, was any successor of these prophets to make of the course of events during the first years of the Maccabean revolt, when the righteous suffered and died as a result of their uncompromising adherence to the faith of Israel, while the ungodly prospered and even thrived precisely because they forsook the commands of the Torah? To be sure, the Syrians and their foreign allies were also deserving of divine punishment, but God had always had a way of punishing such nations before they could fully enjoy the fruits of their only apparent success. On the other hand, there had been no previous period in which a portion of the Jewish nation achieved analogous power and wealth, which was real and not just apparent, at the expense of their fellow Jews, whose lives, property, and religious convictions they were willing to sacrifice to gain acceptance from pagan peoples, with their foreign religious, cultural, and social patterns.

The author of Daniel affirmed in 12:2a that through the process of resurrection many of the dead will awaken at some time. Thus far he stands firmly in a tradition especially (but not solely) visible in Isaiah 26, from which the author of Daniel apparently drew the language and imagery he used here. (The clear parallels between Dan 12:2a and Isa 26:19 will be noted below.)

The unparalleled degree of criminal activity on the part of so many Jews, however, cried out for chastisement even greater than the exclusion from resurrection that Isa 26:14 envisioned for the dead overlords of Israel, and this in spite of the obvious severity of such punishment. In like manner, one might have dared to hope that the future status of those who suffered undeserved deaths would be of special concern to God, and most markedly different from and superior to the state of those who purchased prosperity on earth at the cost of their own religion, Land, and people.

In this connection, it is probable that the writer of Daniel had in mind the divine rewards and punishments graphically portrayed in the last chapters of the book of Isaiah (Trito-Isaiah). George Nickelsburg has convincingly demonstrated that many passages in Third Isaiah bear striking resemblances to the actual situation at the time of Daniel, especially with respect to the apostasy of the wicked. From the perspective of the author of Daniel, these Isaianic passages read like a prophetic description of just what contemporary Israel was undergoing.

Third Isaiah went beyond description of the actions of the wicked to the inescapable divine reaction against those who thus provoked Him. Third Isaiah is likewise rich in illustrations of the ample rewards to be bestowed on those whose faith in God stood firm against all adversity and temptation. Such punishment and vindication had not yet been experienced (i.e., on earth), however, when the author of Daniel wrote, in spite of the fact that the wicked had acted in precisely that manner

which Third Isaiah (and other prophets) had spoken of as certain to
provoke divine wrath and then retribution. Firmly convinced that ultimate divine reward and punishment were no less sure than the human
actions already witnessed, the author of Daniel could state with certitude
that exactly what Third Isaiah had foreseen as the fate of the righteous
and ungodly would indeed be measured out when the dead were re-
awakened by God through the process of resurrection.

Nickelsburg is able to point to one particular lexical item that in
effect seals the link between Daniel 12 and the Isaianic material. We
noted earlier that *dērā'ôn*, which formed part of the authentic text of
Dan 12:2b and stands in antithetic parallelism to "life," is extremely rare
in the Hebrew Bible. In fact, that word occurs in but one other verse, Isa
66:24 (the last verse of the book of Isaiah). Its appearance both there and
in Daniel in the context of the punishment of the wicked can hardly be a
coincidence.

We can summarize as follows the elements that make up the belief
expressed in Daniel. Like others before and contemporary with him, the
author of Daniel envisioned a bodily resurrection of (some of) those who
lay in the sleep of death. His portrayal of the reawakening of the
righteous to a full vitality worthy of the term "life" is in line with, for
example, Isa 26:19. His certainty that the wicked, whose earthly prosperity seemingly made a mockery of divine retribution, would indeed
receive their deserved punishment is the product of an unwavering faith
that what the prophets, here especially (Trito-) Isaiah, had spoken in
God's name must ultimately come true.

Isa 26:19, 14

Isa 26:19

a   Thy dead shall live, their bodies shall rise. ["their bodies," with
    RSV; Heb.: "my body"]
b   Those who dwell in the dust shall awaken and sing for joy. [For b,
    we accept as original the preceding text, which has been preserved in
    the Qumran (Dead Sea) manuscript 1QIsa³; cf. Heb., as translated in
    RSV: "O dwellers in the dust, awake and sing for joy!"]
c   For thy dew is a dew of light,
d   and on the land of the shades thou wilt let it fall. [Translation of c
    and d from RSV]

One immediately notices the similarities in phrasing between this verse
(especially a-b) and Dan 12:2, of which we spoke earlier. It is hard to
imagine that the author of Daniel worked with no knowledge of this
passage.

Most commentators have sought to date the Isaiah Apocalypse (chapters 24-27) through the analysis of supposed references to historical events contained within these chapters. The fact that such analysis leads to dates varying by several centuries should warn us that either the references are such veiled allusions that no analysis is likely ever to penetrate them satisfactorily or that in the last analysis these reputed references to the course of human history are nothing but scholarly illusions. Unless we are totally in error, the latter alternative is the correct one, in which case we need not greater historical accuracy, but more sensitivity to the literary forms and genres under investigation.

Hanson is one researcher who has approached these difficult questions along the lines suggested just above. Rejecting once and for all the quest for a pattern of historical references in such material as Zechariah 9, Isaiah 34-35, and the Isaiah Apocalypse, Hanson proceeds rather from the recognition that these passages are given shape and substance through the abundant use of themes surrounding the Divine Warrior and Holy War. Using a variety of typologies (including poetic structure, orthography, thematic development, and others), Hanson arrived at a sixth century date for the Isaiah Apocalypse and related material. (While there is admittedly a degree of subjectivity in each of the typological sequences devised by Hanson, the convergence of several such typologies, when applied independently according to Hanson's procedure, carries considerable weight and is convincing to the author.)

The imagery of the Divine Warrior is of course not incompatible with the recitation or recollection of the course of history, as we saw earlier. However, careful study has shown that with the recrudescence of older mythic motifs, during the Exilic and early post-Exilic periods, explicit connections with specific events in human history recede farther and farther into the background. The break with history was never complete; nevertheless, increasingly the writers of this material could use even well-known names and places to illustrate activity of the Divine Warrior that was not thereby limited to a particular time or locale.

Isa 26:19 speaks of the (re-)awakening and rising of dead bodies. Is this a reference to "literal" resurrection or simply "figurative" restoration of the people Israel? The context, replete with imagery and language of the Divine Warrior, strongly suggests the former. Associations with the world of nature abound, and specific elements introduced from that realm, such as "bodies," "dust," and "dew," would seem to serve no function if only some sort of restoration, rather than actual resurrection is involved. Moreover, as we argued above, we are not dealing here with any single event in human history, such as the Exile, with which we are allowed to connect the particular notion of Restoration. Rather, the author of this passage expresses his firmest conviction that the righteous ones, faithful to God and His promises (i.e., *Thy* dead), would in time to come have a part in the natural process of revivification and rejoicing that Biblical (and other) writers had for long associated with the returning march of the victorious Divine Warrior.

Isa 26:14

The contrast between Isa 26:19 and 26:14 is the basis for a further argument in support of our interpreting v 19 in terms of "literal" resurrection. 26:14 states, with reference to wicked overlords who oppressed Israel, that

> They are dead, they will not live;
> They are shades, they will not arise;
> to that end thou has visited them with destruction
> and wiped out all remembrance of them.
> (RSV)

As an indication that the wicked exclude themselves from participation in the "natural" process of resurrection, in effect make themselves "unnatural," this verse fits well into its context and forms a meaningful contrast with v 19. The sentiment expressed in v 14 finds parallels elsewhere in the Bible, as we saw earlier when we looked at Psalm 1 and Jeremiah. If v 19 refers not to resurrection, however, but to restoration, the entire force of any possible contrast is lost. Surely, no one anticipated a restoration, national or otherwise, for Israel's godless oppressors! On the other hand, it would certainly be valuable to fashion a clear statement about the respective *post mortem* fates of the righteous and the wicked, so as to dispel any misapprehension that death severed the link between the just and their God or offered an avenue of escape to a better "life" for those who opposed God while on earth.

In this apocalyptic vision of Isaiah, then, resurrection of the dead, since it is limited to the righteous, is in itself vindication of their righteousness and the initial stage in the process of entry into a revitalized new "life." No further process of judgment is envisioned.

The sixth century Isaiah Apocalypse is full of explicit imagery and language drawn from the Hebrew concept of God as Divine Warrior. This should occasion no surprise when we recall our earlier discussion of the development of the themes associated with the Divine Warrior. In that section we also noted, and attempted to account for, the avoidance of just such explicit language on the part of the classical prophets. In the works of these prophets, the figure of YHWH as Divine Warrior is at times visible, but in general this portrayal is fashioned only in "muted tones." Frequently other, more characteristically prophetic themes are intermingled, as the prophets pressed the concept of Divine Warrior into service as but one weapon in the unceasing battle they fought on God's behalf against their stiff-necked, hard-headed fellow Hebrews.

Jer 51:39, 57

We are able to discern just this sort of intermingling of themes twice in Jeremiah 51, which was composed sometime in the sixth century. What makes these observations relevant to our present inquiry is the fact that two statements concerning resurrection are set in the midst of imagery that has its origins in the Biblical concept of God as Divine Warrior. As we shall see, both of these statements affirm, as did Isa 26:14, that wicked overlords are to be excluded from the process of the resurrection of the dead.

The first of these statements (v 39) is contained in an oracle which runs from v 34 through v 40. Language of the Divine Warrior can be detected even in the initial description of the Babylonian king's capture and destruction of Jerusalem:

> Nebuchadrezzar the king
> of Babylon has devoured me,
> he has crushed me;
> he has made me an empty vessel,
> he has swallowed me like a monster;
> he has filled his belly with my delicacies,
> he has rinsed me out.
>
> (RSV; all following citations from
> Jeremiah 51 are also from the RSV)

Such action was sure to provoke divine wrath and ultimately God's severest punishment. First, God's care for His people is portrayed in language drawn from the law-court (imagery frequently found in the classical prophets):

> Behold, I will plead your cause
> and take vengeance for you.
> (v 36a)

Language connected with the Divine Warrior comes to the fore again when Jeremiah begins to describe the manner in which God takes vengeance on behalf of His people:

> I will dry up her sea
> and make her fountain dry;

and Babylon shall become a heap of ruins,
the haunt of jackals,
a horror and a hissing,
without inhabitant.
                                            (vv 36b f)

This imagery is highly suggestive of the portrayal (in Isaiah 34 and
elsewhere) of the wilting and languishing of nature when the Divine
Warrior marches off to engage his foes in battle. It is then significant
that the following statement denying resurrection to Israel's (and God's)
present enemies is found in this context:

[they shall] sleep a perpetual sleep
and not wake, says the Lord.
                                            (v 39b)

As in Isa 26:14, the wicked oppressors of Israel have locked themselves,
through their own evil deeds, in the permanent aridity and sterility of
their own death, from which no re-awakening is possible.

Between the description of God's activity as Divine Warrior and the
condemnation of the wicked to death everlasting, Jeremiah interposes
another of his favorite symbolic representations: the cup of divine wrath,
whose contents are as "poisoned water" (Jer 8:14) to those who drink it.
Jer 51:38-39a reads as follows:

They shall roar together like lions;
They shall growl like lions' whelps.

While they are inflamed I will
prepare them a feast
and make them drunk, till they
swoon away
["swoon away," with the Septuagint and Vulgate; Heb.: "rejoice"]

In the oracle found in vv 50-58, the very same statement is made
with regard to the Babylonians and in a similar context. In this latter
oracle, however, much of the imagery drawn from the various themes
referred to above is left behind, as the actual historical situation receives
greater prominence. Citation of but a few verses from this second oracle
should suffice:

For the Lord is laying Babylon waste,
and stilling her mighty voice.
Their waves roar like many waters,
the noise of their voice is raised. . . .

for the Lord is a God of recompense,
he will surely requite.

I will make drunk her princes and
her wise men,
her governors, her commanders,
and her warriors;
they shall sleep a perpetual sleep
and not wake,
says the King, whose name is the
Lord of Hosts.

(vv 55, 56b, 57)

Since Jeremiah's purpose in these passages is to portray, as boldly and graphically as possible, the certainty of divine punishment against the Babylonians through their destruction on earth and their exclusion from the process of resurrection thereafter, he does not deal with the "positive" side of resurrection (as in, for example, Isa 26:19). We have no doubt that Jeremiah was as familiar with the full Biblical concept of resurrection as the author of the Isaiah Apocalypse. While it suited the purposes of the latter, however, in a grand apocalyptic vision, to deal specifically with the fate of both the wicked and the righteous, Jeremiah's purposes were achieved through the evocation of but part of the fuller belief in resurrection and its connection with the theme of the Divine Warrior.

Job 14:12

Before turning to Ezekiel 37, where the portrayal of the bodily resurrection of the people of Israel is carefully designed to give a prophetically-conditioned hope to the exiles in whose midst Ezekiel dwelled, we want to look briefly at one of the passages in the book of Job which contains a categorical denial of the possibility of human resurrection. In Job 14 the protagonist, in a reply to one of his fair-weather friends, states:

so man lies down and rises not again;
till the heavens are no more he
will not awake,
or be roused out of his sleep.

(v 12; all citations from Job 14
are from the RSV)

Earlier in the same chapter he expresses the same conviction:

But man dies, and is laid low;
man breathes his last, and where
is he?

(v 10)

Elsewhere Job makes the same point in a variety of contexts and with a variety of imagery (see, for example, 3:13 and 7:7ff). What is interesting in chapter 14 is that Job constructs a context with language at least reminiscent of that associated with the Divine Warrior. For example, in contrast to man as described in v 10, "there is hope for a tree . . ." (v 7):

> Though its root grow old in the earth,
> and its stump die in the ground,
>
> yet at the scent of water it will bud
> and put forth branches like a young plant.
>
> (vv 8-9)

According to Job, the perpetual dormancy of man after death (v 12) can be compared to certain phenomena of nature:

> As the waters fail from a lake,
> and a river wastes away and dries up. . . .
>
> (v 11)

We ought not to make too much of any connection between Job's "negative" statements here about resurrection and these images drawn from nature, especially since elsewhere Job says the same thing without any reference to this language. This passage at least raises the possibility, however, that certain statements excluding all humans from the process of resurrection arose as an extension of the belief that the wicked had no part in this process, such an extension itself stemming from the appraisal that no human is worthy of the designation "righteous."

Ezek 37:1-14

The "Vision of the Valley of the Dry Bones" (Ezek 37:1-14) is one of the most popular and oft-cited passages in the entire Hebrew Bible, and justifiably so. In the hands of many groups, these verses have become a proof text to support the reality of a resurrection of the dead. Our concern here is to determine just how justifiable such a use is; in other words, does this vision indeed refer to "literal" resurrection, or has this belief simply been read into it by later generations?

As this vision begins, the prophet is transported through divine agency to a valley or plain filled with "very dry" bones. Ezekiel is commanded by God to speak thus to the bones:

> O dry bones, hear the word of the Lord.
>
> Thus says the Lord God to these bones:

Behold, I will cause breath to enter you,
and you shall live.

And I will lay sinews upon you,
and will cause flesh to come upon you,
and cover you with skin,
and put breath in you,
and you shall live;
and you shall know that I am the Lord.

[vv 4b-6; these verses (as well as other sections in this
vision) were originally composed in the form of poetry;
numerous prosaic elements should not obscure this fact.
We have not attempted to reconstruct the poetic original,
but have simply laid out the RSV translation in a way
that allows the poetry to peek, if not shine, through.]

As a result of the prophet's initial address, the bones "came together, bone to its bone"; all else was also accomplished at once, except
for the (re-)introduction of the divine force of (re-)vitalization, spoken of
here as breath/spirit (recall Gen 2:7). After a further prophecy on the
part of Ezekiel,

the breath came into them,
and they lived,
and stood upon their feet,
an exceedingly great host.

(v 10)

V 11 makes it clear that the preceding vision should serve as a
message of renewed hope to those who lived as exiles in Babylon:

Then he said to me,
Son of man,
these bones are the whole house of Israel.
Behold, they say,
Our bones are dried up,
and our hope is lost;
we are clean cut off.

As we learn elsewhere in the book of Ezekiel (e.g., chapter 18), the exiled
were profoundly concerned with the question of guilt and responsibility.
Ezekiel nowhere suggests that the people did not deserve the exile and
other divine judgment which they received; on the contrary, it is a sign
of God's exceeding love for His people that they did not suffer far worse.
Ezekiel does take pains, however, to point out to the people that their
strength ("bones") has not permanently ebbed, nor are they without

hope forever, if they will but return to the true worship of YHWH. In this connection, the Vision of the Valley of the Dry Bones graphically portrays, to those who will but listen, that God will indeed restore His people, who in their present condition are as enfeebled as those already dead, to that vitality and relationship with Him that alone are worth calling "life."

Vv 12-14 add to this the picture of raising from the grave and especially the understanding that the restoration to which the prophet refers also includes a return to the Land of Israel. Even though we are not sure just how these latter three verses were originally linked to the earlier vision, it is clear that they can be fitted into the prophet's overall portrayal of God's restoration of His exiled people.

Most scholarly commentators are agreed in limiting the application of this Vision to the idea of restoration, even if they arrive at this conclusion through widely varying approaches. However, when one approaches this same Vision from the perspectives we have been developing, significant connections with the theme of the Divine Warrior can be discerned, and these very connections serve to make clear that Ezekiel was acquainted with the concept of the resurrection of the dead.

First of all, the scene in which the vision is set emphasizes the parched and lifeless condition not only of the bones themselves; by extension all of the surrounding natural features are drawn into the bones' aridity and lack of purposeful activity. In the background of this description lies the portrayal of nature's wilting and languishing during the period that the Divine Warrior marches out in his wrath to do battle against his enemies. As the result of divine initiative, the bones that had lain lifeless are re-awakened, joined again into the form proper to them, and finally re-established as complete, vital beings possessed of all the potentialities of life. It is not difficult to recognize here the life-giving activity of the Divine Warrior, whose victorious return leads to fertility and joyous, productive activity throughout nature.

From the above we can see that Ezekiel did make use of the mythic pattern that is by now quite familiar to us. In so doing, Ezekiel carefully selected for his Vision only those aspects that would most dramatically illustrate the determinative role of God in any re-awakening of the people to life.

There is a further detail within the vision itself that points to Ezekiel's fuller association of Divine Warrior imagery with resurrection. Several times the prophet is asked by God to play an important role. After being questioned first merely about the possibility that the dry bones could live, the prophet is instructed to speak the words which transform this possibility into reality. We have not previously seen such an explicit statement on the specific role of a human being in facilitating the general work of God as Divine Warrior or His specific activity in bringing about the resurrection of His people. Time and again, we read in the Hebrew Bible, God did select certain humans through whom to work His will; elsewhere we can detect a certain appropriateness in each choice, and such is also the case here with respect to God's actions as Divine Warrior.

A prophet's first encounter with YHWH is obviously of great importance in shaping the entire course of his prophetic vocation. In connection with Ezekiel, it ought not to be overlooked that his call to prophecy came during a manifestation of God as Divine Warrior, with storm-chariot, attendants, and all of the elements of nature that accompanied YHWH when He appeared in this role. Thus it is that Ezekiel could view himself as a participant with God in the activities described in Ezekiel 37.

We shall see that Ezekiel was not the first human "vehicle" through whom God as Divine Warrior acted. Elijah and Elisha, each of whom is credited with playing decisive roles in the process of resurrection, were both linked to other activities of the Divine Warrior and the Heavenly Hosts.

We have attempted to show that Ezekiel viewed both God's and his own actions in the Vision of the Dry Bones in terms of a well-defined portrayal of God as Divine Warrior. The precise nature of the joint divine-human action is to be defined then in this context established by the prophet himself. There is little doubt, in our judgment, that the prophet had in mind the process of "actual" resurrection.

We saw above that the affirmation that God would indeed resurrect His righteous people (as well as exclude the "wicked" from this process) arose out of that complex of imagery associated with God as Divine Warrior. Ezekiel's choice of language such as "dry bones," "sinews," "skin," and imagery such as "breath came into them," "that they may live," would seem to function most effectively when placed within the specific context provided by the concept of bodily resurrection from death. Vv 12ff, which speak of God's raising of exiled Hebrews from foreign graves, do lend support to our line of interpretation. Even if they were not originally linked with the Vision contained in vv 1-10, in their present location they cannot be totally disassociated from the preceding text.

We have no doubt that those scholars are correct who see in Ezekiel's Vision a hope for national restoration addressed to his fellow exiles. We also have no doubt that they are incorrect when they limit Ezekiel's message to only this. In bold and memorable language Ezekiel makes use of imagery drawn from the theme of the Divine Warrior to affirm the "literal" resurrection of God's righteous people. Those who had died trusting in God, yes even those who were buried outside the Land of Israel, would share in this process.

Exile from the Land drained off much of the vitality and strength of the people; as such, exile partook of many of the attributes that characterized severe illness or other mental/physical states that kept man from participation in the fullness of "life." Thus it was that Ezekiel could move from the "actual" resurrection of the dead to the "actual" restoration of the exiled Jews. We might say that Ezekiel has transferred the meaning of language associated with resurrection to another realm, and to a certain extent this is true. "Restoration" and "resurrection" are, however, in essence both processes whereby God re-awakens a lifeless, enervated people to vigorous and purposeful activity.

We need not ask whether one or the other of these levels of meaning was more prominent in Ezekiel's thinking as he fashioned his message. It is sufficiently clear that Ezekiel was working with a concept of the resurrection of the dead well enough known to his audience to allow for the simultaneous application of this belief to "literal" resurrection and national restoration. In Ezekiel's own time, we may suppose, it was the promise of restoration from exile that drew the fervent attention of most people; later generations placed far greater emphasis on the belief in bodily resurrection expressed by the prophet through his magnificent Vision. That this passage has thus been able to speak to two different, but related, deeply-felt concerns of humanity is a credit both to the genius of Ezekiel and to the vitality of the concepts which he played a part in shaping.

If we were to restrict ourselves, as we have thus far, to the detailed investigation only of passages which in our opinion make mention, either directly/indirectly, positively/negatively, of the Biblical conception of resurrection, then we would turn at once to the narratives in 1 and 2 Kings dealing with Elijah and Elisha, whom we mentioned just above. However, since we have been concerned in large measure with prophetic material from the sixth century, we ought to introduce into our discussion at this point one passage from that period which, although it says nothing at all about the process of resurrection itself, is nevertheless routinely cited as a (valuable) source of information on just that topic. We have reference to Isaiah 53, especially vv 10ff.

Isaiah 53

Isa 53:10ff have generally been interpreted as the last scene in a drama being played out by the "servant" (a figure whose career, so it is argued, can be followed in four songs contained in Second Isaiah: Isa 42:1-4; 49:1-6; 50:4-11; 52:13-53:12). In the verses just preceding we read that this individual "was despised and rejected by men" (v 3), and then "he was oppressed, and he was afflicted" (v 7). Although we share many of the reservations expressed by Harry M. Orlinsky and others in regard to the entire procedure which created both the "Servant Songs" and the problem of the "Servant" to go with them, we cannot agree with those who argue that the text of Isaiah 53 does not speak of actual death. The language used to depict each step in the tripartite structure of condemnation, death, and burial is admittedly ambiguous. Nevertheless, the overall impression is that the text speaks of an individual's death and burial. If that is the case, then vv 10-12 deal with what happens to this individual after his death; namely, his *post mortem* vindication and exaltation above those who had failed to perceive the true worth of this man and thus had repeatedly humiliated him while he was yet on earth. In what ways was this individual to "be exalted" and "lifted up" (52:13)? Among other things,

> He shall see his offspring,
> he shall prolong his days;
> the will of the Lord shall prosper in his hand;
>
> he shall see the fruit of the travail
> of his soul and be satisfied. . . .
>
> I will divide him a portion with the great,
> and he shall divide the spoil with the strong;
> because he poured out his soul to death. . . .
> (parts of 53:10-12, RSV)

As with the preceding verses, these also have been subjected to intense analysis with widely varying results. For our purposes, the precise nature of this vindication is far less important than the context in which this activity, however understood, is set. We agree with those who argue that the scene has shifted from the earthly plane, the location of this individual's humiliation, to what we might call the heavenly court, which becomes the location of his exaltation. In other words, God reserved all the rewards due this man until after his death.

As we have noted repeatedly, however, the Biblical writers generally spoke of death as a dormant state from which one could or could not (re-) awaken. Since the individual whose fate is described here did die, we can assume that he too entered into the sleep of death and was subsequently re-awakened through the process of resurrection to a vitality of "life" he had never enjoyed on earth. Like the righteous mentioned in Dan 12:2 or Isa 26:19, this individual also participated in that process by which God rewards the faithful with "everlasting life" and the fruits of their travail.

Reference to the passages from Daniel and Isaiah should alert us to the very significant difference which exists between those verses (and others we have looked at) and Isaiah 53. Whereas in the previous contexts the various authors did make mention, in one way or other, of the process we have described as re-awakening through resurrection, the author of this passage says absolutely nothing about the way in which the "servant" arrived at the scene of his vindication. In v 9 he is buried; in v 10 his vindication commences. On this point, if on no other, the text speaks, or rather does not speak, as clearly as could be desired.

Thus we learn nothing about the Biblical concept of resurrection itself from this passage. The author of this passage was not interested in describing how the "servant" re-awakened from the sleep of death to everlasting life. Having arrived at these conclusions, we must nevertheless insist that this passage retains its relevance in any discussion of the Biblical concept of resurrection, precisely because of what it does not say. The author of this passage *assumes* knowledge, and acceptance, of the concept of resurrection on the part of his audience. This confident "assumption" allowed him to omit all reference to the resurrection, as he passed directly from the description of death and burial to the "servant's" exaltation. The reader or hearer would surely supply what was so clearly understood that it did not need to be explicitly stated.

There are those who construct an argument diametrically opposed to our own. According to them, this author did not yet possess the linguistic sophistication to express what was still the rather vague notion of resurrection. If this were the case, then all the more would we expect this author to have striven, no matter how difficult the labor, to introduce his audience to a concept of which they were completely, and he partially, ignorant.

In addition to our displeasure with any line of argumentation which seeks to "explain" what may indeed be only a modern problem through a supposed lack of ability or discernment on the part of a given author, we must also point out that here such an assertion of "ignorance" flies in the face of the evidence we have been accumulating throughout the present work. In passages from no less than two major prophetic figures, Jeremiah and Ezekiel, as well as in the Isaiah Apocalypse—all of which date from the sixth century, in which Isaiah 53 was in all likelihood also composed, the language and imagery associated with the resurrection of the dead find clear expression. More to the point, Ezekiel was able to move from this belief to the idea of restoration, and to be sure that his audience was equipped to make the move with him. Thus, the author of Isaiah 53, be he (Second) Isaiah or another, was not likely to be unaware of this concept, unable to express it, or unsure that his audience would understand it. In saying nothing, he bears eloquent testimony to just how well- and widely-known the belief in bodily resurrection was.

We should conclude our discussion of this passage where we began it, for we cannot overemphasize the fact that the author of Isaiah 53 after all tells us nothing about how he envisioned the process of resurrection or its scope beyond this particular case. To this degree, he deprives us of a potentially valuable source of information that would enable us further to round out the contours of development with respect to the belief in resurrection. What he has provided us, however, and more importantly, what he provided his original audience, is a richly-textured portrayal which has full significance within the context of the Hebrew Bible itself, prior to and independent of its re-use in the early Christian community. To the extent that the modern reader of this passage moves along the paths laid out by its author himself and refrains from straying onto roads, however broad and attractive, that the author did not take, to that extent will he come to a fuller and deeper understanding of the message of hope that the writer of Isaiah 53 conveyed to both his and succeeding generations.

Elijah and Elisha (1 and 2 Kings)

When we turn to the texts that relate the activities of the prophet Elijah and his disciple Elisha, we encounter material that differs in several ways from the passages we have considered thus far. All of the previous references to resurrection are found either in passages that have retained their original poetic form or in those where the original poetic structure can at least still be discerned. On the other hand, the exploits of Elijah and Elisha are contained in prose narratives that extend from 1 Kings 17 through 2 Kings 13. These stories may well have had their origins in orally composed and transmitted poetry, but it is likely that they were already in the form of prose at the time of their inclusion into the earliest written forerunner of the present books of Kings. At least it can be said that no poetic substratum for these narratives is easily recoverable.

The passages previously considered were composed in the sixth century or later and reflected contemporary concerns, even when the material used was much older. In our opinion it is not possible to determine when the stories concerning Elijah and Elisha were first set down in the form in which they appear today. It is generally agreed that the books of Kings are part of the work of the Deuteronomistic historian, who was active in the last part of the 7th century B.C.E. Like "historians" of all ages, he used, with varying degrees of skill, sources which themselves varied considerably as to date, Tendenz, reliability, etc. Among these sources was a collection of stories centering on these two great prophetic heroes of Northern Israel.

The Deuteronomistic historian, presumably working in the Judaean capital of Jerusalem, apparently made extensive use of this collection.

For him, anyway, they constituted a reliable witness to old traditions that he deemed worthy of preservation. On that score, we are in agreement with this historian's judgment; moreover, in his incorporation of this material into his larger work, the Deuteronomistic historian appears to have retained in large measure both the substance of this collection and something of the religious and other attitudes that characterized it.

This is not to say that everything the Deuteronomistic historian set down, on the basis of his own interpretation of his sources dealing with Elijah and Elisha, *really* happened, even though it is beyond doubt that these two figures were active as prophets in Northern Israel during the 9th century. Rather than attempt in some arbitrary fashion to separate "fact" from "fiction," we prefer to emphasize that the contents of these narratives reflect what people felt to be significant about these two prophets, in a context where "event" and "interpretation" could not be separated and any distinction between "the hard-to-believe miraculous" and "the easy-to-accept everyday occurrence" would not be comprehensible.

In short, we are dealing with traditions that had gained rather wide acceptance by at least the 7th century. In the absence of any contrary indication, we may seek the origins of these traditions in events and interpretations contemporary with, or only shortly after, the 9th century dates during which these prophets themselves lived. Thus, these narratives can be viewed as a rich source of information concerning the beliefs and attitudes of people several centuries earlier than the period during which the Deuteronomistic historian was at work.

If then we find a belief in the concept of bodily resurrection expressed in this material, these expressions may well go back to the 9th century. The possibility of such an early date for this belief is increased if (a) the manner in which the belief is expressed seems less developed than later formulations we have looked at; or (b) a link can be established between the prophets through whom God brought about the resurrections described in the narratives and imagery connected with YHWH as Divine Warrior; or (c) further references to the resurrection of the dead appear in other early texts, preferably those preserved outside of the Deuteronomistic circle. If all three of the above can be substantiated, then the "possibility" of which we just spoke verges on certainty. Let us now turn to the texts themselves.

We are plunged into the prophetic activities of Elijah the Tishbite precisely at the point where he declares to Ahab that it is in accordance with the will of YHWH (not Baal or any other) that Northern Israel suffer a severe drought. This admittedly abrupt introduction to the prophet in 1 Kings 17 serves to establish from the first a close link between Elijah and the natural phenomena through which God as Divine Warrior manifests His power. Further, Elijah himself is enlisted as a "warrior," to lead the combat against all those who falsely claimed that the Divine Warrior's power over these phenomena belonged to Baal, and not the Lord God of Israel.

Mt. Carmel is the scene in chapter 18 for the well-known contest between Elijah and the assembled masses of pagan prophets, over the question of whose deity did in fact control the rains and, by extension, all the forces of nature. Between the first mention of Elijah and the dramatic events at Mt. Carmel the author of the books of Kings placed a lengthy narrative (17:8-24) that recounts the adventures of the prophet at the home of a widow in the non-Israelite town of Zarephath. Through the aid of the Lord, the small amount that this woman had proved sufficient to provide food for herself, her son, and the prophet, in spite of the drought that ravished the land. At a certain point her son was stricken with an illness "so severe that there was no breath left in him" (v 17). The distraught mother feared that the prophet had come "to cause the death of" her son because of her own sinfulness (v 18). Elijah himself cries out to God, "hast thou brought calamity even upon the widow with whom I sojourn, by slaying her son?" (v 20). Stretching himself upon the child three times, Elijah prays that God may "let this child's soul come into him again" (v 21). God accepted this petition from Elijah, and as a result "the soul of the child came into him again, and he revived" (v 22). Elijah is then able to return the child to his mother with these words, "See, your son lives" (v 23).

Should this incident be placed in the category of the bodily resurrection of the dead? In our opinion this placement is fully justified by the text itself. First of all, careful attention to the wording should leave no doubt that the child did die. Through the accumulation of phrases—"no breath left in him," "cause the death of her son," "slaying her son," "your son lives"—the author of this passage provides an unambiguous picture of the ultimate "pouring out" that is death and the "re-awakening to life" that is the result of resurrection. It is certainly beside the point to argue that a panicky woman of the 9th century might have mistaken a severe illness for death, since the text is not presented to us through the mother's perspective but from that of the author. And, as we noted just above, the language chosen here is clear and straightforward. One may admit that the child did die, but view the work carried out by Elijah as something other than resurrection. After all, it may be argued, the child was not buried and then brought back from the grave, but simply restored to life in his own home. As we pointed out earlier, however, there is nothing in the Biblical concept of resurrection to indicate that prior burial is a necessary condition to the process of bodily resurrection.

The result of Elijah's activity differs in an important respect from the other examples at which we have looked, for here the child was not re-awakened to "everlasting life," but simply allowed the possibility of living out a longer and fuller earthly existence prior to his (second and "real") death. Is this then a case of "actual" resurrection? Such an observation could, admittedly, place our interpretation in some doubt, if this passage dated from the sixth century or later by which time, as we have seen, the concept of bodily resurrection had undergone considerable development and refinement.

In the earlier period reflected in 1 and 2 Kings this belief could be expressed in ways that would seem inappropriate, almost crude, to later generations. Nevertheless, this understanding of resurrection as encompassing cases in which the process results in the restoration of the dead to the full vitality of life that they had previously enjoyed is in keeping with the origins of this concept in the themes associated with the Divine Warrior. If a people conceives of the struggle of the Divine Warrior in terms of more than one round of combat and victory, then the revitalization that is nature's response also recurs. In this context, what Elijah carried out could be termed a preliminary resurrection, but a resurrection nonetheless. After the widow's son died (again), he would/would not (depending on the view of resurrection held) be eligible for the resurrection to "everlasting life" to which clear expression is given only in subsequent periods.

In later contexts, such as the grand (proto-)apocalyptic visions we have looked at, this earlier aspect of the Biblical concept no longer served a meaningful purpose. Moreover, it was far too susceptible to abuse on the part of false men of God (or men of false gods) who wished in this way to show that divine power flowed through them.

Returning to the narrative in 1 Kings, we discover that the overall purpose of this incident is precisely to authenticate Elijah's claim as a true prophet of God. Thus chapter 17 closes with these words of the widow addressed to the prophet: "Now I know that you are a man of God, and that the word of the Lord in your mouth is truth" (v 24). We should not overlook the additional significance that the woman's remark carries for the whole course of Elijah's prophetic career: this man, through whom God as Divine Warrior acted in this one "private" case, is in every way a legitimate vehicle for the dramatic and "public" demonstration of His complete control over all natural phenomena that occurs shortly after (in chapter 18, at Mt. Carmel).

Nor are Elijah's associations with the theme of God as Divine Warrior limited to the earlier events in his career. In the first chapter of 2 Kings Elijah confronts messengers of Ahab's successor Ahaziah on their way to inquire of a pagan deity, "Baal-zebub, the god of Ekron, whether" the king would "recover from this sickness" (2 Kgs 1:2). The prophet orders the royal emissaries to return to the impious monarch who dispatched them and to reveal to Ahaziah the following divine decree: "You shall not come down from the bed to which you have gone, but you shall surely die" (vv 4, 6).

Distressed by these words, Ahaziah three times ordered "a captain of fifty men with his fifty" to convey to Elijah the king's command that the prophet descend from the hill on which he was sitting. Such a descent, which would surely have resulted in Elijah's death, stands in contrast to the forbidden act of "coming down from the bed," which would have signaled the ailing King's return to the fullness of life. The first two times Elijah's response takes the identical form: "If I am a man of God, let fire come down from heaven and consume you and your fifty" (vv 10, 12). As in the contest on Mt. Carmel, this request for divine assistance on the part of Elijah was a call for aid from one "warrior" in God's army, that is Elijah, to another "warrior," in this case one of the natural phenomena (heavenly fire) that served in the legions that attended God as the Heavenly Hosts. That Elijah was justified in considering himself a companion in arms, as it were, with such natural phenomena is proved by the fact that "fire came down from heaven, and consumed him [that is, the captain] and his fifty" (twice: vv 10, 12). Truly, as the widow had already concluded on an earlier occasion, the prophet Elijah was "a man of God."

Rarely does the Hebrew Bible supply us with any information concerning the end of a prophet's career or life. Thus we are all the more fortunate that the Deuteronomistic historian has preserved for us the traditional account of Elijah's final activities on earth. Elijah is one of only two individuals (the other is Enoch, Genesis 5) whose life on earth, as recorded in the Hebrew Bible, did not end in death. At the very beginning of 2 Kings 2, we are alerted to the imminent occurrence of something extraordinary: "Now when the Lord was about to take Elijah up to heaven by a whirlwind . . ." (2 Kgs 2:1). Later as Elijah and Elisha, who was soon to inherit the mantle of his master, talked together for the last time, "a chariot of fire and horses of fire separated the two of them. And Elijah went up by a whirlwind into heaven" (v 11). At this Elisha cried out: "My father, my father! the chariots of Israel and its horsemen!" (v 12).

Associations at this point with the imagery of God as Divine Warrior are numerous and obvious. He who had fought so long and gallantly on earth against all attempts to dilute or compromise the true worship of the true God would be privileged hereafter to continue that struggle for as long as even a few refused to acknowledge the Lord God as the one all-powerful Divine Warrior.

In many ways the prophetic career of Elisha represented a continuation of Elijah's work (see 1 Kgs 19:16ff). From start to finish (and beyond) there are notable parallels in the activities through which each in turn demonstrated the validity of his claim as one of God's chosen prophets. It is possible that the tradition reflected in the Hebrew Bible had already filled out the prophetic careers of these two towering figures by crediting both with outstanding deeds which had originally been associated with only one of the two.

Be that as it may, it is sufficiently clear that the Biblical narratives do have their origins in two separate and distinct 9th century prophets, whose careers followed similar, but by no means identical, courses. Therefore, we ought not to dismiss as mere "doublets" those accounts which narrate activities of Elisha which are similar to those of Elijah. On the contrary, each account should be viewed as a valuable witness to beliefs that tradition associated with Israelites of the period when Elijah and Elisha lived. Indeed, when tradition accords prominence to certain attitudes or themes in its portrayals of both Elijah and Elisha, such matters are all the more deserving of our closest attention.

In our discussion of Elijah we pointed to a number of features, including his role in the resurrection of the widow's son, that linked this prophet to the theme of God as Divine Warrior. Elijah's insistence that God alone had full power over all the phenomena of nature placed him in direct opposition to the pagan prophets of Baal and their powerful allies in the royal household of Northern Israel. While Elijah did enjoy some success (most notably at Mt. Carmel) in his never-ceasing struggle against the worshippers of Baal and the pervasive influence they exercised at all levels of Israelite society, it remained the case at his death that the supporters of the pagan deity were still numerous, and, what made their extirpation all the more difficult, the royal "house of Ahab" continued to provide a climate favorable to the growth of the worship of Baal.

It was therefore necessary for Elisha, as it had been for his predecessor, to maintain, and demonstrate in the face of all claims to the contrary, that the Lord God of Israel alone was powerful to act as the Divine Warrior. Elisha was to become another "warrior" in the service of God; moreover, all the natural phenomena that fought in the ranks of the Heavenly Hosts, and even God Himself, were prepared to aid the prophet in authenticating his message by the timely manifestation of those powers that only the Lord could unleash or contain. Through his links with such powers, Elisha sought not self-glorification, but rather greater recognition for YHWH in whose name he spoke and acted. As with Elijah, this held true for "private" acts, such as resurrection, as well as "public" acts, such as revolution.

After Elijah and Elisha crossed the Jordan River, in what were to be their final moments together on earth, Elisha asked as his inheritance from the prophet whom he followed, "a double share of your spirit" (2 Kgs 2:9). Such a gift, as they both surely recognized, was not Elijah's to bestow; at the same time, the departing prophet was able to perceive the means by which Elisha's worthiness to receive what he desired could be tested: "You have asked a hard thing; yet, if you see me as I am being taken from you, it shall be so for you; but if you do not see me, it shall not be so" (v 10). As we noted above, Elisha did see it (v 12), and thereafter "the sons of the prophets who were at Jericho . . . said, 'The spirit of Elijah rests on Elisha'"(v 15).

In other words, the beginning of the period of Elisha's active prophetic career was made to coincide with his being granted a privileged view of some aspects of God's work as Divine Warrior and of the relationship of Elijah, and of himself, to that work. In some ways, this reminds us of the inaugural vision of Ezekiel, to which we referred earlier. However, Elisha's closest ties with any human figure are with Elijah. This is clearly brought out in the statement uttered by Joash king of Israel, when he saw that Elisha "had fallen sick with the illness of which he was to die" (2 Kgs 13:14). The king's words on this occasion, "My father, my father! The chariots of Israel and its horsemen!" (cf. 2 Kgs 13:7), are precisely those which Elisha himself had cried out when Elijah departed from the earth.

In our earlier discussion of Elijah we pointed to those incidents in his career which showed that he was indeed a vehicle with whose aid God manifested His power as Divine Warrior. We now look at certain events in Elisha's career that serve the same purpose. At one point, the Syrian king became concerned because the Israelite army anticipated each of his tactical moves and thus eluded the traps he had prepared with obvious care. Convinced that he had a fifth column in his midst, he called together his "servants" and demanded of them, "Will you not show me who of us is for the king of Israel?" (2 Kgs 6:11). From one of his servants the king learned that it was not a Syrian, but "Elisha, the prophet who is in Israel, [who] tells the king of Israel the words that you speak in your bedchamber" (v 12). Informed by his intelligence agents that the prophet Elisha was then in the city of Dothan, the Syrian leader dispatched "there horses and chariots and a great army; and they came by night, and surrounded the city" (v 14).

These moves apparently went undetected by the inhabitants of the city of Dothan. At least, Elisha's servant, when confronted the following morning by the unexpected sight of enemy forces, was sufficiently agitated to seek assurance from his master (v 15). For his part, Elisha remained calm, as he sought to convey to his servant that their position was not the precarious one it seemed to be: "Fear not, for those who are with us are more than those who are with them" (v 16). Elisha had seen something which other humans had not been privileged to view. When Elisha prayed that the Lord open his servant's eyes "that he may see," the nature of this "something" became clear to him as well: "Behold, the

mountain was full of horses and chariots of fire round about Elisha"
(v 17). The Heavenly Hosts appeared to Elisha, and at his request to his
servant as well, exactly as Elisha had viewed them when Elijah was
taken up to heaven (in chapter 2). This prophet, like his predecessor,
could rest assured that his fellow "warriors" would assist him when foes
threatened to bring his career to a premature end.

The story does not conclude here, however. The defeat of the Syrian
forces came about not through any military adventure on the part of
human or Heavenly armies, but rather through the direct intervention of
God in response to a request from Elisha. Elisha prayed that God "strike
this people . . . with blindness . . . so He struck them with blindness in
accordance with the prayer of Elisha" (v 18). This divine action stands in
contrast to the opening of the eyes by which Elisha's servant came to
recognize the role of God as Divine Warrior. When later God was led to
open the eyes of the captured Syrian forces, they ceased, at least temporarily, to initiate hostilities against Israel. Are we not to see in their
decision a recognition, however ephemeral and half-hearted, of the same
eternal truth that Elisha's servant had glimpsed when his eyes also had
been opened? After all, in the words of the prophet, at the return of the
victorious Divine Warrior, "the eyes of the blind shall see" (Isa 35:5).

The single most famous action that tradition associated with Elijah
is the contest with the prophets of paganism on Mt. Carmel. The issue
centered on which deity, YHWH or Baal, was due praise and worship as
the Divine Warrior with power over all the phenomena of nature. In like
manner, Elisha is remembered for his decisive role in stirring up the
revolution through which Jehu, with full support from the prophet,
"wiped out Baal from Israel" (2 Kgs 10:28; chapters 9 and 10 provide a
description, often in bloody detail, of the course of this prophetically-
inspired revolution). In the case of Elijah, the grand "public" demonstration of his links with the Heavenly Hosts and with God, who as
Divine Warrior commanded these vast Armies, was preceded by a "private" demonstration through the prophet's role in effecting the resurrection of a young boy. The same holds true for his successor Elisha.

At 2 Kgs 4:8 we are introduced to a wealthy woman, who spared no
expense or effort in providing hospitality to the prophet Elisha whenever he came to her home. When Elisha sought some suitable reward for
this woman, his servant Gehazi pointed to what surely was the most
deeply-felt disappointment in her life: "Well, she has no son, and her
husband is old" (v 14). Upon hearing from Elisha that within a year she
would be embracing her own son, she was understandably somewhat
skeptical: "No, my lord, O man of God; do not lie to your maidservant"
(v 16). Of course, all took place as Elisha had foretold, for "she bore a
son . . . as Elisha had said to her" (v 17).

All of this only serves to heighten the sense of tragedy and loss that we feel when we read of the child's illness and subsequent death. After being stricken in the fields and brought in to his mother, "the child sat on her lap till noon, and then he died" (v 20). She rushed to Elisha, approaching the prophet on Mt. Carmel over the strenuous objections of Gehazi, and upbraided him in the following manner: "Did I ask my lord for a son? Did I not say, Do not deceive me?" (v 28). Elisha responded immediately by dispatching Gehazi, with the prophet's staff in hand, to bring the child back to life. Meeting with no success ("Gehazi . . . laid the staff upon the face of the child, but there was no sound or sign of life"), Gehazi was forced to return to Elisha with this message: "The child has not awakened" (v 31). Therefore, Elisha himself went to the house, where "he saw the child lying dead on his bed" (v 32). After praying to God, the prophet placed himself in contact with the lifeless body of the boy, with the result that "the flesh of the child became warm" (v 34). When Elisha again stretched himself over the body, "the child sneezed seven times, and the child opened his eyes" (v 35).

The arguments we developed earlier in favor of placing the similar activity of Elijah in the category of the bodily resurrection of the dead are equally valid here and need not be repeated. The language in 2 Kings 4 is unambiguous, just as that found in 1 Kings 17 in connection with Elijah. Furthermore, we have additional references to Elisha's action in 2 Kings 8. In 8:1, there is mention of something that Elisha said to the woman "whose son he had restored to life." Later in this chapter, while Gehazi was in the midst of "telling the king how Elisha had restored the dead to life, behold, the woman whose son he had restored to life" came into the king's presence (v 5). Then Gehazi identified the woman who had just entered as the one of whom he was speaking "My lord, O king, here is the woman, and here is her son whom Elisha restored to life" (also v 5).

The words with which Gehazi reported his failure to Elisha are significant: "The child has not awakened" (4 :31). In a prior section we showed that the term "to awaken," especially when expressed through the verb $hqys$ as here, takes us to the very heart of the process of resurrection we have been investigating in the Hebrew Bible. Gehazi is thus admitting his failure to bring about the child's resurrection. In other words, Elisha, however well-intentioned, cannot appoint a surrogate through whom God's power as Divine Warrior is to be made manifest. While the prophet is able to open his servant's eyes wide enough to share in a single vision of the "horses and chariots of fire," Elisha alone is the chosen vehicle for his generation and thus the only one through whom God acts to effect the re-awakening or restoration to life of one of His dead.

Elijah's life on earth did not end in his death. Without experiencing death, he was to continue his struggle on behalf of God. In short, his active influence would not cease with his departure from earth. Elisha did die, but we learn that he also continued to play a role as God's "warrior" even after his life on earth came to an end. This is the point of the following story, which presents the process of resurrection stripped to the bones, as it were:

> So Elisha died, and they buried him. Now bands of Moabites used to invade the land in the spring of the year. And as a man was being buried, lo, a marauding band was seen and the man was cast into the grave of Elisha; and as soon as the man touched the bones of Elisha, he revived, and stood on his feet.
>
> (2 Kgs 13:20-21, RSV)

In and of itself, this narrative does not yield a teaching which anyone is likely to characterize as lofty. As we now have this story, however, it does not appear in isolation, but in a definite historical and theological context. Therefore, we can properly judge its worth only in relation to that context. In this connection, we ought to note that this story is preceded by two full accounts of the process of bodily resurrection, both of which amply demonstrate the theological and other ramifications of this Biblical concept. Moreover, this account illustrates that Elisha's links with God as Divine Warrior were not severed by the prophet's death; rather, God continued to work through the prophet, even through his dead and buried bones, to bring about that re-awakening to life which is resurrection. Thus, this episode forms a fitting and apt parallel to the story of Elijah's ascension to heaven by a whirlwind.

This baldly physical and essentially "untheological" account of a significant divine activity must have puzzled, even embarrassed, later generations. The prophets of the sixth century would surely not have produced such a narrative. Yet, it remains the case that such a seemingly crude and inappropriate account, by its very power to puzzle, shock, and move the otherwise complacent reader/hearer, often leads to the framing of profounder questions and more meaningful answers than would be possible through any other means. Within the Hebrew Bible itself it is a distinct possibility that Ezekiel had this episode in mind as he fashioned the great vision of Ezekiel 37, especially the image of "raising from the grave" in vv 12ff. From all of this, we can see that the Deuteronomistic historian's retention of this narrative served a far more important purpose than that of providing a proof text to shore up lagging trade in "miraculous" saints' bones.

Hos 6:1-3

In the introduction to our analysis of the relevant material from 1 and 2 Kings, we formulated three criteria by which we could gauge the possibility that the belief in resurrection set in the historical context of the 9th century was in fact that old, if not older. Thus far, our investigation of the first two members of this triad has yielded positive results, for (a) the manner in which this belief is expressed in 1 and 2 Kings is distinctly less developed than later formulations; and (b) there are unmistakable links between the prophets, Elijah and Elisha, and imagery associated with God as Divine Warrior.

In order to discover whether there are references to the bodily resurrection of the dead in other early texts, we turn first to Hos 6:1-3, which dates from the third quarter of the 8th century:

> Come, let us return to the Lord;
> for he has torn, that he may heal us;
> he has stricken, and he will bind us up.
>
> After two days he will revive us;
> on the third day he will raise us up,
> that we may live before him.
>
> Let us know, let us press on to know the Lord;
> his going forth is sure as the dawn;
> he will come to us as the showers,
> as the spring rains that water the earth.
>
> (RSV)

In the section immediately preceding these verses the prophet Hosea recalls to the people of Northern Israel many of the losses and troubles they had suffered at the hands of foreign invaders. He forces them to recognize that in these actions it is God at work, bringing punishment on those who refuse to serve Him faithfully in spite of the words addressed to them by His true prophets. Nor is there any hope for the people, unless "they acknowledge their guilt and seek my [God's] face" (Hos 5:15).

The people responded to this urgent appeal from the prophet with a prayer or psalm (6:1-3), the penitential nature of which is clearly indicated by the opening words, "Come, let us return to the Lord." Apparently, the people envisioned this process of "repentance" as a grand *quid pro quo*: they return to God, who in His turn is expected, even ordered, to "heal" them, "bind" them, "revive" them, "raise [them] up," so that they "may live before him." Yes, these people did long to "know" God, sure as they were in their own minds that such knowledge brought with it immediate ("two days . . . third day") and automatic rewards. From the prophetic viewpoint the only thing that was "automatic" was the negative response of God to such a gross misunderstanding of the ways of God and what ought to be the ways of man:

> What shall I do with you, O Ephraim?
> . . .
> Your love is like a morning cloud,
> like the dew that goes early away.
> (Hos 6:4)

So-called repentance of this sort is hardly what the Lord desires!

Most scholarly commentators would have little disagreement with the analysis I have offered thus far. This consensus breaks down, however, precisely at the point of determining exactly what it is the people expect God to do for them. In what context, it has often been debated, is the language of "reviving," "raising up," and "living" to be placed? We are in full agreement with those who interpret the verbs of v 2 in the context of "literal" resurrection. The portrayal in terms of "healing" and "binding" (v 1) forms a prelude to the concepts expressed with greater specificity in v 2. The people, whose weakened form of existence amounted to only the smallest part of that vitality which alone is worth calling "life," fully expected to be the beneficiaries of a process of divine revitalization which they felt justified in describing in terms of bodily resurrection.

For those who make what we believe is the correct connection between the expectation voiced in Hos 6:1-3 and a belief in resurrection, a question then arises concerning the source from which the people derived the language with which they express their hope. For the most part, scholars argue that people of Northern Israel drew their imagery from the pagan cults of the dying-and-rising god, of which we spoke earlier. According to this view, the very words that the nation speaks are tainted, and it is that taint, combined with the attempt to manipulate God into acting how and when His human subjects desire, that reveals the abject spiritual poverty of this rebellious people.

The attempt to see the belief in resurrection expressed here, however, as a rather thinly veneered foreign import just won't do. As we pointed out earlier, there is no clear and convincing evidence of a connection between the belief in a periodically dying-and-rising god and the Biblical concept that God has power to revive His dead. And, on this point the text is unambiguous, it is to this Biblical concept of resurrection that the people have reference ("*he* will revive us . . . *he* will raise us up").

Further, we have been able to locate the Biblical belief in material which tradition associated with the prophets Elijah and Elisha, who lived not many years prior to the period in which Hosea was active. When we recall that the prophetic activity of Elijah and Elisha also took place in Northern Israel, it becomes highly likely that the people of Hosea's time knew of, and were influenced by, the accounts that described the resurrections God effected through these prophetic figures. There is little doubt, moreover, that the relevant traditional material available in Northern Israelite circles of the 8th century far exceeded the amount that the Deuteronomistic historian was able to pass on to us.

Thus, against the prevailing view, we would argue that these northern Israelites derived their imagery and language from a concept of resurrection that was already widely known in Israel, and what is more, associated with prophets whose authority as men of God could not be questioned. Nevertheless, when these people sought to express their own expectations in these terms, their efforts were rejected as unacceptable by God. If their belief *per se* was not sacrilegious, in what way had they erred? As we indicated above, their sinfulness was evident in their attempted manipulation of God's activity to their own advantage.

Much has been made of the temporal expression "after two days . . . on the third day," found in v 2. When these figures are interpreted literally, they are supposed to supply the key which points to the connection of this passage with the agricultural cults of the dying-and-rising god. From an assortment of data, none of which relates directly to the period or locale of Hosea, it seems that the deities worshipped in such cults made their re-appearance on earth precisely three days after their descent. If the people of Northern Israel were pictured as worshipping a dying-and-rising god, then this bit of information would be relevant. As we have seen, however, such is not the charge levelled against them. It is clear to us that this temporal reference is not to be understood literally, but is rather an example of "impressionistic" parallelism, a poetic device whereby an author creates an impression or mood through the use of successive numbers or other related phenomena. Just as elsewhere, both within and outside of the Hebrew Bible, the power of this imagery is sapped through the attempt to find a single referent for each item. The overall impression we gain here is of a people who demand immediate satisfaction from God and, when this is denied them, impatiently stamp their collective feet, with all of the petulance that we are wont to associate with children.

Although the people who speak in Hos 6:1-3 misuse the Biblical concept of bodily resurrection, their very misuse is valuable evidence for the existence of this concept during the 8th century. They were probably dependent at least in part on traditions which associated Elijah and Elisha with the process of resurrection. References to natural phenomena in Hosea 6 may also point in the same direction.

Deut 32:39 and 1 Sam 2:6

This one passage, together with the other evidence already accumu-
lated, may well be sufficient to establish the certainty of an early date for
the Biblical belief. Nevertheless, we think that it is appropriate to bring
in two further passages, both of which take us back to a time as early as
or even earlier than the 9th century.

The first passage is Deut 32:39, which is part of the Song of Moses
(Deut 31:30-32:47):

> See now that I, even I, am he,
> and there is no god beside me;
>
> I kill and I make alive;
> I wound and I heal;
>
> and there is none that can deliver
> out of my hand.
> (RSV)

Cross indicates that a 9th century date for the Song as a whole is a
distinct possibility; he also notes that Albright, Eissfeldt, and others
presented strong arguments in favor of an 11th century dating for this
psalm.

The second passage comes from the psalm (1 Sam 2:1-10) which
Hannah addressed to the Lord when she brought her son Samuel to
Shiloh in accordance with her vow that Samuel would "appear in the
presence of the Lord, and abide there for ever" (1 Sam 1:22). Few would
claim that this song in its present form goes back as far as the mid-11th
century, when Samuel rose to prominence as a judge-prophet, but there
is no reason to deny that certain of its parts, including the verse quoted
just below, are of an antiquity equal to that of the Song of Moses:

> The Lord kills and brings to life;
> he brings down to Sheol and raises up.
> (1 Sam 2:6, RSV)

Before subjecting these verses to separate analysis according to their
individual contexts, we may observe two points at which they are in
significant agreement. First, in both Deut 32:39 and 1 Sam 2:6 the
causative of the Hebrew verb *ḥyh*, "to make alive/bring to life," is
found. In certain contexts, for the Hebrew Bible most notably Isaiah 26,
this verb is to be connected with the concept of resurrection. If the two
passages under discussion here can also be placed in such contexts, then
it would be appropriate to translate "make alive *again*/bring to life
again."

These two verses not only show the same verbs, but also place them in the same order: The Lord (a) kills and (b) brings about life. The order of the next verbs ("wound . . . heal" in Deuteronomy; "bring down . . . raise up" in 1 Samuel), which stand in some form of parallelism with the preceding, follows from this. To us this order is significant, inasmuch as it places the life-stimulating activity of God after the reference to death. Were the poet simply pointing to God's role in the birth and death of each individual, then we would expect these verbs to appear in the reverse order, which would then correctly reflect the sequence in which every human experiences these two aspects of divine power. As it stands, these verbs suggest that it is as a result of death that God must (re-)introduce that vitality which marks one's existence as "life," in the same way that "healing" is only necessary after "wounding" has taken place. At this point let us look at the overall structure and contents of each Song, in order to arrive at as precise an understanding as possible of the verses in which we have a particular interest.

Deuteronomy 32 is presented as next to the last address Moses spoke "in the ears of all the assembly of Israel" (Deut 31:30).[28] It is set in the form of a "covenant lawsuit," whereby the speaker indicts Israel through the use of language and terminology drawn from the realm of legal procedure. Through such lawsuits, which were used with great effectiveness by certain classical prophets as well, Israel stands convicted, or rather convicts itself, of one act of apostasy after another. Turning away from the Lord, "the Rock . . . a God of faithfulness and without iniquity, just and right" (Deut 32:4), the Hebrews preferred to sacrifice "to demons which were no gods, to gods they had never known, to new gods that had come in of late, whom [their] fathers had never dreaded" (v 17). In short, they were a people "unmindful of the Rock that begot" them (v 18). The inevitable divine verdict of "guilty" is followed by the imposition of a sentence, which Israel brought on itself through a history of sinfulness that could not go forever unpunished.

It is not only Israel that has acted against the one God, who alone is the Rock in whom man can take refuge (cf. v 37), for the other nations are to be condemned as well for their imbibing "from the vine of Sodom" and partaking of sin-producing fruit "from the fields of Gomorrah" (v 32). However, while Israel's chastisement will lead to its cleansing and ultimate vindication, the punishment of the foreign

[28] On this chapter see especially G. Ernest Wright, "The Lawsuit of God: A Form-Critical Study of Deut 32," *Israel's Prophetic Heritage, Muilenburg Festschrift* (eds. B. W. Anderson and Walter Harrelson; New York: Harper, 1962) 26-67.

nations, who in opposing Israel also opposed the Lord, means their total destruction, in and through which the power of God as the avenger of the "blood of his servants" (v 43) will be manifest.

Throughout this Song then, the power of God is set in dramatic contrast with the powerlessness of the "no gods" worshipped at some periods by the people of Israel and at all periods by the nations outside of Israel. The Song of Moses in its entirety forms a grand challenge to those who believe that the idols in which they place their trust can indeed save these adherents:

> Let them [i.e., the "no gods"] rise up and help you,
> let them be your protection!
>
> (v 38)

Verse 39, which we quoted earlier, immediately follows this taunt. As such, it is meant to be a summary statement of faith in the one all-powerful God, against whom no act of rebellion or presumption can be effective. In God, there resides all power; He alone is the agency of "death," "life," and all stages of weakness and strength that fall in between the ultimate "pouring out" and the greatest possible "filling up." Since there is perhaps no other action of God's which displays the totality and uniqueness of His power more forcefully than the process by which He restores His dead to life, a reference to bodily resurrection is surely in keeping with the context at this point.

But is it certain that the author of this passage had any such reference in mind? He may have been thinking not of any particular divine action, but rather of the limitless scope of God's power. In this regard, it has been noted that elsewhere in the Hebrew Bible an expression emphasizing totality can be formed through the use of two antithetical terms that serve to define the totality in question. In such an expression, known technically as "merismus," the emphasis is placed not on the extremes (here "death" and "life") that stand at each end of the scale, but on the totality (in this case, of God's power) that is the scale itself. Such a "more general" reference would also be appropriate at this point in the Song of Moses.

Even though no firm decision can be reached on this question, the context certainly does not rule out an understanding of this as a reference to the process of "literal" bodily resurrection. Such an understanding does account for the ordering of the verbs (of which we spoke earlier), which otherwise seems arbitrary and un-"natural." God's action in "wounding" and "healing" is not identical with the process of death and resurrection, but does form an apt parallel to the latter, for in both cases it is a question of God's holding back or granting that vitality over which He alone as creator of all holds sway.

After reflecting on various possible interpretations of this passage, we feel that it is appropriate to see in Deut 32:39 an expression of the Biblical concept of resurrection we have found elsewhere. As is the case in other passages, this author does not elaborate on the process of resurrection, but limits himself to those aspects that are relevant to his larger argument. Here the argument centers on God's power (vs. the lack of power on the part of the "no gods"), as revealed through, but by no means limited to, His ability to restore the dead to life.

In its present location the Song of Hannah is a psalm of thanksgiving and praise, offered joyfully by a mother who had previously grieved for many years "because the Lord had closed her womb" (1 Sam 1:6). Within the Song itself, the particular situation of Hannah is addressed in the following line, which appears to anticipate the birth of further children to her (see 1 Sam 2:21):

> The barren has borne seven,
> but she who has many children is forlorn.
> (1 Sam 2:5b)

Throughout this song God, like unto whom "there is no rock" (v 2), is particularly praised for His ability to transform situations that, from the human perspective, would appear to have attained a certain permanency. Thus, in v 5 quoted just above God opened the womb of one who had been unable to conceive; the very fact that Hannah had been barren for so long would make each pregnancy and birth all the more occasion for rejoicing and thanksgiving.

God's activity in this respect is not limited to the reward of elevating the once barren to motherhood, for the second part of v 5b speaks of the mother of many children who is made forlorn. In the context of the story of Hannah and Samuel, this has specific reference to Peninnah, the other wife of Elkanah, who had children (1 Sam 1:2, 4) and as Hannah's "rival used to provoke her sorely, to irritate her" because of Hannah's childlessness (1 Sam 1:6). More generally, this statement is directed against any woman who would presume to use a gift of God, in this case her own children, to raise herself over another, for it is the Lord alone who "brings low" and "also exalts" (1 Sam 2:7).

Similar cases of "reversal of fortune" are found throughout human society, such that those who "talk . . . very proudly," from whose mouth "arrogance" comes (1 Sam 2:3), are knocked down from what they had considered as unassailable positions of wealth and power; while the "faithful ones," who appear locked out of such positions, find their strength ultimately "exalted in the Lord" (1 Sam 2:9, 1). The author of this psalm provides several illustrations of sudden, dramatic changes in social, economic, or other status; he observes, for example, that some of

> those who were full have hired
> themselves out for bread,
> but those who were hungry have
> ceased to hunger.
>   (v 5a)

Lest anyone think that the dynamics for such change are to be discovered in an economic analysis of the workings of the market or a sociological study of class struggle, this author points beyond the characteristics of any particular human society to the one God who alone is responsible for reversals which otherwise might seem arbitrary:

> The Lord makes poor and makes rich;
> he brings low, he also exalts.
>
> He raises up the poor from the dust;
> he lifts the needy from the ash heap.
>   (vv 7, 8a)

From the fertility of any one individual or family to the order of any society, God effects His will in ways that are quite startling to all, but clearly understood by those whose faith teaches that

> There is none holy like the Lord,
> there is none besides thee.
>   (v 2)

Nothing and no one of this world is of such permanence as to stand unchanged in defiance of God, by whose actions all creation takes place.

This Song is not limited in reference to the individual or society on earth, for at a central point (v 6) the poet introduces the role of God in the process of "life" and "death" (or rather, "death" and "life," in the same order as in Deut 32:39), by which he appears to designate aspects of divine activity which extend beyond the confines of what happens in this world alone. If this is the case, then v 6 is indeed an expression of faith that death is not to be viewed as a permanent situation any more than earthly power or wealth. By His power to effect change, God can "reverse the fortune" of those weak from the sleep of death through the introduction of the vitality of life.

Does the text of v 6 itself support such an interpretation? In the first place, the order of God's actions, "kill" and then "bring to life," seems as significant here as it was in Deut 32:39. While it is true that in the majority of the statements surrounding this verse, the "negative" activity precedes the "positive" one, the example just preceding (v 5b: fertility, then being made forlorn) shows that the author was not bound to present each case in that manner. Further, if we read v 6 in close connection with the two verses which come just before, then it emerges that it is one and the same human who is the object of God's "killing" and "bringing to life." Who is it that the Lord brings down but he that is already mighty? Who is she for whom children are a special blessing but the very one who had been barren for so long? In like manner, God's life-producing action is all the more to be praised in connection with those whom, it might be thought, death had emptied of all that vitality which alone makes life possible.

This understanding is also consistent with the overall structure of this section of the Song of Hannah. We move from society at large to the question of barrenness and fertility within the context of human society (vv 4 and 5). At v 6a the vision is enlarged to encompass God's decisive role as the one who both terminates and (re-)introduces life; such activity obviously extends beyond the bounds of any society, but at the same time it is the means by which an individual is either denied or granted access to full participation with other humans.

At v 6b the author returns the focus to the individual on earth, and does so in language that is suggested by, and parallel to, v 6a, but not synonymous with it. As with similar wording found in Mesopotamian texts looked at earlier, it is to wounding/illness/some other serious distress that "brings down to Sheol" has reference. In this context, God's "raising up" indicates the divine role in whatever restoration is necessary to restore the individual to his fullest capabilities. Thus 6b functions in the same way as the "wounding" and "healing" of Deut 32:39. In addition, this line forms a bridge to vv 7 and 8, which return to the theme of reversals within human society as a whole.

We have sought to show that an interpretation of the divine activity described in 1 Sam 2:6a in terms of the Biblical concept of bodily resurrection is appropriate in the overall context provided by the Song of Hannah. Moreover, this interpretation explains the choice of vocabulary and its ordering in this particular verse and, at the same time, allows for a more profound understanding of the Song as a whole.

If we are correct that the Samuel passage under discussion bears witness to the concept of resurrection, then it may be possible to extract from it something of this author's belief concerning the scope of that process. In all the other cases of "reversal," we are to understand that God's activity involves a judgment on the worth or worthlessness of those affected. After all, it is not every wealthy person who is to be abased, or every poor individual who will be raised to "sit with princes" (v 8). The author of this Song has in mind those who abuse, or are abused by, the various forms of power and wealth to which humans can attain; otherwise, the divine activity he relates becomes unconscionably arbitrary. If this is the case in respect to God's actions on earth, it follows that the same will hold true for the process of resurrection. In other words, 1 Sam 2:6 appears to limit resurrection to those righteous individuals deserving of the "reversal" afforded by this divine activity. In previous discussions we developed the idea that such a "limitation" was in fact part of the Biblical concept at the earlier stages of its development.

1 Kgs 18:27

There is one other passage that ought to be included in our consideration of the Biblical belief in resurrection and its development. As far as we know, no previous researcher has investigated this verse (1 Kgs 18:27), especially the reference to "sleeping" and "awakening," as a source of evidence concerning the Biblical concept of resurrection. This is somewhat surprising in view of the fact that (1) the narrative of Elijah's contest with the pagan prophets on Mt. Carmel (1 Kings 18) is extremely well-known and has been frequently commented upon; (2) the previous chapter (1 Kings 17) contains the account of a resurrection God brought about through the actions of this same Elijah; (3) Baal, as a dying-and-rising god, is certainly to be associated with some beliefs in "resurrection"; and (4) "sleep" is a frequent Biblical designation for the state of death, out of which one might be "(re-)awakened" through the process of resurrection.

However, the force of the imagery of "sleeping" and "awakening" has been obscured at this point by scholarly consideration of other themes in this extremely rich chapter (18), and especially by efforts to understand Elijah's previous action in some context other than "literal" resurrection, efforts at least partly occasioned by that conventional schema which established direct links between the Biblical concept of resurrection and Canaanite beliefs associated with the prominent "dying-and-rising" functions of the deity Baal. Throughout this paper we have sought to cut the knot that bound Israel's belief to such Canaanite practices, thus freeing the way for a fuller appreciation of Elijah's role as champion of God the Divine Warrior. In this role, the prophet worked to demonstrate both the unique powers of YHWH, through such actions as the re-awakening of the dead child (1 Kings 17) and calling down the Heavenly Hosts (2 Kings 1), and the utter impotence of His chief rival Baal, through the events leading up to and including the contest at Mt. Carmel.

The results of that contest made clear that it was God alone who held sway over the phenomena of nature, and thus only He could initiate or bring to an end the drought which had for so long plagued the kingdom of Northern Israel. At the same time that contest was meant to consign not only the prophets of Baal, but Baal himself, to "death," for even the most "pious" adherents of the Canaanite god would be struck by his inability to supply even the slightest token in support of his prophets (whose deaths are reported in 1 Kgs 18:40). That the people of Israel did not complete Elijah's work was hardly his fault, for he provided them with stirring examples not only in the form of action, but also through words. It is in this latter context that we may turn to v 27.

In accordance with Elijah's challenge, the prophets of Baal had prepared a bull for sacrifice, but had "put no fire to it" (v 25). If Baal were indeed the mighty deity that his worshippers proclaimed, it would be a simple matter for him to provide a fire with which to ignite their offering. Baal's prophets "called on the name of Baal from morning until noon, saying, 'O Baal answer us!' But there was no voice, and no one answered. And they limped about the altar which they had made" (v 26). At this point "Elijah mocked them, saying,

> Cry aloud, for he is a god;
> either he is musing,
> or he has gone aside,
> or he is on a journey,
> or perhaps he is asleep and must be awakened."
> (1 Kgs 18:27, RSV)

The annotation in the new Oxford edition of the RSV is surely correct in terming this verse "one of the sharpest satires on paganism ever penned." Nor was it premature on the part of Elijah, who as "a man of God" knew that the efforts of these prophets were as doomed to failure as his were assured of success.

The prophet offers four "alternatives" to account for the seeming inattentiveness of this so-called god to what would appear to be legitimate requests on the part of his "true" prophets. (It is probable that the remark concerning the god's "going aside" is "a euphemism for attending to natural needs" [so the New Oxford Annotated Bible].) We confine our analysis here to the fourth, which is directly relevant to our topic. In this final suggestion for what might otherwise be occupying the "god" Baal, we are able to detect Elijah's concern for a proper understanding of the process of resurrection:

What, is it to Baal that you look when you consider the fertility of land, animals, and fellow humans? Do you carry your apostasy even further and dare to pin your hopes for "life after death" on this deity who does not deign to support his Canaanite worshippers with "life on earth"? What folly, what dangerous folly! Don't you see, the prophet asks, that this "no god," on whose rising all of nature is supposed to depend, is locked, as it were, in the nether-world, unable to awaken =resurrect himself?

How great is the contrast between this one, who could not be roused to action by all the gushing blood and frantic ravings of 450 of his assembled prophets, and the one God of Israel, who showed through His chosen vehicle that He is ever mindful of those who worship Him in truth and faithfulness. Look, listen, and learn, we can hear the prophet pleading to his fellow Israelites, that your God is in no way bound by the processes of nature, but rather has dominion over each and every process of this world which He alone created.

Choose, for you must, between a pagan deity utterly devoid of power, whose adherents yet claim him as warrior and source of fertility, and the God of Israel, who demonstrated before the eyes of all that His vitalizing power as Divine Warrior truly does extend from the provision of fertility throughout the earth to the re-awakening of His dead that is the only authentic resurrection for which one can hope. As we begin to perceive the full import of the language and imagery on which Elijah drew to fashion his verbal arsenal of weapons in the battle he waged on God's behalf, we can only repeat that indeed it was hardly the prophet's fault that so many Hebrews, blinded and deafened beyond even Elijah's ability to heal, chose to follow Baal into that death from which neither the deity nor his followers would ever be resurrected.

There is perhaps another sense in which Elijah may have intended his audience to understand the imagery of Baal's "sleeping" and "awakening." In Genesis 9 it is related that Noah as "first tiller of the soil . . . planted a vineyard . . . drank of the wine, and became drunk" (Gen 9:20). His return to sobriety is described in terms of "awakening from his wine" (Gen 9:24). Is it possible then that the last of Elijah's satirical "alternatives" is meant to portray the great Canaanite warrior god as too drunk to attend to his followers' needs? Some further support for this interpretation is furnished by a Ugaritic text (24.258), which speaks of crying "to awaken the gods (most likely from a drunken sleep/stupor)." In the last analysis, however, such a referent would only dull the sharp edge of the prophet's barb, for the issue here is not Baal's intemperance, but rather his impotence.

CONCLUSIONS

Throughout this paper we emphasized what the Hebrew Bible itself has to say about the topics under consideration. To achieve this purpose, we have felt the need to place each passage in the proximate context provided by the material immediately surrounding and in an overall Biblical context, which can be determined only by drawing as many connections as possible with all types of material wherever found in the Hebrew Bible. Finally, there is the context, both theological and historical in nature, that can be fully appreciated only through a study of the other cultures and societies that made up the ancient Near East.

Few scholars would view their work otherwise, for no one would wish to stand convicted of having imposed his own, or his age's, presuppositions or biases on those products of Biblical writers that have survived the hazardous process of transmission from the time of their composition to the present. Nevertheless, as we have seen, the very same passages "say" very different things, especially when approached from perspectives and via methodologies that are frequently viewed as mutually exclusive. We do not claim that we have heard *everything* that these passages have to say, but we do feel that in each case we have captured something of the authentic message that was aimed both at the original audience and at later generations as well.

As we have charted it, a concept of the bodily resurrection of the dead is expressed in Biblical material that ranges in date of composition from the ninth to the second centuries B.C.E. Expressions of this belief are most prominent in the ninth and eighth centuries (especially in Northern Israel) and in the sixth century.

We have sought to demonstrate that the specific belief in bodily resurrection arose out of the larger themes associated with YHWH as Divine Warrior. Beginning from these themes, various Biblical writers moved in quite different directions. In earlier passages resurrection could be set in this world and resulted in the re-introduction of individuals into the same human society which they had only recently left. In later material within the Hebrew Bible, we do not find examples of such "preliminary" resurrections, although we do meet with them in the New Testament. Except in the very latest Biblical passage dealing with resurrection (Dan 12:2), the scope of this process, when delineated, is limited to those righteous individuals (God's dead) for whom re-awakening from the sleep of death is itself vindication and reward; the evil, identified in these passages in terms of foreign oppressors of Israel, are punished through exclusion from what we have termed, on the basis of evidence from the Hebrew Bible itself, the natural process of resurrection.

On occasion, some of the people of Israel used this belief in an attempt to manipulate God's activity to their own advantage, a dangerous situation to which in our opinion the classical prophets were particularly sensitive. If it is true that some were all too ready to advertise their automatic inclusion among those for whom future resurrection was a virtual certainty, it may also be the case that for other thoughtful observers within Israel the lack of righteousness that seemed to adhere to the human condition presaged the exclusion not only of the foreign oppressors, but of the Hebrews themselves, from the process of resurrection. Finally, in the hands of an Elijah the belief in resurrection could be fashioned into a powerful verbal weapon against the pretensions of those who sought in Baal, rather than in the Lord God of Israel, the all-powerful Divine Warrior, whose control over all natural phenomena was manifest in the process of human resurrection.

Dan 12:2, from the second century B.C.E., marks a significant innovation, in that it envisions the participation of righteous and wicked alike in the process of resurrection. No longer was exclusion alone considered sufficient punishment, especially for those who readily sacrificed their religion and co-religionists as the price for entry into the "sophistication" of the Hellenistic world. In essence, this passage also marks an early stage within the third period during which the belief in resurrection received more than isolated expression. This third period extends beyond the confines of the Hebrew Bible into post-Biblical and Rabbinic Judaism and early Christianity.

Many of the same politico-religious factors that led to the particular expression of belief we find in Dan 12:2 were at work throughout this period. Each of the later traditions was subject to unique historical and theological forces, but these additional elements generally reinforced an already-growing interest in the afterlife, an interest which frequently centered on the process and scope of resurrection.

In this regard, let us look briefly at Rabbinic Judaism. In the Mishnah, which represents a distillation of the earlier period of Rabbinic speculation and debate in c. 200 C.E., the following statement appears:

> All of Israel has a portion in the world to come . . .
> and the following have no portion in the world to come:
> one who says, "There is no resurrection of the dead. . . ."
>
> _m. Sanh._ 10:1

Within a central prayer of the liturgy, the _Amidah_, a clear expression of the belief that God does indeed effect the resurrection of His dead is found. At a later period, the mediaeval Jewish philosopher Maimonides included this concept among his 13 principles of faith. Similar evidence from early traditions within Christianity could equally well be adduced.

For people living in such communities it was not difficult to find references to a belief in bodily resurrection throughout the Hebrew Bible. From our vantage point, we are wont to criticize such ventures as eisegesis (i.e., reading into the text what one wants to find there), rather than exegesis. Such a verdict, however, may well be too harsh.

At certain periods during which the Biblical text was being composed, we can detect an interest in resurrection even when it went largely or entirely unexpressed. At these periods, if not at others, writers could have given shape to such interests through language and imagery that have little or nothing in common with the criteria with which we have been working. If this is the case—and we should be willing to admit the possibility—then we need to give more serious attention to the efforts of those within early post-Biblical communities who might well have retained a sensitivity to the text that is frequently lacking in modern, scientific approaches. As a result, our understanding of the complex process through which the Biblical belief in resurrection developed will undoubtedly be enhanced.

The Samaritan Problem: A Case Study in Jewish Sectarianism in the Roman Era

JAMES D. PURVIS
BOSTON UNIVERSITY

I. THE SAMARITANS AMONG THE JEWISH SECTS

Our understanding of the character of Palestinian Judaism during the last century B.C.E./first century C.E. has changed considerably over the past three decades, largely as a result of the discovery of the Essene library of Qumrân. Judaism in late antiquity now appears to have been more complex and richly variegated than had previously been thought. True, much of the evidence of this complexity had been known to scholars prior to the discovery of the scrolls—from Jewish apocryphal literature, archaeological data, witnesses to varieties of Judaism in classical literary sources, etc. But, for the most part, there had been a tendency to regard the Judaism of that time in terms of what George Foote Moore had called "normative Judaism," that is in reference to the religious traditions of the Pharisaic party which subsequently became normative in Judaism.[1] Other religious traditions tended to be regarded as aberrant or sectarian, in the sense of being representative of the thought of schismatic movements alienated from the mother faith. The sectarian movements of Christian history undoubtedly served as an unconscious model in this distinction, with the theological-sociological analysis of church/sect of Ernst Troeltsch providing a model for understanding the relationship between the two.[2] The availability of the literature of the Essene community stimulated interest in this and in other sects, but at the same time contributed to the breakdown of the older understanding of Jewish sectarianism. Rather than being regarded as aberrant positions, the traditions of the sects (we shall retain the term for convenience) have come to be viewed as components of a greater religious

[1] As set forth in Moore's classic study, *Judaism in the first Centuries of the Christian Era* (3 vols.; Cambridge, MA: Harvard University, 1927-30).
[2] See esp. E. Troeltsch, *Social Teachings of the Christian Churches* (London: George Allen and Unwin, 1931), 1. 331-36; cf. M. Simon, *Les Sectes juives au temps de Jésus* (Paris: Presses Universitaires de France, 1960) 3-16.

complex of which the Pharisaic traditions were themselves a part. It is no longer evident that the religious system of the Pharisaic party represented a normative type of Judaism prior to the last quarter of the first century C.E.

The Samaritans are not *strictly speaking* a Jewish sect, at least *not by their own definition*. Members of the community claim to be descended from the ancient tribes of Ephraim, Manasseh, and Levi, and, accordingly, refer to themselves as Hebrews and Israelites. They reject the traditions associated with Jerusalem and the Judaean branch of the Israelite nation and claim that their faith—based on the Pentateuch and sacred traditions associated with Mt. Gerizim and Shechem—represents the Israelite faith as it has been legitimately practiced from ancient times to the present. They have maintained this theological position and have existed as a distinct religious community since at least the early Roman period. Samaritanism may nonetheless be viewed as a variety of Judaism or as an alternative form of Judaism based on a narrow dimension of the Jewish heritage. Essentially, what the Samaritans claimed about themselves—and continue to affirm to this day—was what the Jewish sects of late antiquity also claimed: that they had correctly interpreted the Mosaic faith and put it into practice (compare the Pharisees and Sadducees), that they were the true Israel of God (compare the Essenes and the early Christian Church), and, in the case of the Dosithean branch of the Samaritan community, that their faith was the eschatological fulfillment of the ancient faith following a Mosaic-like teacher (compare the Essenes, the Christians, and some Baptist sects). Thus, even though the Samaritans understood themselves to be a community distinct from the Jews, they were very much a part of the milieu of Jewish sectarianism of the Roman period.

Although the Jewish sects of that time (including the Samaritans) were distinguished from one another by their individualistic postures and *raisons d'etre*, they frequently shared much in common: halakic interpretation, theological concepts, religious rites, etc. The reasons for this were varied. In some cases commonality of traditions was due to common origins, in other cases to the direct or indirect influence of one group upon another, in yet others to the sharing of an intellectual tradition which was not limited to any one particular sect. Useful comparative studies of traditions preserved by the different sects are thus possible, provided that they are critical and take into account the peculiarly sectarian dimensions of any one tradition. This is particularly true in those instances where a tradition imperfectly known from the surviving literature of one sect is encountered in the literature of another. There are a number of cases in which the study of Samaritan traditions has been helpful in elucidating traditions found in other sects.

To cite but a few examples: halakic practices and calendrical observances of the Sadducees (which are known only from reports of their antagonists),[3] certain theological concepts of the Johannine branch of the early Church which appear unique in contemporary Christian literature,[4] and various beliefs and practices of the Essenes which are alluded to but not fully developed in their literature.[5] Samaritan studies are thus important not only in their own right, but also for what they reveal of Jewish sectarianism in general.

Although it is customary to speak of the Samaritans as a clearly defined sect of the Roman period, it must be kept in mind that there was a variety of religious opinions within the Samaritan community of that time—or *varieties of Samaritanism*. The priests, who appear to have maintained a degree of power after the destruction of the Gerizim temple by John Hycranus in 128 B.C.E., are generally regarded by Samaritanologists as having constituted the orthodox party of that period. As a religious system, the theology of the Samaritan priests was roughly analogous to the theology of the Sadducean party in Judaism. There was also a Samaritan sect known as the Dositheans (some hold there were two distinct Dosithean sects) and a number of smaller groups which were related historically to the Dositheans. Members of this sect regarded Dositheus as a prophet-like-Moses and held a variety of opinions which differed radically from those of the priests (not only in regard to their

[3] J. Bowman, "Is the Samaritan Calendar the Old Zadokite One?" *PEQ* 91 (1959) 23-37; J. Van Goudoever, *Biblical Calendars* (2d ed.; Leiden: E. J. Brill, 1961), *passim*. On Samaritan and Sadducean halakah, see the older study by B. Revel, *The Karaite Halakah and its Relation to Sadducean, Samaritan and Philonian Halakah* (Philadelphia, 1913), I.

[4] J. Bowman, "The Fourth Gospel and the Samaritans," *BJRL* 40 (1958) 298-308; *The Samaritan Problem: Studies in the Relationships of Samaritanism, Judaism, and Early Christianity* (Pittsburgh: Pickwick, 1975) 59-69; "The Identity and Date of the Unnamed Feast of John 5:1," in H. Goedicke (ed.), *Near Eastern Studies in Honor of William Foxwell Albright* (Baltimore: Johns Hopkins University, 1971) 43-56; G. W. Buchanan, "The Samaritan Origin of the Gospel of John," in J. Neusner (ed.), *Religions in Antiquity: Essays in Memory of E. R. Goodenough* (Leiden: Brill, 1968) 149-75; E. D. Freed, "Samaritan Influence in the Gospel of John," *CBQ* 30 (1968) 580-97; "Did John Write His Gospel Partly to Win Samaritan Converts?" *NovT* 12 (1970) 241-56; J. D. Purvis, "The Fourth Gospel and the Samaritans," *NovT* 17 (1975) 161-98; C. H. H. Scobie, "The Origins and Development of Samaritan Christianity," *NTS* 19 (1972-73) 390-414, esp. pp. 401-8; W. Meeks, *The Prophet King: Moses Traditions and the Johannine Christology* (Leiden: Brill, 1967) 216-57, 286-319.

[5] Bowman, *Samaritan Problem*, 91-118; "Contact between Samaritan Sects and Qumran?" *VT* 7 (1957) 184-97; "Did the Qumran Sect Burn the Red Heifer?" *RevQ* 1 (1958) 73-84.

prophet, but also respecting calendar, halakah, and eschatology). Comparisons between the Samaritans and the Essenes, Christians, and Baptist sects are most profitably made with this branch of the Samaritan community. In a recent study, S. J. Isser has demonstrated that in their origins (actually prior to the time of Dositheus himself), the Dositheans or proto-Dositheans represented a Pharisaic-like party among the Samaritans.[6] In addition to the work of Isser, the researches of John Bowman,[7] A. D. Crown,[8] and H. G. Kippenberg[9] have been helpful in clarifying the relationship of the dissident elements within early Samaritanism and in identifying the different branches of the Samaritan community to which the various traditions surviving in Samaritan literature originally belonged. Much of this work is necessarily conjectural, and these scholars do not always agree among themselves, but Samaritan studies have been advanced considerably through their labors.

When James Montgomery produced his classic study on the Samaritans in 1907, the Dositheans and related groups were considered under the rubic "Samaritan Sects."[10] They were indeed sects, but Montgomery appears to have been working with the understanding of church/sect which had prevailed in the study of Jewish sectarianism. The Dositheans were consequently viewed as a movement alienated from the mother faith (the orthodoxy of the Samaritan priests) and as representing an aberrant point of view (compare A. D. Crown's identification of Dosithean traditions as "heterodox"). Traditional modes of understanding are not easily displaced, but it would appear that the situation in Samaritan sectarianism was not unlike the situation in Jewish sectarianism. There is no certainty that the theology of the priests constituted a "normative Samaritanism" during the period under consideration. Normative Samaritan theology (such as that treated by John Macdonald in his *Theology of the Samaritans*[11]) appears to have been standardized in the

[6]*The Dositheans: A Samaritan Sect in Late Antiquity* (Leiden: Brill, 1976), esp. pp. 84-95, 109-10.
[7]See esp. "Pilgrimage to Mount Gerizim," in M. Avi-Yonah et al. (eds.), *Eretz Israel*, vol. VII: *L. A. Mayer Memorial Volume* (Jerusalem: Israel Exploration Society, 1964) 17-28.
[8]"Some Traces of Heterodox Theology in the Samaritan Book of Joshua," *BJRL* 50 (1967) 178-98; "New Light on the Inter-Relationships of Samaritan Chronicles from Some Manuscripts in the John Rylands Library," *BJRL* 54 (1972) 282-313; 55 (1972-73) 86-111.
[9]*Garizim und Synagoge: Traditionsgeschichtliche Untersuchungen zur samaritanischen Religion der aramäische Periode* (Berlin: Walter de Gruyter, 1971).
[10]*The Samaritans, the Earliest Jewish Sect: Their History, Theology and Literature* (Philadelphia: J. C. Winston, 1907; reprinted, New York: Ktav, 1968) 252-65.
[11](London: SCM, 1964).

late Middle Ages and represents a synthesis of priestly and Dosithean elements. The work of H. G. Kippenberg has shown that Samaritanism of the Roman period was even more complex than a simple division of priests and Dositheans.[12]

* * * * * *

The Samaritans have been of interest to western scholars since their rediscovery in the late sixteenth and early seventeenth centuries. A prodigious literature has been produced on the sect since that time. Most recently, Samaritan studies have proliferated, due in part to the renewed interest in Jewish sectarianism but encouraged in particular by the clearer understanding of the Samaritan Pentateuch which has been made possible by the discovery of the Samaritan text-type among the biblical fragments from Qumrân. A recent bibliographical study (1973) indicated that of the many writings on the Samaritans since 1600, approximately twenty-five percent had appeared between 1950 and 1970.[13] As a result of the availability of these materials (including a number of publications and reprintings of primary sources[14]), students of Judaism in late anti- quity (including Christian origins) have become increasingly aware of the importance of the Samaritan traditions for their own researches. Evidence of this may be seen especially in recent studies relating to Samaritan and early Christian traditions.[15] A number of scholars engaged in these researches have expressed surprise in the richness of resources available in Samaritan texts. At least one has ventured the opinion that these materials may prove to be of greater importance for the study of Christian origins than the Qumrân and Nag Hammadi findings.[16] Although this is very much an overstatement, it is at least indicative of the enthusiasm engendered in some quarters by the renewed interest in the Samaritans.

[12]*Garizim und Synagoge,* 175-87.
[13]S. Noja, "Contribution à la bibliographie des Samaritains," *Annal dell'- Istituto di Napoli* 23 (1973) 100 n. 10 — as cited by R. Pummer, "The Present State of Samaritan Studies: I," *JSS* 21 (1976) 39.
[14]See especially the bibliographies of Pummer, "Present State of Samaritan Studies: I," 39-61 and "Present State . . . : II," *JSS* 22 (1977) 27-47; Purvis, "Fourth Gospel and the Samaritans," section I: "The Availability of Samaritan Texts," 162-68. L. A. Mayer's *Bibliography of the Samaritans* (ed. Donald Broadribb; Leiden: Brill, 1964) is flawed by numerous omissions and is already out-of-date.
[15]In addition to the Johannine studies cited in n. 4, see Scobie, "Origin and Development of Samaritan Christianity," 390-414, and the writings to which he refers.
[16]Scobie, "Origin and Development of Samaritan Christianity," 414.

It is the purpose of this essay to indicate how these recent studies have clarified our understanding of the Samaritans and to present in succinct form a picture of this community as a sect of the early Roman period.

II. THE CHARACTER OF SAMARITANISM

Until recently, a clear assessment of the character of early Samaritan religion had been a difficult task. This was due to conflicting testimony on the origin of the sect—how and why it came into being as a distinct religious community and what, consequently, was its theological posture. This state of uncertainty among scholars was reflected as late as 1962 in H. H. Rowley's essay "The Samaritan Schism in Legend and History"[17] (compare his earlier "Sanballat and the Samaritan Temple," 1955[18]). Since that time, much has transpired in research on the Samaritans to clarify this particular issue and make possible a clearer understanding of the nature of Samaritanism.

Almost all investigations of Samaritan origins have begun with the premise that there was a definitive event in the history of relations between Samaritans and Jews which resulted in estrangement between the two communities and the establishment of a distinct Samaritan cultic-religious tradition. Hence the recurrent use of the term *schism* in reference to the origins of the sect. The Samaritans themselves have viewed their beginnings as the result of a schism, but have claimed that it was not they but the Jews who were the schismatics. The Jewish schism, according to their point of view, resulted from the activity of the priest Eli who allegedly transferred Israel's cultic center from Shechem to Shiloh, from whence it was eventually removed to Jerusalem.[19] The Samaritans thus view themselves as the surviving remnant of the Israelites of Shechem who remained loyal to the worship of the Hebrew God and avoided both the heresy of the Judaeans and the paganism of the

[17]Published in B. W. Anderson and W. Harrelson, *Israel's Prophetic Heritage: Essays in Honor of James Muilenburg* (New York: Harper, 1962) 208-22.
[18]Published originally in *BJRL* 38 (1955) 166-98; reprinted in Rowley, *Men of God: Studies in Old Testament History and Prophecy* (London: Thomas Nelson, 1963) 246-76.
[19]On which see the Samaritan traditions preserved in T. G. Juynboll, *Chronicon Samaritanuum, arabice conscriptum, cui titulus est Liber Josuae* (Leiden, 1848) 180-81; E. Vilmar, *Abulfathi Annales Samaritani* (Gotha, 1856) 38-39; E. N. Adler and M. Séligsohn, "Une Nouvelle Chronique samaritaine," *REJ* 44 (1902) 205-6; J. Macdonald, *The Samaritan Chronicle No II (or Sepher Ha-Yamim), From Joshua to Nebuchadnezzar* (Berlin: Walter de Gruyter, 1969) 111-13.

followers of the kings of northern Israel.[20] Jewish traditions on the other hand have maintained that in their origins the Samaritans were neither Israelites nor unalloyed Yahwists. Traditions preserved in the Pharisaic literature claim that the Samaritans were descendants of the Mesopotamian colonists who had been settled in northern Palestine by the Assyrians in the late eighth century B.C.E. and who became half-converts to the Israelite faith (2 Kgs 17:24-41; half-converts in that these settlers were said to have adopted the worship of Yahweh while continuing to worship their former gods, v 41). The Samaritans were accordingly called the *Kûtîm* by the Pharisees (and, we may assume, by other Jews), after *kûtâh*, Cuthah, one of the cities in Mesopotamia from which the colonists had been brought (v 24).[21] Even the appellation Samaritans, *šōmĕrōnîm*, carried an opprobrious connotation for Jews, since the only occurrence of that gentilic in the Hebrew Bible was in reference to these half-pagan, half-Yahwistic people (v 28). The Samaritans themselves generally avoided the term, calling themselves—in addition to Hebrews and Israelites—*haššāmĕrîm*, "the Guardians" (i.e., of the Law).[22] It seems likely that this was a paronomasion designed to avoid the negative associations of *šōmĕrōnîm*. Some scholars have argued, however, that the sectarians originally called themselves the Guardians and that Samaritans was a nickname supplied by their detractors.[23]

The Jewish historian Josephus knew and used the tradition of the Kuthean origins of the Samaritan people and their (supposedly) corrupt Yahwism (*Ant.* 9. 288-291).[24] He also knew of their claim to be descendants of the Joseph tribes, but maintained that this was a fiction which they espoused only when it was to their advantage to be associated with the Jews (9. 291; 11. 341). They were not above denying this association, he said, when kinship with the Jews proved disadvantageous (11. 341; 12. 257-264). He also claimed that religious similarities between the Samaritans and the Jews were due to the Gerizim based community having absorbed renegades and outcasts from Jerusalem (11. 346-347). Indeed, according to Josephus, the Samaritans were indebted to the

[20]On the Samaritan claim to have been disassociated from the paganism of Jeroboam and his followers, see esp. Macdonald, *Samaritan Chronicle No II*, 157-59.

[21]The Rabbinic citations are found in Rowley, "Samaritan Schism in Legend and History," and in Montgomery, *Samaritans*, 165-203.

[22]As, for example, in Macdonald's *Samaritan Chronicle No II, passim.*

[23]So A. Mikolášek, "Les Samaritains Gardiens de la Loi contre les Prophètes," *Communio Viatorum* 12 (1969) 139-48; cf. Macdonald, *Theology of the Samaritans*, 18.

[24]References to Josephus are from the *Loeb Classical Library* edition, *Josephus* (9 vols.; Cambridge, MA: Harvard University, 1926-1965).

priesthood and temple of Jerusalem for their basic cultic institutions. This was explained through an account of the expulsion of priests from the temple of Jerusalem and their attachment to the shrine on Gerizim. (11.302-325). Again, the origins of Samaritan religion were understood as the result of a schism. But for Josephus, and the sources upon which he was dependent, the Samaritans were the schismatics.

Briefly stated, Josephus' account of the Samaritan schism was as follows: Manasseh, the brother of Jaddua, high priest in Jerusalem, was expelled from the temple in Jerusalem because of his marriage to Nicaso, the daughter of Sanballat. Because Manasseh held the priestly office in esteem, he considered divorcing Nicaso. Sanballat then sought permission from Alexander the Great—who had just arrived in Palestine —to build a temple on Mt. Gerizim at which his son-in-law could function as high priest. The shrine was erected and Manasseh was joined by other Jewish renegades. Thus, according to Josephus, the Samaritan schism occurred in 332 B.C.E. Samaritan religion was a deviant form of Judaism to which the Samaritan people adhered when it was advantageous. (Compare Josephus' account of the Samaritans willingly accepting Hellenization in the time of Antiochus IV, 12. 257-264.)

The difficulty with Josephus' account is that Sanballat was represented as a contemporary of Alexander the Great whereas the biblical Sanballat (Sanballat the Horonite) was a contemporary of Nehemiah. Moreover, Josephus' story bears a striking resemblance to an account in Nehemiah's memoirs of how he had expelled a priest who was Sanballah's son-in-law. The priest was unnamed, but was said to have been one of the sons of Jehoiada, nephew of the high priest Eliashib (Neh 13:28). The Bible, however, does not connect this incident with either a schism or the construction of a Samaritan temple. Nonetheless, some scholars were inclined to interpret Josephus' story as a variant account of the incident of Nehemiah 13 and to date the alleged Samaritan schism in the Persian period. This seemed to coincide with Jewish traditions of Jewish-Samaritan antipathies in the time of Sheshbazzar (1 *Esdr* 2:16-24) and Zerubbabel (Ezra 4:1-4; 1 *Esdr* 5:66-73), and with Samaritan traditions representing Ezra as an arch-heretic. Other scholars argued that the incidents of Nehemiah 13 and *Antiquities* 11. 302-325 were unrelated and that Josephus had correctly dated the Samaritan schism in the early Greek period.[25] Scholarly opinion was about equally divided between these two views, but in either case it was generally agreed (following Josephus) that Samaritan religion was a Jewish heresy whose basic institutions (temple, priesthood, Scriptures) were derived from the Jerusalem cultus. The alternative viewpoint, that the Samaritan religion was

[25]The opinions of the two schools of thought are summarized in Rowley, "Sanballat and the Samaritan Temple."

the continuation of a cultic tradition which had existed in ancient times parallel to the Jewish tradition (the view of the Samaritans themselves), had few supporters.[26]

Scholars were left then with several possibilities concerning Samaritan origins and the character of early Samaritan religion. The Samaritans were either (1) the surviving remnant of the Joseph tribes perpetuating the ancient northern Israelite religion (the apology of the community) or (2) the descendants of foreigners who had adopted the Israelite-Jewish faith (the polemic of their enemies). If they were the latter, their Israelitic character was the result of a schism in which they had broken away from the Jews and established a rival community. Such a schism was thought to have occurred either in the Persian period (following Neh 13:28 interpreted in the light of *Antiquities* 11. 302-325) or the early Greek period (following Josephus and disregarding Nehemiah 13). But in the absence of external data by which the theories derived from conflicting literary witnesses could be tested, it was impossible to determine which position was correct. At least this was the state of the problem until recently, when new data began to appear which put the question of Samaritan sectarian origins in a new perspective.

Josephus' account of the construction of the Samaritan temple on Mt. Gerizim in the early Greek period has been clarified by the excavations of Tel Balâṭa (Shechem) and Tel er-Ras (Mt. Gerizim) as well as by the discovery of the papyri of Wâdī Dâliyeh.[27] It has been learned that Shechem was rebuilt in the early Greek period after a time of inactivity and virtual abandonment, and that the foundations of the Roman temple on Mt. Gerizim also date from the Hellenistic period. It had been previously known that Samaria had been rebuilt as a Greek *polis* at this time, as a punitive measure following an abortive revolt against Macedonian rule. The discoveries from Wâdī Dâliyeh indicate the extent of the repressive measures taken by the Greeks. A large number of the leading families of Samaria (several hundred people) fled the city and

[26]Moses Gaster was generally inclined towards this view. See his *The Samaritans: Their History, Doctrine, and Literature* (Schweich Lectures, 1923; London: British Academy, 1925). This is also the position of J. Macdonald in his *Theology of the Samaritans.*

[27]See F. M. Cross, "Aspects of Samaritan and Jewish History in Late Persian and Hellenistic Times," *HTR* 59 (1966) 201-11; "Papyri of the Fourth Century B.C. from Dâliyeh," in D. N. Freedman and J. Greenfield (eds.), *New Directions in Biblical Archaeology* (Garden City, N.Y.: Doubleday, 1969) 45-69; P. W. Lapp and N. L. Lapp (eds.), *Discoveries in the Wâdî ed-Dâliyeh* (*AASOR*, 41; Cambridge, MA: American Schools of Oriental Research, 1974); G. E. Wright, "The Samaritans at Shechem," in *Shechem: Biography of a Biblical City* (New York: McGraw-Hill, 1965) 170-84; R. J. Bull, "The Excavation of Tell er-Ras on Mt. Gerizim," *BA* 31 (1968) 58-72.

332

JAMES D. PURVIS

took refuge in caves in the Wâdī. They were pursued to their hiding place and mercilessly slaughtered to the last woman and child. The suggestion that Shechem was repopulated by the disenfranchised citizens of Samaria provides the best explanation for the renascence of that site. It was a logical place to resettle: time-honored by the most ancient Hebrew traditions, adjacent to the holy mountain of the north, strategically located and offering a good environment for the cultural and economic redevelopment of the community. The erection of a temple was a logical adjunct to this development, and not with precedence. As Elias Bickerman has noted, "It often happened that when a Greek colony was established, native villages under its control formed a union around an ancestral sanctuary."[28]

These new data support Josephus' claim that the Samaritan temple had been built in the early Greek period. But there would have been no reason to doubt him in this were it not for the fact that he associated the event with Sanballat, a person otherwise known from the Bible to have been a contemporary of Nehemiah. Some scholars had postulated a Sanballat II, but this was purely speculative. The papyri from the Wâdī Dâliyeh now give evidence of another Sanballat, the father of one Hananiah, governor of Samaria in 354 B.C.E. This could scarcely have been the biblical Sanballat (the Horonite), because it is known from the Elephantine papyri that he had been succeeded by his sons Delaiah and Shelamiah by the last decade of the fifth century. He was most likely the grandson of Nehemiah's contemporary. We thus know of two Sanballats, Sanballat I and II. The latter would not qualify to be the Sanballat of *Antiquities* 11. 302-325, but he could well have been his grandfather. Thus, although the Samaria papyri do not identify the Sanballat of the early Greek period of whom Josephus wrote, they do give evidence that papponymy (naming a child after his grandfather) was practiced in the ruling house of Samaria and present a chronological sequence in which it appears evident that Josephus' Sanballat was Sanballat III.[29]

Thus we now know that the Samaritans began to develop a distinct community around a Gerizim sanctuary in the last quarter of the fourth century B.C.E. But we do not know that Josephus was correct in claiming that the priesthood of that temple was derived from that of the Jerusalem temple. Nor would we be justified on the basis of this evidence in asserting that this activity represented a schism from the Jewish community. The Samaritan priest-lists represent their priestly chain as independent of the Jerusalem cultus, and many Samaritan scholars are inclined to agree with this tradition of sacerdotal independence.[30]

[28]*From Ezra to the Last of the Maccabees* (New York: Schocken, 1962) 43-44.
[29]So Cross, "Papyri of the Fourth Century B.C. from Dâliyeh," 61-63.
[30]So Mikolášek (n. 23) and Macdonald (who generally accepts the veracity of the Samaritan traditions concerning their origins). But see esp. Kippenberg,

We might be inclined, then, on the basis of the evidence surveyed above, to date the origins of the Samaritan sect which is known from the Roman period to around 332 B.C.E. and to understand its peculiar features as having taken shape at that time or shortly thereafter. Two considerations militate against this. The first is the tradition preserved in Josephus of the Hellenization of Samaritan religion in the time of Antiochus IV (*Ant.* 12. 257-264). The second is the evidence supplied from the biblical fragments from Qumrân which help us understand better the character of the Samaritan Pentateuch and the time of its redaction. I have argued elsewhere that the situation of Hellenization at Shechem under Antiochus IV was the reverse of what occurred in Jerusalem. At Shechem, the Hellenistic party (which I have tentatively proposed called itself the "Sidonians of Shechem"—see *Ant.* 12. 258-259) won out over the "orthodox," whereas in Jerusalem the Hellenistic party was resisted by the revolt of the Maccabees and their supporters.[31] I have also argued that the cumulative evidence now available concerning the Samaritan Pentateuch indicates that it underwent a sectarian redaction in the late Hasmonaean period, roughly contemporaneous with the destruction of the Samaritan temple under John Hyrcanus (128 B.C.E.) and the subsequent destruction of Shechem (ca. 107 B.C.E.).[32]

It now appears evident that the Samaritan sect (as it is known from the Roman period) was a community whose self-understanding was not clearly defined until around 100 B.C.E., much later than the earlier studies had proposed. The chief monument of this self-definition was the distinctively sectarian redaction of the Pentateuch which the Samaritans promulgated at that time.

The concurrence of the dates of the destruction of the Gerizim sanctuary and the city of Shechem with the production of a distinctively sectarian biblical text was certainly not coincidental. The latter was clearly a reaction to the former. The Samaritans found themselves at the end of the second century B.C.E. in a predicament very much like that which they had faced two centuries earlier where they had been expelled

---

Garizim und Synogoge, 60-68, 91-93. Bowman on the other hand, accepts Josephus' tradition of the Zadokite origins of the Samaritan priesthood in his treatment of early Samaritan priestly theology. See, for example, "The Importance of Samaritan Researches," *Annual of Leeds University Oriental Society* 1 (1958-59) 43-54; "Is the Samaritan Calendar the Old Zadokite One?"

[31]In "The Samaritans," forthcoming in *Cambridge History of Judaism*, vol. 1 (eds. W. D. Davies and L. Finkelstein).

[32]See *The Samaritan Pentateuch and the Origins of the Samaritan Sect* (*HSM* 2; Cambridge, MA: Harvard University, 1968). This position has been argued as well by Professor Cross (see n. 34), under whose encouragement and direction my study was undertaken. My indebtedness to my teacher is gratefully acknowledged.

from Samaria. At the earlier time they had been forced to reevaluate their status when they had been deprived by the Macedonians of political leadership of Samaria and its environs. Their response had been to establish a new base (Shechem) through which they could continue to play a prominent cultural role in the area. Their relations with their Judaean neighbors to the south—with whom political and cultural antipathies extended back into the early Persian period—deteriorated progressively in the following centuries.[33] Of the many factors contributing to this estrangement, the Hellenization of Samaritan religion in the time of Antiochus IV appears to have been particularly significant. With the destruction of their sanctuary and devastation of their city by the Hasmonaean prince Hyrcanus, the Samaritans were now faced with a more serious crisis—that of defining their relationship with Jerusalem and clarifying their status as a Hebrew people. This was no easy task, for it necessitated substantiating the legitimacy of their independent existence, and there was little in their immediate past of which they could be justifiably proud. The Samaritans responded by steadfastly maintaining their Israelitic roots and by affirming that their understanding and practice of Yahwistic faith were in accordance with classical Israelite traditions and norms. They could, of course, receive no support for this contention from those Jewish scriptures which represented Jerusalem as the divinely chosen cultic center (i.e., writings in the second and third divisions of the Hebrew Bible), but the Pentateuch and traditions relating to Joshua could be construed as maintaining the sanctity of Gerizim and Shechem. It was precisely these traditions which the Samaritans needed to employ to substantiate their legitimacy, and if these were in any way ambiguous as to the true center of the Israelite faith (Shechem or someplace else), then that point needed to be clarified, *textually.*

It was through their edition of the Pentateuch that the Samaritans were able to demonstrate (at least to their own satisfaction) that it was they and not the Jews who worshipped the Hebrew God in accordance with the most ancient and sacred Israelite traditions. It was not they who were heretics but the Jews. They worshipped God at Mt. Gerizim/ Shechem where Abraham had built his first altar in the land of Canaan, where he had prepared Isaac for sacrifice (identifying Moriah with Gerizim), where Melchizedek had blessed Abraham (identifying Salem with a site near Gerizim), where Jacob had built his sanctuary (identifying Beth-el with Gerizim), and, most importantly, where Moses had commanded the Israelites to build an altar, the place which God had chosen (from the time of the Patriarchs on) as the place where his name

[33]See, for example, Purvis, "Ben Sira? and the Foolish People of Shechem," *JNES* 24 (1965) 88-94.

would dwell. It was at Shechem that Joshua gathered the tribes for a ceremony of covenant renewal in accordance with Moses' command. There the Samaritans (supposedly) continued to worship the Hebrew God, in spite of the heretical activity of Eli in establishing an illegitimate sanctuary at Shiloh, in spite of Solomon's construction of a false temple in Jerusalem, and even in spite of the activities of the kings of northern Israel (from Jeroboam on) in establishing a corrupt and syncretistic Yahwism in the north.

The Samaritans chose for their redaction of the Pentateuch a text-type now known (from biblical fragments from Qumrân) to have been in use in Palestine in the late Hasmonaean period.[34] They also used the palaeo-Hebrew script and a full orthographic tradition for the writing of their Pentateuch, both of which are known to have been in use among Palestinian Jews during the Hasmonaean and Roman periods.[35] In fact, the distinctive letters used by the Samaritans from Roman/Byzantine times to the present day are now seen as having evolved from the Palestinian palaeo-Hebrew of the late Hasmonaean/early Roman period.[36]

Most of the variants of the Samaritan Pentateuch from the standard Jewish text (MT, the Masoretic text)—about six thousand variances— are the result of the adoption of a different textual type and different orthography from that followed by the Jews in their *textus receptus*.[37] Specific sectarian alterations are few but significant in what they imply. The most important is found in the expanded text of the Decalogue in Exodus 20 and Deuteronomy 5. In the case of the Exodus passage, the Samaritans employed a textual tradition which had already been expanded by parallel passages from Deuteronomy. That is, the Palestinian

[34]Purvis, *Samaritan Pentateuch*, 69-87. See also F. M. Cross, "The History of the Biblical Text in the Light of Discoveries in the Judean Desert," *HTR* 57 (1964) 281-99, esp. p. 285; "Contribution of the Qumrân Discoveries for the Study of the Biblical Text," *IEB* 16 (1966) 81-95, esp. pp. 88-89; "The Evolution of a Theory of Local Text," in F. M. Cross and S. Talmon (eds.), *Qumran and the History of the Biblical Text* (Cambridge, MA: Harvard University, 1975) 306-20, esp. pp. 309-11; P. W. Skehan, "The Biblical Scrolls from Qumran and the Text of the Old Testament," *BA* 28 (1965) 87-100, esp. p. 99.

[35]Purvis, *Samaritan Pentateuch*, 52-69.

[36]Ibid., 18-52.

[37]The standard critical edition of SP is A. F. von Gall, *Der hebräische Pentateuch der Samaritaner* (5 vols.; Giessen: Alfred Töpelmann, 1914-1918; reprinted, 1966). A new critical edition has begun to appear in the *Biblia Poliglota Matritense* series, under the direction of F. Perez Castro. See L.-F. Giron Blanc, *Pentateuco Hebreo-Samaritano, Genesis* (Madrid: Textos y Estudios "Cardinal Cisneros," 1976). See also the following editions prepared by Samaritan scholars: A. Sadaqah, *ḥămiššâ ḥûmmĕšê tôrâ* (Tel Aviv, 1959); A. Sadaqa and R. Sadaqa, *ḥămiššâ ḥûmmĕšê tôrâ, nôsaḥ yehûdî, nôsaḥ šômĕrônî* (Tel Aviv, 1961-65).

text was considerably longer than that which was later employed by the
Jews in the establishment of their received text. It had been filled out by
passages from Deut 5:24-27 (within Exod 20:19) and Deut 5:28-31 and
18:18-22 (following Exod 20:21). These were not sectarian interpolations,
but parallel readings derived from Deuteronomy and believed to have
been a part of the original speech of Moses at Sinai. Such editorial
revision of Exodus to bring it in line with the text of Deuteronomy was
justified by statements of Moses in Deut 5:24, 28; 18:17 that he was
repeating words spoken earlier. That these particular additions were not
the result of the Samaritan sectarian redactions is evident from the fact
that the expanded text was known and used by Jews at Qumrân.[38] The
longer Palestinian text (the proto-Samaritan) was later to be rejected by
the Jewish community in favor of a more restrictive textual tradition
(the proto-Masoretic). But to these non-sectarian readings, the Samaritans added one more which was clearly of their own devising. They
included also a passage from Deut 27:2-3a, 4-7 and 11:30 (following
Exod 21:17), with the command to build an altar on *Mt. Gerizim*—their
text of 27:4 read, or was made to read, Gerizim rather than Ebal (MT has
Ebal) and their text of 11:30 stated that the Oak of Moreh was near
Shechem (lacking in MT). They also added this passage to the Decalogue text in Deuteronomy 5, following verse 21. This was clearly
textual manipulation for promoting the theological apologetic of the
sect, and not editorial harmonization as was the case with other additions in Exodus 20. Considering the character of the textual tradition
they employed (an expanded text) their alterations probably did not
seem egregious. But in comparison with the text of Exodus 20 in the
Masoretic textual tradition, the tampering with the biblical text appears
blatant.

In addition to the Decalogue expansion, evidence of sectarian alteration in the biblical text is evident in Deuteronomy in the twenty-one
occurrences of the phrase "the place which the Lord thy God has
chosen" (in reference to the divinely ordained cultic center). The received
Jewish text reads, "the place which the Lord thy God will choose" (Deut
12:5, 11 *et passim*). The difference between the two readings is of only
one letter—the presence or absence of the *yod*-prefix on the verb *bahar*,
to choose. The *yod* indicates an imperfect tense (so the MT, *yibhar*, "will
choose"), the absence of the letter indicates a perfect tense (so the SP,
bāhar, "has chosen"). For the Samaritans, Moses was understood as
referring to Shechem, the place chosen for worship as early as Abraham

[38]P. W. Skehan, "Exodus in the Samaritan Recension from Qumran," *JBL*
74 (1955) 182-187; "The Scrolls and the Old Testament Text," in Freedman and
Greenfield, *New Directions in Biblical Archeology*, 99-112, esp. pp. 101-3;
"Qumran and the Present State of Old Testament Text Studies: the Masoretic
Text," *JBL* 78 (1959) 21-25, esp. pp. 22-23.

(so Gen 12:6-7). For the Jews, the divinely appointed sanctuary site (Jerusalem) had not yet been designated—but would be in time. We see Samaritanism, then, as a type of Israelite religion standardized around 100 B.C.E. by the priests of the devastated Gerizim temple and espoused by the residents of that area (most of whom were eventually to reside in the nearby new city Neapolis, Nablus). These people claimed to be descended from the Joseph tribes which had lived in that region in ancient times. Their chief sectarian monument was an edition of the Pentateuch in which the supremacy of Gerizim/Shechem as the legitimate place of Hebrew worship had been stressed through deliberate textual manipulation.[39] Their religion was thus set forth as an alternative to the Jerusalem based Israelitic religion espoused by the Jewish people. Their autonomy from the Jewish community was not the result of a schism from Judaism (as their Jewish enemies insisted), but was rather derived from their self-definition as the true Israel and their claim that the Jerusalem temple was not a legitimate sanctuary.[40] Any hope of compromise between this northern Palestinian sect and the Jewish sects which accepted the sanctity of Jerusalem had been ruled out by the long history of hostility between Jerusalem and Samaria and, subsequently, Jerusalem and Shechem—punctuated finally and decisively by John Hyrcanus.

There were, and would yet be, a number of Jewish sects differing radically from one another in terms of what they affirmed to be essential in the understanding and practice of the traditional covenant faith. But there was none so radical as this, to affirm that almost all of the Israelite nation had erred from the time of Eli on in worshipping at some place other than Shechem (Gerizim). Others might argue, as did the Essenes, that the temple in Jerusalem had fallen into the hands of a corrupt and illegitimate priesthood; or that the temple in Jerusalem did not correspond to the heavenly archetype, as the Hellenist Christian Stephen maintained (Acts 7); or that the true worship of God transcended the sanctity of a particular place, be it Gerizim or Jerusalem, as the author

[39]Compare the thesis of Kippenberg that the chief sectarian monuments of the Samaritans were their distinctive Pentateuch *and* their priest-list. Kippenberg suggests that both were produced in the early second century B.C.E. concurrently with the loss of the Zadokite priesthood in Jerusalem, and represented an attempt by the Samaritans to embarrass the Jews by stressing their own theological and sacerdotal legitimacy. Kippenberg thus dates the final breach between the Samaritans and the Jews slightly earlier than we have argued. See *Garizim und Synagoge*, 60-93.

[40]This point is forcefully argued, and perhaps overstated, by R. J. Coggins, *Samaritan and Jews: The Origins of Samaritanism Reconsidered* (Oxford: Basil Blackwell, 1975) *passim*, esp. pp. 162-65. See the author's review of Coggin's study in *JTS* 27 (1976) 163-65.

of the Fourth Gospel argued (John 4:20-24); or that the new age called for a return to the desert, as such groups as the Essenes and the followers of John the Baptist affirmed. However, none of these sects denied the sanctity of Jerusalem as it was represented in the ancient Jewish scriptures. Within the broad spectrum of Judaism in late antiquity (i.e., the manifold expressions of Israel's faith of that late time) Samaritanism appeared as an ironic anomaly—an anti-Jewish Jewish sect.

III. ALTERNATIVE TYPES OF SAMARITANISM

Early Christian heresiologists and medieval Samaritan historians bear witness to the existence of sects and parties within the Samaritan community during the Roman period. These have been traditionally understood—following the church/sect model—as sectarian movements representing aberrant positions from the established orthodoxy. But our understanding of what orthodox Samaritanism of that time might have been has been derived from theological and liturgical writings of a later period (none earlier than the fourth century C.E. and all preserved in late medieval and modern manuscripts). It is evident that even these contain traditions of diverse provenience and that if Samaritanism became a unified theological system it was only as a result of the community's coming to terms with its own diversity and reconciling divergent positions. It would be preferable, therefore, to regard the Samaritan sects and parties of the early Roman period as alternative types of Samaritanism. It would appear that these diverse points of view existed from the very beginning of the autonomous life of the Samaritan community and that they developed around distinct groups within that community—priests, laypeople, etc. We may assume that the priests of the Gerizim shrine maintained some degree of power after 128 B.C.E. (indeed, they retain leadership of the community to this very day), so that if we are at all justified in speaking of a Samaritan orthodoxy of that period it would be the theology of the priests. But it is not entirely clear what that theology included (or excluded) and how it may have been related (either positively or adversely) to the theologies of other groups.

Whereas a previous generation of scholars had addressed the dual problem of the origin of the Samaritans and the essential character of Samaritan religion, the present direction of Samaritan studies is inclined towards the resolution of the problem of unity and diversity in early Samaritan religion: What were the relationships of the various Samaritan groups to one another? What were the distinctive theologies of the respective parties? What were the internal social dynamics of the community which caused distinct groups to come into being? To which of these various groups may we attribute diverse traditions preserved in

Samaritan literature? etc. A number of recent studies have led to a clearer understanding of the theological positions of the various parties and the sociological context in which they most likely functioned. But it is still not clear how or when the Samaritan community resolved the problem of its diversity and incorporated disparate elements into its standardized theology. It may have been as early as the fourth century C.E. (certainly no earlier than this) or as late as the fourteenth.

It is necessary to review briefly some of the major conclusions of these recent studies to indicate what has become increasingly clear about the theologies of the respective sects and parties of early Samaritanism.

Studies in Samaritan sectarianism (we shall retain the terms sects and sectarianism for convenience) have centered around the Dositheans, the sect most frequently mentioned by the ancient writers (primarily Christian heresiologists) and the medieval Samaritan historians.[41] The Dositheans were followers of Dositheus (Dusis), a prophet of the first century C.E. (a contemporary of Simon Magus) who claimed to be the prophet like Moses who was anticipated in Deut 18:15-18. Some Samaritan traditions inaccurately date Dusis to the fourth century C.E., most likely because the sect was vigorous at that time. Yet other texts speak of a Dustan sect which came into being in the time of the Jewish ruler Arkia (i.e., John Hyrcanus). We shall see that the sect described as Dustan (i.e., anachronistically called "Dosithean") was most likely the Samaritan party out of which Dositheus came, and which became, after his time, the Dositheans.[42] There were also a number of Dosithean subsects, or groups generated by the Dosithean movement. As early as 1907, James Montgomery succeeded in laying out the various literary witnesses to the several Dosithean groups, but he was unable to clarify the relationship of the parties to one another or to what he tended to regard as the mainline Samaritanism of that time.[43]

Most recently, John Bowman turned his attention to the Dositheans and concluded that they represented a lay-centered party which used the synagogue as an institutional base and which found themselves at odds with the priests who represented the older Samaritan orthodoxy.[44] Differences of opinion between the Dositheans and the priests were most heated in respect to worship (in the synagogue or on Mt. Gerizim), the calendar, halakah, and, most importantly, the doctrine of the resurrection (with the priestly party denying the concept). Bowman was also of

[41]The primary sources have been published, in text and translation, by Isser, *Dositheans*.
[42]As correctly argued by Isser, ibid., 108-10.
[43]*Samaritans*, 252-65.
[44]See esp. "The Importance of Samaritan Researches"; "Pilgrimage to Mount Gerizim."

the opinion that the theology of the Dositheans included an eschatological figure who would be a new Joshua, in contrast to the prophet-like-
Moses anticipated (supposedly) by the priests.[45] Although Bowman
would not be followed strictly in all of his arguments and reconstructions, his major conclusions—especially in respect to lay/priestly tensions—laid the groundwork for subsequent studies on the Samaritan
parties.

Bowman also pointed out—correctly, we think—that although the
Samaritan historians represented Dusis and the Dositheans as heretics,
the long-range reaction of the community to the heresy was not simply
one of rejection, but of interaction and, eventually, of accommodation. He
concluded that the available evidence indicates that the Dositheans
began to gain ascendancy in the fourth century C.E., in the time of the
theologian Marqah (whom he believed to have been a convert to the
Dosithean party), and that some sort of synthesis was achieved at that
time between the priestly and Dosithean theologies. He further suggested
that the two groups remained in tension with one another until the
fourteenth century, when a new and final accommodation was made
(represented in a revised liturgy and in subsequent theological writings
which incorporated both priestly and Dosithean theological elements,
especially in regard to eschatology). Although the question of when the
lay/priestly accommodation was finally made will remain a point of
contention, most scholars are inclined to agree with Bowman that what
Samaritan theology eventually became (and what it is today) was due to
the interaction of the priests with the Dositheans.[46]

Bowman's analysis of the Dositheans was amplified by the work of
his student A. D. Crown, whose investigations centered on materials
which Bowman had not utilized extensively, primarily the Samaritan
chronicles which contain traditions on Joshua.[47] Although agreeing in
general with Bowman, especially in regard to the Dosithean eschatological Joshua, Crown's research moved beyond Bowman's in that it attempted to identify specific materials in Samaritan texts which could be
assigned to Dosithean theology, or, if not clearly Dosithean, to "heterodox" elements in Samaritanism, using the theology of the priests as an
orthodox norm. He also felt that it was possible to identify materials
which represented specific reactions of the priests to the Dositheans. For
example, he suggested that the priestly community developed a new

---

[45]See esp. "The Identity and Date of the Unnamed Feast of John 5:1."
[46]John Macdonald remains an exception in this regard. See Bowman's
comments in *Samaritan Problem*, xvi.
[47]See above, n. 8. See also "Dositheans, Resurrection and a Messianic
Joshua," *Antichthon* 1 (1967) 70-85.

tradition of Joseph-messiah in reaction to the Joshua-messiah of the Dositheans.[48]

It will be noted that a major subject of interest in these investigations was the eschatology of early Samaritanism: the doctrine of the resurrection (supposedly denied originally by the priests but later accepted under Dosithean influence) and the eschatological agent (supposedly Moses in the priestly theology and Joshua in the eschatology of the Dositheans, with a Joseph-messiah later developing, by reaction, among the priests). What these scholars were attempting to do in these constructions was to make sense out of the plethora of Samaritan traditions honoring Joseph, Moses, and Joshua as heroes of the history of salvation (as it was understood by the Samaritans). They assumed that eschatological concerns underlay these glorifications; they may have assumed too much.

As for the doctrine of the resurrection, it is evident from a variety of sources that the concept was lacking in Samaritan theology at an earlier time.[49] It would appear that the priests of the community held a conservative position on this doctrine as did the Sadducean party in early Judaism. It was undoubtedly due to Dosithean influence that the Samaritans as a whole came in time to embrace this concept. As for the eschatological agent (or agents) of early Samaritanism, the problem is much more complex. Late Samaritan texts refer to the eschatological figure under the name or title of the *Taheb*.[50] But neither scholars nor the Samaritans themselves have been able to agree on the original meaning of the term (derived from the root *tûb*, *šûb*, to turn, return, repent). It has been variously interpreted as "the returning one" (usually understood as a returning Moses), "the restorer" (either of the age of divine favor or of the ancient cultic establishment), and as "the penitent one." Because of the preeminence of Moses in the theological texts of the

---

[48]"Some Traces of Heterodox Theology in the Samaritan Book of Joshua," 196-97. See also the critique of this position in Purvis, "Joseph in the Samaritan Traditions," in G. W. E. Nickelsburg, Jr. (ed.), *Studies on the Testament of Joseph* (SBLSCS 5; Missoula: Scholars, 1975) 147-53, esp. pp. 149-50; "Fourth Gospel and the Samaritans," 178-81.

[49]See, for example, the famous dictum preserved in the extra-Talmudic tractate *m. Kut*: 2:28, "When shall we take them back? When they renounce Mount Gerizim and confess Jerusalem and the resurrection of the dead. From this time forth he that robs a Samaritan shall be as he who robs an Israelite."

[50]On which see esp. J. Bowman, "Early Samaritan Eschatology," *JJS* 6 (1955) 63-72; Macdonald, *Theology of the Samaritans*, 362-71; Kippenberg, *Garizim und Synagoge*, 276-305; M. Gaster, *Samaritan Oral Law and Ancient Traditions*, vol. I: *Samaritan Eschatology* (London: Search, 1932) 221-77; A. Merx, *Der Messias oder Ta³eb der Samaritaner* (BZAW 17; Giessen, 1909).

Samaritans, and because of the inclusion of the prophet-like-Moses text of Deut 18:15-18 in the expanded Decalogue of Exodus 20 in the Samaritan Pentateuch, it has been generally understood that the concept of the *Taheb* developed out of the ancient prophet-like-Moses concept. The understanding that it was Moses who was promoted as the eschatological agent by the Samaritan priests rests upon the assumption that the inclusion of Deut 18:15-18 in Exodus 20 in SP was a deliberate sectarian alteration comparable to the readings promoting the Gerizim cultus. Since it was the Samaritan priests who were responsible for the sectarian redaction, it was assumed that the theology of the priests included also the anticipation of an eschatological Moses or Moses-like figure. There are several difficulties with this interpretation. First, it is now known that the inclusion of the Deut 18:15-18 text in Exodus 20 of SP was not a distinctively sectarian action; the reading belonged to the pre-sectarian Palestinian recension which was used by the Samaritans. Second, the passage is not in and of itself an eschatological text. That is, it could be understood as such, but it could also be understood as having had its fulfillment in history. Joshua, for example, could have been viewed (and most likely was by some segments of the Samaritan community) as having fulfilled this role *in history*. Third, one might ask why the priests would have been active in promoting an eschatological agent when they otherwise appear to have been conservative and restrictive in regard to eschatology, denying the concept of the resurrection. What would have been the function of such an eschatological figure?

Clearly, something more was necessary for the clarification of early Samaritan theologies than the simple isolation of variant traditions in later Samaritan literature and the assigning of these to one or another of the early parties, priestly or Dosithean. What was needed was the establishment of sound criteria by which such judgments could be made based upon the emergent knowledge of early Samaritan history. An investigation which took these considerations into account was H. G. Kippenberg's *Garizim und Synagoge: Traditionsgeschichtliche Untersuchungen zur samaritanischen Religion der aramäischen Periode*.[51] As the subtitle indicates, Kippenberg utilized the methodology of "the history of tradition" for the establishment of his criteria. The materials he utilized were for the most part, but not exclusively, Aramaic texts. He also prefaced his study with a lengthy history of the ancient Samaritans based upon recent studies (such as those indicated in section II, above). Essentially, what Kippenberg sought to demonstrate was that specific traditions in the Aramaic texts could be understood as having had their origins in sociologically identifiable segments of the early Samaritan community.

[51]Published as vol. 30, *Religionsgeschichtliche Versuche und Vorarbeiten* (eds. W. Burkert and C. Colpe; Berlin: Walter de Gruyter, 1971).

Beginning with Bowman's thesis that the Dositheans were a lay-centered movement, Kippenberg took as the two basic sources of distinct traditions the Gerizim-based priests and the synagogue-based Dositheans (hence the main title of his study). But he further distinguished groups of lay people around whom particular traditions would have clustered: teachers of the Law, political leaders (*Stammesfürsten*), and judges (whom he suggested played a more significant role in the community in the Byzantine than in the Roman period).[52] He regarded the Dositheans as having emerged out of the community of lay teachers, and as having received the support of most of these, but as having been resisted by the lay governors. It was the Dositheans, Kippenberg maintains, who developed the concept of the *Taheb* as the eschatological agent of the day of judgment and the resurrection of the dead. Kippenberg suggests that the *Taheb* was a concept originally distinct from the prophet-like-Moses concept, but that the two were eventually merged.[53] The priests, in contrast, were concerned with the restoration of the Gerizim cultus through the recovery of the hidden tabernacle, which had supposedly been secreted away by God when Eli transferred the cultus to Shiloh.[54] Their eschatology was not originally one of judgment day and resurrection, but of the restoration of the ancient age of divine grace when Israel had worshipped at the legitimate cultic center of Shechem. The answer to our earlier question concerning the function of an eschatological figure promoted by the priests would be, then, the restoration of the ancient cultic order and the return of the age of divine favor (understanding that we are now living in an age of divine disfavor). In time, Kippenberg suggests, the restoration of the age of grace (which the Samaritans called the *Raḥûtâ*) came to be associated with a returning Moses. Kippenberg rejected Bowman's thesis of a Dosithean Joshua-messiah and argued (correctly we think) that the promotion of Joshua as Moses' successor in history was essentially an anti-Dosithean polemic (i.e., against the claim that Dusis was the prophet-like-Moses).[55] As for the alleged Joseph-messiah, Kippenberg saw some evidence that the political leaders looked to Joseph as an archetypal model of secular leadership. He suggested that this would have been the source of the Messiah ben Joseph concept known from some medieval Jewish sources (a moot point at best) and that it probably was the inspiration of later Samaritan revolts against Byzantine rule (which it may well have been).[56]

In surveying Kippenberg's work, this writer would offer the judgment that he advanced the investigation of early Samaritan traditions

[52]Ibid., 175-87.
[53]Ibid., 300-305.
[54]Ibid., 234-54.
[55]Ibid., 314-23.
[56]Ibid., 273-74.

considerably and corrected some of the mistaken judgments of Bowman and Crown—especially in regard to the Joshua-messiah, but that if he erred it was in being too confident that he had isolated the sources of all of the traditions he investigated. Nonetheless, his major conclusions, as noted above, appear sound. As for his analysis of the Dositheans and their theology, his study included a comprehensive review of the archaeological data relating to the Samaritan synagogues (including inscriptional materials) but, curiously, avoided a careful analysis of the literary materials by which the Dositheans are known to us. These are beset with many difficulties but fortunately have been the subject of a skillful study by S. J. Isser.[57] It is with his work that we conclude our survey of recent research relating to divergent types of Samaritan theology of the Roman period.

Isser's contribution to the understanding of the Dositheans was twofold: first in sorting out the various, often conflicting literary sources relating to the prophet Dositheus and, second, in defining (more carefully than earlier researchers) the character of the particular variety of Samaritanism out of which Dositheanism emerged. Bowman had identified the milieu of Dositheanism as the laity of the Samaritan community. Kippenberg had identified these more precisely as teachers of the Law. It remained for Isser to demonstrate that in its interpretation of the Law this party functioned very much as the Pharisaic party of the Jewish community. The priestly party, by contrast, invites comparison with the Jewish Sadducees. Isser equated this "Pharizaizing group" with the Dustan sect known from the Samaritan historiographer Abu ᵓl Fath.[58] The Dustan party had been known to scholars for some time, but it had not been clear exactly what relationship the sect had to the Dositheans. Isser demonstrated convincingly that this ancient party represented the original stage of what became the Dosithean sect, the branch of the Samaritan community which accepted Dositheus as the prophet-like-Moses in the first century C.E. (what we may appropriately call the "proto-Dositheans").

In addition to analyzing the particular teachings of the Dustan party on the basis of what Abu ᵓl Fath had reported, and finding these to represent a tendency which may be called Pharisaic, Isser also compared Jewish (i.e., Pharasaic) traditions which discussed Samaritan *halakah*. He found in many of these an indication that there was a branch of the Samaritan community which had interpretations of the Law which were consistent with those of the Pharisees. One such tradition, treating a hypothetical legal case, used the term *ḥābēr* to identify a Samaritan

---

[57] *The Dositheans: A Samaritan Sect in Late Antiquity* (*SJLA*; Leiden: Brill, 1976).

[58] Ibid., 84-93.

whose halakic interpretations were acceptable, one who would presumably "observe the law as did the Pharisaic *ḥăbērîm*."[59] Isser felt that the evidence pointed to the Dustan group and their successors as the Pharisaic-like party of the Samaritans.

It was not only in matters of legal interpretation that this Samaritan group had affinities to the Pharisees. There were affinities as well in matters of sacred calendar and in liberalizing tendencies which allowed the acceptance of such novel concepts as the resurrection of the dead and of the age to come. It is reported that the sect worshipped away from Gerizim, in the (enigmatic) *Zawila*. Isser compares here the worship in "Damascus" of the Essene literature, and suggests that the so-called Dustan party did not deny the sanctity of Gerizim but rather felt that the site had been profaned, either by the cultic establishment of that place (compare the Essenes' relationship to Jerusalem) or by the desecration of the holy site by John Hyrcanus.[60]

As for Dusis, Isser found the traditions preserved in the Christian writer Epiphanius and the Samaritan Abuʾl Fatḥ to represent the best sources available for reconstructing the Dosithean beliefs concerning their prophet. These are found now in the testimony of the avowed enemies of the Dositheans, but they indicate, he felt, the existence of an early aretalogy (an account of a sacred hero based on standardized models or paradigms) which set forth the case for Dositheus' prophethood (both Epiphanius and Abuʾl Fatḥ preserve a sort of reverse aretalogy in which the sectarian claims were rejoined).[61] According to Isser's reconstruction, Dositheus was a miracle worker of the first century C.E. who applied the prophet-like-Moses text of Deut 18:15-18 to himself and who also authored texts advancing new interpretations of biblical Law. He was accepted as the Mosaic prophet by the Pharisaic-like segment of the Samaritan community (the Dustan group) which then developed an aretalogy for their prophet utilizing Moses traditions. Dositheus was apparently an ascetic and a martyr from his asceticism. His teachings included a temporary rejection of worship on Gerizim. Religious practices of the disciples of Dositheus included baptismal rites. The followers of Dosithius probably anticipated his return as the *Taheb*. Not long after the time of Dositheus, a variety of Dosithean sub-sects came into being— to cite those specifically mentioned in Samaritan sources, the Baʿunay, a group of ascetics and celibates who removed themselves to Transjordan; the Qilatay, an antinomian group which felt that all religious duties had been abolished and which rejected the sanctity of Gerizim; the Saduqay, which had some peculiar teaching on resurrection and the Serpent but

[59]Ibid., 87.
[60]Ibid., 91.
[61]Ibid., 151-58.

which kept its doctrines secret; the followers of Abiyah and Dosa, also an antinomian group; the followers of Shalīh, a prophet whom many of the Dositheans followed; and the followers of Julian of Alexandria, another prophet of the Dosithean tradition who, his desciples believed, had inaugurated the age of divine favor with his death.[62] The similarity of these Dosithean groups to various Palestinian baptist sects, to the Essenes, and to the Ebionite Christians will not go unnoticed to the observant reader. In recent times it has been suggested that there may have been points of contact between these various sects (one influencing another, etc.).[63] It seems more likely that the similarities were due to diverse groups with similar points of view reacting in analogous ways to comparable situations.

A much more complex problem is the relation of Samaritanism, especially Dositheanism, to the Syro-Palestinian gnostic sects. The Christian heresiologists suggested some such connection when they represented Simon Magus as the archheretic of Gnosticism. Simon is known from both Christian and Samaritan sources to have been from Samaria. But was he a Samaritan (of any one of the various parties of the Gerizim-centered community) or merely a resident of the area? It has long been noted that the distinctive features of Gnosticism are lacking in Samaritan theology, although some of the gnostic vocabulary occasionally appears. However, all this indicates is that if some of the Samaritan sects had gnostic tendencies (or developed gnostic systems) these were not incorporated into the standardized theology of the Samaritans (as were some of the teachings of the Dositheans—resurrection of the dead, the *Taheb*, etc.). Thus the answer to the question, was Simon Magus a Samaritan? cannot be determined by simply comparing what is known of Simonian gnosticism with the theological system represented in the surviving Samaritan literature.[64]

In fact, there are several things which would link Simon to early Samaritanism. One is the tradition preserved in both Christian and Samaritan sources that Dositheus and Simon were related to one another as teacher/student (although there is some confusion as to which was teacher and which was student); another is the so-called gnostic terminology preserved in some Samaritan texts. Kippenberg devoted the concluding section of his major study to one of these terms, "The Great Power" (*hē dýnamis megálē*), as it was used in the Samaritan Aramaic texts and in the Simonian system;[65] Isser considered another term, "The

[62]Ibid., 80-84.
[63]So Bowman, "Contact between Samaritan Sects and Qumran?" See also J. M. Ford, "Can we Exclude Samaritan Influence from Qumran?" *RevQ* 6 (1967-69) 109-29.
[64]Compare Macdonald, *Theology of the Samaritans*, 453.
[65]*Garizim und Synagoge*, 328-49.

Standing One" (*ho hestōs*), as it was used in the Samaritan Moses tradition and, as far as it can be determined, by Dositheus.[66] Kippenberg concluded that Simon was a Samaritan gnostic who applied the Samaritan divine epithet "The Great Power" to himself. He did not think that Dositheus was a gnostic, but he did regard Meander, another of Simon's students, as a gnostic, as well as one other sect derived from Simon (the Sabuaoi).[67] He considered these as only having been peripherally related to the Samaritan communities. Isser concluded that if Dositheus used the epithet "The Standing One" it was not for the purpose of claiming Divinity (as did Simon) but rather to identify himself with Moses, to whom the title was given in the Samaritan Moses tradition.[68] Isser did, however, see some gnostic association in the Dosithean sub-sect the Saduqay,[69] and noted the possibility that later gnostic writers may have attributed writings to Dositheus (such as the Revelation of Dositheus known from the Nag Hammadi library) because of the tradition that he was Simon's teacher/predecessor.[70] It would not be surprising if the gnostics regarded Dositheus as one of their own. He was thus regarded by some Christian heresiologists; at least they considered Dositheus, Simon, and Meander as being of the same ilk.[71]

The problem of the relation of gnosticism to early Samaritan thought, with Simon as the connecting link, has been the subject of much investigation.[72] However, the most that can be said on the subject is that Simon may have included some elements of a particular Samaritan tradition in the development of his system. Kippenberg has noted one of these, the Divine epithet, "The Great Power," which Simon applied to himself. So, too, the title, "The Standing One," which both Simon and Dositheus appear to have used, although Dositheus probably claimed less for himself in this than did Simon. The particular branch of Samaritanism out of which Simon came was clearly that of the Dosithean party, as is attested by the Dositheus/Simon linkage in both Samaritan and Christian traditions. But we would not be justified on the basis of the available evidence to call the Dositheans a gnostic sect. It does not appear that Dositheus understood himself after the cosmological-mythological pattern of Simon's self-understanding. But if Dositheus understood himself as a neo-Moses, there was a sufficient amount of

[66]*Dositheans*, 138-40; cf. Kippenberg, *Garizim und Synogoge*, 347-49.
[67]*Garazim und Synagoge*, 122-28.
[68]*Dositheans*, 139.
[69]Ibid., 104.
[70]Ibid., 118.
[71]So Pseudo-Tertullian, Epiphanius, and Philaster. See Isser, *Dositheans*, 11-69, 165-66.
[72]See the summary of these researches in Pummer, "Present State of Samaritan Studies: II," 27-33.

mythological language in the Samaritan Moses tradition upon which Simon could have drawn in the development of his distinctive system (i.e., distinct from Dositheanism). There are numerous Samaritan texts which identify Moses as a near-Divine figure—the embodiment of the Eternal Light, vested with Prophethood by his ascent at Sinai, received by the angels at his death to reign as king of the celestial paradise, etc.[73] It is not clear whether the development of this Moses tradition in Samaritan theology was due to Dosithean influence or was the result of the reaction of the priests to the Dositheans (i.e., the promotion of Moses against the Moses-like Dositheus).[74] The Moses theology was clearly a major part of Dositheanism and would have passed into Simon's gnostic system if the tradition of the teacher/student relationship is accurate and not contrived. This is not to say that this was the only source of Simon's theology, but one need not look further than the Samaritan locale for the remaining sources. The region had been extensively Hellenized during the pre-Roman period. Simon appears to have drawn not only on the intellectual traditions of the Israelitic Gerizim-based Samaritan community (as expressed in the Dosithean party), but also on that segment of the population which had closer affinities to Hellenistic mythologies. In so doing he produced a religious system which was inimical to the vast majority of Samaritans, certainly to the priests and most likely to most of the Dositheans.

We would conclude by suggesting that although Dosithean Samaritanism may have contributed to the development of Simonian gnosticism, and thus indirectly to other gnostic systems, Simonianism in turn (unlike Dositheanism) made virtually no impact upon the developing theology of the Samaritan community.

SUMMARY AND CONCLUSION

The Samaritans may be seen as an Israelitic sect which developed out of that northern Palestinian community which had rebuilt Shechem in the late fourth century B.C.E. The devestation of the Gerizim shrine by Hyrcanus in 128 and the final destruction of Shechem in 107 B.C.E. resulted in the community's defining self (vis à vis the Jewish community) as the only surviving branch of the ancient Israelite community

---

[73] See especially the treatment of the Samaritan Moses traditions in Meeks, *Prophet King*, 216-57. Compare G. Widengren, *The Acension of the Apostle and the Heavenly Book* (UUÅ 5; Leipzig: Harrassowitz, 1950) 40-58; Purvis, "Samaritan Traditions on the Death of Moses," in Nickelsberg, Jr. (ed.), *Studies on the Testament of Moses* (SBLSCS 4; Cambridge, MA: Society of Biblical Literature, 1973) 93-117; Macdonald, *Theology of the Samaritans*, 147-222.

[74] Kippenberg suggests the latter, but Isser argues (we think correctly) that the Dositheans drew upon a previously existing Moses theology. See Isser, *Dositheans*, 137.

remaining loyal to the Pentateuchal traditions which held Shechem/ Gerizim to be the legitimate center of Hebrew life and worship. The vehicle through which this affirmation was expressed was the Samaritan sectarian redaction of the Pentateuch. The Samaritan religious community did not come into being as the result of a schism from Judaism, but rather from their self-definition as a community apart from the Jews and their alleged heresy (maintaining the sanctity of Jerusalem). The social dynamics which resulted in this affirmation are to be seen in the long history of mutual antipathies between Samaria and Judah terminating in Hyrcanus' actions.

The essential character of Samaritanism of the early Roman period may be seen in the loyalty of the community to Gerizim and to the Torah in its possession. Unlike the Jewish community, which had a wealth of traditions of patriarchs, seers, and prophets, the Samaritans had only the patriarchs (including Joseph), Moses, and Joshua upon which to construct their *Heilsgeschichte*. Chief among these was Moses, the Law Giver. As for the interpretation of that Law, at least two major schools of thought developed from an early time. The one was represented by the priests of the Gerizim community who continued to exercise leadership after the destruction of their temple through pilgrimage festivals to Gerizim and through the continued practice of the blood sacrifice of Passover, an observance which continues to this day. The priestly theology was characterized by a conservative interpretation of biblical Law and by a conservative approach to such new religious concepts as resurrection of the dead and calendar reform. Their eschatological concerns centered on the restoration of the ancient cultic system and the return of the age of divine favor. In addition to honoring Moses as the Law Giver, the priests also viewed Joshua as an important hero of the history of salvation—it was he who had established the cultus on Gerizim after the entry into Canaan. The other school of biblical interpretation was represented by a lay-based party which favored more liberal interpretations of the Law. This party was receptive to changes in established religious practices and to such concepts as the day of judgment, the resurrection of the dead, and the age to come. In the development of its eschatology, it drew upon the tradition of the coming of a prophet-like-Moses. The lay-based liberal party of the Samaritan community was similar in many respects to the party of the Pharisees among the Jews; the priestly party was similar to the Jewish Sadducean party. However, whereas the Pharisees emerged as the dominant party in Judaism following the destruction of the Jerusalem temple in 70 c.e., the situation among the Samaritans was otherwise. There the priests continued to exercise leadership. Nonetheless, the Samaritan lay party remained vigorous and, through a process which is not altogether clear, eventually influenced the theology of the Samaritans to a considerable degree. The use of the synagogue as an institutional base was undoubtedly a major factor in their influence.

Sometime in the first century C.E. the Samaritan lay-based party came to be known as the Dositheans, after Dositheus, a miracle worker-teacher whom many Samaritans accepted as the Mosaic eschatological prophet. Not all of the followers of Dositheus agreed on the meaning of his prophethood or teachings, and thus the movement was fractured by a variety of Dosithean or Dosithean-like sects. Some of these sects followed teachers in the succession from Dositheus, e.g., Simon, Meander, Abiyah, Dosa, Shalīh, and Julian (the latter four being known only from Samaritan sources, and in a rather confused account). Some of the movements generated by Dositheanism had gnostic tendencies, others an ascetic character, yet others were antinomian. The situation was not unlike that in the Jewish community, where sects came into being following particular teachers (the Essenes following the enigmatic Righteous Teacher; baptist sects following teachers of repentance, such as John; etc.). The situation was similar also to that which existed in early Christian history, when diverse groups proliferated prior to the establishment of a catholic orthodoxy.

In the course of time, Samaritanism produced its own orthodoxy and the Dosithean party ceased to exist as an opposition party to the priests. By that time (most likely the fourteenth century), the majority of Samaritans had come to accept many of those teachings which had once been peculiar to the Dositheans. Thus even when faith in Dositheus as the eschatological prophet ceased as a popular opinion, Dositheanism survived within the theology of the Samaritans. The theology of the Dositheans was not so much eradicated as absorbed.

Patterns of Eschatology at Qumran

JOHN J. COLLINS
DEPAUL UNIVERSITY

I N his pioneering study of the Qumran scrolls Frank Moore Cross, Jr. noted the unique importance of the phenomenon of an "apocalyptic community" or "community life lived in anticipation of the Kingdom of God."[1] On the one hand, the "eschatological existence" of the early Christian Church could no longer be regarded as a unique phenomenon. On the other hand "the Essene literature enables us to discover the concrete Jewish setting in which an apocalyptic understanding of history was living and integral to communal existence."[2] The potential value of Qumran for the study of apocalypticism has even now, a quarter of a century later, scarcely been realized. Not only does Qumran make possible the study of the social organization which accompanied an intense eschatological expectation,[3] but it also provides an exceptional opportunity for studying the nature and logic of apocalyptic thinking. The scrolls present a diverse corpus of eschatological doctrines which were formulated and maintained side by side within a highly compact community.[4] Further they show that even the same doctrines

---

[1] F. M. Cross, Jr., *The Ancient Library of Qumran and Modern Biblical Studies* (rev. ed.; Garden City, New York: Doubleday, 1961) 78, 204.

[2] Ibid., 203. The appropriateness of the adjective "apocalyptic" might be questioned, since there is no clear case of an apocalypse actually composed within the community, although the sectarian writings share several basic conceptions with the apocalypse. See J. J. Collins, "The Jewish Apocalypses" in *Apocalypse: The Morphology of a Genre. Semeia* 14 (1979) 48-49. See also H. Stegemann, "Die Bedeutung der Qumranfunde für die Erforschung der Apokalyptik," *Proceedings of the International Colloquium on Apocalypticism* (Uppsala, Aug 12-17, 1979), and J. Carmignac, "Apocalyptique et Qumrân," *RQ* 37 (1979) 163-92. Both Stegemann and Carmignac question the customary use of "apocalyptic" in connection with Qumran.

[3] See S. R. Isenberg, "Millenarianism in Greco-Roman Palestine," *Religion* 4 (1974) 26-46.

[4] We may take as established that the history of the Qumran community extends from approximately the middle of the second century B.C.E. to the first Jewish revolt against Rome. See Cross, *Ancient Library*, 58-63, 119-22, J. T. Milik, *Ten Years of Discovery in the Wilderness of Judaea* (SBT 26; London: SCM, 1959) 44-98, and, more recently, H. Stegemann, *Die Entstehung der*

can be understood in different ways and on different levels. In short, the scrolls attest a complex system of symbolic thought and show that Jewish apocalypticism cannot be conceived as a consistent and univocal set of beliefs, even within a single community. Rather the eschatological doctrines of Qumran are concerned to disclose patterns and structures which can be expressed in diverse formulations. These patterns and structures do not pertain to the future alone, but posit a coherent web of relationships between past, present and future. Accordingly, the eschatological concepts of Qumran are used to express not only future hopes but an understanding of the entire structure of human life and community, which also determines the present. In this study we will examine the polyvalent, multi-dimensional character of some key eschatological concepts from the scrolls: the messianic expectations, the war of Light and Darkness, and the eschatology implied in 1QH 3. Finally we will suggest that a proper understanding of the complexity of eschatological symbolism is an essential prerequisite for any attempt to understand the social phenomenon of apocalypticism.

Qumrangemeinde (Bonn: published privately, 1971) and J. Murphy-O'Connor, "The Essenes and Their History," *RB* 81 (1974) 215-44. The recent attempt of B. E. Thiering (*Redating the Teacher of Righteousness.* Australian and New Zealand Studies in Theology and Religion 1; Sydney: Glenburn, 1979) to lower the dates of all the documents to the Roman period and identify the Teacher of Righteousness with John the Baptist is unlikely to win much support, but a refutation of her views must be left for another occasion. The major documents of the sect with which we are concerned here are 1QS (the Community Rule), CD (the Damascus Document), 1QM (the War Scroll) and 1QH (the Thanksgiving Hymns). The oldest copies of 1QS date to the first quarter of the first century B.C.E. and CD to the first half of that century. None of these copies are autographs. Cross suggests that 1QS "reflects the discipline of the first community in the wilderness of Qumran at a time when its practices had been systematically worked out" (*Ancient Library*, 121). CD dates to "the late second century B.C., or better, perhaps, the early first century B.C." (ibid., 82). Both these documents may be end-products of a redactional process and may have existed in earlier stages. (See Murphy-O'Connor, "The Essenes and Their History," 217). The manuscript of 1QM is from the Herodian period. The document is evidently composite, as can be seen by contrasting col. 1, where the battle is concentrated in a single day, with col. 2, which envisages a period of 40 years. Yadin's argument for a date after the Roman conquest is based on the military data in cols. 2-7, which are largely independent of the rest of the work. (Y. Yadin, *The Scroll of the War of the Sons of Light against the Sons of Darkness* [Oxford: Oxford University, 1962] 246). Opinions on the date of the framework, 1QM 1, 15-19, differ sharply. P. R. Davies (*1QM, The War Scroll from Qumran* [Biblica et Orientalia 32; Rome: PBI, 1977] esp. 89-90) argues for a complex history of composition in which the framework is a late stage. Davies maintains the Maccabean date of cols. 2-9 and assumes "a fairly long period" before the final

1. MESSIANIC EXPECTATIONS

Jewish eschatology in the Second Temple period has traditionally been divided into two main types. In the words of Sigmund Mowinckel: "The one side is national, political, this-worldly, with particularistic tendencies, though universalistic when at its best. The other is super-terrestrial, other-worldly, rich in religious content and mythological concepts, universalistic, numinous, at home in the sphere of the 'Holy' and the 'wholly Other.'"[5] The eschatology of Qumran cannot be contained within either of these types outlined by Mowinckel. Rather, both are found side by side, even within a single document in the case of 1QS. The aspect of Qumran eschatology which has received most scholarly attention is Mowinckel's "national, political, this-worldly" eschatology. Much of the discussion here has focused on the peculiarity that the scrolls refer to not one but two messiahs.[6] The so-called Damascus

---

revision. Even if one grants the early date of cols. 2-9, which is very doubtful, the appeal to "a fairly long period" is hopelessly vague. More specifically, Davies argues that the cosmic scope of the dominion of Belial must have its earthly counterpart in Rome, but in fact cosmic imagery was commonly used for lesser kingdoms in the Ancient Near East; so this argument is worthless. Finally, Davies identifies the "king of the Kittim" as a Roman consul, an identification which has no parallel. Davies' extreme use of source criticism has been severely but rightly criticized by J. Carmignac in his review in *RQ* 36 (1978). G. Vermes (*The Dead Sea Scrolls. Qumran in Perspective* [Cleveland: Collins, 1978] 51-54) argues for a still later date on the assumption that the king of the Kittim is the Roman emperor. Other scholars consider the framework of 1QM to be one of the oldest of the sectarian documents because of its close parallels with Daniel and its affinities with 1 QS among other reasons. See L. Rost, "Zum Buch der Kriege der Söhne des Lichts gegen die Söhne der Finsternis," *TLZ* 80 (1955) col. 206, P. von der Osten-Sacken, *Gott und Belial* (SUNT 6; Göttingen: Vandenhoeck & Ruprecht, 1969) 28-41, 116-22, 214-38, and Collins, "The Mythology of Holy War in Daniel and the Qumran War Scroll," *VT* 25 (1975) 610-11. 1QH is very widely thought to be in large part the work of the Teacher of Righteousness himself. See G. Jeremias, *Der Lehrer der Gerechtigkeit* (SUNT 2; Göttingen: Vandenhoeck & Ruprecht, 1963) 168-77. All these documents were still copied in the last phase of the history of the sect (Milik, *Ten Years*, 96). It appears, then, that all these documents circulated side by side for much of the history of the sect.

For a recent survey see Vermes, *The Dead Sea Scrolls*. For data on the publications and bibliography see J. A. Fitzmyer, *The Dead Sea Scrolls. Major Publications and Tools for Study* (Sources for Biblical Study 8; Missoula: Scholars, 1975).

[5] S. Mowinckel, *He That Cometh* (Nashville: Abingdon, 1954) 281.

[6] See especially A. S. van der Woude, *Die messianischen Vorstellungen der Gemeinde von Qumran* (Assen: van Gorcum, 1957). Also K. G. Kuhn, "The Two Messiahs of Aaron and Israel," in *The Scrolls and the New Testament* (ed.

Document (CD) refers in several places to the coming of the messiah of Aaron and Israel.[7] When this document was first discovered in the Cairo Geniza at the beginning of this century, Louis Ginzberg realized that it implied two messiahs rather than one.[8] This interpretation was supported by the reference in 1QS 9:11 to the coming of a prophet and the messiahs of Aaron and Israel. The scriptural basis for this expectation is laid out in 4Q Testimonia, where we find juxtaposed the prediction of a prophet like Moses (Deut 18:18-19), Balaam's oracle in Num 24:15-17 ("A star shall come out of Jacob and a sceptre shall rise out of Israel") and the blessing of Levi in Deut 33:8-11 ("Give Thy Tummim to Levi"). The texts suggest, respectively, the coming of an ideal prophet, king and priest.[9] Finally, in 1QSa, the rule for the community "at the end of days" we read that "the priest" will take precedence over "the messiah of Israel." Here again the priest is clearly the messiah of Aaron and a dual messiahship is envisaged.

K. Stendhal; New York: Harper, 1957) 54-64, and R. E. Brown, "The Messianism of Qumran," *CBQ* 19 (1957) 53-82.

[7]CD 12:23-13:1; 14:19; 19:11. CD 20:1 refers to a messiah from Aaron and from Israel. Note also the prophecy of the Star and the sceptre in 7.18-20. In CD 2:12 and 6:1 the word *mšyḥ* is used with reference to the prophets. See Kuhn, "The Two Messiahs," 59-60.

[8]L. Ginzberg, *An Unknown Jewish Sect* (New York: Jewish Theological Seminary, 1976) 209-56 (trans. of the German edition of 1922). Kuhn ("The Two Messiahs," 59) assumes that the text, as found in the Geniza has been altered by "medieval Jewish copyists," but this is unnecessary. The phrase "messiah of Aaron and Israel" can grammatically refer to two messiahs. See van der Woude, *Die messianischen Vorstellungen*, 29, R. Deichgräber, "Zur Messiaserwartung der Damaskusschrift," *ZAW* 78 (1966) 333-43. J. Starcky, ("Les quatres étapes du messianisme à Qumrân," *RB* 70 [1963] 481-505) proposed that CD reflects a distinct stage in the history of the sect when the two messianic figures had merged into one. (So also A. Caquot, "Le messianisme Qumrânien," in M. Delcor, ed., *Qumrân. Sa piété, sa théologie et son milieu* [BETL XLVI; Paris-Gembloux: Duculot & Louvain University, 1978] 231-47 and Thiering, *Redating the Teacher of Righteousness*, 191-97). For a refutation of Starcky see Brown, "J. Starchy's Theory of Qumran Messianic Development," *CBQ* 28 (1966) 51-57. See also the cautious comments of M. de Jonge, "The Role of Intermediaries in God's Final Intervention in the Future according to the Qumran Scrolls," in O. Michel, et al. *Studies on the Jewish Background of the New Testament* (Assen: van Gorcum, 1969) 44-63.

[9]Van der Woude, *Die messianischen Vorstellungen*, 184. Balaam's oracle also occurs in CD 7:18-20, where the star and sceptre appear to refer to two distinct individuals. Here the oracle most probably refers only to the kingly messiah, since the priestly messiah is evidently the subject of Deut 33:8-11. The inconsistency is not surprising, given the exegetical methods of Qumran. Balaam's oracle is also cited in 1QM 11:6.

The expectation of two messiahs is not such an anomaly as it first appeared. It is paralleled in the Testaments of the Twelve Patriarchs, which predict a messiah from Levi and a messiah from Judah.[10] More significantly, perhaps, it corresponds to the organization of the post-exilic community, under the twin leadership of the governor Zerubbabel and the high-priest Joshua, the two "sons of oil" of Zech 4:14.[11] The dual messiahship of Qumran has rightly been seen as an eschatological idealization of this post-exilic organization. Accordingly, it reflects what Shemaryahu Talmon has called "restorative" eschatology.[12] It is modelled on an actual historical situation of the past. It involves an idealization of that situation, but is not entirely different from it. There is nothing to suggest that the messiahs are other than human. They will fill institutional roles within the community. They are eschatological figures, in the sense that they imply a definitive change in the course of history, but they do not imply an end of the historical process. As Talmon has perceptively noted, the difference between the dual messiahship of Qumran and the single messiahship of Christianity is qualitative as well as quantitative.[13] What is involved at Qumran is an ideal community structure. There is no emphasis on the personalities of the

[10]Especially T. Levi 18:2-14 and T. Judah 24. See G. R. Beasley-Murray, "The Two Messiahs in the Testaments of the Twelve Patriarchs," *JTS* 48 (1947) 1-12. The date of the Testaments is a notoriously vexed question and the possibility of Christian influence on the messianic passages cannot be ruled out. However, the basic conception of two messiahs is certainly pre-Christian. See A. Hultgård (*L'Eschatologie des Testaments des Douze Patriarches. I. Interprétation des textes.* [Acta Universitatis Upsaliensis, Historia Religionum 6; Uppsala: Almqvist & Wiksell, 1977] 305), who argues that the analogies between the Testaments and the Scrolls should be understood against the background of a common priestly ideology.

[11]Caquot ("Le messianisme qumrânien," 233) would restrict the term messiah to Zerubbabel since the hope of a future transformation was linked to him rather than to Joshua, but the restriction is scarcely justified in view of the expression "sons of oil." Hultgård (*L'Eschatologie*, 65-66) rightly points out that Zechariah 4 is atypical of post-exilic Judaism. The more typical tendency was for the High Priesthood to absorb the royal power and attributes and become the sole leadership. Hultgård suggests that the revival of the Davidic messiahship beside the priestly in the Testaments and at Qumran was a reaction against the monopolization of power by the Hasmonean priest-kings.

[12]S. Talmon, "Typen der Messiaserwartung um die Zeitenwende," *Probleme biblischer Theologie* (Gerhard von Rad zum 70. Geburtstag, ed. H. W. Wolff; München: Kaiser, 1971) 571-88. See also Carmignac, "La future intervention de Dieu selon la pensée de Qumrân," in Delcor, ed., *Qumrân*, 219-29. Carmignac, however, gives a one-sided view of the eschatology of Qumran, which ignores the elements of otherwordly eschatology which we shall discuss below.

[13]Ibid., 583.

messiahs as savior figures. In fact, the scrolls are tantalisingly reticent on the activities of the messiahs and in most cases merely assert that they will arise. The activity of the messiahs in 1QSa takes place within the eschatological age and is not envisaged as saving action which brings that age into being. The focus is on the community of which the messiahs are part, rather than on the exaltation of the messiahs themselves.[14]

The different dimensions of Messianism

The expectation of the two messiahs then would seem to fit a realistic and univocal expectation of the future, and indicate a specific way in which the community should be organized. However, precisely because of its realism, the messianism of Qumran takes on a certain ambiguity. The sectarians considered themselves to be already an eschatological community. Hence their present institutions already anticipate those of the messianic age.

The organization of the sect may be seen at two levels. In addition to the overall structure of authority, both CD and 1QS provide for smaller groups of at least ten men (CD 13; 1QS 6). Both documents require that every group include a priest, who is presented as the supreme authority. Beside him, a second superior is also required. In CD 13:6-7 this figure is called the *Měbaqqēr* or overseer of the community and is clearly distinguished from the Priest. 1QS 6:12 also refers to *Měbaqqēr*, and while he is not explicitly distinguished from the Priest, there is nothing to suggest that they are identified. Both CD and 1QS may be understood to require a dual leadership in the groups: a priest, who is the highest authority and an overseer, or governor. The latter figure is also referred to as *pāqîd* (1QS 6:14), the equivalent term to the Greek *episkopos*.[15] The overall stucture of the sect shows the same dual

[14]Two other possible instances of messianic activity should be noted. In CD 14:19 Rabin translates: "until there shall arise the Messiah of Aaron and Israel and he will make conciliation for their trespass . . ." (C. Rabin, *The Zadokite Documents* [Oxford: Clarendon, 1958] 70). However, the passage is very fragmentary and the verb for "make conciliation" *ykpr* could also be read as a Pual, taking "their trespass" as subject, so: "their trespass will be covered over." See van der Woude, *Die messianischen Vorstellungen*, 32. Second, in 1QM the chief priest may possibly be viewed as a priestly messiah, but he is not the agent of the military victory, which rests with God and Michael.

[15]See the succinct summary of this material by Vermes, *The Dead Sea Scrolls in English* (Harmondsworth: Penguin, 1968) 18-25. Some scholars (e.g. Milik, *Ten Years*, 100) suggest that 1QS need only imply one official, a priest who is also *Měbaqqēr*. It is of course possible that the two offices were combined in some groups. However, in view of the clear distinction in CD and the distinct terminology in 1QS, the ideal structure appears to call for 2 figures. Vermes

leadership. In CD 14 we find "a rule for the assembly of all the camps."
Two individuals are singled out: a priest who is appointed over the
congregation and who must be from thirty to sixty years old, and the
Měbaqqēr (Overseer) of all the camps, who must be from thirty to sixty
years old. In 1QS the requirements for the smaller groups must also be
presumed to apply to the entire community.[16]

The dual leadership of the priest and *Měbaqqēr* (Overseer) at the
various levels of the community is clearly analogous to that of the
messiahs of Aaron and Israel. The messiahs are still expected in the
future, and so cannot be identified simply with the present rulers, but
the offices they will fill are presumably the same (quite certainly so in
the case of the priestly messiah). The ambiguity entailed by this situation becomes clear in 1QSa.[17] This brief document is introduced as "the
rule for all the congregation of Israel in the last days." It is largely
concerned with the different stages of initiation and authority in the
community and restrictions on membership of the assembly. Then in
1QSa 2:11-22 we find instructions for a time "when [God] sends the
messiah to be with them."[18] The passage first describes the entry of the
congregation in which the Priest enters at the head of the Aaronids and
then the Messiah of Israel and the rest of the congregation.[19] Then at the
common table, the Priest is the first to bless the bread and wine, then the
Messiah of Israel "shall stretch out his hand to the bread and then all the
congregation shall give thanks and partake." Thus far the text might be
read simply as a prescription for the future messianic age. However, the
passage concludes: "And they shall act according to this prescription
whenever (the meal) [is arr]anged when as many as ten solemnly meet
together."[20] Now if "the Priest" and the "Messiah of Israel" were specific

---

further identifies the *Měbaqqēr* with the *Maskîl* and with the *ʾîš dôrēš battôrâ* of
1QS 6:6 (*Dead Sea Scrolls*, 22).

[16] 1QS describes at length the role of the *Maskîl* which corresponds to that of
the *Měbaqqēr* in CD, and consists primarily of instruction (see Vermes, *Dead Sea
Scrolls*, 20). Since 1QS repeatedly stresses the priority of the priests, we may
safely presume that a priest held the highest position in the community as a
whole, just as in the smaller group. 1QS refers also to a special council of 12
men and 3 priests (8:1). The relation of this body to the priest and the *Měbaqqēr*
is not specified.

[17] In the opinion of Barthélemy, 1QSa reflects an earlier stage of the
community than 1QS (DJD I:108) but van der Woude more plausibly contends
that it presupposes 1QS and is therefore later (*Die messianischen Vorstellungen*, 97).

[18] 1QSa 2:11. Trans. Cross, reading *ywlyk* (sends) for *ywlyd* (causes to be
born) (*Ancient Library*, 87-88). The text is fragmentary.

[19] The word *hkwhn*, the Priest, is restored, but is not disputed.

[20] Trans. Cross, *Ancient Library*, 89.

(eschatological) individuals they could scarcely be present at every meal at which ten sectarians assembled. We must conclude that the messianic roles could be assumed by the current leaders of the community or group. Indeed there is already a close parallel between the messianic meal of 1QSa and the community meal in 1QS 6:4: "and when they prepare the table to eat or the wine to drink, the priest will first stretch out his hand to bless the bread and the wine." All of 1QSa before the introduction of the messiahs is concerned with matters which apply to the present regulation of the community (stages of initiation, restrictions of membership, etc.) We must conclude that the "messianic" rule also, in the words of Cross, "obviously applies to the current practice of the sect."[21]

It would seem then, that the expectation of the two messiahs is already actualized in the institutions of the sect. The actualization is undoubtedly proleptic, and does not preclude the expectation of further fulfillment in the future. Yet it shows that even the "restorative" eschatology of Qumran is not so univocal as it first appears. The doctrine of the two messiahs refers to a recurring pattern, which can be discerned in Israel's historical past, in the present structure of the community and will be fully manifest in the future. Even the eschatological fulfillment of the pattern can however be encountered, in some degree, in the present ritual of the community. Accordingly, the messianic language may be used to describe not only the future but also an aspect of the present.

A similar ambiguity in eschatological language is evident in a controversial passage in CD 6:2-11. The passage applies Num 21:18 to the history of the community and concludes "And the Staff (mĕḥôqēq) is the expositor of the Law (dôrēš hattôrâ) . . . and the nobles of the people are those that have come to dig the well with precepts (mĕḥôqĕqôt) which the Staff laid down, that they might walk in them during the whole epoch of wickedness. Except for them they cannot grasp (the Law) until the Righteous Teacher arises in the end of days."[22] The "Righteous Teacher" is well-known from other passages as the key figure in the founding of the sect.[23] Here, however, he is preceded by an "expositor of the Law" who sets out the precepts which are apparently still in force. There are two possible interpretations of this figure. Either he is "an early Hasidic leader, a precursor of the Teacher at the earliest beginnings

---

[21]Ibid., 90.

[22]Trans. ibid., 226.

[23]The phrase here is yôrēh haṣ-ṣedeq, while it usually appears as môrēh haṣ-ṣedeq or mwrh ṣdq. The difference, however, is too slight to carry weight in the interpretation.

of the sect,"[24] or he is the one elsewhere called the "Righteous Teacher," and the "Righteous Teacher" here is a messianic figure. It is important that the "Righteous Teacher" here appears to be expected in the future. Yet in CD 20:1, 14 the "unique teacher"[25] is already dead, and in 20:32 the voice of the "Righteous Teacher" is the normative way to salvation.[26] It seems more likely then that the "expositor of the Law" in CD 6 is the historical Teacher, while the Teacher who is to arise at the end of days is a messianic figure.[27] This ambiguous use of the phrase "Righteous Teacher" is understandable if we bear in mind that Qumran is concerned with offices rather than personalities. There is no reason to infer from this passage that the historical Teacher would return from the dead.[28] Rather "Righteous Teacher" is a role, which was exercised by the founder of the sect and will be exercised again by one of the messiahs (almost certainly the Messiah of Aaron, since the historical Teacher was presumably a Zadokite).[29] If the historical Teacher was the chief priest of the Community he could be viewed as a proleptic Messiah of Aaron.

In summary, then, our examination of messianic expectations shows that the distinction betwen historical present and eschatological future is blurred at Qumran. The eschatological terminology overlaps with that used to describe the current institutions. Ultimately, the messianic assertions should be understood, not as simple predictions, but as attempts to discern a pattern which binds together the past and present and will be fully manifest in the future.

[24]Cross, *Ancient Library*, 227-28.

[25]*mwrh hyḥyd*. Possibly the phrase should be read as *mwrh hyḥd* (the teacher of the community).

[26]*mwrh ṣdq*. CD 20:28 refers to the same individual simply as *mwrh* (teacher). See Jeremias, *Der Lehrer der Gerechtigkeit*, 162-66.

[27]So also van der Woude, *Die messianischen Vorstellungen*, 67-74. The complexity of the passage is compounded by the ambiguity of the phrase "expositor of the law" (*dôrēš hattôrâ*), which in CD 7:18 can be understood to refer to either (or both!) a historical figure "who came to Damascus" or a future messiah (since the reference is in conjunction with a quotation of the Oracle of Balaam, and the expositor is identified with the Star). See van der Woude, *Die messianischen Vorstellungen*, 43-61. Starcky ("Les Maîtres de Justice et la chronologie de Qumrân," in Delcor, ed., *Qumrân*, 249-56) also concludes that at least two Teachers of Righteousness were envisaged.

[28]The theory of the resurrection of the Teacher is espoused by J. Allegro, A. Dupont-Sommer, C. Rabin, J. Hempel, C. T. Fritsch and others. For references and refutation see van der Woude, *Die messianischen Vorstellungen*, 71-72.

[29]Cross, *Ancient Library*, 228, van der Woude, *De messianischen Vorstellungen*, 67-74.

2. THE WAR OF LIGHT AND DARKNESS

The expectation of the two messiahs is representative of Mowinckel's "national, political, this-worldly" eschatology. By contrast, the great eschatological tableau of 1QM (the War Scroll) fits rather the second "super-terrestrial, other-worldly" type, which "is found particularly in the apocalyptic literature."[30] 1QM anticipates a conflict of cosmic forces, the Sons of Light under the leadership of Michael, and the Sons of Darkness led by Belial. The atmosphere of the work may be indicated by a passage from 1QM 12:7-8:

> Mighty [men and] a host of angels are among those mustered with us, the Mighty One of War is in our congregation, and the host of His spirits is with our steps.[31]

The language and concepts of the scroll are clearly drawn from different streams of tradition from those of national eschatology.[32] The difference between the two conceptual worlds is so striking that some scholars have sought to explain 1QM as a late development, in response to the disappointment when messianic expectations failed to materialize.[33] While the actual scroll as we have it is certainly from Roman times, its basic conceptions find their closest parallels in the canonical book of Daniel and in 1QS, and several scholars have argued that at least in its framework the War Scroll is one of the oldest of the Qumran documents.[34] While different degrees of emphasis may have been placed on

---

[30]Mowinckel, *He That Cometh*, 282. We should note that the absence of any reference to the "Son of Man" cannot be regarded as an indication that "Qumran eschatology was messianic but not apocalyptic" (so W. S. LaSor, *The Dead Sea Scrolls and the New Testament* [Grand Rapids: Eerdmans, 1972] 104). The "one like a son of man" in Daniel 7 is not a title and should be understood to refer to a heavenly, angelic figure, closely analogous to Michael in 1QM and quite probably identified with Michael in Daniel. (See Collins, *The Apocalyptic Vision of the Book of Daniel* [HSM 16; Missoula: Scholars Press, 1977] 144-46.) Similar figures are found in other Qumran documents, most strikingly Melchizedek in 11QMelch.

[31]Trans. Yadin, *The Scroll of the War*, 316. All translations of 1QM in this article are from Yadin.

[32]1QM, nonetheless, draws on predominantly Israelite traditions (see von der Osten-Sacken, *Gott und Belial*, 28-41), while some influence of Persian dualism must also be admitted (Collins, "Holy War," 604-12).

[33]So Talmon, "Typen der Messiaserwartung," 586-87. Starcky ("Les quatres étapes") also assigns 1QM to a late phase of the sect.

[34]Above, n. 4. See Collins, "Holy War," 610-11. The critique of that article by P. R. Davies ("Dualism and Eschatology in the Qumran War Scroll" *VT* 28 [1978] 28-36) is based on several major misunderstandings of my argument. See

one or another type of eschatology at different periods, both the this-worldly conception of the messiahs and the cosmic war of 1QM are features of Qumran eschatology throughout.

In fact, the conceptions of 1QM are not totally incompatible with this-wordly eschatology. The outcome of the battle has two levels: "to raise amongst the angels the authority of Michael and the dominion of Israel amongst all flesh" (1QM 17:7). The state of salvation of the Sons of Light is never clearly described. It will extend "unto all appointed times of [eternity] for peace and blessing, glory and joy, and long life for all Sons of Light"(1:9). The hymnic passage in 1QM 12:11-15 uses a string of biblical phrases to paint a picture of this-worldly glory in Zion. These passages are at least compatible with a this-worldly view of salvation.[35] 1QM envisages the "eternal annihilation of all the lot of Belial" (1QM 1:5), but there is no reference to the destruction of the world and the historical process is not necessarily brought to an end. No mention is made of the messiahs of Aaron and Israel, but the citation of Balaam's prophecy (the Star and the Scepter) in 1QM 11:6 may be read as a reference either to both messiahs or to the kingly messiah alone.[36] Further, it is possible that the chief priest, who is prominent throughout the scroll and "the Prince of the Whole Congregation" in 1QM 5:1 should be interpreted respectively here as the messiahs of Aaron and Israel.[37] As we have noted, however, it is difficult to distinguish between the historical leaders of the community and their eschatological successors. The question here is whether the definitive messianic state has arrived in the War Scroll. Ultimately, we must admit that the scroll simply does not speak of messiahs of Aaron or Israel. However, these passages show that 1QM can in fact be correlated with messianic expectations. They also put those expectations in perspective: the messiahs, like the Priest and the Prince in the eschatological war, can have no more than a subordinate position in a greater system. The victory is not in their hands, but in those of God and his angels.

---

my reply, "Dualism and Eschatology in 1QM. A reply to P. R. Davies," *VT* 29 (1979) 212-16.

[35]Compare J. Becker, *Das Heil Gottes* (SUNT 3; Göttingen: Vandenhoeck & Ruprecht, 1964) 82: "Das Heil ist also ein irdischer Glückzustand aufgrund einer theophanen Gegenwart Gottes."

[36]Van der Woude (*Die messianischen Vorstellungen*, 118) sees a reference only to the kingly messiah here. He also sees a single reference when the prophecy is cited in the Testimonia, but contends that the quotation in CD 7:19 alludes to both messiahs.

[37]Van der Woude, *Die messianischen Vorstellungen*, 124-44. The chief priest appears in 1QM 2:1; 15:4-7a; 16:11-14; 18:5-6; 19:9-13 and is probably implied in 13:1. The term, *mšyhykh* (thy anointed ones) is used with reference to the prophets in 1QM 11:7.

The War Scroll is not only concerned with the conflict of other-worldly beings. There is a human component on both sides: the members of the sect on the one hand and their adversaries (such as the Kittim) on the other. I QM envisages a synergism of the earthly and the heavenly. It is concerned with a conflict between the faithful Israelites and their enemies on earth. However, it sees this conflict as only one dimension of a cosmic event. Corresponding to the earthly war, and determining its outcome is the war between the angelic sons of light and sons of darkness. This correspondence of earthly and heavenly events is a common feature of ancient Near Eastern thought. In the Bible it is found in the oldest traditions of the "Wars of Yahweh" and again comes to prominence in the Hellenistic age.[38] It is particularly prominent in apocalyptic writings. A good example is found in Daniel 10.[39] There the history of the Persian and Macedonian empires is tersely expressed from a Jewish viewpoint as a conflict between the angelic "princes" of Persia and Greece and the angels Michael and Gabriel. In the same way the conflict of Michael and Belial in the War Scroll may be presumed to express a human conflict in the eschatological future. The War Scroll does not focus its expectations on human messiahs, but at least it shares with the messianic passages the central concern with the future exalta-tion of the community.

However, the other-wordly dimension of the War Scroll cannot be simply reduced to a figurative device for expressing an earthly conflict. There is no exact correspondence between Michael and Belial and their human counterparts. The idea that the war is ultimately controlled by conflicting supernatural powers entails an admission that the human agents are not masters of their fate. Accordingly, the language of the scroll carries with it a sense of determinism which is not suggested by the doctrine of the two messiahs.[40] It also gives expression to a super-natural power of evil, personified in Belial. Since this power is evenly matched with Michael, the "Prince of Lights" until the time of divine intervention, the War Scroll presents a dualistic vision of the world which is unparalleled in the biblical tradition.[41] The messiahs of Aaron and Israel could be accommodated within this system, but they evidently could be no more than a subordinate component.

[38]See P. D. Miller, The Divine Warrior in Early Israel (HSM 5; Cambridge: Harvard, 1973) 156-59; B. Albrektson, History and the Gods (Lund: Gleerup, 1967) 27; P. D. Hanson, "Jewish Apocalyptic against its Near Eastern Environ-ment," RB 78 (1971) 39-40; Collins, "Holy War," 598.

[39]Collins, The Apocalyptic Vision, 115-16, 133-38.

[40]Ibid., 87-88 (on apocalyptic determinism) and 175-78 (on the significance of otherworldly imagery).

[41]See Collins ("Holy War," 603-12) on the probability of Persian influence on 1QM.

The implications of the terminology used in the War Scroll are, however, more far-reaching still. The primary designation used for the adversaries in the War are neither ethnic nor national, nor even social. They are "Sons of Light" and "Sons of Darkness." These terms may be taken as metaphysical or as moral, but in any case they cannot be assumed to coincide with external human distinctions. The sectarians may have tended to assume that the Sons of Light were co-terminous with their community. However, they allowed for the future conversion of others and made regulations to govern the departure of present members.[42] It follows that the identity of the Sons of Light is not absolutely public and certain at any given time. The term "Sons of Light" expresses not only, then, membership of the community, but more precisely, a certain state of the individual which is presumed to be constitutive of members of the community. The adoption of this terminology in preference to the traditional, national and social affiliations opens up considerably the range of application of the eschatological language. Specifically, it invites the correlation of the eschatological drama with the state of the individual. The implications of this are seen more fully in 1QS.

The conflict of the spirits in 1QS

1QS does not speak directly of the battle between Michael and Belial. However, it gives elaborate expression to the dualism of the Sons of Light and Sons of Darkness. Again, the conflict is not simply on the human level. Rather:

> in the hand of the prince of lights is the rule over all the sons of righteousness, and in the ways of light they walk. In the hand of the angel of darkness is all the rule over the sons of deceit and in the ways of darkness they walk. By the angel of darkness (comes) the aberration of all the sons of righteousness, . . . but Israel's God and His true angel help all the sons of light.[43]

The human Sons of Light have a heavenly counterpart in the "Prince of Lights" while their adversaries are led by an Angel of Darkness. As is widely recognized, these titles are variants for Michael and Belial.[44] However, the variation is significant. The angels in 1QS are "two spirits" in which humanity must "walk until the time of visitation"

---

[42]E.g., 1QS 7:16-27.

[43]1QS 3:20-25. Trans. P. Wernbert-Møller, *The Manual of Discipline* (STDJ 1; Leiden: Brill, 1957) 25.

[44]Von der Osten-Sacken, *Gott und Belial*, 116-20, H. G. May, "Cosmological References in the Qumran Doctrine of the Two Spirits and in Old Testament Imagery," *JBL* 82 (1963) 1-14, O. Betz, *Der Paraklet* (Leiden: Brill, 1963) 66-69.

(1QS 3:18). They are personifications not, or not only, of national or
social groups, but of life-styles, characterized by such qualities as humil-
ity, patience, compassion, goodness, on the one hand, and impiety,
falsehood, pride and haughtiness on the other (1QS 4:2-6, 9-12). Further,
"the spirits of truth and deceit stuggle in the heart of man. . . . According to his share in truth and righteousness, thus a man hates deceit, and
according to his assignment in the lot of deceit (and ungodliness) thus
he loathes truth"(1QS 4:22-24). The location of the conflict is now "in
the heart of man." The cosmic conflict of the Prince of Light and the
Angel of Darkness is now taken to express not only the social antithesis
of the Qumran sect and its opponents but also the moral conflict of good
and evil within every individual.[45]

The eschatological dimension of the conflict is not entirely suppressed. God "has put down a limited time for the existence of deceit. At
the time fixed for visitation He will destroy it for ever, and then the truth
of the earth will appear forever" (1QS 4:18-19). The outcome for the
Sons of Light involves "healing and great peace in a long life, multiplication of progeny, together with all everlasting blessings, endless joy in
everlasting life, and a crown of glory together with a resplendent attire
in eternal light" (1QS 4:7-8) and for the Sons of Darkness "eternal
perdition by the fury of God's vengeful wrath, everlasting terror and
endless shame, together with disgrace of annihilation in the fire of
murky Hell" (1QS 4:12-13).[46] The contrasting fates of the Sons of Light
and Sons of Darkness are seen as the consistent working out of the
dualism inherent in creation, when God created the two spirits (1QS
3:18).[47] The conflict of Light and Darkness is also a feature of creation
from the beginning. The full consequences of the division between the
two spirits will be evident only at "the time fixed for visitation" (1QS
4:19). However, those consequences are already determined for each
individual according to "his share in truth" or "his assignment in the
lot of deceit" (1QS 4:24).

Here again the distinction between the present of the community
and the eschatological future has been blurred. The juxtaposition of the
War Scroll and 1QS suggests a series of homologies: the dualistic

[45] See further Wernberg-Møller, "A Reconsideration of the Two Spirits in the
Rule of the Community (1QSerek III,13-IV,26)," *RevQ* 3 (1961) 413-41.
[46] Trans. Wernberg-Møller, *The Manual*, 26. The word for "murky Hell"
(*mḥškym*) is perhaps better translated "dark regions" (Vermes).
[47] The idea that the eschatological future is built into the order of creation is
widespread in the Hellenistic age. See Collins, "Cosmos and Salvation: Jewish
Wisdom and Apocalyptic in the Hellenistic Age," *History of Religions* 17 (1977)
121-42.

conflict may be envisaged at once on several different levels.[48] The social, and perhaps military conflict between the sect and its adversaries is only one manifestation of a more fundamental dualism, which is expressed at the cosmic level as the conflict of two spirits or angelic powers. This conflict is also manifested in the moral struggles in the hearts of individuals. The single dualism of Light and Darkness is found then on a series of distinct levels—the individual heart, the political and social order, and the cosmic level embracing earth and heaven. The cosmic conflict of the two spirits may be used to express this dualism on any other level. The resolution of the conflict by the intervention of God to aid the Sons of Light may also indicate the anticipated resolution of the conflict at any level.

It appears then that the eschatological War of the Sons of Light against the Sons of Darkness is even less univocal than the expectation of two messiahs. The war itself may refer to either present or future conflict on either the individual political or cosmic level. It functions as a polyvalent symbolism which articulates a dualistic structure in diverse aspects of the cosmos. It is at once a pattern discerned in the present and an expectation for the future.

The symbolic versatility of the eschatological language in 1QS is all the more striking since that document also contains an allusion to the coming of the prophet and the messiahs of Aaron and Israel. In 1QS the realistic expectation of the messiahs is not abandoned, but it is put in perspective as only one aspect of a complex multi-dimensional view of the eschatological age.

3. ESCHATOLOGY IN THE HODAYOT

The adaptability of eschatological language to express more than one level of experience or expectation is most clearly visible in 1QH (Hodayot, Thanksgiving Hymns). As is widely recognized, these Hymns use the eschatological language of resurrection and exaltation to express the present experience of the members of the community. So we read in 1QH 3:19-22:

> I thank thee O Lord, for Thou has released my soul from
> the grave,
> and from the abyss of Sheol Thou hast raised me up to an
> eternal height
> so that I can wander in the plain without limit,

---

[48] So H. W. Huppenbauer (*Der Mensch zwischen zwei Welten* [Zürich: Zwingli, 1959] 103) speaks of the plural "Dualismen" of the Qumran texts.

and so that I know that there is hope for him whom Thou hast
formed out of dust unto an eternal fellowship.
And the perverted spirit Thou hast cleansed from the great
transgression
to stand in the assembly with the hosts of the saints
and to come into communion with the congregation of the sons
of heaven.[49]

The Hymns attest the belief that the members of the community already
live in the presence of the angelic host.[50] This belief is one aspect of the
conviction that the eschatological age has begun. Accordingly, the
pattern of events foretold in eschatological prophecies can already be
experienced in the actual present of the community.[51] Further, the
otherworldly cosmology associated with eschatological events is accessible in the present. So the hymnist can claim to have been resurrected
from Sheol and to walk on the "everlasting heights" in the company of
the angels. Such metaphorical use of language is, of course, found
already in the canonical book of Psalms,[52] but it acquires a new realism
in the heightened context of Qumran.

The language of individual afterlife is not the only eschatological
language used in a metaphorical sense in 1QH. The third column of the
scroll contains two striking hymns which ostensibly refer to a more
public eschatology, specifically the "messianic woes" and the destruction of the world by fire.

The "messianic woes"

The first of these hymns extends from the beginning of the column
(which is fragmentary) to line 18. The hymnist gives thanks for deliverance and proceeds to use a series of analogies for his previous distress:

[49]Trans. S. Holm-Nielsen, *Hodayot: Psalms from Qumran* (Aarhus:
Universitets-vorlaget, 1960) 64.
[50]This idea is also found in 1QSa 2:3-11, 1QM 7:4-6; 12:7-8. See especially
H. W. Kuhn, *Enderwartung und gegenwärtiges Heil* (SUNT 4; Göttingen: Vandenhoeck & Ruprecht, 1966). Also H. Ringgren, *The Faith of Qumran* (Philadelphia: Fortress, 1963) 127-32 and G. W. Nickelsburg, *Resurrection, Immortality
and Eternal Life* (HTS 26; Cambridge, MA: Harvard, 1972) 152-56.
[51]This is precisely the presupposition of the exegesis we find in the Pesharim.
So Cross writes: "Two major assumptions characterize apocalyptic exegesis. All
biblical prophecy is normally taken to have eschatological meaning. . . . Secondly, it must be understood that the apocalyptist understood himself to be
living in these days of final crisis, at the end of days and the beginning of the
New Age, so that the events of his own times were recognized as precisely those
events forecast by the prophets of old as coming in the last days." (*Ancient
Library*, 112).
[52]See C. Barth, *Die Errettung vom Tode in den individuellen Klage-und
Dank-liedern des Alten Testaments* (Zollikon: Evangelischer, 1947) 117, 145, 152.

and they set the soul in affliction in the depths [of the sea],
and like a besieged city [in the face of her enemies].
And I am in distress, as a woman giving birth for the first time.[53]

The latter analogy is then developed at length in lines 7-12. This passage
is, in the words of Holm-Nielson, "almost impossible to translate on
account of the double meaning of the words."[54] Discussion has focused
especially on lines 9-10:

for in the breakers of death she giveth life to a man,
and in the pangs of Sheol there goeth forth from the womb of
    the pregnant
one a wonderful counsellor with his strength
and a man child is brought forth from the birth canal.

Then in line 12 reference is made to one who is pregnant with $^{\circ}p^c h$,
which is variously translated "wickedness" (Holm-Nielson), "nought"
(Mansoor),[55] or "asp/viper" (Dupont-Sommer).[56] The last is the most
common biblical meaning of the word, but the ambiguity is undoubtedly intentional, as in line 18 one pregnant with $^c wl$ (wickedness) is used
in poetic parallelism with the spirits of $^{\circ}p^c h$ (nought, or asp). In any
case this pregnant woman must suffer pain and terror:

And the foundations of the wall shake as a ship upon
    the waters . . .
and both they that dwell in the dust and they that go down
    to the sea are terrified by the roar of the waters.

The imagery of sinking in the depths is continued and merges into a
descent to Sheol. Finally in line 18:

[53]Trans. Holm-Nielson, *Hodayot*, 51.
[54]Ibid., 53. Some examples of the ambiguities: *ḥbl* means pain, especially
with childbirth, but can also mean "bond, snare" and be associated with death
and Sheol (so *ḥbly š^cwl* in 1QH 3:9). The meaning of *nmrṣ* (1. 8) is uncertain,
but it may mean "quick, hasty" or "incurable."
    mšbrym can be understood as *mašbēr*, "birth-canal" or *mišbār*, "breaker."
(Holm-Nielson takes it as "breakers" in lines 8b, 9, 11, and 12, but as "birth-
canal" in 1. 10.)
    bkwr may be from the root *bkr*, "first-born," but can also be understood as
the preposition *b* with *kwr*, "furnace." Van der Woude (*Die messianischen
Vorstellungen*, 55) takes "furnace" as a metaphor for "womb." Holm-Nielson
thinks "furnace" is related to child-birth "through the idea of suffering."
[55]M. Mansoor, *The Thanksgiving Hymns* (STDJ 3; Grand Rapids: Eerdmans, 1961) 114.
[56]A. Dupont-Sommer, *The Essene Writings from Qumran* (trans. G. Vermes;
Gloucester, Mass: Peter Smith, 1973) 208; "La mère du Messie et la mère de
l'Aspic dans un hymne de Qoumrân," *RHR* (1955) 174-88.

the doors of the pit close behind her that is pregnant
  with mischief
and the bars of eternity behind all the spirits of wickedness.[57]

Most commentators agree that the hymn falls into two sections,
with the division in line 12, where the second pregnant woman is
introduced.[58] Lines 7b-12a are completely taken up with the birth of a
boy-child. The pregnancy with the asp/wickedness does not occupy as
much space, but it provides the framework for lines 12b-18a. This
section begins with the travail of the one pregnant with the asp/wicked-
ness and ends with her confinement in "the pit." The extensive storm
imagery of lines 13-16 is framed by these two references and only serves
as supplementary elaboration of this pregnancy. The hymn then is
largely taken up with the contrast between a painful labor which issues
in the birth of a *geber*, man, and another painful labor which culmi-
nates with imprisonment in Sheol.

The issue of the first pregnancy is described in line 10 as "a
wonderful counsellor" (pl° $yw^c s$).[59] The phrase is taken, of course, from
Isa 9:5. In its original context it referred to a child who would sit on the
throne of David, and it was understood as a messianic prophecy in
Christianity. Consequently, Dupont-Sommer and others have assumed
that a reference to the (a?) messiah is intended here.[60] The majority of
scholars deny that the passage envisages a specific individual but "there

[57]So Holm-Nielsen. The word translated "mischief" is $^c wl$ and "wickedness" is $^\circ p^c h$ (which could be asp/viper).

[58]Van der Woude, *Die messianischen Vorstellungen*, 150. G. Hinson
("Hodayoth, 3:6-18: In What Sense Messianic?" *RQ* 2 [1960] 183-203) argues that
the hymn is structured around three images: a ship in distress, a beleaguered city
and a woman in travail. These images are first introduced and then expanded in
reverse order. However, neither the ship nor the city is proportional in prominence to the imagery of childbirth, and Hinson fails to explain the contrast
between the two pregnancies.

[59]The majority of commentators agree that the phrase pl° $yw^c s$ is descriptive
of the child here. So Holm-Nielsen, Mansoor, Dupont-Sommer, Vermes, Hinson,
and M. Delcor (*Les Hymnes de Qumran* [Paris: Letouzey, 1962] 111-12). Van der
Woude (*Die messianischen Vorstellungen*, 154; following L. H. Silberman,
"Language and Structure in the Hodayot [1QH 3]," *JBL* 75[1956] 105) takes pl°
as a substantive referring to God, and $yw^c s$ as a participial predicate. It is most
unlikely that a biblical phrase would be used in a way so sharply at variance
with its meaning in its original context.

[60]Dupont-Sommer, "La mère du Messie," 174-88. See M. Burrows (*More
Light on the Dead Sea Scrolls* [New York: Viking, 1958] 317-20) for a summary
of the various positions. Van der Woude (*Die messianischen Vorstellungen*, 153)
objects that the phrase is never applied to the messiah in rabbinic literature. The
objection is not decisive, since the rabbis might have avoided the messianic
interpretation because of its use by Christians. See Delcor, *Les Hymnes*, 120-21.

is tolerable agreement among them that the background for lines 7-12 is a sketch of the Messianic woes, i.e. signs and warnings of the dawn of the Messianic era."[61] Birth imagery is found in an eschatological context in the NT and the Jewish apocalypses.[62] More significantly, the fate of the woman pregnant with the asp/wickedness in the second half of the hymn has clear eschatological connotations. She will be confined in Sheol with "all the spirits of the asp/wickedness" (1QH 3:18). The destruction of the forces of wickedness is a recurring feature of the eschatology of Qumran.[63] Since the outcome of the evil pregnancy is clearly eschatological, parallelism suggests that the outcome of the good pregnancy is eschatological too. Accordingly, even if we follow the majority of scholars who reject the identification of the "wonderful counsellor" as "the messiah," we must still recognize that the two pregnancies are metaphorical sketches of the eschatological tribulation and its outcome.

However, the purpose of the hymn is not to prophesy the messianic age. Rather it is a thanksgiving hymn, which describes the distress and deliverance of the author.[64] The birth imagery is specifically introduced as an analogy in line 7: "And I am in distress, as a woman giving birth for the first time." It follows on two other analogies—the ship at sea and the besieged city, which are not specifically eschatological. This consideration does not remove the eschatological reference of the birth imagery. Rather, the experience of the author is being illustrated at once by a double analogy: that of childbirth itself and that of the eschatological

[61]Holm-Nielsen, Hodayot, 61. So also van der Woude, Die messianischen Vorstellungen, 156.

[62]The most obvious and frequently discussed parallel is Revelation 12. There too a woman brings forth a male child, and the chapter also refers to a dragon, "the ancient serpent" (Rev 12:9). The parallel with 1QH 3 is significant in so far as it provides an instance of birth imagery in an eschatological context and personifies the eschatological adversary as a snake. However, the imagery of Revelation 12 cannot be understood against the background of 1QH 3 and no historical connection can be maintained. See the thorough discussion by A. Yarbro Collins (The Combat Myth in the Book of Revelation [HDR 9; Missoula: Scholars, 1976] 67-69, 92). Instances of birth imagery in the apocalypses in an eschatological context are 4 Ezra 4:42 and 1 Enoch 62:4-5. Neither provides a close parallel to 1QH 3. Finally, we should note that birth imagery is very common in all sorts of contexts and is not necessarily eschatological.

[63]1QM 1:5, 15; 1QS 4:12-13, 19; Book of the Mysteries 5 (Dupont-Sommer, The Essene Writings, 327). See van der Woude, Die messianischen Vorstellungen, 156.

[64]See S. Mowinckel, "Some Remarks on Hodayoth 39:5-20," JBL 75 (1956) 265-76. On the Gattung of the Hodayoth see further Günter Morawe, Aufbau und Abgrenzung der Loblieder von Qumrân (Berlin: Evangelische Verlagsanstalt, 1960).

process evoked by the birth imagery. The purpose of the psalm is not to prophesy either the messiah or the messianic age. The eschatological reference serves as a metaphor for the psalmist's experience. It is inadequate, however, to say that it is "only a simile."[65] The fact that eschatological language can be used in this way in an "apocalyptic community" such as Qumran is highly significant. It presupposes the discernment of a pattern on several different levels. The distress of the righteous individual which issues in deliverance is like the pain of childbirth, which issues in the birth of a child, and which in turn is analogous to the eschatological trials of the community which issue in the messianic age. Conversely, the distress of the wicked is like a malignant labor, which, in turn, is analogous to eschatological disaster. The eschatological future is known by analogy with other patterns and can in turn serve as an analogy for other areas of experience. Eschatological language here presupposes and renders explicit a common pattern in present and future and so can be applied to the present situation, just as the language of eschatological war is applied in 1QS to the ongoing battle in human hearts.

The destruction by fire

The second hymn in 1QH 3 extends from lines 19-36. In lines 19-23 the author gives thanks to God for elevating him from "the abyss of Sheol" to "an eternal height," although he is only "a creature of clay" who stands "within the border of ungodliness and with the vicious by lot." The hymn goes on to describe the tumults that surround "the soul of the poor." These include "the arrows of the pit" (l. 27), "the period of wrath for all Belial" and the snares of death (l. 28). Then follows a description of the eruption of the fiery floods of Belial, which devour "right down to the great deep" and "break through into the abyss" (31-32), and finally the thundering of God and the "war of the heroes of heaven" which sweeps the world "until the appointed consummation" which is for eternity (36).

The hymn is evidently giving thanks for deliverance already accomplished.[66] Yet at least the last verse is undisputably eschatological and must refer to the future. Also the fiery flood of Belial would seem to be eschatological, since it involves the destruction of the physical universe, and the motif has extensive parallels in Persian, Jewish and Christian eschatology.[67] Translators and commentators disagree as to how much of

---

[65]Mowinckel, "Some Remarks," 276.
[66]See Kuhn, *Enderwartung*, 44-66.
[67]See Ringgren, "Der Weltbrand in den Hodajot," *Bibel und Qumran* (Hans Bardtke Fs., S. Wagner ed.; Berlin: Evangelische Haupt-Bibelgesellschaft, 1968)

the hymn refers to the tumults experienced by the author in either present or past. There is general agreement that lines 25-28 refer to the actual experience of the author. Vermes translates the eruption of the floods of Belial (l. 29) as future.[68] However, it is difficult to draw a line between the "floods of Belial" and the "arrows of the pit" (l. 27) and the "period of wrath upon all Belial" which precede that line.[69] Others translate by the past or present tenses for lines 29-33 and only use the future for the final consummation.[70]

The solution to this problem lies in the appreciation of the deliberate ambiguity of eschatological language which we have found throughout the Qumran documents. The primary reference here, as in 1QH 3:1-18, is clearly the deliverance of the individual which is already realized. However, both the nature of the deliverance (communion with the sons of heaven, l. 22) and that from which deliverance is required (the grave, Sheol) are expressed in eschatological language throughout. The tumults which surround the author in lines 25-28 are located in "the period of wrath upon all Belial," which is the final period envisaged throughout the scrolls. In the context of the intense apocalypticism of Qumran, such language cannot be dismissed as "merely" metaphorical. It is certainly metaphorical but it expresses the conviction of the author that the eschatological drama is already underway. If the "arrows of the pit" can refer to the present experience of the author, the "floods of Belial" can too.[71] Even the war of the heroes of heaven, which clearly corresponds to that described in 1QM, may be conceived as already in progress.

However, the eschatological language of the hymn is not exhausted by, or co-terminous with, the experience of the individual or his community. In fact, the author claims that he has already been raised to the eternal height. His victory is secure. Yet the eschatological tumult is certainly not finished. The deliverance of the individual from "the snares of the pit" (26) is only part of a wider process on the cosmic level.

177-82. On the motif see further Collins, *The Sibylline Oracles of Egyptian Judaism* (SBLDS 13; Missoula: Scholars, 1974) 101-10.

[68]Vermes, *The Dead Sea Scrolls*, 159. The use of tenses in the hymn is confusing since it vacillates between imperfects with Waw-Consecutive and simple imperfects.

[69]Holm-Nielsen translates the phrase *qṣ ḥrwn lkwl blyᶜl* as "the moment of anger upon all corruption." *blyᶜl*, however, occurs in "the floods of Belial" in the following line and the juxtaposition is surely deliberate. ("All Belial" should be understood as "all the forces of Belial"). *qṣ ḥrwn* very probably implies a pun on *qṣ ᵓḥrwn*, the last age.

[70]Holm-Nielsen uses the present tense down to line 36b; Delcor and Mansoor vacillate between past and present.

[71]So also Ringgren, "Der Weltbrand," 182.

The afflictions which beset the individual are only part of a wider cosmic tumult occasioned by the warring of Belial and the heavenly host. On the wider level that tumult is even thought to involve the destruction of the physical universe. Here again the underlying assumption is that there is a common pattern between human affairs and cosmic processes. Accordingly, cosmic language can be used metaphorically to express the state of the individual. The space in which the author of this hymn moves is the cosmic space of Sheol and the eternal height. The time in which he moves is the eschatological period of wrath against Belial. The pattern of future tumult and deliverance is already manifest in his own experience.

4. CONCLUSIONS

The foregoing review of some of the main eschatological ideas of Qumran reveals a two-fold complexity. First, there is a plurality of ways in which the eschatological age can be described. Second, even individual eschatological doctrines can be understood on several different levels simultaneously.

The diversity of expectations

We have seen above that expectations of the "national, political, this-wordly" type, such as the two messiahs, are not necessarily incompatible with "super-terrestrial, otherwordly" conceptions such as are found in the War Scroll. However, they undeniably reflect different modes of eschatological thinking. Further, the idea of a fiery destruction of the world found in 1QH 3 is quite incompatible with the political, this-worldly type of messianism. Accordingly, we agree with Morton Smith's assertion that the expectations of the sect should not be harmonized into a systematic body of doctrines.[72] Rather, we must reckon with the persistence of diverse conceptions side by side in the same community.

In his study of this phenomenon, Smith concluded that the importance of eschatological doctrine for the sect had been exaggerated: "If a group had no single eschatological myth, it cannot have been organized as a community of believers in the myth it did not have. . . . If the variety of eschatological prediction is any evidence, eschatology was, for the members of these groups, a comparatively arbitrary and individual matter."[73] Now it is certainly true that Qumran did not have a systematic body of doctrine analogous to what later developed in Christianity. Smith seeks to explain the diversity of eschatological doctrines, however,

[72]M. Smith, "What is implied by the Variety of Messianic Figures?" *JBL* 78 (1959) 66-72.
[73]Smith, "What is implied," 71-72.

by assuming that different beliefs were held by different people.[74] This assumption is unsatisfactory. We have seen that diverse eschatological views, the ongoing war of the spirits and the expectation of the messiahs of Aaron and Israel, are found side by side in a single document in 1QS. Further, it is typical of apocalyptic writings that a series of eschatological visions which are logically incompatible are placed side by side.[75] Recent analysis has shown clearly that such juxtaposition is not a result of the combination of different sources, but is a device well known from myths and folklore. The repetition of different formulations draws attention to the basic structure they have in common. That structure is not exhausted by any one way in which it is expressed but emerges from the juxtaposition of a number of formulations which differ in detail.[76] The variety of eschatological doctrines at Qumran does not, then, suggest that eschatology was an arbitrary and individual matter, but that the underlying structure was more important than any specific formulation.

Disclosure models

This conclusion throws light on the nature and logic of eschatological belief at Qumran. In the well-known terminology of Ian Ramsey, the eschatological doctrines are "disclosure models" rather than "scale" or "picture models."[77] In picture modelling "a model is thought of as a replica, a copy picture, . . . reproducing identically those properties common to model and original which, for a particular purpose in mind, are importantly relevant."[78] If the eschatological doctrines of Qumran were understood as picture models, this would imply that the events predicted were expected to happen in precisely this way. In this case views which could not be reconciled with each other in detail must be

[74]Ibid., 72: "the opinions of different members might, and did, differ quite widely."

[75]See Yarbro Collins, *The Combat Myth*, 11-44 (on the NT book of Revelation), Collins, *The Apocalyptic Vision*, 117 (on Daniel), Collins, *The Sibylline Oracles*, 37, 74 (on Sib Or 3 and 5) and E. Breech, "These Fragments I have Shored against my ruins: the Form and Function of 4 Ezra," *JBL* 92 (1973) 267-74 (on 4 Ezra).

[76]See C. Lévi-Strauss, "The Structural Study of Myth," *Structural Anthropology* (New York: Basic Books, 1963) 229, E. Leach, "Genesis as Myth," *Myth and Cosmos* (John Middleton, ed.; Garden City: Natural History, 1967) 1-13; P. Ricoeur, *The Symbolism of Evil* (Boston: Beacon, 1969) 167-68; W. Meeks, "The Man from Heaven in Johannine Sectarianism," *JBL* 91 (1972) 48.

[77]I. T. Ramsey, *Models and Mystery* (London: Oxford University, 1964) 1-21. Ramsey's terminology is adapted from M. Black, *Models and Metaphors: Studies in Language and Philosophy* (Ithaca: Cornell, 1962).

[78]Ramsey, *Models*, 2-3.

presumed to be held by different people. By contrast, "disclosure" or "analogue models" are "designed to reproduce as faithfully as possible the *structure* or web of relationship in an original."[79] In this case differences in detail are not important, since the doctrines do not give exact literal descriptions of the future in any case. Instead, the emphasis is on "the structure or web of relationship"—the division of the world between two forces, symbolically called "Light and Darkness," and the conviction that "Light" will prevail.

The understanding of the eschatology of Qumran as "disclosure" or "analogue" modelling also throws light on the fact that doctrines can be understood on several different levels at once. The leadership of the messiahs of Aaron and Israel can be enacted by the present leaders of the community. The war of Light and Darkness is already raging in the hearts of humanity. The author of the *Hodayot* can claim to have already experienced the "messianic woes" and the "floods of Belial" and even the deliverance which follows them. We have noted that this application of eschatological language to the present rests on the assumption of a common pattern between the historical present (and past) and the eschatological future.[80] The expectation of the two messiahs is modelled on the dual leadership of the post-exilic community and reflected in the present organization of the sect. The dualistic conflict of light and darkness is inherent in the cosmos in creation and goes on perpetually within human hearts. The messianic woes are modelled on the experience of childbirth and the same pattern is found in the trial and deliverance of an individual. The eschatological assertions of Qumran presuppose a coherence in the structure of the universe, past, present and future. Their purpose is to disclose the structure or web of relationship that constitutes that coherence. Insights into the pattern of present experience can then be used to illuminate the future and eschatological doctrines can disclose meaning in the present.

An alternative order

The disclosure of structural patterns is not in itself peculiar to Qumran or to apocalyptic writing. Jonathan Z. Smith has argued persuasively "that Wisdom and Apocalyptic are interrelated in that both are essentially scribal phenomena. They both depend on the relentless quest for paradigms, the problematics of applying these paradigms to new situations and the *Listenwissenschaft* which are the characteristic

[79]Ibid., 9.
[80]The idea of a recurring pattern in history and in the eschatological future is found in some, though not all, Jewish apocalypses. See Collins, "Pseudonymity, Historical Reviews and the Genre of the Revelation of John," *CBQ* 39 (1977) 337-38.

activities of the Near Eastern scribe."[81] The distinctive aspect of Qumran, and of apocalypticism in general, lies in the patterns they disclose and the projection of those patterns into the eschatological future. While ancient wisdom is generally recognized to presuppose a unified cosmic order,[82] the world of Qumran is divided between two conflicting orders.[83] It is significant to note, however, that the eschatology of Qumran is, like wisdom, an attempt to find order and structure in the world. Apocalypticism, as represented by Qumran, is not only a cry of protest against the dominance of the hostile order of Belial and Darkness. It is also an affirmation of an alternative order which is eclipsed in the present, but is already experienced by the elect community and will be fully manifest in the future. The stance of Qumran cannot be understood in terms of rejection of the established order alone. It involves equally the assertion of a positive counter-structure which has its own coherence.[84]

Finally, by way of an epilogue, we may note that the latter observation is of some significance for the social phenomenon of Qumran. Qumran is characterized by an elaborate hierarchical structure and ritual practice. This fact has been perceived as anomalous for an "apocalyptic community," since millennial groups are often presumed to be anti-structural and anti-ritual.[85] However, we have seen that the eschatology of Qumran presupposes a complex world order, which we should then expect to find reflected in the community structure. In fact, we have noted a close correspondence between the actual community structure and ritual and its messianic expectations. Eschatology and community structure appear to go hand in hand at Qumran, and neither can be regarded as secondary to the other. Structure and ritual cannot be regarded as misplaced relics of the priestly antecedents of the community, but are inherently related to the apocalypticism or millennarianism of the sect. Further study of the social phenomenon of apocalypticism will have to take full account of this fact.

[81] J. Z. Smith, "Wisdom and Apocalyptic," *Religious Syncretism in Antiquity: Essays in Conversation with Geo Widengren* (ed. Birger Pearson; Missoula: Scholars, 1975) 154.

[82] See H. Gese, *Lehre und Wirklichkeit in der alten Weisheit* (Tübingen: Mohr, 1968); H. H. Schmid, *Wesen und Geschichte der Weisheit* (BZAW 101; Berlin: Töpelmann, 1966) 17-22; G. von Rad, *Wisdom in Israel* (Nashville: Abingdon, 1972) 144-76; J. J. Collins, "The Biblical Precedent for Natural Theology," *JAAR* 15/1 (1977) Supplement, B: 35-67.

[83] For the analogies and contrasts between wisdom and apocalypticism see further Collins, "Cosmos and Salvation."

[84] Compare the use of such expressions as "alternative symbolic universe" and "symbolic counter-universe" with reference to apocalypticism by P. D. Hanson, "Apocalypticism," *IDBSup*, 31.

[85] See S. Isenberg and D. E. Owen, "Bodies, Natural and Contrived: The Work of Mary Douglas," *RelSRev* 3 (1977) 10-13.

Myth And History In The Book Of Revelation: The Problem Of Its Date

ADELA YARBRO COLLINS

MCCORMICK THEOLOGICAL SEMINARY

METHODS of interpretation tend to reflect the presuppositions and questions of the interpreters. That principle partly explains the variety of approaches used by students of the book of Revelation over the centuries. It cannot, however, fully account for the widely differing techniques applied to this book. The enigmatic character of Revelation's overall structure and individual images make its intended and actual relation to reality problematic.

The earliest approach for which we have evidence accepted Revelation as a divinely inspired prophecy of the immediate future.[1] The focus was on the reign of a thousand years (20:4-6), which was expected to be earthly and temporal. This was the perspective of the Montanists. Their claims that prophecy was still alive and that its fulfillment was near apparently evoked two kinds of reaction. A more moderate chiliasm (from the Greek *chilioi*, a thousand) was maintained by Irenaeus and Hippolytus. They held to the earthly messianic reign but did not believe it to be imminent. In Alexandria Revelation was interpreted allegorically by Clement and Origen. They emphasized its revelation of spiritual and moral truth in the present. These two basic points of view never died out in the history of the interpretation of Revelation and are still held by some today.

The moderate chiliasts were convinced that the book of Revelation revealed God's plan for human history. As time passed, it was difficult to maintain the intensity of expectation reflected in the book while seeing it as a prophecy of one's own time. This tension seems to have elicited the church-historical or world-historical approach, which flowered in the medieval period. Whereas other interpreters, especially the allegorists, had understood each of the series of seven as recapitulating one another, the practitioners of this method saw them as predictions of

---

[1]For the history of the interpretation of Revelation, see W. Bousset, *Die Offenbarung Johannis* (MeyerK 16; 5th ed.; Göttingen: Vandenhoeck und Ruprecht, 1896) 51-140 and I. T. Beckwith, *The Apocalypse of John* (New York: Macmillan, 1922) 318-36.

different historical events. Taken together, they predict the course of history from the time Revelation was written to the interpreter's situation.

In the hands of Protestant exegetes, the church-historical method was used to identify Babylon and the beast with contemporary Rome and the papacy. Perhaps in an attempt to defend Catholicism against this identification, a Jesuit commentator of the sixteenth century interpreted Revelation entirely in terms of its original historical context. This approach, which came to be called the contemporary-historical method, gradually won the day, at least among those committed to the historical-critical method of Biblical interpretation.

The principle that Revelation must be interpreted in terms of its historical context provides a necessary limit to the exercise of the imagination in seeking appropriate meanings and applications of its images. The contemporary-historical method, however, has its limitations and can be abused, like any other. When narrowly and mechanically applied, it leads to a flat and simplistic kind of allegorical interpretation: this image equals that historical figure and that is the end of the matter. Near the end of the nineteenth century, Hermann Gunkel published a study of Revelation which polemicized against the excesses of the contemporary-historical method and introduced a new approach.[2] He presented the author as the heir to a rich and ancient tradition of mythic images and narratives, who composed his work within this traditional framework. He was not, according to Gunkel, a lone genius who created his images intuitively out of his historical experience.

Gunkel's method belongs to the history-of-religions approach and has also been called the tradition-historical method. These two methods, the contemporary-historical and the tradition-historical, are essential for any responsible interpretation of Revelation. Each complements the other. The tradition-historical method determines the author's raw materials and their conventional meanings. The contemporary-historical sheds light on how and why he shaped these raw materials into a new and distinctive composition. Both methods have something to contribute to the task of defining the date of the book. At the same time, a fairly precise knowledge of the book's date allows a more finely honed application of each of these methods. If a particular tradition which appears in Revelation is known elsewhere, the other occurrences may provide a fixed point either before or after which the book should probably be dated. On the other hand, a particular motif may have several possible

---

[2]H. Gunkel, *Schöpfung und Chaos in Urzeit und Endzeit: Eine religionsgeschichtliche Untersuchung über Gen 1 and Ap Joh 12* (Göttingen: Vandenhoeck und Ruprecht, 1895).

origins and thus meanings. Knowledge of the date (and of course the place) of composition can help in deciding which of these the author intended and readers recognized. By using the contemporary-historical method, the interpreter can discern historical events reflected in the book's images and narratives. When the date has been fixed as nearly as possible, the interpreter, by means of the same method, is able better to understand and to assess the author's purpose in writing the book and its function for the earliest readers.

EXTERNAL EVIDENCE FOR THE DATE

Determining the date of Revelation is a complex task for which there is evidence of different kinds and of varying weight. One type of evidence is external to the book of Revelation itself, namely, the testimony of the Church Fathers and other early Christian writers. The earliest witness is Irenaeus (*Adv. haer.* 5. 30. 3) who says that the apocalypse was seen at the end of the reign of Domitian.[3] Since Domitian ruled from 81-96, Irenaeus' comment refers to about 95. The wording leaves open the possibility that Irenaeus believed the book to have been written down somewhat later, especially since he says elsewhere that John lived in Ephesus until the times of Trajan. Victorinus (who died in 303) and Eusebius say that Revelation was written during the reign of Domitian.[4] They add that John was banished to Patmos by Domitian and that he was released when Domitian died. Several other writers support the Domitianic date. A few late sources date Revelation to the time of Claudius, Nero or Trajan. These texts show that there were traditions about the date of Revelation which were apparently independent of Irenaeus. Their historical reliability, however, is doubtful.

Irenaeus' testimony has been questioned recently on the grounds that he believed also that the gospel of John was written by the same author and that the author in question was the apostle John.[5] Few scholars today believe that the gospel and Revelation were written by the same person, because of their linguistic and theological differences.

[3]For an English translation of the passage and its context, see A. Roberts and J. Donaldson, eds., *The Ante-Nicene Fathers* (Buffalo: Christian Literature Publishing, 1886) 1. 559-60. The original Greek text is quoted by Eusebius *Hist. eccl.* 3. 18. 3; The Latin and Greek texts, along with a French translation are available in A. Rousseau, L. Doutreleau and C. Mercier, eds., *Irénée de Lyon: Contre les hérésies, livre V* (Paris: Les Editions du Cerf, 1969) 2. 384-85.

[4]The ancient texts are quoted by H. B. Swete, *The Apocalypse of St. John* (3rd ed.; New York: Macmillan, 1909) lxxxix-xc and R. H. Charles, *A Critical and Exegetical Commentary on the Revelation of St. John* (ICC; New York: Scribner's, 1920) 1. xcii-xciii.

[5]By J. A. T. Robinson, *Redating the New Testament* (Philadelphia: Westminster, 1976) 222.

Another problem is that the apostle John, if he survived that long, must have been an extremely old man by the end of Domitian's reign.

Another objection to Irenaeus' dating could be raised on the basis of Domitian's portrayal as the second persecutor, a new Nero, in Christian tradition. There is extremely little evidence that such was actually the case. The earliest explicit evidence for this tradition is Eusebius' quotation of a passage from Melito's book, *To Antoninus* (Eusebius *Hist. eccl.* 4. 26. 5-11). This book was an apology for Christianity dedicated to Marcus Aurelius. Melito's presentation of the emperors' attitude toward Christians is not very accurate. It appears that he wanted to show that only those emperors who had a bad reputation among Romans themselves persecuted Christians, not because Christians deserved punishment, but because those emperors were evil. Nero had indeed persecuted Christians. Domitian was called a second Nero by some Roman writers,[6] so that it would have been easy for Melito to assimilate the later to the earlier. Once the comparison was made, it seems, it became traditional. Details were added and particular names associated with Domitian's persecution.[7] So one might argue that Irenaeus, knowing that Revelation was not written under Nero or judging on the basis of internal evidence that it could not have been, concluded that it must have been written under Domitian.

Neither of the two objections described above to Irenaeus' dating is persuasive. In fact, the evidence discussed tends to support Irenaeus. A number of considerations make it more likely that Irenaeus was wrong about authorship than about the date. It is well known that John was a common name among Jews and Christians in the first century. The potential for confusion a few generations later is obvious. Secondly, in the process of the canon's formation, there was a tendency to associate respected and long used writings with apostles. If clear evidence to the contrary was not available, Irenaeus would thus be inclined to link Revelation with the apostle John. The fact that he dated the book as he did, in spite of the difficulty about the apostle's age, implies that he had independent and strong evidence for the date.

Irenaeus' reason for dating Revelation to the reign of Domitian does not seem to be the tradition that Domitian was the second great persecutor of Christians. He does not mention any persecution in connection with the book or with the emperor. Further, he does not mention even John's exile to Patmos. If Irenaeus knew the tradition that Domitian was a second Nero, he shows no interest in it. It is likely that

[6] Juvenal *Sat.* 4.38, Pliny *Paneg.* 53.3-4.
[7] J. Moreau argued that Eusebius used one or more pagan sources listing Roman aristocrats exiled by Domitian and claimed these as Christian victims of persecution ("A propos de la persécution de Domitien," *La Nouvelle Clio* 5 [1953] 125).

he had another reason for dating the book to Domitian's reign, perhaps information he received from other Christians of Asia Minor when he lived there.

INTERNAL EVIDENCE FOR THE DATE

Irenaeus' testimony is crucial because the later writers who date Revelation to Domitian's reign could be dependent on him. There seems to be no good reason for doubting Irenaeus' date on grounds external to the book of Revelation. His dating can be accepted, however, only if it is harmonious with the evidence found within the book itself.

The Name Babylon

The book of Revelation announces and describes in several places the destruction of a city called Babylon (14:8; 16:19; 17:5; 18:2, 10, 21). It is inconceivable that an early Christian author was so interested in the fall of the actual, historical Babylon. The reader is given a clear hint that the name is not to be taken literally. In chap. 17 the city is seen in a vision as a woman. V 5 says, "and upon her forehead a name was written, a mystery, Babylon the great, the mother of prostitutes and of the abominations of the earth." The word "mystery" (*mystērion*) is used in a similar way in chap. 1. The author sees a vision of Christ in the midst of seven golden lampstands with seven stars in his hand. The stars and lampstands are called a mystery; the secret is revealed by Christ, "the seven stars are angels of the seven congregations and the seven lampstands are seven congregations" (1:20). Similarly, in chap. 17 the interpreting angel tells the seer, "I will tell you the mystery of the woman and of the beast which carries her, which has the seven heads and the ten horns" (v 7). A rather lengthy discourse follows. Two remarks in it make clear that the woman represents the city of Rome: "the seven heads are seven mountains upon which the woman sits" (v 9)[8] and "the woman whom you saw is the great city which holds rule over the kings of the earth" (v 18).

A few extreme proponents of the tradition-historical method have denied that the woman "Babylon" can be identified with a particular, historical city.[9] Most commentators, however, agree that Babylon is a symbolic name for Rome. It is not by any means the case that Babylon was the obvious or only name which might be taken from the Hebrew

[8]Rome as "the city of seven hills" was a common expression in classical writers; for references see Charles, *Revelation of St. John*, 2.69. See also G. B. Caird, *A Commentary on the Revelation of St. John the Divine* (HNTC; New York: Harper & Row, 1966) 216.

[9]For example, E. Lohmeyer, *Die Offenbarung des Johannes* (HNT; 2d ed.; Tübingen: Mohr, 1953) 145-47.

Bible to designate Rome as the enemy of the people of God. Egypt, Kittim, and Edom appear along with Babylon in Jewish sources as pseudonyms for Rome. In fact, Edom is the most common in the rabbinic literature.[10] Most of the occurrences of Babylon as a symbolic name for Rome are in 2 Esdras, the Syriac Apocalypse of Baruch, and the fifth book of the Sibylline Oracles. In each case where it occurs in these three works, the context makes it abundantly clear why the name Babylon was chosen.[11] Rome is called Babylon because her forces, like those of Babylon at an earlier time, destroyed the temple and Jerusalem. It is probable that the author of Revelation took over this identification from the Jews, and that it had already become traditional by the end of the first century.[12]

The use of the name Babylon for Rome in Revelation is a rather weighty internal indication of the date. It is highly unlikely that the name would have been used before the destruction of the temple by Titus. This internal element then points decisively to a date after 70 C.E.

The Seven Kings

The speech of the interpreting angel in chap. 17 contains another passage which, at first sight, seems to offer important evidence for the date of Revelation. After remarking that the seven heads of the beast are seven mountains, the angel continues, "And they are seven kings; five have fallen, one is, the other has not yet come, and when he comes, he must remain a little while. And the beast which was and is not, he himself is also an eighth and is one of the seven, and he goes to destruction" (vv 9-11). It would appear that Revelation was composed under the ruler referred to in the remark, "one is," and that the interpreter need only calculate who that ruler was to discover the work's date. Few commentators have found that calculation to be an easy matter!

First of all it is necessary to understand the image of the beast. Gunkel's masterful study showed conclusively that the beast is a traditional motif which has its roots in ancient Near Eastern myths.[13] The

[10]The texts are quoted and discussed by C. -H. Hunzinger, "Babylon als Deckname für Rom und die Datierung des I. Petrusbriefes," in *Gottes Wort und Gottes Land: Hans-Wilhelm Hertzberg zum 70. Geburtstag* (ed. H. G. Reventlow; Göttingen: Vandenhoeck und Ruprecht, 1965) 67-77.

[11]2 Esdr 3:1-2, 28-31; 2 *Apoc. Bar.* 10:1-3; 11:1; 67:7; *Sib. Or.* 5:143, 159.

[12]Hunzinger makes the same point and concludes that I Peter must have been written after 70 C.E. (see 1 Pet 5:13; Hunzinger, "Babylon als Deckname für Rom," 73-77).

[13]Gunkel, *Schöpfung und Chaos*.

implication is that the beast in Revelation is not a two-dimensional historical allegory or a simple metaphor. It may well have allegorical and metaphorical characteristics, but it carries with it a rich heritage of connotations which derive from the function of the creation and combat myths in which it traditionally appears. The same commentators who deny a contemporary-historical reference to the city-woman "Babylon" argue against the identification of the beast with the Roman empire.[14] They are right that the association of the two does not exhaust the meaning of the image, but they go too far in disputing that the beast represents the Roman empire on at least one level of meaning and in the author's intention.

A comparison of the attributes and especially the functions of the beasts mentioned in 11:7, 13:1-10 and chap. 17 shows that they are equivalent in meaning.[15] Like the beasts of Daniel 7, this beast some-times represents a kingdom (the Roman empire) and sometimes a king (the emperor Nero).[16] It is clear that these visions in Revelation have been shaped by the legend of Nero's return. That legend had already been used in Jewish literature to portray Nero as the eschatological adversary of God. The author of Revelation apparently took over the Jewish form of the legend and adapted it, so that the Neronic eschato-logical adversary became an Antichrist in the precise sense of the word: a dying and rising destroyer, rather than savior.[17]

It may be taken as established that the beast of 13:1-10 and chap. 17 represents both the Roman empire and Nero (the historical as well as the eschatological) and that one of the beast's seven heads is Nero. The beast who will return as the "eighth (head)" is the eschatological Nero, the Antichrist. One must conclude that Revelation was written after the death of Nero (68) since the parallel between him and Jesus requires it. Given the prominence of the Nero legend, it is very likely that the ten kings (17:12-14, 16-17) are the allies from the East whom Nero was expected to bring with him to regain his throne.[18]

The identity of the other heads is difficult to determine. There are three basic positions on the issue. (1) The seven heads include all the Roman emperors who had ruled up to the author's time, starting at the beginning and counting consecutively. Revelation was thus written under the sixth emperor. Some who take this position begin with Julius Caesar, others with Augustus. Some include Galba, Otho and Vitellius;

[14]Lohmeyer, *Offenbarung des Johannes*, 141.
[15]This point is argued in detail in A. Yarbro Collins, *The Combat Myth in the Book of Revelation* (HDR 9; Missoula: Scholars, 1976) 170-72.
[16]Ibid., 171-76.
[17]Ibid., 176-86.
[18]Ibid., 175.

others do not.[19] (2) This position is the same as (1), except that the author is not actually writing under the sixth emperor. Some hold (a) that an earlier source was used and not updated;[20] others think (b) that the author antedated his work.[21] (3) The seven heads do not represent all the Roman emperors, but only selected ones.[22] There are several different theories about the principle of selection.

The assumption that the seven heads are intended to include all the Roman emperors who reigned up to the writer's time has little to recommend it. The conclusion seems to be drawn by analogy with

[19]Few recent interpreters take this position. C. C. Torrey (*The Apocalypse of John* [New Haven: Yale, 1958] 66) begins with Augustus and includes Galba. J. M. Ford (*Revelation* [AB 38; Garden City: Doubleday, 1975] 290) begins with Julius Caesar and omits Galba, Otho and Vitellius. Robinson (*Redating the New Testament*, 248-53) begins with Augustus and includes Galba, Otho and Vitellius. A. A. Bell ("The Date of John's Apocalypse. The Evidence of Some Roman Historians Reconsidered," *NTS* 25 [1979] 93-102), in effect, begins with Augustus and considers Revelation to have been written under Galba, the sixth head.

[20]Charles, *Revelation of St. John*, 2. 69; Bousset, *Offenbarung Johannis*, 478-80; T. F. Glasson (*The Revelation of John* [Cambridge: Cambridge University, 1965] 99) thinks that a source was used but that the author reinterpreted it, so that the first head became Caligula and the sixth, Domitian; P. Carrington (*The Meaning of the Revelation* [London: SPCK, 1931] 283-84) posits a source dating to the time of Vespasian, which the author reinterpreted, so that the eighth was Domitian.

[21]A. Feuillet, *L'Apocalypse: Etat de la question* (Paris: Desclée De Brouwer, 1963) 77-79; W. Barclay, *The Revelation of John* (Philadelphia: Westminster, 1960) 2. 190; L. Cerfaux and J. Cambier, *L'Apocalypse de saint Jean lue aux chrétiens* (LD 17; Paris: Les Editions du Cerf, 1955) 152; A. Wikenhauser, *Die Offenbarung des Johannes* (RNT 9; 3rd ed.; Regensburg: Pustet, 1959) 131. H. B. Swete (*The Apocalypse of St. John*, 221) held that the author used a source, reedited his own, earlier work, or antedated this passage.

[22]E. -B. Allo, *Saint Jean: L'Apocalypse* (EB; 4th ed.; Paris: Gabalda, 1933) 281; L. Brun, "Die römischen Kaiser in der Apokalypse," *ZNW* 26 (1927) 128-51; A. Strobel, "Abfassung und Geschichtstheologie der Apokalypse nach Kap. XVII. 9-12," *NTS* 10 (1964) 433-45; B. Reicke, "Die jüdische Apokalyptik und die johanneische Tiervision," *RSR* 60 (1972) 173-92. A number of commentators hold that the motif of the seven heads has no precise contemporary-historical meaning, but is symbolic, namely, Beckwith, *Apocalypse of John*, 708; E. Lohse, *Die Offenbarung des Johannes* (NTD 11; 8th ed.; Göttingen: Vandenhoeck und Ruprecht, 1960) 87; Caird, *Commentary on Revelation*, 218-19; M. Kiddle and M. K. Ross, *The Revelation of St. John* (MNTC; London: Hodder and Stoughton, 1940) 350-51; J. Bonsirven, *L'Apocalypse* (VS 16; Paris: Beauchesne, 1951) 269-70. Others are cited by Robinson, *Redating the New Testament*, 245, n. 125. H. Kraft (*Die Offenbarung des Johannes* [HNT 16a; Tübingen: Mohr, 1974] 222) holds that the sixth head is Nerva and the seventh Trajan.

Suetonius' *The Twelve Caesars*, the list of rulers in *Sib. Or.* 5:12-51, and the eagle vision of 2 Esdras 11-12. Suetonius' work belongs to a quite different genre. The interest in completeness and consecutive order is explicit. The Sibylline oracle also has a different literary form and interest. It begins by calling itself the chronicle of the sons of Latium. A chronicle by definition must relate events in chronological order and be relatively complete. A very brief sketch of previous history is given and then a list of the Roman emperors (with a characterization of each) up to Hadrian.

The comparison of Revelation 17 with the eagle vision of 2 Esdras is very instructive. The eagle vision seems to have been influenced by Daniel 7, as was Revelation 13. 2 Esdras 11 and Revelation 13 both portray a single beast rather than Daniel's four. The eagle seems to have been chosen to represent the Roman empire, since Rome's military emblem was the eagle.[23] The animal is described as having twelve wings, eight little opposing wings, and three heads. The twelve wings clearly represent Roman emperors, beginning with Julius Caesar, since the second is unmistakably Augustus (2 Esdr 11:13-17, 12:14-15). The identity of the little opposing wings is very difficult to establish.[24] If the vision has any interest in completeness, it is expressed in these two series of wings. The heads, on the other hand, represent three emperors selected from the total list. The descriptions of the heads (2 Esdr 11:29-32, 12:22-28) indicate that they stand for Vespasian, Titus and Domitian. It is quite clear then that these three emperors are represented both by three of the twelve major wings and by the three heads.

Revelation 17 and 2 Esdras 11-12 are certainly of the same literary genre. The use of imagery in 2 Esdras, however, does not support the assumption that the seven heads of Revelation 17 represent all the emperors of Rome up to the actual or supposed time of writing. If there is an analogy between the two, the ten horns might be taken as a complete list of emperors and the seven heads as a selection. But the similarity between the two should not be pressed, and one cannot assume that the author of Revelation was following the example of 2 Esdras 11-12 or that he used traditional images in exactly the same way.

A further problem with the theory that the seven heads represent all the emperors is that, if one begins counting with Julius Caesar, Nero is the sixth. Since Nero's death is presupposed in the imagery, he cannot be the "one (who) is." Holders of this position who recognize this problem

[23]Each Roman legion had an *aquila* ("eagle") of silver or gold; H. M. D. Parker, "Signa militaria," *Oxford Classical Dictionary* (Oxford: Clarendon, 1949) 838.

[24]See the discussion by J. M. Myers, *I & II Esdras* (AB 42; Garden City: Doubleday, 1974) 299-301.

solve it by beginning with Augustus rather than Caesar.[25] To justify this
some point to Tacitus, saying that he regarded the empire as beginning
with Augustus. In Hist. 1.1 Tacitus says:

> I shall begin my work with the year (69 C.E.) in which Servius Galba and
> Titus Vinius were consuls, the former for the second time. My choice of
> starting point is determined by the fact that the preceding period of 820
> years dating from the foundation of Rome has found many historians. So
> long as republican history was their theme, they wrote with equal elo-
> quence of style and independence of outlook. But when the Battle of
> Actium had been fought and the interests of peace demanded the concen-
> tration of power in the hands of one man, this great line of classical
> historians came to an end.[26]

Tacitus is making a critical judgment about Roman historians and not
defining the beginning of the empire as such. He does not mention
Julius Caesar and one can conclude at most that he was a borderline
figure. Tacitus' failure to mention him in this context may be due
simply to the fact that his rule was too short to be of significance for the
practical matter Tacitus is discussing. Furthermore, Tacitus does not
begin his own history with Augustus but with Galba.[27] The more
significant parallels for Revelation (Sib. Or. 5:12-51 and 2 Esdras 11-12)
begin with Julius Caesar.[28] If the theory that the seven heads represent

[25]See note 19 above.
[26]The translation cited is by K. Wellesley (Baltimore: Penguin, 1964) 21.
[27]The opening passage of the Annals also does not support the theory that
Tacitus considered Julius Caesar to belong to the republic and the empire to
begin only with Augustus:

> Neither Cinna nor Sulla created a lasting despotism: Pompey and Crassus quickly
> forfeited their power to Caesar, and Lepidus and Antony their swords to Augustus,
> who, under the style of "Prince," (princeps) gathered beneath his empire a world
> outworn by civil broils (translation from the Loeb edition).

Their titles were certainly different, but Tacitus seems to be drawing a parallel
between the two in this passage. Bell ("The Date of John's Apocalypse," 98)
argues that "Tacitus clearly considers the assumption of this title Princeps to be
the major distinction between the emperors and all the earlier magistrates of the
Roman state. Julius never held that title, and throughout his work Tacitus
pointedly differentiates dictatorem Caesarem aut imperatorem Augustum." But
the passages he cites do not support this conclusion. Yes, Tacitus distinguishes
their titles, but not their functions. In Ann. 4.34 the deified Julius and the
deified Augustus are called "the Caesars" (in a speech by Cremutius Cordus),
and in 13:3, both are included in a list of masters of the empire.
[28]Josephus also apparently considered the empire to begin with Julius
Caesar. In Ant. 18.32, he refers to Augustus as "the second emperor (autokratōr)
of the Romans."

all the emperors in succession leads to an impossibility (that Revelation was written under Nero), one should seek another interpretative principle, rather than make a weakly justified modification in the theory.

The theory that the seven heads represent all the emperors in sequence has yet another flaw. If one avoids making Nero the sixth by beginning with Augustus, Galba becomes the "one (who) is." Galba's reign (68-69), however, ran its course before the temple in Jerusalem was destroyed. It is quite unlikely, therefore, that Revelation was written under Galba. Some interpreters who begin the series with Augustus do not accept the logical conclusion that Galba is the sixth. They omit Galba, Otho and Vitellius on the grounds that Suetonius describes their reigns as "a revolution of three emperors" (*rebellio trium principum*; *Vesp.* 1). But Suetonius' point is not that their reigns were in any way illegitimate, only that they were unstable and that the Flavians brought stability once again. If, therefore, one holds the position that the seven heads represent all the (legitimate) emperors in sequence, one may not leave Galba, Otho or Vitellius out. All three were recognized as emperor by the senate. Suetonius includes them in *The Twelve Caesars*, and they also appear in *Sib. Or.* 5:12-51 and 2 Esdras 11-12.

The first basic position, then, that the seven heads include all the Roman emperors up to the time of the author of Revelation, involves insurmountable difficulties. The second basic position is that the author was not actually writing under the "one (who) is." Most holders of this position assume that the seven heads represent all the emperors in sequence. One form of this theory is that the writer of Revelation made use of a source which had been written under the sixth emperor. Wilhelm Bousset and R. H. Charles both held this view.[29] Bousset's major argument in support of this conclusion is that two stages of the Nero legend appear side-by-side in this chapter. Now it is very likely the case, as was suggested above, that the author of Revelation took over the Nero legend and modified it. But it is not so easy to separate two different forms of the legend in chap. 17. According to Bousset, the source contained an older form of the legend, involving the return of the living Nero from the East with Parthian allies to regain power over Rome. But Nero is consistently referred to in this chapter as "the beast." This designation implies Revelation's own depiction of the eschatological Nero who ascends from the abyss. Revelation 17 certainly reflects an older form of the Nero legend, but it has already been absorbed by a new conception.

Charles posited two sources; one constituting the bulk of vv 1-10 and 18, the other found in vv 11-13, 17 and 16.[30] One of his stronger

[29]See note 20 above.
[30]Charles, *Revelation of St. John*, 2. 59-60.

arguments is that the word order of vv 11-17 is distinctly non-Semitic, whereas in most of Revelation it is quite Semitic.[31] This argument does not affect the passage about the kings. In terms of content, he argues that the twofold interpretation of the seven heads (mountains and kings) is a sign of dual authorship.[32] He implies that an image could not possibly have more than one meaning for a single author. The same reasoning underlies his other prominent argument on the basis of content: the beast seems to represent the Roman empire in vv 3 and 7, whereas later in the chapter, it represents Nero.[33] These arguments presume that the author of Revelation and his contemporaries used images in a simple manner involving exclusive, one-to-one relationships between signifier and thing signified. It is unlikely that such was the case.[34] The very fact that the author could compose or edit chap. 13 in such a way that the beast represents both Nero and the Roman empire makes such an assumption unlikely.

The arguments in favor of recoverable sources in chap. 17 do not seem very strong. It is, on the other hand, highly probable that earlier traditions were used in its composition. The motif of a beast's seven heads representing seven kings may be such a traditional element.[35] It is unlikely, however, that the author simply took over this tradition without applying it to his own situation, as both Bousset and Charles suggest.[36] The remark that the beast who will return is the eighth and belongs to the seven implies that the author has made some calculations and that the numbers are meaningful for him.

The theory that the author was not actually writing under the "one (who) is" takes another form, namely, that he antedated his work. The main argument supporting this theory (apart from the desire to harmonize chap. 17 with Irenaeus' dating) is that such antedating is a common device in apocalyptic literature. Many Jewish apocalypses are indeed antedated. But usually the entire work is clearly set in an earlier time and the seer is a venerable figure of the distant past. Revelation does not have these characteristics. The function of antedating is usually to allow for prophecies after the fact, so that the book gains authority. It is unlikely that Rev 17:10 has such a function. No other passage in the book clearly functions in that way. This passage is too minor and too obscure to be an impressive example of predictive reliability.

[31]Ibid., 56.
[32]Ibid., 68-69.
[33]Ibid., 58-59.
[34]See J. J. Collins, "The Symbolism of Transcendence in Jewish Apocalyptic," *BR* 19 (1974) 5-22.
[35]At least the motif of a seven-headed beast is traditional; Yarbro Collins, *The Combat Myth in the Book of Revelation*, 77, 79.
[36]Charles, *Revelation of St. John*, 2.70; Bousset, *Offenbarung Johannis*, 479.

The two forms of the second position are both untenable. There is little evidence for the use of sources in chap. 17. Even if the motif of the seven kings is traditional, the context implies that the numbering was understood by the author in a way meaningful for his own situation. The theory that the author antedated his work is not persuasive, because no plausible function for such a technique is apparent.

The third basic position is that the seven heads do not represent all the emperors who reigned up to the author's time, but only a selection. E.-B. Allo argued that the heads represent consecutive emperors beginning with Nero, the first to show open hostility to the Church.[37] A. Strobel theorized that the first head is Caligula. He argued that Rev 17:9-12 reflects a theology of history in which the death and exaltation of Christ constitute the turning point from the old to the new aeon. The list of emperors could only begin, therefore, with the first to come to power after Jesus' death, Caligula (37-41 C.E.).[38] Lyder Brun also concluded that the first head is Caligula. In support of this contention, he pointed to the fact that Caligula was the first emperor to instigate serious trouble for the Jews.[39] The attempt to set his statue up in the temple must have reminded the Jews of the sacrilege of Antiochus Epiphanes. Both Josephus and Philo witness to the deep impression Caligula's policy made.

Some form of this third position is the most likely explanation of the meaning of the seven kings for the author of Revelation. The analogy of 2 Esdras 11-12 makes it plausible that the heads represent selected emperors who were particularly feared and hated. Caligula is a natural starting point, given the close affinities between Revelation and contemporary Jewish anti-Roman literature. Nero, hated by Jews and Christians alike, would obviously be included. Vespasian and Titus, as the destroyers of Jerusalem, would certainly have been included. Domitian would probably have been included, at least as the son of Vespasian. It is impossible to say with certainty what the author had in mind. The most likely hypothesis is that he began counting with Caligula and included the following emperors in sequence, omitting Galba, Otho and Vitellius, as reigning too short a time to cause trouble for the saints. The five would then be Caligula, Claudius, Nero, Vespasian and Titus. Domitian would be the "one (who) is." A seventh was expected to fill out the traditional number seven. The prediction that the last emperor would have a short reign probably arose from the intense expectation of the eschatological climax in the near future.

[37]Allo, *Saint Jean: L'Apocalypse*, 281.
[38]Strobel, "Abfassung und Geschichtstheologie der Apokalypse nach Kap. XVII. 9-12," 437-39.
[39]Brun, "Die römischen Kaiser in der Apokalypse," 136-38.

The motif of the seven kings does not by any means point decisively to a date earlier than the reign of Domitian. It is improbable that the kings mentioned are intended to include all the emperors up to the writer's time. The motif may be traditional, but the context shows that it was meaningful for the author. If the "list" was not meant to be exhaustive, it could easily be updated by subsequent reinterpretation. This passage, therefore, does not establish a Domitianic date, but is compatible with it.

The Temple in Jerusalem

Rev 11:1-13, especially vv 1-2, seems to imply that the earthly, historical temple in Jerusalem is still standing. Before the technique of source-criticism was applied regularly to Revelation, that is before 1882, this passage was used to date the book as a whole before 70 C.E.[40] J. A. T. Robinson has attempted recently to revive that argument.[41] He sees 11:1-13 as a unity, composed by the author of Revelation. He interprets the measuring as a command that the temple be purified. That purification is part of the final call to repentance issued by the two witnesses. Robinson finds it incredible that the passage was written after the destruction of Jerusalem in 70, since only a tenth of the city falls (v 13) and by an earthquake, not an enemy's attacks.

The first question is whether vv 1-2 and vv 3-13 are a unity, that is, whether they were originally composed as a continuous passage. The alternative is that the passage (vv 1-13) was composed by joining two sources or two separate traditions. The latter alternative is the more probable. The connection between the two is loose and external. The only obvious link is that the scene is Jerusalem in both. The time periods mentioned in each section are equivalent, but the repetition is a seam, as it were, joining the two sources. The first section focuses on the temple, but the second does not mention the temple at all.

The next question which must be raised in considering Robinson's theory is whether the two sections were rather freely formulated by the author of Revelation on the basis of tradition, or whether he adapted oral or written sources whose wording was relatively fixed. In both cases, it is likely that the author was using a source. The references in v 2 to the outer courtyard and to the Gentiles trampling the courtyard and city make it probable that the first section originally referred to the historical temple in Jerusalem. It is conceivable that v 1 was originally composed with an allegorical or spiritual meaning. The temple of God, the altar and the worshippers in it (presumably the temple) could easily have several layers of meaning. It would not be surprising if a figurative

---

[40]Bousset, *Offenbarung Johannis*, 128, 147.
[41]Robinson, *Redating the New Testament*, 238-42.

meaning were primary. V 2, on the other hand, has much too concrete and historical a surface meaning to have been composed with any other sort of primary reference.[42]

If it is the historical temple which is being discussed, one must then determine what is being said about it. A. Feuillet has argued that the wording of v 2 makes a historical or literal meaning impossible.[43] How, he asks, could a courtyard be "cast out"?; in any case it is already said to be "outside." *Ekbale exōthen* need not, however, be translated in the physical sense. According to Liddell-Scott-Jones, *ekballō* can have the sense "reject."[44] In this context, "leave out," or "leave aside," would seem to be legitimate translations.

The symbolic act of measuring was used in the Hebrew Bible to express a wide variety of meanings: rebuilding, restoring, judgment, destruction, and preservation.[45] Since the image was used for opposite meanings in different contexts, the meaning here must be determined primarily from the context. The outer courtyard is not measured and it is given over to the Gentiles; they will trample the holy city for forty-two months. So the courtyard is at least to be controlled by the Gentiles. Perhaps it is to be profaned or even destroyed as well. Since the outer courtyard is not measured and the temple, altar and worshippers are measured, the destiny of the latter must be the opposite. So the temple, altar and worshippers are to escape the control of the Gentiles (and possibly profanation and destruction as well).

The language implies a situation of military conflict.[46] It fits well the situation described by Josephus in book six of *The Jewish War*, when Titus and his legions had broken through the walls of the outer temple, by firing the gates. After establishing access to the outer temple, Titus ordered the fire put out and held a council of war with his generals to decide whether or not to destroy the sanctuary itself. The insurgents had made the temple their citadel and had been resisting the Romans from there. Titus decided not to destroy the temple, but his soldiers were carried away by passion and set fire to it against his orders. When the sanctuary was in flames, the soldiers decided they might as well set fire to what remained of the outbuildings. Josephus records the following incident which occurred in the process:

> Next they came to the last surviving colonnade of the Outer Temple. On this women and children and a mixed crowd of citizens had found a

[42]So also Bousset, *Offenbarung Johannis*, 373-75.
[43]A. Feuillet, "Essai d'interpretation du chapître XI de l'Apocalypse," *NTS* 4 (1957-58) 186-87.
[44]LSJ 501 (9th ed., 1940).
[45]Charles, *Revelation of St. John*, 1. 274-76.
[46]This was seen by J. Wellhausen; his work is cited by Charles, ibid., 270.

refuge—6,000 in all. Before Caesar could reach a decision about them or instruct his officers, the soldiers, carried away by their fury, fired the colonnade from below; as a result some flung themselves out of the flames to their death, others perished in the blaze: of that vast number there escaped not one. Their destruction was due to a false prophet who that very day had declared to the people in the City that God commanded them to go up into the temple to receive the signs of their deliverance. A number of hireling prophets had been put up in recent days by the party chiefs to deceive the people by exhorting them to await help from God, and so reduce the number of deserters and buoy up with hope those who were above fear and anxiety (*J.W.* 6. 283-86).[47]

Josephus' negative interpretation of the motives of the prophets he mentions may be due, at least in part, to his negative judgment on the Jewish resistance. It is likely that some of those prophets spoke and acted in good faith. This general context provides a plausible background for the prophecy of Rev 11:1-2. When the prophecy was not fulfilled on the literal level, it seems to have been handed on with one or more new interpretations.

It is unlikely that the author of Revelation in its present form could have composed 11:1-2. There is no positive interest in the historical, earthly temple elsewhere in the book. In 3:12 the phrase "the temple of God" (*ho naos tou theou*) is used in quite a different way. Christ promises that he will make the one who conquers a pillar in the temple of God. This language implies that the author of Revelation conceives of the Christian community, either in his own time or in the new age, as the real or new temple of God. Such a conception is most understandable after the historical temple had been destroyed. In the visions of the body of the book, apart from 11:1-2, the temple of God refers to the temple in heaven (7:15; 11:19; 14:15, 17; 15:5, 6, 8; 16:1, 17). In the final vision, the vision of the new Jerusalem, it is explicitly stated that there is no temple in the city (21:22). The lack of a temple probably reflects the destruction of the historical temple, as well as the attitude that no restoration of the temple is necessary.

It is also unlikely that the author of Revelation, composing freely, would have referred to the earthly, historical Jerusalem as "the holy city" (11:2). The writer's positive concern is for "the new Jerusalem, which comes down out of heaven" (3:12). It is the heavenly Jerusalem which the author calls the holy city (21:2, 10). The earthly Jerusalem is referred to later in chap. 11 as Sodom and Egypt, the place where the Lord was crucified (v 8).

[47]The translation cited is by G. A. Williamson (rev. ed.; Baltimore: Penguin, 1970) 348.

The evidence, therefore, is strongly against the theory that Rev 11:1-2 was composed by the author of the book as a whole. There are also good reasons for holding that a source was used in 11:3-13. The passage contains a significant number of linguistically distinctive elements, compared with the rest of the book.[48] The content of the passage is best understood as the author's adaptation of traditional material about the conflict between two eschatological prophets and the eschatological adversary.[49]

The task of dating the source used in 11:3-13 is made difficult by the fact that it was edited by the author of Revelation.[50] Little certainty can be achieved about precisely what should be attributed to the source and what to the author. Reasonable certainty about the use of a source does not imply the ability to reconstruct the source. Robinson argues that the passage presupposes a pre-70 situation; Jerusalem is assumed to be standing.[51] Bousset and Charles were of the same opinion.[52] This assumption is questionable. Much of Jerusalem was indeed leveled by Titus and his troops in 70. But a legion was stationed there, probably with an ancillary civilian population.[53] It is likely that a considerable number of Jews and Christians returned to the city after the war, and that some rebuilding took place.[54] In fact, a setting in Jerusalem after 70 makes sense of the description of the witnesses' foes as (some) from the peoples and tribes and tongues and nations (v 9) and as those who dwell upon the earth (v 10). Such descriptions fit Jerusalem better after 70 than before. There is no compelling reason to date either the source or Rev 11:3-13 in its present form to a time prior to 70 c.e.

Even if the author of Revelation was using sources in 11:1-13, he must have interpreted them in a way that made sense for his own situation. It is likely that the opposition between the Church as the true Jews and those Jews who did not accept Jesus as the Christ played some role in the author's understanding of the prophecy of 11:1-2. The references to Jews as a synagogue of Satan in 2:9 and 3:9 attest to the

[48]Charles, *Revelation of St. John*, 1. 271-73; see the discussion of his arguments in Yarbro Collins, *The Combat Myth in the Book of Revelation*, 195 n. 60.

[49]Bousset, *Offenbarung Johannis*, 382-87.

[50]Yarbro Collins, *The Combat Myth in the Book of Revelation*, 196 n. 61.

[51]Robinson, *Redating the New Testament*, 240-42.

[52]Bousset, *Offenbarung Johannis*, 386; Charles, *Revelation of St. John*, 1. 271.

[53]E. M. Smallwood, *The Jews under Roman Rule* (SJLA 20; Leiden: Brill, 1976) 346, 433.

[54]G. Stemberger ("Die sogenannte 'Synode von Jabne' und das frühe Christentum," *Kairos* 19 [1977] 17) wants to minimize the evidence, but cites it nevertheless.

vehemence of the author's feelings on this subject. But Feuillet seems to go too far in identifying the worshippers in the temple with the Church and the outer courtyard with the unbelieving Jews.[55] There is little support for such an explicit allegorical interpretation elsewhere in the book. It seems more likely that the author reinterpreted the inner/outer distinction of the text with his own heavenly/earthly polarity. The outer courtyard would then represent the earthly Jerusalem and temple which have been given over to the Gentiles. The temple itself, the altar and worshippers would represent the heavenly temple which the Gentiles cannot control, profane or destroy. In the background looms the tragic events of 70 c.e. But the symbolic measuring is still a source of hope; not any longer for rescue from the military power of the Romans, but for heavenly vindication.

This passage about the fate of the earthly Jerusalem introduces the appearance of the two witnesses. The narrative of vv 3-13 also reflects tragic events, the death of Jesus and the rejection of his message. But hope is expressed here also. As Jesus was raised, so will the two witnesses. But this time, the resurrection will take place in view of the enemies and they will repent (11:11-13). The narrative of the witnesses probably functioned as a paradigm of their own destiny for the earliest readers of Revelation.

Domitian and the Christians

The date a commentator is inclined to assign to Revelation has a good deal to do with his or her understanding of the function of the book. J. A. T. Robinson, for example, dates the book to 68 or 69 c.e. One of his reasons is that the author must have experienced the Neronian persecution firsthand, in Rome itself. He writes "One thing of which we may be certain is that the Apocalypse, unless the product of a perfervid and psychotic imagination, was written out of an intense experience of the Christian suffering at the hands of the imperial authorities, represented by the 'beast' of Babylon."[56] Robinson makes a large assumption and seems to forget how relative "an intense experience" can be. Other interpreters date the book of Revelation to the time of Domitian and argue that there was or must have been massive and systematic persecution of Christians during his reign.[57]

The evidence for persecution of Christians under Domitian is rather slight. Doubt is cast on the early Christian tradition about Domitian as

[55]Feuillet, "Essai d'interpretation du chapître XI de l'Apocalypse," 187.

[56]Robinson, *Redating the New Testament*, 230-31.

[57]W. G. Kümmel, *Introduction to the New Testament* (14th ed.; Nashville: Abingdon, 1966) 327-29 and the commentators listed by E. S. Fiorenza, "Apocalyptic and Gnosis in the Book of Revelation and Paul," *JBL* 92 (1973) 565 n. 3.

the second persecutor by its probable apologetic function.[58] The persons named as victims of this persecution seem to have been, at most, sympathizers of Judaism or God-fearers. The conclusion that they were Christians is unwarranted.[59] Suetonius praises Nero for his repression of the Christians. If Domitian also had taken steps against Christians as such, Suetonius would probably have mentioned the fact.[60]

A number of other early Christian texts are referred to often as further evidence for a persecution under Domitian. 1 Peter clearly reflects some degree of persecution, but its date is uncertain.[61] The allusion to Rome as Babylon shows that it was written after 70 C.E.[62] But there is no compelling reason to prefer a Domitianic date to other possibilities. Nothing in Hebrews points to more than the usual harassment to which Christians were exposed from time to time in the first two centuries. The allusion to misfortunes and calamities (*symphoras kai periptōseis*) in 1 Clement 1 is so vague that it need not refer to persecution at all.

There seems, therefore, to be no reliable evidence which supports the theory that Domitian persecuted Christians as Christians. Nevertheless, as indicated in connection with the letter to the Hebrews above, Christians were harassed sporadically from time to time in the first two centuries. The fact that the founder of The Way had been crucified by the Romans already in itself made the earliest Christians and their communities suspect. The letters of Paul and the book of Acts attest to a pattern of events which begins with controversy between Christians and Jews and leads, via Jewish initiative, to the involvement of Roman officials. Acts 16:16-24 and 19:23-41 show that Gentiles sometimes took the initiative in either unofficial harassment or denunciation of Christians to Roman authorities.[63]

The study of the relationship between the early Christians and Roman officials in the first century is very complex and controversial

[58]See the discussion of Melito above in the section on the external evidence; see also Moreau, "A propos de la persécution de Domitien," 121-29; E. M. Smallwood, "Domitian's Attitude Toward the Jews and Judaism," *Classical Philology* 51 (1956) 1-2; G. E. M. de Ste. Croix, "Why Were the Early Christians Persecuted?" *Past and Present* 26 (1963) 15.

[59]Smallwood, "Domitian's Attitude Toward Jews and Judaism," 1, 7-9; Bell, "The Date of John's Apocalypse," 94-96.

[60]So also Bell, "The Date of John's Apocalypse," 96.

[61]E. G. Selwyn, "The Persecutions in I Peter," *Bulletin of the Studiorum Novi Testamenti Societas* I (1950); reissued in a single volume with nos. 2-3 (1963) 39-50.

[62]So also Hunzinger, "Babylon als Deckname für Rom und die Datierung des I. Petrusbriefes," 67-77.

[63]See the discussion of Acts 16:19-40 by A. N. Sherwin-White, *Roman Society and Roman Law in the New Testament* (Oxford: Clarendon, 1963) 78-83.

because of the scarcity of evidence.[64] What evidence there is supports the theory of G. E. M. de Ste. Croix that the sporadic actions of the Roman "government" against Christians during this period were due primarily to the pressure of public opinion.[65] This negative public opinion was owing, ostensibly, to the belief that Christians were guilty of certain abominations (*flagitia*), such as incest and cannibalism. De Ste. Croix argues plausibly that such accusations only masked a deeper, truer reason, namely, that the Christians' refusal to worship any god but their own aroused pagan hostility. The pagans feared that this exclusiveness alienated the goodwill of the gods and endangered the wellbeing of nature and society. Such an attitude is easily demonstrated for the later period and it fits the discussions of Christians by Tacitus, Suetonius, Pliny and Trajan.

Few passages in Revelation clearly look back on persecution in the past. One of these is 1:9, which implies that the author was banished to Patmos because of his activities as a Christian prophet. Another is 2:13 which refers to Antipas' death at Pergamum, probably an execution ordered by the governor of the province of Asia.[66] The vision of the souls under the altar in 6:9-11 may refer to Christians who died before the moment of writing, but such a reference is not certain. The other allusions to persecution in the book cannot be used as evidence for events which have actually occurred or are occurring. The form of the vision account and the use of tenses in the book foreclose any easy conclusions about the relation of these texts to historical reality. It seems safest to conclude that most of the rest of the book expresses the author's expectation of persecution.

The passages which do refer clearly to cases of persecution in the past involve only two people. Further, these events could have taken place at almost any time in the first two centuries after the death of Jesus. There is, therefore, no compelling reason to understand Revelation

[64]See the summary of the history of scholarship and the suggested solution by A. N. Sherwin-White, "The Early Persecutions and Roman Law," Appendix V of *The Letters of Pliny: A Social and Historical Commentary* (Oxford: Clarendon, 1966) 772-87.

[65]De Ste. Croix, "Why Were the Early Christians Persecuted?" 6-38. See also the response by Sherwin-White ("Why Were the Early Christians Persecuted?—An Amendment") and the reply by de Ste. Croix ("Why Were the Early Christians Persecuted?—A Rejoinder") in *Past and Present* 27 (1964) 23-27 and 28-38.

[66]See the detailed discussion of these two passages by Yarbro Collins, "Persecution and Vengeance in the Book of Revelation," an essay which will be published in a volume of proceedings of the International Colloquium on Apocalypticism at Uppsala in August, 1979, edited by D. Hellholm.

as a reaction to any new or significant initiative of Roman authorities against Christians.

The theme of persecution in Revelation allows a date during the reign of Domitian, but does not establish it in and of itself. Another element in the book which has often been used to date it to Domitian's rule is the motif of ruler cult.[67] It is well known that Augustus followed a moderate policy on this score.[68] He allowed himself to be worshipped (while still living) in the provinces, as long as the cult included the worship of Rome as well. He did nothing to check private expressions of veneration. In Italy divinity could be ascribed to him only after death. Tiberius followed Augustus' precedent. Caligula, on the other hand, presented himself as a god even in Rome and had temples and sacrifices dedicated to his own divinity. He demanded oaths by his own genius and insisted that he be honored by the ritual of *proskynēsis*. The latter was a gesture of greeting offered by a social inferior to his superior. It originated in Persia and was considered as self-abasement by free Greeks and Romans. The act would probably have had connotations of worship as a gesture to a supposed god. Because of the allusions to Nero, Revelation cannot be dated to the time of Caligula. But the prominence of ruler cult in chap. 13 and the fact that Caligula was the first to exploit it increase the likelihood that he is the first king of 17:10.

Claudius attempted to return to the policy of Augustus, but apparently Caligula had set a new precedent, irresistible for some. Perhaps as flattery, certain Roman writers gave Claudius divine epithets. Nero associated himself closely with Hercules and Apollo and encouraged flattery of himself as divine. A date under Nero for Revelation is excluded by its reflection of his death and the legend of his return. Vespasian and Titus returned to Augustus' example.

Domitian took a position on ruler cult similar to those of Caligula and Nero. He let it be known that he wished to be called "our lord and god" (*dominus et deus noster*). This address apparently was used in both speech and writing.[69] It is perhaps no coincidence that Revelation uses that particular phrase for God ([*ho*] *kyrios kai ho theos hēmōn*; 4:11, 19:6) and other similar phrases (1:8, 4:8, 11:17, 15:3, 16:7, 18:8, 21:22, 22:5). The practice of *proskynēsis*, introduced by Caligula, was revived by at least one person who wished to flatter Domitian. According to Dio

---

[67]So, for example, Bousset (*Offenbarung Johannis*, 162-63) used the ruler cult to date Revelation to the reign of Domitian, at the earliest.

[68]For a summary of ruler cult from Augustus through Domitian, see M. P. Charlesworth, "Some Observations on Ruler-Cult Especially in Rome," *HTR* 28 (1935) 26-42.

[69]M. P. Charlesworth, *CAH* 11. 41; idem, "Some Observations on Ruler-Cult," 34-35.

Cassius, a certain Juventius Celsus was suspected of conspiracy by Domitian and saved himself by performing *proskynēsis* and calling the emperor "lord and god."[70] The gesture encouraged by Caligula and Domitian may be alluded to in Revelation's statements that people worship (*proskyneō*) the beast (13:4, 8, 12; 14:9, 11; 20:4).

From the time of Augustus it had been the custom to take an oath by the genius of the emperor. This act was voluntary and not official. There is evidence that under Domitian for the first time people began to swear by the genius of the living emperor in public documents. Flatterers apparently began to offer sacrifice voluntarily to Domitian's genius.[71]

When Christians were denounced before Pliny, the governor of Bithynia and Pontus, in about 112 C.E., some of them denied that they were Christians. Using what was apparently a standard test, Pliny asked them to repeat after him an invocation of the gods, to offer wine and incense to images of Trajan and of the gods, and to curse Christ (*Epist. ad Traj.* 10.96). M. P. Charlesworth hypothesized that Domitian made the voluntary action of sacrificing to the genius of the living emperor into a test of loyalty. Anyone accused or suspected of disloyalty could save himself or herself by offering sacrifice before the image of the emperor. If a person refused, he or she could be charged with *atheotēs* (neglect of the worship of the gods).[72] If, however, de Ste. Croix is correct that the reason Christians were persecuted was their neglect of the worship of the gods, the test described by Pliny could have originated quite spontaneously in the provinces. Then the worship of the emperor, from the pagan point of view, would have been quite an incidental matter. The practice of Caligula, Nero and Domitian would probably have encouraged the inclusion of the living emperor's image among those of the other gods, but the worship of the emperor would not have been the central point.

The persecution reflected in Revelation, the banishment of the author and the execution of Antipas, seems to be nothing more than an example of the usual, sporadic repression suffered by the Christians from time to time in the first two centuries. It is doubtful that the emperor cult was forced upon Christians at any time during the first and early second centuries, including the reigns of Domitian and Trajan. The book of Revelation cannot be understood as a response to a new initiative against the Christians taken by Roman authorities. A more

[70]Kenneth Scott, *The Imperial Cult under the Flavians* (Stuttgart: Kohlhammer, 1936; reprinted, New York: Arno, 1975) 111; Charlesworth, "Some Observations on Ruler-Cult," 18-19, 33.

[71]Charlesworth, *CAH* 11. 42; idem, "Some Observations on Ruler-Cult," 33.

[72]Charlesworth, *CAH* 11. 42; idem, "Some Observations on Ruler-Cult," 32-34.

plausible view of its function is that it was written to awaken and intensify Christian exclusiveness, particularly vis-à-vis the imperial cult. The remark in Rev 13:15, that the beast from the land caused to be slain those who would not worship the image of the beast from the sea, is probably a purposely selective view of the standard cultic test described by Pliny. It is well known that the cities of Asia Minor supported the imperial cult enthusiastically.[73] After persistently seeking the honor, Ephesus was allowed to establish a temple and cult of Domitian as a god (*theos*) during his lifetime.[74] Domitian's heightened claims to divinity and his encouragement of the worship of his person was probably the occasion for the author of Revelation to view the Roman emperor as the adversary of God on the model of Antiochus Epiphanes.

The Seven Messages

Before considering the evidence of the seven messages for the date of Revelation, one must discuss the question of their literary relationship to the rest of the book. R. H. Charles concluded that they were written by the same author as the body of the work, because of the similarity in diction and idiom. He also concluded that they were written earlier than the other portions of Revelation.[75] His major warrant for this conclusion was that the messages contain two conflicting expectations of the end of the world. On the one hand, the congregations are expected to survive until Christ's last advent. This idea, according to Charles, is expressed in the exhortation to some in Thyatira "to hold fast what you have until I come" (2:25) and in the warning "I will come as a thief" (3:3).[76] On the other hand, the promise to the congregation in Philadelphia, "I will keep you from the hour of trial which is about to come upon the whole earth to test those who dwell upon the earth," presupposes, according to Charles, a world-wide persecution in which all the faithful would suffer martyrdom.[77] Charles interpreted 3:10 in light of chap. 7 and other passages. He argued that the 144,000 are sealed to preserve them from demons, but not from physical death. Charles felt that the expectation of survival until the parousia and the expectation of universal martyrdom were mutually exclusive. Therefore, 3:10 must be a later addition to the messages from a time when the author's expectations had changed.

Charles was probably correct in concluding that certain statements in the seven messages reflect the expectation that some Christians would

[73]Swete, *The Apocalypse of St. John,* lxxxix-xci.
[74]Scott, *The Imperial Cult under the Flavians,* 96.
[75]Charles, *Revelation of St. John,* 1. 37-46.
[76]Ibid., 43.
[77]Ibid., 44.

survive until the parousia. But his thesis that chaps. 4-22 presuppose the martyrdom of all Christians goes beyond the evidence.[78] If the author did not expect all Christians to die in a world-wide persecution, the contradiction evaporates.

Charles also put forward a supporting argument for the theory that the messages are earlier than the rest of the book. He interpreted Revelation to mean that a world-wide persecution was to arise in connection with the imperial cult. He found no reference to that cult in the messages, a fact which led him to conclude that they must have been written "before the fundamental antagonism of the Church and the State came to be realized. . . ."[79]

In the discussion of the imperial cult above, it was argued that the persecutions already experienced by Christians were not due primarily to conflict between Christians and Roman authorities over the imperial cult. The punitive actions of the Roman officials had the usual, more general causes. The emphasis on the imperial cult in Revelation is probably due to the author's selection of that issue as a negative rallying point for Christians. If the imperial cult was not an objectively significant problem for the congregations in Asia Minor, it is not surprising that it receives little emphasis in the messages. It was suggested above that the author's intention in polemicizing against the ruler cult was to heighten the exclusiveness of Christians vis-à-vis pagan culture. If that suggestion is correct, then the function of the body of the book and the messages are similar. A major concern of the messages is to refute the position of the Nicolaitans, Balaam and Jezebel. These people apparently were teaching the Christians in Ephesus, Pergamum and Thyatira to accommodate themselves to the pagan culture for economic, political and social reasons.[80]

Charles's theory that the messages were composed earlier than the rest of the book led him to incline toward the theory that they were originally seven letters actually sent to the seven congregations.[81] To make this theory plausible, he had to hypothesize that the endings and parts of the beginnings of the messages were added later to link them with the rest of the book.[82] There is little evidence to support such a theory and its correlative hypothesis. The messages lack the conventional opening and closing of contemporary letters. They are highly

[78]See the discussion by I. H. Marshall, "Martyrdom and Parousia in the Revelation of John," *Studia Evangelica* 4 (ed. F. L. Cross; TU 102; Berlin: Akademie, 1968) 332.
[79]Charles, *Revelation of St. John*, 1. 44.
[80]See the discussion by Yarbro Collins, "Persecution and Vengeance in the Book of Revelation."
[81]Charles, *Revelation of St. John*, 1. 46-47.
[82]Ibid., 44-46.

stylized and all have the same form. It seems more reasonable to suppose that they were composed for their present context.[83]

The seven messages contain little that points to a date with any precision. In his letter to the Philippians, Polycarp states, "For concerning you he (Paul) boasts in all the Churches who then alone had known the Lord, for we had not yet known him" (11:3). Polycarp, bishop of Smyrna in the first half of the second century, implies that the congregation in Smyrna was founded later than the one in Philippi. Some commentators argue on this basis that the message to Smyrna, and thus Revelation as a whole, could not have been written as early as the 60s.[84] This argument is not compelling, but Polycarp's remark does favor a date after 70 for Revelation.

In the message to Smyrna, the following remark is made in reference to the local Jews: "and (I know) the blasphemy of those who say that they are Jews, and are not, but are a synagogue of Satan" (2:9). A similar comment is made about the Jews of Philadelphia (3:9). These comments imply great hostility between at least some Christians and Jews of Asia Minor. At the same time, the author of Revelation, and perhaps other Christians also, claimed the name "Jew" for himself and his fellow Christians. Robinson argues that such a claim presupposes a time when "the final separation of Christians and Jews had not yet taken place."[85] He apparently believes that the final separation occurred in 70 C.E. with the destruction of the temple. Günter Stemberger argues that the definitive break, from the Christian point of view, took place already with the acceptance of the Gentile mission.[86] Other scholars consider the so-called Synod of Jamnia, dated between 80 and 90, to be the turning point.[87] The separation between Jews and Christians cannot be understood as a simple event which took place at a single moment in time and which held for every locality. The separation was gradual and very likely relative to individual perceptions and to the particular circumstances of each geographical area. The indirect claim in Rev 2:9 and 3:9 that Christians are the true Jews is not a reliable indication of date.

---

[83]So also F. Hahn, "Die Sendschreiben der Johannesapokalypse," in *Tradition und Glaube. Das frühe Christentum in seiner Umwelt. Festgabe für Karl Georg Kuhn zum 65. Geburtstag* (ed. G. Jeremias. H. -W. Kuhn and H. Stegemann; Göttingen: Vandenhoeck und Ruprecht, 1971) 362.

[84]This argument is criticized by Robinson (*Redating the New Testament*, 229-30).

[85]Ibid., 227-28.

[86]Stemberger, "Die sogenannte "Synode von Jabne" und das frühe Christentum," 19.

[87]J. L. Martyn, *History and Theology in the Fourth Gospel* (New York: Harper & Row, 1968) 31-41; R. E. Brown, *The Community of the Beloved Disciple* (New York: Paulist, 1979) 22.

Laodicea suffered a serious earthquake in 60/61 C.E. Nevertheless, it is addressed in Revelation as an affluent Church. The earthquake is not mentioned or alluded to in Revelation. These facts have been used by different scholars to support widely differing dates.[88] The fact that the citizens did not need imperial help to rebuild is an indication that a date in the late 60's is not impossible. This bit of evidence is of no help in dating the book.

CONCLUSION

The strongest external evidence for the date of Revelation is the testimony of Irenaeus. He says that the Apocalypse was seen at the end of the reign of Domitian. He probably considered it to have been written down at about the same time. Irenaeus' comment refers to a date of approximately 90-95 C.E.

The clearest internal evidence in Revelation is the use of the name Babylon for Rome. In Jewish literature this name is explicitly associated with Rome as the second destroyer of Jerusalem. The symbolic name Babylon for Rome was probably taken over by the author of Revelation from Jewish tradition. Its use thus indicates a date after 70 C.E.

The motif of the seven kings in chap. 17 can be interpreted in a variety of ways. The usual assumption that they represent all the emperors up to the author's time leads to insurmountable difficulties. Further, it is not necessarily supported by the parallel texts usually cited. There are insufficient grounds for holding that the author used an earlier source for 17:10 or that he antedated his work. The most likely interpretation is that the seven kings are selected emperors, beginning with Caligula, the first emperor to come into significant conflict with the Jews and the first to present himself as a god in his own lifetime in Rome. The king "(who) is" is probably Domitian.

The prophecy in 11:1-2 that the temple would in some sense be preserved from the Gentiles refers to the historical temple in Jerusalem and constitutes a source taken over by the author of Revelation. It dates just prior to the destruction of the temple. The author of the book as a whole interpreted it in terms of the heavenly temple. The narrative about the two witnesses (11:3-13) is also based on a source, but that source need not be dated prior to 70.

There is insufficient evidence to warrant the conclusion that Domitian persecuted Christians as Christians. The past incidents of persecution reflected in Revelation are best explained as typical of the sporadic opposition encountered by Christians in the first two centuries. It is doubtful that the emperor cult was forced on Christians at any time in the first or early second centuries, including the reigns of Domitian and

[88]See the discussion by Robinson (*Redating the New Testament*, 230).

Trajan. But Domitian's policy on ruler cult seems to have been the occasion for the author of Revelation to call for intensified Christian exclusiveness over against the surrounding pagan culture.

The seven messages were probably composed by the author of the book as a whole at about the same time as the rest of the work. Their lack of emphasis on the imperial cult is not surprising, if that cult was not being forced on Christians systematically. The messages nevertheless function in a way similar to the visions. They attack the policy of accommodation apparently supported by the Nicolaitans, Balaam and Jezebel and thus reinforce Christian exclusiveness.

The use of the name Babylon for Rome and the use of temple language for phenomena other than the physical temple are internal indications of a date after 70. No compelling reason exists to reject Irenaeus' testimony to the date. Ambiguous passages with relevance for the date can be interpreted plausibly against the background of Domitian's reign. That background provides a credible context for the book's content and function.

The tradition-historical method helps the interpreter discover mythic elements in Revelation, such as the chaos beast in 11:7, 13:1-10 and chap. 17. Appreciation of these elements and their function helps one sense the depth of Revelation's images and their wide spectrum of nuances. The contemporary-historical method allows a more precise reconstruction of the historical context of the book than mere inference from the text itself. The results achieved by applying this method to Revelation in this study suggest that the author was taking a much more active role than is usually thought. Rather than simply consoling his fellow Christians in a situation of grave crisis, he wrote his book to point out a crisis which many of them did not perceive.

Bibliography

of the writings of

FRANK MOORE CROSS

HANCOCK PROFESSOR OF
HEBREW AND OTHER ORIENTAL LANGUAGES

HARVARD UNIVERSITY

December, 1979

1947

1. "The Tabernacle: A Study from an Archaeological and Historical Approach," *BA* 10 (1947) 45-68.
2. "A Note on Deuteronomy 33:26," with D. N. Freedman, *BASOR* 108 (1947) 6f.

1948

3. "The Blessing of Moses," with D. N. Freedman, *JBL* 67 (1948) 191-210.
4. "Review of the *Westminster Study Edition of the Bible*," *McCormick Speaking* 2:3 (Dec., 1948) 12f.

1949

5. "The Newly Discovered Scrolls in the Hebrew University Museum in Jerusalem," *BA* 12 (1949) 36-46.

1950

6. "Notes on a Canaanite Psalm in the Old Testament," *BASOR* 117 (1950) 19-21.
7. "Review of *The Bible and Modern Belief* by H. Wallis," *Religious Education* 45 (1950) 121f.

1951

8. "The Third-person Pronominal Suffix in Phoenician," with D. N. Freedman, *JNES* 10 (1951) 228-30.
9. "Review of *Hebrew Origins* by Theophile Meek," *Journal of Bible and Religion* 19 (1951) 156.
10. "The Blessed Poor," *McCormick Speaking* 5:3 (Dec., 1951) 7-10.

1952

11. *Early Hebrew Orthography: A Study of the Epigraphic Evidence*, with D. N. Freedman (AOS 36; New Haven: American Oriental Society, 1952), vii + 77 pp.

12. "Ugaritic DB²AT and Hebrew Cognates," *VT* 2 (1952) 163f.

13. "Notes on the *Revised Standard Old Testament*," *McCormick Speaking* 6:2 (Nov., 1952) 7-10.

14. "Review of *The Hebrew Scrolls from the Neighborhood of Jericho and the Dead Sea* by G. R. Driver," *CH* 21 (1952) 273.

1953

15. "Josiah's Revolt Against Assyria," with D. N. Freedman, *JNES* 12 (1953) 56-58.

16. "A Royal Psalm of Thanksgiving: II Samuel 22 = Psalm 18," with D. N. Freedman, *JBL* 72 (1953) 15-34.

17. "Review of *Beginning in Archaeology* by Kathleen M. Kenyon, and *Die Welt des Alten Testaments: Einführung in die Grenzgebiete der alttestamentlichen Wissenschaft* by Martin Noth," *BA* 16 (1953) 43f.

18. "The Council of Yahweh in Second Isaiah," *JNES* 12 (1953) 274-77.

19. "A New Qumran Biblical Fragment Related to the Original Hebrew Underlying the Septuagint," *BASOR* 132 (1953) 15-26.

1954

20. "The Manuscripts of the Dead Sea Caves," *BA* 17 (1954) 2-21.

21. "Inscribed Javelin-heads from the Period of the Judges: A Recent Discovery in Palestine," with J. T. Milik, *BASOR* 134 (1954) 11-14.

22. "The Evolution of the Proto-Canaanite Alphabet," *BASOR* 134 (1954) 15-24.

23. "Notes on Recent Research in Palestine," *McCormick Speaking* 7:8 (May, 1954) 11, 14.

24. "Les rouleaux de la Mer Morte," *Evidences* 6:41 (Juin-Juillet, 1954), 5-12 [translation of no. 20].

25. "Review of *The Biblical Doctrine of Man in Society* by G. Ernest Wright," *McCormick Speaking* 8:2 (Nov., 1954) 16.

26. "The Banquet of the Kingdom," *McCormick Speaking* 8:3 (Dec., 1954) 7-10.

1955

27. Articles: "Inscriptions, Ancient Hebrew and Related Syro-Palestinian," "Writing, Ancient Hebrew," and "Yahweh," with D. N. Freedman, *Twentieth Century Encyclopedia of Religious Knowledge* (2 vols.; ed. L. A. Loetscher; Grand Rapids, 1955).

28. "The Scrolls from the Judean Wilderness," *The Christian Century* 72:31 (August 3, 1955) 889-91.

29. "The Scrolls and the Old Testament," *The Christian Century* 72:32 (August 10, 1955) 948ff.

30. "The Essenes and Their Master," *The Christian Century* 72:33 (August 17, 1955) 954f.

31. "The Scrolls and the New Testament," *The Christian Century* 72:34 (August 24, 1955) 968-71.

32. "The Oldest Manuscripts from Qumran," *JBL* 74 (1955) 147-72.

33. "Geshem The Arabian, Enemy of Nehemiah," *BA* 18 (1955) 46f.

34. "Archaeological News and Views," *BA* 18 (1955) 79f.

35. Translation, with J. S. Hazelton, of *"The Nabateans: a Historical Sketch,"* by Jean Starcky, *BA* 18 (1955) 82-106.

36. "From Manuscripts Found in a Cave," a review article of *The Scrolls from the Dead Sea*, by Edmund Wilson, *The New York Times Book Review* (Oct. 16, 1955) 1, 31.

37. "The Song of Miriam," with D. N. Freedman, *JNES* 14 (1955) 237-50.

38. "A Footnote to Biblical History," *McCormick Speaking* 9:2 (Nov., 1955) 7-10.

1956

39. "A Footnote to Biblical History," *BA* 19 (1956) 12-17, [reprinted from no. 38].

40. "A Report on the Biblical Fragments of Cave Four in the Wâdî Qumrân," *BASOR* 141 (1956) 9-13.

41. "The Scrolls from the Judaean Desert," *Archaeology* 9:1 (Spring, 1956) 41-53.

42. "La Lettre de Simon ben Kosba," *RB* 63 (1956) 45-48.

43. "La travail d'édition des fragments manuscrits de Qumran," *RB* 63 (1956) 49-67, esp. 56ff. (Communications by the several members of the Jerusalem staff editing scroll fragments.)

44. "Chronique archéologique: El Bouqei ͨah," with J. T. Milik, *RB* 63 (1956) 74-76.

45. "Explorations in the Judaean Buqei ͨah," with J. T. Milik, *BASOR* 142 (1956) 5-17.

46. "The Dead Sea Scrolls, Their Significance to Religious Thought: A Symposium," with M. Burrows, E. P. Arbez, W. F. Albright, A. Wilder, *et al.*, *The New Republic* (April 9, 1956) 12-25, esp. 17ff.

47. "Qumran Cave I," *JBL* 75 (1956) 121-25.

48. "The Boundary and Province Lists of the Kingdom of Judah," with G. E. Wright, *JBL* 75 (1956) 202-26.

49. "Review of the *Ancient Near East in Pictures* . . . , by J. B. Pritchard,"
    Archaeology 9 (Summer, 1956) 150f.
50. "Lachish Letter IV," *BASOR* 144 (1956) 24-26.
51. "McCormick's Rehnborg Collection of Dead Sea Scrolls," *McCormick
    Speaking* 10:4 (Dec., 1956) 7-10.
52. "Editing the Manuscript Fragments of Qumran," with P. Benoit, *et al.*,
    BA 19 (1956) 75-96, esp. pp. 83-86 [translation of no. 43].

1957

53. "The Dead Sea Scrolls," *IB* (Abingdon: Nashville, 1957) 12.645-67.
54. "Review of *Biblical Archaeology*, by G. Ernest Wright," *BA* 20 (1957) 79f.

1958

55. *The Ancient Library of Qumran and Modern Biblical Studies* (New York:
    Doubleday; London: Duckworth, 1958), xx + 196 pp.
56. "Epigraphik, semitische," *RGG*³ (ed. K. Galling, 1958) 2. cols. 523-26.
57. "Will you lie for God?" Convocation Address, Sept. 24, 1958, Occasional
    publication of the *Harvard Divinity School Bulletin.*

1959

58. "A Typological Study of the El Khaḍr Javelin and Arrow-heads," with
    J. T. Milik, *ADAJ* 3 (1956) 15-23.
59. "Report from the Dead Sea 'Scrollery'," *McCormick Speaking* 13:2 (Dec.,
    1959) 20-23.

1960

60. "Will Ye Speak Falsely for God?" *Contemporary Accents in Liberal
    Religion* (Boston: Beacon, 1960) 92-105.
61. "A Ugaritic Abecedary and the Origins of the Proto-Canaanite Alphabet,"
    with T. O. Lambdin, *BASOR* (1960) 21-26.

1961

62. "The Priestly Tabernacle," *BAR* 1 (ed. G. E. Wright and D. N. Freedman;
    Garden City: Doubleday, 1961) 201-28 [Revised form of No. 1].
63. "The Development of the Jewish Scripts," *The Bible and the Ancient
    Near East: Essays in Honor of William Foxwell Albright* (ed. G. E.
    Wright; New York: Doubleday, 1961) 133-202.
64. *The Ancient Library of Qumran*² (Garden City: Doubleday, 1961) xxii +
    260 pp. [cf. No. 55].
65. "The Study of the Old Testament at Harvard," with G. E. Wright,
    Harvard Divinity School Bulletin (April-July, 1961) 14-20.
66. "Epigraphic Notes on Hebrew Documents of the Eighth-Sixth Centuries
    B.C.: I. A New Reading of a Place Name in the Samaria Ostraca," *BASOR*
    163 (1961) 12-14.

1962

67. "Epigraphic Notes on Hebrew Documents of the Eighth-Sixth Centuries B.C.: 2. The Murabbᶜât Papyrus and the Letter Found Near Yabneh-yam," *BASOR* 165 (1962) 34-46.

68. "An Inscribed Seal from Balâṭah (Shechem)," *BASOR* 167 (1962) 14-15.

69. "Yahweh and the God of the Patriarchs," *HTR* 55 (1962; Nock Volume; ed. F. M. Cross and K. Stendahl) 225-59.

70. "An Archaic Inscribed Seal from the Valley of Aijalon [Soreq]," *BASOR* 168 (1962) 12-18.

71. "Epigraphic Notes on Hebrew Documents of the Eighth-Sixth Centuries B.C.: 3. The Inscribed Jar Handles from Gibeon," *BASOR* 168 (1962) 18-23.

72. "Excursus on the Palaeographical Dating of the Copper Document," *Les 'Petites Grottes' de Qumran* (*DJD* 3; ed. M. Baillet, J. T. Milik, *et al*; Oxford, 1962) 217-21 and Fig. 12.

1963

73. "The Discovery of the Samaria Papyri," *BA* 26 (1963) 110-21.

74. "The Discovery of the Samaria Papyri," *Christian News from Israel* 14 (1963) 24-35 [*manu secunda*; cf. No. 73].

1964

75. "The Name of Ashdod," with D. N. Freedman, *BASOR* 175 (1964) 48-50.

76. *Studies in Ancient Yahwistic Poetry*, with D. N. Freedman, (Johns Hopkins Dissertation, 1950; Photo-print; Ann Arbor, 1964), 358 pp.

77. "The History of the Biblical Text in the Light of the Discoveries in the Judaean Desert," *HTR* 57 (1964) 281-99.

78. "An Ostracon from Nebī Yūnis," *IEJ* 14 (1964) 185f., pl. 41H.

1965

79. "The Origin and Early Evolution of the Alphabet," Hebrew Abstract in *Mᶜrbw šl glyl wḥwp hglyl* (Jerusalem: I. E. S., 1965) 17-19. [The Nineteenth Archaeological Convention, ed. Israel Exploration Society].

80. *Scrolls from the Wilderness of the Dead Sea*: Catalogue of the Exhibit, The Dead Sea Scrolls of Jordan. Editor and contributor. [Published by the University of California for the American Schools of Oriental Research, 1965; Canadian edition (French and English) by the University of Toronto, 1965; British edition, by the British Museum, 1965]. 30 pp. + 19 plates.

1966

81. "The Divine Warrior in Israel's Early Cult," *Studies and Texts 3: Biblical Motifs* (ed. A. Altmann; Cambridge: Harvard University, 1966) 11-30.

82. "The Contribution of the Discoveries at Qumran to the Study of the Biblical Text," *IEJ* 16 (1966) 81-95.

83. "Aspects of Samaritan and Jewish History in Late Persian and Hellenistic Times," *HTR* 59 (1966) 201-11.

84. "An Aramaic Inscription from Daskyleion," *BASOR* 184 (1966) 7-10.

85. "Yahvé y el dios de los patriarcas," *Selecciones de teologia* 17 (1966) 56-60 [translation of no. 69].

86. "The History of the Biblical Text in the Light of Discoveries in the Judaean Desert"; "The Oldest Manuscripts from Qumrân"; and "A New Biblical Fragment Related to the Original Hebrew Underlying the Septuagint" [reprinted essays, nos. 77, 32, 19], *Readings on the History of the Bible Text in Recent Writing* (ed. S. Talmon; Jerusalem, 1966) 77-95, 217-54.

1967

87. "The Origin and Early Evolution of the Alphabet," *Eretz Israel* 8 [Sukenik Memorial Volume] (1967) 8*-24*.

88. "Piety and Politics," *CCar Journal* [Central Conference American Rabbis] (June, 1967) 28f.

89. *Die Antikebibliothek von Qumran und die moderne Biblische Wissenschaft* (Neukirchen-Vluyn: Neukirchener 1967), 232 pp. [German edition revised from 2nd English edition of no. 55 (+ Anhang, pp. 219-29)].

90. "The Scrolls from the Judaean Desert," *Archaeological Discoveries in the Holy Land* (New York, 1967) 157-67 [republication of No. 41].

1968

91. "Mesopotamia," "Egypt," "Syria-Palestine," "Anatolia" and "The Dead Sea Scrolls," *An Encyclopedia of World History* (4th ed.; ed. W. L. Langer; Boston, 1968) 27-50, 115-17.

92. "The Structure of the Deuteronomic History," *Perspectives in Jewish Learning* 3 (Annual of the College of Jewish Studies; Chicago, 1968) 9-24.

93. "The Song of the Sea and Canaanite Myth," *Journal for Theology and the Church* 5 (1968) 1-25.

94. "The Canaanite Cuneiform Tablet from Taanach," *BASOR* 190 (1968) 41-46.

95. "The Early History of the Qumrân Community," *McCormick Quarterly* 21 (1968) 249-64.

96. "The Priestly Tabernacle," *Old Testament Issues* (ed. S. Sandmel; New York, 1968) 39-67 [cf. No. 62].

97. "The Phoenician Inscription from Brazil: A Nineteenth Century Forgery," *Or* 37 (1968) 437-60.

98. "Jar Inscriptions from Shiqmona," *IEJ* 18 (1968) 226-33.

1969

99. "Judaean Stamps," *Eretz Israel* 9 [W. F. Albright Volume (Jerusalem, 1969)] 20-27; pl. V.

100. "New Directions in the Study of Apocalyptic," *Journal for Theology and the Church* 6 (1969) 157-65.

101. "A Christian Understanding of the Election of Israel," *The End of Dialogue and Beyond* (ed. S. Seltzner and M. L. Stackhouse; New York: Friendship, 1969) 72-85.

102. "Papyri of the Fourth Century B.C. from Dâliyeh," *New Directions in Biblical Archaeology* (ed. D. N. Freedman and Jonas Greenfield; New York: Anchor, 1969) 41-62; figs. 34-39.

103. "The Early History of the Qumran Community," *New Directions in Biblical Archaeology* (ed. D. N. Freedman and Jonas Greenfield; New York: Anchor, 1969) 63-79 [republication of No. 95].

104. "Epigraphic Notes on the Ammân Citadel Inscription," *BASOR* 193 (1969) 13-19.

105. "Two Notes on Palestinian Inscriptions of the Persian Age," *BASOR* 193 (1969) 19-24.

106. "An Ostracon from Heshbon," *Andrews University Seminary Studies* 7 (1969) 223-29; pl. XXV.

107. Associate Editor and Translator, *The New American Bible* (Paterson, N.J.: St. Anthony Guild Press, 1969-70) [I, II Samuel, with P. W. Skehan].

1970

108. "The Cave Inscriptions from Khirbet Beit Lei," *Near Eastern Archaeology in the Twentieth Century* [Glueck Volume] (ed. J. A. Sanders; New York: Doubleday, 1970) 299-306.

109. "The Dead Sea Scrolls," *Encyclopedia Britannica* (Chicago: Benton, 1970) Vol. 7, 117-19.

110. "Phoenician Incantations on a Plaque of the Seventh Century B.C. from Arslan Tash in Upper Syria," with R. J. Saley, *BASOR* 197 (1970) 42-49.

111. "William Foxwell Albright: Orientalist," *BASOR* 200 (1970) 7-11.

1971

112. "An Inscribed Jar Handle from Raddana," with D. N. Freedman, *BASOR* 201 (1971) 19-22.

113. "Buqeiᶜah," *Encyclopedia of Archaeological Excavations in the Holy Land* [Hebrew] (ed. B. Mazar, et al.; Jerusalem: Israel Exploration Society, 1971), 1. 99-100.

114. Editor, with John Strugnell, *Studies in Memory of Paul Lapp* [*HTR* 64, 2-3] (Cambridge: Harvard University, 1971).

115. "The Old Phoenician Inscription from Spain Dedicated to Hurrian Astarte," *HTR* 64, 2-3 [Lapp Memorial Volume (1971)] 189-95.

116. "אֵל [ʾēl]," *Theologisches Wörterbuch zum Alten Testament* (ed. G. J. Botterweck and H. Ringgren; Berlin: Kohlhammer, 1971), I. Sp. 259-79.

1972

117. "The Stele Dedicated to Melcarth by Ben-Hadad of Damascus," *BASOR* 205 (1972) 36-42.

118. Editor, with J. C. Trever, D. N. Freedman, and J. A. Sanders, *Scrolls from Qumran Cave I* (Jerusalem: Albright Institute of Archaeological Research and Shrine of the Book, 1972), 163 pp.

119. "Introduction" to *Scrolls from Qumran Cave I* [item 118] 1-5.

120. "Some Observations on Early Hebrew," with D. N. Freedman, *Biblica* 53 (1972) 413-20.

121. "An Interpretation of the Nora Stone," *BASOR* 208 (1972) 13-19.

122. "The Evolution of a Theory of Local Texts," *Septuagint and Cognate Studies* 2 (1972) 108-26.

123. "William Foxwell Albright," *Yearbook of the American Philosophical Society* 110-15.

1973

124. *Canaanite Myth and Hebrew Epic: Essays in the History of the Religion of Israel* (Cambridge: Harvard University, 1973), xvii + 376 pp.

125. "Heshbon Ostracon II," *Andrews University Seminary Studies* 11 (1973) 126-31.

126. "Two Archaic Inscriptions on Clay Objects from Byblus," with P. K. McCarter, Jr., *Revista di Studi Fenici* 1 (1973) 3-8.

127. "W. F. Albright's View of Biblical Archaeology and its Methodology," *BA* 36 (1973) 2-5.

128. "ʾēl [Dios]," *Diccionario teologico del antiquo Testamento* (ed. G. J. Botterweck and H. Ringgren; Madrid: Ediciones Cristianidad, 1973) cols. 256-75 [Translation of No. 116].

1974

129. Editor of posthumous article by W. F. Albright, "The Lachish Cosmetic Burner and Esther 2:12," *A Light Unto my Path. Old Testament Studies in Honor of Jacob M. Myers* (ed. H. N. Bream, R. D. Heim, and C. A. Moore; Philadelphia: Temple University, 1974) 25-32.

130. "The Contribution of the Qumrân Discoveries to the Study of the Biblical Text," *The Canon and Masorah of the Hebrew Bible: An Introductory Reader* (ed. S. Z. Leiman; New York: Ktav, 1974) 334-49 [reprint of No. 82].

131. "Prose and Poetry in the Mythic and Epic Texts from Ugarit," *HTR* 67 (1974) 1-15.

132. "אֵל [ʾēl]," *Theological Dictionary of the Old Testament* (ed. G. J. Botterweck and H. Ringgren; tr. J. T. Willis; Grand Rapids: Eerdmans, 1974), 1. 242-61 [Translation of No. 116].

133. "Notes on the Ammonite Inscription from Tell Sīrān," *BASOR* 212 (1973) 12-15.

134. "George Ernest Wright: A Tribute to him at his Death," *Harvard Divinity School Bulletin* 5:1 (October, 1974) 4, 6.

135. Editor, with D. N. Freedman and J. A. Sanders, *Scrolls from Qumran Cave I* from photographs of J. C. Trever (Jerusalem: Albright Institute of Archaeological Research and the Shrine of the Book, 1974) [Student Edition of No. 118].

136. "Inscriptions from Idalion in Greek, Cypriote Syllabic, and Phoenician Script," *American Expedition to Idalion, Cyprus. First Preliminary Report: Seasons of 1971 and 1972* (Supplement to *BASOR* 118; Cambridge: ASOR, 1974) 77-81.

137. "Leaves from an Epigraphist's Notebook: 1. A Second Phoenician Incantation Text from Arslan Tash; 2. The Oldest Phoenician Inscription from the Western Mediterranean; and 3. A Forgotten Seal," *Patrick W. Skehan Festschrift* [*CBQ* 36:4 (October, 1974)] 486-94.

1975

138. "William Foxwell Albright, Orientalist" and "William Foxwell Albright," in *The Published Works of William Foxwell Albright: A Comprehensive Bibliography* (ed. D. N. Freedman; Cambridge: ASOR, 1975) 14-23 [republications of nos. 111 and 123].

139. "A Reconstruction of the Judean Restoration," *JBL* 94 (1975) 4-18 [The Presidential Address, delivered 25 October, 1974, at the Annual Meeting of the Society of Biblical Literature held in Washington, D.C.].

140. "A Reconstruction of the Judean Restoration," *The History of Israel and Biblical Faith in Honor of John Bright* [*Interpretation* 29 (1975)] 187-203 [republication in a corrected version of No. 139].

141. "Ammonite Ostraca from Heshbon," *Andrews University Seminary Studies* 13 (1975) 1-20, pls. I, II.

142. Editor, with S. Talmon, *Qumran and the History of the Biblical Text* (London and Cambridge: Harvard University Press, 1975), iii + 415 pp.

143. "The Oldest Manuscripts from Qumran," *Qumran and the History of the Biblical Text* [Item No. 142] 147-76 [republication of No. 32].

144. "The History of the Biblical Text in the Light of Discoveries in the Judaean Desert," *Qumran and the History of the Biblical Text* [item no. 142] 177-95 [republication of No. 77].

145. "The Contributions of the Qumran Discoveries to the Study of the Biblical Text," *Qumran and the History of the Biblical Text* [item no. 142] 278-92 [republication of No. 82].

146. "The Evolution of a Theory of Local Texts," *Qumran and the History of the Biblical Text* [item no. 142] 306-20.

147. *Studies in Ancient Yahwistic Poetry*, with D. N. Freedman (Missoula, Montana: Scholars Press, 1975), vii + 191 pp. [publication of Item No. 76, with a postscriptum written in 1975].

148. "El-Buqei^ca," *Encyclopedia of Archaeological Excavations in the Holy Land* (ed. M. Avi-Yonah; Jerusalem: IES, 1975), 1. 267-70. (Cf. No. 113).

1976

149. Contributor with P. and N. Lapp, *et al., Discoveries in the Wâdī ed-Dâliyeh*, *AASOR* 41 (Cambridge: ASOR, 1974) 17-29, 57-60; pls. 59-63, 80, 81.

150. "Presidential Report to the American Schools of Oriental Research," *BASOR* 219 (1975) 1-3.

151. "Heshbon Ostracon XI," *Andrews University Seminary Studies* 14 (1976) 145-48.

152. Editor, with P. D. Miller and W. E. Lemke, *Magnalia Dei. Essays on the Bible and Archaeology in Memory of G. Ernest Wright* (New York: Doubleday, 1976), xii + 611 pp.

153. "The Olden Gods in Ancient Near Eastern Creation Myths," *Magnalia Dei* [item 152] 329-38.

1977

154. *Scrolls from the Wilderness of the Dead Sea*, reprinted with slight revisions by the School of Theology at Claremont (Claremont, 1977), 30 pp. [see item 802].

155. "The Dead Sea Scrolls and the People Who Wrote Them," *BARev* 3 (1977) 1, 23-32, 51 [*manu secunda*].

156. "George Ernest Wright," with P. D. Hanson, W. L. Moran, and K. Stendahl, *Harvard University Gazette* 72:27 (April 15, 1977).

1978

157. "David, Orpheus, and Psalm 151:3-4," *BASOR* 231 (1978) 69-71.

158. "The Historical Importance of the Samaria Papyri," *BARev* 4 (1978) 25-27 (*manu secunda*).

159. "The People Who Wrote the Dead Sea Scrolls," *Jewish Digest* 24:2 (October, 1978) 63-70 [*manu secunda*].

1979

160. Editor, *Symposia Celebrating the Seventy-fifth Anniversary of the Founding of the American Schools of Oriental Research (1900-1975)*: Volume 1 *Archaeology and Early Israelite History*; Volume 2 *Archaeology and the Sanctuaries of Israel* (Cambridge: ASOR 1979) ix + 183 pp.

161. "Early Alphabetic Scripts," *Archaeology and Early Israelite History* [item 160] 95-123.

162. "A Newly-Published Inscription of the Persian Age from Byblus," *IEJ* 29 (1979) 40-44.

163. "Problems of Method in the Textual Study of the Hebrew Bible," *The Critical Study of Sacred Texts* (ed. W. D. O'Flaherty; Berkeley: Berkeley Religious Studies Series, 1979) 31-54.

164. Volume editor with K. Baltzer, *Ezekiel I* by Walther Zimmerli, trans. R. E. Clements. *Hermeneia. A Critical and Historical Commentary on the Bible* (Philadelphia: Fortress, 1979).

165. "Phoenicians in Brazil?" *BARev* 5 (1979) 36-43 [*manu secunda*].

In Press

166. "The Samaritans. From the Fall of Samaria through the Hasmonean Era," *Encyclopedia Biblica* [Hebrew] (ed. B. Mazar and H. Tadmor; Jerusalem: Bialik Institute) Vol. 8.

167. "Two Offering Dishes with Phoenician Inscriptions from the Sanctuary of Arad," *BASOR* 235 (1980).

168. "An Aramaic Ostracon of the Third Century B.C.E. from the Excavations of Jerusalem," *EI* [Aharoni Volume].

169. "The Fixation of the Text and Canon of the Hebrew Bible," *Cambridge History of Judaism*, ed. W. D. Davies, Volume III.

170. "Newly-Found Inscriptions in Old Canaanite and Early Phoenician Scripts," *BASOR* 237.

171. "Inscriptions form the Buqêᶜah," in L. E. Stager, *Ancient Agriculture in the Judaean Desert: A Case Study of the Buqêᶜah Valley in the Iron Age* (Chicago: University of Chicago, 1979).

172. "The Priestly Tabernacle in the Light of Recent Research," *Temples and High Places in Biblical Times*, ed. A. Biran.

173. "Phoenician Tomb Stelae from Akzib," *Tombs at Akzib*, ed. M. W. Prausnitz.

174. "Fragment of a Monumental Inscription from the City of David," *BASOR*.

175. *The Ancient Library of Qumran* (4th ed.; Grand Rapids: Baker, 1980).

176. "Heshbon Ostracon XII," *Siegfried Horn Volume*, ed. L. Geraty.

INDEXES

SUBJECT INDEX

Micaiah 102-3
Michael 360, 361, 362, 363
Moses 117, 119, 130, 171, 172, 173, 185,
187, 193, 194, 195, 196, 200, 201, 202,
203, 204, 205, 206, 207, 208, 209, 210,
211, 341, 342, 343, 348, 349
—prophet-like 340, 341, 342, 343, 344,
345, 349, 350
monologue 196, 197, 198, 199, 204, 205,
211
Mot 233, 234, 266, 269
myth and history (see Date of Revelation)
myth and ritual 258, 259

Nabataean inscriptions 38
Nag Hammadi 327
Name theology 175, 176, 177, 178
nature/natural phenomena 266, 268, 270,
271, 272, 275, 276, 277, 278, 279, 280,
285, 288, 290, 292, 293, 298, 300, 301,
302, 309, 316, 318, 320
Nero 380, 383, 387, 388, 389, 394, 395, 397,
398
Nerva 384
Nineveh 215, 222, 225, 236, 237, 238, 239,
241, 243, 245
normative theology 33-34, 44-57
—developmental approaches to revelation
48-51
—non-religious approaches 54-56
—primitive revelation 46-48
—relativizing the biblical traditions 51-
54
northern league 74-75

oath (see also authenticating prophecy)
100-103, 105
Otho 383, 384, 387, 389

Palestinian text 335-36
Palmyrene inscriptions 38
paranomasia 131
parousia 399, 400
Passover 190
Persia/Persian 257, 259, 260, 261, 362
Persian period 330, 331, 334
Pharisees 247, 323, 329, 344, 345, 349
Philistia/Philistine 61, 62, 85-86, 89-90
priest/priesthood 76-78, 83
Prince of Light 362, 363, 364
prophecy 83
prophecy/fulfillment 174, 187, 194, 195
prophetic messenger word (see also divine
word) 97

prophetic message (see also divine word)
103-4
prophetic office 83

Qumran 323, 327, 335, 336
—eschatology of (see also eschatology)
351-75
—Hodayot (see Hodayot)
—messianic expectation (see also messiah)
352, 353-59, 360, 361
—war of Light and Darkness 352, 360-
65
—1QS 352, 354, 356, 357, 358, 360, 363-
65, 369, 373
—1QSa 354, 356, 357, 358, 366
—CD 352, 353-54, 356, 357, 358, 359,
361
—1QM 352, 356, 360, 361, 362, 366, 369
—1QH 365-72, 373
—1QH3 352
—4Q Testimonia 354
—11Q Melch 360
—4QSam 5
—IQIsa^a 284

radical editing 9-31
rationalism 19-31
redaction 152, 153
—pre-exilic 152, 157
—exilic 152, 153, 155, 156, 157, 158, 159,
160, 161, 162
redaction criticism (see also Redaktionsgeschichte) 26, 28
Redaktionsgeschichte 9-31
—concealment of editorial handiwork
11
—incomplete editing 11
—uniqueness of the Bible 11
—proto-logical 12
redemptive work 112-13
repentance 161, 162
reporting/reported speech 193-211
resurrection 247-321, 341, 342, 343, 345,
349, 365, 394
restoration 285, 286, 292, 293, 294, 296,
300
redaction (see also normative theology,
primitive revelation) 44, 46-50, 52-
53
Revelation, Book of
—Antichrist 383
—beast 382-83, 388
—eagle vision 385

AUTHOR INDEX

SCRIPTURE INDEX

Psalms

Extra-biblical Sources

LANGUAGE INDEX